FALAISE ROLL

COMITÉ "GUILLAUME LE CONQUÉRANT"

À L'ÉPOQUE DE L'INAUGURATION DU MÉMORIAL

Présidents d'honneur.

M. Henry Chéron, sénateur, ancien ministre.
Honourable M. Jackson Crispin, de New York.
Right honourable lord Eustace Percy, m.p., ancien ministre.
M. le général Gouraud, gouverneur militaire de Paris.
M. A. Bussière, préfet du Calvados.

Membres d'honneur.

The most noble the marquess of Crewe, k.g.
M. le comte d'Harcourt, sénateur.
M. Boivin-Champeaux, sénateur.
Mme la baronne Ernest de la Grange.
M. le marquis de Voguë, président de France-Grande-Bretagne.
His worship, alderman G. Ormerod, maire d'Hastings.
M. Maigron, recteur de l'université de Caen.
Colonel F.-G. Langham, m.a., ll.b., o.a.
M. le marquis d'Eyragues, président du syndicat d'initiative.
M. Engerand, député du Calvados.
M. Guilloteau, maire de Falaise.
M. le professeur Prentout, de l'université de Caen.
M. Detolle, maire de Caen.
M. Dodeman, maire de Bayeux.
M. Thomas, maire de Ouistreham.
M. Duval, adjoint au maire de Falaise (trésorier).
M. Macary, professeur au collège de Falaise (secrétaire général).

SEAL.

COUNTERSEAL.

SEAL OF WILLIAM KING OF ENGLAND AND DUKE OF NORMANDY PRESERVED IN THE ARCHIVES PHOTOGRAPHIQUES D'ART ET D'HISTOIRE, PARIS

THIS PROVES THAT ARMORIAL BEARINGS WERE NOT THEN IN USE, FOR IF SO CHARGES WOULD HAVE APPEARED ON THE COUNTERSEAL AS THEY DO ON THE OTHERS HEREIN REPRODUCED. IT IS THE ONLY SEAL OF THE CONQUEROR IN EXISTENCE

CHÂTEAU OF WILLIAM THE CONQUEROR AT FALAISE, NORMANDY

FALAISE ROLL

RECORDING

PROMINENT COMPANIONS

OF

WILLIAM DUKE OF NORMANDY

AT THE

CONQUEST OF ENGLAND

BY

M. JACKSON CRISPIN
Princeton University, 1896, A.B., Officier d'Académie,
Chevalier de la Légion d'Honneur

AND

LEONCE MACARY
Professor of the College of Falaise O.I.

WITH ADDITIONS AND CORRECTIONS BY
G. ANDREWS MORIARTY
from *The American Genealogist*
Volume XVI, Number 1, July, 1939

Southern Historical Press, Inc.
Greenville, South Carolina

Please direct all correspondence and book orders to:
SOUTHERN HISTORICAL PRESS, Inc.
PO Box 1267
Greenville, SC   29602-1267

Originally Published 1938 London
ISBN #978-1-63914-252-1
Printed in the United States of America

Table of Contents

BRONZE TABLET ERECTED IN THE CHAPEL OF THE CHÂTEAU OF WILLIAM THE
CONQUEROR AT FALAISE, NORMANDY, 21 JUNE 1931. (Rabiant, fondeur d'art)

Falaise Roll

ADAM DE RIE
ACHARD D'AMBRIÈRES
AMAURY, VICOMTE DE THOUARS
ALAIN FERGANT, COMTE DE BRETAGNE
ALAIN FITZ FLAALD
LE COMTE ALAIN LE NOIR
LE COMTE ALAIN LE ROUX
ALRIC LE COQ
ANDRÉ DE VITRIE
ANSCOUL DE PICQUIGNI
ANSGER DE MONTAIGU
ANQUETIL DE ROS
ANSGOT DE ROS
ARNOUL D'ARDRE
AUBRI DE COUCI
AUVRAI LE BRETON
AUVRECHER D'ANGERVILLE
AVENEL DES BIARDS
LE SIRE D'ARGOUGES
LE SIRE D'ANISY
LE SIRE D'AUBIGNY (ROGER)
LE SIRE D'AUVILLERS
BAUDOIN DE MEULES ET DU SAP
BERENGER GIFFARD
BERNARD DE NEUFMARCHÉ
BERNARD DE ST-OUEN
BERNARD DE ST-VALÉRY
BERTRAN DE VERDUN
LE SIRE DE BAILLEUL
LE SIRE DE BEVILLE ET D'YVELIN
LE SIRE DE BOLLEVILLE
LE SIRE DE BONNEBOSQ
LE SIRE DE BOSC-ROARD
LE SIRE DE BOUTTEVILLAIN
LE SEIGNEUR DE BRECEY
LE SIRE DE BRUCOURT
CORBET LE NORMAND
LE SIRE DE CANOUVILLE
LE SIRE DE CINTHEAUX
LE SIRE DE CLINCHAMPS
LE SIRE DE COUVERT
LE SIRE DE CUSSY
DREU DE LA BEUVRIÈRE
DREU DE MONTAIGU
DURAND MALET
LE SIRE DE DRIENCOURT
ENGENOULF DE L'AIGLE
ERRAND DE HARCOURT
ETIENNE ERARD
EUDES, EVÊQUE DE BAYEUX
EUDES, COMTE DE CHAMPAGNE
EUDES DAPIFER, SIRE DE PRÉAUX
EUDES DE FOURNEAUX
EUDES LE SENESCHAL, SIRE DE LA HAIE
EUSTACHE, COMTE DE BOULOGNE
LE SIRE D'EPINAY
LE SIRE D'ESCALLES
FOUQUE D'AULNAY
FOUQUE D'AUNOU
LE SIRE DE FRIBOIS
GAUTIER D'AINCOURT
GAUTIER D'APPEVILLE
GAUTIER DE CAEN
GAUTIER LE FLAMAND
GAUTIER GIFFARD, COMTE DE LONGUEVILLE
GAUTIER HACHET
GAUTIER DE LACY

GAUTIER LE POITEVIN
GAUTIER DE VERNON
GEOFFROI ASCELIN
GEOFFROI DU BEC
GEOFFROI DE COMBRAY
GEOFFROI, EVÊQUE DE COUTANCES
GEOFFROI DE LA GUIERCHE
GEOFFROI DE MANDEVILLE
GEOFFROI, SEIGNEUR DE MORTAGNE
GEOFFROI MARTEL
GEOFFROI DE PIERREPONT
GEOFFROI RIDEL
GEOFFROI TALBOT
GILBERT D'ASNIÈRES
GILBERT LE BLOND
GILBERT DE BRETTEVILLE
GILBERT DE COLLEVILLE
GILBERT CRISPIN 2E SEIGNEUR DE TILLIÈRES
GILBERT DE GAND
GILBERT MALET
GILBERT DE NEUVILLE
GILBERT TISON
GILBERT DE VENABLES
GILES DE PICQUIGNI
GONFROI DE CIOCHES
GUI DE LA VAL
GUILBERT D'AUFAY
GUILLAUME ALIS
GUILLAUME D'ALRE
GUILLAUME D'ANNEVILLE
GUILLAUME L'ARCHER
GUILLAUME D'ARQUES
GUILLAUME D'AUDRIEU
GUILLAUME BACON, SIRE DU MOLAY
GUILLAUME DE BEAUFOU
GUILLAUME BERTRAM
GUILLAUME LE BLOND
GUILLAUME DU BOSC
GUILLAUME DE BOURNEVILLE
GUILLAUME DE BRAI
GUILLAUME DE BRIOUSE
GUILLAUME DE CAHAIGNES
GUILLAUME DE CAILLY
GUILLAUME LA CHIÈVRE
GUILLAUME DE COLLEVILLE
GUILLAUME DE COLOMBIÈRES
GUILLAUME CRISPIN 1ER COMTE DU VEXIN
GUILLAUME BIGOT
GUILLAUME DE GOUVIX
GUILLAUME COMTE D'EVREUX
GUILLAUME DE FERRIÈRES
GUILLAUME FITZ OSBERNE
GUILLAUME DE LACELLES
GUILLAUME LOUVET
GUILLAUME MALET DE GRAVILLE
GUILLAUME DE LA MARE
GUILLAUME DE MONCEAUX
GUILLAUME DE MOULINS S. DE FALAISE
GUILLAUME DE MOYON
GUILLAUME DE ST-JEAN
GUILLAUME DE PANTOUL
GUILLAUME PATRY, DE LA LANDE
GUILLAUME PÉCHÉ
GUILLAUME DE PERCY
GUILLAUME PEVREL
GUILLAUME DE PICQUIGNI

GUILLAUME LE POITEVIN
GUILLAUME DE REVIERS
GUILLAUME DE ROS
GUILLAUME DE ROUMARE
GUILLAUME SAYE
GUILLAUME DE SEMILLY
GUILLAUME TAILLEBOIS
GUILLAUME TALBOT
GUILLAUME DE TOENI
GUILLAUME DE VIEUXPONT
GUILLAUME DE WARREN
GODEFROI DE VILLERS
GUINEBOUD DE BALON
LE SIRE DE GACÉ
LE SIRE DE GLANVILLE
LE SIRE DE GLOS
HAMELIN DE BALON
HAMON DE LA VAL
HAMON LE SENESCHAL
HASCOUF MUSARD
HENRI DE DOMFRONT
HENRI DE FERRIÈRES
HERBERT D'AIGNEAUX
HONFROI DE BOHON —
HONFROI DE CARTERET
HONFROI VIS DE LOUP
HUARD DE VERNON
HUBERT DE PORT
HUBERT DE RIE
HUGUE L'ASNE
HUGUE DE BEAUCHAMP
HUGUE DE BERNIÈRES
HUGUE DE BOLBEC
HUGUE DE CARBONNEL
HUGUE DE GOURNAY
HUGUE DE GOURNAY "LE JEUNE"
HUGUE DE GRENTEMESNIL
HUGUE DE MACEY
HUGUE DE LA MARE
HUGUE DE MONTFORT LE CONNESTABLE
HUGUE DE MORTEMER
HUGUE MUSARD
HUGUE DE PORT
HUGUE DE ROUSSEL
HUGUE DE ST-QUENTIN
HUGUE DE WANCI
HUGUE D'HÉRICY
HUGUE D'HOUDETOT
IBERT DE LACY
INGELRAM DE LIONS
IVE TAILLEBOIS
IVE DE VASSY
JACQUES LE BRABANÇON
JEAN D'IVRI
LE SIRE DE JORT
LE SIRE DE LITHAIRE
MARTIN DE TOURS
DE MUSCAMP
MATHIEU DE LA FERTÉ-MACÉ
MAUGER DE CARTERET
MICHEL DE BURES
MILE CRISPIN
DE MATHAN
DU MERLE
NÉEL VICOMTE DE ST-SAUVEUR
OSBERNE D'ARQUES
OSBERNE DE SASSY
OSBERNE GIFFARD
OSBERNE DE WANCI
OSMOND BASSET
OURS D'ABBETOT

ADDITIONAL NAMES ACCEPTED

STATUE OF WILLIAM THE CONQUEROR ERECTED IN THE PLACE DE L'HÔTEL
DE VILLE AT FALAISE IN 1851 BY A DONATION OF THE KING AND BY
PUBLIC SUBSCRIPTION. (Rochet, sculptor)

INTRODUCTION

THE 900th anniversary of the birth of William, duke of Normandy, afterwards king of England, in 1927, was the occasion for celebrations at Falaise, Bayeux, Caen, and Hastings. Many notabilities from America, England, and France, met together to show their appreciation of that valiant warrior and to commemorate the momentous event of 1066, which has so greatly influenced the history of the English-speaking peoples of the world.

From July 1927 dates the formation of the "Committee Guillaume le Conquérant," whose aim has been to give a new impetus to the historical study of the period of the conquest of England.

The ambition of this international body was to enrol a list of those companions of duke William for whose presence at Senlac strong presumption existed, although not absolutely substantiated by documentary evidence.

How great the difficulties confronting this undertaking and the tremendous amount of research required was fully realized, but it was believed a credible selection could be made by a careful perusal of the works of the historians and antiquarians of the past who had given the subject profound thought.

Scanty information is offered by the contemporary historians, since William of Jumièges, William of Poitiers, Guy of Amiens and Orderic Vital have mentioned only a few of the greatest nobles.

We agree with Fowke, Steenstrup, Freeman and Planché that the Bayeux tapestry was woven not long after the victory of duke William at Hastings, wherefore we have accepted the names appearing upon it as well as all of those deduced therefrom by the abbé de La Rue in his *Researches* of this marvellous relic.

His conclusions were approved by the great modern antiquarian and member of the French institute, Léopold Delisle.

The controversy concerning the historical value of the poem of Robert Wace, whom we found it impossible to ignore, is ages old and will probably continue indefinitely. We have chosen to credit him because his sources of information seem the most highly acceptable, considering the relative proximity of his *Roman de Rou* to the time of the invasion of England. We could not withhold approval from a writer who had collected oral information from the witnesses or at least from the sons of witnesses of this momentous event. Finding it impossible to contradict him excepting in some small details and a few duplications, we made his poem the basis of our roll.

Wace says at the conclusion of his list of participants at the battle : "Many other barons there were whom I have not even mentioned, neither can I give the names of all the barons nor the surnames of all whom the duke brought from Normandy and Brittany in his company."

Benoît de Sainte-More, who composed his *Chronique des Ducs de Normandie* on these events when the *Roman de Rou* was written, offers little additional information. From these sources 144 names were secured.

The remaining names were taken from acts, charters and documents attesting presence in England in 1066 or shortly thereafter, and from the recorded opinion of the learned and distinguished students of the subject. Eadmer's *Life of St.-Anselm*, the *Interpolations of Jumièges* by Robert de Torigny (du Mont) and his *Chronique* offer valuable information concerning families in the last half of the 11th and the first part of the 12th centuries. The volumes of Camden, Hearne, Fox, Duchesne, Dugdale, De Gerville, La Roque, Père Anselme, Le Prevost, Lobineau, Edgar Taylor, Stapleton, Fuller, John Bernard Burke, Thierry, *Recherches sur le Domesday*, Delisle, Dupont, Freeman, Planché, Cleveland, *Norman People* and many others have been critically examined in this connection.

Domesday tenancy naturally does not signify participation at Senlac, but is proof of land ownership in England at or before 1086. This, taken in conjunction with other facts, demands recognition, and the majority of the names accepted are inscribed in that survey.

We will not attempt to discuss the merits of the various rolls published in the past centuries commencing with that of Battle abbey, which hung upon its walls for hundreds of years. It has long since disappeared, no one knows where; probably the monks themselves destroyed it to prevent detection of the insertions perpetrated in that document which had been entrusted to their care. Only copies of it remain made by Leland, Holinshed and Stowe, later published by Duchesne, who received it from Camden, concerning which the latter remarks : "Whosoever considers well shall find them always to be forged, and those names inserted which the time in every age favoured, and were never mentioned in that authenticated record."

Neither are we prepared to vouch for the authenticity of the legend that the original was copied on parchment from the muster-roll of the Norman knights prepared before embarkation, which was called the morning after the battle, to ascertain who had been slain.

Nevertheless, wherever our selection has been corroborated by this roll or those of Guillaume le Tailleur, William of Worcester, John of Brompton, Scriven, and the Dives roll of Léopold Delisle, while admittedly not authentic, we have recorded it, since it is difficult to overlook the conclusions of these eminent antiquarians.

The work of the committee has thus materialized into a list of 315 names which have been engraved upon the bronze memorial erected on 21 June 1931, in the chapel of the castle of Falaise. These companions were chosen from the thousands who fought by the side of duke William, because a sum of well-grounded probability had been gathered which permitted the acceptance of their presence at the battle of Hastings as most likely. The late and much-regretted professor Prentout, distinguished specialist in Norman history of the university of Caen, a member of the committee, rendered invaluable service in the compilation of this roll. The attempt has not been made to give other than a few of the principal facts concerning those personages whose history has been widely recorded. This can be readily ascertained by consulting the authorities named in the general references at the conclusion of each biography.

Our researches will continue and may in the process of time justify the publication of additional names.

The 315 names inscribed upon the tablet were compiled by taking 18 from Vital among which are included 13 by William of Poitiers. All but 3 of these are chronicled by Wace, from whose poem were acquired 114 occurring or implied therein. To this 117 the Bayeux tapestry itself offers 3 not elsewhere referred to and the Researches of La Rue 24, while Professors Macary and Prentout procured 88. The remaining 83 were obtained by Jackson Crispin as well as the 91 additional names [1] accepted, making a total of 406.

It was decided at the time of the dedication of the tablet to publish the reasons for the selection which devolved upon the latter who carried out the research, compiled the biographies and the entire work.

The 315 biographies after their compilation were reviewed by Richard Holworthy archivist and genealogist, London.

---

[1] Of these additional names one was enrolled by Guy of Amiens (Gui comte de Ponthieu), one by Vital (Robert de Vitot), and two by Wace (Fitz Bertran de Peleit and De Tournières).

LIST OF ABBREVIATIONS

Gui of Amiens . . . . *Widonis Carmen de Hastingæ Proelio*, anonymous, ascribed to Gui de Ponthieu, bishop of Amiens, almoner to queen Matilda, died *c.* 1074. (*Chronique Anglo-Normands*, Michel, III, 1 to 38.)

Père Anselme . . . . *Histoire Généalogique et Chronologique de la Maison Royale de France*, Père Anselme, 1730.

Opera S. Anselmi, Epist. . *Sancti Anselmi ex Beccensi Abbate Cantuariensis Archiepiscopi Opera Omnia*, Gerberon, 1731. (St. Anselme, died 1109.)

Banks . . . . . . *Dormant and Extinct Baronage of England*, Banks, 1809–1820

Benoît . . . . . . *Chronique des Ducs de Normandie*, Benoît de Sainte-More, ed., Michel, 1836–44. (Benoît contemporary with Wace.)

Bérée . . . . . . *La généalogie des Seigneurs et Dames d'Etrépagny*, Robert Bérée, 1658, pub. by Legay in the *Bulletin de la Société de l'Histoire de Normandie*, 1884.

Bouquet . . . . . *Grand Recueil des historiens français*, Bouquet, 1738.

Chron. John of Brompton . "*Chronicon Joannis Brompton*," pub. in "*Historiæ Anglicanæ Scriptores*," Twysden, 1652. Brompton was abbot of Jervaulx (1437).

Burke . . . . . . *The Roll of Battle Abbey Annotated*, Burke, 1848.

Cle. . . . . . . *The Battle Abbey*, Duchess of Cleveland, 1889.

Des Bois . . . . . *Dictionnaire de la Noblesse*, Des Bois la Chesnaye, 1773.

Introd. Domesd. . . . *General Introduction to Domesday Book*, Ellis, 1883.

Rech. Domesd. . . . . *Recherches sur le Domesday*, D'Anisy and de Sainte-Marie, 1842.

Dugdale . . . . . *The Baronage of England*, Dugdale, 1675.

Duchesne . . . . . "*Foeda Normanniæ*" in *Historiæ Normannorum scriptores antiqui*, Duchesne, 1619.

Dupont . . . . . *Recherches historique et topographique sur les Compagnons de Guillaume le Conquérant*, Dupont, 1907.

Eadmer. Hist. Nov. Rolls . *Eadmeri Historia Novorum in Anglia, De Vita Sancti Anselmi*, Rule, 1884. (Eadmer, a monk under St. Anselme at Canterbury, who died 1124.)

Dict. de l'Eure . . . *Dictionnaire de l'Eure*, Charpillon et Caresme, 1868–79.

Hist. Litt. de la France . . *Benedictins de la Congrégation de Saint Maur*, 1756.

Gall. Christ. . . . . *Gallia Christiana.* 16 vols., between 1716 and 1869.

Rech. de Gerville . . *Recherches sur les anciens Châteaux du département de la Manche*, De Gerville, 1825–30.

Bibl. nat. lat. 13905 . . *Le Recueil de Jouvelin*, Bibl. nat. lat. 13905. (Monk at Bec after 1690, died St-Cyprien de Poitiers, 1713.)

Jumièges . . . . . *Gesta Normannorum Ducum*, Guillaume de Jumièges, Marx, 1914. (Jumièges died 1090.)

Jumièges Interp., Ord. Vit. . *Interpolations of Jumièges*, by Orderic Vital, ed., Marx.

Jumièges Interp., de Torigny *Interpolations of Jumièges*, by Robert de Torigny, ed., Marx.

Chart. Abb. Jumièges. . . *Chartes de l'Abbaye de Jumièges*, Vernier, 1916.

Opera Lanfranci . . . *Beati Lanfranci Archiepiscopi Cantuariensis Opera Quae Supersunt Omnia*, Giles, 1844.

De nob. Crispin. gen. . . *Miraculum quo beata Maria subvenit Willelsmo Crispino seniori, ubi de nobili Crispinorum genere agitur*, Milo and Gilbert Crispin, ed., Giles, 1844. (Milo died *c.* 1150.)

Lib. Nig. . . . . . . *Liber Niger Scaccarii*, Hearne, editio altera 1774.

Lobineau . . . . . Contenant les preuves de l'Histoire de Bretagne, Lobineau, 1707.
Mabillon . . . . . Annales Ordinis Sancti Benedicti, Mabillon, ed., 1707, 1739.
M.R.S. . . . . . " Magni rotuli scaccarii Normanniæ " sub regibus Angliæ in the Mémoires de la Soc. des Antiquaires de Normandie, t. 15–17.
M.S.A.N. . . . . . Mémoires de la Soc. des Antiquaires de Normandie.
Mon. . . . Monasticon Anglicanum, Dugdale, ed., 1846.
Moreri . . . . Le Grand Dictionnaire Historique, Moreri, 1759.
Morice . . . . Mémoires pour servir de Preuves à l'Histoire de Bretagne, Morice, 1742.
Neustria Pia. . . . Neustria Pia, Du Monstier, 1663.
Nor. Peo. . . . . Norman People, 1874.
Plan. . . . . . The Conqueror and his Companions, Planché, 1874.
William of Poitiers . . Willelmi Conquestorie Gesta, a Willelmo Pictaviensi Lexoviorum archidiacons in Patrologiæ, Migne, t. CXLIX. (Poitiers wrote before 1089.)
Porée . . . . . Histoire de l'Abbaye du Bec, le chanoine Porée, curé de Bournainville, 1901.
Le Prevost Mem. . . . Mémoires et Notes de M. Auguste Le Prevost du Département de l'Eure, Delisle and Passy, 1862–72.
Le Prevost, Notes, Wace . Le Roman de Rou et des Ducs de Normandie, by Robert Wace, pub. by Frédéric Pluquet, with notes by Auguste Le Prevost, 1827. (Wace, b. early 12th cent., d. circa 1184.)
R.C. . . Rotulus Cancellarii (Record publication).
R.C.R. . . Rotuli Ciriæ Regis Palgrave, from 1194 to 1200, 2 vols., 8vo (Record publication).
R.H. . . . Rotuli Hundredorum, 2 vols., fo., C 1272 (Record publication).
La Roque . . . . Histoire généalogique de la maison de Harcourt, La Roque, 1662.
L'abbé de La Rue . . Recherches sur la Tapisserie de Bayeux, l'abbé de La Rue, 1824.
Stapleton . . . . Observations on the Great Rolls of the Exchequer of Normandy, "Magni rotuli scaccarii Normanniæ", sub regibus Angliæ, Stapleton, 1840.
Guillaume Tailleur . . Cronieques de Normendie, Guillaume le Tailleur, 1487.
Wace, Taylor . . . Master Wace, his Chronicle of the Norman Conquest from the Roman de Rou, Edgar Taylor, 1837.
Bibl. nat. vol. 12884 . . Chronicon Beccense, Thibault, Bibl. nat. lat. 12884. (Died a monk at Bec, 1684.)
Chron. de Torigny . . Chronique de Robert de Torigny, abbé du Mont-Saint-Michel, Delisle, 1872–3. (Torigny, died 1186.)
Ord. Vit. . . . . The Ecclesiastical History of England and Normandy, Orderic Vital, ed. Forester, 1854. (Vital, 1075–1141.)
Ord. Vit. Le Prevost . Orderici Vitalis Angligenæ, Coenobii, Monachi Hist. Eccl., Le Prevost, 1833–55.
Roger of Wendover . . Roger of Wendover's Flowers of History, Giles, 1849. (Roger died 1237.)
G.E.C. . . . . Cokayne's Complete Peerage.
C. . . Charter.
T. . . Genealogical Table.
App. . . Appendix.
Add. . . . . . Addenda.

A MAP OF
NORMANDY,
ILLUSTRATIVE OF WACE,
with the principal
Religious establishments
(marked +)

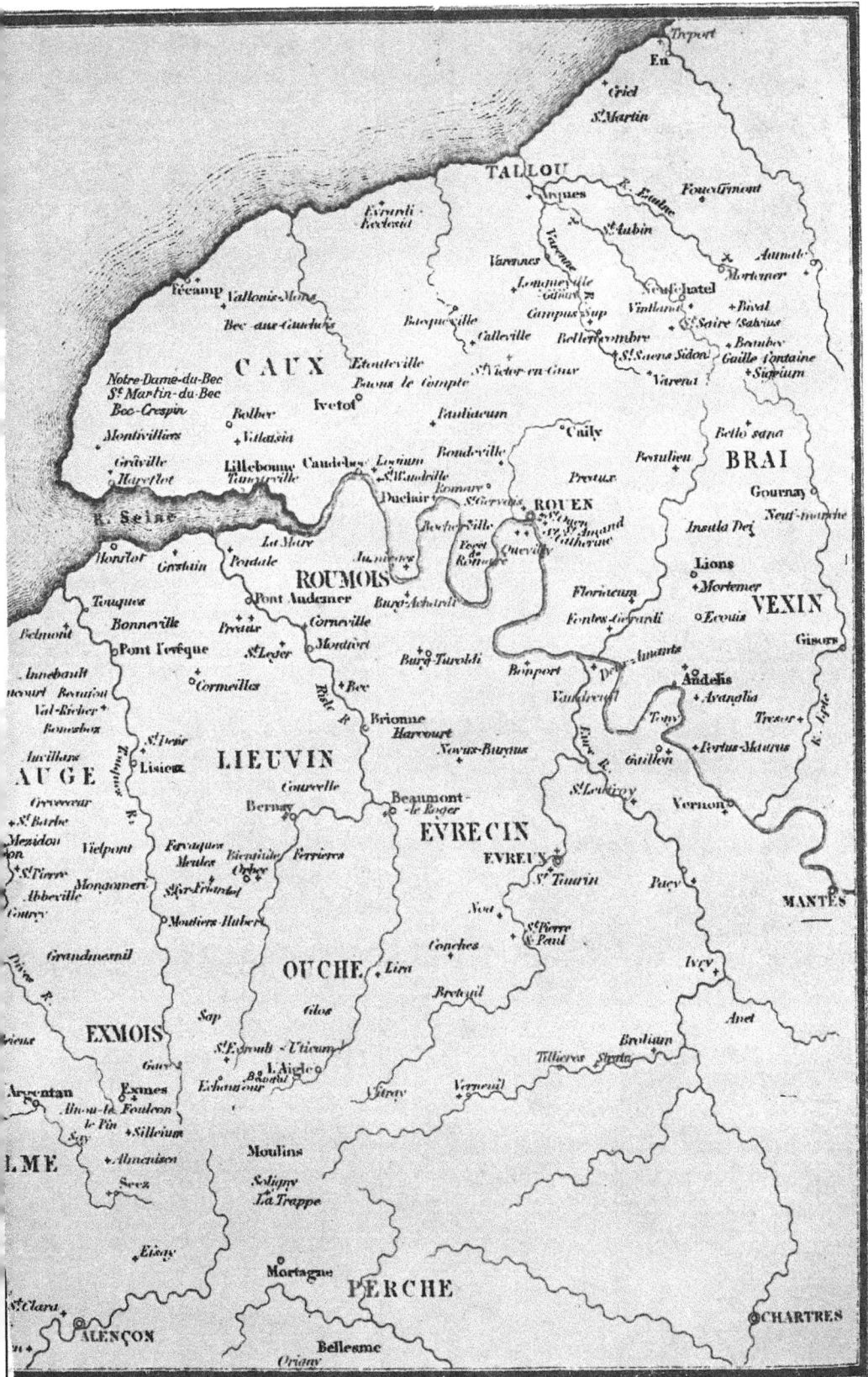

Treport

En

Criel

TALLOU

St. Martin

Foucarmont

Dieppes

R. Eaulne

Varenne

St. Aubin

Arcanes

Arques

Aumale

Mortemer

Longueville-Gilbert

Neufchatel

Bival

St. Saire Sabrus

Fécamp

Vallonis Mons

Campus Sup

Vintland

Bec aux Cauchois

Basqueville

Calleville

Bellencombre

St. Saens Sidon

Boubuy

Gaille Fontaine

Varena

Sigrium

C A U X

Etouteville

Bauns le Comte

St. Victor-en-Caux

Notre-Dame-du-Bec

St. Martin-du-Bec

Bec-Crespin

Ivetot

Pauliacum

Cailly

Bello sana

Bestlieu

B R A I

Montivilliers

Bolbec

Villatsia

Boudeville

Pretaus

Gournay

Neuf-marche

Graville

Havetlot

Lillebonne

Tancarville

Candebec

Loyium

St. Wandrille

Romare

St. Gervais

R O U E N

St. Ouen

St. Amand

St. Catherine

Insula Dei

Lions

Mortemer

Ecouis

V E X I N

R. Seine

Duclair

Jecher-ville

Forest de Romare

Quevilly

Horstot

Goustain

La Mare

Foudale

Jumieges

R O U M O I S

Burg-Achatali

Florineum

Fontes Gerardi

Gisors

Tourques

Bonneville

Pont Audemer

Corneville

Burg-Turoldi

Bonport

D. Amant

Andelis

Avanglia

Tresor

Belmont

Pont l'eveque

Preaus

St. Leger

Mordtort

Bec

Vaudreuil

Tony

Guillon

Pertus-Maurus

R. Apte

Innebault

Beciulon

Val-Richer

Romesbos

Cormeilles

St. Desir

Brionne

Harcourt

Novux-Burgus

St. Leufroy

Vernon

Juvillans

St. Pierre

AUGE

Lisieux

L I E U V I N

Courcelle

Beaumont-le-Roger

Groveccur

St. Barbe

Mezidon

St. Pierre

Abbeville

Bernay

Faruques

Meules

Orbey

Ferriera

E V R E C I N

E V R E U X

St. Taurin

Pacy

MANTES

Vielpont

Mongommeri

St. Ger-Friardel

Bieuville

Noat

St. Pierre

Paul

Grandmesnil

Moutiers-Hubert

Conches

Lion

O U C H E

Ivry

Dive R.

E X M O I S

Sap

Glos

Bretoyil

Brolium

Anet

Argentan

Exmes

St. Evroult-Uticum

L'Aigle

Echaufour

Vstroy

Verneuil

Tillieres Spina

Almenisou

Moulins

L M E

Seez

Soligny

La Trappe

Elsay

Mortagne

P E R C H E

CHARTRES

St. Clara

ALENÇON

Bellesme

Origny

FALAISE ROLL OF THE COMPANIONS OF
WILLIAM THE CONQUEROR

ADAM DE RIE. *Vide* Eudes Dapifer, Sire de Préaux.

ACHARD D'AMBRIÈRES. This family, seated in the Passais Normand and Achard d'Ambrières, were probably descended from Achard the castellan of Domfront, Normandy, in 1020, who was a witness to a charter of the abbey de Lonlay in 1025. Achard d'Ambrières distinguished himself at the siege of the castle of Mayenne and Ambrières, where he defeated Geoffroi de Mayenne,[1] for which reason duke William gave him the custody of the castle of Ambrières, which previously had been under the guardianship of Robert d'Estouteville. Two years later he was at the conquest of England with Henry de Domfront.[2] Domesday records him as an under-tenant of Roger de Montgomery in Sussex and William Fitz Ansculf in Buckinghamshire and Worcestershire. William Achard, his son or younger brother, was constable of Domfront from 1091–1102, and received a grant of seven manors in Berkshire from Henry I. Goisbertus filius Achardi occurs in a charter in favour of the abbey of Jumièges in 1069[3] and may have been another son of Achard the elder. Achard appears in l'abbé de La Rue's *Researches of the Bayeux Tapestry*, as well as on the rolls of Worcester and Dives.

Rech. Domesd., 48. Plan., II, 253–85. *Nov. Peo.*, 134. Cle., II, 195.
[1] Jumièges, 127; Ord. Vit., I, 449.
[2] *Vide* Henri de Domfront. [3] *Chart. Abb. Jumièges*, I, 81.

AMAURY VICOMTE DE THOUARS. Amaury came from the district located between the river Sèvre which flows to Mortagne and the Dives which passes to Moncontour.[1] Wace, Orderic Vitalis, Benoît de St-More

and William of Poitiers have recorded Amaury, vicomte de Thouars, as having been present at the battle of Hastings, in which engagement he was appointed by duke William to lead with Alain le Roux of Brittany the left wing of the army. Amaury was the eldest son of Geoffry II, vicomte de Thouars and Aldearde, and married first Aserengarde, sister of Raoul de Maulgon, by whom he had Herbert, Geoffry and Ildegarde who married Henry VI, sire de Lezingen. Amaury married second Ameline, by whom he had, according to Père Anselme, four sons, Savary, Raoul, Hugues and another Geoffry. He died in 1093 and was buried in the church of St-Nicolas de la Chèze, which he had just built. His name appears on all the rolls. Wace (l. 13598) records " E li Visquens cil de Toarz."

Plan., I, 242–6.
[1] Letter by De Besly to André Duchesne, May 23, 1620.

ALAIN FERGANT, COMTE DE BRETAGNE. Alain Fergant was the son and heir of Houel V, duke of Brittany, by Havoise of Brittany, sister and heir of duke Conan II. Alain married first Constance of Normandy, the second daughter of William the Conqueror, and secondly Ermengarde, daughter of Foulques (IV) Le Réchin, count of Anjou. He was sent by his father to join duke William in Normandy in 1066, with a very strong contingent of knights to participate in the invasion of England, for which he was magnificently rewarded with all the lands that before the conquest had belonged to earl Morcar, held in barony and chief with the rights and title of palatine count. He has sometimes been confounded with the brothers, count Alain Le Roux and count Alain Le Noir, both of Brittany. "Alain Felgan," as he is recorded in Wace (l. 11508), did not succeed his father as duke of Brittany until 1084, and died in 1119 a monk at the abbey of Rhedan.

Plan., I, 264. Cle., III, 81. *Rech. Domesd.*, 71 and fol.

ALAIN FITZ FLAALD.

Alain Fitz Flaald came to England at the conquest and was baron of Oswaldestre, Salop and Mileham, Norfolk. He received the shrievalty of Shropshire from Henry I and died *c.* 1114. Wace (l. 11511), in recording " Sire de Dinan," undoubtedly referred to him. While his parentage is more or less obscure, there is evidence to show that Flaald, his father, lived in Brittany and was a brother of Alain, seneschal of Dol, descended from the old Armorican counts of Dol and Dinan. Alain Fitz Flaald was the father or grandfather of Walter Fitz Alan, steward to David I, king of Scotland, ancestor of the Stuarts, kings of that country. Alain Fitz Flaald was also the father of William Fitz Alan, to whom Henry II gave in second marriage Isabel de Say, baroness of Clun, the greatest heiress of Shropshire. He was ancestor of John Fitz Alan, who married Isabel, sister and co-heiress of Hugh d'Albigny.[1] Upon a division of Hugh's property at his death in 1243, the castle of Arundel was assigned to John, son of the aforementioned John and Isabel, who thus became the first earl of Arundel of the Fitz Alan line. This property eventually passed to Mary, daughter and heiress of Henry Fitz Alan, who carried it, together with the earldom and the barony of Maltravers, to her husband Thomas Howard, duke of Norfolk,[2] in which family it still remains. Alain Fitz Flaald and his wife Adeline were benefactors to the Norfolk priory of Castle Acre, early in the reign of Henry I. Turchil Rufus or le Rous, who came to England in 1066, held lands from Alain in Norfolk.[3]

Cle., I, 38–41 ; II, 2–42 ; III, 63–265. *Nor. Peo.*, 408.
[1] *Vide* Le Sire d'Aubigny and Roger de Montgomeri.   [2] *Complete Peerage*, by G. E. C., I, 239. This differs from the pedigree of " Blauw's Barons' War " quoted by

Cleveland (I, 41), which affirms that Edmund Fitz Alan, great-grandson of John and Isabel Fitz Alan, was the first earl of this line summoned to parliament.
[3] *Mon.*, i, 627.

LE COMTE ALAIN LE NOIR.

Alain Le Noir was the brother of Alain Le Roux and succeeded him as earl of Richmond.[1] He received as his reward for participation at Senlac, 120 manors, principally in Suffolk and Norfolk. Lobineau[2] affirms that he had an elder brother, Brient or Brian of Brittany, comte de Vannes, who attended his brothers at the conquest. This Brian accompanied William Fitz Osberne in 1068 to relieve Exeter, which was being besieged by the Welsh and disaffected men of Cheshire, Devonshire and Cornwall, under Edric the Wild. The rebels were defeated and nearly all put to the sword. Brian also is reported to have defeated twice in one day (24th June 1069) two sons of Harold with great slaughter, when they landed at the north of the river Tivy with a large force from Ireland. The *Norman Chronicle* declares the comte de Vannes (Brian) with Odo, bishop of Bayeux, after the battle of Cardiff, in which the Normans were victorious but suffered great loss, retired with the remainder of the forces to Caerleon. Count Brian was quite probably the father of Brian FitzCount, by Lucie, sister of Hamelin de Balon.[3]

Cle., I, 126. Plan., I, 178–267 ; II, 116.
[1] *Vide* Le Comte Alain Le Roux.
[2] *Hist. de Bretagne*, Lobineau.   [3] *Vide* Hamelin de Balon ; Robert d'Ouilli.

LE COMTE ALAIN LE ROUX.

Alain Le Roux was the second son of Eudes, count de Penthièvre and Agnes, daughter of Alain Cagnart, comte de Cornowaille, and great-grandson of Richard I, duke of Normandy. He was created the first earl of Richmond by the Conqueror and received the domain of earl Edwin, son of Algar, in the county of York, as his reward for participation in the conquest. He built the castle of Richmond and died unmarried in 1089, being succeeded in his possessions by his brother, count Alain Le Noir.

Vide references to Alain Fergant.

ALRIC LE COQ. Alricus Coquuis held lands in Buckinghamshire in 1086 (Domesday), and derived his name Le Coq, or Coquuis, from the office of comptroller of the Conqueror, whom he followed to the conquest of England. Rodbertus Cocus held lands at Estraites in Kent from Hugh de Montfort in 1086 (Domesday), and Hugh his grandson witnessed a charter of Folkestone priory in 1137.[1] Guillelmus Cocus witnessed a charter in favour of the abbey of Jumièges in 1077[2] and also two c. 1080.[3] Another William Cocus occurs in one to the same abbey between 1177 and 1183.[4] The family appears until the 15th century, at which period a branch settled in Gloucestershire and Worcestershire, from whom descended the earls Somers.

Rech. Domesd., 119, 263-7. *Nor. Peo.*, 203.
[1] *Mon.*, i, 560.   [2] *Chart. Abb. Jumièges,* I, 83.   [3] *Ibid.*, I, 106-7.   [4] *Ibid.*, II, 41.

ANDRÉ DE VITRIE. There is a Vitré, Vitrie or Vitry in Brittany, and a Vitray-sous-l'Aigle, arrd. of Mortain, Normandy. Wace mentions "cil de Vitrie" (ll. 13604 and 13705), but there is nothing to indicate whether he refers to the same or different persons. André de Vitrie married Agnes, daughter of Robert, comte de Mortain, the half-brother of the Conqueror,[1] and is probably the companion of duke William to whom Wace refers. He therefore doubtless came from Vitray-sous-l'Aigle. Their son Robert received from his grandfather, comte de Mortain, all the land the latter held in Trugny, Nicey and Vercreuil, Normandy. His son, Robert de Vitrie, called the younger, married Emma, daughter of Alain de Dinan ; and Eleanor, their only daughter, married, 1, William, son of Fulk Painel ; 2, Gilbert Crispin V, baron de Tillières, who was killed in the Crusades in 1191, before St-Jean d'Acre; 3, William Fitz Patrick, earl of Salisbury ; and, 4, Gilbert de Malmaines, who had a son Thomas by a former marriage, who married Joanna, a daughter of Eleanor and Gilbert Crispin de Tillières.[2] Eleanor is generally believed to have been the mother of Ella, sole daughter and heir of her third husband

the earl of Salisbury, who became the wife of William Longuespee, son of the Fair Rosamond, by Henry II. André de Vitrie was a benefactor of Hambie and Robert de Vitrie possessed half the fief of Rye-en-Bessin, and other lands in le Bocage, at the end of the 12th century. William de Vitrie appears in a charter recorded in the *Monasticon Anglican.* The historians of Brittany claim that Robert, seigneur de Vitrie (Ille-et-Vilaine), grandson of Rivallon-le-Vicaire, is the person indicated by Wace. It is quite possible that both André and Robert were at Senlac, since Wace has recorded the name in two different places. There is considerable information on this family in Bowles' *History of Laycock Abbey.*[3]

Wace, Taylor, 221. Le Prevost, *Notes, Wace,* II, 243. Cle., II, 247. Plan., II, 300.
[1] *Chron. de Torigny,* I, 319 ; II, 46.   [2] Stapleton, II, xlvi.   [3] Bowles, 264.

ANSCOUL DE PICQUIGNI. Picquigny in Picardy is near Amiens where a castle dating from the 8th century was the head of a barony from which this family, descending in the female line from Charlemagne, took its name. It was one of the greatest houses in that part of France, and some centuries later was elevated to a duchy for the Chaulnes. Anscoul, his brother Giles, and his son William de Picquigni, followed duke William to the conquest. Anscoul became sheriff of Surrey and died before 1086, but his son William Fitz Anscoul held 100 manors in different counties, including eleven baronies. William is variously reported to have died without issue, or to have had a daughter Beatrice, who married Fulk Painel. Giles is entered in Domesday as "Gilo frater Ansculfi," holding in capite in four counties. His barony of Wedon in Northamptonshire was called Wedon-Pinkney and consisted of fourteen and a half knights' fees. He founded there a cell to the monastery of St-Lucien, France. The name appears on the lists of Guillaume Tailleur and Léopold Delisle.

Nor. Peo., 363. Cle., III, 8. Dugdale, Banks, Bouquet. *Mag. Brit. Berksh.*, 178. *Collect. on Worcesters.*, Nash, I, 358. *Rech. Domesd.*, 173-4. *Introd. Domesd.*, I, 215.

ANSGER DE MONTAIGU. From the parish of Montaigu-les-Bois, in the arrondissement of Coutances, commune of Gavray. Ansger de Montaigu, with his brother Dreu, came to England at the conquest in the train of the earl of Mortain. The former held lands in chief in the counties of Devon and Somerset, and as an under-tenant of the count of Mortain in Dorset, and of the bishop of Coutances in the same county. It is apparent that he died without posterity, as there is no record of any in England. Dreu, his brother, held several manors in Somerset, among which were Shipton and Sutton. The first was his seat, which was later called Shepton-Montague, and the latter was designated Sutton-Montague. He was the father of William de Montagu, who succeeded him towards the end of the reign of Henry I. He left much posterity in England, among whom were the earls of Salisbury as well as the dukes of Montagu and Manchester. The name appears on the Dives roll, as well as that of Leland.

Rech. Domesd., 179 and fol. Cle., II, 284. *Nor. Peo.*, 336. *History of Somersetsh.*, Collinson, I, 49–93, 99, 312. *Ext. Baron*, Banks, III, 649. Dupont, I, 60.

ANQUETIL DE ROS. The name Ros is derived from the parish of Ros, now Rots, near Caen. The family was numerous at the time of the conquest, when five of the name, Anquetil, Ansgot, Goisfrid, Serlo and Guillaume, followed duke William to England. All are entered in Domesday, but their relationship has not been determined. William, to whom the Conqueror gave a small barony in Sussex with the abbey of Fécamp in 1079, of which he became the third abbot, was the only tenant-in-chief; the others were under-tenants. Anquetil was an under-tenant of the bishop of Bayeux in the counties of Kent and Surrey, and possessed the manor of Holtune. He held in Herefordshire under Lanfranc, archbishop of Canterbury and from Alain, count of Brittany, in the same county which depended also from the archbishop. He was also a sub-tenant of Robert de Guernon in this county.

Cle., III, 50. *Nor. Peo.*, 382. *Rech. Domesd.*, 161 and fol.

ANSGOT DE ROS. *Vide* Anquetil de Ros.

ARNOUL D'ARDRE. Baldwin I, count of Flanders, built at Ardes a castle of the same name, which is situated in the county of Guines near Saint-Omer and Boulogne (Pas de Calais). This branch of the family became extinct in France c. 1293. Arnoul d'Ardre accompanied count Eustache of Boulogne, probably his kinsman, to the conquest of England in 1066, and held large estates under him in Cambridge and Bedford in 1086 (Domesday). In 1165 William de Arden held a fief in Kent, Helias de Arden held in Somerset and Thomas de Arden in Essex,[1] while in the 13th century Ralph de Arden of Essex held a fief from the honour of Pevrel.[2] The family was connected with the barons of Ixworth in Suffolk.[3] M. Léopold Delisle carries the name of Arnoul d'Ardre on the Dives list.

Rech. Domesd., 205. Cle., I, 29. *Nor. Peo.*, 171. Dupont, I, 163.
[1] *Lib. Nig.* [2] *Testa*, III, 64. [3] *Mon.*, ii, 184.

AUBRI DE COUCI. From Coucy near Laon, dept. Aisne, Normandy. Alberic de Coucy had issue Drogo, sire de Coucy, and Boves. He was living in 1059, and had Eguerrand, Robert, Anselm, and Alberic de Coucy or Cocy. The latter held lands in Yorkshire in capite and in Buckinghamshire, and Berkshire as an under-tenant in 1086 (Domesday). Alberic was the father of Ingenulf, whose son Geoffry de Cocy was in Gloucestershire in 1130, and a Richard Cocy or Cose appears in the 12th century. Delisle gives in his list Aubri de Couci, and Duchesne also registers the name.

Nor. Peo., 212. Dupont, II, 104. *Rot. Pip. Mon.*, i, 496.

AUVRAI LE BRETON. This Breton family beyond doubt came to England at the conquest under the banner of Alain Le Roux. Nine of the name are written in Domesday, in consequence of which it is impossible to trace the different genealogies. Auvrai Le Breton held twenty-two lordships of the king in Devon, and is the only member of the family Delisle has recorded as having been present at Hastings. Oger held in Leicester and Lincoln and Goselin, in the counties of Buckingham, Gloucester and Bedford ; Rainald in Sussex ; Tihel in Essex and Norfolk ; Waldeve in Lincoln and Cheshire ; Maigno or Manno in Buckingham and Leicester, and Roger and Thomas in Somerset and Huntingdon. From this family descended Francis Annesley, viscount Valentia, in the reign of James I, and the earls of Anglesey, Mountnorris and Annesley.

Cle., I, 111. *Nor. Peo.*, 140. *Rech. Domesd.*, 131–40.

AUVRECHER D'ANGERVILLE.

From Angerville in the Cotentin. The name appears in abbé de La Rue's *Researches of the Bayeux Tapestry* and on the list of Leopold Delisle. Hubertus de Ansgeville and Rogerius his son are witnesses to a charter in favour of the abbey of Jumièges concerning the fief of Colombrères in 1069.[1] Walter de Angerville occurs in England in 1130. Raoul d'Angoville is recorded in a charter of Mont-St-Michel in 1187.[2] Benedict de Angervilla, the castellan of Osmanville on the river Vire in the Bessin, died in 1180.[3] William d'Angerville received lands at Mesnil in the bailiwick of Orimin in the county of Evreux from King John in 1202,[4] and Robert d'Angerville also occurs in Normandy at this time.[5] The family was among the oldest of Normandy.

Traité de l'Origine des Noms, La Roque, 29. *Nor. Peo.*, 221.
[1] *Chart. Abb. Jumièges*, I, 81. [2] *Chron. de Torigny*, II, 337. [3] Stapleton, I, lxiii. [4] *Ibid.*, II, clxxv. [5] *M.R.S.*, vol. 15.

AVENEL DES BIARDS.

From Les Biards, canton of Isigny, arrondissement of Mortain. This was one of the great houses of Normandy, the Avenels being the hereditary seneschals of the counts of Mortain. The castle of Les Biards in ancient times was a very powerful one, commanding the country round Mortain, but its importance lessened gradually as time wore on. The name appears twice in Wace (l. 13600) as " cil de Biarz " and again as " Des Biarz i fu Avenals " (l. 13632).

According to Vincent de Beauvais, an historian of the 13th century, Harold Avenel was a companion of duke Rollo, and the first of the family to settle in Normandy. His descendant Hervé Avenel, baron of Biards, *c.* 1035, witnessed a charter in favour of the abbey of Marmoutiers and in 1067 another with his son, Sigemberg des Biards. Hervé was the father also of Ormellinus, surnamed Avenellus, who, with the consent of his wife in 1060, made a donation to the church of St-Martin de Say.[1] Sigemberg died without issue and the sons of his brother Ormellinus joined the name of Biards to that of Avenel. William was the eldest son and was the William Avenal, seigneur des Biards, who was seneschal to Robert, count of Mortain, the half-brother of duke William. He was a benefactor to the abbey of St-Pierre-de-la-Couture at Mans [2] and is assumed to have been the companion of the Conqueror referred to by Wace. He was the father of four sons, namely : William, Richard, Robert, and Hugh Avenel. From William descended the Avenals of France, the elder branch of which family became extinct with the death of his great-grandson in the 14th century. His daughter Guillenine brought the barony of des Biards to the family of Le Sotherel. Just how the Avenel of Domesday was connected with this William Avenel is unknown. The name is carried by Guillaume le Tailleur ; Leland, Brampton, Worcester and the Dives' roll record Avenel des Biars.

Plan., II, 198. Cle., III, 353. *Nor. Peo.*, 145–363. *Rech. Domesd.*, 234 and fol. Dupont, I, 16. Le Prevost, *Notes*, *Wace*, II, 247. *Wace*, Taylor, II, 19.
[1] *Gall. Christ.*, Instr. Col., 153. [2] *Ibid.*, IX, Instr., 107.

LE SIRE D'ARGOUGES.

Argouges is on the frontier of Normandy and Brittany. The name is mentioned on the list of l'abbé de La Rue, in his *Researches of the Bayeux Tapestry*, as well as by Delisle. Robert de Harcourt, first of the name called le Fort, married Colette d'Argouges, as is stated by La Roque.[1] In this parish is the Logis du Gault, probably expressed in a charter of duke Robert I under the name of Goolt ; Matthew Paris says that one Gaunt was at the conquest: "M. de Gaunt qui venerat in Angliam ad conquestum et acceperat in sorte retributionis post victorim." [2] Argouges being located on the frontier explains why no names of the seigneurs belonging to this locality are to be found in Domesday [3] as Normandy was always on the point of being invaded by Brittany.[4] For this reason the duke-king built a strong fortress at Saint-James (Manche).[5] This seignior de Gault may be the d'Argouges here indicated. There is not a great deal on record concerning the family, but the French genealogists claim that it extended from the time of the conquest. Roger d'Argences appears in a manuscript of this period ; Robert d'Argences is positively known to have existed in 1106 [6] ; Robert d'Argences was elected cellarer of the abbey of Jumièges in 1177,[7] probably identical with Robert d'Orgences who was abbot there in 1182 [8] ; Richard d'Argences occurs in Normandy in 1197,[9] and Raoul d'-Argouges was living in 1209.[10] Raoul d'Argences, abbé of Fécamp, died in 1219.[11]

[1] La Roque, V, 305 ; vide Robert de Harcourt.　[2] Matthew Paris ; Dupont, I, 5.　[3] Hist. du Mont-Saint-Michel et du Diocèse d'Avranches, Desroches. [4] Dupont, ibid.　[5] Cartulaire du Mont-Saint-Michel, Bibl. d'Avranches MS., 210. [6] Le Prevost, Notes, Wace, Supplement. III, 26.　[7] Chron. de Torigny, II, 75. [8] Chart. Abb. de Jumièges, II, 71.　[9] Ibid., II, 112 ; Stapleton, II, xliv.　[10] Ibid., II, 181 ; Le Prevost, ibid.　[11] Ibid., Note.

LE SIRE D'ANISY. Wace (l. 13551) records "la jovente d'Anisie," which young men came from Anisy near Caen. About 1042 Turstan de Anisy granted certain lands to the monastery of Saint-Vigor, Cherisy, with the consent of Eudo, Ralph and Ranulph his sons.[1] There appears in acts existing in the Norman archives Godefroy d'Anisy, living in 1066 and in 1096. Jean d'Anisy, knight, without doubt his brother or son, accompanied duke Robert Courteheuse to the Crusade in 1096. Ranulph d'Anisy his son who, following an inquiry made by the order of Henry I, held a knight's fee, which was part of the seven held by Roger, viscount of Saint-Sauveur, and

in the same inquiry Turstain d'Anisy under-held from Ranulph, viscount of Bayeux, the parishes of Saint-Manvieux and de Marcellet.[2] We also find members of this family among the benefactors of the abbey of Longues in 1166 and 1189. In most of these acts, they are designated as seigneurs d'-Anisy, de Ver, de Brecy, de Villons and de Feuguerolles. They figure as knights to the court of Caen, and in the exchequer of Normandy.

La Roque, I, 996-7. Des Bois, 1-300. Le Prevost, Notes, Wace, II, 234. Dumoulin, App., 10. Wace, Taylor, 211. Nor. Peo., 220. Rech. Domesd., 270. Anc. Abb. de Norm., Léchaudé d'Anisy, I, 269-71.

[1] Mon., ii, 961.　[2] Arch. du Calvados, II, 427-30.

LE SIRE D'AUBIGNY. This family derived its name from Aubigny, near Periers, in the Cotentin, and Wace (l. 13603) mentions "li boteillier d'-Aubignie." The pedigree commences with Grimoult du Plessis, the traitor of Valognes and Val-Des-Dunes, who died in a dungeon 1047. William d'Aubigny, first of the name, married the sister of Grimoult and had issue Roger, who married Amicia, sister of Geoffry, bishop of Coutances, and of Roger de Montbray (i.e. Mowbray). The latter had issue, William d'Aubigny II, pincerna to Henry I, who married Maud Bigot, daughter of Roger Bigot, and died 1139 ; 2, Richard, abbot of St-Albans ; 3, Nigel, whose son took the name of Mowbray on inheriting the estates of that family ; 4, Humphrey, and finally, Ralph. William d'Aubigny II had issue William III, who married Adeliza, widow of king Henry I of England, in whose right he became the first earl of Arundel of this family,[1] which died out in the male line with Hugh d'-Aubigny, the fourth earl, in 1243, when the earldom passed to his sister, Isabel Fitz Alan.[2] Nigel d'Aubigny, the third son of Roger, became one of the greatest landowners in England and is the only member of the family recorded in Domesday, having received grants of several lordships in Buckingham, Leicester, Bedford and Warwick, as he succeeded to the estates of his father and grandfather. He is reputed to have possessed 120 manors in Normandy and as many in England, including the great domain of the earl of Mowbray, which came to him through his wife, confiscated from his cousin, Robert de Mowbray, earl of Northumberland, given by Henry I, on the condition that their eldest son would take the name of Mowbray. He lived to a very great age, and died in 1138. Opinion differs regarding whom Wace intended. Le Prevost favours Roger, Taylor prefers William I or Roger, and Planché believes both were at Hastings, which is undoubtedly correct. Burke and other genealogists erroneously state it was William II Pincerna, but he was a child, if indeed born, in 1066. Roger made a donation to the abbey of Lessay in 1084 [3] and died about this time, for he is not entered in Domesday.

Plan., II, 93. Burke, 16. Cle., I, 38; III, 265. *Wace*, Taylor, 221. Le Prevost, *Notes, Wace*, II, 243. *Rech. Domesd.*, 96, 218-19.
[1] *Roger of Wendover*, 491. [2] *Vide* Alain Fitz Flaald and Roger de Montgomery. [3] *Gall. Christ.*, XI, c. 236, D, and 247, C; *Mon.*, i, 593.

LE SIRE D'AUVILLERS. There is an Auvillers in the arrondissement of Pont Lévêque, and one in Mortimer-sur-Eaulne. The "sire d'Auviler" of Wace (l. 13748), the companion of the Conqueror, undoubtedly came from the latter place, since the sires d'Auvillers were vassals and companions in arms of the family of Mortimer, and Wace describes this personage as "charging in company with Hugh de Mortemer." The family then settled in the former place was allied to the house of Tournebu. Hugh d'Auvillers was a benefactor of the priory of Eye and is mentioned in the foundation charter in the reign of the Conqueror. He appears as a vassal of Robert Malet in Suffolk and was probably the warrior at Senlac.

Le Prevost, *Notes, Wace*, II, 264. Plan., II, 281. La Roque, I, 782.

BAUDOIN DE MEULES ET du SAP. Meules is in the arrondissement of Lisieux and Sap in that of Argentan,

Normandy. Wace (l. 13668) mentions "cil de Sap," which he undoubtedly intended for Baudoin de Meules et du Sap, variously styled Baldwin Fitz Gilbert, Baldwin the viscount, Baldwin of Exeter, and Baldwin de Brionne or Brionis, since he possessed Sap at the time of the conquest, also this name almost immediately follows that of Richard d'Orbec (et de Bienfaite) his brother. He is not referred to elsewhere by Wace, although Le Prevost believes he was, as "sire de Riviers," but this supposition has been thoroughly refuted.[1] Baldwin was the younger son of Gilbert, count of Brionne and Eu, whose father Godfry, also count of Brionne and Eu, was the son of Richard I, duke of Normandy.[2] When Baldwin was a youth, his father, one of the guardians of young duke William, was murdered between 1036 and 1040, at which time he and his brother Richard fled to the court of Baldwin, count of Flanders, where they remained until 1053-4, when the marriage of duke William to Mathilda, the daughter of count Baldwin, occurred. The duke then, at the solicitation of his father-in-law, gave Meules and Sap to Baldwin to recompense him for the loss of his proportion of his father's estates, which had been confiscated and joined to the ducal possessions.[3] For his participation in the battle of Senlac and his other just claims upon duke William he was granted vast domains in the west of England, consisting of 164 manors, 159 of which were in the county of Devon; besides 19 houses in Exeter, and a site within the walls, where he built the great Rougemont castle which required the removal of 48 houses. He was appointed governor of the city and hereditary sheriff of Devonshire, receiving also the barony of Okehampton, where he built his castle, which Albreda his wife, the daughter of an aunt of the Conqueror, (et filiam amitæ suæ uxorem dedit,) brought to him in marriage. Baldwin was of great service to king William in keeping this part of England in subjection, a very large benefactor to the church both in England and Normandy, and died about 1090. He had issue by his wife Albreda, Richard, Robert, and William, and was the father of a natural son, Guiger, who was shorn a monk, and is said also to have had three daughters. His wife having predeceased him, he married secondly Emma, mentioned by the Conqueror in two charters of Holy Trinity of Caen, one in 1066 and the other in 1082. Which of his wives was the mother of his three daughters is unrecorded. His son and heir, Richard Fitz Baldwin, succeeded him as sheriff of Devon, and in the barony of Okehampton. He died without issue in 1137, when Adeliza his sister became invested with the family possessions and estates. She married Randolph Avenel by whom she had an only child Maud, who inherited the estates, and was married twice, first to Robert d'Avranches (de Abrancis) and secondly to Robert Fitz Edith, a natural son of Henry I; by her first husband, she had one daughter Hawise; by her second another named Maud. These children were committed to the custody of Reginald de Courtenay, by king Henry II. Reginald himself married the elder and the other daughter he gave to his son William by a former wife.[4] These possessions and estates were joined with those of the Redvers-Vernon family, by the marriage of Robert de Courtenay to lady Mary, daughter of William de Vernon, 6th earl of Devon. Lady Mary married secondly sir Peter Prouz of Eastervale, afterwards of Changford, Devonshire, from whom descended Thomasine Prouz or Prouse, who married c. 1330 sir John de Chudleigh.[5] This genealogy differs slightly from that recorded by Edmonson, while Pole asserts that the register of Ford abbey, which contains the family records, is false. Cleaver in his *History of the House of Courtenay* points out that Richard, son of Baldwin de Brionis, died without issue and that Dugdale has confounded the two families of de Brionis and Redvers, the first being hereditary sheriffs of Devon, and the latter created earls of Devon by king Henry I. Nevertheless, these authors name Hawise and Maud as the eventual heiresses of Baldwin, who conveyed their estates to the Courtenays through marriage. Banks in the *Dormant and Extinct Baronage* has apparently followed Dugdale, for he has fallen into the same error.[6] They both ignore

altogether Richard de Redvers[7] who died in 1107.[8]

Stapleton, II, cxxxvi. *Cokayne's Complete Peerage of England*, Vicary Gibbs, I, 269. Plan., II, 40. Le Prevost, *Notes, Wace*, II, 255. *Wace*, Taylor, 233. Cle., II, 307; III, 60. *Nor. Peo.*, 145. *Mag. Brit. Devon*, Lysons, 1, note. *Introd. Domesd.*, I, 377, note.
[1] *Vide* Richard de Reviers.   [2] *Vide* Richard de Bienfaite.   [3] Ord. Vit., Le Prevost, III, 340. Forester, II, 490.   [4] Plan., II, 40. Cle., II, 307; III, 60.   [5] *Cokayne, ibid.*, IV, 309, 315, 316, 335; *The Baronage of England*, Dugdale, I, 255, 636, 732. *Harleian MS.* printed in *Lipscomb's Hist. of the County of Buckingham; Visitation of the County of Devon*, Vivian, 189–90.   [6] *The Baronage of England*, Dugdale, I, 254; *Baronag. Genealog.*, Edmonson. Banks, D. & E., III, 243–4 and note; *Some Account of the Barony and Town of Okehampton*, Wright, 15–16.   [7] *Ibid.*, note 1.   [8] *Vide* App. 24.

BERENGER GIFFARD.   *Vide* Comte de Longueville.

BERNARD DE NEUFMARCHÉ.
From the castle of Neufmarché, in the canton of Gournay en Bray arrondissement of Neufchâtel, Normandy. Turquetil de Neufmarché was murdered in the civil wars of Normandy, c. 1035,[1] probably at the instigation of Raoul de Gacé. The strong castle of Neufmarché was seized, c. 1060, by duke William to the prejudice of its inheritor, Geoffrey de Neufmarché.[2] Bernard de Neufmarché was a companion in arms of the Conqueror whom he accompanied to the battle of Hastings and c. 1088 subdued the territory of Brecknock in Wales. In the same year he granted lands in Brecknock to sir Reginald Aubrey.[3] Bernard "continued in the career of arms till an advanced age and served in the wars under three kings of England with great bravery."[4]

Nor. Peo., 144–344. Cle., II, 351.
[1] Ord. Vit., II, 403.   [2] *Ibid.*, I, 455.   [3] *Ibid.*, II, 267.   [4] *Ibid.*

BERNARD DE SAINT - OUEN.
This family came from Saint-Andoen, near Arques, Normandy, which was held by William de Saint-Andoen, under the baron of Tancarville c. 1150. Nicholas, abbé of Saint-Ouen (Sancto

Audoeno), furnished twenty ships and one hundred men to the fleet of the Norman duke.[1] The brothers Bernard and Germond de Saint-Ouen followed duke William to the conquest of England, probably under the banner of William d'Arques (viscount of Arques and Rouen), the chief seat of William's barony was Folkestone in Kent. Bernard (Bernardus de Andoeno Sancto) in 1086 (Domesday) held under the latter in this county as well as in Suffolk, where he left posterity which obtained for several generations. Germond held under the barony of Geoffry de Mandeville in Herefordshire and at the time of the formation of Domesday figured in the hundred of Odesy in the same county as a juror, which document still exists. There was a Saint-Ouen among the commissioners who presided at the compilation of the Domesday book,[2] and Gilbert Saint-Ouen was a witness of Philip de Briouse concerning an agreement made at Salisbury in January, 1103, between the latter and William de Ros, third abbot of Fécamp.[3]

L. Delisle carries Bernard de Saint-Ouen on the Dives roll. *Rech. Domesd.*, 228–30. *Nor. Peo.*, 199.
[1] *MS. list of Taylor.* Le Prevost, *Notes, Wace*, II, 531.   [2] *MS. Cotton*, Brit. Mus., A. VI, fo. 38.   [3] *Mon.*, iii, 972.

BERNARD DE SAINT-VALÉRY.
From Saint-Valéry-sur-Somme, Normandy. Gilbert, advocate of Saint-Valéry, married Papia, daughter of Richard II, duke of Normandy, by whom he had two sons, Bernard and Richard. Bernard is positively stated by August Le Prevost, which opinion is concurred in by Edgar Taylor and Delisle, as having been the "sire de Saint Galeri" whose presence at Hastings is mentioned by Wace (l. 13827). This conclusion is supported by the fact that Walter de Saint-Valéry, his son, held extensive estates in 1086 (Domesday), among which was the manor of Isleworth, Middlesex. Since Bernard does not appear in Domesday, it is assumed that he died before the compilation of that survey. Orderic Vital has recorded considerable information concerning this family because they were great benefactors to the abbey

of Saint-Evroult, where he spent his life and Guillaume Tailleur records him on his roll. Ranulph de Saint-Valéry, reported to have accompanied Jean d'Ivri and Robert d'Ouilli to the conquest, was the father or brother of Guy de Saint-Walery (Valéry), who received in 1110 by gift of Henry I the barony of Waleries (Saint-Valéry) with Ambrosden, Beckley and other places which had reverted to the crown on the death of Geoffry of Ivry, son of the above mentioned Jean.[1]

Plan., II, 207. *Nor. Peo.*, 429. Cle., 1–342. Le Prevost, *Notes, Wace*, II, 272. *Wace*, Taylor, 246. Ord. Vit., II, 262 to 266.
[1] *Hist. of Wallingford*, Hedges, I, 227.

BERTRAN DE VERDUN. A
Norman baronial name from Verdun, near Avranches. Bertrand de Verdun came to England in 1066 and in 1086 was a Domesday baron, holding Farnham Royal in Buckinghamshire. On the day of the coronation he provided a glove for the king's right hand and supported his right arm during the service so long as his monarch held the royal sceptre. In 1095 he attested a charter of William Rufus to St-Mary's abbey, York, and served as sheriff of that county in 1100. William and Bertran de Verdun (sons of Normand) appear in a charter of the abbey of Mont-Saint-Michel in 1158 [1] and William, probably the same, occurs in two of the abbey of Jumièges, one in 1187 and the other in 1188.[2] The name appears in the *Researches of the Bayeux Tapestry* by l'abbé de La Rue, and on the Dives list.

Cle., III, 221. *Nor. Peo.*, 431.
[1] *Chron. de Torigny*, II, 240.   [2] *Chart. Abb. Jumièges*, II, 87–97.

LE SIRE DE BAILLEUL. There
seems to be very little on record concerning this sire de Bailleul, whose name appears in the *Researches of the Bayeux Tapestry* of the abbé de La Rue. Léopold Delisle mentions Renaud de Bailleul on the Dives roll and Guillaume Tailleur chronicles Pierre de Bailleul, seigneur de Fécamp. Remigius almoner of Fécamp, afterwards bishop of Lincoln, and one of the

itinerant commissioners for the compilation of the Domesday survey, for the vicinity of Berkshire, Oxfordshire, etc.,[1] may or may not have been the personage here intended.[2] He contributed, according to Taylor's list, one ship and twenty men-at-arms to duke William's fleet,[3] and died in 1091.[4] Whatever was the christian name of this de Bailleul, however, it appears that he was the seigneur of Fécamp at the time of the conquest, if the statement of Guillaume Tailleur can be credited.

Cle., II, 73. Plan., II, 238.
[1] *The Baronage of England*, Dugdale, I, 59. [2] *Roger of Wendover*, Giles ed., I, 350. [3] Le Prevost, *Notes, Wace*, II, 530. [4] *Roger of Wendover*, 362. *Vide* Gautier d'Aincourt.

LE SIRE DE BEVILLE et d'YVELIN. From Beuville, near Caen. The name is variously spelled : Beaville, Bevill, Beville, Boiville, Biville, Boville, Boeville, Beeville and Buvilla. Humphrey de Buiville held a barony in Herefordshire and William de Bocvilla was an under-tenant in Suffolk. Léopold Delisle, in recording these personages as present at Senlac, spells the name Biville. Gilbert's *Cornwall* states " The first Bevill at the conquest was an officer under the earl of Morton and Cornwall, one of whose descendants married a Gwairnick heiress. Philip de Boville, perhaps the son of William, the mesne-lord here mentioned, gave lands to Wykes priory in Essex during the reign of Henry I, and a William de Boville occurs in Essex and Hertfordshire in 1130.[1] Paul de Boville lived in the following reign and in 1165 Otwell de Boville held lands in Essex. Helias de Boyvill and William de Buiville appear in Gloucester and Buckinghamshire.[2] Matthew de Beyvill witnessed a charter of Henry II.[3] Richard de Bevill was seneschal to the archbishop of York in 1301.[4] The family was widely spread in England, having been located in at least eleven different counties. The name occurs on the lists of Holinshed, Leland and Brompton, while Worcester records Butevile.

Cle., I, 157. *Nor. Peo.*, 155, 169–70.
[1] *Rot. Pip.* [2] *Lib. Nig.* [3] *Mon.*, ii, 247. [4] *Ibid.*, 45.

LE SIRE DE BOLLEVILLE. From Belleville, or Bella Villa near Dieppe, now called Belle-ville-sur-Mer. This family in the latter part of the last century was represented by the marquis de Belleville, who was seated at Pont-Tranquart, near Dieppe. In England the name frequently occurs as Boleville and Bolleville. Brompton, in recording the family as present at Senlac, spells it Bolvyle. On the list of Duchesne the name appears as Botvile, and Etienne Dupont, in his *Recherches Hist. sur les Comp. de Guillaume le Conqt.*, states " Les seigneurs de Bolleville took part in the conquest of England." Robert de Boleville, in 1165, held of the earl of Gloucester in that county,[1] and Godfry de Bellavalle is mentioned in Essex, 1194–8.[2] Ralph de Bellavilla in the time of Richard I was a benefactor of Vaudrey Abbey, Lincoln.[3]

Nor. Peo., 156. Cle., III, 360.
[1] *Lib. Nig.* [2] *R.C.R.* [3] *Mon.*, i, 833.

LE SIRE DE BONNESBOSQ. From Bonnesbosq, arrondissement of Pont l'Evêque. The "sire de Bonnesboz" of Wace (l. 13667) has not been satisfactorily identified, for which reason it is possible that he may have fallen in the battle of Hastings. Ralph de Bonnesbosq was a benefactor of St-Stephen at Caen, and under Henry I Gilbert de Bonnesbosq, son-in-law of Morin du Pin, was dapifer of the earl of Mortain. William de Bonnebosq and his son Robert appear in a charter of the abbey of Jumièges in 1138 [1] and Robert de Bonnebosq, possibly the latter, occurs in two in 1171–8 to this abbey.[2] The name appears on the list of Guillaume Tailleur.

Plan., II, 282. Le Prevost, *Notes, Wace*, II, 255. *Wace*, Taylor, 233.
[1] *Chart. Abb. Jumièges*, I, 161. [2] *Ibid.*, II, 9–26.

SIRE DE BOSC-ROARD. Simon de Bosco-Roardo was lord of Stathern in Leicestershire, Clifton in Buckinghamshire and Okley in Bedfordshire at the time of the conquest.[1] De Bois-Robert or Roard, of whom Robert de Bois and his brother held estates in Buckinghamshire in 1086 (Domesday), belonged to one of the numerous branches of this family, one of which, Bois or Bosco, held lands in South Elham from the conquest, as appears by a suit at Ipswich, 1285.[2]

Cle., I, 88 ; III, 80. *Nor. Peo.*, 390. [1] *Leicestersh.*, Nichol. [2] *Coll. Suffolk*, Davy, XXXV. *Vide* Guillaume du Bosc.

SIRE DE BOUTTEVILLAIN. The " Bolevilain " of Wace (l. 13711), companion of the Conqueror at Hastings, is not recorded in Domesday, for which reason it is concluded that he either died in the conflict or before the compilation of that work. The family was seated in Northampton and Norfolk, one of whom, Guillaume Boutevileyn, founded in 1143 the abbey of Pipewell in the former county. Several others are found in this county a little later. Leland has Buttevillain, Brompton, Boutevilain, and Fox and Stow, Boutevillain. M. de Gerville, in his *Recherches*,[1] certifies that sire de Boutteville from the arrondissement of Valognes, was at the conquest, and this family established itself in Somerset and Bedford. It was long of great consequence in England, and the name appears on the roll of Battle abbey as Boutevile. The burden of opinion seems to be that Bouttevillain and Boutteville are separate families.

Plan., II, 282. Cle., I, 87. *Nor. Peo.* 168-83. Le Prevost, *Notes, Wace*, II, 260. *Wace*, Taylor, 237. [1] *Rech.*, de Gerville, 24.

LE SEIGNEUR DE BRECEY. From Brecy, near Caen. Three noble families of this name existed in Normandy and Radulphus de Braceio, who occurred in a Norman charter of 1082,[1] was probably the member of the family at the conquest. William, his son, held Wisteston in Cheshire of the barony of Nantwich, Robert his grandson, held three knights' fees in that county, from William Malbank, baron of Nantwich, his uncle.[2] There were many branches of the family, which spread in different parts of England, from whence the Brasseys of to-day are descended.

Nor. Peo., 171. Cle., I, 136. [1] *Gall. Christ.*, XI, 86. [2] *Chesh.*, Ormerod, III, 177.

LE SIRE DE BRUCOURT. Wace (l. 13773) chronicles " sire de Briencort," but there is no such place in Normandy though Le Prevost supposes it was intended for Brucourt, arrondissement of Pont Lévêque. Very little is known of the family at the time of the conquest. A Robert de Brucourt confirmed grants by Geoffry de Fervaques to Walsingham, and about the same time a Gilbert de Brucourt gave lands at Fervaques to the abbey of Val-Richer. Gilbert de Bruecourt and Hugh, his son, appear in a charter to Troarm.[1] The family long continued in Normandy and " Robertus de Briencurt "[2] and " Robertus de Brincurt,"[3] no doubt the same, appears in different places in the dedication of the fiefs of Mont-Saint-Michel in 1172. Duchesne mentions three of the name one of whom, Henry de Bruecourt, held a fee ; of the Foeda de Hiesmes. It is given as Briencourt in the *Liber Niger*, where we find Robert de Briencourt holding three fees of the honour of Clare in Suffolk, and Geoffry de Briencourt one fee of earl Ferrers in Derby. He also held lands of the Pevrels in Kent, Leicester, Notts and Derby.[4] Baldwin de Brencurt held land in Wytham, Lincolnshire, of the heirs of Hugh Wac[5] and was a benefactor of Spalding priory. His son, John, is mentioned in the time of Edward I.[6]

Plan., II, 282. Cle., III, 360. *Nor. Peo.*, 174. Le Prevost, *Notes, Wace*, II, 267. *Wace*, Taylor, 241. [1] *M.S.A.N.*, VIII, 238. [2] *Chron. de Torigny*, II, 297. [3] *Ibid.*, II, 302. [4] *Rot. Pip.* [5] *Testa de Neville.* [6] *Rotul. Hundred.*

CORBET LE NORMAND. The family came from Pays de Caux, Normandy, and according to Blakely, ascended from a very remote antiquity, probably of Scandinavian origin. Corbet Le Normand had four sons, Hugue, Roger, Reynaud, and Robert, the second and fourth sons, Roger and Robert, came to the conquest of England with their father, while Hugue and Reynaud remained in Normandy, where the former is mentioned in charters of the abbey of Bec, and Reynaud with his sons Robert and Guy were in Palestine in 1096. Roger and Robert were known in Normandy before

the conquest by the surname of Moreton and are so inscribed upon the
Falaise tablet, although after their
arrival in England they were designated
as FitzCorbet or Corbet.[1] With his
two sons, Corbet settled in Shropshire
where they assisted Roger de Montgomery in the government of his earldom of Shrewsbury and the former died
before the compilation of Domesday.[2]
Roger FitzCorbet at that time held
24 lordships, while Robert possessed 14,
all of which were in Shropshire. In
1102 Roger FitzCorbet defended Bridgnorth for Robert de Belèsme against the
forces of king Henry[3] but three months
later was compelled to surrender it to
the king.[4] Roger built a castle at
Alfreton, which was the head of his
barony and named Caux from Pays de
Caux, his former home in Normandy.
It was one of the border fortresses
which stood in a strong position commanding the pass of the valley of the
Rea. From him descended Peter Corbet
of Caux castle, summoned to parliament as a baron by Edward I, and hence
the Corbets of Moreton-Corbet. Robert
FitzCorbet his brother held Longden
and Alcester in Warwickshire, but
his male line died out in the following generation. From him descended
through the female line the Herberts,
earls of Pembroke, Finches, earls of
Winchelsea, and the earls of Huntingdon. Annora, sister of Alice, co-heir
of Robert Corbet, who married William
Botterill, was the mother of Reginald,
earl of Cornwall, by Henry I. The
name appears on the rolls of Worcester,
Brompton, Holinshed, Duchesne,
Scriven and Dives.

Eyton, IV, 351. Cle., I, 219. Nor. Peo.,
135, 167, 209, 348. Burke, 39, and Dugdale.
[1] L'Europe au Moyen-Age, Henry Wal-
lam, French translation by Dudouit and
Borghers in 8vo, 1828, II, 67. Généalogie
de la Maison Guigues de Moreton, de
Chabrillan by Laine. [2] Ord. Vit., For.
ed., II, 48. [3] Ibid., III, 334. [4] Ibid.,
III, 336.

LE SIRE DE CANOUVILLE. This
family probably is identical with Conovill,
and the Walter Conovill who witnessed
the foundation charter of Robert Malet
to the priory of Eye recorded in the
Monasticon Anglican may have been
the companion of the Conqueror. John
de Kenouill of Gloucestershire occurs
in Rotuli Curia Regis of 1200. Gilbert
de Conoville appears in Devonshire in
the time of Edward I.[1] Radulfo de
Keneuvile at about the same period
witnessed a charter of Ralph de Rosei
in Norfolk and Willielmus de Kenovilla
witnessed a grant to the abbey of Saint-
Georges de Bocherville in Normandy
about 1191. The name de Canouville
is recorded in the Researches of the
Bayeux Tapestry of the abbé de La
Rue and is also chronicled on the
Dives roll. The family continued later
in both England and Normandy.

Cle., I, 249.
[1] R.H.

SIRE DE CINTHEAUX. The " de
Sainteals" in Wace (l. 13653) refers to
Cintheaux, a commune now called by
that name, which is near Gouvix,
arrondissement of Falaise, but its
possessor in 1066 has not been determined. In 1081 it belonged to Robert
Marmion, who gave the church there
to the abbey of Barbery, of whom a
Cintheaux may have been an under-
tenant at the time of the conquest.

Plan., II, 294. Le Prevost, Notes, Wace,
II, 251. Wace, Taylor, 230.

LE SIRE DE CLINCHAMPS. This
family appears to have come from
Trévières, between Bayeux and Caen.
The name continued in Normandy
until 1138, when Ranulph de Clin-
champ assumed that of Travers. The
family of Travers was of considerable
importance in England at the time of
the conquest. Le sire de Clinchamps
is recorded as present at Hastings in
the Researches of the Bayeux Tapestry
by l'abbé de La Rue, and Delisle
registers the name on the Dives roll.

Nor. Peo., 422. Cle., III, 203.

SIRE de COUVERT. Couvert in
the Bessin, Normandy, was held by the
service of one knight's fee of the barony
of Braiose, and the Couverts possessed
lands in Sussex from the time of the
conquest, in which battle l'abbé de
La Rue in his Researches of the Bayeux
Tapestry registers the opinion that they

participated. Although the identity of the member of the family here intended has not been established, it may have been the William de Cuvert who witnessed the foundation charter of Barnstable in 1107.[1] William Gubert (Cuvert) held a fee of William de Courcy in Somerset in 1165.[2] Couvert in 1172 was in the possession of William de Braiose, for at that time he returned his services as three knights and one knight.[3] From this family descended lord Heytesbury.[4]

Nor. Peo., 134.
[1] *Mon.*, i, 684. [2] *Lib. Nig.* [3] Stapleton, I, clxxii. [4] *Wiltsh.*, Hoare, Hist. Heytesbury, 120, 129.

LE SIRE DE CUSSY. Le sire de Cussy, from the parish of that name in Normandy, a companion of the Conqueror mentioned by l'abbé de La Rue in the *Researches of the Bayeux Tapestry*, possesses an obscure identity. Léopold Delisle likewise supports the opinion of the presence of an individual of this name at the conquest of England. The fee of Cussy was held by Gislebert de Montfichet in the latter part of the 12th century.

Stapleton, I, lix ; II, cclxiii.

DREU DE LA BEUVRIÈRE. Dreu de La Beuvrière was a Fleming of high standing, who, according to the book of Meaux and the register of Fountains abbey, came to England at the conquest, for which he received the isle of Holderness, where he erected the strong castle of Skipsey. He was the recipient of considerable other estates in various counties, among which was Bytham in Lincolnshire. Dreu is said to have married a kinswoman of the Conqueror, whom he killed in 1086, whether by accident or intent does not appear. However, he hastened to king William and pretending that he needed money to take his wife to Flanders, borrowed what he was able to get from the king and hastily made his exit from England. His possessions were immediately confiscated by king William and he died later dishonoured and in want in his native land.

Plan., I, 127. *Rech. Domesd.*, 95.

DREU DE MONTAIGU. *Vide* Ansger de Montaigu.

DURAND MALET. *Vide* Guillaume Malet de Graville.

LE SIRE DE DRIENCOURT. Wace (l. 13772) chronicles " de Driencourt." The original name of Neufchatel-en-Bray was Drincourt (Driencuria), which was changed when Henry I built a castle there in 1106 to Neufchatel-en-Drincort. A sire de Drincourt was killed in the battle of Hastings,[1] which may account for the fact that the family did not appear in England, unless it is the same as Daincurt, of *Domesday Introd.* Drincourt or Driencourt has sometimes been confused with Drucourt, variously styled Drocourt, Droecourt, Druolcurt, Drolcort and Dricourt, located in the arrondissement of Bernay, canton of Thiberville, which formed part of a vast domain of William Crispin I in the diocese of Lisieux with Livarot as the main seat. His son and heir, William Crispin II, gave the church of Drucourt to the abbey of Bec before 1070, with the tithes, the patrimony and all its dependencies.[2] At the end of the 12th century the seigniory of Drucourt had passed from the Crispin family to Enguerrand de Drucourt, who sold it to Roger de Mortimer in 1195.[3] The Aincourts, from a town of that name in the canton of Magny (Seine-et-Oise), are still another family.[4]

Dugdale, I, 385. *Wace*, Taylor, 241. Stapleton, I, xxxviii. Plan., II, 236. Le Prevost, *Notes, Wace*, II, 267.
[1] *Rec. sur le Bray Normand et le Bray Picard*, I, 233. [2] *Le Prevost Mem.*, II, 17 ; Bibl. nat. lat., 12884, fo. 83, and lat., 13905, fo. 115 ; *Statistique Monumentale du Calvados*, de Caumont, V, 674. [3] Bouquet, XXII, 752 ; *Le Prevost Mem.*, II, 17 ; *Dict. de l'Eure*, I, 955. [4] *Vide* Gautier d'Aincourt ; Porée, I, 384.

ENGENOULF DE l'AIGLE. Engenoulf de l'Aigle was the son of Fulvert de Beine, founder of the castle of l'Aigle, on the river Risle, arrondissement of Mortagne, Orne. Wace (l. 13592) calls him " Engerran de Laigle," and Orderic Vital,[1] confirms his presence at Hastings, saying that he, with many others, in charging the English, fell into an ancient ditch and was killed. He married Richeveride, by whom he was the father of three sons, Roger, who was slain about the year 1060 [2]; Richard, who was at the conquest (sometimes called de Aquila), obtained the barony of Pevensey in Sussex, with other large estates, and was killed by an arrow shot in the eye at the siege of the castle of Saint-Susanne in 1085 [3]; the third son, Gilbert, stood high in the favour of duke Robert Courtheuse, who gave him the castle of Exmes, and made him vicomte of that county. He was mortally wounded when Gerrard Chevreuil and Robert de Ferrers attempted to capture him in 1092 and was buried at Saint-Sulpice.[4] Thus all the sons of Engenoulf met with a violent death.

Plan., II, 159. *Nor. Peo.*, 226. Le Prevost, *Notes, Wace,* II, 242. *Wace,* Taylor, 218.

[1] Ord. Vit., I, 486.   [2] *Ibid.,* I, 427.
[3] *Ibid.,* II, 379.   [4] *Ibid.,* II, 485.

ERRAND DE HARCOURT. This family is one of the most illustrious in both France and England. Errand is mentioned by La Roque, the French historian of this great house, Père Anselm, and other genealogists as the personage referred to by Wace (l. 13769) which reads "sire de Herevourt was there also, riding a very swift horse." They are not supported in this conclusion by Le Prevost, as he favours Anchetil, the father of Errand, or Robert, his younger brother. The burden of opinion is, however, against this eminent historian. Turquetil, seigneur de Turqueville, and de Tanqueraye, *c.* 1001, appears in several charters concerning the abbeys of Fécamp and Bernay. He was lord of Neufmarché-en-Lions, governor of the boy duke, William, and was treacherously assassinated between 1035 and 1040 by hirelings of Raoul de Gacé. Turquetil was the second son of Torf, the son of Bernard the Dane, which latter was governor and regent of Normandy in 912, from whom descended the sires de Beaumont, comtes de Meulent, the barons of Cancelles and Saint-Paer, the lords of Gournay and Milly, the barons of Neubourg, the vicomtes of Evreux, the earls of Leicester, and many other noble French and English houses. Turquetil married Anceline, sister of Toustain, seigneur de Montfort-sur-Risle, and had issue Anchetil, and Walter de Lescelina who married Beatrice, abbess of Montivilliers, natural daughter of Richard I, duke of Normandy,[1] as well as Leceline de Turqueville, the wife of William, comte d'Exmes (later d'Eu), an illegitimate son of the same duke. Anchetil was the first to assume the name of Harcourt from the bourg of Harcourt, near Brionne, and married Eve de Boessey-le-Chapel, by whom he had seven sons and one daughter. The eldest was Errand, who predeceased his father, and was succeeded by Robert as head of the house. Jean, Arnoul, Gervais, Yves, and Renauld were the other sons. Errand de Harcourt commanded the archers of Val de Ruel at the battle of Hastings, but returned to Normandy in 1078 and probably died soon after. His younger brother, Robert, who accompanied him to the conquest, was the ancestor of this distinguished house, concerning whom a paragraph follows.

Hist. Geneal. Maison de Harcourt, G. A. de La Roque. *Thury-Harcourt Essai hist. et Stat.*, Chapolin. Père Anselme. Plan., II, 229. Cle., II, 148. Le Prevost, *Notes,* *Wace,* II, 266. *Wace,* Taylor, 241. Burke, 66.

[1] *Vide* Gilbert Crispin, App. 15.

ETIENNE ERARD. Orderic Vital [1] remarks "Thomas, son of Stephen, had obtained an audience of the king (Henry I) and offering him a gold mark, said to him, Stephen, son of Airard (Erard), was my father and during his whole life he was in your father's service as a mariner. He it was who conveyed your father to England in his own ship, when he crossed the sea to make war on Harold." This Thomas was chosen captain of the ill-fated Blanche-Nef (White Ship), which was wrecked on its voyage from Normandy to England in December, 1120. The two sons of Henry I, with several hundred of the flower of the younger nobility of England, perished in this catastrophe. This ancient family was established in Normandy from 868, and Erard, a descendant, in command of a Danish army, came to the rescue of

Richard I, duke of Normandy.[2] The "Stefanus Eiraidi filius," written in Domesday, is beyond doubt identical with the subject of this paragraph. He appears as a tenant-in-chief in Berkshire and in Dorsetshire under-held of Aiulf the Chamberlain, and *Recherches sur le Domesday* affirm he was the head of this house in Normandy. Duchesne mentions Etienne, fils d'Erard, as one of the seigniors who accompanied the duke to England, and Etienne Erard appears on de Magny's addition to the Dives roll.

Rech. Domesd., 67.
[1] Ord. Vit., IV, 33.   [2] *Hist. de France*, Robt. Gaguin, V, 41.

EUDES, EVÊQUE DE BAYEUX.

Odo, bishop of Bayeux and earl of Kent, son of Herluin de Conteville, and Arlette, the mother of the Conqueror, was the half-brother of the latter and participated in the battle of Hastings. Wace refers to him thus : " l'Eveske Odun " (l. 11130), and Orderic Vital remarks : " Many of the clergy had followed the norman army, among whom were two bishops, Odo of Bayeux and Geoffry of Coutances, with attendant clerks and monks, whose duty it was to aid the war with their prayers and councils." His life and movements after the conquest are so well known that they will not be here repeated. Opinion differs as regards the date of Odo's birth. Mr. Freeman remarks that " a son of Herluin and Herleva (Arlette) could not be born before 1036," assuming that the marriage of Arlette did not take place before the death of duke Robert in the Holy Land. He is supported in this statement by Jumièges, but the facts point to the contrary. William of Malmesbury places the date of the birth of Odo in 1030, which would make him nineteen when he was consecrated in 1049 (Hugh, bishop of Bayeux, died in October of this year, while attending the council at Rheims). Orderic Vital informs us that duke William procured the bishopric for his half-brother while he was very young (in adolescentia) and that he functioned during fifty years (really forty-eight) in this dignity, which agrees fairly well with the date of his death in 1097 at Palmero.[1]

Duke Robert (I) the Magnificent married shortly after 1025 Estrith, sister of Canute the Great, widow of Ulf, a distinguished Dane, who was murdered in that year. Robert ill treated and repudiated her, by whom he had no issue, which was probably the cause of his anger. By Arlette he had two children, William the Conqueror, born *c*. 1027–8 and a daughter, Adelaide, born *c*. 1029, who married Eudes, comte de Champagne.[2] Arlette then married Herluin de Conteville, by whom she had issue besides Odo, Robert, count of Mortain, Emma who married Richard vicomte d'Avranches, and Muriel, the wife of Eudo al Chapel. Emma, who could not have been born before 1030, was probably the oldest, for if she was only sixteen at the time of her marriage, Hugh Lupus (d'Avranches) her son could not have been more than nineteen in 1066. Odo was born, therefore, *c*. 1031, and Robert and Muriel shortly thereafter, probably before 1035.

William of Poitiers, Migne, col. 1252. Ord. Vit., I, 483. Plan., I, 88. Le Prevost, *Notes, Wace*, II, 185. *Wace*, Taylor, 101, 108, 194, 278.
[1] Ord. Vit., Forester, II, 428 to 430 and n. ; *Ibid.*, Le Prevost, III, 263 n.   [2] *Vide* Eudes, comte de Champagne.

EUDES, COMTE DE CHAMPAGNE.

The castle of Aumale, which was built by Guerinfroi *c*. 1000, who became the first sire d'Aumale. He left an only daughter and heiress, Berta, who married Hugh II, comte de Poithieu, by whom she had a son Enguerrand, who became sire d'Aumale and married Adelaide, sister or half-sister of duke William. Hugh was killed in 1053, after having settled Aumale upon his wife in dower. Adelaide married secondly in 1054, Lambert, count of Lens, brother of Eustache II, count of Boulogne. Lambert was killed in 1055 and a daughter also named Adelaide was born from one of these husbands. Adelaide, the mother, married thirdly Eudes, comte de Champagne. If this occurred prior to 1066, which seems likely, then Eudes was undoubtedly sire d'Aumale in right of his wife before the conquest and therefore the "sire d'Aubemare" of Wace (l.

13552). But if the marriage took place thereafter, Aumale would still have been in possession of Adelaide. It was created a county by king William and came into great prominence, for which reason Wace can be excused for having designated Eudes by this title in his poem. Edgar Taylor in his translation of Wace asks whether it is possible that Gui, comte de Ponthieu, uncle of Adelaide the daughter, who was released after the battle of Mortimer, on doing homage to William, held Aumale during her minority, which possibly extended to 1066. This query is predicated on the assumption that Adelaide, Eudes' step-daughter, had inherited Aumale from her mother, Adelaide, before the conquest, which seems quite improbable. Eudes received from the Conqueror the island of Holderness (Meaux) shortly after the compilation of Domesday which had previously been in possession of Dreu de La Beuvrière and espoused the cause of William Rufus after the death of king William I. His castle of Aumale received an English garrison, which was enlarged and strengthened by him and his son, Stephan, at the expense of the royal treasury, on the invasion of Normandy by William Rufus in 1090. Later he conspired with Robert de Mowbray and other powerful nobles to depose the king and place his son, Stephan, on the throne. The plot having failed, Eudes and Stephan were captured and thrown into prison, in 1094,[1] where Eudes remained until his death, c. 1108. Stephan was condemned to have his eyes put out, but by the intercession of his wife and family and the payment of a large sum of money was liberated.

Plan., I, 118. Le Prevost, *Notes, Wace,* II, 235. *Wace,* Taylor, 210. Cle., I, 1. *Archives of Rouen Foundation Charter, Abbaye de St. Martin d'Auchy-Lez-Aumale* and *Betterrima Notitia* of the same abbey. Stapleton, II, xxx, xxxi. *Collectanea Topographica et Genealogica,* IV, 265. *Rech. Domesd.,* 78.
[1] *Roger of Wendover,* 366.

EUDES DAPIFER, SIRE DE **PRÉAUX.** From Rye, near Bayeux. Geoffry de Rie was living *c.* 980 and his son, Odo FitzGeoffry, gave half the

church of Rie to Fécamp abbey, which was confirmed in 1027 by duke Richard II.[1] Hubert de Rie in 1047 saved the duke's life, when young William was fleeing from Valognes, where the conspirators of the Cotentin were attempting to capture him. Hubert placed him on a fresh horse and giving misleading information to his pursuers, commanded his three sons, Ralph, Hubert and Adam (the fourth son, Eudo, was apparently too young) to conduct him to Falaise, which they succeeded in doing. Later on, duke William assembled some of his principal lords at a time when he wanted a messenger to go to England to attend Edward the Confessor, on behalf of his claim to the English crown. It was considered a very dangerous undertaking and Hubert alone of those present volunteered to make the perilous journey, on which he immediately departed. He returned with the promise of the kingdom for William with tokens confirming it from king Edward. Prior to 1060 he witnessed a donation to the abbey of Saint-Peter at Chartres.[2] Hubert attended the duke at the conquest of England with his sons, and a short time later was sent to Normandy to quell a disturbance there and was not heard of again in England. He died before 1086, as he is not mentioned in Domesday. His four sons, however, were all magnificently rewarded by the Conqueror and appear in that survey. The eldest, Ralph, generally called FitzHubert, was castellan of Nottingham and held lands in Leicester, Stafford, Nottingham and Lincoln, but the head of his great barony was in Derby in which he possessed the whole estates of the rich Saxon, named Levenot, comprising 36 manors. His male line died out with his grandson, Hubert, in about the third year of the reign of Henry III, who left two daughters. Hubert, the second son, held the honour of Hingham, in Norfolk, comprising 40 knights' fees, and became castellan of Norwich, in 1074. His wife, Agnes, daughter of Robert de Todeni, the first baron of Belvoir, was richly endowed and brought him several manors. He founded and made great donations to the cathedral of Norwich, and his line also expired with his grandson, Hubert, baron of Hingham, in 1188, who left two co-heirs,

Aliva and Isabel, both of whom married and left issue. Adam, the third son, held large estates in Kent, under bishop Odo, and was one of the compilers of Domesday. Little is known of him or his descendants, excepting that a Robert de Rie of Kent, probably one of that family, is mentioned in the Pipe roll of 1189. Eudes de Rie, dapifer, sire de Praels (Préaux), the youngest son, was by far the ablest and most distinguished. He received enormous possessions in Essex, where his principal estates were, but he also held lands in Norfolk, Suffolk, Hertford, Cambridge, Berks, Bedford, Northampton, as well as the great hereditary office of seneschal or dapifer, to which he succeeded William FitzOsberne. He was with the Conqueror when he died at Caen and following the last wishes of his monarch, hurried to England to secure the succession for his son, William Rufus. Eudo concealed the king's death on his arrival and, clothed with the proper authority, went direct to Winchester, where he secured the keys of the treasury. He then visited the principal strongholds on the coast adjoining Normandy, whose castellans he made swear not to open their gates except at his expressed command; after which he returned to Winchester, announced the king's death, handed the keys of the treasury to William Rufus, who was at once proclaimed king. This monarch confirmed him in the office of dapifer and gave him the town of Colchester, where he built a castle, the keep of which was the largest in England. He founded a magnificent abbey, dedicated to Saint-John the Evangelist, and living to a ripe old age, died in 1120, in his castle of Préaux, Normandy. By his wife, Rohesia, daughter of Richard de Bienfaite,[3] he had issue an only daughter, Margaret, who married William de Mandeville, whose son, Geoffry, earl of Essex, was Steward of Normandy, in her right.

Plan., II, 126. Nov. Peo., 387. Cle., III, 71. Le Prevost, Notes, Wace, II, 251. Wace, Taylor, 229. Rech. Domesd., 53. Wace, Pluquet, II, 23.
[1] Neustria Pia, 218. [2] Stapleton, II, cclxx. [3] Vide Richard de Bienfaite et d'Orbec.

EUDES DE FOURNEAUX. From Fourneaux near St-Lo and Coutances. Ralph de Fornelles witnessed a charter of St-Evroult, Normandy, in 1070.[1] Eudes de Fourneaux, who accompanied the duke to the conquest, held in capite in Somerset in 1083 (Ex. Domd.) where he occurs as Odo de Furnell. The family appears in several counties and were later of considerable consequence. One of their seats was at Kentisbere and another at Fenn Ottery in Devon, which Henry I granted to Allen de Fourneaux, whose son, Galfrid de Furnell, was sheriff of Devon in 1154. His son sir Allen Forneaux in 1165 was one of the justiciaries,[2] and also sheriff of Devon in 1199. The name is carried on the rolls of Holinshed, Duchesne, Leland, Brompton and Dives.

Cle., II, 32. Nov. Peo., 248. Burke, 56.
[1] Ord. Vit., II, 187. [2] Mon., i, 999.

EUDES LE SENESCHAL, SIRE DE LA HAIE. Eudes Le Seneshal came from the castle and barony of La Haie-du-Puits, arrondissement of Coutances, which dates to the time of the partition of Normandy by duke Rollo. The annals of the family, however, commence with Turstain Haldub, probably a younger son of Turstin de Bastembourg, whose eldest son, Eudo, by his wife, Emma, founded with him the abbey of Lessay, shortly before the conquest. Wace (l. 13701) calls him "sire de la Haie." His full title was Eudo Haldub, surnamed al Chapel, sire de la Haie, le seneschal, and as he has been alluded to under these different designations, it has caused considerable confusion. He married Muriel, a daughter of Herluin de Conteville, and Arlette, the mother of the Conqueror. He was at the council of the chief men of the duchy before the one called at Lilleboune in 1066, and accompanied duke William to the conquest of England in that year. He became a great baron and possessed vast estates in Sussex, Essex, Suffolk, etc., in 1086 (Domesday). He was among the largest donors to the church of his day. He died in 1098 and was buried in the chapter house of his abbey of Lessay, having left an only daughter, Muriel, who married Robert, son of Ralph de la Haie, dapifer to

C

Robert, count of Mortain, her cousin, to whom she brought her vast possessions.

Nor. Peo., 282. Plan., II, 124. Cle., III, 366. Le Prevost, *Notes, Wace*, II, 258. *Wace*, Taylor, 102, 212, 235. *Rech.*, de Gerville, 41. Dupont, I, 48.

EUSTACHE, COMTE DE BOULOGNE.

Eustache II, comte de Boulogne, was the son of Eustache I and Mahaut, daughter of Lambert the Bearded, count of Louvain, and succeeded his father about 1047. In 1050 he married Goda, daughter of Ethelred II, king of England, and widow of Dreu, the count of Vexin, Pontoise, Chaumont, and Amiens. He joined duke William in the conquest of England, and is expressly named by William of Poitiers and personally depicted as *Eustatius* on the Bayeux Tapestry.[1] Guy, bishop of Amiens, author of *Carmen de Bello*, states that Harold's body was mutilated by Eustache, Walter Giffard, Hugh de Montfort and " the heir of Ponthieu." The latter was Gui, count of Ponthieu and Montreuil,[2] who captured Harold on his visit to Normandy before the conquest and who died in 1100. Wace chronicles " Wiestace d'Abeville " (l. 13562), but if this does not refer to him, which both Le Prevost and Taylor seem to doubt, he is certainly not mentioned in the *Roman de Rou*. However, there is plenty of evidence that he was at Senlac. Orderic Vital tells us that he was severely wounded at the duke's side, while advising him to retreat, and Benoît de Saint-More speaks of him as taking part in the battle. For his services in the engagement he received large grants of lands in various parts of England.

Plan., I, 148. Cle., I, 28. *Nor. Peo.*, 164. Ord. Vit., I, 484–6 ; II, 79, 399.
[1] William of Poitiers, Migne, 1254.
[2] *Vide* App. 1.

LE SIRE D'EPINAY.

Wace (l. 13616) chronicles " cil de Epine," of which name there are a number of fiefs in Normandy. Epinay-Tesson in the arrondissement of Bayeux is favoured by Edgar Taylor, since Enguerandus de Espineto appears in the Bayeux inquest, and points out that Hardy's *Rot. Norm.*[1] leads one to suppose that the fief of Epinay was vested in Roger de Saint-Sauveur. On the other hand, Le Prévost thinks the Epinay-sur-Duclair in the arrondissement of Rouen is intended, whose lords appear in charters of the abbey of Jumièges. Lamberto de Espineto was a witness to a donation of lands in Espinay-sur-Duclair by Rotrou, archbishop of Rouen, to that abbey, 1165–83,[2] and Willelmo de Spineto occurs in one of Roger de Mortemer, 1192–8.[3] The companion of this name who accompanied the Conqueror to Senlac has not been identified, but we find under Henry I a Richard and Gilbert de Spineto among the vassals of Pierre de Valognes in the county of Norfolk.

Plan., II, 285. Le Prevost, *Notes, Wace*, II, 244. *Wace*, Taylor, 222, 301.
[1] Hardy, 16.   [2] *Chart. Abb. Jumièges*, I, 224.   [3] *Ibid.*, II, 115.

LE SIRE D'ESCALLES.

The d'Escalles, Scales, Chaleys and Challières family was apparently not Norman, but derived from Aquitaine from the viscounts of Scales, who were of great importance from the time of Charles Martel, *c.* 730. Harduin d'Escallers or de Scallariis had extensive grants in Hertford and Cambridge in 1066, and he and his posterity also held three knights' fees in York by the gift of Alain La Roux, earl of Richmond.[1] Soon after 1086 Smydeton, or Smithton (now Smeaton), part of the demesne of earl Alain near Richmond, York, was granted to Malger, son of Harduin de Scelers. The family continued of much importance in various parts of England for many years, and the Smithson's changed their name to Percy when they acquired the dukedom of Northumberland. The name Scales appears on the list of Brompton and Delisle carries Harduin d'Escalles on the Dives roll.

Nor. Peo., 401. Cle., III, 362. *Rech. Domesd.*, 125.
[1] Gale, *Hon. Richmond*, App. 26.

FOUQUE D'AULNAY.

There are four communes of this name in Normandy, as well as Anet, a little south of Ivri. Fouque d'Aulnay was descended from Bathel, or Basset, duke of the Normans of the Loire, *c.* 895–905,[1] who acquired Ouilly-Basset and Normanville in 912. His son Norman was the father of Osmond de Centville, or Basset, viscount of Vernon. The latter married a niece of the duchess Gonnor, by whom he had Fulco de Alneio I and several daughters, one of whom was the mother of Baldwin de Redvers or Reviers I.[2] This Fouque d'Alneio, Alnei, Aneto, Anet or Aulnay, as he is variously called, was the father of Osmond[3] Basset, Robert d'Ouilli,[4] William de Lisors (Willelmi de Linsorens), ancestor of the house of Lisors, Fouque d'Alnet, or d'Aulnay II, ancestor of the Dawnays, and possibly Toustain Basset.[5] The second Fouque is probably the "cil d'Alnei," whom Wace (l. 13775) mentions as having been present at Senlac, whom he records as one of the five knights who challenged king Harold to come forth and fight. The name de Alneto occurs in the foundation charter of the abbey of Aumale, 1115, and is frequently seen in others of the 12th and 13th centuries.[6] Hugo de Alneto is recorded as a witness to a charter of the abbey of Jumièges in 1138[7] while Simon de Aneto and Joscelinus de Alneto occurs in one of 1172,[8] and Walterius de Alneto at the commencement of the 13th century.[9] Fouque d'Aulnay has frequently been confused with Fouque d'Aunou on account of the similarity of the name, and from the fact that they were contemporary. They were, however, the representatives of separate and distinct families.

Le Prevost, *Notes, Wace*, II, 264. *Wace*, Taylor, 242. Plan., II, 203. Cle., I, 24. *Nor. Peo.*, 151, 222, 355. [1] Boquet, VII, 360; VIII, 317. [2] *Jumièges Interp.*, de Torigny, 329. [3] *Vide* Osmond Basset. [4] *Vide* Robert d'Ouilli. [5] Great charter of the abbey of Montivilliers, lat. 1035, Rouen. [6] *Mon.*, ii, 999. [7] *Chart. Abb. Jumièges*, I, 162. [8] *Ibid.*, II, 14–15. [9] *Ibid.*, II, 223.

FOUQUE D'AUNOU. This name is derived from Aunou-le-Faucon or Foulcon in the arrondissement of Argentan, Normandy.[1] Fouque d'Aunou I or his son Fouques d'Aunou II was present at the battle of Hastings, whom Wace (l. 13559) designates "sire d'Alnou," and the accepted opinion is that it was

the latter. The elder Fouque is stated in Taylor's manuscript list of Norman ships[2] to have furnished 40 vessels for duke William's fleet, that is if the Fulco Claudo therein mentioned refers to him. According to Orderic Vital[3] Fouque d'Aunou I was the son of Baldric le Teuton, whose estates depended from the monks of Saint-Evroult, and " was a man of high birth to whom Gilbert, count of Brionne, grandson of duke Richard I gave his niece in marriage, who came into Normandy with his brother Viger to take service under the duke." From this marriage sprung six sons, namely: Nicholas de Bacqueville, Fouque d'Aunou, Richard de Courcy, Richard de Neuville, Baldric de Bauquencey and Viger de Apulia and several daughters. Two of them were Gonnor, who married Gilbert Crispin I,[4] and Hawise who became the wife of Erneis, the parents of Robert Fitz-Erneis, killed in the battle of Hastings, who also married a lady by the name of Hawise.[5] Concerning the sons of Baldric, Vital says: "They all distinguished themselves by great valour under duke William from whom they received great riches and honours and left their heirs vast possessions in Normandy."[6] Regarding this marriage, there is every reason to believe that Vital's statement is substantially correct, as he was a monk at St-Evroult and therefore fully informed concerning Baldric and his family. This niece, if Vital really intended to say niece, undoubtedly was the daughter of an unrecorded sister of Gilbert, count of Brionne, since he did not have a brother. For the marriage to fit in with all of the known facts, the sister of count Gilbert must have been about twenty years his senior. At least enough older to make his niece about his own age, for it has been established that grand-children of this union fought in the battle of Hastings, namely Robert FitzErneis, Fouque d'Aunou II, Richard de-Courcy II and William Crispin I. Assuming that Fouque d'Aunou II was twenty-three years of age at the battle of Hastings, this would crowd five generations in about 110 years, as Richard I, duke of Normandy, was born in 933; possible, but highly improbable. It is more likely that Vital intended to say that Baldric married an aunt or sister of count Gilbert. If an aunt, it might have been one of the two unnamed daughters of Richard I,[7] possibly full sisters of Godefroy, count of Brionne and d'Eu, and his brother William, count of Exmes, both natural sons of duke Richard. Either of these suppositions would fit in perfectly with the proper number of generations required to make the pedigree normal. Prior to 1060, Fouques d'Aunou witnessed a donation to the abbey of St-Pere de Chartres.[8] In 1066 and 1082, Fouques d'Aunou was a donor to the abbaye-aux-Dames at Caen, and in 1070–7 he and his sister Albereda occur in a charter of the abbey of Bec. He also appears in numerous acts and documents of this epoch. With the exception of the charter executed in 1082 the individual here recorded was probably Fouque the first.[9] Early in the 12th century there is a seal of Fulconis de Alnuio, on a charter of the abbey of Goufferin.[10] In 1124, Fulco de Alnou is mentioned in a charter of Henry I to Dives, Normandy.[11] Fulco de Alnou in 1165 was one of the most powerful lords in Normandy, his barony consisting of thirty-eight fees,[12] and Fucone d'Alnou appears in a charter of the abbey of Jumièges in 1180.[13] The family of Fouque d'Aunou I and Fouque d'Aulnay I, Aneio or Anet have been constantly confounded particularly in England, but in France they remained distinct as d'Aunou and d'Anet, and it existed for several centuries in both countries. William d'Alno held lands of Robert Guernon in Suffolk in 1086 (Domesday), and settled in Somerset, from whom descended the Alno family of that county. He belonged to the house of Bricqueville, which possessed the castle of Alno or l'Aune in the Cotentin, canton of Lessay. William d'Alno or any member of his family would without doubt have taken the name of the castle, under which he appears in Domesday. M. de Gerville in his *History of the Chateaux de la Manche* [14] says that this branch of the Bricqueville family established itself in England for several centuries under the name of l'Aune or de Alno. This William may be the Bricqueville mentioned in the *Researches of the Bayeux*

Tapestry, by the abbé de La Rue, as having been present at Senlac.

Rech. Domesd., 114. Plan., II, 132. *Nor. Peo.*, 222, 355. *Wace*, Taylor, 213. Le Prevost, *Notes, Wace*, II, 236, 531.
[1] *Feod. Norm.*, Duchesne, 1046.
[2] Taylor's *Anon. MS.*, Littleton, i, 464.
[3] Ord. Vit., I, 427. [4] *Opera Lanfranci*, I, 341. [5] *Gall. Christ.*, XI, Inst. 334.
[6] *Ibid.*, 428. [7] *Jumièges Interp.*, de Torigny, 229. [8] Stapleton, II, cclxx.
[9] *Gall. Christ.*, XI, 61, 330, and Bibl. nat. lat. 13905, fo. 115, and lat. 12884, fo. 85.
[10] *Mem. des Ant. Norm.* in the Atlas to Vol. VIII. [11] *Gall. Christ.*, XI, 159, Inst. 330. [12] *Chart. l'Abb. de Jumièges*, II, 56. [13] *Feod. Norm.*, Duchesne. [14] *M.S.A.N.*, II, 241.

LE SIRE DE FRIBOIS. The name appears in the *Researches of the Bayeux Tapestry*, by abbé de La Rue, and Delisle likewise affirms that he was present at Hastings. Whether the Ferebrace of Brompton refers to the same individual is open to conjecture. The family occurs frequently in Yorkshire and Normandy in the time of Philip Augustus.

Nor. Peo., 250. *Mon. Ebor.*, Burton.

GAUTIER D'AINCOURT. Gautier d'Aincourt probably came from the parish of Aincourt, situated in the Norman Vexin, whose patronage was given by one of his descendants to the abbey of Bec. The information on the family in Normandy is scant. There are towns bearing the name Aincourt, Encourt, Eincourt and others in the Haute Normandy, as well as in the Beauvoisis. He accompanied duke William to England at the conquest and served him with great zeal, for which he was rewarded with sixty-seven manors in different counties, among which was the domain of Blankney, in Lincolnshire, which became the chief seat of his barony. An epitaph to the memory of his son William in Lincoln cathedral on a leaden plate found in his grave in the churchyard there, states that he was of royal blood and a kinsman of Remigius, almoner of Fécamp, later bishop of Lincoln.[1] Ralph d'Eyncourt, William's younger brother, founded Thurgarton priory, Nottinghamshire, and was a great feudal baron. The family was powerful and prominent down through the centuries, the male line becoming extinct in the reign of Henry VI, when the estates were carried in the female line to the families of Cromwell and Lovel.

Plan., II, 237. Cle., I, 6. *Rech. Domesd.* 66. Burke, 12. Dugdale.
[1] *Roger of Wendover*, Giles ed., Vol. I, 350. *Vide* Le Sire de Bailleul.

GAUTIER D'APPEVILLE. From one of the three following communes in Normandy : Appeville, canton of Mont-fort-sur-Risle, arrondissement of Pont-Audemer ; Appeville-les-Petit, canton of Affranville, arrondissement of Dieppe, or Appeville-la-Haie, canton of La Haie-du-Puits, arrondissement of Coutances. There were a number of families of prominence of this name in Normandy in the 11th, 12th and 13th centuries, and there is reasonable assurance that an Appeville fought at Senlac. Since Walter held the manor of Folkestone in 1086 (Domesday) from the barony of Odo, bishop of Bayeux, under William d'Arques, in Kent, there is a strong probability that he was identical with this individual.

Rech. Domesd., 190. Plan., II, 277. Cle., I, 26.

GAUTIER DE CAEN. From Caen, Normandy. Walter de Caen held great estates in Norfolk in 1086 (Domesday). His son, Robert Fitzwalter, was a knight of William Malet, by whom he was enfeoffed of Horsford, where he built his castle. He married Sibyl, the daughter and heiress of Ralph de Canieto (Cheney), lord of Ling in Norfolk, which latter Dugdale affirms " came into England with king William the Conqueror." Ralph gave the manor of Coxford, according to Blomfield, to his daughter at the time of her marriage. Mauritius de Cadomo (Caen) held lands in barony in Devonshire, 1083 (Ex. Domesday), and William de Cadomo held in Norfolk, 1086 (Domesday). Renebald de Caen occurs in 1130.[1] The family is frequently mentioned later in England and occurs often in Normandy in the 12th century. Fouque and Maurin appear on the Dives list. A natural son of Henry I, Robert de Caen was created earl of Gloucester and

married the heiress of Robert Fitz Hamon.

Ord. Vit., II, 473. *Nor. Peo.*, 185. Cle., I, 257 ; II, 60.
[1] *Rot. Pip.*

GAUTIER LE FLAMAND. The family was Flemish, descending from the castellans of Cambray, of whom Walter de Lens is mentioned in the *Chronicle* of Baldric of Noyon, *c.* 950. Walter II, his son, was castellan of Cambray, *c.* 990, and had Walter, who was succeeded by his nephew Walter D'Oissy, castellan, in 1049. He had Hugh, father of Hugh II, viscount of Meaux, living 1096.[1] Walter de Cambray, or D'Oissy, surnamed " le Flamand," a younger brother, came to England at the conquest in 1066, and was a great Domesday baron in Buckingham, Hertford, and Wadhull in Bedford, where he had his chief seat. MM. Léchaudé d'Anisy et de Sainte-Marie, in their *Recherches sur le Domesday*, state that Robert d'Armentières and Adelolfus de Mert from the town of Armentières in Flanders came to England under his banner, he being their suzerain. From Walter descended the barons of Wadhull and the celebrated earl of Strafford. The Wentworth family also descended from him. Mr. Edgar Taylor, in his *Wace*, likewise registers the opinion that he was at the conquest. Six of the name appear on the Dives roll.

Nor. Peo., 145, 229, 244, 245, 347, 444. *Wace*, Taylor, 113.
[1] Des Bois.

GAUTIER GIFFARD, COMTE DE LONGUEVILLE. Walter Giffard I was lord of Longueville in Caux, whom Jumièges [1] tells us was the son of Osberne de Bolbec and Wevie, a sister of Gonnor, the wife of Richard I, duke of Normandy, but as the duchess Gonnor was the great-grandmother of the Conqueror, this seems impossible ; consequently it is necessary to be contented with the conclusion that he was descended from this union. In 1035 with Hugh de Gournay he joined in the attempt of Edward, son of king Ethelred, to recover the crown of England, and in 1053 he was left by duke William in command of the forces blockading the castle of Arques, at which time he was lord of Longueville and already past the prime of life. He was, in 1054, one of the four commanders entrusted with the defence of Caux, in which Longueville was situated, which developed into the battle of Mortimer. Walter later made a pilgrimage to St-Iago de Compostella, Spain, where he received the gift of a horse from the king, who had a great friendship for him. This horse Walter presented to duke William, and was the first one he used in the battle of Hastings, to which engagement Walter, then an old man with "white and bald head," accompanied him. His brothers, Berenger and Osberne, also followed the duke to England. Walter contributed thirty vessels and a hundred men to the fleet, according to Taylor's list. Benoît de St-More affirms that he was struck down during the engagement and rescued by duke William himself. His reward for participation in the conquest was the earldom of Buckingham, which he received in 1070, together with large possessions, and he appears to have founded the priory of St-Michel de Bolbec in 1079. He married Ermengarde, daughter of Gerrard Flaitel, by whom he had a son, Walter, who succeeded him in the earldom. Another son was chancellor to William Rufus and made bishop of Winchester by Henry I. A daughter, Rohesia, married Richard de Bienfaite, eldest son of Gilbert, count of Brionne, from which union sprung the great house of Clare. His death occurred about 1084, and William of Poitiers, Orderic Vital, Wace, Benoît de St-More and all other writers of the period subscribed to his presence at Senlac.

Plan., I, 160. Cle., II, 120. Nor. Peo., 177.
[1] Jumièges Interp., de Torigny, 325.

GAUTIER HACHET. (Achet, Hackett, Hacket, Hageth, Hachett, Hatchett or Haget.) The name Ache or Achet appears in 1040 in the list of the household of Thiboult (Theobald) III, comte de Chartres. The existence of two parishes of the name of Achet in the department of Pas-de-Calais would lead to the supposition that Achet belonged to the Picard family. Walter

Achet held lands from Walter Giffard in Buckingham in 1086 (Domesday), in whose train he doubtless came to the conquest. He was a witness to a charter made to Trinité-du-Mont, Rouen. A Geoffry Haget is mentioned in the great charter of Beaubec as having given to that abbey possessions in Beaubec itself. In Worcester, William Hacket held lands in Claines in the time of Henry I. The family was long settled in Yorkshire and Gloucestershire and spread to many parts of England and Ireland. Ricardi Hacket occurs in a charter of the abbey of Jumièges in 1170.[1]

Rech. Domesd., 50. Ord. Vit., III, 453. Nor. Peo., 274. Cle., II, 156.
[1] Chart. Abb. Jumièges, II, 2.

GAUTIER DE LACY. This member of a prominent Norman family was from Lassy on the road from Vire to Auvray. Walter de Lacy subscribed his name to a charter of William Fitz-Osberne, and it appears certain that a Walter and Ibert de Lacy were at the conquest, from which it can be surmised that "cil de Laci" of Wace (l. 13604) was meant for Walter and that "chevalier de Lacie" (l. 13657) was intended for Ibert. Their relationship has not been established definitely, but it is supposed they were brothers. In 1069 Walter was sent into Wales with William FitzOsberne against the people of Brecknock; subsequently he assisted Wulstan, bishop of Worcester, and Ours d'Abetot, then sheriff of that county, in preventing the passage of the Severn by the earls of Hereford and Norfolk. He founded the church of St-Peter at Hereford, during the building of which he fell from a ladder and was killed in 1084. Walter married Emmelin, by whom he left three sons, Roger, Hugh and Walter, as well as two daughters, Ermeline and Emma. Roger his heir possessed ninety-six lordships in 1086 (Domesday), sixty-five of which were in Gloucestershire, the balance being in Shropshire, Herefordshire, Worcestershire and Berkshire. He lost his estates because he conspired with bishop Odo against William Rufus and later attached himself to Robert de Mowbray. His nephew Gilbert, by his sister Emma, became the ancestor of the lords of

Ulster, conquerors of the greater part of Ireland. The branches of the house were so numerous that forty coats of arms are recorded.

Plan., II, 153-6. Cle., II, 176. Nor. Peo., 304. Le Prevost, Notes, Wace, II, 243-52. Wace, Taylor, 220. Freeman, IV, 215, 284, 297-8.

GAUTIER LE POITEVIN. Vide Guillaume Le Poitevin.

GAUTIER DE VERNON. Vide Richard de Vernon.

GEOFFROI ASCELIN. The name Ascelin appears in Normandy and Brittany from the year 943. Robert Pincerna, son of Ascelin, appeared in a charter of duke William, and executed one which indicates his descent from the family of Dinan in Brittany, on which castle he held certain rights. (Ego Rotbertus Pincerna filius Ascelini . . . fratrisque mei Galteri . . . omnem meam Consuetudinem quam jure hoereditario tenebam in Castello de Dinam.[1]) It is presumed that Ascelin was a younger or natural son of this family and the father of Geoffry Asceline or Alselin, Robert Pincerna and Walter. Geoffry attended the conquest of England in 1066 and was a tenant-in-chief in Northamptonshire and Lincolnshire, and held estates in Leicestershire, Derbyshire, Nottinghamshire, where he appears under the name of Alselin in 1086 (Domesday). He possessed four manors and twenty-four houses with a church in the town of Nottingham and in Lincoln. In 1065, William Hansel held two fees in Lincoln from Ralph Alselin or Hansell, his kinsman, from whom descended the Ancells. The Dives list carries Geoffroi Alselin.

Rech. Domesd., 120. Cle., I, 58. Nor. Peo., 139.
[1] Ducange, at the word Patella, Book I.

GEOFFROI DU BEC. " Goisfrid de Bech," a great baron in Hertfordshire, where he held as tenant-in-chief, 1086 (Domesday),[1] has sometimes been erroneously confused with Goisfrid Mareschal, ancestor of the Marshals and earls of Pembroke. Ralph " de Bech," who held under him in the aforesaid county, and Gilbert Crispin, abbot of

Westminster, are said by Norman People to have been his brothers and the sons of William Crispin I, who was the son of Gilbert Crispin I, Seigneur de Tillières. From what source this information was derived is not disclosed, but so far as abbot Gilbert is concerned, it is known to be true.[2] The conclusion that Geoffry and Ralph were brothers is plausible because they bore the same surname and the one held from the other. If they were brothers of Gilbert Crispin, the abbot, it could account for Ralph having held Pelham and Eldedrie, Hertfordshire, from the see of London in 1086 (Domesday), which came under the former's jurisdiction, but the statement of relationship requires documentary substantiation. M. Planché asserts that Geoffry du Bec may have been identical with Geoffry Crispin, lord of Chateauceaux, now Champtoceaux, overlooking the Loire in Anjou on the border of Brittany. It was alternately possessed by both, but at the time of the Crispin occupation belonged to the counts of Anjou.[3] Geoffry Crispin did not live until the latter half of the 12th century, when he executed a charter without date as lord of Chateauceaux, to which dom. Morice incorrectly appended two confirmations of the period of the conquest, accordingly misleading Planché.[4] Mr. Stacy Grimaldi is of the opinion that Geoffroi du Bec and Toustain Fitz-Rou Le Blanc, occasionally designated du Bec, the standard-bearer at Senlac,[5] were brothers and the sons of Rolf, who, he states, was the brother of Gilbert Crispin I, seigneur de Tillières.[6] Toustain's father was certainly named Rou or Rolf from Bec-aux-Couchois as recorded by Orderic Vital[7] and Wace,[8] who could well have been the brother of Gilbert Crispin I, for there is nothing on record which conflicts with this assumption, but it needs proof. The surname of Geoffry and Ralph du Bec suggests that they were rather the brothers of Toustain than abbot Gilbert Crispin, for it still remains to be shown that the Crispin family held a barony of Bec at this time. However this may be, Ralph du Bec held, in addition to his estates, depending from the see of London, possessions in Cambridge from Picot de Cambridge in 1086

(Domesday), and from the former descended the Pelhams, lords Pelham,
dukes of Newcastle and earls of Chichester. Walter du Bec or Beke, a
very powerful lord who, Burke says,
was at Hastings, received Eresby in
Lincoln and was an under-tenant in
Buckingham. By his wife Agnes,
daughter of Hugh Pincerna, he left
with other issue Henry, ancestor of the
lords Willoughby.

Nor. Peo., 358. Plan., II, 196–7. Cle.,
I, 120. *Rech. Domesd.*, 178. Burke, 25.
[1] *Introd. Domesd.*, II, 293.   [2] *Vide*
Guillaume Crispin.   [3] *Vide* App. 15.
[4] *Ibid.*   [5] *Vide* Toustain FitzRou.
[6] *Vide* Mile Crispin.   [7] Ord. Vit., I, 483.
[8] Pluquet, *Wace*, II, 198.

GEOFFROI DE COMBRAY.

From the lordship of Cambrai, near
Falaise, Normandy. Wace (l. 13775)
mentions " cil de Combrai," one of the
knights who challenged Harold to come
forth at Senlac. This was probably
Geoffroi de Cambrai, who held lands in
capite in Leicestershire in 1086 (Domesday). The lords of Combray at a later
period were among the benefactors of
St-Barbe-en-Auge and Fontenay, and
Robert de Conbrai occurs in Normandy
in 1180. Henry de Combray held in
Derbyshire in 1165, while a Ralph
de Cambray paid fees in Sussex and
Hampshire in 1199 and 1203. It became corrupted into Chambreys and
Chambreis. His name appears on the
Dives roll of Delisle and that of
Guillaume Tailleur.

Plan., II, 285. Cle., I, 241. *Nor. Peo.*,
186. *Wace*, Taylor, 242. Le Prevost,
Notes, Wace, II, 267. Stapleton, I, lxxviii,
Sub. Lib. Nig.

GEOFFROI, EVÊQUE DE COU-
TANCES. From Montbrai (Montrai)
in the canton of Percy, arrondissement
of Saint-Lo. Geoffroi de Montbray,
bishop of Coutances, was at the battle
of Senlac. Dugdale remarks, " This
Geoffroi being of noble Norman extraction and more skilful in arms than
divinity, knowing better to train up
soldiers than to instruct clergy, did good
service at the battle of Hastings," for
which he received vast possessions in
Somerset and other counties, amounting
to 280 manors, and dedicated his

immense wealth to the building of the
cathedral of Coutances. In 1069 he
marched against the insurgents of
Dorset and Somerset and raised the
siege of Montacute. Two years later he
represented the king in a suit between
bishop Odo and archbishop Lanfranc,
and in 1074, with bishop Odo, suppressed the rebellion of the earls of
Hereford and Norfolk, at which time he
was appointed earl of Northumberland
but soon relinquished the earldom to
his nephew Robert, who became his
heir. He assisted at the coronation of
the Conqueror and died 1093–4.

William of Poitiers, Migne, Vol. I, 1252.
Ord. Vit., I, 483. Plan., II, 25. Cle., II,
235. *Nor. Peo.*, 339. Le Prevost, *Notes,
Wace*, II, 259. *Wace*, Taylor, 236.
Wace (l. 12491) records " Giffrei,
Eveske de Constances."

GEOFFROI DE LA GUIERCHE.

Geoffry de la Guierche derived his name
from La Guerche, a town near Rennes
on the border of Brittany. His father
Sylvester, lord of La Guerche, was a
churchman, and on the death of his
wife was consecrated bishop of Rennes,
in 1075. When he entered the church
his son succeeded to his estates.[1]
Geoffry is entered in Domesday under
the anglicized form of Wirce or Lawirce.
He was a great landowner in Domesday,
having obtained twenty-six manors in
Leicester; twelve in Warwick; the
entire isle of Axholme, with the manors
of Gainsborough, Somerby and Bly-
borough, in Lincoln, and Adlingfleet in
York. At the time of the survey he
had also custody of count Alberic's
lands in Warwick. His principal residence is believed to have been Melton,
and he was a benefactor to Selby abbey
and St-Mary's, York. From these
charters it is evident that he had no
issue. In 1093 he witnessed a deed of
Hervey, son of Goranton,[2] and died
soon afterwards, as the next year,
his heir, Walter, surnamed Hay,
founded a priory at Pouence.

Cle., II., 127.
[1] *Hist. Gene. de Plu. Maisons Illus. de
Bretagne*, Père du Paz.   [2] Lobineau, II,
217a.

GEOFFROI DE MANDEVILLE.

Geoffry de Mandeville apparently came
from either Magneville, near Valognes,

or Mandeville le Trevières. Wace (l. 13562) calls him "sire de Magnaville." For his part in the battle of Hastings he was rewarded with 118 lordships, his chief seat being Walden in Essex. He held the shrievalties of London, Middlesex and Hereford, and was the first constable of the tower of London after the conquest, which office was held by his grandson, who was created earl of Essex. Geoffry founded the Benedictine monastery at Hurley in Berkshire as a cell of Westminster abbey, where he desired to be buried.[1] He married first Adeliza de Balto (Bauté), who was the sister of Turstain Haldub,[2] father of Eudo al Chapel, by whom he had first, William, his heir; second, Stephen, father of Roger de Mandeville, castellan of Exeter, an ancestor of the Mandevilles of Devon; third, Geoffry, who had grants consisting of fifteen knights' fees from Henry I, of which Mersewood, Dorset, was his seat. Geoffry de Mandeville married second Leceline, by whom he seems to have had no issue.

Devon, Pole, 233. Testa de Neville, 183. Le Prevost, *Notes, Wace*, II, 238. *Wace*, Taylor, 214. Plan., II, 73. Cle., II, 226. *Nor. Peo.*, 204, 321.
[1] Dean Stanley.   [2] Stapleton, II, cxi, clxii.

GEOFFROI SEIGNEUR DE MORTAGNE. Geoffroi, son of Rotrou, seigneur de Mortagne, comte du Perche, is the individual referred to by Wace (l. 13582) as "De Meaine li vieil Gifrei." He is mentioned by both William of Poitiers and Vital as having been at the conquest, which statement can be accepted as authentic. His father, Rotrou I, vicomte de Chateaudun and comte de Mortagne, was living in 1079 at the time of the dedication of the church of St-Denis de Nogent. The nobility of the birth of Geoffroi and that of his wife Beatrice, daughter of Hilduin, fourth comte de Montdidier and Ronci, rendered him illustrious above all his compeers, and he had amongst his subjects warlike barons and brave governors of Cailly. His son Rotrou succeeded him and gave his daughters in marriage to men of the rank of count. Margaret married Henry, earl of Warwick, and Johain was given to Gilbert de l'Aigle, while Matilda married first Raymond I, vicomte de Turenne and second, Gui de las Tours in Limousin, from whom sprang a noble race. Rotrou assumed the habit of a Cluniac monk and died in 1100 and was buried in the church of the monastery of St-Dionysius the Areopagite, founded by his grandfather, Geoffroi I, in 1030, and which he richly endowed.

Plan., I, 261. *Nor. Peo.*, 137. *Wace*, Taylor, 216. Le Prevost, *Notes, Wace*, II, 240.

GEOFFROI MARTEL. From Bacqueville, arrondissement of Dieppe. It has been stated by Le Prevost that Geoffry Martel is the individual whom Wace records as "de Basquevile i fu Martels" (l. 13651) and he must not be confused with Geoffry Martel, count of Anjou. The same commentator adds that Geoffry Martel was not, as is commonly believed, the son of Nicholas de Bacqueville, the head of the family of that name, one of the sons of Baldric the Teuton, who married a niece of the duchess Gonnor, which is stated by the continuator of William of Jumièges. He was instead the brother of the son-in-law of Nicholas de Bacqueville, namely, Hughes de Varhan, or Varvannes, from the arrondissement of Dieppe. This latter was the son of Gripon, as shown in a charter of Montivilliers.[1] Le Prevost suggests that Geoffry Martel may also have been a son-in-law of Nicholas de Bacqueville; this would account for the land of Bacqueville being in the family. He occurs as Goisfrid Martel, an under-tenant in the *Introduction of Domesday*,[2] and in the *Red* book as Gaufridus Martel. Rogerus Martel also appears there. A descendant, William Martel, was dapifer to king Stephan and was captured by the earl of Gloucester at Wilton and obliged to give his castle for his ransom. The family made donations and were witnesses to several charters recorded in the *Monasticon Anglicanum*, one of which, in 1109, was Robert de Baskerville, who on his return from the Palestine, granted lands to Gloucester abbey.[3] The name of Bacqueville appears on the rolls of Holinshed, Scriven, Brompton, Worcester, Guillaume Tailleur, Leland and Dives. That descendants of Nicholas de Bacqueville were in England at the time of the conquest, or shortly thereafter, there can be little doubt, for although the name is not written in Domesday, unless indeed the surname Ralph, a sub-tenant of Roger de Laci, in Gloucestershire, was a de Bacqueville. At the beginning of the 13th century their name occurs in Hertfordshire, Northamptonshire, Shropshire, Warwickshire, Norfolk, Buckinghamshire, Wiltshire, etc., and continued for several centuries. Pending further information, it can be assumed that Geoffry Martel and Martel de Bacqueville are one and the same and that he should be styled Geoffroi Martel de Basqueville.

Le Prevost, *Notes, Wace*, II, 250 ; III, 20. *Wace*, Taylor, 229. Plan., II, 133. Cle., I, 83. *Nor. Peo.*, 155.
[1] *Gall. Christ.*, XI, App. C, 329 E.
[2] *Introd. Domesd.*, II, 352. [3] *Mon.*, i, :15.

GEOFFROI DE PIERREPONT.

From Pierrepont, near Saint-Sauveur, in the Cotentin, which up to the 17th century remained in the family, or from Pierrepont, near Falaise. Three brothers occur as under-tenants in Domesday, Reginald, Geoffroi and Robert. The first, Reginald, held property in Norfolk, while Geoffry and Robert occur in Suffolk. Reginald's name appears as Reinaldus de Perapund, and Geoffry and Robert as de Petroponte. The two latter held about 9,000 acres in Sussex, under earl Warren, and there is reason to believe that they were closely related to him.[1] Reginald's son, William, held 4,000 more acres in the county and founded the family of Poynings, a very renowned house. Robert, the founder of the great house of Pierrepont in England, probably held the largest manor in this county, Hurst-Pierpoint, extending over several different parishes, which he transmitted to his descendants in unbroken male succession for nearly three centuries. A Simon and Robert de Pierrepont went to the siege of Acre with Richard Cœur de Lion. A descendant of Robert de Pierrepont was created by Charles I, baron Pierepont of Holme-Pierrepont and viscount Newark in 1627. In the following year he

became earl of Kingston. The name appears in the *Researches of the Bayeux Tapestry* by the abbé de La Rue, and upon the Dives roll.

Cle., II, 55, 381. Dupont, I, 91 ; II, 57.
[1] *Sussex Archæologia*, W. S. Ellis, Vol. 9.

GEOFFROI RIDEL.

The family originated from the ancient counts of Angoulême, who received their fiefs from Charles the Bald in 866 ; Gerard, baron of Blaye, c. 1030, granted lands to the abbey of Fons Dulcis, near Bordeaux, which was confirmed by his brother Gerald de Blavia, his sons, Geoffry Rudelli (Ridel) and William Frehelandus.[1] The last named, living 1079-99,[2] was ancestor of the Scottish branch of the family. The surname was first assumed about 1048 by Geoffry, the second son of count Geoffry, who inherited the barony of Blaye in Guienne, and married the heiress of Perigord. By this countess he had two sons, Helias, the elder, forefather of the counts of Perigord, and the second Geoffry, who fought in Apulia, and came from thence to the conquest of England with William Bigot. He appears in Domesday as the possessor of large grants of land and succeeded to his father's barony of Guienne. In the next generation, another Geoffry married Geva, the natural daughter of Hugh Lupus ; was crown commissioner in 1106 with Ralph Basset, whom he succeeded as lord judiciary,[3] and was drowned in the shipwreck of the *Blanche Nef* with his brother-in-law, the young earl of Chester.

Nor. Peo., 377. Cle., III, 57. Burke, 94.
[1] *Gall. Christ.*, II, 484 Instr. [2] *Ibid.*, 459 Instr. [3] *Mon.*, i, 172.

GEOFFROI TALBOT. *Vide* Guillaume Talbot.

GILBERT D'ASNIÈRES.

Wace (l. 13663) chronicles " Gilbert li viel d'Asnières." This ville and Colombières are in the arrondissement of Bayeux. M. Le Prevost was of the opinion that the name should not be Gilbert but Raoul, who probably succeeded Gilbert and witnessed a charter of 1082 in favour of the abbaye-aux-Dames of

Caen, where also appears the name of Colombières. Ralf de Columbels occurs in Kent in 1086 (Domesday). In the Bayeux inquest the Malevriers, a well-known Anglo-Norman family, are found to hold half a knight's fee in Asnières. They also were prominent in England. Helto Malevrier held lands in Kent in 1086 (Domesday), and Helto his son witnessed a charter of Bolton, York, in 1120.[1] From this time the name appears continually in York and Nottingham ; William d'Asnièrs occurs in the acts of Robert de Torigny, abbot of Mont-Saint-Michel, in 1155-9 ; Rénaud in 1180,[2] and another William d'-Asnières was bishop of Lisieux from 1285 to 1298.[3]

Plan., II, 280. Cle., II, 312. Nor. Peo., 236. Le Prevost, Notes, Wace, II, 254. Wace, Taylor, 232.
[1] Mon., ii, 101.   [2] Chron. de Torigny, II, 244, 323.   [3] Ord. Vit., IV, 262-3.

GILBERT LE BLOND. The lord of Guisnes is said to have had three sons in the Conqueror's army, Robert, William and Gilbert. The latter returned to France while Robert and William held baronies in the eastern counties and are entered in Domesday, the name being variously given as Blon, Blondus and Blundus. Robert Le Blond was in possession of manors in England in the time of Edward the Confessor [1] and may be the same Robert, son of Raoul Le Blond, described in a strange *vision of purgatory* related by Orderic Vital concerning departed spirits in 1091.[2] Robert was baron of Icksworth in Suffolk, having held Oxford castle and several other manors in the same county. He married Gundred, daughter of the earl Ferrers, and their son Gilbert founded in 1100 the priory of Icksworth in Suffolk. The family was large and the name occurs frequently in Essex, Suffolk, Wiltshire, Nottingham, etc. Richard Blond witnessed a charter of Richard de Vernon in favour of the abbey of Jumièges in 1174.[3] The name is carried on the lists of Leland and Delisle.

Cle., I, 152. Nor. Peo., 162.
[1] Ord. Vit., II, 518, ed. note.   [2] Ibid., II, 517.   [3] Chart. Abb. Jumièges, II, 36.

GILBERT DE **BRETTEVILLE.** The barony of Bretteville was near Caen and had been granted by the duchess Gonnor to Mont-St-Michel. The name is variously given as Betevile, Bertevile, Bretteville. Gilbert de Bretteville was a Domesday baron, holding lands in Hampshire, Wiltshire, Oxfordshire and Berkshire. The Hampshire estate was in the hundred of Andover, for the most part on the border of Wiltshire. He owned three houses at Southampton, of which the Conqueror granted him the customs.[1] The name appears on the rolls of Duchesne, Leland and Dives.

Cle., I, 172. Rech. Domesd., 91.
[1] Hants, Woodward.

GILBERT DE **COLLEVILLE.** From Colleville near Bayeux. Gilbert and William de Colleville came to England at the conquest ; the former held lands in Suffolk in 1086 (Domesday), and the English barons of Colville descended from him. William held lands in Yorkshire (Domesday), and his son, William, in the time of Henry I, was lord of Colleville in Normandy.[1] It was held from Ranulph the vicomte and from the church of Bayeux.[2] From Philip, his eldest son, descended the lords of Colville of Scotland. Mackenzie remarks " they were the most ancient possessors of land that are recorded at Ancroft, in Northumberland." Renouf de Colleville occurs in the acts of Robert de Torigny in 1158 and Guimond in 1186.[3] The name appears on the rolls of Holinshed, Duchesne, Scriven, Worcester, and Delisle records both Gilbert and Guillaume de Colleville on the Dives roll. M. de Zeppeler has published a study in Danish on the English and French Collevilles to establish their Scandinavian origin.

Cle., I, 206. Nor. Peo., 206, 405. Dugdale.
[1] M.S.A.N., VIII, 430.   [2] M.S.A.N. [3] Chron. de Torigny, II, 256, 337.

GILBERT CRISPIN 2e SEIGNEUR DE TILLIÈRES. Tillières-sur-Avre is in the department of the Eure, arrondissement of Evreux and canton of Verneuil. The ruins of the great walls of the ancient castle, overlooking the valley of the Avre, remain to show how vast was the site of this fortress. It was built *c.* 1014 by Richard II, duke of Normandy, and *c.* 1030 was given to Gilbert Crispin I, in hereditary custodianship by duke Robert (I) the Magnificent.[1] Gilbert, renowned for "his race and nobility," who first assumed the name of Crespin or Crispin and Crispinus, as is anglicized and latinized, was born *c.* 995[2] and has usually been incorrectly referred to as count of Brionne.[3]

Concerning his ancestry, different theories have been advanced, one of which claims that he was descended from Rongwald, the Norwegian viking, father of duke Rollo, through Hrolf Turstan (living 920), the former's grandson. Hrolf followed Rollo to Neustria, where he married Gerlotte, daughter of Thibaud (I) le Tricheur, count of Blois, Chartres and Tours, and became the ancestor of the powerful Norman houses of Avranches, Briquebec, Crispin, and Montfort-sur-Risle. This opinion is expressed by d'Anisy and de St-Marie in their *Recherches sur le Domesday*, wherein they are supported by *Norman People*, Cleveland, and partially by Planché, but the two generations immediately preceding Gilbert need clarification and substantiation.[4]

Mr. Stacy Grimaldi records his descent from Crispina, a supposed daughter of duke Rollo,[5] and others accord him Roman descent which he may have had from some unknown ancestor.[6]

The generally accepted opinion that Gilbert (I) was descended from the ducal family of Normandy possibly through one of the numerous children of duke Richard I or a female offspring of William Longswood, second duke, persists, in which event he married a near relative.[7] The many historical references to his lofty ancestry,[8] the important fortresses which he possessed in heredity, his vast domains and the high esteem in which he was held by duke Robert I, signifies a very close connection. Certain it is, however, that his children were descended from duke Richard I since Gilbert's wife Gonnor was the daughter of Baldric the Teuton, and a niece of Gilbert, count of Brionne.[9] This fact and the names of his immediate family and descendants have been historically recorded.[10] St-Anselme

confirms it by referring to one of his grandsons as of the "first blood of Normandy."[11] They had issue, Gilbert II, hereditary custodian of Tillières,[12] William, count of Vexin,[13] Robert, who distinguished himself in Constantinople, where he was a famous general and greatly honoured by the emperor, on which account he was poisoned through jealousy by the Greeks before 1073, leaving no issue,[14] Emma, mother of Pierre de Condé, and Esilia, wife of William Malet.[15] A second marriage between Gilbert Crispin and Arlette, the mother of the Conqueror, is constantly referred to by various historians which could have occurred after 1035; whether true or not, it is significant that his grandson, William Malet II, gave the manor and church of Conteville to the abbey of Bec.[16] Gilbert Crispin I was a witness to a charter of the monastery of Montivilliers in 1035 by duke Robert I,[17] and shortly after attested the consecration of its abbess Beatrice, aunt of the aforesaid duke and a natural daughter of duke Richard I, who had married Gautier de Lescelina.[18] Gilbert emanated from Livarot or Blangy,[19] in the vicinity of Lisieux, where the Crispins had vast domains,[20] and when he became seated at Tillières he possessed in heredity, in addition to the latter, the fortress of Damville, then built and had the guardianship of the surrounding country.[21] He was specifically entrusted by duke Robert I before he started for the Holy Land to hold Tillières at any sacrifice for his young son William, as it was the principal fortress opposing France on that frontier. King Henry I of France besieged it *c.* 1040, whereupon Gilbert shut himself within his castle with a strong garrison and stoutly defended it against the combined forces of the French king and the Normans, accompanied by young duke William who, desiring peace at any price, had joined in the assault. Gilbert, immovable alike to persuasion and threats, refused to surrender, but "at length yielding to the prayers of the duke, Gilbert regretfully gave up the castle" (Jumièges), saying to William, according to Benoît, "I would have let myself be burned or hanged therein, but you are my absolute lord and I can not defend against you, your own castle." The fortress was demolished, king Henry promising not to rebuild it, but a short time afterwards, he treacherously broke his solemn oath and, having fortified it, the castle became the greatest thorn in the side of Normandy.[22] After the battle of Mortimer in 1054,[23] in which the French were defeated and massacred, king Henry abandoned Tillières and Normandy[24] to duke William, who then gave Tillières to Gilbert Crispin II,[25] his father having died,[26] in whose family it remained for three centuries. King Henry again invaded Normandy in 1058, but, having been decisively defeated at Varaville,[27] arranged terms of peace with duke William at Fécamp[28] in 1060, formally ceding Tillières to Normandy. In the interim, to compensate Gilbert I for the loss of the fortress, he was granted by duke William the fief of Hauville.[29] His son Gilbert II, in the same year that he received Tillières, donated this fief of " an inestimable value because of its great extent " to the monks of Jumièges.[30] Gilbert II participated in the conquest of England, regarding whom and sire de Ferrières, Wace (l. 13499) remarks : " E cil ki dunc gardoit Tillières," and further that " both these barons brought large companies and charged the English together, dead and captive were all who did not flee before them and the earth quaked and trembled." Gilbert returned to Normandy after the conquest and became the ancestor of the powerful seigneurs de Tillières, whose male line became extinct in the 15th century. He witnessed many acts and charters of the period and made large donations to the Church, especially to the abbeys of Bec, Jumièges and St-Père de Chartres. One of the latter abbey, dated 1107, and another of Jumièges in 1109 establishes his death about the former year.[31] He confirmed to the abbey of St-Evroult (1071–89) with his sons and William de Breteuil lands originally belonging to Raoul, comte d'Ivri, attesting their relationship to this powerful lord[32] and witnessed the foundation charter of Holy Trinity at Caen 1082.[33] His heir by

his wife Hersinde, Gilbert Crispin III, in 1119, ambushed and captured William de Chaumont, son-in-law of king Louis le Gros, when he, with 200 followers, made a clandestine advance upon Tillières, who was released upon the payment of a heavy ransom.[34] Gilbert III married Laurentia, by whom he had Gilbert IV, who succeeded him at his death in 1154. Gilbert Crispin V, the latter's son, by his wife Julienne de Laigle, followed in 1171, and in 1185 married Eleanor de Vitrie, great-great-granddaughter of Robert, count of Mortain, the half-brother of the Conqueror.[35] This same Gilbert entertained at Tillières in 1189 Richard Cœur de Lion and Philippe Auguste, which monarchs held an interview there with reference to their Crusade. Gilbert took the Cross at the meeting in Nonancourt in 1190 and having raised a strong contingent, followed the two kings to the Holy Land, where he was killed 13 July 1191 at the taking of St-Jean d'Acre, while planting the colours upon the walls, leaving three small children.[36] His son Gilbert VI died without issue in 1222, when his sister Juliana succeeded, dealt with in the addenda. Gilbert Crispin VII, the next baron, executed a charter in 1259, kept among those of St-Père de Chartres, bearing his seal. These arms were emblazoned upon the ceiling of the church at Tillières by Jean Goujon about 1525, which edifice was erected at the beginning of the 16th century, where they still appear : a lion rampant or upon a field azure scattered with billitts of the first.[37] This indicates that a lion rampant was the original coat of the Tillières, the senior branch of the Crispin family of Normandy. The ancient church of Saint-Hilaire de Tillières was donated c. 1070 by Gilbert Crispin II to the abbey of Bec.[38]

Jumièges, 84. De nob. Crispin. gen., I, 342 and fol. Père Anselme, VI, 342. La Roque, I, 268 and fol. Nor. Peo., 297, 333. Plan., II, 191.
[1] Jumièger, 84 and n. ; vide vicomte Neel de St-Sauveur, App. 16. [2] Vide Guillaume Crispin, n. 1 ; vide App. 16. [3] Mabillon, IV, 367, 391–9, 520, ed. 1707 and 1739 ; Le Prevost, Notes, Wace, II, 232 ; vide App. 11, 16. [4] Rech. Domesd., 241 ; Cle., I, 44 ; Nor. Peo., 297–333 ;

Plan., II, 18 ; Benoît, II, 171 n. ; *vide*
Richard d'Avranches for their complete
genealogy.   [5] *Vide* Mile Crispin for
Crispin-Grimaldi genealogy.   [6] *Ibid.* ;
vide App. 16.   [7] *Vide* p. 81 aud App.
11 ; for children of duke Richard I.
[8] *Chart. Abb. Jumièges,* I, 69 ; *De nob.
Crispin. gen.,* I, 340 ; Bibl. nat. lat. 13905
et 12884.   [9] Ord. Vit., I, 152 ; *vide*
App. 16.   [10] *Vide* Guillaume Crispin,
n. 1.   [11] *Opera S. Anselmi, Epist.,* I, 18,
p. 318 ; *vide* App. 16.   [12] *De nob.
Crispin. gen.,* I, 341.   [13] *Vide* Guillaume
Crispin, n. 8 ; *vide* Raoul de Gael, App. 8.
[14] *De nob. Crispin. gen.,* I, 341 ; *Hist.
de l'Empire Byzantin,* Diehl, I, 80.
[15] *De nob. Crispin. gen.,* I, 341 ; *Charters
of the Monastery of Eye* ; *Wace,* Malet,
185.   [16] *Dict. de l'Eure,* II, 914 ; *vide*
App. 3, 16.   [17] Mabillon, IV, 400 ; *vide*
App. 16.   [18] Bibl. lat. Rouen, 1035 ;
vide App. 16.   [19] *Chron. du Bec.* Porée,
192 n.   [20] Bibl. nat. lat. 13905, fo. 115,
et 12884, fo. 83 ; *Statist. Monum. du Calvados,* de Caumont, V, 674.   [21] *Dict. de
l'Eure,* I, 927 ; *vide* App. 16.   [22] Jumièges,
117 ; *Wace,* Pluquet, II, 5 to 7 ; Benoît,
III, 16.   [23] Ord. Vit., I, 152.   [24] *Le
Prevost Mem.,* III, 277.   [25] *De nob.
Crispin. gen., ibid.* ; Mabillon, IV, 566.
[26] *De nob. Crispin. gen., ibid.* ; *Chart. Abb.
Jumièges,* I, lxxix ; *Le Prevost Mem.,* III,
277 ; *vide* App. 16.   [27] Jumièges, 131 n.
[28] *Hist. Litt. de la France,* XI, 364.
[29] Mabillon, IV, 565 ; *Dict. de l'Eure,* II,
342.   [30] *Chart. Abb. Jumièges,* I, lxxix ;
photograph of this charter appears in the
Monographie Paroissiale de Hauville, l'abbé
Paul Eudeline, plan., II ; *vide* App. 16.
[31] *Ibid.,* I, 142–3 ; original (Arch. Seine
Inférieure fonds de Jumièges, série H, non
classé) ; *Cart. de St-Père de Chartres,*
518–19, 545–64 ; *vide* App. 16.   [32] Ord.
Vit., II, 399, ed. Le Prevost, and n. ; *vide*
App. 16.   [33] *Opera Lanfranci,* Giles, I,
400 ; *Neustria Pia,* 661 ; *vide* App. 16.
[34] Ord. Vit., III, 490 ; *vide* App. 16.
[35] *Vide* André de Vitré ; *vide* App. 16.
[36] Stapleton, II, xliv and fol. ; *Dict. de
l'Eure,* II, 914 ; *vide* App. 16.   [37] *Arch.
Eure et Loir,* H, 409 ; *Le Prevost Mem.,*
III, 278.   [38] Bibl. nat. lat. 13905 et 12884.

GILBERT DE GAND. Few among
the companions of the Conqueror were
so splendidly rewarded as was Gilbert
de Gand, who held 172 English manors,
and became baron of Folkingham ; yet
there is much difference of opinion as
to his identity. Dugdale, sir Henry
Ellis and others have called him a
younger son of Baldwin, count of
Flanders, which would make him a
nephew of the queen Matilda. This

opinion now seems exploded. Freeman rejects it, calling him a Flemish
adventurer. This latter seems scarcely
true, in view of the great possessions he
received. *Norman People* traces him
from Witikind, duke of Angria,[1] the
opponent of Charlemagne, *c.* 780, which
pedigree seems more reasonable. From
Witikind descended Bruno, duke of
Saxony, whose second son, Wickman,
was created count of Gand in 940 by
the emperor Otho, his nephew. Wickman's second son, Adalbert, was the
father of Ralph, who was the father of
Baldwin de Gand, count of Gand or
Alost, whose younger brother, Gilbert
de Gand, the subject of this paragraph,
became baron of Folkingham in England. Gilbert with William Malet and
Robert Fitz Richard, followed the
Conqueror on his expedition to the north
of England in 1068 and took charge of
the conquered city of York, with its
new Norman garrison. In the following
year, they were in command of the
city when the Danes landed in England
and he was one of a small number who
escaped that massacre. He was the
restorer of Bardney abbey in Lincolnshire, and is supposed to have died in
1094.[2] He married Alice, daughter of
Hugh de Montfort-sur-Risle, who had
(1) Gilbert, who died without issue
during the lifetime of his father ; (2)
Hugh, married Adeline, sister of Waleran,
count of Meulent ; (3) Walter de Gand,
ancestor of the earls of Lincoln ; (4)
Robert de Gand, provost of Beverly,
and possibly Ralph. Walter succeeded
to all his father's English possessions,
and married Maud, the daughter of
Stephen, count of Brittany and earl of
Richmond. He died in 1138, leaving
Gilbert, Robert and Geoffroy. Gilbert became earl of Lincoln upon his marriage
with a daughter of Ranulph Gernons,
fourth earl of Chester and Lincoln.[3]

Cle., II, 99, 262 ; III, 307–8. *Nor. Peo.,*
207. *Mon.,* v, 491. *Norman Conquest,*
Freeman, IV, 204. *Wace,* Taylor, 113.
[1] *L'Art de Verif. les Dates,* XVI, 145.
[2] Ord. Vit., II, 21–2, 506, and ed. note.
[3] Stapleton, II, clvii.

GILBERT MALET.   *Vide* Guillaume Malet de Graville.

GILBERT DE NEUVILLE. *Vide*
Richard de Neuville.

GILBERT TISON. *Vide* Raoul Tesson.

GILBERT DE VENABLES. From Venables, canton of Gaillon, arrondissement of Louviers, near Evreux, Normandy, which was the ancient seat of the barony of Le Veneurs, so named for their hereditary office of veneur or venator (huntsman) to the dukes of Normandy. They appear as far back as the 10th century in charters of the *Gallia Christiana.* Walter Le Veneur fought at the battle of the Fords in 960 between Lothaire, king of France, and Richard I, duke of Normandy. Gilbert Venator, or de Venables, held the barony of Kinderton, Cheshire, in 1086 (Domesday), where he was a palatine baron of Hugh Lupus. From him descended the barons of Kinderton and many other families in England, as well as a French line.

Cle., III, 228. *Nor. Peo.*, 271, 431.

GILES DE PICQUIGNI. *Vide* Anscoul de Picquigni.

GONFROI DE CIOCHES. Chucks, Chokes or Chioches from Choques in Flanders. Gunfrid de Cioches, a great Flemish noble, held an extensive barony in Buckingham, Northampton, Hertford, Gloucester and Bedford, comprising sixteen lordships at the time of the general survey in 1086 (Domesday).[1] This passed by marriage to the Bethunes, advocates or protectors of Arras, but the male line continued as Cheokes, Chokes or Choke.

Nor. Peo., 198.
[1] *History of Somersetsh.*, Collinson ; *Historic Peerage*, Nicolas.

GUI DE LA VAL. The family came from Laval Guion in the province of Maine. At the time of the conquest, Guy II, seigneur de la Val, was quite an old man and confirmed grants made to the abbey of Marmoutiers by a son Jean, who at an early age had become a monk there. Hamon, his second son, was the father of Guy, afterwards third of the name, called "the young" and "the bald," who were both present at the conquest of England. Hamon received lands, which were inherited by his descendants and remained in the family until the reign of king John.

He succeeded his father, Guy II, the year after the conquest in the lordship of Laval, and died in 1080. Guy III, his son, received in 1078 from the Conqueror in marriage his niece Denise, daughter of Robert, count of Mortain and Cornwall. On the death of Denise,[1] he married Cecile, a kinswoman of the counts of Anjou, and died in 1095 and was buried at Marmoutiers. Gui de la Val, a descendant in 1189, witnessed a marriage contract of Waleran de Meulan.[2]

Plan., I, 145.
[1] *Chron. de Torigny*, I, 319. [2] Stapleton, II, cxcix. The name of the wife of Gui II was Bertha (*Hist. de Marmoutiers*, vol. I, dom le Michel, Bibl. munici de Tours, no. 1387).

GUILBERT D'AUFAY. Guilbert d'Aufay was the son of Richard de Heugleville, lord of Aufay, whose father Guilbert, the advocate of St-Valeri, had married Papia, a daughter of Richard II, duke of Normandy, hence Guilbert d'Aufay was a blood relative of the Conqueror. He married Beatrice, daughter of Christian de Valenciennes who, Vital states, was the cousin of queen Matilda, and adds that Guilbert fought by the side of the duke in all the principal actions during the English war until he became king and peace was restored, when he returned to Normandy. Notwithstanding the fact that king "William offered him ample domains in England, with innate honesty he refused to participate in the fruits of rapine. Content with his patrimonial estates, he declined those of others and piously devoted his son, Hugh, to a monastic life in the abbey of St-Evroult."

Ord. Vit., II, 268 ; III, 80. Plan., II, 212. Cle., I, 342. Le Prevost, *Notes, Wace*, III, 272.

GUILLAUME ALIS. From Alis near Pont-de-l'Arche, Normandy. In 978 Hugh d'Ales witnessed a deed of the abbey of Chartres and was a favourite of Fulco Nerra, the count of Anjou.[1] William Alis followed duke William into England, for which he received lands in Hampshire (Domesday), where he was a tenant-in-chief, holding the barony of Ellatune. He was one of the principal vassals of the lords of Breteuil, and this family gave its name to two mills, one at Breteuil, the other at Carentonne, near Bernay, an estate which it held for a long period. He witnessed the confirmation by William de Breteuil and Gilbert Crispin II of the grant of Guernanville to St-Evroult [2] as well as a charter by Raoul de Toeni II in favour of the abbey of Jumièges in 1080.[3] William de Breteuil died leaving no son born in wedlock and Eustache, his natural son, claimed his possessions and estates, in which he was supported in 1103 by William Alis, either the companion of the Conqueror or his son. Two legitimate nephews of William de Breteuil, namely William de Guader, who lived in Brittany, and Reynold de Grancei, of the house of Burgundy, disputed this succession, but the Normans favoured Eustache, preferring a countryman of their own, although illegitimate, to a Breton or Burgundian. Eustache secured the aid of king Henry I, who not only supported him in his claim but gave him his daughter Juliana in marriage.[4] This William Alis was probably the donor of lands to the canons of the priory of Denys, near Southampton, confirmed a long time afterwards by Geoffry Laci, bishop of Winchester.[5] Philip Alis in 1165 held a fief in Hereford, and a daughter of sir Roger Alys or Halys married Thomas, earl of Norfolk, son of king Edward I.

Rech. Domesd., 109. *Nor. Peo.,* 235.
[1] Des. Bois. [2] Ord. Vit., II, 187.
[3] *Chart. Abb. Jumièges,* I, 105. [4] Ord. Vit., III, 344. [5] *Mon.,* v, xi, 110.

GUILLAUME D'ALRE. The name Aure, Alre, or Aure was derived from Auray in Brittany, of which this family were hereditary castellans. William d'Aure, or Alre, held lands in Devon in 1083.[1] Though it is evident that this William was present at the conquest, his name is not written in the Domesday book, nor is he a tenant-in-chief. Nevertheless, the family later occurs in England. There are several citations, which without doubt are sufficient to justify the abbé de La Rue in adding him to his supplementary list of the companions of duke William at Hastings. A William d'Alure witnessed a charter of Robert Malbere, granting his estate of Cheddok to his son. This

William was sheriff of Salop in 1199. Hubert d'Aure witnessed the charter of Emma d'Auvers to Thames abbey, Oxford. From him descend the baronets Hoare of England and Ireland.

Rech. Domesd., 61, 117. *Nor. Peo.,* 286.
[1] *Ex Domesd.,* fol. 61.

GUILLAUME D'ANNEVILLE. This was a noble Norman family which gave its name to, or received it from, the canton of Val-des-Saire, which has at various times been called Ansleville, Ansneville, Aundevyle, and Anneville. Samson d'Ansneville, the first of the family mentioned prior to 1050, was commissioned by duke William to drive from the island of Guernsey, which then belonged to Normandy, some pirates who had established themselves there. He succeeded in doing this, in consequence of which, according to an entry of 1061 in an Exchequer roll at Rouen, duke William gave to Samson d'-Ansneville " his squire " and to the abbey of Mont-St-Michel, half the isle of Guernsey, in equal proportions. In 1066 a seigneur d'Ansneville was governor of the Val-de-Saire. Samson had issue first, Guillaume d'Anneville, who was probably the " sire Val-de-Saire " referred to by Wace (l. 13604) as being present at the conquest and who was an under-tenant of Roger de Montgomery in Hampshire, and a second son, Humphrey, who was a sub-tenant of Eudo Dapifer in Hertfordshire. The name d'Annerville occurs in the *Researches of the Bayeux Tapestry* by the abbé de La Rue.

Rech. Domesd., 187. Plan., II, 240. Cle., I, 30. *Nor. Peo.,* 277.

GUILLAUME L'ARCHER. The family took its name from the office which it held under the dukes of Normandy before the conquest. Willelmus Archairus (general of bowman) held by barony and in chief, in the hundred of Sunburne in Hampshire 1086 (Domesday). Barlow in his *Peerage of England* [1] as well as Léchaudé-d'Anisy and de Ste. Marie subscribe to the opinion that William L'Archer and Robert L'Archer were both at the conquest of England. Fulbert L'Archer, son of William, witnessed a charter of

Geoffry de Clinton during the reign of king Henry I.[2] "Robert filius Willelmi" was a tenant-in-chief in the counties of Derby and Nottingham. Herbert L'Archer of Warwick occurs in the 12th century in a charter of Henry II.[3] A family of L'Archer still exists in Brittany.

Nor. Peo., 142. *Rech. Domesd.*, 203. Cle., I, 22.
[1] *Peerage*, Barlow, 339.   [2] *Mon.*, i, 465.
[3] *Ibid.*, 519.

GUILLAUME D'ARQUES.

Guillaume d'Arques held estates in 1086 (Domesday) under Odo, bishop de-Bayeux, and Lanfranc, archbishop of Canterbury, in Kent and Suffolk, in which latter county Bernard St-Ouen held under him. He also possessed the great barony of Folkestone and had two daughters, one of whom, Emma, married Ralph de Monneville, son of Nigel de Monneville, a tenant-in-chief in Yorkshire in 1086 (Domesday), whose only child, Mathilda, inherited the whole barony of Folkestone and was given in marriage by king Henry I, soon after he ascended the throne, to Ruallon d'Avranches. Their son William apparently lost his estates, for in 1141 the empress Matilda gave to Alberic III, earl of Guisnes, the lands of William d'Avranches together with the inheritance he claimed on the part of his English grandmother, Emma de Monneville, daughter and one of the rich co-heiresses of William d'Arques. The other daughter of William d'Arques, Mathilda, married by command of the same king, William de Tancarville, his chamberlain,[1] who inherited the Norman estates of her father. Cleveland quoting Rous states Mathilda was the daughter of Richard d'Arques, but this is manifestly an error. There has been considerable controversy concerning the identity of this William d'Arques of Folkestone. It has been said that he was William, comte d'Arques, son of Richard II, duke of Normandy, which is intenable since he revolted against duke William in 1054, by whom he was banished from Normandy, and having taken refuge with his brother-in-law Gui de Ponthieu and later with Eustache de Boulogne, is not believed to have survived long after. It has also been suggested that

the William d'Arques of Folkestone was count William's son, but he is not known to have had one. The personage here referred to was William, vicomte d'-Arques, who resided most of his time after the conquest at his castle of Arques in Normandy, which accounts for his not having been mentioned more frequently in England. He was the son of Geoffroi de Bolbec, son of Osberne Giffard, sire de Bolbec and Wevie, sister of the duchess Gonnor.[2] Geoffroi became viscount of Arques and Rouen through marriage with Beatrice, the daughter of Gosselin, viscount of Rouen and Arques. The latter after he had founded the abbeys of La Trinité du Mont (later changed to that of St-Catherine) of Rouen and that of St-Amand, in 1030, was made viscount of Arques with the guardianship of that county which name he assumed.[3] William his grandson succeeded his father Geoffroi in that dignity in 1053. William, vicomte d'Arques, received king William for a few hours on 6 September, 1067, at the castle of Arques, when the Conqueror was on his return to England. In 1074, he was a witness at Vernon, Normandy, to a confirmation of a charter of Hugh de Vernon by his nephew Richard de Vernon, in favour of the abbey of Jumièges.[4] He took in 1088 the monastic robe in the abbey of Pré, situated in the bourg of Ermaudreville, to-day St-Sever of Rouen, and died about 1090. Osberne d'Arques, his younger brother, also a warrior at Hastings, held in barony and in chief in both the West and North Riding of Yorkshire in the former numerous domains in thirty-two different localities, with several houses under the bishop of Coutances. In Lincolnshire he was a tenant-in-chief under the name of " Osborn de Arcis." The erroneous statement that William d'Arques of Folkestone was the son of Osberne was caused by the following entry in Domesday : "Willelmus filius Osberni," but Osberne had a son William to whom it refers. This William founded Nun-Monkton, Yorkshire, during the reign of Stephen, and his brother Thurstan was pincerna of the barony of Sandal to whom William gave Kettlewell and lands in Yorkshire. From Thurstan descended the family of

Saville.[5] Gosselin, viscount of Rouen and Arques, had two sons, William and Hugues, as inscribed on his tomb in St-Catherine's where he is buried, who predeceased him. It has been stated that they left children who were very young at the time of Gosselin's death, which explains why the viscountcy of Arques passed to Gosselin's son-in-law, Geoffroi de Bolbec. William, the son of Gosselin, is said to have been the father of Osberne d'Arques above mentioned, whose son was the William d'Arques of Folkestone. This latter deduction can be discarded since it lacks proof and as Osberne and William of Folkestone were brothers.

Rech. Domesd., 196–8. Cle., I, 47 ; II, 321 ; III, 194–207. *Nor. Peo.*, 141, 392. La Roque, I, 194. *Dict. de la Noblesse*, Des Bois, *vide* App. 22.
[1] *Jumièges Interp.*, de Torigny, 325 ; *Chron. de Torigny*, II, 197. [2] *Jumièges Interp.*, de Torigny, 325. [3] *Ord. Vit.*, I, 382 ; II, 106 ; *Chron. de Torigny, ibid.* [4] *Chart. Abb. Jumièges*, II, 36. [5] *Mon. Ebor.*, Burton, 174.

GUILLAUME D'AUDRIEU. From Audrieu, canton of Tilly-sur-Seulles, near Caen, which the family held from the see of Bayeux. In 1083 William de Aldreio (Audrieu) held lands in Wiltshire, where he was a sub-tenant holding under William d'Eu (*Ex. Domesd.*). D'Anisy and de Ste-Marie in the *Recherches sur le Domesday* are of the opinion that he followed duke William to the conquest from which time the family occurs in England ; Roger de Adrieu held lands in Durham in 1183,[1] also in Normandy. The foundation charter of the prebend de Aldreio made in 1153 by Philip, bishop de Bayeux, was confirmed by the pope Eugene III in 1154. It is presumed that this feudatory was a descendant of the first lords of Audrieu. The Dives roll records Guillaume d'Audrieu.

Rech. Domesd., 104. *Nor. Peo.*, 145.
[1] *Boldon Book*, 580.

GUILLAUME BACON, SIRE DU MOLAY. From Mollei-Bacon, arrondissement of Bayeux. Bacon or Bacco occurs in Maine in the 11th century, but this family was Norman. Anchetil Bacon made grants at his lordship of Molay to St-Barbe-en-Auge before the conquest.[1] In 1082 William Bacon, lord of Molay, made donations to Holy Trinity at Caen, wherein his sister had taken the veil, and is conceded to have been the " del Viez Molei " mentioned by Wace (l. 13654) as present at Senlac. The English family of Bacon, which includes the great lord chancellor and the premier baronets of England, claimed descent from Grimbold, a cousin of William de Warren, whose great-grandson, according to genealogists, assumed the name of Bacon in Normandy. It would be logical, however, that the lords of Molai, who came over at the conquest, were the progenitors of the English family of Bacon. Richard Bacon, nephew of Ranulph, earl of Chester, founded the priory of Roncester in the county of Stafford. Roger Bacon, mentioned 1154 as of Vieux Molay, held estates in Wiltshire.[2] In 1165 Robert, William and Alexander Bacon held in Essex of the barony of Montfichet.[3] M. Le Prevost wonders why the English family prefer to derive their descent from Grimbald rather than the Norman family of Bacon du Molay.

Plan., II, 287. Cle., I, 139. *Nor. Peo.*, 146. Le Prevost, *Notes, Wace*, II, 269. *Wace*, Taylor, 242.
[1] *Des Bois.* [2] *Rot. Pip.* [3] *Lib. Nig.*

GUILLAUME DU BEAUFOU. *Vide* Robert de Beaufou.

GUILLAUME BERTRAM. *Vide* Robert Bertram, Le Tort.

GUILLAUME LE BLOND. *Vide* Gilbert Le Blond.

GUILLAUME DU BOSC. Guillaume de Bois or Bosc, of Caux, possessed estates in 1086 in Essex.[1] The family held lands in South Elmham from the time of the conquest, as appears by a suit at Ipswich in 1285.[2] There were numerous branches of the Bois family which appear to have come to England about the period of the invasion, of which le sire de Bosc-Roard [3] was one. Delisle carries the name of Guillaume du Bosc on the Dives roll.

Nor. Peo., 390. Cle., I, 88–9.
[1] *Domesd. Ess.*, 81. [2] *Suffolk Coll.*, Davy, Vol. XXXV. [3] *Vide* Le Sire Bosc-Roard.

GUILLAUME DE BOURNE-VILLE. There is a Bourneville in the arrondissement of Pont-Audemer, canton of Quillebœuf, and a Bournainville in the arrondissement of Bernay, canton of Thiberville, which have been variously called Bornanville, Bromevile, Burnenville, Bernwell, Burneville, Berneville, Bornenille and Burnaville. Delisle and Passy in their *Memories and Notes of Auguste Le Prevost* [1] point out that the diversified spelling of these names and places in the middle ages caused great difficulty in classifying them under the proper commune. The one here intended is the former, as the seigniory of Bournainville belonged to the Crispin family from a very early date. William Crispin II made a donation of property from Bournainville to the abbey of Bec before 1070 which was confirmed by his grandson Joscelyn in 1155 and in the first years of the 13th century it passed into the possession of Roger of Essarts, near Damville.[2] The participant at Hastings was William de Bournaville who held in Norfolk and Suffolk in 1086 (Domesday), and settled in the latter county. " This most ancient family of Burnaville," says the Jermyn Mss. for Suffolk, " was seated in Livingston, in Colens hundred, and was very early extinct, for sir William Burnaville died without male issue in the reign of Edward I and left Margaret his sole daughter and heir married to Jo Weyland." Robert and William de Bernwell occur in 1165 [3] and the former in the time of Stephan witnessed a charter of Briset abbey, Suffolk.[4] The presence of members of this family at Senlac has been subscribed to by Holinshed, Duchesne, Leland, Brompton, and Delisle carries the subject of this paragraph.

Cle., I, 176. *Nor. Peo.*, 157.
[1] Vol. I, 406–7; Vol. II, 19. [2] Bibl. nat. lat. 13905, fo. 115, and lat. 12884, fo. 85; La Chesnayes-des-Bois; *Dict. de l'Eure*, I, 526. [3] *Lib. Nig.* [4] *Mon.*, ii, 871.

GUILLAUME DE BRAI. From Bray, near Evreux, Normandy. Milo de Brai, Milo the Great or Miles, lord of Mont Cheri and Brai-sur-Seine, father of Guy Troussel, married *c.* 1070 Litheuil, hereditary viscountess of Troyes, and founded in 1064 the priory of Longpont.[1] This family was related to the Gournays and Guillaume de Brai is probably the "sire de Brai" who accompanied old Hugue de Gournay and his son Hugue to Hastings. While he is not mentioned in Domesday, he was one of the subscribing witnesses to the charter of Battle abbey in 1088. The family appears in England for several centuries thereafter in Winchester, Cambridge, Bedford and Devon.

Cle., I, 133; II, 74. Plan., II, 210. *Nor. Peo.*, 172.
[1] Ord. Vit., III, 78.

GUILLAUME DE BRIOUSE. This great baronial family originated from Briouze, near Argentan, Normandy. William de Briouse was one of the most powerful barons in the Conqueror's army. He received large possessions, chiefly in Sussex, including the whole Rape of Bramber, where he built Bramber castle, which was his seat. In 1075 he executed the foundation charter of Sele abbey, Sussex,[1] founded the abbey of Braiose in the time of William I [2] and made grants to St-Florent Saumur. Gunnora, his mother, in 1082 held lands from Hugo Pincerna and Roger de Cuilli.[3] The date of his death is not known, but he was succeeded by his son Philip, during the reign of William Rufus; he increased the vast estates of his father by marriage with Berta, sister and co-heir of William, earl of Gloucester. He is mentioned by Orderic Vital [4] in 1096 as supporting William Rufus against his brother Henry, who held the strong castle of Domfront in Normandy, from which he carried on his operations. Philip was the ancestor of the great house of Braose, barons of Bramber, Brecknock, Gower and Totness, and of William de Braose, who obtained from king Henry II a grant of the " whole kingdom of Limerick " in Ireland for the service of sixty knights' fees. Numerous branches existed also in Sussex, Bedford, Hampshire, Norfolk, Suffolk, Wales, and from him descended also the Wingfields, viscounts Powerscourt. The family must not be confused with that of Brius, Bris or Brix, of which Robert de Brix was the representative at Hastings.[5]

Cle., I, 52. *Nor. Peo.*, 173, 448. *Rech. Domesd.*, 127.
[1] *Mon.*, i, 581.   [2] *M.S.A.N.*, xxii, 81.   [3] *Gall. Christ.*, XI, 71.   [4] Ord. Vit., III, 74.   [5] *Vide* Robert de Brix.

GUILLAUME DE CAHAIGNES.

Le sire "de Cahaignes," chronicled by Wace (l. 13664), was Guillaume, whose family came from Cahagnes in the arrondissement of Vire, which was held of the count of Mortain in whose train he, beyond doubt, came to England at the conquest. Guillaume was one of the count's principal feudatories in Normandy as well as England, where he held lands in Buckingham, Sussex, Cambridge and Northampton.[1] He was tenant-in-chief in the latter two counties, his seat having been at Dodford in Northamptonshire. His son Ralph occurs in Domesday as Radulfus de Caisned, holding Horsted-Keynes in Sussex; he was a benefactor to Lewes priory, as was his grandson Ralph, between 1091 and 1097.[2] The latter Ralph married a Kentish heiress and was granted by Henry I, Tarent and Combe in Dorsetshire and also Somerford in Somersetshire, while Tarent-Keynes was his seat. The lords of Cahagnes were among the benefactors of the abbey of Grestin in Normandy, and were prominent in that country during the 12th century and in England for many years.

Le Prevost, *Notes, Wace,* II, 254. Plan., II, 285. Cle., II, 169. *Nor. Peo.*, 185. *Wace*, Taylor, 232.
[1] *Introd. Domesd.*, I, 390; II, 360.   [2] *Sussex Archæ.*

GUILLAUME DE CAILLY.

The name "de Caillie" is mentioned by Wace (l. 13649). Cailly is in the canton of Clères arrondissement of Rouen, and it is quite certain that one or more members of this family came to the conquest. William de Calso (Cailly), who held lands in capite in Berkshire in 1086 (Domesday), was present on that occasion, as was probably Osberne de Cailly and his son, Roger, who in 1080 made a donation to St-Ouen.

They were of importance in England through their alliance with the Giffards and Tateshalls. Thomas de Cailly married Emma, one of the co-heirs of sir Robert de Tateshall, and succeeded through her to the barony of Buckingham, which at his death without issue passed through his sister and heir Margaret, to the family of Clifton, in the tenth year of the reign of Edward II. The lords of Préaux in Normandy formed a branch of this family. Guillaume Tailleur has the name and the Dives list records Guillaume de Cailly.

Plan., II, 283. *Nor. Peo.*, 192. Le Prevost, *Notes, Wace,* II, 249. *Wace,* Taylor, 228.

GUILLAUME LA CHIÈVRE.

From la Chièvre or Capra, in Normandy. William Capra, or la Chièvre, occurs in Normandy, 1070,[1] and held forty-seven lordships in barony in 1086 (Domesday) in Devon. Anschitillus held from William de Chièvre in his barony as an under-tenant in this county (*Ex. Domesd.*). William and Gosfred Capre witnessed a charter at Montacute, Somerset, c. 1100.[2] William Capre was one of the chief barons of William Rufus and was a judiciary.[3] The seat of the barony was at Bradninch, Devonshire, which was lost during the time of Henry I, but the family remained. They became viscounts of Mount Leinster in Ireland.

Nor. Peo., 197. Cle., I, 276. *Rech. Domesd.*, 157.
[1] *Gall. Christ.*, XI, 64.   [2] *Mon.*, ii, 910; Ord. Vit., IV, 118, ed. n.   [3] *Ibid.*, i, 997.

GUILLAUME DE COLLEVILLE.
Vide Gilbert de Colleville.

GUILLAUME DE COLOMBIÈRES.

Of the baronial family which came from Colombières, near Bayeux, Normandy, on which seventeen fees were dependent.[1] Guillaume de Colombières was mentioned as a baron in 1082 in a charter in favour of the abbaye-aux-Dames, Caen,[2] and is probably the Willame de Columbières mentioned by Wace (l. 13662). Since he does not appear in Domesday he probably died before its compilation.

However, Ranulphus de Columbières, his son, held much land in Kent and elsewhere in capite in 1086 (Domesday). The family appears in Normandy later when Philip de Colombières held the forest of Roumare in 1180.[3] Guillaume Tailleur and most of the rolls carry the name.

Plan., II, 251. Cle., I, 216. *Nor. Peo.*, 143. Le Prevost, *Notes, Wace,* II, 253. *Wace,* Taylor, 232.
[1] Des Bois. [2] *Gall. Christ.*, XI, 71.
[3] Stapleton, I, cx, cxiv.

GUILLAUME CRISPIN Ier, COMTE DU VEXIN.

William Crispin I, count of Vexin, seignior of Neaufles, Livarot and Blangy, second son of Gilbert Crispin I, "for his moral standards and military prowess became the most famous of the Crispins."[1] He was apparently born c. 1015–20[2] and came from the vicinity of Lisieux, where his castle at Livarot was the principal seat of his vast barony.[3] He first appears in history as a witness, with Gilbert Crispin either his father or brother, to a charter of duke Robert I in 1035, in favour of the abbey of Montivilliers.[4] Duke William c. 1045 appointed William Crispin hereditary viscount of Vexin because of the frequent invasions of that territory by the French under Gautier le Vieux, count of Pontoise, Chaumont and Mantes.[5] He had not then succeeded his father Dreu as count of Vexin.[6] The duke gave to William Crispin the fortified camp of Melfia (Neaufles), where he immediately built his castle, and also placed him in command of the fortresses which guarded that border, including Estrepagny, Dangu and Pacy.[7] He held the title of count of Vexin c. 1048, at which time he so subscribed himself (Willelmi Comitis Vilcasini) to a charter of Roger de Montgomery in favour of the abbey of Jumièges. This was executed in the presence of duke William, who attested the document, and all the witnesses were descendants of duke Richard I or the duchess Gonnor. The title however was not hereditary.[8] William Crispin acquired vast possessions in the Norman Vexin, from whence he regularly journeyed to his barony at Livarot, always stopping at the abbey of Bec to see the abbot Herluin when going and returning, to which he was one of the largest donors of property.[9] On one of his visits he had a miraculous escape from the French and around this incident the family history for several generations was written, which has been substantiated by historical records and charters. William, with his men-at-arms, was hastily summoned to Caux by duke William in 1054, where he distinguished himself in the battle of Mortemer, in which engagement he was one of the four commanders with Robert, comte d'Eu, Gautier Giffard and Hugue de Gournay.[10] He accompanied duke William to the battle of Hastings, to whom Wace (l. 13564) refers as "Williame ke l'en dist Crespin," and his name appears on the roll of Guillaume le Tailleur. William returned to Normandy after the conquest, and just previous to his death, 8 January 1074,[11] received the monastic garb and last rites from the abbot Herluin. He was buried at the abbey of Bec and thereafter the monks held a special service on the anniversary of his death.[12] He married lady Eve de Montfort,[13] who, after her husband's death, retired also to that abbey where she received the veil and died 23 January 1099.[14] They had issue among other children William II, Gilbert, who became abbot of Westminster in 1085, which he ruled for thirty-two years,[15] Manasses, usually styled de Dangu,[16] and possibly Fouque.[17] William II succeeded his father, and in addition to the possessions aforementioned held Estrepagny, with Bournainville, Duranville, Drucourt and Thiel-Nolent.[18] The latter comprised an extensive domain in the Lieuvin and he had the guardianship of Dangu c. 1090.[19] He made large donations to the abbey of Bec and witnessed its grand charter c. 1070–7, if the document was executed after 1074, otherwise the William Crispin there recorded was his father.[20] He attested a title deed of Saint-Evroult, 1081, the foundation charter of Saint-Stephen, Caen, in 1082, and later a confirmation to the same abbey as well as the confirmation of the privileges of the abbey of Fontenville at the council held at Oistel, near Rouen, in 1082.[21] He was viscount of the Norman Vexin and is so called in a charter of Marmoutiers 1084–1095 witnessed by him and his sons William and Simon, at which time Neaufles was a barony.[22] He successfully prevented c. 1093–1101 the usurpation of the rights of the monks of Bec by the powerful count of Meulent,[23] and in 1105 with his brother Manasses witnessed a charter of Sainte-Marie at Rouen.[24] He was one of the commanders in the battle of Tinchebrai in 1106 on behalf of Robert, duke of Normandy, against his brother, king Henry I of England, was captured with duke Robert and several others and thrown into prison,[25] where he probably suffered terrible punishment and died.[26] William Crispin II married Agnes, daughter of Godfry d'Estrepagny,[27] by whom he had the following issue: William III,[28] who succeeded, Simon, probably Amaury, seigneur de Chateauceaux,[29] and Milo, author of the ancient Crispin genealogy.[30] William III, prior to 1112, had joined Fulk the Younger, count of Anjou, his cousin, in his war against king Henry, on which account he was banished in December 1111 or January 1112, from Normandy[31] but was pardoned by the king when peace was arranged at Pierre-Percée in February 1113, together with William, count of Evreux, and Amaury de Montfort.[32] In 1118 he joined Louis-le-Gros, king of France, with other Norman lords in an attempt to give Normandy to William Clito, son of duke Robert, to whom it rightfully belonged. He fought in this year before the castle of l'Aigle, which was captured and placed in his custody with Amaury de Montfort and Hugh Château-Neuf.[33] During the battle of Noyon or Bremule, 20 August 1119, between king Henry and the French, William Crispin III, " at the head of 80 knights, catching sight of king Henry, whom he mortally hated," possibly on account of the cruelties inflicted upon his father by him,[34] " charged at the king and struck him fiercely on the head with his sword twice," from which " the blood flowed forth abundantly " although protected by his helmet and mail. Roger de Bienfaite, a partisan of king Henry and William's cousin, " bore the bold assailant to the earth and throwing himself

upon him, protected him from the king's friends, who would have killed him on the spot."[35] He was free again before 1123, because he joined the league of powerful Norman barons at La Croix Saint-Leufroy in another attempt to make William Clito duke of Normandy.[36] For this purpose he was before the castle of Gisors with his great-uncle Amaury de Montfort in an unsuccessful attempt to wrest that fortress from Robert de Chandos II, king Henry's castellan.[37] William was also beyond doubt in the disastrous battle of Bourgtheroulde, the following year, which ruined William Clito's cause.[38] William supported his cousin Geoffry, count of Anjou, in December 1135 in subduing the revolt of Robert de Sablé, wherein he had a miraculous escape from death,[39] but was later captured and thrown into prison, where he suffered miserably. After a long time he was released, and upon starting for the Holy Land, in fulfilment of a vow that he would make a pilgrimage there if liberated, he died and was buried in the abbey of Bec, to which monastery he was a large benefactor.[40] The identity of the wife of William III[41] has not been established unless she was the lady of Lisors. He had at least three sons, William IV, Joscelyn and Robert, who are recorded in a charter of the abbey of Mortemer.[42] William IV followed and apparently died without male issue, for his brother Joscelyn had succeeded him by 1140.[43] Joscelyn Crispin confirmed in 1155 with his young son William the donations of his ancestors to the abbey of Bec, wherein he recites the family pedigree.[44] He left descendants in Essex and Hertford,[45] and was a large donor to the abbey of Mortemer, where he was buried at his death, c. 1197.[46] His son and heir, William Crispin V, is generally said to have married lady Eve d'Harcourt, which is very doubtful, for at the time of his death his wife was Amicie de Roye.[47] He executed a document in 1216 attaching an equestrian seal charged with fusils, which are the first recorded arms of the Norman Crispins.[48] He died between this date and 1223,[49] and his son and successor William VI was deceased before 1254.[50] The latter was in turn followed by his oldest son, William VII, baron of Neaufles, Dangu and Estrepagny, one of the most powerful lords of his time. Through his wife, Jeanne de Mortemer, he became the hereditary constable of Normandy, 11 January 1254,[51] and acquired La Luthumiére, Varanguebec, Bretterville, Vareville, and Bec-Mortemer, then changed to Bec-Crispin. The title of barony was attached to the ground of the latter, of which he thus became the first baron.[52] He accompanied king Louis to northern Africa in 1269,[53] was created marshal of France 1281–3, at which period there were only two.[54] He died in 1313 and was buried in the abbey of Mortemer.[55] By his wife he had issue among other children two sons, William VIII, who succeeded, and Jean. The former had only daughters, Jeanne, the eldest, married Jean de Meulan II, count of Tancarville and grand chamberlain of France, through whose descendants Estrepagny eventually passed to the illustrious house of Orléans-Longueville. Marie, the other daughter, espoused Jean III de Chalons, count of Auxarre and Tonnerre, high cup bearer of France.[56] The family was continued by Jean, younger brother of William VIII, with whose great-great-grandsons, the brothers Jean and Antoine, this male branch become extinct.[57] Jean Crispin, baron of Bec-Crispin, Mauny, Plasnes and Auvricher, hereditary marshal of Normandy, grand master inspector of waters and forests in Normandy and Picardy, councillor and chamberlain of the king, captain of Pont de l'Arche, died without issue in 1453,[58] when his titles and estates went to his brother Antoine, successively bishop of Paris, bishop and duke of Laon, a peer of France, archbishop of Narbonne, and at the same time abbot of Jumièges, who died in 1472.[59] He was succeeded in his possessions by his eldest sister Jeanne Crispin who married the celebrated Pierre de Brézé.[60] The male line now reverted to Hugues, younger brother of William Crispin VII, the marshal who was the progenitor of the seigneurs de Bourri and de Villebon and also the marquis de Vardes.[61] Elizabeth, daughter and sole heiress of François-René du Bec-Crispin de Grimaldy, marquis de Vardes, comte

de Moret, etc., the last of this illustrious branch of the Crispin family, carried its possessions by marriage, 28 July 1678, to Louis de Rohan-Chabot, duke of Rohan, peer of France, and prince of Laon.[62]

De nob. Crispin. gen., I, 342 and fol. La Roque, I, 268 and fol. Père Anselme, VI, 632 and fol. *Le Prevost Mem.*, II, 17, 58. Plan., II, 191. *Nov. Peo.*, 297–333. Porée, I, 30 and fol. [1] *Vide* Gilbert Crispin and App. 17. [2] *Gilbert Crispin, Abbot of Westminster*, Robinson, I; *vide* App. 17. [3] *Statist, Monum. du Calvados*, de Caumont, V, 672; La Roque, I, 269; *vide* App. 17. [4] *Vide* Gilbert Crispin, n. 17. [5] *Ibid.*, n. 1. [6] Le Prevost, *Notes, Wace*, Sup., III, 5. [7] *Dict. de l'Eure*, I, 934; II, 622; *ibid.*, n. 1. [8] *Vide* App. 8; *Chart. Abb. Jumièges*, I, 69; Original, Arch. de la Seine-Inf., fonds de Jumièges, Serie H, non classée; Le Prevost, *Notes, Wace*, Sup., III, 5; *Opera S. Anselmi*, Dom Gerberon, 599 n. [9] Bibl. nat. lat., 13905, fo. 115, et lat. 12884, fo. 85. [10] William of Poitiers, Migne, CXLIX, col. 1231; Benoît, III, 209; *Wace*, Pluquet, II, 73; *Chron. Henry of Huntingdon*, Forester, 205; Ord. Vit., I, 152; *Chron. William of Malmesbury*, Giles, 284. [11] *Anselm.*, I, 226 n., Martin Rule; *Gilbert Crispin, Abbot of Westminster*, Robinson, 15; *vide* App. 17. [12] *Vide* App. 17; Bibl. nat. lat., 1208, fo. 108 v⁰. [13] *Vide* App. 17. [14] *Opera S. Anselmi, Epist.*, Gerberon, II, 51; III, 138; *MS.* 499 du fonds de la Reine de Suède at the Vatican, fo. 157 v⁰; Porée, I, 183; Robinson 15. [15] *De nob. Crispin. gen.*, I, 342; *Jumièges Interp.*, de Torigny, 255. [16] Arch. Seine-Inf. G. fonds du ch., 8740; *Dict. de l'Eure*, I, 934; *vide* App. 17. [17] *Bath Chartularies* [Somerset Rec. Soc.], I, No. 37. [18] *Le Prevost Mem.*, II, 17, 58, 235; Bibl. nat. lat., 13905, fo. 115, etc.; *vide* Le Sire de Driencourt; *vide* Guillaume de Bourneville. [19] *Dict. de l'Eure*, I, 934. [20] *Ibid.*, n. 9; *vide* App. 17. [21] *Opera Lanfranci*, Giles, I, 380; Moreri, II, 287; La Roque, I, 630; *Etudes Critiques sur l'Abb. de St. Wandrille*, Ferdinand Lot, 90. [22] *De nob. Crispin. gen.*, I, 342; Bibl. nat. lat., 5441, fo. 100; *vide* App. 17. [23] Mabillon, V, 229; *Hist. de St. Anselme*, Le P. Ragey, I, 481. [24] Arch. Seine-Inf. G. fonds du chap., 8740; *Dict. de l'Eure*, I, 934; *vide* App. 17. [25] *Eadmer. Hist. Nov. Rolls*, Martin Rule, 184; *Henry of Huntingdon*, Forester, 243; *Florence of Worcester*, Forester, 215; Ord. Vit., III, 381. [26] *Vide* Robert d'Estouteville; Ord. Vit., III, 359 n., 381, and 430; IV, 26; Freeman, V, 174, 843, 849; *vide* App. 17. [27] Bibl. nat. lat., 13905, etc.;

Mabillon, IV, 367 ; Père Anselme, VI, 632 ;
La Gene. des Seig. et Dames d'Etrepagny,
Robert Beree, published by Ch. Legay in
the *Bulletin de la Soc. de l'Hist. de Norm.,*
22 and fol. ; *vide* App. 17.   [28] *De nob.
Crispin. gen.,* I, 348 ; Bibl. nat. lat., 13905,
fo. 19 v°, 48 ; *Le Prevost Mem.,* II, 19 ;
Porée, I, 657 ; *vide* App. 17.   [29] *Vide*
Geoffroi du Bec., App. 15.   [30] *Ibid.,* n. 1.
[31] Ord. Vit., III, 443 and n. ; *Chron. de
Torigny,* I, 142 ; *Chron. Henry of Huntingdon,* Forester, 245 ; *Chron. John of Brompton,* Twysden, I, 1004.   [32] Ord. Vit.,
ibid., says they were in banishment fourteen
months.   [33] *Ibid.,* III, 456.   [34] *Vide*
Robert d'Estouteville ; *vide* App. 17.
[35] Ord. Vit., III, 484 ; *Roger of Wendover,*
Giles, I, 470 ; *Henry of Huntingdon,* Forester,
247 ; *Robert of Gloucester,* Hearne, II, 436–7 ;
John of Brompton, I, 1007 ; *vide* App. 17.
[36] Ord. Vit., IV, 62 ; *Dict. de l'Eure,* II,
52.   [37] Ord. Vit., IV, 70 ; *vide* Robert
de Chandos.   [38] Ord. Vit., IV, 71–8.
[39] *Ibid.,* IV, 156 ; *De nob. Crispin. gen.,*
I, 348 ; Porée, I, 182 ; Robinson, 22 ; *vide*
App. 5.   [40] *De nob. Crispin. gen.,* I,
348 ; Bibl. nat. lat., 13905, fo. 19 v° ;
Porée, I, 656.   [41] *Dict. de l'Eure,* II, 440 ;
Le Prevost Mem., II, 315, App. 17.   [42] *Commanderie de Bourgoult,* l'abbé C. Guéry,
aumônier du lydée d'Evreux, in *Revue
Catholique de Norm.,* Evreux, 15 September
1901, 114 ; *vide* Robert de Chandos ; *vide*
App. 17.   [43] *Cart. de Mortemer,* 12 and
fol., Bibl. nat. lat., 18369 ; *vide* App. 17.
[44] *Ibid.,* n. 28 ; App. 17.   [45] *Lib. Nig.* ;
Testa de Neville ; *Rot. Canc.* ; *R.C.R.* ; *Rot.
Pip.* ; *vide* App. 17.   [46] *Cart de Mortemer,*
20–60 ; *Le Prevost Mem.,* II, 58 ; *Grands
Rôles des Echiquieres de Norm.,* second
part, 12[2] ; Stapleton, II, liii, xliii ; *vide*
App. 17.   [47] Bibl. nat. lat., 17048, fo
704 ; *vide* App. 17.   [48] The seal is of
white wax five and one-half centimetres in
diameter whereon William Crispin is represented armed and on a horse carrying a
fusiled shield with saddle cloth bearing the
same charges, with the legend " Sigil.
Guillelmi Crispini." Fusils appear also on
the Counter Seal (Bibl. nat. lat., 5441; I,
fo. 101) ; *vide* Mile Crispin, App. 18, n. 31.
[49] *Ibid.,* n. 47 ; *vide* App. 17.   [50] *Cart.
Norm.,* Delisle, 519 ; *vide* App. 17.
[51] *Norm., ibid.* ; Père Anselme, VI, 632 ;
Moreri, II, 288 ; *Le Prevost Mem.,* II, 7 ;
Rich. de Gerville, 18 ; *Cart. de Abb. de St.
Wandrille,* fo. 290 ; *vide* App. 17 ; *Arch. de
l'Empire,* J. Boutaric, I, J. 217, No. 20 ;
Cart. ; *vide* App. 22.   [52] *Ibid.,* Anselme ;
vide App. 17.   [53] *Ibid.* ; Moreri, II, 287 ;
ibid., Le Prevost Mem.   [54] *Ibid.* ; *Dict.
hist. des instit. Moeurs et Coutumee de la
France,* A. Cheruel, I, 211 ; II, 733 ;
William le Breton (book VIII) of the
Philippeide ; *vide* App. 17.   [55] *Le Prevost*

Mem., II, 58 ; *vide* App. 17.   [56] *Ibid.,*
Père Anselme, Moreri, and Le Prevost ;
La Roque, II, 1460 ; *vide* App. 17.
[57] *Ibid.,* Père Anselme, Moreri ; *vide* App.
17.   [58] Pieces Originales 928, charter
no. 30 and fol. ; Bibl. nat. fr., 27412 ;
Père Anselme, VI, 635 ; Moreri, *ibid.* ;
Les Chron. de Norm., A. Hellot, 283 ;
Hist. de Charles VII, Beaucourt, IV, 411 ;
V, 67 ; *vide* App. 17, 18.   [59] *P.O.* 928, No.
43 ; Père Anselme, II, 112 ; *Hist. de Rouen,*
Dusouillet, II, part 6, p. 46 ; *Hist. Abb.
Royal St. Pierre de Jumièges,* Loth, II, 233 ;
Gall. Christ., VI, 104 ; *Hist. de Charles VII,*
Vol. II, 1458 ; App. 17.   [60] La Roque,
I, 630 ; Moreri, II, 287 ; *vide* App. 17.
[61] Moreri, II, 288 ; Père Anselme, II, 84 ;
Dossier Blews, vol. 78.   [62] Père Anselme,
II, 88 ; IV, 564 ; Moreri, *ibid.* ; *vide*
App. 18.

GUILLAUME BIGOT.

William Bigot was the brother of Roger Bigot and second son of Robert Wigot, Fitz Wigot, or Bigot. He went to Apula, but returned with Geoffroi Ridel and fought at the conquest of England. He received large grants of land from king William, among which were Dunmow and Finchingfield, Essex, where he made gifts to Thetford abbey.[1] He had a son Ilger, who in 1096 was chief com- mander in Palestine under Tancred, who left him with 200 knights to defend Jerusalem.[2] The name is mentioned by Holinshed, Duchesne, Leland, Bromp- ton and Dives.

Nor. Peo., 318–77. Cle., III, 57. *Vide* Roger Bigot.
[1] *Mon.,* i.   [2] Ord. Vit., III, 178–9.

GUILLAUME DE GOUVIX.

From Gouvix near Falaise. The castle stood on the rocks on the banks of the Laise, where its ruins are still visible. The " cil de Goviz " of Wace (l. 13653) was probably Guillaume de Gouvix, who witnessed a charter of king William in 1082,[1] in which he is styled baron. Alured his son held from the honour of Senlis in Cambridge in 1086 (Domesday). Richard de Guiz was granted lands in Yorkshire in 1130 by Hue de Laval, and Robert de Guiz held lands in Cambridge in 1165 and witnessed a charter for Bernwale priory in that country.[2] He held Gouvix in Normandy, where he made grants to St-Barbe-en-Auge.[3]

Ralph, his son, had Andrew de Guiz of Cambridge in 1199.[4] Richard de Guiz held in Gloucestershire from the earl of Gloucester in the year 1165.[5] The family remained prominent in both England and Normandy.

Rot. Norm., Hardy, 93, etc. *Nor. Peo.*, 218, 272. Le Prevost, *Notes, Wace*, II, 251. *Wace*, Taylor, 230. *M.S.A.N.*, VII, 363; IV, 406.
[1] *Gall. Christ.*, XI, 74 instr. [2] *Lib. Nig.* [3] *Foed. Norm.*, Duchesne, i; *M.S.A.N.*, VII, 97. [4] *R.C.R.* [5] *Lib. Nig.*

GUILLAUME, COMTE D'EVREUX.

From Evreux, Normandy. Robert, comte d'Evreux, archbishop of Rouen, was the son of Richard I, duke of Normandy, who had by his wife Herleva, three sons, Richard, comte d'Evreux, Ralph d'Evreux, sire de Gacé,[1] and William d'Evreux, who married first the widow of Robert de Grentemesnil, by whom he had a daughter, who married Robert, count of Sicily. By a second marriage, according to Jumièges, he had two sons, William and Roger d'Evreux, who came to England in 1066. The latter, Roger, held in Norfolk in 1086 (Domesday), and married the sister of Walter de Lacy of Hereford.[2] Richard, comte d'Evreux, the eldest son of the archbishop and count, was the father by his wife Adele, widow of Roger de Toeni, slain in 1038, of William, comte d'Evreux, who succeeded him, and a daughter, Agnes. The latter was abducted by Simon de Montfort and became his third wife, from which union sprung Amaury de Montfort, who succeeded his uncle William as count of Evreux. Count William contributed 80 ships to duke William for the invading army, and appears in Domesday as "Eberoicensis comes," holding a great barony in Hampshire, Berkshire and Oxfordshire. About 1070 his castle of Evreux was taken from him by king William I, in which was placed a royal garrison. It was however returned to him in 1087 at the death of the Conqueror. He was constantly in trouble with king Henry I, by whom he was banished from Normandy several times, but always had his rank and property restored. He died without issue 18 April 1118. It is conceded by all historians on this subject, including William

of Poitiers, Vital, Wace, etc., that he was at the battle of Hastings.[3]

Plan., I, 248. Cle., I, 325. *Nor. Peo.*, 225.
[1] *Vide* Le Sire de Gacé. [2] Père Anselme, II, 477, etc. [3] *Vide* App. 2.

GUILLAUME DE FERRIÈRES.

Vide Henri de Ferrières.

GUILLAUME FITZ OSBERNE

William Fitz Osberne was the son of Osberne de Crépon, who was murdered by William de Montgomery, when he was guarding the young duke William in his bedchamber, and the grandson of Herfast, a brother of the duchess Gonnor. He was seignior of Breteuil and Pacy, where were located strong fortresses opposing the frontier to France. William was the closest personal friend and chief officer of the duke's household, having succeeded his father as dapifer. Although he is not particularly mentioned, he must have attended his lord in the various battles in which he was engaged, prior to the conquest of England. He, it was, who first advised duke William to go to England and take vengeance on Harold, and later at the assembly of the barons of Normandy, whom William had called together at Lillebonne, when they were demurring and making objections about crossing the sea, contrived to become their spokesman to the duke. He announced to their utter astonishment that they were unanimous in their determination to support the expedition and would do so by doubling the number of knights which their feudal fealty required of them on this occasion. The duke immediately sent for each baron individually and held him to this declaration. William Fitz Osberne at Senlac commanded the wing composed of the men of Poix and Boulogne, for which he received as his reward the earldom of Hereford and the lordship of the isle of Wight, the manor of Hanley in Worcestershire and a number in Gloucestershire and elsewhere. In 1067 he was made governor of the recently built castle of Winchester, and he and bishop Odo were vice regents of the realm during king William's absence in Normandy in that year. After the defeat of Edgar Ethelin at York by the Conqueror in 1068, he was appointed governor of that city and in the following year, in conjunction with count Brian of Brittany, slaughtered the Welsh before Exeter. King William sent him to Normandy in 1070 to assist queen Matilda in the government of the duchy, which was at that time much disturbed. Simultaneously war broke out in Flanders between Richilde, widow of count Baldwin VI and Robert the Frison. Queen Matilda espoused the cause of the former and sent William to her support, who being a widower at that time, became a suitor for her hand. She married him and made him titular count of Flanders. He was killed the following year, on the 22nd of February, at Ravenchoven, near Cassel, by the forces of Robert the Frison, with the young count Ernulph, his step-son. The earl was buried in the abbey of Cormeilles of Normandy, which he had founded in 1060. He married first Adelina de Toeni, daughter of Roger de Toeni, by whom he had three sons and two daughters. William, the eldest, succeeded him as lord of Breteuil and Pacy and all his other possessions in Normandy. Ralph, the second son, was shorn a monk in the abbey of Cormeilles, and the third son, Roger de Breteuil, received the earldom of Hereford and the lands of his father in England. Emma, his eldest daughter, married Ralph, earl of Norfolk, and the name of his other daughter is unknown. His presence at Hastings is recorded by William of Poitiers, Orderic Vital, Wace, Benoît de St-More and other contemporary writers.

Plan., I, 173. Cle., II, 69 and fol.

GUILLAUME DE LACELLES.

The family of de Lacelles, barons of Messie, came from Lacella, near Falaise, which, with its church, belonged, in 1154, to the abbey of St-Sauveur, Evreux.[1] They were seated in Yorkshire from the time of the conquest and during the reign of Henry I were divided into two powerful branches, concerning whom Dugdale writes : " Of this ancient family, seated in the county of York, were divers persons of great note, many ages since " ; the first branch were the Lacelles of Kirby, who were represented by Roger in 1130, Picot, 1139-65,

Roger in 1165, Robert Fitz Picot, and Roger, which latter was summoned to parliament as a baron in 1295. " Radolphus de Lacelles " was the head of the other branch, the Lacelles of Horlsey, who held lordships in Yorkshire of Ilbert de Lacy in 1086 ; soon afterwards Horlsey, Bingeley and Buskerby were granted to the family by the king. Radolphus was a benefactor to Nostel priory [2] ; he had issue Jordan and Turgis of Yorkshire in 1130.[3] The former was a benefactor to the same priory and in 1154 Henry II confirmed his grants.[4] Simon de Lacelles held two knights' fees from the de Lacys in 1165,[5] and in Norman People it is affirmed that the earls of Harewood are descended from him. The present house differ from this statement, recognizing as their undoubted progenitor John Lacelles, seated at Hinderskelfe, now called castle Howard, in the time of Edward II. The present viscount Lascelles, earl of Harewood, married Princess Mary, daughter of king George V. The name is carried on the rolls of Duchesne, Leland, Holinshed and Dives.

Cle., II, 208. Burke, 71. Nor. Peo., 303. [1] Gall. Christ., XI. [2] Mon., ii, 35. [3] Rot. Pip. [4] Ibid., 37. [5] Lib. Nig.

GUILLAUME LOUVET.

William Louvet was a great Domesday baron, having held large possessions in capite in Berkshire, Bedford, Northampton and Leicester, in which counties the family long continued of great prominence. The honourable Neville Lovett, bishop of Portsmouth, is a descendant of this companion of the Conqueror. Guillaume de Louvet appears on the Dives list and that of Worcester.

Nor. Peo., 315. Stemmata Lovettana. Landed Gentry, Burke. Banks. Hist. of the County of Buckinghamsh., Lipscomb.

GUILLAUME MALET DE GRA-VILLE.

Wace (l. 13472) chronicles "Guillaume ke l'en dit Mallet," who stands out as one of the most imposing figures at the conquest. There can be no doubt of his presence there, which is subscribed to by William of Poitiers, Guy of Amiens, Orderic Vital, and all historians of this epoch. So much has been placed on record concerning him that just a few facts of his life will be

recited here. He was probably descended from Gerard, a Scandinavian
prince and companion of duke Rollo,
which gave the name to their fief of
Gerardville or Graville, near Havre.
Robert, the son of Malet, occurs in a
document of c. 990 in Normandy.[1] On
his mother's side William Malet was of
Anglo-Saxon origin, for she was probably the daughter of Leofric, earl of
Mercia, and Godwa or Godgifu, the
supposed sister of Thorold the Sheriff
in the time of Edward the Confessor,
and therefore the aunt of Edwin and
Morcar, earls of Northumberland.[2] He
was nearly killed in the battle of
Hastings but was rescued by the sire
de Montfort and Guillaume de Vieuxpont, and was appointed by the Conqueror to take charge of the body of
Harold, a statement that has been disputed. The consensus of opinion favours it, and it is most logical if William
Malet's mother was as stated the sister
of Algar II, seventh earl of Mercia, who
was the father of Alditha, wife of Harold.
He accompanied king William at the
reduction of Nottingham and York in
1068, for which he was rewarded with
the shrievalty of Yorkshire and large
grants of land in that county. Gilbert
de Gand and Robert Fitz Richard were
also commanders in this expedition.
The former was at the conquest as was
undoubtedly the latter. The following
year he was besieged in the castle of
York by Edgar, the Saxon prince, and
was only saved from surrender by the
timely arrival of the Conqueror. In the
same year he was attacked by the
Danes, who captured the city of York
with great slaughter and took William
Malet, his wife and children, prisoners,
but their lives were spared, as was that
of Gilbert de Gand, for the sake of their
ransoms.[3] There is evidence that he
was slain in this year, but it is uncertain and the date of his death is
unknown. An entry in Domesday that
" William Malet was seized of this
place (Cidestan, co. Suffolk), where he
proceeded on the King's service where
he died," would indicate that his death
occurred during the compilation of that
book.[4] He was a witness to a charter
of king William to the church of St-
Martin-le-Grand, in London, and is
there styled " princeps," which title,

however, was honorary and not hereditary, having ceased with his death.
He married Esilia, daughter of Gilbert
Crispin I, baron of Tillieres,[5] by whom
he had a number of children, and after
his death his widow most probably married Alured de Lincoln, as shown in Appendix 20. Robert Malet, his eldest son,
succeeded him, and was amongst the
greatest landowners of England. With
the honour of Eye, he held over 221
manors in Suffolk alone. He was lord
great chamberlain to Henry I and lost his
life and fortune in the battle of Tinchebrai, where he espoused the cause of
duke Robert. His younger brother
William held the Norman barony of the
family and died a monk at the abbey
of Bec, to which he gave Conteville.[6]
A Gilbert was the ancestor of the Malets
of Somersetshire and held possessions
in Suffolk concerning whom Glover has
recorded a charter, where he styles
himself " dapifer regis." He is variously said to have been the son or
brother of Guillaume Malet I. The
same applies to Durand Malet who
appears in 1086 (Domesday), as a
tenant-in-chief in Lincolnshire and both
are reported at the conquest of England.
William Malet had a daughter Beatrix,
married to William d'Arques, possibly
the viscount, and another, Lucia, who
became the wife of Ive Taillebois.[6]

Plan., II, 94. Cle., II, 261. Nor. Peo.,
141, 320. Le Prevost, Notes, Wace, II, 229 ;
Wace, Taylor, 206. Rech. Domesd., 133 ;
Conquest of England, Wace, sir Alexander
Malet, 181, 269. Vide sup. Auvrai de Lin-
coln.
[1] Vide App. 3.   [2] William of Malmes-
bury, Giles, 285 ; Henry of Huntingdon,
Forester, 206 ; Arch. Inst., Lincolnsh.,
Nicholas, 255 ; Ellis, I, 490 ; Cle., II, 344.
[3] Freeman, IV, 268.   [4] Introd. Domesd.,
II, 322b.   [5] Vide Fouque d'Aunou ; vide
Alured de Lincoln, sup. Gilbert Crispin, and
App. 3.   [6] Vide App. 3.

GUILLAUME DE LA MARE. The
" cil de La Mare " of Wace (l. 13555)
came from Lamare at St-Opportune,
arrondissement of Pont-Audemer, where
the castle was built on piles on the
border of a lake. Guillaume de la
Mare, or Fitz Norman, as he is variously
styled, was the son of Norman de La
Mare, who lived c. 1030. William
came to England at the conquest, a

tenant-in-chief in Gloucestershire and Herefordshire; he was head of the house. He appears also as a sub-tenant in Wiltshire and Hertfordshire in 1086 (Domesday), under the name of William de La Mare. He married a daughter of Hugh Lupus, earl of Chester, from whom descended the barons of Braybrooke, viscounts Doneraile. Hugh de La Mare, also called Hugh Fitz Norman, lord of Lea, his brother, occurs in a Breton charter in 1070,[1] and also held under Hugh Lupus in Cheshire. His line became extinct with his grandson and his estates reverted to the palatinate barons of Montalt, descended from his brother Ralph, who was the earl's dapifer, and ancestor of this branch of the family. The fourth brother, Roger, is mentioned in a charter of Hugh Fitz Norman to St-Werburgh's abbey, Chester, 1107–20.

Le Prevost, *Notes, Wace*, II, 235. Plan., II, 287. Cle., II, 192. *Nor. Peo.*, 216, 223, 307. *Wace*, Taylor, 212.
[1] Morice, I, 434.

GUILLAUME DE MONCEAUX.

The family of Monceaux was descended from the ancient lords of Maers and Monceaux, counts of Nevers. Landry I was from Poitevin, Normandy, who married Hildesende and was the hereditary count of Nevers. He lived in 868 and was succeeded by his son and heir, Landry II, who became the hereditary seignior of Maers, c. 880, which seigniory he received from Richard le Justiciar, duke of Burgundy, for his services at the siege of Maers in Nevernois. His son and successor, Landry III, married a lady of Anjou, and he was followed by Bodo I, seigneur de Maers and de Monceaux. The name of the latter seigniory was derived from a castle which he built and named in honour of his godfather, Bodo des Monts. Landry IV, his son and heir, seigneur de Maers and de Monceaux, appears in a charter of 986, in favour of the church of St-Cyr de Nevers, of which he became count, either by concession from Henry the Great, duke of Burgundy, or by that of Otho William, son of Adalbert II, duke of Lombardy, called by some, king of Italy, who gave him this county in marriage with his elder daughter Matilda. Before the year 992 he took the title of count of

Nevers and died between 1015 and 1028. His second son, Landry de Nevers, was seigneur de Monceaux and was the father of another Landry, who was seigneur de Monceaux, living in 1100, who must have been quite an old man at the time, for his son, William de Nevers and de Monceaux, was mentioned by Wace (l. 13654) as "de Monceals." He is presumed to have been the William de Moncellis of Exeter (Domesday), and the William de Noers, Denoiers,' or de Nuers, recorded as an under-tenant in Norfolk in 1086 (Domesday), where he received thirty-three manors from the Conqueror, in whose favour he is said to have stood very high. At the compilation of Domesday, the manors of Gothurst, or Grayhurst, as it was later called, in Buckingham, were held under bishop Odo by Robert de Nodariis or Nowers, which family afterwards possessed it in their own right. Ralph de Nuers held Swanton Nuers, *temp*. Henry II. Milo de Nuers sold part of it in the time of Richard I and Robert de Nuers appears in 1327 and his son John in 1361. A branch of the family also retained the name de Monceaux, from whom descend the lords of Monson, viscounts Castlemaine, and the lords Sondes. Both names appear on nearly all the rolls.

Père Anselme, III, 195, 196, 197. Ord. Vit., II, 346. Hardy, *Lit. Calus*, 376. *Nor. Peo.*, 336–47. Plan., II, 288. Cle., II, 336–41. Le Prevost, *Notes, Wace*, II, 251. *Wace*, Taylor, 230. *Norfolk*, Blomfield.

GUILLAUME DE MOULINS, SIRE DE FALAISE.

This personage was lord of Moulins-la-Marche, arrondissement, of Mortagne, and son of Walter de Falaise, who is considered to have been the brother of Arlette and therefore the uncle of the Conqueror. The duke rewarded him for his services by giving him in marriage Alberede, daughter and heiress of Guitmund, lord of Moulins-la-Marche, whom he repudiated, after having had by her two sons, William and Robert. He then married Duda, daughter of Waleran de Meulent, by whom he had Simon and Hugh. In 1075 he was sent to the relief of Jean la Fleche.[1] As William de Falaise he witnessed a charter by William de Briose and its confirmation by the Conqueror,[2] and under the same name held in 1086 (Domesday) the barony of Dartington, Devon, as well as twenty-nine lordships. The families thereafter of Molines and Falaise were spread in all parts of England. D'-Escures or Shore was a branch of this house. Alured de Falaise was of York, *temp.* king William I,[3] and was the father of Alan de Escures or Falaise, to whom the estates of Escures belonged, *temp.* Henry I,[4] who was the ancestor of William de Scures of York, 1165.[5] Henry I gave to Baldwin de Bollers the barony of Montgomery with the hand of Sybil de Falaise, his niece.[6] He was the son of Stephen de Boularia, who, in 1096, witnessed a charter of Manassas, bishop of Cambray, and joined in the first Crusade.[7] The barony of Boulers or Boulaia was one of the principal fiefs in Flanders.

Plan., II, 106. Le Prevost, *Notes, Wace,* II, 239. Cle., III, 281. *Nor. Peo.*, 177, 238, 335, 398. *Wace,* Taylor, 215. *Rech. Domesd.,* 140. *Vide* App. 24.
[1] Ord. Vit., II, 192. [2] *Ibid.,* III, 328, ed. note ; *Mon.,* i, 541. [3] *Mon. Ebor.,* Burton, 340. [4] *M.S.A.N.,* VIII, 428 ; *Rot. Pip.,* 31 Henry I. [5] *Lib. Nig.* [6] Dugdale. [7] *Opera Diplom.,* Miraei, I, 166.

GUILLAUME DE MOYON.

Moion, near St-Lo, Normandy, was the seat of "Le viel Williame de Moion" of Wace (l. 13620). In 1026 it belonged to the ducal domain and in that year was granted by duke Richard III to his countess. It was afterwards conveyed to an ancestor of the Moyon family, one of whom, William, accompanied duke William to the conquest of England. Leland [1] records a list of the companions he had with him in his train, which staggers belief and which is apparently an error. William obtained a great barony of fifty-five lordships in Somersetshire (Domesday), with the lordship of Clehangre in Devonshire and Sutton in Wiltshire. Dunster castle was his principal seat and caput baroniæ. He was buried in the priory of Bath and his grandson William, son of his son William, became the first earl of Somerset. From this family descended also the earls of Dorset in the time of

Stephen and a branch of the barons [2] of Okehampton.

Plan., II, 121. Cle., II, 223. *Nov. Peo.*, 334. Le Prevost, *Notes, Wace,* II, 246. *Wace,* Taylor, 223.
[1] In *Collectanea de Rebus Britannicis,* edited by Hearne, I, 202. [2] de Gerville ; *Mem. Russell,* Wiffen, 185 ; Dugdale ; Banks.

GUILLAUME DE SAINT-JEAN.

William de St-John came from St-Jean-le-Thomas, near Avranches. Wace (l. 13642) remarks " The men of Saint Johan " were at Hastings. Their leader, according to a tradition of the St-John family, had charge of the transports and munitions of the invading army, for which reason his posterity ever afterwards bore the horse-hemes, or collars, as their cognizance. This was probably William de St-John, who married Olivia, daughter of Raoul de Fougères of Normandy,[1] and had issue Thomas, who died childless, and John de St-John, who succeeded his brother as lord of Staunton-St-John in Oxfordshire and who was a benefactor of St-Peter's abbey, Gloucester, in 1112. He was one of twelve knights who invaded Glamorgan with Robert Fitz Hamon and received the castle of Falmont or Faumont as his share of the conquest. He had two sons, Roger the eldest and Thomas. The latter inherited Staunton-St-John. Roger married the great Sussex heiress Cecily, daughter of Robert de la Haie, and had two sons, with whom the male line became extinct. Muriel, a daughter, married Reginald de Orival, whose daughter Mabel became the wife of Adam de Port, and their son assumed the name of St-John. Hence the lords St-John of Basing, the baron St-John of Beltshoe, the viscounts Grandison, the earls of Jersey, the earls and viscounts Bolingbroke, the marquesses of Winchester and dukes of Bolton. The name occurs on the rolls of Holinshed, Brompton and Guillaume Tailleur.

Burke, 97. *Nov. Peo.*, 388. Plan., II, 250. Cle., III, 116. Le Prevost, *Notes, Wace,* 249. *Wace,* Taylor, 227.
[1] *Vide* Raoul de Fougères.

GUILLAUME DE PANTOUL.

Guillaume de Pantoul occurs in Domesday as baron of Wem, holding great estates in Shropshire, in which county he was one of the chief officers in the administration of the earldom of Shrewsbury, for Roger de Montgomery. He came to England at the Conquest and in 1077 made an expedition to the court of Robert Guiscard, duke of Salerno, "who received him with distinguished honours and tried to retain him in his service having offered him three towns if he would remain in Italy." William refused and returned to England, where he encountered considerable hostility from Mabel de Belèsme, wife of earl Roger de Montgomery ; she was afterwards murdered by Hugh d'Ige, a close friend of William, who was accused of implication in the deed, by the earl and his sons, who seized and confiscated his estates. Later he was acquitted of the charge and reinstated in all his possessions, after which he again journeyed to Apulia, from whence he returned with a tooth from St-Nicholas, which he bestowed on the monks of St-Evroult. He took arms against Robert de Belèsme, third earl of Shrewsbury, who disinherited him, but going over to king Henry I, William was largely instrumental in crushing de Belèsme at Bridgenorth, on which account he was given the custody of the castle of Stafford and his estates were restored to him. He was succeeded in England by his son Robert, from whom descended the barons of Wem, and his son Philip inherited his estates in Normandy. He was a great benefactor to the abbey of St-Evroult, and his name appears in Dugdale and is on the rolls of Holinshed, Worcester, and Dives.

Ord. Vit., II, 48, 196, 207 and fol., 334, 397. Cle., III, 39. Nor. Peo., 237.

GUILLAUME PATRY DE LA LANDE. This family came from La Lande-Patry, arrondissement of Domfront, near Avranches. Wace (l. 13715) records "Willame Patric de la Lande," "who called aloud ' For king Harold,' " charging him with perjury. He had been present when Harold had sworn fealty to duke William at La Lande, where Harold stopped on his way to Brittany before the death of Edward the Confessor. William of Poitiers states that duke William received Harold's oath at Eu, which seems to

be borne out by the *Bayeux Tapestry*, but this is irrelevant, as Patry could very easily have witnessed the ceremony there as well, especially since he is said to have been held in high esteem by the duke. William received from the Conqueror a barony of fifteen fees in Norfolk and Suffolk. William his son witnessed a charter of William I to Savigny abbey. He had issue Ralph, whose son William joined Ralph de Fulgeres and the sons of Henry II in their revolt. This house existed for about five centuries after the conquest.

Plan., II, 188. Le Prevost, *Notes, Wace*, II, 261. Nor. Peo., 354. Cle., I, 334. Wace, Taylor, 237.

GUILLAUME PÉCHÉ. Péché is the French word for sin, and was probably acquired in the early annals of the family. William Péché the companion of the Conqueror at Senlac occurs as Willielmus Peccatum in Domesday, where he is listed as an under-tenant in Norfolk, Suffolk and Essex. In the latter county he held Netherhall of Richard de Bienfaite, son of Gilbert, count of Brionne, whose kinsman he is believed to have been. Ralph Péché, perhaps his son, about 1113 received from Robert de Clare, the second son of Richard de Bienfaite, the manor of Birdbrook in Essex. The relationship of these families is borne out by the fact that some of the sons of Robert bore the name of Peche or Peccatum. Hamon Péché was ancestor of the barons of Brunne, which barony he acquired in 1134 in right of his wife Alice, a co-heir of William Pevrel. He held one of his own of twelve knights' fees in Suffolk and was sheriff of Cambridge from 1164 to 1166. Another son of Robert Fitz Richard named Robert Peche was bishop of Ely and still another, Simon Peche or Péccatum Fitz Robert, possessed estates in Suffolk and Norfolk in 1130,[1] including probably Trillawe, Suffolk, which had belonged to Richard de Bienfaite in 1086. Simon was baron of Daventry by his father's gift [2] and was the ancestor of the Thurlows of Burnham, Norfolk, lord chancellor Thurlow and the lords Thurlow.

Cle., II, 395. Nor. Peo., 417.
[1] *Rot. Pip.* [2] Dugdale.

GUILLAUME DE PERCY. The amazing deeds of this noble and illustrious family, so well known in English history, uninterruptedly occurring since the time of its arrival from Normandy, form a part of the annals of that country. From the period of the conquest a Percy has been found fighting in the front ranks of almost every war and insurrection, down through the intervening years. They have given their lives in battle and, on account of their political beliefs, have died in prison and suffered execution upon the scaffold; their titles and estates were from time to time forfeited but ultimately regained. Of its origin a theory has been advanced by Glover, the herald, who contends that they were descendants of Manifred the Dane, who had preceded Rollo into Neustria. Geoffry, the son of Manifred, followed him in the service of Rollo, whose descendants succeeded in the order here given : William, Geoffry, William, and finally Geoffry, all born in Normandy, the latter being the father of the William de Percy the first of the family who, with his brother Serlo, first abbot of Whitby, and Ralph, followed duke William to England. This genealogy is disputed in *Norman People* on the ground that Percy did not belong to a private family but was part of the ducal domain of Normandy until 1026, when it became the property of a branch of the powerful baronial house of Tesson, and so continued until the reign of Richard I.[1] This history derives the family of Percy from Erneis Tesson, brother of Raoul Tesson of Val-des-Dunes' fame, with whom he was co-founder of the abbey of Fontenay in 1050. It asserts that the three aforesaid brothers were his sons, all of whom came to England and were the progenitors of the Percys of that country.[2] William de Percy held at the compilation of Domesday thirty knights' fees, part of which had belonged to Emma de Port, a lady of Saxon descent, whom he later married.

Hugh d'Avranches and his sworn companion-in-arms, William de Percy, came to England together.[3] When Hugh became earl of Chester he transferred to William the great domain of Whitby in the East Riding of York,

where the latter re-founded the abbey of St-Hilda and appointed his brother Surlo the first prior.[4] The brothers, it would seem, were in continual disagreement, so that finally Surlo, receiving lands in Hakenas and Northfield from William Rufus, had transferred thither part of the community of Whitby. William was distinguished among his contemporaries by the addition of Algernons (with the whiskers) and his posterity constantly bore the name Algernon. He followed duke Robert to the Holy Land in the First Crusade in 1096, and died at Mountjoy, near Jerusalem. By his wife, Emma de Port, he had four sons and two daughters. The eldest, Alain de Percy, married Emma, daughter of Gilbert de Gand, with whose son William the eldest branch of the first Percys from Normandy became extinct, when the great inheritance devolved upon his daughters Maud and Agnes.[5] The former became the wife of William, earl of Warwick, by whom she had no issue and upon her death in 1204-5 the entire possessions of the Percys were inherited by Agnes, who married Joscelyn of Louvain, brother of queen Adeliza, second wife of Henry I and son of Godfry Barbatus, duke of Lorraine and count of Brabant, who was descended from the emperor Charlemagne. Agnes only consented to the marriage with the understanding that Joscelyn would adopt either the Percy surname or arms. He chose the former, so as to retain his claim to the principality of his father, should the line of the reigning duke become extinct. Queen Adeliza as a wedding gift granted them the honour of Petworth, Sussex, comprising twenty-one knights' fees. Henry, the eldest son of this illustrious alliance, was the ancestor of the Percys of Northumberland, whose fame on the field of battle and brilliant marriages occurred with each of the eighteen succeeding generations, covering a period of nearly 500 years. The first baron by writ was Henry de Percy, summoned to parliament by Edward I in 1299. He purchased the great northern barony of the de Vescis with the strong frontier fortress of Alnwick from the bishop of Durham. His son secured the barony and castle of Warkworth from Edward

III and was a brilliant soldier. He was victorious at Halidon Hill and was one of the commanders in the battle of Nevill's Cross, where David III was captured.

The next lord Percy married lady Mary Plantagenet, the great-grand-daughter of Henry III, who had issue two sons, Henry and Thomas. The latter, a companion-in-arms of the Black Prince, was in 1397 created earl of Worcester by Richard II, whom, and his successor, he served with much distinction, until joining in the rebellion of his brother he was captured at the battle of Shrewsbury and beheaded, leaving no issue. His elder brother Henry was by the same monarch at the time of his coronation created earl of Northumberland in 1377, but later he dethroned Richard, for which he received a grant of the isle of Man, to be held by the tenure of carrying at each coronation the sword with which the new king had landed at Holderness. He afterwards attempted to remove the king and supplant him with the young earl of March, but was defeated at Shrewsbury. Henry was pardoned, but again rebelled in the year following, and was killed at Bramham moor in 1403. His head was set up on London bridge and his quarters were hung over the gates of London, Newcastle, Berwick and Lincoln. Hotspur, his son, immortalized by Shakespeare, was slain in the same battle. The latter's son, the second earl, was killed at St-Albans in support of the house of Lancaster, and the third earl, his grandson, was likewise slain leading queen Margaret's army at Towton.

Three other brothers of the latter lost their lives in the same cause. Sir Richard at Towton, lord Egremont in the king's tent at Northampton, and sir Ralph at Hedgeley moor. The third earl, through marriage with Eleanor, granddaughter and heiress of the last lord Poynings, acquired the baronies of Poynings, FitzPayne and Brian, but all the estates were confiscated by Edward IV of the house of York, his son confined in the tower of London and his earldom transferred to lord Montague in 1467. However, after two years, the son having sworn allegiance to the king, he was liberated and reinstated in the family possessions; lord Montague in lieu of the Percy earldom received the marquessate of Montague. Sir Thomas Percy of the next generation was executed in 1537 at Tyburn for participation in the Pilgrimage of Grace. Consequently, his son being attainted in blood, was unable to succeed to the earldom on the death of his uncle the sixth earl (Anne Boleyn's lover) without issue. John Dudley, earl of Warwick, received the Percy estates, and was created by Edward VI, duke of Northumberland. But about twenty years later, having conspired to place his daughter-in-law upon the throne, the duke was beheaded. The son of sir Thomas Percy was thereupon reinstated by queen Mary in 1557 in the family estates and newly created earl of Northumberland. He, with the earl of Westmorland, were the leaders in the great Catholic conspiracy of the Rising of the North, which met with disaster, whereupon the earl fled to Scotland, but was betrayed and delivered to queen Elizabeth, and he was beheaded at York in 1572. His brother succeeded him, but conspired on behalf of Mary queen of Scots, with whom he had fallen deeply in love. For this reason he was imprisoned in the tower in 1584, where he was found dead in bed of three pistol wounds the following year. The ninth earl, for participation in the Gunpowder plot, in which one of his nephews was implicated, was fined £30,000 and thrown into the tower by order of the Star chamber. He was kept there for fifteen years, where sir Walter Raleigh was his companion, and having interested himself in scientific studies, earned the name of the "Wizard earl." His son supported Oliver Cromwell. With his grandson, Joscelyn, the eleventh and last earl, who died at the age of 26 at Turin in 1670, the male line of the Percy-Louvain family came to an end. Joscelyn left an only daughter, lady Elizabeth, aged four, three times married and twice a widow before she was seventeen. Charles Seymour, duke of Somerset, was her third husband, by whom she had thirteen children, of whom an only son Algernon, earl of Hertford, and one daughter, lady Catherine, wife of sir William Wyndham, left offspring. Algernon married a

Thynne and had issue, a son George, viscount Beauchamp, who died at Bologne in 1744, aged 19, and a daughter, lady Elizabeth, who married sir Hugh Smithson of Stanwick, in north Yorkshire. Sir Hugh, having adopted the name and arms of Percy, was created in 1766 duke of Northumberland, and was the direct ancestor of the present duke. The arms of the family consist of nearly 900 quarterings, among which are those of king Henry VII, several of the younger branches of the blood royal of the sovereign houses of France, Castille, Leon and Scotland, and of the ducal houses of Normandy and Brittany. M. l'abbé de La Rue, in his *Researches of the Bayeux Tapestry*, records the name of Percy and it appears on the rolls of Leland, Scriven, Brompton, Worcester and Dives, also on that of Battle abbey if Perceley is intended for Percy as sir Bernard Burke believes.

The distinguished lord Eustace Percy, minister in the British cabinet, is a younger brother of the present duke of Northumberland.

Cle., II, 374 and fol. Burke, 92. Plan., II, 182 and fol. *Nor. Peo.*, 270, 360.
[1] Stapleton, I, lxxxiii; *vide* Raoul Tesson.
[2] *Gall. Christ.*, XI, 413. [3] *Mon.*, i, 72; *vide* Richard d'Avranches and App. 10.
[4] *Introd. Domesd.*, I, 465. [5] *Ibid.*

GUILLAUME PEVREL. Guillaume Pevrel is generally conceded to have been a natural son of duke William by Maud, a daughter of Ingleric, an Anglo-Saxon nobleman, who was a benefactor to the Collegiate church of St-Martin-le-Grand, London. Freeman and Eaton dissent; however, the weight of opinion is against them, as voiced by Camden, Glover, and others. The latter's deduction is substantiated by the vast possessions which he received and the trust imposed in him. While Wace does not mention him in connection with Senlac, he was most probably there, for he appears in 1068 in charge of the newly built castle of Nottingham, and at the compilation of Domesday was the possessor of 162 manors in England, including the honour and forest of the Peak in Derbyshire, besides sixty-nine houses and cottages in Nottingham alone. Ranulph Pevrel also

appears in Domesday as holding sixty-four manors.[1] He was the half-brother of William, whose father Ranulph married Maud, the daughter of Inglerich, either before or after the birth of William, the natural son of the duke, who assumed the name of Pevrel. From this marriage descended the powerful baronial family of Pevrel of Nottingham, of London and Dover, Kent, Pevrel of Brunne in Essex and Salop. William Pevrel witnessed in 1075 the foundation charter of Sele abbey, Sussex, by William de Braiose.[2] He married Adelina de Lancaster, reported to have been a daughter of Roger de Poitou, son of Roger de Montgomery, sometimes called earl of Lancaster, by whom he obtained large possessions in this county and from which union he had a son William who died during his lifetime, and another, also named William, who succeeded him.

Burke, 90. Plan., II, 258. Cle., III, 1. *Nor. Peo.*, 438. Ord. Vit., II, 19; III, 440.
[1] Ranulph was doubtless at Senlac, which Delisle believes. [2] *Mon.*, I, 581.

GUILLAUME DE PICQUIGNI.
Vide Anscoul de Picquigni.

GUILLAUME LE POITEVIN.
Guillaume and Roger appear in Domesday as Pictavensis or Peteunius; the former was an under-tenant in Kent and in Yorks, and also occurs in a grant to St-Clements, Pontefract, under the name of Pictavus. He held of Ralph de Pomerai under the name of William Pictavensis, a manor called Odeordi, which has not been identified. Roger was an under-tenant in Suffolk and must not be confused with Roger le Poitevin, son of Roger de Montgomery. These Peytevins, Pictavi, or Pictaviensis emigrated from Poitou in the train of the Lacys and held great possessions in the West Riding of York. They became extinct at a rather early period. Walter Paytfen, lord of Hedingley, where he was seated, came to the conquest of England. He married Lettice, daughter of Hugh Morker, lord of Normanton, Clayton, and Carlston, by whom he acquired half the town of Normanton. The name appears on the rolls of Holinshed, Duchesne, Leland;

E

and Delisle carries both William and Roger de Poitevin.

Cle., III, 28. *Rech. Domesd.*, 51.

GUILLAUME DE REVIERS. *Vide* Richard de Reviers.

GUILLAUME DE ROS. *Vide* Anquetil de Ros.

GUILLAUME DE ROUMARE. The exact identity of the " E Dam Willame de Romare " of Wace (l. 13553) is uncertain. It has been stated that he should have chronicled Roger, the son of Gerold de Roumare, as affirmed by Le Prevost, but Roger was living and lord of Spalding in 1100, at which period he was young and newly married to Lucia, daughter of Ivo Taillebois.[1] He died some time previous to 1110 for by that time Lucia had become the wife of Ranulph le Meschin, earl of Chester. William would therefore not have been born at the time of the Conquest. Peter de Blois claims that Roger Fitz Gerald had an elder brother named William, which, if true, and assuming that he died unmarried before the compilation of Domesday, no trace would be left of him, so he could well have been this companion of the Conqueror. However, there is nothing to show that Robert de Roumare, elder brother of Roger, could not have been at Senlac. About 1065 duke William confided the frontier fortress of Neufmarché-en-Lions to Gerold and Hugh de Grantemesnil.[2] Gerold made a donation to the abbey of St-Amand of the church of Roumare for the redemption of his soul and that of his wife Albreda, then deceased, with the consent of his son and heir, Robert, and the attestation of Ralph, brother of Gerold.[3] He had another wife Helisenda, but whether she was the mother of Roger or any other children he may have had is not known.[4] This Robert Fitz Gerold is written in Domesday, in Dorsetshire, Somersetshire, Wiltshire, Hampshire and Berkshire.

Plan., II, 144. Cle., III, 344. Le Prevost, *Notes, Wace,* II, 235. *Wace,* Taylor, 211. *Hist. of Laycock Abbey,* Bowles, 69. Concerning Agnès and Guillaume de Semilly, *vide* addenda.

[1] Stapleton, II, cliii. [2] *Ibid.* [3] *Ibid.* ; *Hist. de l'Abb. de St-Amand de Rouen,* fol. 1662. [4] Stapleton, *ibid.*

GUILLAUME DE SAYE. This Norman family emanated from Say, west of Exmes in the Norman viscountcy of Roger de Montgomery, and was a branch of the Avenel family descended from Picot de Say, living in 1030, whose son, Robert Fitz Picot, lord of Aunay, was co-founder of Saint-Martin of Seez in 1060. He had three sons, all of whom came to England at the conquest, namely : 1, Picot (de Say), baron of Clun and Stoke-Say, Salop, who received twenty-nine manors, and was in 1083 one of the principal men summoned by Roger de Montgomery to witness the foundation charter of his abbey of Shrewsbury. His male line ended with his grandson, Helias, whose daughter and heiress, Isabel, married William Fitz Allen, through whose descendants it passed to the dukes of Norfolk, who still possess it ; 2, Robert Fitz Picot, an officer and follower of Roger de Montgomery,[1] who became baron of Brunne, Cambridge (Domesday), from whom descended the lords Seaton, earls of Wintoun and Dunfermline, viscounts Kingston, marquesses of Huntley, and dukes of Gordon ; 3, William de Say, who gave his name to Hamme-Say, now Hamsey, in the county of Sussex. He married Agnes, daughter of Hugh de Grentmesnil,[2] whose grandson William married Beatrice, a sister of Geoffry de Mandeville, earl of Essex, from whom descended lords of Say and the dukes of Newcastle. The name appears on the roll of Guillaume Tailleur, as well as that of Holinshed, Scriven and Brompton, and is referred to by Dugdale. Wace (l. 13706) chronicles " cil de Saie."

Plan., II, 246. Cle., III, 126. *Nor. Peo.,* 263. *Rech. Domesd.,* 93. Le Prevost, *Notes, Wace,* II, 259. *Wace,* Taylor, 236.
[1] Ord. Vit., II, 201. [2] *Ibid.,* II, 501.

GUILLAUME DE SEMILLY. Semilly is near St-Lo and the castle there was an important one.[1] Wace (l. 13650) chronicles " sire de Semillie," who was probably the Guillaume de Semilly who appears in two charters in 1082. He must have been of high degree, since he witnessed these documents immediately after bishop Odo and Roger de Montgomery.[2] His daughter and heiress, Cecilia, married Enguerrand, son of

Richard du Hommet, constable of Normandy, and their eldest son, Guillaume, assumed the name of his mother, granting as Guillaume de Semilly land to the abbey of Aunay, with the consent of his brothers, Jourdain, bishop of Lisieux, Geoffry and Enguerrand du Hommet.[3] His name is registered by Guillaume Tailleur.

Plan., II, 295. *Nor. Peo.*, 401. Le Prevost, *Notes*, *Wace*, II, 250. *Wace*, Taylor, 229. *Vide* addenda.
[1] *Mem. ant. Norm.*, de Gerville, V, 232.
[2] *Mon.*, ii, 1006.   [3] *Ibid.*

GUILLAUME TAILLEBOIS. *Vide* Ive de Tailleboix.

GUILLAUME TALBOT.

The claim is advanced that the family of Talbot is descended from Hugh, bishop of Lisieux,[1] said to have been surnamed Taleboth. He was the younger son of William, count of Exmes, who some time after the death of his brother Godfry, count of Brionne and Eu, came into possession of the latter comté, by which name he was thereafter known.[2] Hugh " Taleboth," *c.* 1035, granted a charter in favour of Trinité du Mont, Rouen, which was witnessed by Gilbert d'Eu.[3] The author of *Norman People* states that the latter was Gilbert, count of Brionne and Eu, son of count Godfry, and that he was the brother of Hugh Taleboth. The first part of this statement is correct, since count Gilbert possessed Eu at this time.[4] Nevertheless, he usually designated himself Gisleberti comitis, as he did when he witnessed the charter of the abbey of Fécamp, 1032–5.[5] He was not the brother of Hugh Taleboth, but his first cousin, assuming, of course, that Hugh Taleboth and Hugh the bishop were identical. William Talbot, son of Hugh Taleboth, is mentioned in the foundation charter of Tréport, executed in 1059 by Robert, comte d'Eu,[6] who, *Norman People* affirms, was his cousin, but instead Robert was his uncle. William was a benefactor to that abbey.[7] He witnessed as " Willelmi Tallebot " a charter of St. Marie d'Albuniville[8] and a confirmation of duke William in favour of the abbey of Jumièges before 1079.[9] There is no reason to doubt that Hugh the bishop

had a son by this name, since he is recorded in the cartulary of Trinité du Mont at Rouen, as having had one by the name of Roger (Rogerius Hugonis Episcopi filius).[10] This William Talbot came to England in 1066 with his sons Richard and Geoffry. Richard held as an under-tenant in 1086 (Domesday), in Bedford from Walter Giffard, earl of Buckingham, and was a witness to a charter of the aforesaid earl in the time of the Conqueror.[11] He married the daughter of Gerard de Gournay, baron of Yarmouth, thereby founding the great historical house of Talbot. He had two sons, Gilbert, ancestor of the Talbots of Bashall, and Hugh, castellan of Plessis in Normandy in 1119,[12] and ancestor of the earls of Shrewsbury; he died a monk of Beaubec, Normandy. Geoffry Talbot I, brother of Richard and grandson of Hugh Taleboth was ancestor of the lords Talbot of Malahide, a mesne-lord in Essex in 1086 (Domesday), and a benefactor to the church of Rochester.[13] The name appears on the rolls of Duchesne, Scriven, Leland, Brompton, Worcester, and Dives carries Geoffroi and Richard Talbot. William Aldric held eleven hides of ground of William d'Eu in Wiltshire in 1086 (Domesday). This William d'Eu is possibly identical with William Talbot.

Rech. Domesd., 105. Cle., III, 164. *Nor. Peo.*, 412.
[1] Ord. Vit., I, 400, and I, 462, Forester's note; William of Poitiers, Migne, Col. 1243.
[2] *Jumièges Interp.*, de Torigny, 229; *vide* Richard de Bienfaite.   [3] Ord. Vit., Forester's note, III, 452.   [4] Jumièges, 116; *ibid., Interp.*, de Torigny, 229.   [5] *English Historical Review* of April, 1916, p. 264.
[6] *Vide* Robert, count d'Eu.   [7] *Gall. Christ.*, XI, 15 instr.   [8] Bibl. nat. lat., 1035, Rouen.
[9] *Chart. Abb. Jumièges*, 89.   [10] *Charter of Trinité du Mont*, pp. 442–3.   [11] Ord. Vit., III, 452.   [12] *Ibid.*   [13] *Mon.*, i, 30.

GUILLAUME DE TOENI. *Vide* Raoul de Toeni.

GUILLAUME DE VIEUXPONT.

Guillaume de Vieuxpont was from Vieux-pont-en-Auge, in the arrondissement of Lisieux, and Wace (l. 13480) informs us that " Dam Willaume de Vezpont," in conjunction with the " sire de Montfort," rescued William Malet from the English at the battle of Senlac, thereby saving his life. There is considerable controversy whether it was William or Robert de Vieuxpont who attended the conquest. M. le Prevost is of opinion that it was the latter, because he was sent in 1073 to Normandy to assist Jean de la Flèche. Orderic Vital states that Robert was killed at the siege of St-Susanne in 1085, but Le Prevost quotes a charter of Henry I in favour of the abbey of St-Pierre-sur-Dives, which records him as having become a monk there. However, there is nothing to prove that Robert did not have a father or brother William, who could have been killed at Hastings, or died before 1073, and pending further information Wace's statement can be accepted. There is nothing to dispute the assumption that both Robert and William were in the battle. The family was of great importance in Normandy and possessed a barony in Westmorland.

Cle., III, 409. Plan., II, 99. Nor. Peo., 435. Le Prevost, Notes, Wace, II, 230. Wace, Taylor, 207. Ord. Vit., II, 76, 379.

GUILLAUME DE WARREN. The family derived its name from the fief of Varenne in St-Aubin-le-Cauf, arrondissement of Dieppe. William, count of Warren (*Varenne*) in Normandy, was descended from Gautier de St-Martin and a niece of the duchess Gonnor, who had issue, 1, Raoul de Warren, a benefactor to the abbey of Trinité du Mont in the middle of the 11th century, was the father of William de Warren I and of Roger de Mortemer, father of Raoul de Mortemer, who was present at Hastings ; 2, sire de St-Martin, possibly named Gautier, ancestor of the family of this name in Normandy and England. Orderic Vital [1] styles William the cousin or kinsman (consanguineo ejus) of Roger de Mortemer ; however, this is an error. *Norman People* published this pedigree, Gautier de St-Martin, and a niece of the aforesaid duchess had a son, William de St-Martin, whose issue were : 1, Roger de Mortemer, father of Raoul de Mortemer, a warrior at Hastings, 2, Raoul de Warren, and 3, sire de St-Martin, but this makes too many generations for the known facts (*vide* addenda, 183).

William de Warren is first mentioned in history in connection with the battle of Mortemer in 1054 by Orderic Vital,[3] and again as having attended the council at Lillebonne, where it was determined to invade England.[4] He later was one of the powerful seigniors who attended duke William to the conquest,[5] and Wace (l. 13586) records " De Garenes i vint Willeme," but nothing of importance is chronicled concerning him at Hastings. In 1067 he was one of the nobles entrusted with the government of England during the king's absence in Normandy under the jurisdiction of bishop Odo and William Fitz Osberne. In 1074 he was associated with Richard de Bienfaite in the suppression of the rebellion of the earls of Hereford and Norfolk and as joint-justice-general with him for administering justice throughout the whole realm. His reward was princely, since he held the great baronies of Castle Acre in Norfolk, Lewes in Sussex, where he usually resided, and Coningsburg in Yorkshire, with twenty-eight towns and hamlets in its soke. In all he possessed 300 manors and was created first earl of Surrey by William Rufus. The reason for this enormous reward was probably because he married Gundreda, who is believed to have been the daughter of queen Matilda ; she died in 1085. This theory is supported by a charter of William de Warren to Lewes priory, in which he states that his donations, among others, were for queen Matilda, the mother of his wife. It is conjectured that Grundreda and Gherbod the Fleming, created earl of Chester, her brother, were the children of queen Matilda by a former marriage, probably clandestine, and therefore not reported by the historians of the day. William de Warren I was succeeded by his son, William II, earl of Warren and Surrey, who married Elizabeth, daughter of the great earl of Vermandois, the widowed countess of Meulent, by whom he had, among other children, William III, the last earl of his line, who succeeded him and died in the Holy Land, leaving an only child Isabel, who inherited his vast domain and through whom the family descended.[6] In addition to Wace, William de Warren is reported at Hastings by

William of Poitiers, Orderic Vital and Benoît de St-More.

Cle., III, 262. Plan., I, 131. *Nor. Peo.*, 338, 441. Burke, 105. Le Prevost, *Notes*, *Wace*, II, 241. *Wace*, Taylor, 217. *Introd. Domesd.*, I, 506.
[1] Ord. Vit., II, 408. [2] *Jumièges Interp.*, de Torigny, 328. [3] Ord. Vit., ibid. [4] *Ibid.*, I, 462. [5] *Ibid.*, I, 484. [6] *Vide* App. 4.

GODEFROY DE VILLERS. There are several places named Vilers or Villers, in Normandy. Galdefridus de Vilers accompanied the Conqueror in 1066 to the conquest of England and witnessed a charter of St-Evroult in 1081. He had a son from whom descended the Villiers of Gloucester. Pagan de Villiers, his brother, or son, obtained the barony of Warrington from Roger de Poitou in the time of William I. He was also lord of Crosby, in Lancaster, and had possessions in Nottingham and York.[1] From this family descended the baroness Trafford. There is a difference of opinion whether the Villiers of Brokesby, dukes of Buckingham, which include the great and renowned George Villiers, duke of Buckingham and earl of Coventry, viscounts Purbec, earls of Jersey and of Grandison, were descended from this family, or from another Norman race of Villiers. The name appears on the rolls of Worcester, Scriven, Holinshed and Leland.

Ord. Vit., I, 462. Le Prevost, *Notes*, *Wace*, II, 127. Cle., III, 326. *Nor. Peo.*, 422–34.
[1] *Leicestersh.*, Nichol, 189, 197.

GUINEBOUD DE BALON. *Vide* Hamelin de Balon.

SIRE DE GACÉ. Wace (l. 13656) mentions "cil de Gascie," who came from Gacé in the arrondissement of Argentan in Normandy. Robert de Gacé, son of Rodolph, the son of Robert, archbishop of Rouen, and comte d'Evreux, died without issue in 1063, making his cousin, William, count of Evreux, his sole heir, but duke William seized and confiscated his estates and they apparently remained a part of the ducal domain until 1089.[1] At this time Fulk le Rechin, count of Anjou, sought of William, count of Evreux, the lovely

Bertrade, his niece, in marriage. Count William agreed to grant the request providing duke Robert Courteheuse would restore to him the lands which rightfully were his, including those of "my paternal uncle Raoul, called 'Tête d'Ane,' for Robert de Gassie, son of Raoul, has made me his sole heir." Consequently there was no sire de Gacé at the time of the conquest, nor is it known what member of the house Wace may have referred to. Raoul de Gacé was the instigator of the murder of Gilbert, count of Brionne, which foul deed was carried out according to Jumièges by two of the family of Giroie, Odon le Gros and Robert Fitz Giroie,[2] while Orderic Vital ascribes it to Robert de Vitot—probably all three were concerned in it—regarding which Orderic remarks: "Robert de Vitot was banished for assassinating count Gilbert."[3] This Robert was later pardoned and fought in the battle of Hastings, since Orderic adds: "Robert de Vitot after some time reconciled himself with the duke and was restored to his lordship . . . not long afterwards the war with England, in which he was wounded in the cheek, being ended, he fell sick of a mortal disease."[4] The name appears on the rolls of Guillaume Tailleur, Holinshed and Duchesne.

Plan., I, 16, 19, 251, and II, 33, 286. Le Prevost, *Notes*, *Wace*, II, 252. *Wace*, Taylor, 231.
[1] Ord. Vit., I, 449. [2] *Jumièges Interp.*, Ord. Vit., 155–6 ; Ord. Vit., ed. Le Prevost, II, 25.
[3] Ord. Vit., I, 449 [4] *Ibid*; *vide* App. 5 (The name of Robert de Vitot should have been inscribed upon the Falaise roll but was omitted through an error.)

LE SIRE de GLANVILLE. From Glanville, canton of Dozulé, arrondissement of Pont l'Evêque. About 1064, Rainald de Glanville witnessed a charter of Roger de Mowbray in favour of Holy Trinity at Caen [1] and had issue—1, Robert de Glanville, who held great estates in Suffolk in 1086 (Domesday). 2, Walter, who held possessions in Leyland, Lancaster, in 1086 (Domesday), and is styled "his knight"[2] in a charter of Warin Bussel, baron of Penwortham, in favour of Evesham abbey. He probably held from him Rouchcliffe and Weeton, which descended to his posterity.[3] From him descended the family of Butler, marquesses of Ormond, earls of Carrick, viscounts Mountgarret and barons Dumboyne. Ranulph de Glanville was a powerful favourite of king Henry II [4] and Roger de Glanville occurs in Normandy c. 1175.[5] Guillaume Tailleur, as well as Delisle and Duchesne, carries the name.

Cle., III, 299. *Nor. Peo.*, 182.
[1] *Gall. Christ.*, XI, 60, Instr.   [2] *Mon.*
[3] *Lancash.*, Baines, I, 117; Testa 411.
[4] Stapleton, II, xxxiv, c, clxxxiii.   [5] *Ibid.*, I, cxxviii.

LE SIRE de GLOS. Gloz-la-Ferrière, now Glos-sous-Laigle, in the arrondissement of Argentan, canton of Lisieux, and county of Ouche, Normandy, belonged at the time of the invasion of England to William de Breteuil, eldest son of William Fitz Osberne, whose family had possessed it from a very early date. Barnon de Gloz was dapifer of the latter, between 1036 and 1040, which position he probably had previously held under William Fitz Osberne's father, Osberne de Crépon, whose vassal he was. Osberne was murdered by William de Montgomery while sleeping in the same bed with young duke William, and Barnon in revenge for this dastardly act, assembled one night some followers and surprising William de Montgomery and his accomplices in a house where they were resting, fell upon and killed them all.[1] After Barnon's death William de Gloz, his son, before the conquest, succeeded as dapifer in the service of William de Breteuil, which position he held until his death shortly before 1091. It is therefore highly probable that Wace, in recording "cil de Gloz" (l. 13668), referred to him, especially as he was considered quite an important individual by Orderic Vital, although he did not possess Gloz. He married Beatrice, by whom he had issue several sons, the eldest of whom was Roger de Gloz, who in 1119 was castellan of the castle of Gloz.

Ord. Vit., I, 390–7; II, 191, 516; III, 466–91, 492. Le Prevost, *Notes, Wace*, II, 255. *Wace*, Taylor, 232. Plan., II, 292.
[1] *Jumièges Interp.*, Ord. Vit., 157.

HAMELIN DE BALON. The strong fortress of Balon or Baladon, near Le Mans, Sarthe, had its defences increased by Robert de Belesme in 1099, when he held it for William Rufus in his war with Elias, count of Maine, and in 1201 it was besieged by Philip Augustus.[1] Drogo de Baladon held a barony in the Welsh marches in 1086 (Domesday), and from him descended the de Balaons, barons of Monmouth. He had three sons who are said to have come to the conquest of England, Hamelin, Guionech and Wynebald or Guinebaud. Hamelin received vast grants in Wales and Cornwall, and erected a strong castle at Abergavenny. This was one of the most important fortresses of the lords marcher. He founded here a priory of Black monks (Benedictine), and having died childless, was buried there in 1090. His castle and vast barony of Abergavenny went to Brian Fitz Count, the son of his sister Lucie, who was already baron of Wallingford in the right of his wife Maud, the widow of Milo Crispin. Of Guionech, the second son of Drogo, little is known, but Guinebaud was a great baron and benefactor to religious houses during the reign of Henry I.[2] He obtained either from his brother or the earl of Cornwall the three fees of Trehampton, Tredrea, and Trelawney. His sons were Roger of Trehampton, seated in Lincoln, Hoel of Trelawney and Jordan of Tredrea. The Huntleys are a branch of this family.

Cle., I, 126. *Nor. Peo.*, 148, 423.
[1] Ord. Vit., II, 455; IV, 258.   [2] *Mon.*, i, 590.

HAMON DE LA VAL. *Vide* Gui de La Val.

HAMON LE SENESCHAL. From Crèvecœur, arrondissement of Lisieux, where a strong castle still remains in the valley of Auge.[1] Hamon le Sénéschal, or Hamo vice-comte, was the "sire de Crèvecœur" of Wace (l. 13772). Hamon-aux-Dents, lord of Thorigny and Creulli, was killed in the battle of Val-es-Dunes in 1045. He had two sons, Hamon, the eldest, who would therefore be sire de Crèvecœur, and who became dapifer, or seneschal, of king William, and Robert de Crèvecœur, who was seigneur of Thorigny and died without issue before the compilation of Domesday. Both brothers were present at the battle of Senlac and appear as witnesses to a charter of the Conqueror to the abbey of St-Denis, extant in Paris (Ego Haimo Regis dapifer—Ego Robertus frater hujus Haimonis).[2] Hamon was sheriff of Kent in England and one of the judges in a dispute between archbishop Lanfranc and Odo, bishop of Bayeux. He had two sons, the eldest, Robert Fitz Hamon, founder of Tewkesbury, the father of Mabel, who became the wife of Robert de Caen, earl of Gloucester, an illegitimate son of king Henry I. The second son, Hamon, was the ancestor of the family of Crèvecœur, of which one was Hamon de Crèvecœur, who married Maud d'Avranches, the great heiress of Folkestone in the time of Richard I, king of England.[3]

Plan., II, 243, 280. Cle., I, 217. Nor. Peo., 215. Le Prevost, Notes, Wace, II, 264–7; III, 24. Wace, Taylor, 239–41.
[1] M.S.A.N., XXIV, 90, etc. [2] Introd. Domesd., 1–432. [3] Vide App. 6.

HASCOUF MUSARD. The pedigree of this family starts with Roald, a Breton noble living c. 1000, father of Hasculph, viscount of Nantes, Bretagne, c. 1050,[1] whose four sons came to England at the conquest in the train of Alain Le Roux of Brittany, later earl of Richmond; Hanscouf Musard, the eldest, possessed of the great barony of Staveley in Derbyshire as well as lands in Berkshire, Buckinghamshire, Oxfordshire, Gloucestershire and Warwickshire; Hugh, the next son, held in Lincolnshire of the countess Judith, and in 1086 Saxeby in Leicestershire was held partly by him; Enisand, the third brother, held vast possessions in Yorkshire of Alain Le Roux, with the feudal dignity of constable of Richmond. The seat of his seigniory was at Burton near Richmond. His grandson, Roald, founded Easby priory in 1152,[2] whose son Alan, constable of Richmond, witnessed a charter of duke Conan of Bretagne, temp. Henry II.[3] From this branch of the family descend the marquesses Conyngham, barons Londesborough and baronets Burton, as well as John Wycliffe, the great

reformer, and the de Rupierres. Ruald, the fourth son, was surnamed Abode, and held three lordships in capite in Devonshire in 1086. His son Ruald was the father of Alan Fitz Ruald; married lady Alis de Dodbroke, through whom he acquired extensive estates.[4] From him descended Theobald Roualt, who became seated in France, temp. Edward II, as sire de Boismenard, from whom descended Joachim Rouault, marshal of France. He died in 1478 and his posterity became settled in England, during the reign of Charles I, and were the ancestors of the barons of Northwick. Lechaudé d'Anisy and de Sainte-Marie, in their Recherches-sur-le-Domesday, derived the family from the Musards, who were lords of Sauxelles and Issoudun-sur-Creuse in La Marche, but the Brittany descent fits in better with the surrounding circumstances, since they appear to have been vassals of count Alain Le Roux. The name appears on the rolls of Holinshed, Duchesne, Scriven, Leland and Dives.

Cle., II, 272. Rech. Domesd., 222. Nor. Peo., 180, 382, 385, 396 and 450.
[1] Lobineau, II, 117. [2] Mon., ii, 649. [3] Ibid., 883, 903. [4] Devon, Pole; called Ruaud l'Adoube.

HENRI DE DOMFRONT. The castle of Domfront, situated in the department of the Orne, was one of the strongest and most celebrated in the early history of Normandy. It belonged to the family of Talvas, who were, prior to 1048, constantly in conflict with Geoffry Martel, count of Maine, for its possession. At this period duke William, giving his support to the Belesmes, intrenched them in its custody. Prince Henry, later king of England, possessed the castle in 1094, from which fortress he operated against his brother William Rufus and held it until he became king. Warin de Domfront, eldest son of William I, lord of Domfront, Mortain and Nogent, and viscount of Chateaudun in the right of his wife Melisende, treacherously murdered Gunheir de Bellesme about 1027,[1] for which dastardly deed, according to a fable recorded in Jumièges,[2] he was "strangled by a deamon in the presence of his friends." It would seem very probable that Henri de Domfront was descended from this family, who brought under his banner to the conquest of England eighty knights from the Passais-Normand in company with Archard d'Ambrières, Mathieu de la Ferté-Macé and Raoul Taillebois.

Rech. Domesd., 48 and 250.   Plan., II, 285. *Essai sur l'hist. ant. de ville et arrd. de Domfront,* Caillebotte, p. 11.
[1] Ord. Vit., IV, 110.   [2] Jumièges, 102.

HENRI DE FERRIÈRES. Henry de Ferrières is referred to by Wace (l. 13499) thus: "Henri li sire de Ferrières," and he who then held Tillières (Gilbert Crispin II) " brought large companies," etc. He was seigneur de Saint Hilaire de Ferrièrs near Bernay and the son of Walkelin de Ferrers, who fell in a contest with Hugh de Montfort I early in the reign of duke William, in which both of these noblemen were killed. He had an elder brother William, also reported at Hastings, undoubtedly well advanced in years at that time, who died before the compilation of Domesday, where his name does not appear. Henry de Ferrers received 210 manors, 114 of which were in Derbyshire. The seat of his chief barony was Tutbury castle in Staffordshire, which had previously belonged to Hugh Lupus, but upon the latter becoming the earl of Chester in 1071, it was granted to Henry de Ferrers, who founded nearby a Cluniac monastry. Henry was appointed one of the commissioners for the general survey in 1085 and richly endowed the priory of Tutbury in 1089. He married Berta, whose identity is unknown, by whom he had three sons, Enguenulf, William and Robert. The two eldest died during his lifetime without issue and Robert succeeded him, becoming the first earl of Derby (Rodbertum Siquidem de Stotesburia (de Ferrariis) probum militem legitimumque, Comitem Derbiciae Constituit)[1] in 1138. His son Robert, the second earl of Derby or earl of Ferrières was probably the Robert who distinguished himself at the battle of Northallerton, known as the battle of the Standard. The third earl rebelled against Henry II, was subdued and surrendered his castles of Tutbury and Duffield, which were demolished. William, the next earl was a great favourite of king John, from whom he received vast grants of land, amongst which was the great Northampton estate of William Pevrel, whose daughter one of his ancestors had married. Earl William was largely instrumental in placing Henry III on the throne and took an important part in the siege of mount Sorrel and the battle of Lincoln. In 1230 he was one of the three chief counsellors recommended to the king by the barons and died in 1240. William, the next earl, married two great heiresses, first, a daughter of William Marshal, earl of Pembroke, and second, the heiress of Roger, earl of Winchester. From the latter marriage sprung two sons, Robert the sixth earl, and William, who received the lordship of Groby from his mother and founded this still existing family. The fifth earl, William, died in 1254, whose eldest son was the last earl of Derby of this branch, although his male line continued for six generations. Robert, the last earl, revolted in Worcester, was defeated at Evesham and pardoned on payment of a heavy ransom, but the next year taking up arms again in north Derbyshire, he was routed at Burton bridge, wherefore he was deprived of the earldom which was given to the king's son Edmund Crouchback. His son John was summoned to parliament as lord Ferrers of Chartley, Staffordshire, in 1299. This barony in 1450 passed through the female line to the house of Devereaux on the death of the last male heir. Robert, a descendant, was created lord Ferrers of Chartley in 1677, and viscount Tamworth and earl Ferrers in 1711. A branch of the family of Ferrers, represented by lord Eggington in Derbyshire, is mentioned by Dugdale, and another was seated in Bedfordshire.

Plan., II, 69. Burke, 52. Cle., II, 25. *Nov. Peo.,* 241. Le Prevost, II, 32. *M.S.A.N.,* IV, 434. *Wace,* Pluquet, II, 2 n. *Wace,* Taylor, 208–8. *Mon.,* i, 354. *Feudal Hist. of Derbysh.,* Yeatman.
[1] Ord. Vit., ed Le Prevost, V, 111–12.

HERBERT D'AIGNEAUX. This family came from the viscountcy of Caen in the Cotentin and gave its name to the parish of Aigneaux. It must have existed before the beginning of the

Norman invasion; its power, great belongings and donations from the year 1066 show that it had been established for a long time. It was evidently represented at the conquest, but is not mentioned in Domesday unless under the first name (Petrus) de Agnellis. The representative at Senlac was probably Herbert, from whom bishop Odo of Bayeux acquired property which he gave to his church in 1074, and in the same year he also purchased lands from Corbin, son of Herbert. A branch settled at an early date in Scotland and held the hereditary shrievalty of Wigton, from whom descended the baronets Agnew. The Aïgneauxs had a very important barony, which constituted a great number of fiefs and sub-fiefs for seven miles along the river La Vire. They also possessed the domain of St-Contest at Amfreville, on the island of Marie and other places. They were benefactors to almost all the religious establishments in this part of Normandy. The name appears in the *Researches of the Bayeux Tapestry* by l'abbé de La Rue and occurs on the Dives roll.

Rech. Domesd., 259. *Nor. Peo.*, 136.

HONFROI de BOHON. This family originated from Bohon in the arrondissement of St-Lo in the Cotentin, Normandy, where there still exists St-André and St-Georges de Bohon. The mound of the old castle is still visible. Wace (l. 13583) chronicles "E de Bohun li vieil Onfrei," the companion of the Conqueror at Senlac, who at that time held the fief. He is reputed to have been a near kinsman of duke William, but how or to what degree is not clear. The fact remains that the witnesses to the Benedictine priory at St-George's in 1092, were all members of king William's immediate family or branches thereof. He was married three times, the names of his wives being unknown, and died prior to 1113, leaving three sons, Robert, who died unmarried during his lifetime, Richard de Meri, sire de Bohun, 1070 to 1113, whose daughter and heir carried his Norman barony to Engelger and Angevin. From him descended also in the female line the Bohuns of Midhurst in Sussex. The third son, Humphrey II, was the

ancestor of very illustrious nobility, as from him descended the earls of Hereford, Sussex and Northampton, the former of whom were hereditary constables of England. Alliances in the female line were made with Thomas of Woodstock, earl of Gloucester, son of Henry III, and with Henry Bolingbroke, son of John of Gaunt, duke of Lancaster, and subsequently king Henry IV.

Rech., de Gerville. *Introd. Domesd.*, I, 383. *Herald and Genealogists*, VI, 481. Burke, 20. Plan., II, 63. Cle., I, 71. Le Prevost, *Notes, Wace,* II, 240. *Wace,* Taylor, 216.

HONFROI DE CARTERET. The family of Carteret were seigniors of Carteret near Barneville in the arrondissement of Valognes, Normandy, and Wace (l. 13584) mentions "De Cartrai Onfrei e Maugier," a newly made knight. Regnaud de Carteret, son of Honfroi, living *c.* 1000, accompanied duke Robert the Magnificent to the Holy Land in 1035.[1] Gui L'Oiseleur, who founded the Norman abbey of Fontenelles, was the father of Geoffroi, sire de Carteret, who in turn is supposed to have been the father of the two Carterets at Senlac. There is very little known or on record concerning these brothers. Roger de Carteret is mentioned on the Dives roll, but does not appear on any of the others. Reginald de Carteraye accompanied duke Robert Courtheuse to the Holy Land in 1096 and was present at the capture of Jerusalem under Geoffry de Boullion. His son Phillip de Carteret held the barony of Carteret and considerable lands nearby, as well as possessions in Guernsey, where he built the church of Torteval in 1129, and may have been the Phillip de Carteret, who appears in a charter of Mont-St-Michel, executed between 1155 and 1159.[2] He also held "Le grand fief Haubert de St-Ouen" in Jersey with the governorship of its island fortresses, which remained for generations in the family, from whom descended the earls of Granville, the marquesses of Bath and Tweeddale and the earls Dysart and Cowper.

Le Prevost, *Notes, Wace,* II, 240. *Wace,* Taylor, 217. Plan., II, 284. Cle., I, 266. *Rech.*, de Gerville, 14.
[1] *Peerage*, Collins.   [2] *Chron. de Torigny,* II, 237.

HONFROI VIS DE LOUP. This seigneur emanated from Vis-de-Lou in Normandy. He held a barony in Berkshire, and in addition was a mesne lord in the same county, as well as in Hampshire. Ralph, his brother, held in Norfolk, in 1086 (Domesday), from whom descended William de Vis-de-Lou, lord of " Visdelieus " in Shelfhanger in 1170.[1] A member of the Berkshire line, Walkelin Vis de Lou, held a barony in 1165 [2] and sir William Vis de Lou likewise appears there c. 1300.[3] Sir Thomas occurs c. 1350, and a branch was seated for seven generations at Shotley, Suffolk. The family remained in these counties for many centuries.

Cle., III, 324. Nor. Peo., 242, 433. Rech. Domesd., 147.
[1] Blomfield, I, 114–17.   [2] Lib. Nig.
[3] Parliamentary Writs, Palgrave.

HUARD DE VERNON. Vide Richard de Vernon.

HUBERT DE PORT. Vide Hugue de Port.

HUBERT DE RIE. Vide Eudo Dapifer, Sire de Preaux.

HUGUE L'ASNE. The family came from l'Asne, near Argentan, Normandy. Hugo de l'Asne witnessed a charter of William Fitz Osberne to the abbey of Lire, Normandy, in 1066,[1] and one of Fulk, dean of St-Evroult, made between 1071 and 1089, to that abbey, which was confirmed by William de Breteuil. Hugh was a vassal of William on his domains in the county of Hereford.[2] He came to the conquest apparently with William Fitz Osberne under whom he settled in the west of England, where he was actively employed in the defence of the border of this lord, then earl of Hereford. He held in capite Kentchester in Herefordshire, with twenty manors, and claimed the great lordship of Radnor at the time of the survey, when he must have been advanced in years. He also possessed Knighton and Norton in Shropshire, Brockworth and the lands of Wluuard in Shipton, Salperton and Bagendon in Gloucestershire.

The barony was lost during the reign of Henry I, but the family continued.

Rech. Domesd., 225. Nor. Peo., 140. Cle., II, 221.
[1] Gall. Christ., XI, 125 Instr.   [2] Ord. Vit., II, 187, and ed. n.

HUGUE DE BEAUCHAMP. Beauchamps, near Avranches, in the Cotentin, was part of the barony of St-Denis le Gaste.[1] Hugo de Belcamp is written in Domesday as holding a great barony, comprising thirty-seven lordships in Bedford, Buckingham and Hertford. The name appears on all of the lists of the companions of the Conqueror, but none of the contemporary historians mention it. Hugh is said to have had three sons, Simon, who died without issue, Pagan, the possessor of the whole barony of Bedford with its castle, and Milo. Another Milo, a member of this family, whose identity is obscure, defended this castle against the assault of king Stephan, to whom he was eventually compelled to surrender. This great family, one of whom was amongst the founders of the order of the Garter, was the same race as the Grenvilles, Meurdracs, Montagues and were the ancestors of the earls of Warwick.

Burke, 26. Plan., II, 172. Cle., I, 127. Nor. Peo., 154. Rech., de Gerville.
[1] Rech., de Gerville.

HUGUE DE BERNIÈRES. Bernières is in Normandy, near Falaise. Hugue de Bernières was a sub-tenant in Essex, Cambridge and Middlesex in 1086 (Domesday). He held Bernston and Roding Bernères under Geoffry de Mandeville in the former county. Eversdon in Cambridge was his chief seat and that of his posterity. William de Bernières in 1093 witnessed a charter of Robert Fitz Hugh to Chester abbey. Ralph Berniers held six knights' fees, and Richard de Berniers seven, in 1165. In 1264 Ralph de Berners, one of the rebellious barons, was reinstated and pardoned and served later as the sheriff of Berks. He died in 1296, possessed of Islington in Middlesex, West Horsley in Surrey, Icklingham in Sussex, and the old Domesday manor of Berners' Berwick in Essex. A descendant, Margery, the sole heir of Richard de Bernières, married sir John Bourchier, eventually summoned to parliament in 1454, as lord Berners. This sir John was the fourth son of William, earl of Eu, by Anne Plantaganet, his wife. The title fell into abeyance and descending through heiresses to Robert Wilton, of Didlington, and to Luisa Strangways as co-heirs, and was eventually conferred on the former.

Burke, 19. Cle., I, 98. Nor. Peo., 149. Lib. Nig.

HUGUE DE BOLBEC.

HUGUE DE BOLBEC. From Bolbec, arrondissement of Havre. The printed text of Wace gives " Li Viel Luce de Bolbec " (l. 13665), but the manuscript of Duchesne reads, " le filz Hue de Bolbec," while the British museum manuscript reads " vielz Hue," which may be presumed to be correct. Le Prevost, Taylor, Delisle and Stow all take this view. He held a barony in Buckingham, etc., in 1086 (Domesday) under Walter Gifford, lord of Bolbec and Longueville, whom he accompanied to England at the conquest, and whose brother he is said to have been. They joined in 1061 in the donation of the church of Bolbec to the abbey of Bernay.[1] He had two sons, Hugh and Walter, and the family also possessed a barony in Northumberland.

Nor. Peo., 177. Le Prevost, Notes, Wace, II, 254. Wace, Taylor, 232. Rech. Domesd., 176.

[1] Introd. Domesd., I, 383 ; Essai hist. de Bolbec, Collen Castaigne, in 8vo ; Hist. de Bolbec, Duval, in 16mo.

HUGUE DE CARBONNEL.

HUGUE DE CARBONNEL. The Carbonnels were sires of Cerisy, arrondissement of St-Lo. Their ancient castle, Château Robert, was on the river Avre, of which the foundations still remain. According to the genealogy of the family, it was Hugue de Carbonnel, sire de Cerisy, who was at the conquest. He followed duke Robert to the Holy Land and distinguished himself at the taking of Jerusalem. He may have been the Carbonnel who held a Hereford manor of the king in capite in 1086 (Domesday). In the reign of Henry II the family of Carbonnel possessed property in Brevands, a parish in the deanery of Carentan, in the Cotentin, and William Carbonel owned

an extensive tract of land within the diocese of Rouen on the left bank of the Seine at the same period. Cerisy was elevated into a marquessate in favour of René de Carbonnel in 1643. In England the family long flourished in Hereford, Buckingham and Oxford. The name appears in the Researches of the Bayeux Tapestry by l'abbé de La Rue, as well as on the Dives list of Léopold Delisle.

Cle., I, 251. Nor. Peo., 188. Stapleton, I, lxxxiv, cxvii.

HUGUE DE GOURNAY.

HUGUE DE GOURNAY. Hugue de Gournay, second of the name, was sire of Gournay in the district of Le Brai, in Normandy, and is assumed to be the individual to whom Wace refers (l. 13588) as " E li Viel Hue de Gornai." He attended duke William to the conquest of England accompanied by his son, Hugue (III) le Jeune and the sire de Brai. This family is presumed to have followed Rollo to Neustria, where it was allotted part of the district of Le Brai, in which the principal places were Gournay and La Ferté. Eudes, whose son Hugh I erected a strong castle there, is the first of the name appearing in Normandy. The latter was succeeded by Renaud de Gournay, who by his wife, Alberada, had issue, Hugh II, born c. 1000, and Gautier. The elder became lord of Gournay and the younger lord of Le Ferté-en-Brai. The former was one of the Norman leaders of the fleet of forty ships which accompanied Edward, the Saxon prince, son of king Ethelred to England in 1035, when Edward made an attempt to recover the kingdom on the death of Canute. The expedition, not being well received, returned to Normandy. Hugh II again appears as one of the leaders in the battle of Mortimer in 1054, and is reported to have died at the abbey of Bec in Normandy from wounds received in the battle of Cardiff, which is variously reported as having been fought in 1074 and 1092 to 1094 ; the latter date fits in better with the known facts and is generally accepted. This statement concerning him is probably incorrect as he is not entered in Domesday from which it can be assumed that he died before 1086. Hugh left most distinguished posterity, the Mowbrays, dukes of Norfolk, the Talbots, earls of Shrewsbury, etc. The history of this great and noble house is so well known that further details are unnecessary.

Burke, 57. *Nor. Peo.*, 274. Plan., II, 109. Cle., II, 74. Le Prevost, *Notes, Wace*, II, 241. *Wace*, Taylor, 217. *Record of the House of Gournay*, Daniel Gurney. *Vide* Vicomte Néel de Saint-Sauveur.

HUGUE DE GOURNAY, le Jeune. *Vide* Hugue de Gournay.

HUGUE DE GRENTEMESNIL. From Grandmesnil in the arrondissement of Lisieux. Wace (l. 13570) chronicles " Un vassal de Grentemesnil" as having been present at Senlac, which is supported by William of Poitiers and Orderic Vital. He was the son of Robert de Grentemesnil by Hawise de Giroie, and was banished from Normandy by duke William in 1058 for very little cause, but was pardoned in 1063, at which time he was given the custody of the castle of Neufmarché-en-Lions. In 1067 he was one of those who, with William Fitz Osberne and bishop Odo, were invested with the government of England during the king's absence. Hugh received 100 manors, mostly in Leicester, of which county he was sheriff. He was one of the Normans who interceded with king William on behalf of his son, Robert Courteheuse. On the ascension of William Rufus to the throne he supported duke Robert, but later becoming dissatisfied with the conduct of the young duke, he left his cause and attached himself to the king. In 1090, though quite an old man, he was in Normandy opposing Robert de Belesme in his strongholds at Fourches and La Conebe on the river Orne. Having died in England 22 February, 1094, his body was taken to Normandy, where it was buried on the south side of the chapter house of St-Evroult next to his wife, who had previously been interred there. Hugh married Adeliza, daughter of Ivo, count of Beaumont-sur-l'Oise, who brought him Brokesbourne in Herefordshire, and three lordships in Warwickshire. They had issue, Robert, William, Hugh, Ivo, Aubrey and five daughters,

Hawise died unmarried, Adeline married Roger d'Ivri, Rohais became the wife of Robert de Courci, Matilda espoused Hugh de Montpincon, and Agnes married William de Say.[1]

Cle., I, 146. Plan., II, 75. Le Prevost, *Notes, Wace*, II, 239. *Wace*, Taylor, 216.
[1] Ord. Vit., II, 506.

HUGUE de MACEY. From Macey, near Pontorson and Mont-St-Michel, arrondissement Avranches, Normandy. Macey is mentioned in a charter of William Longsword of 917, " Macei dimidium cromerai."[1] Hugo de Maci held in Huntingdonshire in 1086, and Hamo de Macy possessed nine lordships in Cheshire from Hugh Lupus, having been one of the palatinate barons, who built his castle at Dunham Massey. In 1093, he subscribed to the foundation charter of Chester abbey to which he granted lands.[2] Robert de Macey witnessed a charter of Ranulph Meschines in the 12th century.[3] Hamon and Roland (Rualend) de Macey are mentioned in several declarations of fiefs to the abbey of Mont-St-Michel in 1172.[4] The family remained prominent in England, and from them sprung the barons Massey. Delisle carries Hugue de Maci and the name appears on the rolls of Scriven, Leland and Worcester.

Nor. Peo., 325. Cle., III, 391.
[1] *MS.* 210 *Cormerai, section of that district.* [2] *Mon.*, i, 985–6. [3] *Ibid.* [4] *Cartulaire du Mont-St-Michel*, fo. 132 v⁰. *Chron. de Torigny*, II, 299–300.

HUGUE DE LA MARE. *Vide* Guillaume de La Mare.

HUGUE DE MONTFORT LE CONNESTABLE. The famous house of Montford emanated from Montfort-sur-Risle, near Brionne, arrondissement of Pont-Audemer, Normandy, and were the hereditary marshals of that duchy. According to Wace (l. 13612), " Hue le' sire de Montfort" and "sire de Vez-Pont " rescued William Malet from death at the battle of Hastings. Oslac, baron of Briquebec, living in the 10th century, the progenitor of the family, was the father of Turstan de Bastenburg, the father of Hugh Barbatus (with the beard), who had a son, Hugh de Montfort II. The latter was a companion of the Conqueror and furnished fifty ships and sixty knights for the expedition. He is referred to by Orderic Vital in this connection as "earl Hugh the constable" and William of Poitiers and Benoît de St-More also affirm his presence at Senlac. Hugh came into prominence at the battle of Mortimer in 1054, in which engagement he was one of the leaders. The Conqueror for his part in the conquest of England rewarded him with 113 manors in Essex, Suffolk, Norfolk and Kent, with a large portion of Romney marsh, and he was one of the noblemen whom the Conqueror entrusted with the government of England when that monarch visited Normandy in 1067. The governorship of the castle of Dover, the chief fortress in the earldom of Kent belonging to bishop Odo, was entrusted to him by that prelate. The exact date of his death is unknown but he died at the abbey of Bec. William of Jumièges informs us that he was twice married, one wife having been the daughter of Richard de Bellofogo (Beaufoe) by a daughter of the count of Ivry. He had issue Hugh and Robert, both of whom died without issue and a daughter Alice, who eventually became their heir, and married Gilbert de Gand. The name appears on all of the rolls.

Cle., II, 293. Burke, 80. Plan., I, 167. Le Prevost, *Notes, Wace,* II, 244. *Wace,* Taylor, 206. *Vide* Gilbert de Gand. *Ord. Vit.,* I, 484. Wm. of Poitiers, Migne, 1254. *Rech. Domesd.,* 177.

HUGUE DE MORTEMER. *Vide* Raoul de Mortemer.

HUGUE MUSARD. *Vide* Hanscouf Musard.

HUGUE DE PORT. Hugue de Port derived his name from Port, a commune in the Bessin, near Bayeux, whom Wace (l. 13613) records as "cil de Port." He may have referred to either Hugue or Hubert, for both are conceded to have been at Senlac by Le Prevost, Planché and Taylor. In 1086, Hugh held seventy manors in capite, chiefly in Hampshire, of which Basing was his seat, and twelve others under bishop Odo, whom he probably followed to

the conquest of England. The priest Anschil de Presbyter held under him. Hugh made donations to the monks of Gloucester in 1096, and becoming a monk, died at Winchester, leaving a son and heir Henry, who founded the priory of Shirebourn near Basing. Adam de Port, a grandson of Henry, married Mabel de Aurevalle, daughter and heir of Muriel de St-John, whose son assumed the name of St-John, from whom descended the marquesses of Winchester, dukes of Bolton, viscounts Grandison, earls of Jersey and earls and viscounts of Bolingbroke.

Hubert de Port, as well as Gilbert de Port, appear in a number of charters between 1080 and 1082. Gilbert is also reported as having been at Hastings

Plan., II, 249. Cle., III, 116. *Nov. Peo.,* 367. Le Prevost, *Notes, Wace,* II, 244. *Wace,* Taylor, 222. Dugdale and Banks, *Rech. Domesd.,* 156.

HUGUE DE ROUSSEL. The family came from the seigniory of Rosel in the Cotentin, Normandy. They were a branch of the baronial house of Bertram, barons of Briquebec.[1] William, surnamed Bertram, baron of Briquebec, living 1012, had Hugue who received the castle and fief of Rosel and in 1077 having reached an advanced age granted as Hugh de Rosel, with the consent of his son Hugh, lands in Normandy to St-Stephen at Caen, which he had received from the Conqueror.[2] Hugh de Roussel II followed the duke to Senlac and is mentioned in a charter in the time of Stephen, as the father of Robert Russel.[3] He held possessions in Dorset in 1086 (Domesday), by the serjeantry of being marshal of the butlery of England, a feudal dignity, which conferred rank and was hereditary. The family occurs in Normandy, 1180–95; also the fief of Russel.[4] The name appears on the lists of Holinshed, Duchesne, Scriven and Worcester.

[1] *Mem., House of Russell,* Wiffen, I, 531. [2] *Mon.,* ii, 937. [3] *Ibid.,* Wiffen. [4] *M.R.S.*

HUGUE DE SAINT-QUENTIN. This family is from Saint-Quentin, near Coutances, in the Cotentin, or Saint-Quentin, the capital of lower Picardy. Hugh de Saint-Quentin, who came to

England at the conquest and held lands in capite in Essex, Dorsetshire and Hampshire in 1086, was the son of Wido de St-Quentin, who, during the reign of the Conqueror,[1] granted lands to Cerisy on assuming the monastic habit, and Hugh's brother Alured made a donation to the same abbey.[2] The former had issue, 1, Robert, who was at the conquest of Glamorgan in 1090, and whose descendants sat in parliament as barons ; 2, William, living in Normandy in 1120 ; 3, Herbert, who held estates in Lincolnshire and Yorkshire in 1149,[3] and was ancestor of Catherine Parr, the last wife of Henry VIII. The name appears on the rolls of Holinshed, Duchesne, Scriven and Brompton.

Burke, 96. Nor. Peo., 389. Cle., III, 96.
[1] Mon., i, 190. [2] Ibid. [3] Ibid., 198.

HUGUE DE WANCI. This family derived from Vanci, or Wancy, Neufchatel, Normandy. Hugh and Osborn de Wanceio each held fiefs in Suffolk in 1086 (Domesday), and Hugh held also as a mesne-tenant at West Borsham, in Norfolk, under William de Warren whom they accompanied to the conquest. Leland chronicles Warenne et Wauncy. In 1085 Hugh was a witness to one of earl Warren's charters to Castle Acre priory to which both he and his descendants were liberal benefactors. A descendant in the retinue of the Black Prince at Poitiers in Poitou took prisoner Philip of France, afterwards duke of Burgundy. The family continued in Norfolk for about 300 years and also appears in Wiltshire, Buckingham, Devonshire, Northamptonshire, Rutland and Suffolk. The name is enrolled on the lists of Leland, Scriven and Dives.

Nor. Peo., 269, 440. Cle., III, 242.

HUGUE D'HÉRICY. Landric de Baugency of Baugency in the Orléanois had issue John and Hericus or Hercie, who, in 1022, were prohibited by king Robert of France from making inroads on the estates of a neighbouring abbey.[1] Landric witnessed a charter of king Robert in 1028 [2] and was the ancestor of the barons of Baugency. In Norman People it is stated that Hercius was the father of Ancelin de Beaumont, styled

Alselin in Domesday, who held a great barony in Nottingham, etc., in 1086 (Domesday), but this latter Alselin was a descendant of the house of Dinan in Brittany.[3] Ivo Fitz Hercie, or de Heriz, was viscount of Nottingham before 1130. Ralph Herice occurs in 1178 in Normandy.[4] The name appears in the Researches of the Bayeux Tapestry by l'abbé de La Rue and upon the roll of Léopold Delisle.

Nor. Peo., 278. Burke, 65.
[1] Grand Recueil des historiens français, Bouquet, X, 607. [2] Gall. Christ., VIII, 297 Instr. [3] Vide Geoffroi Ascelin.
[4] Stapleton, II, c.

HUGUE D'HOUDETOT. The identity of Hugue d'Houdetot is obscure, and since his name is not written in Domesday it is supposed he was either killed in the battle of Hastings or died before its compilation. His name appears in the Researches of the Bayeux Tapestry by l'abbé de La Rue and is supported also by Léopold Delisle on the Dives list.

IBERT DE LACY. For his services at Senlac, Ibert de Lacy was rewarded by the Conqueror with the whole district of Blackburnshire in Lancashire, with 170 lordships, of which nearly 150 were in Yorkshire. He held the town and castle of Pontefract, a great stronghold, which became his seat, the remainder was in Lincolnshire and Nottinghamshire. Ibert founded inside his fortress a Collegiate chapel, dedicated to St-Clement, and also built the foundation for the abbey of St-Oswald at Nostall, completed by his eldest son and heir. He married Hawise by whom he left two sons, Robert, who succeeded him, called de Pontefract, and Hugh. Vide Gautier de Lacy.

INGELRAM DE LIONS. The name is derived from the castle and forest of Lions in Normandy. Ingelram de Lions came to England in 1066 and held Corsham and Culington from the king.[1] He had Ranulph, and another son William de Lions received a grant in Norfolk from earl Walter Gifford and left descendants there. Ranulph had Ingelram de Lions named Parcar, from being forester of Croxton, Leicester, by exchange with the king.[2] William Parcarius de Lion was a benefactor to Croxton abbey during the reign of Henry II and was brother of Hugh de Lion, who was deprived of his estates in 1203.[3] From him descended the family of Parcar or Parker and earls of Macclesfield ; hence also the lords Lyon and Glamis, earls of Strathmore and Kinghorn. King George VI married lady Elizabeth Bowes-Lyon, daughter of present earl of Strathmore, whose eldest daughter the little princess Elizabeth is heir-apparent to the throne.

Cle., II, 216. Nor. Peo., 317.
[1] Mon., ii, 604.   [2] Ibid.   [3] Leicestersh., Nichol.

IVE TAILLEBOIS. There is very little known of the family excepting that they were Angevin. Three of the name are written in Domesday 1086. William Taillebois was an under-tenant in Bedford and Hereford, as well as Lincoln. He was probably the brother of Ivo who held a barony in Lincoln and Norfolk and was lord of the whole district of Hogland. He was the sheriff of Lincoln, in which county he was a great prince, holding court with much pomp and splendour at his castle of Spalding. He held large portions of the north of Lancaster as well as that part of Westmorland which came under the barony of Kendal. He is said to have been a relative of the Conqueror, which is most unlikely, and was the husband of Lucia, daughter of William Malet,[1] concerning whose birth and parentage there has been much controversy. Ivo died in 1114.[2] Ethelred, or Fitz Renfrid, is variously claimed to have been his brother, son, or nephew, which assertions are all disputed. However, this Ethelred, whoever he was, inherited the barony of Kendal, Westmorland, whose descendant, William Taillebois, took the name of Lancaster, as constable of Lancaster castle, from whom descended the Prestons, viscounts Gormanston and lords Tara. Ivo did have a daughter Lucia who was his heiress, first married to Roger de Roumare and second to Ranulph, earl of Chester.[3] Ralph Taillebois, whose name is also in Domesday, was of another family.[4] Guillaume and Ivo Taillebois are written in the Dives roll

of Léopold Delisle and both Scriven and Duchesne have enrolled the name.

Rech. Domesd., 251.   Cle., III, 344.   Nor. Peo., 369.
[1] Vide Guillaume Malet and App. 3.   [2] Lincolnsh., Allen.   [3] Ibid., n. 1.   [4] Vide Raoul de Taillebois.

IVE DE VASSY. Vide Robert de Vassy.

JACQUES LE BRABANÇON. Belonged to a family of Brabant, which settled in Normandy. From this house descended Jacques de Brabançon, who followed duke William to the conquest of England, and was called the " Great Warrior." His descendants settled in Surrey at Betchworth and later appear in Leicestershire. The family flourished in England for many centuries, from whom descended the earls of Meath and the baronets Brabazon. The name appears on the list of Guillaume Tailleur.

Burke, 18.   Nor. Peo., 171.   Cle., I, 82.
Chron. de Torigny, II, 44.

JEAN D'IVRI. This family took its name to the castle of Ivry in Normandy and not from Raoul of Ivry, the half-brother of duke Richard I, by the same mother, Sprota, mistress of William Longsword, and of Asperleng, the wealthy miller of Vaudreuil, whom she married after the death of the duke. Alberade, wife of count Raoul, built the famous castle of Ivry, which when completed, was so unequalled in construction in Normandy that the countess Alberade, to prevent another being built of similar or greater strength, had Lanfred, the architect, beheaded. This noble lady eventually met the same fate at the command of her husband.[1] They had issue two sons, Hugh, bishop of Bayeux, and John, bishop of Avranches, later archbishop of Rouen. The fief of Ivry passed to William Fitz Osberne and then to his son, William de Breteuil. John of Ivry, here recorded, was probably the son of Waleran of Ivry, who held one knight's fee in Tinchebrai, Normandy, by service of cup bearer to the duke, and eight and one-half knights' fees in the town and castle of Ivry. This family were not the lords of Ivry but its hereditary castellans. John of Ivry and Robert d'Ouilli, mutually engaged to share in each other's fortunes at the conquest of England. Robert having married the daughter of the wealthy Wigod de Wallingford, gave to John of Ivry the entire barony of Waleries, of which Beckley was the chief seat. This included Ambrosden and its hamlets, Blackthorn, and Arncott, with the villages of Hodley, Notbrook, Mixbury, etc., afterwards known as the honour of St-Valery. John died *c*. 1079, leaving three sons, Roger, Hugh who received the manor of Ambrosden, and Geoffry.[2] Roger, the eldest, who succeeded to the barony and office of cup bearer, has frequently been confused with his father, John, and has also been called the latter's brother. There appears a memorandum in the *Introduction to Domesday* that " Robert d'Ouilli and Roger d'Ivri came to the conquest as sworn brothers in arms, pledged to each other by their mutual solemn oaths." [3] This undoubtedly should read John instead of Roger, since Robert d'Ouilli actually ceded the barony of Waleries (St-Valery) to " his very familiar Friend John de Ivery who had accompanied him in the Wars as his Sworn Brother." Roger's name frequently occurs with that of Robert d'Ouilli as joint owners in Domesday, under Abingdon abbey and in Buckinghamshire, as well as in the annals of Oseney.[4] Roger married Adeline, daughter of Hugue de Grentemesnil,[5] and founded in 1071 the abbey of Ivry. In 1078 he held the town of Rouen for king William against his son duke Robert [6] and defended Ivry against the French in 1087.[7] During the same year he supported duke Robert Courteheuse against his brother William Rufus for the throne of England, for which reason he was banished, had his possessions confiscated and died almost immediately afterwards, for his brother Geoffry held all of his estates and those of his deceased brother, Hugue, in 1088.[8] At this time, duke Robert gave the castle of Ivry to William de Breteuil, which had been erected by his grandmother, Alberade.[9] Asceline Göel de Percival, son of Robert of Ivry, lord of Breval, in 1089, seized the castle of Ivry and returned it to duke Robert Courteheuse, from whom William de Breteuil redeemed it for a large sum of money.[10] Later, in 1091, Asceline de-

feated William in battle, took him prisoner, eventually compelling him to give to him for his freedom the castle of Ivry and his illegitimate daughter, Isabel, in marriage.[11]

[1] Ord. Vit., III, 25 ; Plan., II, 220. [2] *Hist. of Wallingford*, Hedges, I, 202 ; *Osney Register*. [3] *Introd. Domesd.*, I, 458 ; Ord. Vit., II, 506. [4] *Mon.*, vi, 251 and viii, 146 ; Leland ; *Hist. of Wallingford*, Hedges, I, 202 ; Plan., II, 220 ; Cle., I, 330 ; *Hist. of Abingdon*, II, 25, 143 ; *Ann. Mon.*, iv. 10. [5] Ord. Vit., II, 213. [6] *Ibid.*, II, 109. [7] *Ibid.*, II, 398. [8] Hedges, *ibid.*, I, 202 ; *Osney Register*. [9] Ord. Vit., II, 428. [10] *Ibid.*, II, 484. [11] *Ibid.*, II, 487.

LE SIRE DE JORT. Jort is near Courci in the arrondissement of Falaise, which belonged to Lesceline, countess d'Eu, but the possessor of it at the time of the conquest is not clear. It was probably held by someone under the de Courcis, as "cil de Courci e cil de Jort" (Wace, l. 13614) are named together. Roger de Jauri appears in a charter of king William I and Anchetil de Jorz occurs in England in 1110.[1] Goel de Jurieo figures in a document of St-Evroult in 1128 while John de Jort, a man-at-arms of Robert, earl of Caen, was killed outside that castle in 1138.[2]

Nor. Peo., 264. Plan., II, 220. Le Prevost, II, 245. *Wace*, Taylor, 222. [1] *Wint. Domesd.* [2] Ord. Vit., IV, 200.

LE SIRE DE LITHAIRE. The family of Lithaire came from a town of that name, commune of La Haie du Puits, in the Cotentin, on the coast opposite Jersey. Eudo al Chapel, sire de la Haie, was seignior of it in 1066 from whom it passed to Robert de Haie, who married Muriel, his only daughter and heir. He might have held it under Eudo at that time and have been the personage referred to by Wace (l. 13554) as "sire de Litehare," since this individual has not otherwise been identified. Rainaldus de Orivallo was contemporary with Robert Courteheuse and Henry I and founded a cell in 1115 at Orval in the church of St-Helen. His son, William, held Lithaire and Orval in 1172, whose daughter, Mabilia, became the wife of Adam de Port. Their son, William de Portu, held the honour of Lithaire in the second year of the reign of king John.[1]

Rech., de Gerville, 39. Le Prevost, Notes, Wace, II, 235. Wace, Taylor, 211–20. Plan., II, 287.
[1] Stapleton, I, clx, clxi, lxxxvii.

MARTIN DE TOURS. The Norman family of Martin probably came from Tor or Tour in the vicinity of Bayeux. The individual here indicated was Martin d'Amfreville, sire de Tour, who came to England at the conquest and conquered Cameys in Wales. It was erected into a palatine barony, which he governed as lord marcher, having his castle at Newport, where the ruins still exist. He was a great benefactor to religious houses and began the foundation of a Benedictine abbey at St-Dogmael's, annexing it as a cell to the monastery of Tyrone in France. His son Robert Fitz Martin gave the endowment, which charter was witnessed by Henry I. Shortly after the compilation of Domesday he was in possession of the honour of Dartington and other lands, formerly belonging to William de Falaise. William Fitz Martin of the next generation married the daughter of Rhys-ap-Griffith, sovereign of South Wales. William's grandson acquired the honour of Barnstaple by marriage with Maud, daughter of Guy de Brian and Eva his wife, heiress of Henry de Tracey, lord of that barony. She brought him large possessions in Devonshire, where he already had great estates. The family later held considerable possessions in different parts of England, among which were Seaborough and Althelhampton in Dorset; Compton-Martin in Somerset; Comb-Martin in Devon, and Long Melford in Suffolk, etc.

Nor. Peo., 325. Cle., II, 256. Devon, Pole. Vide Robert d'Amfreville. Burke, 76.

DE MUSCAMP. From Muscamp, Normandy, which was held by the Tillys.[1] This family established itself in the north of England at the time of the conquest. Roger de Muscamp held Wilgebi, in Lincoln in 1086 (Domesday), and Robert de Muscam, his son, was seneschal to Gilbert de Gand. The latter had issue [2] Robert, whose son Hugh was a benefactor of Nostel priory

in the time of Henry I.[3] This Hugh appears in Liber Niger as a landowner in York and Lincoln and gave his name to Muscam in Nottingham. A very important branch of the family was settled in Northumberland, where Reginald de Muscamp is mentioned in 1130.[4] Robert de Muscamp, perhaps his brother, received from Henry I a barony of four knights' fees in Bamborughshire, and Wooler was the head of his honour. His son Thomas joined prince Henry's rebellion in 1172; he married Maud de Vesci, the daughter of the lord of Alnwick, whose grandson, another Robert, was considered the greatest baron in the north of England. He died in 1249, leaving three daughters as co-heiresses. From this family descended sir William de Willoughby, who married the heiress of Du Bec, baron of Eresby [5]; and hence sprang the lords Willoughby of Eresby, so renowned in the French wars, and the lords Middleton, Willoughby of Broke and Willoughby of Parham. The name occurs on the rolls of Brompton and Duchesne.

Nor. Peo., 447. Cle., III, 325.
[1] M.R.S., XV, 175. [2] Mon., i, 963.
[3] Ibid., ii, 35. [4] Rot. Pip. [5] Vide Geoffroi du Bec.

MATHIEU DE LA FERTÉ-MACÉ. Wace (l. 13707) designates this personage, "sire de la Ferté," who came to England at the conquest from La Ferté Macé in the arrondissement of Domfront, department of the Orne, in the Passais-Normand, in the contingent of Henri de Domfront. Turulph, a companion of Rollo, obtained in 912 the barony of La Ferté (Firmitas) near Evreux, now la Ferté-Fresnel. His grandson of the same name lived in the time of Richard I. Radulphus de la Ferté lived before 1000; William his son gave the forest of Notre Dame des Bois to St-Evroult abbey. Hugh de la Ferté is considered by Norman People and Cleveland as the personage referred to by Wace, but this is an error, as pointed out by Le Prevost, who establishes that Hugh II, seignior of Fêrté-en-Bray, became a monk in the abbey of St-Ouen in Rouen before the conquest, without leaving issue. William de la Ferté, who with Turgis

F

de Tracie were governors of Main in 1073, were perhaps of this family. A William de la Feritate held Weston and Stokes by barony from the conquest of England. A sire de Ferté Macé, probably either Mathieu or William, married a sister of Odo, bishop of Bayeux, and his son William is mentioned in a charter of an archbishop of Tours, *temp.* St-Louis, from which it may be assumed that William also was present at Senlac. Richard de la Ferté accompanied duke Robert of Normandy to Palestine in 1096. From this family descended the marquesses of Sligo, barons Kilmaine and viscounts Montague.

Stapleton, I, lxxvii, lxxix. *Rech. Domesd.*, 48. Le Prevost, *Notes, Wace,* I, 260. *Wace,* Taylor, 237. Plan., II, 285. Cle., I, 115. *Testa de Neville*, 286.

MAUGER DE CARTERET. *Vide* Honfroi de Carteret.

MICHEL DE BURES. The origin of this family was Bures near Bayeux, who owned an important castle there. Michel de Bures was, according to the Egerton manuscripts in the British museum,[1] the first of the name who came to England. He accompanied duke William to the battle of Senlac, by whom he was given two manors in Somersetshire, one in Hertfordshire, mentioned in the Domesday survey. The two manors in Somersetshire are known as East Bower and West Bower, Bridgwater. Walter, his son, held a small manor near Calne in Wiltshire, to which he gave the name of Bures. Erenis de Burun was a tenant-in-chief in Yorkshire and Lincolnshire, in 1086 (Domesday), and Radulfus de Burun occurs at that time in Derbyshire and Nottinghamshire. Pierre de Bures was viscount of Dieppe and Arques during the war of 1173-4. The family prevailed in England in the counties of Stafford, Somerset, Berks, Gloucester, and others, for several centuries, and the name is mentioned on the rolls of Holinshed and Duchesne.

Cle., I, 86. Dupont, II, 33. Stapleton, I, cii.
[1] No. 1075.

MILE CRISPIN. Milo Crispin possessed in capite in 1086 (Domesday) a barony of 88 lordships in the counties of Buckingham, Berks, Wilts, Surrey, Gloucester, Bedford and Oxford, 28 were in the former, 33 the latter, and the remainder distributed among the others. King William gave to him in marriage Matilda, daughter and heiress of Robert d'Ouilli, who had married Algitha, the daughter and heiress of the rich and influential Wigod de Wallingford, through whom he received the honour and castle of that name, then one of the strongest fortresses in England.[1] They were married prior to 1084, since in that year Robert d'Ouilli entertained king William at Wallingford at Easter,[2] when Milo is mentioned as his son-in-law (Milo de Wallingford cognomento Crispinus) who with Osborne, bishop of Sarum, were the only persons permitted to dine at the king's table. Matilda was then very young.[3] The exact parentage of Milo is unknown as he is not named in the *De nobili Crispinorum genere*[4] among the children of Gilbert Crispin I, consequently, it is supposed that he was either his natural son or the son of William Crispin I or Gilbert Crispin II.[5] He apparently received the English possessions which his family obtained for having participated at Hastings, and is the only Crispin written in Domesday. Milo was in high favour with king William and his sons, kings William Rufus and Henry, for the former not only gave to him in marriage one of the greatest heiresses of the kingdom but showered upon him great possessions and honours, while the latter had him witness numerous charters executed by them. He remained loyal to these English sovereigns, although his family in Normandy espoused the cause of duke Robert Courteheuse, and later, his son William Clito. He was a witness to the Grand charter of the abbey of Bec about the year 1070[6] and gave to that monastery in 1087 Swyncombe, a lordship in Oxford with all the tithes of his demesne of the honour of Wallingford.[7] Milo and Alain, earl of Richmond, were the only witnesses of William Rufus' foundation charter of the abbey of Saint-Mary's York, 1090, which they alone later confirmed.[8] Milo attested two others of William Rufus to his kinsman Gilbert, abbot of Westminster between 1087 and 1100, and

1086 and 1102, a grant of abbot Gilbert to Gunter and his heirs was also witnessed by his dapifer Gislebertus Pipardus.[9] He witnessed the confirmation of king Henry I to the church of St-Mary's at Tewkesbury in 1100,[10] and the terms of an alliance between Robert, count of Flanders, and Henry I, made at Dover in 1101.[11] He confirmed gifts made by himself in favour of the monks of Abingdon in 1107,[12] placed on the altar by Gillebertus Pipardus, his dapifer.[13] Milo was a councillor of the king and died in 1107 without legitimate issue.[14] His own estates reverted to the crown, but the honour of Wallingford remained by right of birth with his widow, henceforth called Matildis Domina de Walingford.[15] Sometime thereafter Gillebertus Pipard occurs with "Hugo fil Milonis" at Waddesdon, co. Buckingham, where a grant was made to the abbey of Abingdon.[16] The query naturally arises, was Hugo the illegitimate offspring of Milo Crispin? Howbeit, Milo's widow in 1113 married Brian Fitz Count,[17] and during the reign of Henry II Wallingford, lacking heirs, was seized by the crown.[18] Stacey Grimaldi in the *Gentleman's Magazine* of October 1832, published the following genealogy.[19] Crispina, a supposed daughter of Rollo, first duke of Normandy, married Grimaldus I, prince of Monaco, c. 920, and had issue Guido, prince of Monaco, Giballinus, a celebrated warrior against the Saracens, and Ansgothus Crispinus, who settled in Normandy and possessed the barony of Bec. The latter married Heloise, daughter of Rodulph, count of Guynes and Boulogne, by Roselle, daughter of the count Saint-Paul, whose children were Herluin,[20] abbot of Bec, Gilbert, baron of Bec, lord of Tillières, constable of Normandy and marshal of the army,[21] who relinquished the surname Grimaldi to assume that of Crispin, Odo and Roger, both named in a charter by abbot Herluin as his brothers,[22] and Rollo or Rolf. This pedigree asserts that Gilbert Crispin was the father of William Crispin, baron of Bec, Gilbert Crispin, lord of Tillières, and Milo Crispin. It further records that Rolf had two sons, Goisfrid Fitz Rou or du Bec,[23] the Conqueror's marshal, and Toustain Fitz Rou le Blanc,[24] the stan-

dard bearer, sometimes called du Bec. Duke Rollo had only one daughter mentioned in history, Gerlotte, later called Adele, who married William, count of Poitou and duke of Aquitaine (932–63),[25] and if he had another by the name of Crispina, it has nowhere else been recorded. There was no barony of Bec in the Crispin family before *c.* 1250 which has been identified,[26] and no prince of Monaco until the 13th century. The first authentic ancestor of this family was Otto Canella (died 1142), whose son Grimaldo was thrice consul of Genoa from 1162 to 1184. These great Genoese lords did not come to Monaco until 1270, whence they were then driven by the Gibelins.[27] This genealogy was composed in 1646 by Charles de Venasque-Ferriol, secretary of Honoré II, prince of Monaco, and Jean Le Laboureur, the historian of Renée du Bec-Crispin,[28] and her husband Jean Baptiste de Budes, comte de Guébriant, and Perigord, vicomte de Limoges, marshal of France, under the title of *Historica et genealogica Grimaldæ gentis Arbor*. Although it was published by Venasque-Ferriol, the clever work of Le Laboureur can easily be detected.[29] Countess Renée in 1645 escorted the queen of Poland from Paris to her estate, on which account she was granted the title of ambassadrice extraordinaire de France, an honour never accorded to any other lady; she was also lady of honour to Marie-Thérèse. Renée lies buried with her husband in the cathedral of Notre-Dame, where an inscription to this effect appears upon their tomb.

These powerful families with the desire to obtain a Carlovingian descent through Grimoald, duke of Brabant, son of Pepin d'Héristal (slain 714), imagined a fabulous Grimaldus to whom, according to an apocryphal manuscript exhumed at the library of Ambroise at Milan, the emperor Otho gave, about 960, the sovereignty of Monaco. It was thus recorded Grimaldus (700), count of Flanders and mayor of the palace, son of Pepin, by his wife Theodesinde had Théobald (750) married to Aliarde, whose son Hugo Grimaldus (800) had Passanus (850), who was the father of Grimaldus I, prince of Monaco, married to Crispina. Charles III, prince of Monaco (1856–89), branding this pedigree as untrue, gave an order to his successive archivists, Cais de Pierlas, Saige and Labande, to write a correct one founded on authentic documents and not falsified as this one and the famous donation of the gulf de Sambracie, later called gulf de Grimaud (Saint-Tropez in 980) admittedly were.[30] Nevertheless, the Grimaldi found their arms were identical with those of the Crispins of Normandy which had been on record before their advent to Monaco, both of whom bore fusily argent and gules.[31] It is a very strange coincidence that such distinguished and influential families had the same armorial bearings, but with so simple a coat great importance cannot be attached to it unless fortified with other evidences of relationship. Milo Crispin appears on the Battle abbey roll under the name of Valingford.

Introd. Domesd. Parochial Antiquities, Bishop Kennet, vol. I. *Hist. of Wallingford,* Hedges, vol. I. Cle., I, 126–329; III, 251.
[1] *Introd. Domesd.,* I, 458, II, 361; *vide* Robert d'Ouilli. [2] *Ibid.,* I, 402; Robert d'Ouilli; *History of Abingdon,* Roll S, II, 12. [3] *Vide* Robert d'Ouilli, n. 6; *Parochial Antiquities,* Bishop Kennet, I, 94; Freeman, IV, 728. [4] *De nob. Crispin. gen.,* I, 343. [5] Freeman, IV, 45; *Dict. de l'Eure,* I, 927; *vide* App. 18. [6] *Bibl. nat. lat.,* 13905, fo. 115, et lat. 12884, fo. 85. [7] *Mon.,* ii, 954; Bishop Kennet, 95, *Hist. of Wallingford,* Hedges, I, 216. [8] *Introd. Domesd.,* I, 182; *Mon.,* iii, 547; Dep. Keeper's rep., XXIX, 46. [9] *Faustina,* Aiii, fo. 55; *Lib. Nig.,* fo. 25; *West. Domesd.,* fo. 129. [10] *Mon.,* ii, 65*b*; Dep. Keeper's rep., XXX, App. 6, p. 202; from *Charter roll Edward I,* m. 3. [11] *Lib. Nig.,* Hearne, I, 7; *Foedera* (*Rec. Com.*), I, 7. [12] *History of Abingdon,* II, 107. [13] Bishop Kennet, 105; *Hist. of Abingdon,* II, 97. [14] *An Outline Itinerary of King Henry I,* Farrer, 46; *Mem.,* Walt de Coventry; *Hist. of Abingdon,* II, 97; Roger of Hovenden. [15] *Mon.,* I, 582*a*. [16] *Hist. of Abingdon,* II, 109. [17] Hamelin de Balon; *Hist. of Wallingford,* Hedges, I, 216. [18] *Ibid.,* I, 265; Roger Dodsworth ms., vol. 4. [19] *Gentleman's Magazine,* London, Oct. 1832, vol. I, 26–30. [20] *Vide* App. 18. [21] *Ibid.* [22] Bibl. nat. lat. 13905; *Le Prevost Mem.,* I, 234. [23] *Vide* Geoffroi du Bec. [24] *Vide* Toustain Fitz Rou. [25] Jumièges, 24–35; *Royal Genealogies,* Anderson, 391, 741; *La Normandie,* Frere, 23; *Hist. de Norm.,* Licquet, **I,** 105. [26] *Vide* App. 18.

[27] *Ibid.; Monaco ses Origines et son Histoire,* Gustave Saige, Introd., IX–X; 40–1, 224–5; *Hist. Véridique, etc.,* Word Grimaldi, baron du Roure; *Cart. de Lérins édit.,* Moris et Blanc; Arch. des Alpes Maritimes, fonds ecclésiastiques; Arch. du palais de Monaco (Arch. secrètes a, 17 no. 2, pièce 6). [28] *Ibid.;* Pièces Originales, 259, 96, 110, 111, 112; *vide* App. 18. [29] *Ibid.,* n. 27. [30] *Ibid.;* Letter 27 March 1928 of the Labande archevist, palace of Monaco; also of the present marquis de Grasse. [31] *Ibid.,* n. 27; *vide* App. 18.

DE MATHAN. The abbé de La Rue in his *Researches of the Bayeux Tapestry* mentions de Mathan, and Delisle also chronicles the name on the Dives roll. There seems to be little on record concerning this companion of duke William, for which reason it may be assumed that he possibly died at the battle of Hastings, or at least before the Domesday survey. Robert, William and Samson de Maton appear in Normandy in 1180. Richard and Thomas de Mathan appear in England *c.* 1272.

Nor. Peo., 325. *M.R.S. R.H.*

DU MERLE. Du Merle is recorded in the *Researches of the Bayeux Tapestry* by the abbé de La Rue, which is also subscribed to by Léopold Delisle, who carried the name on the Dives roll. This warrior was probably deceased before the compilation of Domesday as his name is not written therein and he is one of the many followers of duke William whose identity is difficult to establish, but the family appears in documents later in Normandy. Simon Merle is recorded in Normandy 1180–95 and Adam de Merlene occurs there at the same time. There was a fief of Merlai in Normandy which was undoubtedly another family.

Nor. Peo., 329. Cle., III, 390. *M.R.S.*

NÉEL VICOMTE DE SAINT-SAUVEUR. Saint-Sauveur-le-Vicomte is a canton in the arrondissement of Valognes in the department of Manche. Richard, sire de Saint-Sauveur, le vicomte, in 920 gave to Néel, his son, the lordship of Nehou, which castle had belonged to the barony of Saint-Sauveur for about a century, and he was made hereditary constable of the

Cotentin in 938.[1] A descendant, also named Néel de Saint-Sauveur I, was vicomte of Cotentin, whom Jumièges informs us with Raoul de Toeni I and his son Roger were given the custody of the newly built castle of Tillières, c. 1014, after the battle fought there between duke Richard II and his brother-in-law, Hugh, count of Chartre, whom the duke vanquished in that engagement. They remained governors of this castle until c. 1030, when it was given by duke Robert in hereditary custodianship to Gilbert Crispin I, in whose family it remained for many centuries.[2] Néel de Saint-Sauveur, vicomte de Cotentin, called for his valour "Chef de Faucon," fought at the battle of Val-des-Dunes in 1047 in the army of king Henry of France against duke William, for which reason he was banished and took refuge in Brittany, but was subsequently pardoned and his estates returned before the conquest. Since Néel I must have been at least twenty-five to thirty years of age at the time he was entrusted with the co-guardianship of so important a castle as Tillières, the strongest fortress on the border between France and Normandy, he would probably have been in 1047 about sixty years of age. Consequently, it is possible that it was his son Néel II who participated in this battle, but it surely was the latter who fought at Senlac. Le Prevost disagrees with the opinion of a Saint-Sauveur having been at Hastings because of the animosity which had existed, but as their possessions had been returned and the duke needed all the assistance he could secure, he was doubtless very glad to obtain the services of so valiant and powerful a vassal. In substantiation of this, Wace informs us that Néel " exerted himself much to earn the love and goodwill of his lord and assaulted the English with great vigour." He has not been identified in Domesday, although eight Néels are entered therein. This Néel is reported to have been killed in the battle of Cardiff in Wales, 1092-4, with Roger de Montgomery, Hugue de Gournay, Arnoul de Harcourt and other prominent nobles, who are on record as having died at this period.[3] Howbeit, he died in 1092, which gives support to the theory that the battle of Cardiff

was fought at about this time, as his relative Geoffry, bishop of Coutances, expressed a desire to attend his funeral in that year.[4] One of his daughters married Jourdain Tesson and the other was the mother of Fulk de Partis.[5]

Ord. Vit., II, 404. *Rot. Norm.*, Hardy, 16. Le Prevost, *Notes, Wace*, II, 231-6. *Wace*, Taylor, 207-12. Plan., II, 143-206. Cle., II, 360 ; III, 213. *Vide* Richard de Vernon.
[1] *Rech.*, de Gerville, 17. [2] Jumièges, 84. [3] *Vide* Hague de Gournay. [4] *M.S.A.N.*, I, 286 ; II, 46. [5] *Vide* App. 7.

OSBERNE D'ARQUES. *Vide* Guillaume d'Arques.

OSBERNE DE SASSY. From Sacey, arrondissement of Avranches, near Pontorson. Wace (l. 13659) mentions "cil de Sacie," but two members of the family entered in Domesday are generally conceded to have been at Senlac : namely, Osbernus de Salceid, who held a barony in Devonshire, and Radulphus de Salceit, possessor of one in Hereford, both of whom left descendants in many parts of the country. Jourdain de Sassy appears in a charter of Richard de Subligny, bishop of Avranches, about the middle of the 12th century.[1] The family held considerable lands in Oxford, Buckingham, Nottingham, Derby, Hereford and Northampton.[2] They had estates in Normandy, 1180-95,[3] and also in England, c. 1198.[4] Planché observes that duke Robert I built a castle in 1030 on the banks of the Coesnon, a river dividing Normandy and Brittany, about a league from the bourg of Sassy, called Charruel, or Cheruel, which gave the name to the Norman family of Kyriel. This family was of importance in England from Domesday, as Kyriell, de Croil de Cruel and Ashburnham. The name Sassy appears on the rolls of Guillaume Tailleur, Scriven, Holinshed, Worcester, and Delisle mentions both Osborn and Raoul de Saussi on the Dives list.

Plan., II, 294. Cle., III, 137. *Wace*, Taylor, 231. *Nor. Peo.*, 391. Le Prevost, *Notes, Wace*, II, 252.
[1] *Rech.*, de Gerville, 93. [2] *Antiquities of Kiddington.* [3] *M.R.S.* [4] *R.C.R.*

OSBERNE GIFFARD. *Vide* Gautier Giffard, comte de Longueville.

OSBERNE DE WANCI. *Vide* Hugue de Wanci.

OSMOND BASSET. The name Basset is derived from its ancestor Bathet, or Baset, duke of the Normans of the Loire, 895-905,[1] and the family came from Ouilly le Basset, near Falaise. Osmond Basset, the eldest son of Fouque d'Aulnay I, was at the conquest and is mentioned in the Great charter of Montivilliers.[2] He had six sons, the eldest of whom, Hugh Fitz Osmond, held in Hampshire in capite in 1086 (Domesday) and another, Anchetil Fitz Osmond, lord of Cosham, occurs there at the same period. He went to Palestine in 1096 and appears in 1110 as Anchetil Palmarius at Winchester in Hampshire [3] and became the progenitor of the Palmer family. Osmond witnessed an act in Normandy in 1050 concerning the foundation of the abbey of St-Evroult.[4] Thurston Basset, possibly another brother, held at Drayton in Staffordshire in 1086 (Domesday) and Raoul, the celebrated judiciary, also recorded in Domesday, were at the conquest, though the latter must have been very young at that time and advanced in years at his death, which occurred in the year of 1120. Dugdale mentions William Basset who, he says, was a Benedictine abbot at Hosme in Suffolk.[5] The family held large possessions in Oxfordshire, some of which were granted to them by Milo Crispin.[6] The name appears on the rolls of Guillaume Tailleur as well as Holinshed, Duchesne, Leland, Brompton, Worcester and Dives.

Nor. Peo., 151, 351. Cle., I, 61.
[1] Bouquet, VII, 360 ; VIII, 317 ; *vide* Fouques d'Aulnay. [2] Ord. Vit., III, 328, ed. note ; Great charter of duke Robert II to the abbey of Montivilliers, latin 1035, Rouen. [3] *Winchester Domesday.* [4] Ord. Vit., I, 395. [5] Dugdale, I, 378. [6] *History of Wallingford*, Hedges, I, 226.

OURS D'ABBETOT. The name came from St-Jean d'Abbetot, canton of Colbose, arrondissement of Havre, of which the seigniory belonged to the chamberlain of Tancarville, indicated in the foundation charter of St-George de Bocherville. Its founder, Raoul, the first chamberlain of duke William, son of Gerold, the first known branch of the house of Tancarville, gave the church of Abbetot in 1050 for the use of the chanoines of this collegiate church. Ours d'Abbetot was the elder brother of Robert le Despensier, the son of Amaury d'Abbetot (younger brother of Raoul aforementioned) and grandson of Gerold, sire de Tancarville.[1] Ours accompanied duke William to the conquest of England, after which he became a great power, having been created sheriff of Gloucester and Worcester, and held a great barony as tenant-in-chief in Hereford and Warwick. In 1073 he was one of the king's council and rendered great service in the suppression of the rebellion of the earls of Hereford and Norfolk. Ours was a despoiler of the lands of the church of Worcester, as well as the abbeys of Evesham and Pershore, and terribly oppressed the tenants of Droitwich. Great power had been granted to him as hereditary sheriff, making it his duty to keep the county in subjection, in almost all parts of which he held manors. On the other hand, he founded Malvern priory, which became a cell to Westminster abbey. Ours was alive during the reign of Henry I, but the exact date of his death is unknown. By his wife, Atheliza (parentage unrecorded), he had Robert d'Abbetot, who succeeded him, but who shortly afterwards had his inheritance and properties confiscated because he killed a servitor of the king. His sister, Emeline, recovered from Henry I the hereditary shrievalty of Worcester with the confiscated possessions of her brother on her marriage with Walter de Beauchamp. Their son William was despensier to the king and sheriff of Worcester and adjoining counties. In the 13th century the barony of Hanslope and the famous earldom and castle of Warwick were obtained by the family through marriage. The Abbetots prevailed in Normandy until the time of Philippe Auguste and in England for six hundred years.

Rech. Domesd., 46. Plan., II, 150. *Nor. Peo.*, 266. Cle., I, 129, 283, 349. Stapleton, II, cli, cclxxvi.
[1] *Vide* Le Chamberlain de Tancarville.

LE SIRE D'ORIGNY. Wace (l. 1705), chronicles "cil de Urinie." It is supposed that he intended to mention Origny, of which there are two communes in Normandy, one near Belesme, the other near Mamers. The sire d'Origny who attended the conquest is another of those obscure personages whom it is difficult to locate, especially as his name does not appear in Domesday. He must, therefore, pending further information, be classed among those who died at or near the time of the conquest and who left no known posterity.

Plan., II, 300. Le Prevost, *Notes, Wace*, II, 259. *Wace*, Taylor, 236.

LE SIRE D'ORGLANDE. Orglandes (Egglandes), located in the county of Coutances, was granted to Adela, wife of Richard III, duke of Normandy, as future dowry in 1026–7, at which time the city of Coutances with the entire county was ceded to her with the exception of the land of Robert, archbishop of Rouen, and of the city of Caen "in comitatu Bajocense." The marriage never having been consummated, the dowry reverted to duke Robert, who succeeded his brother, Richard III.[1] The companion of duke William at Hastings of this name, mentioned in the *Researches of the Bayeux Tapestry* by the abbé de La Rue and by Delisle on his Dives roll does not appear in Domesday. Herbert d'Orglander was a witness to a donation to the abbey of Montebourg, Normandy, by Adeliza, widow of Richard de Redvers,[2] executed between 1142 and 1155.[3] Geoffry, priest of Orlandes, appears as a witness to an act concerning the abbey of St-Père de Chatres between 1132 and 1150.[4] The family was represented in England by the baronets Oglander. In Normandy, the barony of Orlandes was in existence as late as 1180–95, at which time Roger and Alan de Orglandes occur there.

Nor. Peo., 348.
[1] Stapleton, I, lxxxii, xxiv, lvii.
[2] *Vide* Richard de Redvers. [3] Stapleton, II, cclxxiv. [4] *Ibid.*, II, cclxx–cclxxi.

PAISNEL DES MOUTIERS-HUBERT. From les Moustiers-Hubert, canton of Livarot, arrondissement of Lisieux, Calvados, named by Wace (l. 13630) "Des Moustiers-Hebert Painals." William Paisnel is mentioned by Orderic Vital,[1] as subscribing to a charter of the cathedral of Bayeux in 1073, who, Orderic states, died about the same time as the Conqueror. It must have been prior to 1085, for he is not written in Domesday. He was probably the member of the family present at Senlac. Ralph Painel, or Paganel, supposed to have been his younger brother, is there recorded possessing forty-five lordships as tenant-in-chief in Lincolnshire and Yorkshire. His residence, Drax, was situated in the latter county, of which he was sheriff.[2] Lambert, a Norman chief, held Witham, Lincolnshire, under him in 1086.[3] He founded in 1089 the priory of Holy Trinity at Yorkshire. William probably remained in Normandy and received as his reward lands in the Cotentin, which his descendants inherited. The Conqueror also gave his wife as a dowry the fief of Briqueville-sur-Mer.[4]

Nor. Peo., 304, 446. Plan., II, 234. Cle., II, 390. Le Prevost, *Notes, Wace*, II, 248. *Wace*, Taylor, 226.
[1] Ord. Vit., II, 426. [2] *M.S.A.N.*, de Gerville, II, 280, 308. [3] *Vide* Raoul Lambert. [4] *Cart. Mont-St-Michel.*

PICOT DE SAYE. *Vide* Guillaume de Saye.

LE SIRE DE PACY. From Pacy-sur-Eure, arrondissement of Evreux. Pacy, which anciently belonged to the Frank kings and the Carlovingians, came into the possession of duke Rollo, who annexed it to the ducal domain. Richard I, duke of Normandy, granted it to Herfast, the brother of his wife, who was the father of Osberne de Crépon, and grandfather of William Fitz Osberne. A strong castle existed there from a very early date, which as time wore on came into increasing prominence, and as late as 1222 king Philippe Auguste of France sojourned there. William Crispin I was the possessor of a large amount of property in Pacy which is made evident by his many donations to the abbey of Bec before 1070.[1] When he was appointed hereditary viscount of the Norman Vexin by duke William, about

1045, the castle of Pacy came under his command, it being one of the border fortresses in this district.[2] The seigniory of Pacy was in possession of William Fitz Osberne at the time of the conquest, consequently there could not have been another sire de Pacy then, as affirmed by Wace (l. 13655), unless he meant to chronicle William de Breteuil, eldest son of William Fitz Osberne, who succeeded to this seigniory at the death of his father in 1074. If this assumption is incorrect, then he referred to someone who held under Fitz Osberne, though probably not entitled to be designated "sire de Pacy." There was at that time a William de Pacy (Willelmus de Paceio) apparently of considerable importance, who with his mother Hadwis gave lands to the abbey of Bec c. 1070.[3] He would appear to be the same William de Pacy, possibly castellan of Pacy, who was among the witnesses of a charter in favour of St-Evroult, by Raoul de Toeni II, between 1087 and 1099.[4] Ranulf Flambord, bishop of Durham, deprived of that see by king Henry I, acquired the bishopric of Lisieux for his son Thomas, a mere child. He governed it himself, not as a bishop, but as a prévost, and was compelled to relinquish it after three years. The bishopric of Lisieux was then purchased by his clerk, William de Pacy, for a large sum of money paid to duke Robert Courteheuse, "but being condemned for his simony, first at Rouen and afterwards at Rome, he paid dearly for his presumption."[5] Another William de Pacy c. 1135, son of Matilda, made a donation to the abbey of St-Taurin, with the consent of his suzerain, William de Breteuil.[6]

Plan., II, 288. Le Prevost, *Notes, Wace,* II, 251. *Wace,* Taylor, 230. *Nor. Peo.,* 350. Porée, I, 625. *Le Prevost Mem.,* II, 515.
[1] *Dict. de l'Eure,* II, 622. William Crispin I gave to the abbey of Bec before 1070 one-sixth of the mills at Pacy, one-half of the forest there belonging to it, and 100 solidi of the customs of that citadel. (Sertam partem Molendinorum Pacei, dimiduim silvae ibidem ad se pertinentis, C solidos de Paceio.) Bibl. nat. lat. 13905, fo. 115, et lat. 12884, fo. 85. [2] *Omnia Lanfranci, De nob. Crispin. gen.,* I, 343 ; *Dict. de l'Eure,* II, 622. [3] Bibl. nat., *ibid.*

[4] Ord. Vit., II, 189 ; *Cartulaire St. Evroult,* II, 685. [5] Ord. Vit., III, 287–8. [6] *Cart. de Saint-Taurin,* fo. 147. If Le Prevost was correct in placing this charter in 1135, then this William de Breteuil was the son of Eustache de Breteuil, known as William de Pacy, seigneur de Pacy and de Breteuil, who died in 1152 (*Le Prevost Mem.,* II, 513).

LE SIRE DES PINS. The "sire des Pins" of Wace (l. 13567) from Pin-au-Haras, arrondissement of Argentan, recorded at Senlac, has not been identified, but the family was seated in England from the time of the conquest. Fouque des Pin is named in a charter to St-Pierre-sur-Dives as a contemporary of the Conqueror and Gilbert du Pin commanded the troops for duke Robert Courteheuse in an attack on the castle of Brionne in 1090, which surrendered, but Gilbert was killed.[1] Odard du Pin was captured in the battle of Bourg-teroude in 1124 by the forces of king Henry I, by whose order his eyes were put out. Morin du Pin, steward and castellan of Walern II, count of Meulent, who had been the governor and tutor of the young count by the king's appointment, held his castle of Beaumont after the count's capture in that battle by the king. On the order of the count he reluctantly surrendered the castle, which still held out against the king, for which Morin was banished from Normandy for life and died in exile.[2] He was probably the same who witnessed a charter granting Guernani-ville to the abbaye of St-Evroult c. 1080.[3]

Plan., II, 289. Le Prevost, *Notes, Wace,* II, 239. *Wace,* Taylor, 215. Dunstaple.
[1] Ord. Vit., II, 492. [2] *Ibid.,* IV, 75, 77, 78. [3] *Ibid.,* II, 187.

LE CHEVALIER DE PIROU. Wace records "un chevalier de Pirou" (l. 13557), who came from Pirou, near Lessay, arrondissement of Coutances in the Cotentin, as having been present at the conquest. William, lord of Pirou, presumably his son, is said by Orderic Vital,[1] whom he calls the king's dapifer (Henry I), to have perished on the White Ship in 1120. His son William appears in a charter of Henry I with the subscription " ego Gulielmus Pirou-dapifer," which signature follows that of queen Adelaide of Louvain.[2] In 1165 another William Pirou held a barony of eleven fees in Normandy, and a William Pirou also held five fees from earl Bigot in Norfolk and one from Montfichet. William Fitz Humphrey, also of this family, held a fee of the honour of Eye,[3] and another William Pirou appears in 1198.[4] From this family descended the earls of Longford and the Packenhams of Suffolk.

Plan., II, 289. Nor. Peo., 350. Le Prevost, Notes, Wace, II, 236. Wace, Taylor, 212. Dupont, I, 71.
[1] Ord. Vit., IV, 41.   [2] Mon., ii, 7.
[3] Lib. Nig.   [4] R.C.R.

LE SIRE DE POER. Poher, Poncar, or Power descended from the lords of Poncar in Brittany, of whom Rivallon was living in 846.[1] From him descended the viscounts of Poncaer or Poher, of whom Tanegui occurs c. 1100. A branch of the family settled in Devon in 1066, with Alured de Mayenne, and in 1165 Ranulph Poher held three fees of this barony.[2] Bartholomew Poher at the same time was lord of Blackborough, Devon, and was father of Robert Poher.[3] This Robert Poher, or Poer, settled in Ireland and was ancestor of the lords Poer, barons of Dunnoyle and Curraghmore. Hence descended the earls of Tyrone, ancestors in the female line of the marquesses of Waterford, the lords of Decies and also baronets Poer. The name is carried on the rolls of Holinshed, Duchesne, Leland and Worcester.

Nor. Peo., 368. Cle., II, 387. Burke, 89.
[1] Morice, I, xi.   [2] Lib. Nig.   [3] Devon, Pole, 165.

LE SIRE DE PRAÈRES. This family came from Presles, near Vire, and Wace (l. 13661) mentions "sire de Praères" as having been present at the conquest, but this personage has not been identified. In 1119 a sire de Praèrs is recorded a vassal in England of the earl of Chester. This was Richard de Praers, who gave Kanockmirton at that time to Chester abbey. He was a tenant of the baron of Wich-Milbank at Barthomley in Cheshire, held by the family shortly after 1086. They possessed great estates and from them descended the branches which had settled in Baddeley, Badington, Checkley, Duddon and Stoke, all of which became extinct at an early period. The principal line, that of Barthomley, expired with Thomas de Praers in 1349. The name is found in several parts of England.

Plan., II, 289. Cle., III, 37. Le Prevost, Notes, Wace, II, 253. Wace, Taylor, 231.

RAOUL BASSET. Vide Osmond Basset.

RAOUL BOTIN. Raoul Botin was a kinsman of count Alain Le Roux of Brittany, earl of Richmond, in whose train he came to England at the conquest. He is entered in Domesday as the holder of an immense estate in Yorkshire, including Tanfield, which was one of the most beautiful in the earldom of Richmond, and possessed there also Kirkby-Ravensworth, where he built his castle. He died a monk in the abbey of St-Mary, York, having transferred his vast estates to his younger brother Bardolf, whose posterity remained there for 400 years. They ranked among the foremost barons of Yorkshire, where they possessed the large moorlands of Arkendale and Hope, and were the progenitors of the family of Fitz Hugh. Bardolf bestowed the churches of Patrick, Brompton and Kirkby-Ravensworth on the abbey of St-Mary, where, at the end of his life, he was shorn a monk. His son Akaris founded Fors abbey, called the abbey of Charity, in Wensleydale. The family remained prominent for many generations and Petrus Bodin occurs in Normandy in the 12th century.[1] The Beadons of Gotton house, Somerset, claim descent from the Devonshire Beaudins. The name is inscribed on the rolls of Holinshed, Duchesne and Dives.

Burke, 32. Nor. Peo., 169. Cle., I, 170.
[1] M.S.A.N., V, 90.

RAOUL L'ESTOURMI. Vide Richard l'Estourmi.

RAOUL DE FOUGÈRES. The family of Fougères came of very ancient Breton stock. Alan, baron of Fougères, Brittany, c. 900, was father of Maino, the direct progenitor of the family. Maine II was baron of Fougères in Brittany at the time of the conquest, and could himself have been present. He was the son of Alfred I, whom he succeeded in 1048 and survived the battle of Hastings by sixteen years. By his wife, Adelaide, he had three sons, Judhael, Eudes and Raoul. The former died during his lifetime without issue, and Raoul succeeded him, c. 1084.[1] The latter held in chief in Devonshire and occurs in Buckinghamshire, Norfolk, Suffolk and Surrey in 1086 (Domesday). He was a great benefactor to the church, having in 1112 founded the abbey of Savigny [2] and made donations to the abbey of Risle from his vast domains in Normandy, as well as to the abbey of Marmoutiers. Raoul married Avicia, daughter of Richard de Bienfaite, from whom he had seven children. Having died in 1124, he consequently must have been eighty-eight years of age at that time. From this family descended the lords Bohun of Midhurst.[3] A William Fougères, who was a sub-tenant in Buckinghamshire in 1086 (Domesday), has not been identified.[4] Delisle carries on his list both Raoul and Guillaume de Fougères, and Guillaume Tailleur mentions the latter.

Nor. Peo., 248. Cle., II, 218. Plan., II, 225. Le Prevost, *Notes, Wace*, II, 231. *Wace*, Taylor, 208.

[1] Morice ; *Hist. of the Barons of Fougères*, De Pommerel (*l'Art de verifier les dates*, vol. XIII, 270). [2] *Les grandes seigneuries de Bretagne*, G. de Corson, II, 188. [3] *Herald and Genealogist*, VI, 441. [4] *Introd. Domesd.*, I, 418. Wace (l. 13496) chronicles " cil de Felgieres."

RAOUL DE GAEL. Raoul de Guader, or de Gael, surnamed " le Breton," mentioned by Wace (l. 13627), was a very powerful baron in Brittany, lord of the castle of Guader and Montfort-sur-Mer, from Gaël, canton of Saint-Méen, arrondissement of Montfort in the department of Ile and Vilaine, near Rennes.[1] There is much controversy concerning his parentage, but he was probably the son of Ralf, earl of Hereford (or earl of the East Angles), and Getha, an English heiress, which Ralf was the son of Goda, sister of Edward the Confessor, by her first husband, Dreu, count of Vexin, Pon-

toise, Chaumont and Amiens.[2] Raoul commanded a great company of Bretons at the battle of Hastings, for which he received the earldoms of Norfolk and Suffolk and part of Cambridge. He married, 1075, Emma, daughter of William Fitz Osberne, in defiance of the expressed wishes of the Conqueror while the latter was absent in Normandy, at which time he conspired with his brother-in-law, Roger de Breteuil, Waltheof, earl of Northumberland, and other nobles against king William. The plot was revealed by Waltheof, who repented and advised Lanfranc, archbishop of Canterbury, and later the king, of the conspiracy. The revolt speedily ended. Roger de Breteuil was cast into prison, where he remained for the balance of his life, but Raoul de Gael, earl of Norfolk, escaped to Denmark. His wife defended the castle of Norwich until she could make satisfactory terms for herself and followers, when she joined the earl in Brittany, where they found refuge under Hoel V, count of that country. Banished from England, he long flourished in Brittany, and attended duke Robert Courteheuse on the Crusade to the Holy Land in 1096, accompanied by his wife, both of whom died on the journey to Jerusalem. He was succeeded by his son in his Brittany estates of Gauder and Montfort, and his daughter, having married Robert, earl of Leicester, returned to England.

Plan., II, 1. Cle., III, 267. *Wace*, Taylor, 225. Freeman, III, 460. *Les grand. seig. de Bretagne*, G. de Corson, 2° Serie, 200.

[1] Le Prevost, *Notes, Wace*, II, 247. [2] *Vide* App. 8.

RAOUL LAMBERT. This ancient family derives from Lambert, count of Mons and Louvain. He was born about 940 and died in 1004, leaving three sons. The eldest succeeded him in his estate, while the second, Baldwin, settled in Flanders and from him descended the Lambertine family of Bologna, always considered one of the most illustrious in that duchy. The third son, Ralph de Lambert, was born about 980 and settled in Normandy on the estate of his mother, where he married. Their son Ralph de Lambert was born about 1010 and accompanied the Conqueror to England at the battle of Hastings. He was succeeded by Hugh Fitz Lambert, who married Mathilda, daughter of Peter de Roos. William de Lambert, their son, married Gundred, widow of Roger de Beaumont, second earl of Warwick. This lady was the daughter of William, count of Warren in Normandy and the first earl of Surrey, by his wife Gundred (died 1085), believed to have been the daughter of queen Matilda.[1] William Fitz Lambert, William, Peter and Flodus Lambert occur in Normandy between 1180 and 1198.[2] Robert, Walter and William Lambert appear in England c. 1272.[3] In 1086 (Domesday) a Norman chief, Haco or Lambert, is registered as holding Witham from Ralph Paganel. He occurs in 1091 as Haco de Multon.[4] Thomas de Multon, his son, a benefactor to Spalding, had Lambert de Multon living in the time of Stephen.[5] From his eldest son descended the lords Multon of Egremont. His younger son Henry Fitz Lambert was a benefactor to the church in Lincoln, and had Richard Fitz Lambert living in 1235.[6] A branch became seated in Surrey, from whom descended the distinguished general sir Oliver Lambert in the time of Elizabeth, ancestor of the lords Lambert, earls of Cavan.

The House of Hervelson in Ireland, verified by Greenbank. *Nor. Peo.,* 304.
[1] *Vide* Guillaume de Warren. [2] *M.R.S.* [3] *R.H.* [4] *Mon.,* ii, 100, new ed. [5] *Lib. Nig.* [6] Robert's *Excerpt.*

RAOUL DE LIMESI. The family of Limesy from the pays de Caux, near Pavilly, five leagues north-west of Rouen, was a branch of the powerful family of Toeni, Hugh de Toeni, younger brother of Roger d'Espagne, the sons of Raoul de Toeni, one of the castellans of Tillières in 1027, was surnamed de Limesi, from his seigniory of that name in Normandy. He was living in 1060, and his sons, Raoul and Balderic de Limesi, were at the conquest of England. Raoul de Limesi obtained forty-one lordships in Somerset, Hertford, Devon, Gloucester, Northumberland, Warwick, Nottingham, Essex, Norfolk and Suffolk, which he held as tenant-in-chief, including the barony of Wolverley in Warwick, where he built a strong castle which was

the seat of his posterity. Kelham in his *Illustrations* says he was the son of one of the half-sisters of the Conqueror.[1] He died towards the end of the reign of king William, after founding the priory of Hertford, where he and his wife Hadewisia, were admitted towards the end of their lives. His branch of the family is recorded for many generations, and his descendants, through the female line, the comtes de Frontbosc and marquesses de Limesay, were flourishing at the time of the French revolution. Balderic de Limesay, his brother, held lands from the earl of Chester and was the ancestor of the family of Lindsay, Limesy or Limesay in Scotland, including the earls of Crawford and Balcarres, and the dukes of Montrose. Leland and Worcester carry the name and Delisle inscribes Raoul de Limesi.

Nor. Peo., 312. *Cle.,* II, 182. *Lives of the Lindsays,* lord Lindsay. *Rech. Domesd.,* 134.
[1] *Introd. Domesd.,* I, 446.

RAOUL DE MALHERBE. The house of Malherbe is one of the most ancient in Normandy, descended from a Danish noble, companion of duke Rollo. Raoul de Malherbe was at Senlac and from him descended seven principal branches : Seigneurs de Bouillon d'Arry, de Missy, du Bois d'Escure, de Tresnay, d'Armanville, de la Pigacière, de Digny, and finally the marquesses de Malherbe. They held in Devon at Feniton and at Winton-Malherbe and later possessed lands in Somerset, Bedford, Norfolk, Lincoln, Dorset, Northampton, Kent, etc. The Candels and Anstruthers are of this family. Hugh Malherbe occurs in a number of acts and charters of the abbey of Mont-Saint-Michel between 1155 and 1172.[1] Raoul de Malherbe is inscribed on de Magny's *Addition to the Dives List* and the name also appears on the rolls of Holinshed, Duchesne and Brompton.

Nor. Peo., 140. *Cle.,* II, 268. *Nobiliaire de Normandie. Hist. of Vincentius.*
[1] *Cart. du Mt.-St.-Michel,* fo. 112, v° 118; *Chron. de Torigny,* II, 258, 298, 303.

RAOUL DE MORTEMER. The family of Mortemer derives its name from Mortemer (Mortuo-Mari) in Pays-de-Caux at the source of the river Eaulne. The castle of St-Victor-en-Caux was the chief barony of the family, which is said to have sprung from a marriage of Walter de St-Martin and a niece of the duchess Gonnor. It was possessed by Roger de Mortemer in 1054, on which date he was one of the commanders of duke William's forces at the battle of Mortemer. He sheltered in his castle after the battle his father-in-law, Raoul (III) the Great, comte de Valois and d'Amiens, by Orderic Vital called de Montdidier, one of the French commanders, until he was able to conduct him safely to his own territories three days later.[1] For this reason Roger was banished by duke William and his estates confiscated. He was later pardoned and his possessions returned with the exception of the castle of Mortemer, which the duke had given to Roger's brother, William de Warren I. He contributed sixty vassals to the fleet of duke William and it is generally conceded that he was too old to have been present at Senlac, although he made a donation to the abbey of St-Ouen in 1074 and died prior to the compilation of Domesday. Wace (l. 13747) mentions "Hue de Mortemer" as having taken part in the battle. Many commentators believe this to be an error, contending that Wace should have chronicled Roger or his only son Ralph, or both, because the only recorded Hugh was the son of Ralph and therefore too young to have participated in this event. There is no proof, however, that if not of this branch of the family a Hugh could not have sprung from another. Furthermore, Eyton says, " There is evidence that Roger had two sons in addition to Ralph, namely, Hugh and William." We have therefore to accept this statement recorded by Wace, pending further information to the contrary. Forester in his notes to his edition of Orderic Vital states that " Roger de Mortemer, son of Roger, fought at Hastings," but gives no references, which is very much regretted.[2] Ralph, nevertheless, was certainly Roger's heir, and if the son of Hawisa, the only known wife of Roger, he must have been young at the time he attended the conquest. He possessed at the

compilation of Domesday 123 manors, in addition to the castle of Wigmore, in Herefordshire, which was the chief seat of his barony. In 1088 Ralph was opposed to William Rufus in favour of Robert Courteheuse, but two years later, being pardoned, he accompanied Robert, count d'Eu, and Walter Giffard to Normandy, where they arrayed themselves against duke Robert. In 1100 he founded the priory of Wigmore, and in the *History* of the foundation of this priory it is stated that Roger de Mortemer, descended from this family, was about 1200 the second founder.[3] Ralph, by his wife Millicent, had issue, Hugh, who succeeded him, William, to whom his brother gave Chelmarsh and who was ancestor of the Mortimers of Attleborough, and Hawise, who married Stephen, comte d'Aumale. From this family descended the lords Wigmore, earls of March, lords Mortimer of Richard's castle, etc.

Burke, 77. *Nor. Peo.*, 338. Plan., I, 232. Cle., II, 248. Le Prevost, *Notes, Wace*, II, 263. *Wace*, Taylor, 238.
[1] Ord. Vit., II, 408. [2] *Ibid.* [3] Stapleton, II, cxxi ; *vide* App. 19.

RAOUL D'OUILLI. *Vide* Robert d'Ouilli.

RAOUL DE LA POMMERAIE. La Pommeraye, is in the canton of Thury-Harcourt, diocese of Bayeux, Normandy. A small portion of this ancient Norman castle still remains in the Cingueleiz, near Falaise.[1] It is called château Ganne. Ralph is written in Domesday as the possessor of sixty manors, principally in Devon, where Berry Pomeroy became head of this barony. His grandson Ethelevard founded Buckfast abbey during the reign of Henry I. Joel de La Pommeraie married an illegitimate daughter of Henry I, the sister of Reginald, earl of Cornwall. Henry, son of Joslin de Pomere in 1124, had charge of the castle at Pont-Antou, Normandy, at the confluence of the Risle with the river Antou, for king Henry.[2] There are several grants made by this Henry de Pomere in the time of Henry I recorded in the *Monasticon Anglicanum*. He was probably the nephew of Ralph de Pommerai of Berry Pomeroy here mentioned.[3] Henry de Pommeraie supported prince John, when king Richard I was imprisoned by the duke of Austria and garrisoned his castle of Berry Pomeroy. The main line became extinct during the reign of queen Elizabeth. Younger branches were at Sandridge and Ingeston, Devon and Pallice, county Cork, from whom descends viscount Harberton.

Burke, 91. *Nor. Peo.*, 366. Cle., III, 10. Dugdale and Banks.
[1] de Gerville.   [2] Ord. Vit., IV, 71.
[3] *Ibid.*

RAOUL DE RIE. *Vide* Eudo Dapifer, sire de Preaux.

RAOUL DE SASSY. *Vide* Osberne de Sassy.

RAOUL TAILLEBOIS. This warrior of Senlac was descended from the family of that name in the arrondissement of Domfront in the department of the Orne, Normandy, and must not be confused with the Angevine family. He was sheriff of Bedfordshire, held by barony and in chief and was undoubtedly the seignior of Taillebois, who came to the conquest under the banner of Henri de Domfront.[1] His wife, Azelina, held from the king in Buckinghamshire and Cambridgeshire as widow and by barony in Bedfordshire. They left one daughter, who was a tenant-in-chief in Hertfordshire. A Raoul Taillebois occurs in the acts of Mont-Saint-Michel in 1172.[2] His name appears on the Dives roll and Taillebois is carried by Duchesne and Scriven.

Rech. Domesd., 146, 251. *Nor. Peo.*, 369. Cle., III, 344. *Hist. du Canton d'Athis* (*Orne*), Hector de la Ferrière, 1 vol. in 8 v°.
[1] *Vide* Henri de Domfront.   [2] *Cartulaire du Mont-Saint-Michel*, fo. 132, v°; *Chron. de Torigny*, II, 296, 302.

RAOUL TESSON. The castle of La Roche Tesson was near St-Lo, the seat of the Tessons, one of the most powerful families in Normandy. It is said at one time to have possessed a third of that duchy, including the forest and seigniory of Cingueleiz. The name of the family was originally Ticio, seated in the vicinity of Angoulême, who distinguished themselves against the Saracens *c.* 725.[1] They were afterwards seated in Anjou.[2] Radulphus Taxo of Angers in 1028 witnessed a charter regarding the abbey of Coulombs.[3] Rodulfi Taisson, probably the same, appears in the foundation charter of the priory of Sigi by Hugh de Gournay before 1035. Raoul Tesson I, lord of Cingueleiz, led 120 knights of his barony to the assistance of duke William at Val-des-Dunes in 1047.[4] He founded the abbey of Fontenay near Caen, and from him descended the powerful Tesson family.[5] Gilbert Tesson, his brother, obtained the barony of Alnwick from Edward the Confessor and was killed at the battle of Hastings, fighting on the side of Harold. Gilbert's son William, lord of Alnwick and Malton in the county of Northumberland, succeeded him, whose only daughter and heir, Alda, married Ivo de Vassy.[6] Their only daughter and heir Beatrice became the first wife of Eustache Fitz-John, whose son William took the name of Vesci. John, grandson of the latter, was the first baron de Vesci summoned to parliament in 1264. Raoul Tesson II, son of the last-named Raoul, whom Wace (l. 13622) speaks of as "De Cingueleiz Roul Tesson," was a companion of the Conqueror at Hastings and married Matilda, daughter of Walter de Falaise, uncle of duke William on his mother's side. He is not written in Domesday, on which account it is assumed that he either was slain in battle or died before 1086. Raoul Tesson III, his son, inherited the great fief of La Roche Tesson in Normandy, and Gilbert, his second son, received the English possessions which would have gone to his father in addition to his own reward, comprising great estates in York, Lincoln and Nottingham (Domesday). He must have been young at the time he accompanied his father at the conquest, since he lived until 1131. The opinion has been expressed that he possessed Alnwick, but this is incorrect as it passed through the heirs of Ivo de Vassy to the dukes of Northumberland by purchase in 1309, where it still remains. Jordan Taisson, another son, married one of the daughters of the last Néel de Saint-Sauveur[7]; her name, as stated by De Gerville, was Letetia.[8]

From this family descends those of Percy, Marmion, vicomtes de Fontenay, Fitz Erneis, etc. Some historians derive the family from Dotho, a kinsman of duke Rollo.

Plan., II, 104, 158. *Nor. Peo.*, 324, 360, 427. Le Prevost, *Notes*, *Wace*, II, 246. *Wace*, Taylor, 208, 239. Cle., III, 163. Stapleton, I, lxxxiii, lxxxvi, clxxvi. [1] Des Bois, *Art. Achard.* [2] *M.S.A.N.* Vaultrier, X, 78, 94. [3] *Gall. Christ.*, VIII, 297, Instr. [4] *Rech.*, de Gerville. [5] *Gall. Christ.*, XI, 413. [6] Dugdale. [7] *Rot. Norm.*, Hardy, 16. [8] *Rech.*, de Gerville.

RAOUL DE TILLY. Tilly is near Caen, where was located the castle and barony of which the lords of this name were castellans and was one of the most illustrious families in Normandy.[1] Haymon de Telleia occurs in Normandy in 960.[2] The castle was held in fee in 1165 by Henry de Tilly.[3] Ralph de Tilly held lands in 1083 (Domesday) and his descendants continued until the time of Richard, Cœur de Lion, when they were seated in Wonford. During the reign of Stephen the greater part of the confiscated barony of Geoffry de Mandeville was granted to de Tilly, consisting of fifteen knights' fees, of which Mersewood, Dorset, was the chief seat.[4] It was, however, regained by Robert de Mandeville in 1205.[5] At the time of the conquest, Muscamp in Normandy was held by a branch of this family.[6] Odo de Tilly granted lands to Troarn Abbey, Normandy, during the reign of Henry I, and appears to have obtained fiefs in Yorkshire, where his descendants long continued. Geoffrey de Wadworth in the time of Stephen,[7] was father of Eudo de Tilly, called also Eudo de Wadworth. This Eudo held land from the barony of Pontefract in 1165,[8] hence the family of Wordsworth, ancestors of the celebrated poet. The name appears in the *Chronicle* of Guillaume Tailleur on the *Researches of the Bayeux Tapestry of l'abbé de La Rue* and the Dives roll of Léopold Delisle.

Cle., III, 399. *Nor. Peo.*, 204, 419, 449. [1] La Roque, II, 1662, 1994, 1999. [2] *Neustria Pia*, 93. [3] *Foed. Norm.*, Duchesne. [4] *Devon*, Pole, 233 ; *Testa de Neuville*, 183. [5] *Abl. and Fin.*, Hardy, 302. [6] *M.S.A.N.*, XV, 175. [7] *Mon. Ebor.*, Burton, 323. [8] *Lib. Nig.*

RAOUL DE TOENI, SEIGNEUR D'ACQUIGNY. The name is derived from Toeny, commune of Gaillon, arrondissement of Louviers, Normandy. The Toenis were the hereditary standard-bearers of Normandy, although Raoul II, referred to here, refused to carry it at Senlac, protesting to duke William that he could perform greater service to him by participating in the actual fighting. Raoul was seigneur de Conches, d'Acquigny and de Portes,[1] and Wace refers to him (1. 12718) as "Raol de Conches." There can be no doubt of his presence at Hastings as it is attested also by William of Poitiers and Orderic Vital.[2] The genealogy of this family started with Mahulc, uncle of duke Rollo, whose son Hugo, lord of Cavalcamp in Neustria, had issue, Ranulph, or Raoul, and Hugo, archbishop of Rouen, 942-80, which latter gave Toeni to his brother Raoul. The grandson of Raoul, also named Raoul, was from *c.* 1014-30 castellan of the castle of Tillières jointly with his son Roger and Néel, viscount of Cotentin, which fortress passed in hereditary custodianship to Gilbert Crispin, *c.* 1030. This Raoul had issue 1, Roger de Toeni, surnamed d'Espagne, founder of the abbey of Conches, who perished in the civil wars of Normandy *c.* 1038,[3] and had issue, Raoul II de Toeni, hereditary standard-bearer, Robert de Toeni, surnamed de Stafford, the first castellan of that newly built castle, and Nigel de Toeni, also surnamed de Stafford. The second son of Raoul de Toeni I was Hugh de Limesi, living 1060, whose sons Raoul de Limesi and Baldwin de Limesi were at Senlac. Raoul I de Toeni had a third son Robert, who spelt his name de Toedni. He was also present at Hastings, and held eighty manors in thirteen counties at the compilation of Domesday. His chief seat was on the border of Lincoln and Leicester, where he built Belvoir castle. He died 1088 leaving issue, William d'Albini Brito, Berenger de Belvoir, who held a great barony in Yorkshire, Geoffrey, whose son assumed the name de Chauveni, and Robert. Raoul de Toeni II was banished in 1058 with several other powerful nobles by duke William for very little cause, but pardoned and reinstated in his possessions in 1063 at the solicitation of Simon de Montfort l'Amauri.[4] Raoul, born *c.* 1024,[5] distinguished himself at Hastings, and was rewarded with thirty-seven lordships, most of which were in Norfolk, but he made Flamstead in Hertfordshire his chief seat in England. According to Orderic Vital he acquired great glory in the wars of duke William and was among his first nobles in honour and wealth. He espoused Isabel,[6] daughter of Simon de Montfort l'Amauri, which marriage he consummated by kidnapping Agnes, his half-sister, daughter of Richard, count of Evreux, and Adele his widowed mother, marrying Agnes to the aforesaid Simon. Isabel " bore him noble children, Roger and Raoul III and a daughter named Godehilde, who was first married to Robert, count of Meulent,[7] and then (before 1090) to Baldwin, son of Eustache, count of Boulogne " (later in 1100 elected king of Jerusalem).[8] Roger died young and was buried in the abbey of Conches, beside his grandfather, Roger, where his father Raoul II was also later interred. Raoul made a donation to the abbey of St-Evroult *c.* 1080 after his safe return from Spain, to which country he made a journey as his father before him had done.[9] The name appears on all of the rolls.

Plan., I, 217. Cle., III, 171. *Nor. Peo.*, 312. Dugdale. Banks. Norman Exchequer roll in the *Red* book.
[1] Ord. Vit., III, 487. [2] William of Poitiers, Migne, 1254 ; Ord. Vit., I, 484. [3] *Introd. Domesd.*, I, 493 ; Jumièges, 159 ; Ord. Vit., I, 149. [4] Ord. Vit., I, 431–41. [5] *Vide* App. 9. [6] *Ibid.* [7] *Ibid.* [8] Ord. Vit., II, 190. [9] *Chart. S. Ebrulfi*, II, No. 685 ; Ord. Vit., II, 188. Matthew Paris says (460) that William d'Albini Brito captured duke Robert at Tinchebrai.

RAOUL LE VENEUR.

The name is derived from the office of veneur, or venator (a huntsman), of the dukes of Normandy and the ancient seat of the family was Venables, near Evreux.[1] Walter de Veneur distinguished himself at the battle of the Fords between Lothaire, king of France, and the Normans,[2] and the name occurs about this time in charters of the *Gallia Christiana*. Three brothers of the family came to England at the period of the conquest. Gilbert Venator, or de Venables,[3]

another brother, probably ancestor of the Butlers of Chester, barons of Warrington, and Raoul, a baron of Chester, who held in capite from Hugh Lupus. He was a witness to the foundation charter of Chester abbey and a benefactor to it,[4] and the ancestor of the celebrated Grosvenor family of Chester, as well as the marquesses and dukes of Westminster, earls of Wilton and lords Ebury. The name occurs on the lists of Holinshed and Leland.

Nor. Peo., 271. Cle., III, 232.
[1] La Roque, II, 1181. [2] *Hist. Norm.*, Palgrave, II, 738. [3] *Vide* Gilbert de Venables. [4] *Mon.*, i, 201.

RICHARD VICOMTE D'AVRANCHES.

There is a difference of opinion whether Richard d'Avranches referred to by Wace (l. 13600) as " D'Avrencin i fu Richarz," or his son Hugh Lupus, later earl of Chester, was present at Hastings. Léchaudé d'Anisy and de Ste-Marie in their *Recherches sur le Domesday*, think it was Richard because, according to the custom of that period, Hugh could not have taken the territorial name of Avranches before the death of his father, who is known to have been living in 1082. He then witnessed a charter of Roger de Montgomery in favour of St-Stephen at Caen, which he signed " Richard, fils Thurstain," and his son as " Hugo Comes." To a charter of king William in 1074, concerning the church at Bayeux, there appears among the witnesses the signature of Richard Goz, vicomte d'Avranches.[1] This contention is considerably supported by a narration of Orderic Vital [2] concerning Hugh after the battle of Hastings and an entry in the cartulary of the abbey of Whitby,[3] both of which imply his advent into England after that engagement, when he was less than nineteen years of age.[4] Regardless of whether Richard or Hugh or both were at Senlac, as they could have been, it is evident that Wace thought it was Richard. Le Prevost, nevertheless, positively states that Wace should have named Hugh instead of Richard, but fails to give his reasons, which view, according to Planché, Cleveland and Taylor, is generally accepted. The family came from Avranches, Normandy, and is descended from Rogn-wald, earl of Maere, the father of Rollo, first duke of Normandy. He had a natural son Hrollager, living in 896, who married Emma, by whom he had Hrolf Turstan, living 920, who married Gerlotte, daughter of Thibaut, count of Blois, Chartres, and Tours. They had issue, 1, Anslac de Bastembourg, branch of Briquebec, living in 943, who died 990 ; 2, Ansfrid de Goz, the Dane, first vicomte d'Exmes, which he held until 978 ; 3, Guillaume, branch of the seigneurs du Bec-Crespin (concerning whom we have no information, neither do we know where D'Anisy and de Sainte-Marie secured this part of the pedigree). Ansfrid, the second son, had 1, Onfroy the Dane, vicomte d'Exmes, in 1013, and 2, Osmont de Goz. The former was father of Turstain de Goz, vicomte d'Exmes from 1035 to 1041, who married Judith Monterolier, and were the parents of Richard, vicomte d'Avranches, who died before the compilation of Domesday. Richard married Emma de Conteville, daughter of Arlette, the mother of the Conqueror, by whom he had, among other children, Hugh surnamed Lupus, whose domains in England were tremendous.[5] He possessed nearly the whole county of Chester, of which he was created palatine count (earl), which made him almost as powerful as a king. He married Ermentrude, daughter of Hugh, comte de Clarmont, by his wife Margaret de Rouci, and had one son, Richard, who succeeded him in the earldom at the age of seven years. Richard married Matilda de Blois, daughter of Stephen, count of Blois, by Adela, daughter of William the Conqueror, and perished with his wife in the wreck of the *Blanche Nef* in 1119–20, leaving no issue.

Plan., II, 16. Cle., I, 44. *Nor. Peo.*, 145. Le Prevost, *Notes, Wace*, II, 242. *Wace*, Taylor, 2, 19.
   [1] *Gall. Christ.*, col. 66.   [2] *Vide* App. 10.
[3] *Ibid.*   [4] *Vide* Eudes Eveque de Bayeux.
[5] *Rech. Domesd.*, 249.

RICHARD DE BEAUMAIS. Bele-

mis, Beaumis, Beaumeys, Beaumetz, from Beaumetz, near Alençon. "Three brothers, William, Richard and Walter, came to England at the conquest.

Richard was a clerk in Holy Orders in the service of Roger de Montgomery and was prominent among the men who attested his charters. He was a witness also of all the charters, genuine and doubtful, which are assigned to earl Hugh, in the register of Shrewsbury abbey." [1] In 1087, Richard de Belmez, sheriff of Salop, witnessed a charter of Salop abbey,[2] and his name is affixed to its foundation charter in 1067. In 1102 Richard de Belmeis was on the king's commission for treating with the Welsh princes wherein he showed such ability that he was appointed viceroy of Shropshire and warden of the Marches. When Robert de Belesme, son of Roger de Montgomery, rebelled against the king, he remained loyal, and in 1108 was elected bishop of London.[3] Roger de Beaumez witnessed a charter of Henry I in 1124 [4] and died in 1127. Hugh, castellan of Beaumitz, married Beatrice, daughter of Arnold de Gand, count of Guisnes, and was living in 1172. Delisle has inscribed Richard de Beaumais on the Dives roll and the name, spelled in various ways, is recorded by Brompton, Scriven, Holinshed and Duchesne.

Nor. Peo., 154. Cle., I, 196.
   [1] *Shropsh.*, Eyton.   [2] *Mon.*, i, 376.
[3] *Roger of Wendover*, 461.   [4] *Gall. Christ.*, XI, 158.

RICHARD DE BIENFAITE ET D'ORBEC.

Bienfaite and Orbec are in the arrondissement of Lisieux, Normandy. Wace says (l. 13666), " E Dam Richart ki tient Orbec," of whose presence at Senlac there can be no doubt. He appears in history under the designation de Bienfaite, d'Orbec, Fitz Gilbert, de Tunbridge, and de Clare, and was the eldest son of Gilbert, count of Brionne and Eu.[1] Count Gilbert has almost unanimously been styled Gilbert Crispin, count of Brionne, by the latter-day historians. Both dom Mabillon and Auguste Le Prevost [2] fell into this error, but later corrected it. Gilbert, count of Brionne, and Gilbert Crispin, seigneur de Tillières,[3] were separate and distinct personages, living at the same period and both connected with the ducal house of Normandy which caused the confusion. They witnessed numerous charters in the first half of the 11th century, but in no single instance did Gilbert, count of Brionne, use the name of Crispin, always signing as count Gilbert (Gislebertus comes) [4] or Gilbert d'Eu,[5] while Gilbert Crispin, seigneur de Tillières, never executed a document as count of Brionne.[6] Jumièges informs us that Richard I had two natural sons, Godfry, count of Brionne and Eu, and William, count of Exmes, as well as two daughters whom he does not name.[7] One of these was Beatrice, abbess of Montivilliers,[8] and the other, probably the wife of Baldric the Teuton.[9] The mother or mothers of these children are unrecorded and, in addition to them, Benoît de St-More mentions two sons by the duchess Gonnor [10] whom he cannot identify ; all of the offspring of the latter by the duke were formally acknowledged at the time of their marriage.[11] Count Godfry died at the age of about forty-eight, soon after 1006, in which year both he and his brother William affixed their signatures to the act of the assembly at Fécamp.[12] Godfry left a son Gilbert of tender years,[13] and if any other children, they are unknown. Gilbert should have inherited both Brionne and Eu ; he did succeed to the former, but the immediate disposition of the latter is obscure. His uncle William, count of Exmes, founded the church of Eu for secular canons in 1001 [14] and revolted against his half-brother, duke Richard II,[15] between 1006 and April 1012–13, when he witnessed a charter of the duke in favour of the abbey of Jumièges, also attested by the duchess Gonnor.[16] Jumièges states that count William, after five years' imprisonment, escaped, and, having repented, was forgiven by his brother, the duke, to whom the latter then gave the beautiful Lesceline, daughter of Turquetil (de Neufmarché), in marriage, with the comté of Eu.[17] He adds that William's son Robert inherited from him, thus signifying Robert's succession immediately following his father (Rodbertum Scilicet Post ejus Mortem Comitatus illius heredem).[18] Jumièges makes no mention of Exmes, which was given by duke Richard II to his son Robert (I) the Magnificent in 1025.[19] It therefore seems this county was not returned to count

William or, if so, was taken away from him again or he died before that date. Dom Mabillon, however, affirms that count William died while his house was in mid-construction and when completed in 1046 his widowed countess bestowed their dwelling at Saint-Pierre-sur-Dives on Ainardus, a monk of Saint-Trinité du Mont at Rouen, to found a monastery.[20] This is supported by the gift of William, count of Eu (Willelmus comes de Augo),[21] made to the abbey of Bec, which would of necessity have been sometime after 1034, the date of its foundation.[22] Should this be correct, then count William lost Eu for a long period, since in 1030 it certainly was in the possession of count Gilbert, who witnessed as Gilbert d'Eu the foundation charter of Trinité du Mont at Rouen in this year.[23] Gilbert still held it c. 1036–40, the date of his murder, because Jumièges and his continuators, Orderic Vital and Robert de Torigny, say so.[24] If count William predeceased count Gilbert, doubtless the latter, on the death of his uncle William, seized Eu, for he probably thought that it belonged to him as his rightful inheritance and it is scarcely possible that he could have taken it forcibly from so powerful a noble as his uncle. In any event, if count William was alive after 1030, he did not possess either Exmes or Eu from that date until after the death of count Gilbert. A plausible solution is offered in the *Dictionnaire de l'Eure*, who say count William was the guardian of count Gilbert during his minority and returned to him his full powers and possessions c. 1020, but cite no proof.[25] However, when count Gilbert died, his estates were seized by duke William, who gave Brionne to Guy of Burgundy and then, beyond doubt, Eu passed to count William if alive, or if not, to his son and heir Robert, who, according to the cartulary of Tréport, held it shortly thereafter.[26] The wife of count Gilbert is not at present known, although he is said to have married Arlette, the mother of the Conqueror, by whom he had sons Richard and Baldwin.[27] Richard de Bienfaite fled to the court of Baldwin, count of Flanders, after his father's death, with his brother Baldwin, and on his return to Normandy, at the time of the marriage of duke William to Matilda of Flanders, was given Bienfaite and Orbec to compensate him for the loss of his inheritance.[28] He possessed at the compilation of Domesday, 189 manors and burgages, thirty-five of which were in Essex and ninety-five in Suffolk, including the honour of Clare. To reimburse him for the loss of the castle of Brionne in Normandy he was granted the same amount of land round Tunbridge in Kent, where he built his castle.[29] He and William de Warren were jointly the high judiciaries of England during the king's visit to Normandy in 1067, and he assisted in the suppression of a revolt of the earls of Hereford and Norfolk. He was high in the councils of his cousin, the king, and was the progenitor of the illustrious house of Clare, the barons Fitz Walter and the earls of Gloucester and Pembroke. He died about 1090, and by his wife Rohesia, the eldest daughter of Walter Gifford, first earl of Buckingham, had issue : Godfry, Robert (from whom the Barons Fitz Walter), Richard a monk of Bec, Walter and Roger, who both died without issue, and Gilbert who succeeded him, from whom descended the earls of Hereford and Gloucester. He had two daughters : Rohesia, who married Eudo dapifer and another, who was the wife of Ralph de Telgers.[30]

Plan., II, 33. Le Prevost, *Notes, Wace,* II, 254. *Wace,* Taylor, 232.
[1] *Jumièges Interp.,* Ord. Vit., 229 ; Ord. Vit., II, 490. [2] Dom Mabillon, IV, 367, 391, 399, 520 ; Le Prevost, *Notes, Wace,* II, 5, 232. [3] *Vide* App. 16, n. 3. [4] *English Historical Review,* Haskins, vol. 31, p. 122, of April 1916 ; *Cart. de la Cathéd. de Rouen,* fo. 33, v°, chart. XXI. [5] Ord. Vit., III, 452, n. [6] *Vita Domini Herluini Abbatis Beccensis Auctore Gilberto Crispino, Omnia Lafranci,* Giles, I, 260 ; *De nob. Crispin. gen.,* I, 341 ; *vide* App. 16, n. 6. [7] *Jumièges,* 74 ; *ibid. Interp.,* de Torigny, 229–55 ; Dudon de Saint-Quentin, lib. III, Duchesne, 152c. [8] *Vide* App. 16, n. 17, 18. [9] *Vide* Fouque d'Aunou. [10] Benoît, II, 321–4. [11] *Jumièges Interp.,* de Torigny, 229, 323 ; *vide* App. 11. [12] *Hist. de la France,* X, 371 ; *Neustria Pia,* 214 and fol. ; *Helgaldi Epist. Vitæ Roberti regis,* 106. [13] Stapleton, I, lvi. [14] *Neustria Pia,* 694 ; Freeman, III, 117. [15] *Jumièges,* 74 ; *ibid. Interp.,* de Torigny, 230, 251. [16] *Chart. Abb. Jumièges,* I, 18. [17] *Jumièges,* 74.

[18] *Ibid.,* 75 ; *Cart. de Notre-Dame du Tréport,* L. de Kermingant, p. 1. [19] *Jumièges,* 97 ; Freeman, I, 468 ; *Hist. de Norm.,* Licquet, II, 1. [20] Stapleton, II, xci. [21] *Bibl. nat. lat.* 12884 et 13905 ; *vide* App. 11. [22] *Jumièges Interp.,* de Torigny, 238 ; Porée, I, 35 ; *vide* App. 11. [23] *Ibid.,* n. 5 ; *Le Prevost Mem.,* II, 520–1 ; *Cart. de la Cathéd. de Rouen,* fo. 33 v°, chart. XXI. [24] *Jumièges,* 116 ; *ibid. Interp.,* Ord. Vit., 155, et de Torigny, 229 ; Ord. Vit., ed. Le Prevost, I, 180 ; II, 25, 37 ; Benoît, III, 5 ; *vide* sire de Gacé, App. 5, 11. [25] *Dict. de l'Eure,* I, 584. [26] *Jumièges,* 122 ; *Chron. de Torigny,* I, 30 ; *ibid.,* n. 16. [27] *Vide* App. 11. [28] Stapleton, II, cxxxvi. [29] *Jumièges Interp.,* de Torigny, 289 ; Ord. Vit., ed. Le Prevost, III, 343, n. 1 ; *vide* App. 11. [30] Ord. Vit., II, 493.

RICHARD DE COURCI. Wace (ll. 13614 and 13656) records "cil de Corcie," which was Richard de Courci II from the arrondissement of Falaise, who was present at Senlac. He was the son of Richard de Courci, one of the six sons of Baldric the Teuton, who received from the Conqueror the barony of Stoke in the county of Somerset, and the manors of Newnham, Setenden and Foxcote in Oxfordshire (Domesday). He defended the castle of Courcy against Robert Courteheuse, at the instigation of Robert de Belesme, when quite an old man. His son Robert married Rohesia, daughter of Hugh de Grentemesnil. The family held a distinguished rank for several centuries in both England and France. In the latter country, Richard de Courcy was abbé of Savigny[1] and Guillelmo de Curci, who died in 1176, was seneschal of Normandy and married the daughter of Richard of Aquila, by whom he left offspring.[2] Richard appears on the Dives roll and the name is carried on those of Holinshed and Brompton. It likewise occurs in the *Researches of the Bayeux Tapestry* by l'abbé de La Rue.

M. Richome's notice in Mem. Ant. Norm., III, 102. *Introd. Domesd.,* I, 403, 412. Plan., II, 83. Le Prevost, *Notes, Wace,* II, 245, 251. *Wace,* Taylor, 222. [1] *Chron. de Torigny,* II, 190. [2] *Ibid.,* II, 63, 308.

RICHARD L'ESTOURMI. Estourmi was a "family that from the most remote antiquity held a high rank among the nobles of the province."[1]

Jean, a younger brother, remained in Normandy and was ancestor of the family there. Richard and Raoul came to England at the conquest, the former held in capite in Hampshire, Wiltshire and Surrey, and Raoul held under him in 1086 (Domesday). Two of Richard's manors were Lysse-Sturmy in Hampshire and Cowsfield-Esturmy in Wiltshire. His descendants were for many generations foresters in fee of Savernake. Hugh l'Estourmi of Sussex occurs in 1176. The great estates of the family of Estourmi eventually went by marriage to Roger Seymour, ancestor of the dukes of Somerset, from whom descend the marquesses of Ailesbury and viscounts Savernake. The family spread to many parts of England and is mentioned on the rolls of Holinshed, Duchesne and Leland, and both Raoul and Richard appear on the Dives list of Léopold Delisle.

Cle., II, 15–16.
[1] *Nobiliaire de Normandie.*

RICHARD DE NEUVILLE. So called from his fief of Neuville-sur-Touques in the department of the Orne, arrondissement of Argentan, and canton of Gacé. Richard de Neuville was the father of four sons, Gilbert, Robert, Richard, and Ralph. Gilbert, styled the Norman, is supposed to have been the admiral of duke William's fleet. It would appear that Leland first made this statement at the close of the 15th century on the authority of " a roulle of the Genealogie of the Erles of Westmoreland," but giving no idea of the date of that roll, or the authorities from which it was compiled. Whether the Richard de Neuville at Hastings was Richard de Neuville I, or his third son, Richard II, is open to conjecture. Robert was one of the supporters of Robert de Belesme entrusted with the defence of Bridgnorth in 1102, against king Henry I.[1] Ralph de Neuville, who held Thrope of Turold, abbot of Peterborough, would appear to be the only member of the family entered in Domesday. It was very distinguished and widely spread in England, and from it, in the female line, descended the earls of Westmorland and Abergavenny. The name appears on the rolls of Leland, Holinshed, Duchesne, Brompton, Worcester, and Dives.

Plan., II, 135. Cle., II, 342. *Nor. Peo.*, 343, Dugdale. Burke, 84.
[1] Ord. Vit., III, 334.

RICHARD DE REVIERS. There is much confusion concerning the identity of the "sire de Reviers" chronicled by Wace (l. 13616), who " brought with him many knights," which family came from Revières, near Creulli, in the arrondissement of Caen. M. le Prevost thinks Wace refers to Baldwin de Meules and du Sap, the younger son of Gilbert, count of Brionne and Eu, basing his assumption on the statement in the *Interpolations of Jumièges* by de Torigny, that Osmond de Centville, viscount of Vernon, and a niece of the duchess Gonnor, had a daughter, who was the mother of the first Baldwin de Redvers.[1] The eminent commentator in this instance is in error, as there was a very prominent and powerful seignior at the time of the conquest by the name of Richard de Redvers, who founded the abbey of Montebourg in 1080, which he richly endowed. In a charter of this abbey appears the name of Richard de Redvers, witnessed by his two sons, Baldwin and William; the former is beyond doubt the Baldwin de Redvers to whom de Torigny refers.[2] Richard de Redvers was probably the son of William de Redvers, as indicated by Stapleton, who held lands in Montebourg, Normandy, by a daughter of this niece of the duchess Gonnor. This would fit in perfectly with the statement in the *Cartulary of Carisbrook*, that Richard was the nephew of William Fitz Osberne, whose son, Roger de Breteuil, he succeeded in the possession of the isle of Wight. He subscribed to a charter of the abbaye-aux-Dames in Caen in 1082 [3] and was one of the chief counsellors and champions of prince Henry during his conflicts with his brothers, William Rufus [4] and duke Robert Courteheuse. On his ascension to the throne, Henry magnificently rewarded Richard.[5] He received the castle and honour of Plympton and Tiverton in Devonshire, with the gift of the " Tertium Denarum "—third penny —of the pleas, by which he became earl of that county. Opinion differs whether he was actually constituted earl because he is not so styled in contemporary documents, which theory is supported by Stapleton [6] in his *Addenda*, though it is evident that his wife so considered him. In a charter to Twinham she gives the church of Holy Trinity for the health of the souls of her lord Richard, earl of Redvers, and of her son earl Baldwin; the grant being made with the consent of "Earl Richard my grandson and heir." Richard died in 1107 [7] and was buried in his Norman abbey of Montebourg, where De Gerville discovered his stone coffin, upon the top of which was inscribed "Fundator." By his wife Adeliza Pevrel he left three sons, Baldwin, earl of Devon, William surnamed de Vernon, both of whom witnessed the foundation charter of Mountebourg, and Robert of St-Mary's Church, Devon; also one daughter Hadewise, countess of Lincoln. Baldwin, his son, succeeded as earl of Devon and lord of the isle of Wight, and strongly supported the empress Matilda. He was followed by his son Richard in 1155,[8] the father of two earls, Baldwin and Richard, both having died without issue, the title and inheritance passed to their uncle, William de Vernon, who thus became the sixth earl.[9] William de Vernon married lady Mabel de Beaumont, the daughter of Robert, count of Meulent,[10] by whom he had one son, Baldwin, and two daughters, Mary and Joan. His son predeceased him, leaving a small son Baldwin, who became the seventh earl. His daughter Mary married 1, Robert de Courtenay, baron of Okehampton, and 2, sir Peter Prouz, the ancestor of Thomasine Prouz, who married sir John de Chudleigh, *c.* 1330.[11] Later the male line of Redvers-Vernon, having become extinct, William de Fortibus, earl of Albemarle, married Isabel, countess of Devon and lady of the isle of Wight, who were succeeded by a daughter, Aveline, their other children having died. Inheriting the two earldoms, the isle of Wight and the vast possessions of these powerful families, she was, by the request of king Henry III, married to his son Edmund Crouchback, afterwards earl of Lancaster, in 1269. Aveline died childless and the earldom of Devon

finally in 1355 passed to sir Hugh de Courtenay, descended from lady Mary de Redvers or de Vernon, the eldest daughter of William de Vernon, the sixth earl. Guillaume de Reviers, perhaps the brother of Richard de Redvers, here chronicled, held a barony in Dorset in 1086 (Domesday), and is claimed by Léopold Delisle to have been at the conquest.

Plan., II, 45. Cle., II, 307; III, 60. Le Prevost, *Notes, Wace,* II, 245. *Wace,* Taylor, 222.
[1] Jumièges, 328. [2] *Gall. Christ.,* IX; Stapleton, II, cclxix and fol. [3] Ord. Vit., II, 498. [4] *Ibid.* [5] *Ibid.,* III, 270, 282. [6] Stapleton, II, cclxxiii. [7] Ord. Vit., III, 418. [8] If it were not for the definite information in a charter to Twinham priory executed by Baldwin's mother, the countess Adeliza, who died sometime between 1155 and 1165, it could be assumed that a generation was missing between Richard and his son Baldwin. [9] *Vide* Baudoin de Meules. [10] *Complete Peerage,* G.E.C., IV, 315. [11] *Visitation of Devon,* Vivian, 189-90; *Vide* App. 12.

RICHARD DE SAINT-CLAIR. This family derived its name from St-Clair, in the arrondissement of St-Lo, in the Cotentin, Normandy. The site of the castle was still in existence during the time of de Gerville as recorded in his *Researches.* The "sire de St-Cler" of Wace (l. 13749) was Richard, who held lands in Suffolk in 1086 (Domesday), and was succeeded by Hamo de St-Clair, living 1130.[1] Britel de St-Clair, brother of Richard, held in Somerset in 1086 (Domesday), and witnessed a charter of the earl of Mortain,[2] and William, probably his son, held in Dorset, 1130,[3] and had a grant of Rosslyn in Scotland from David I. William St-Clair endowed the abbey of Savigny during the reign of Henry I, and in 1139 the priory of Villers-Fossard was founded by a member of the family. A William of this line married Isabel, daughter and heir of Malise, seventh earl of Strathern and earl of Orkney and Caithness. She traced her descent from Rognavald, the uncle of duke Rollo. The first earl of Caithness of this line married, 1, lady Elizabeth Douglas, a granddaughter of Robert III of Scotland. Richard de St-Clair appears on the Dives roll of Léopold Delisle.

Cle., III, 95. *Nor. Peo.*, 388. Plan., II, 290. Le Prevost, *Notes*, *Wace*, II, 264. Burke, 95. *Wace*, Taylor, 239.
[1] *Rot. Pip.* [2] *Mon.*, ii, 910. [3] *Rot. Pip.*, *ibid.*, n. 1.

RICHARD DE SOURDEVAL.

The seigneurs de Sourdeval were a branch of the house of Verdun and took the name of La Moigne in Normandy.[1] Richard de Sourdeval accompanied the count of Mortain to the conquest, having come from Sourdeval-la-Barre, near the town of Mortain. He held in capite fifty-five manors, chiefly in Yorkshire, from the aforesaid earl. It was probably his brother Robert de Sourdeval who went with Mark Bohemond, prince Tarentum, eldest son of Robert Guiscard, to the Holy Land on the first Crusade.[2] Richard does not appear to have been a benefactor to the church and probably died soon after the survey, for, in the reign of William Rufus, some of his manors were vested in Ralph Painel in the right of his wife, Matilda, who was probably the sole heiress of Richard. The family continued in England for several centuries. The name appears on the lists of Holinshed, Leland, Worcester and Dives.

Cle., I, 33.
[1] *Rech.*, de Gerville. [2] Ord. Vit., III, 83.

RICHARD TALBOT. *Vide* Guillaume Talbot.

RICHARD DE VERNON.

The lords of Vernon were of the house of Reviers or Redvers, and their castle of Vernon was located in the arrondissement of Evreux, which was very strong and celebrated in the 11th and 12th centuries. Roger was baron of Vernon *c.* 1030, at which time his daughter, Blithildis, was married, who, in 1082, granted to Holy Trinity at Caen the lands at Vernon, which had been given to her by her father. This grant was made with the consent of her nephew, William, then lord of Vernon.[1] This William had recovered Vernon, formerly granted by duke William *c.* 1040, to count Guy of Burgundy,[2] of which he was the seignior between 1050 and

1052, and from whom descended the barons of Vernon, who held sixty-one knights' fees. M. le Prevost says it was Richard, William's eldest son and heir, to whom duke William gave Vernon in 1050, and that he accompanied the duke to the conquest of England. However this may be, Richard certainly possessed it later when he was head of the family.[3] He and Walter, sons of William, appear in Cheshire in 1086 (Domesday), where the former held sixteen lordships. Walter was a tenant-in-chief in Buckinghamshire and is supposed to have left no heirs, while the third and less known brother Huard or Alured de Vernon was a mesne-lord in Suffolk in 1086 (Domesday). These three members of the family are recorded to have been at the conquest of England, and Richard in 1074 confirmed at Vernon a charter of his uncle Hugh, to the abbey of Jumièges.[4] He was one of the palatine barons of Hugh Lupus and "had a castle at Shipbrook on the Wever, which commanded its passes."[5] Richard is not referred to by Wace, unless the "sire de Neauhou" (l. 13556) is intended for him. Nehou passed from the viscounts of St-Sauveur to the Vernons[6] and a Richard de Vernon in the Red book of the Exchequer is returned as holding the honour of Nehou by the service of ten knights' fees and having the custody of the castle of Vernon, who was beyond doubt this Richard. Delisle has inscribed Richard de Vernon on the Dives roll and the name appears on those of Holinshed, Duchesne, Leland and Brompton.

Nor. Peo., 432. Cle., III, 212. Burke, 104. Plan., II, 205. *Hist. de la Ville et du Canton de Vernon*, Th. Michel.
[1] *Gall. Christ.*, XI, 70 Instr. [2] Ord. Vit., II, 404. [3] *Le Prevost Mem.*, III, 351 ; M. Merlet has considerable information on this subject in the *Cartulaire des Vaux de Cernai*, I, 701. [4] *Chart. Abb. de Jumièges*, II, 36. [5] *Chesh.*, Ormerod. [6] *Vide* Vicomte Néel Saint-Sauveur; *vide* App. 7.

ROBERT D'AMFREVILLE.

There are eight communes of the name in Normandy, but probably Amfreville-sur-Iton in the viscountcy of Evreux,[1] was the residence of this family. M. le Prevost suggests that Toures should read Tourville adjoining the principal seat of the lords of Amfreville-la-Champagne.[2] Umfreville is the English name and Robert de Umfreville " with the beard," lord of Tour, and Vian in Normandy, and a kinsman of the Conqueror, came to England with him at the conquest and received the lordships of Prudhoe and Riddesdale in Northumberland. Robert, his eldest son, was witness to the foundation charter of Kelso abbey in 1076. His second son Gilbert was contemporary with Henry I and joined in the conquest of Glamorgan in 1091, and Odonel, the third son, became baron of Riddesdale and Prudhoe. The great-grandson of the latter, Gilbert, lord Umfraville, was in the right of his wife, earl of Angus [3] in Scotland at the close of the 13th century. The name appears frequently in *Monasticon Anglicanum*.[4] A branch remained in Normandy, which descended from Walter d'Amfreville, who was at the battle of Gisors in 1097,[5] in which county the family flourished in the 13th and 14th centuries and made donations to the abbey of Jumièges.

Nor. Peo., 325, 428. Cle., III, 349.
[1] *Foed. Norm.*, Duchesne. [2] Ord. Vit., III, 209, ed. note. [3] *Complete Peerage*, G.E.C., I, 146 ; *Northumberland*, Hodgson, I, II, 6. [4] *Ibid.* [5] Ord. Vit., III, 209.

ROBERT BANASTRE. The name was derived from Banastre, now Beneter, near Etampes, and Camden says it is the title of office latinized into Balneator, master of the bath. Robert Banastre came to England at the conquest and an ancient pedigree of this family, beginning with Robert down to the time of Edward I, is preserved in the rolls of parliament. He held Prestatyn, one of the hundreds of Flintshire, under Robert of Rhudlaw (de Rodelent), a kinsman of the Conqueror, where a castle was built which was destroyed by the Welsh during the reign of Henry II. The family then withdrew to Lancashire, where they held possessions under the earl of Chester. In a deed of 1106, Richard Banastre, a baron of Cheshire, appears, and in 1128 is a witness to a charter of Robert de Meschines. He also held in capite in Shropshire, under Henry I, as lord of Munslow and Aston-Munslow in 1115. Later on the barony of Newton

and the lordship of Walton-in-the-Dale passed through the female line to the Langtons, where they remained for about 300 years. The family spread to many parts of England. A member of the Lancashire Bannisters was a knight of the order of the Garter. The name appears on the rolls of Holinshed, Duchesne and Leland.

Cle., I, 124. Burke, 21. *Nor. Peo.*, 149.

ROBERT LE BASTARD. Robert le Bastard, sometimes written Baisterd, and Bestard, is reputed to have been a natural son of William the Conqueror, and according to a legend in the family, was in command of a vessel of duke William's fleet. This ship was driven by a gale into Salcomb, and land there is still held by the Bastard family. He received a barony in Devonshire and the Bastards gave their name to Loveton-Bastard and were several times sheriffs of Devonshire. Their original seat, held from the conquest, was Efford in the parish of Egg-Buckland, where the family prevailed until the beginning of the 14th century. Early in the 18th century the head of the house removed to Kitley, when the heiress of Edmund, the last of the Pallexfens, brought it to William Bastard. John Pallexfen Bastard in 1816 represented the county in seven successive parliaments.

Cle., I, 186. *Nor. Peo.*, 151.

ROBERT DE BEAUFOU. This illustrious and ancient barony was in the environs of Pont l'Evêque, called Beaufou, Beaufois, and Belfai, latinized Bellofago.[1] Its lords were descended in the female line from Raoul, comte d'Ivri, uterine brother of duke Richard (I). Wace (l. 13558) informs us that " Robert, sire de Belfou," was present at Senlac, which opinion is concurred in by William of Poitiers, Planche and Cleveland. M. le Prevost, on the other hand, thinks Wace should have recorded Ralph instead, since his name occurs in contemporary documents, and Radulph de Bellofago is entered in Domesday. Guillaume de Beaufou, also at the conquest, was lord of Swanton Morely in Norfolk in 1086 (Domesday), and many other manors in the county. He is said to have been a " near relation, if not the son " of William de Beaufoe, bishop of Thetford, chaplain and chancellor of the Conqueror. William's daughter and heir Agnes married Hugue de Rie, castellan of Norwich, also present at Hastings.

Plan., II, 283. Cle., I, 200. Le Prevost, *Notes, Wace*, II, 236. *Wace*, Taylor, 213.
[1] *Introd. Domesd.*, I, 379–80.

ROBERT DE BEAUMONT. Master Wace (l. 13462) records " Rogier li veil cil de Belmont," but in the manuscript in the British museum the name is Robert, which is correct, since Roger remained in Normandy at the head of the council to assist queen Matilda in the government of that duchy. Roger is conceded to have been the wealthiest, noblest and most trusted of the seigniors of Normandy. He was the son of Humphrey de Viellers, grandson of Thurold de Pontaudemer, a descendant of the kings of Denmark, through Bernard the Dane, the companion of duke Rollo. Lofty as was his ancestry, he adopted the title of the family of his wife, Adelina, countess of Meulent, Meulant, Mellent, later Meulan used by his posterity. He contributed sixty vessels to the fleet of duke William and was represented at Senlac by his son Robert, whom William of Poitiers and Orderic Vital state was " a novice in arms." Robert was rewarded with ninety manors in Warwick, Leicester, Wilts and also Northampton. He and his brother Henry, afterwards earl of Warwick, were among the barons who reconciled king William and his son, duke Robert Courteheuse, in 1081. He was known after the death of his mother as count of Meulent and as such in 1082 sat in the French parliament, as a peer of France. With his brother, he espoused the cause of William Rufus, and after his death that of king Henry, by whom he was created earl of Leicester. He married Elizabeth, daughter of the count of Vermandois, by whom he had issue : Emma, born 1102 ; Waleran and Robert, twins, born 1104, and Hugh the Poor, afterwards earl of Bedford, and the following other daughters, Adeline, Amicia, Albreda and Isabel. Robert de Beaumont married first Godehilde, daughter of Raoul de

Toeni II, who bore him no children and from whom he was separated by 1090. When between fifty and sixty married secondly lady Elizabeth, who was young, and William de Warren II, earl of Warren and Surrey, supplanted Robert in her affections, so that she ultimately deserted him, which affected his mind and hurried him to his death in 1118.

Plan., I, 181, 203. Cle., I, 145. Burke, 29. *Wace*, Taylor, 205. Le Prevost, *Notes, Wace*, II, 229. *Vide* Robert de Montgomeri and Raoul de Toeni; App. 9.

ROBERT BERTRAM LE TORT. Robert Bertram le Tort, whom Wace designates " Robert Bertram ki esteit torz " (l. 13634), was lord of Briquebec, near Valognes, Normandy, which barony consisted of forty knights' fees. He was descended from Anslac de Bastembourg,[1] very renowned in Normandy, whose son Torstin witnessed a charter in favour of St-Denis in 968,[2] and was a benefactor to Fontenelles in 960.[3] William his son, surnamed Bertram, was living in 1012 and was the father of Robert Bertram, baron of Briquebec, living in 1066.[4] This Robert was surnamed le Tort and was present at Hastings, where he was accompanied by his younger brother William, who is entered in Domesday. Robert died before the compilation of that survey having made several donations on his death-bed in 1082 to the abbey of St-Stephen at Caen. From his son Robert, descended the barons of Briquebec, barons of Mitford and Bothal in Northumberland. Wace (l. 13747) chronicles " de Peleit le filz Bertran," about whom nothing is known other than the statement that he was a Briton who joined the army at St-Valéry, with sire de Dinan and Raoul de Gace, which indicates that he was not of the Norman Bertram family.

Plan., II, 247, 281. Cle., I, 47. *Nor. Peo.*, 333. Le Prevost, *Notes*, II, 248. *Wace*, Taylor, 227. Dugdale, 543.
[1] *Vide* Richard d'Avranches. [2] Bouquet, IX, 731. [3] *Mem. Russell*, Wiffen, I, 60. [4] *Gall. Christ.*, XI, 60, 229 Instr.

ROBERT BLOUET. This family came from Briqueville-la-Blouette, in Normandy.[1] Robert Blouet, the chaplain to William the Conqueror, was later promoted to the see of Lincoln, which he held from 1093 to 1123.[2] He witnessed a charter of William I.[3] Richard and William Blouet occur in Normandy in 1084,[4] and Ralph Blouet, an under-tenant in Hampshire in 1086 (Domesday) is mentioned in the *Monasticon Anglicanum* [5] as a benefactor to Gloucester abbey. Godfry Bloet appears in an act of Mont-Saint-Michel in 1185.[6] The family was long prominent in the west of England and in Normandy until the 18th century, when Blouet de Cahagnolles of the bailiwick of Caen was a member of the great assembly of nobles in 1789. From this family descended the lords of Raglan.

Burke, 24. Cle., I, 112. *Nor. Peo.*, 162. [1] *La Roque*, II, 1834. [2] *Ord. Vit.*, III, 201 ; *Roger of Wendover*, 363. [3] *Mon.*, i, 49. [4] *Gall. Christ.*, XI, 228 Instr. [5] *Mon.*, i, 118. [6] *Chron. de Torigny*, II, 382.

ROBERT BOURDET. The family descends from the Bordets, lords of Cuilly in Normandy. Robert Bordet and his son Robert, witnessed a charter of the count of Anjou *c*. 1050. He had issue, besides Robert, another son Hugh, both of whom came to England at the conquest and were mesne-lords in Leicester in 1086 (Domesday), in which county Hugh held considerable estates from the countess Judith. He was the founder of Lowesby in Leicester, the ancient seat of the family,[1] and was ancestor of the Burdetts, baronets, and of baroness Burdett-Coutts. Robert was lord of Cuilly, and died before 1086, at which time his widow held from Hugh de Grentemesnil in Leicester.[2] He was living in 1077 [3] and his son, Hugh de Cuilli, in 1128 witnessed a charter of Richard' de Beauvais.[4] Hugh had issue Robert and Walter de Cuilly ; Robert, sire de Cuilli, married Sibylla, daughter of William de Chievre, a baron of Devon.[5] He, undertaking to rebuild the city of Tarragona in Spain, obtained the suzerainty with rank of prince of Tarragona. At the battle of Fraga in 1133, at the head of his Norman cavalry, he rescued Alfonso, king of Aragon and his army from destruction by the Saracens.[6] Walter, his brother, witnessed the foundation charter of Canwell, Stafford, in 1142.[7] Hugh de Cuilly of the family was in

1309 constable of Kenilworth, and his great-granddaughter married sir John Stanhope of Rampton.[8] A descendant, Walter Colley, went to Ireland, *temp.* Henry VIII, and from him descended the lords of Castle-Carbery, the lineal male ancestors of Arthur Wellesley, the renowned and famous duke of Wellington, one of England's greatest generals. The name appears on the list of Scriven, Holinshed, Duchesne and Leland, while Delisle on the Dives roll carries Robert and Hugh Bourdet.

Cle., I, 191. *Nor. Peo.*, 179, 205. [1] Ord. Vit., VI, 114, Forester's n. [2] *Introd. Domesd.*, I, 232. [3] *Mon.*, i, 562. [4] *Ibid.*, ii, 143. [5] *Vide* Guillaume la Chièvre. [6] Ord. Vit., VI, 114-18. [7] *Mon.*, i, 444. [8] *Rot. Origin.*, II, 351.

ROBERT DE BRIX. The name Bruis, or Brus, comes from the castle of Brus, or Bruis (now Brix), near Cherbourg, where the remains of an extensive fortress built in the 11th century still exists.[1] The family is mentioned by Wace (l. 13643) as "cels de Bruis," while the manuscript in the British museum reads "cil de Bruis." The castle of Brix belonged to the ducal desmesne in 1026, when it formed part of the dowry granted to Adèle, consort of duke Richard III.[2] Robert de Brutz, or Brusce, was counsellor to duke Robert the Magnificent, and his son Robert de Brus, accompanied by his two sons William and Adam, attended the conquest of England. The latter, Robert, died shortly after, when William received the castle of Bramber in Sussex,[3] whose descendants for several generations were barons of the realm. Adam, or Adelm de Brus, the younger brother of William, came to England in 1050, attending queen Emma. Shortly after which he went to Scotland, but joined his father and brother later at the conquest. He was rewarded with ninety-four lordships in Yorkshire, and died in 1079, in consequence of which his son Robert received these possessions and is entered in Domesday. The latter built the castle of Skelton and founded the priory of Guisborough in 1119 ; was at the battle of the Standard 1135 and died in 1141. He had issue, 1, Adam ; 2, Robert, who was the grandfather of Robert de Bruce, lord of Annandale, who married the heiress of David, brother and heir of William, king of Scotland, and whose great-grandson was Robert the Bruce of Bannockburn fame, the most illustrious monarch of Scotland. Hence also the earls Elgin, barons Burleigh, baronets Bruce, etc. This family has frequently been confused with that of de Briouse near Argentan, Normandy. The name appears on the lists of Leland, Fox and Dives.

Cle., I, 102. *Nor. Peo.*, 175. Burke, 33. *Wace*, Taylor, 227. *Monogr. Sur le Chat. d'Adam Bruce a'Brix* (*Mem. de la Soc. Nat. Academ. de Cherbourg*), l'abbé Adam, p. 17. [1] *Rech.*, de Gerville, 9, 10. [2] Stapleton, II, xxix, clxxviii. [3] *Introd. Domesd.*, I, 387.

ROBERT DE BUCI. Buci is in Normandy, and Leland says, "The Gentilmen communely caullid Busseyes cam with the Conqueror owt of Normandie." Robert de Buci held a great barony of the king in Leicester and Northampton in 1086 (Domesday) and left an only daughter, who married Ralph Basset, the great judiciary of England, in the reign of Henry I.[1] There were numerous collateral branches and a member of one of them, William de Bucy, witnessed a charter of Roger de Mowbray in the time of Henry I.[2] The family occurs in Lincoln and Normandy in 1185 and in Norfolk, Suffolk, Sussex, Northampton in the 13th, and in Leicester until the 15th century, as well as in many other parts of England. The Dives list carries Robert de Buci.

Cle., I, 106. *Nor. Peo.*, 181. [1] *Mon.*, ii, 190. [2] *Ibid.*, 90.

ROBERT DE COMINES. Robert de Cuminis, created earl of Durham in 1069, as Orderic Vital[1] informs us, came from Comines in Flanders. "In the third year of his reign king William gave the county of Durham to Robert de Comines, who soon afterwards entered the city, with great confidence, at the head of five hundred men, but the citizens assaulted early in the night and massacred Robert and all of his troops, except two who escaped by flight. The bravest were unable to defend themselves; taken at a dis-

advantage, at such an hour, and overwhelmed by numbers." King William in a discourse on his death-bed says "one thousand troops were slain."[2] The ill-fated earl left either sons or kinsmen, as the name long survived in the north of England. Hugh Cumin witnessed the charter of Rievaulx abbey, York, *temp.* Henry I.[3] Otard Cumin witnessed one in the time of king Stephan.[4] William Comyn became chancellor of Scotland in 1133.[5] John Commin was elected bishop of Dublin in 1181[6] and John Cummin witnessed an accord between Henry II and Robert de Torigny, abbé of Mont-St-Michel, on 14 July 1166.[7] William Cumin attested a charter in behalf of the monks at Bordesley at Westminster, c. 1128,[8] and Baldwin de Comines occurs in Normandy in 1197 as witness to an agreement executed by Philip, count of Namur.[9] William Comyn, son of Richard Comyn, justiciary of Scotland, became, c. 1210, earl of Buchan in right of his second wife, Margaret, countess of Buchan, He died in 1233. His descendants were famous in the annals of Scotland; they included the earls Angus, and the Comyns of Badenoch. Hence the earls of Buchan.

Cle., I, 212. *Nor. Peo.*, 207. Burke, 35. [1] Ord. Vit., II, 21. [2] *Ibid.*, II, 413. [3] *Mon.*, i, 729. [4] *Ibid.*, i, 476. [5] Dugdale's *Peerage*. [6] Benoît, I, 280, 287; *Chron. de Torigny*, II, 118. [7] *Cart. de Mont-St-Michel*, fo. 122 v°; Bibl. nat. lat. 10072, fo. 173. [8] Stapleton, I, xx. [9] *Ibid.*, II, lxxiv.

ROBERT DE CHANDOS. The original seat of the family was a fief, lying at the junction of the communes of Catelon, Illeville, and Flancourt (Eure), the etymology being "Campi Dorsum." Robert de Chandos, founder of this great and illustrious house, companion-in-arms of the Conqueror, won with his sword a princely domain in Caerleon in Wales. He married Isabella, heiress of Auvrai d'Espagne, a very great Domesday baron, according to Eyton's *Domesday Studies*.[1] He had three sons: Robert II, Roger and Gautier,[2] and he or his son Robert II with his wife Isabel founded in 1113 Goldcliff (Goldclive) priory in Monmouth which they very richly endowed with lands, churches and tithes in

Somerset and Devon. He gave this priory to the abbey of Bec on the advice of Henry I. Dugdale says Robert I died 2 November 1120, which makes it uncertain whether the father or son is here involved. It is an established fact that Robert II married Isabel, sister of Gautier Giffard II or III, count of Longueville, as stated in the *Cartulary of Mortemer*, which records their donation for the founding of an abbey at Beaumont, near Estrepagny, in 1130, wherein Robert is called an old man " venab lis." The cartulary also shows that he died before 1134, when the monks removed to Mortemer, where they founded that famous abbey.[3] Consequently both Roberts married ladies of the same name, as Eyton's statement does not seem to be questioned.

Robert de Chandos, son of the Conqueror's companion, was castellan of Dangu in 1119, which the Crispin family had held in hereditary custodianship since the time of William Crispin I. His grandson, William Crispin III had been deprived of it by king Henry I of England, because he was one of a number of Norman seigniors who founded a league with Louis-le-Gros in 1118 in favour of William Cleto, son of duke Robert Courteheuse, when king Henry gave it to Robert de Chandos.[4] Robert was attacked there in 1119 by king Louis of France and when he saw surrender inevitable burned the castle and fled to Gisors, from which fortress he operated against the French.[5] In 1123 Robert was " warden of the king's tower " at Gisors, where a plot was made by Amaury de Montfort, count of Evreux, and his grand-nephew, William Crispin III, both bitter enemies of Henry I, to take Robert de Chandos prisoner or assassinate him and capture the fortress. They made arrangements to meet him in the town, but Robert, hearing the noise made by the invading forces and sensing the plot, fled within the fortress, which he defended successfully until the arrival of king Henry, who brought forces to his succour a short time afterwards from Pont-Audemer.[6] A family of Dangu, owners of the domain, must not be confused with the castle bearing the same name. Robert de Dangu was present in 1135 at the session of the court of common pleas held by Henry I at Sainte-Gauburge, diocese of Seez, to end a dispute between the monks of Marmoutiers and the bishop of Seez concerning the churches of Belesme.[7] Dangu was a grand vavassorie (grand sub-fief), always considered a barony and the first of the four baronies and Franches vavassories (free sub-fiefs) in Normandy. It was held for the service of one knight's fee,[8] and had the seigniorial rights of " low " and " middle justice " (i.e. all rights, save capital punishment).[9] Isabel du Plessis de Dangu, daughter of Robert de Dangu and his wife Eufemie was the wife of Joscelyn Crispin, the son of William Crispin III, who was probably castellan of Dangu at the time of his marriage.[10] Blanche Crispin, lady of Dangu, and Thury by marriage, brought these seigniories to Pierre, seigneur de Preaux, shortly after 1327.[11] Dangu passed through the female line to the seigniors of Ferrières and eventually, 27 November 1554, was sold to Anne de Montmorency, constable of France.[12] The name of Chandos appears on the rolls of Holinshed, Duchesne, Leland and Scriven, while the Dives roll carries Robert de Chandos. Dugdale states that Robert de Chandos came to England with the Conqueror but confuses the first Robert with the second. Robert's descendants carried on for generations the bloody conflicts which devastated the Welsh border. " From him sprang the lords Chandos (whose eventual heiress, Alice Berkely, granddaughter of sir John Chandos, married Thomas Bruges, ancestor by her of James Brydges, the princely duke of Chandos), and the renowned sir John Chandos of Radborne, a great warrior and one of the original knights of the Garter at the date of the foundation of that order."

Cle., I, 223. Burke, 40.
[1] Cle., I, 224. [2] *Mon.*, 155. [3] *Cart. de Mortemer*, pp. 1 and 5. [4] Ord. Vit., III, 446; *Dict. de l'Eure*, I, 934; *vide* Guillaume Crispin. [5] Ord. Vit., III, 479. [6] *Ibid.*, IV, 69–70. [7] *Arch. d'Alencon, Mem. des Antiquaires*, 6. [8] *Register of Philippe Auguste* about 1210, T. Duplessie. [9] *Le Prevost Mem.*, II, 5; *vide* App. 13. [10] *Cart. de Mortemer*, 55–7; *Le Prevost Mem.*, II, 5. [11] *Le Prevost Mem.*, II, 8. [12] *Ibid.*, 10.

ROBERT DE COIGNIÈRES. Conyers or Norton was the elder branch of the family of Conyers, from Coignières, île de France. They took the name Norton from their barony of that name in Yorkshire, the chief seat of the English family, which Robert de Coignières who came to England in 1066 held, from the see of Durham, in 1086 (Domesday). Roger, his son, was made by William the Conqueror constable of Durham castle and keeper of all the arms of the soldiers within it. The descendants of this family were the lords of Stockburn for more than 500 years. This powerful family spread throughout many parts of England, holding vast estates, nearly all having died out in the male line before the 17th century. The name appears on the rolls of Scriven and Duchesne.

Cle., III, 286.

ROBERT DE COURSON. From Courson, near Caen, arrondissement Vire, Normandy. Robert de Curcon, or de Curcun, held estates in Norfolk and Suffolk in 1086 (Domesday) and left descendants in the former county, who prevailed for many generations. Richard and Hubert, his sons, were seated in Derby in the reign of Henry I. Richard and William de Curcun appear in the *Rotuli Curia Regis* (1194-9). John de Courzon was summoned to the great council held in Westminster in 1324 and the next year was a commissioner of Array. Hubert de Courson certified a grant to the church of St-Marie-de-Courson, Normandy,[1] and a member of the family from the bailifry of Orbec attended the great assembly of the nobles in 1789.[2] The name appears on the rolls of Holinshed, Duchesne and Dives.

Nor. Peo., 218. Cle., I, 259. *Rech. Nobil. Norm. gent. Norm.*, de Courson.
[1] *M.S.A.N.* [2] *Nobiliaire de Normandie.*

ROBERT LE DESPENSIER. There are two le Despensiers entered in Domesday. William, an under-tenant in Kent, who occurs on the Dives list, and Robert. What relationship existed between them, if any, is not known. Robert, steward to the Conqueror, was a great baron who held large possessions in Leicester, Lincoln, Warwick and Worcester. He was the younger brother of Ours d'Abbetot,[1] and assumed the surname le Despensier. He was a despoiler of the monks of Worcester, from whom he took the manor of Elmley, which he never returned, and was witness to many of the Conqueror's most important charters. Whether he left posterity is in doubt ; he was however succeeded by William and Thurston le Despensier, stewards to Henry I, who ma*y* be presumed to have been his sons. Whether Hugh, who held the great office of justice of England, in 1259, was descended from Thurston, as sir Egerton Brydges asserts, or from a Hugh, who was sheriff of Shropshire and Staffordshire in 1223, as well as constable of the royal castles of Shrewsbury, Bruges and Bolsover, which Dugdale affirms, is unknown. Another theory is that Hugh was descended from the Duttons of Cheshire, descendants of Otard, a baron of Chester, under Hugh Lupus. However this may be, the fact remains that from this celebrated judiciary descended the earls of Sunderland and Spencer, the dukes of Marlborough and barons Churchill.

Nor. Peo., 404. Cle., I, 283. Plan., II, 151. *Rech. Domesd.*, 46.
[1] *Vide* Ours d'Abbetot.

ROBERT COMTE d'EU. Wace (1. 13828) records "Eli Quens d'Ou," which was Robert, comte d'Eu, the eldest son of William, comte d'Exmes and d'Eu,[1] a natural son of Richard I, duke of Normandy. His younger brothers were William de Busac, count of Hiemois, afterwards of Soissons, and Hugh, bishop of Lisieux. William de Busac rebelled against duke William at the time he held the castle of Eu. When and how he obtained it is unknown, but Robert had it in his possession in 1054.[2] The latter furnished sixty ships to duke William's fleet and received large estates in Sussex and other counties in England, with the custody of the castle of Hastings. He was one of the four commanders at the battle of Mortemer in 1054, and in 1059 founded the abbey of Tréport. He was present at the battle of Hastings and was largely responsible for the slaughter of the Danes in Lindsey in 1069. He died between 1090 and 1095 and was succeeded by his son William, who joining the rebellion against William Rufus in 1096, was captured, deprived of his sight and terribly mutilated. He also had a younger son named Robert. It was at the castle of d'Eu in 1053-4 that duke William married Matilda, daughter of Baldwin, count of Flanders.

Introd. Domesd., I, 463. *Hist. des Comtes d'Eu*, L. Estancelin. Plan., I, 257. *Nov. Peo.*, 412. Cle., III, 164. Le Prevost, *Notes, Wace*, II, 273. *Wace*, Taylor, 246. Ord. Vit., III, 452.
[1] *Jumièges Interp.*, de Torigny, 251, 270 ; Freeman, III, 118. [2] *Vide* Richard de Bienfaite.

ROBERT DE CREVECŒUR. *Vide* Hamon le Seneschal.

ROBERT D'ESTOUTEVILLE. The

"sire d'Estoteville" of Wace (l. 13561) was probably Robert from Estouteville-en-Caux, Normandy, of which country this family was one of the great houses. They held large possessions in many parts of England, especially in Yorkshire and the north. Ten or eleven years previous to the conquest, Robert d'Estouteville I (Front-de-Beouf) was governor of the castle of Ambrières and defended it against Geoffry Martel, count of Anjou, until relieved by the approach of duke William.[1] His name appears as a witness to a confirmation of a charter in favour of St-Evroult between 1066 and 1089. He was succeeded by his son Robert d'Estouteville II, who participated in the battle of Tinchebrai, in 1106, fought between king Henry I and his brother duke Robert, where brothers and kinsmen were aligned against each other in the opposing armies. In this engagement, Robert d'Estouteville II was, with William, earl of Mortain, Robert de Belèsme, William Crispin and William de Ferrers, one of the commanders of duke Robert's army. King Henry's army was superior in numbers, consequently they were defeated and all of them, including duke Robert, captured, excepting Robert de Belèsme, who was in command of the rear of the army, for when he saw the outcome of the battle in doubt he took flight and escaped,[2] treacherously abandoning his partisans to their fate. Orderic Vital

informs us that " the king sent over to England all his enemies taken in the war, throwing into dungeons and condemning to perpetual punishment duke Robert, his brother," William, earl of Mortain,[3] his nephew, Robert d'Estouteville, " and several others." " He was inflexible in his resolution to treat them all with severity and consequently withstood all the influence of entreaties, promises, and gifts from many quarters employed to mollify his resentment."[4] Some of them, including his nephew, earl William, are reported to have had their " eyes torn out "[5] and to have been " exposed to horrible and long-continued cruelties."[6]

Plan., II, 253. Cle., II, 5. *Nor. Peo.*, 410. Le Prevost, *Notes, Wace*, II, 237. *Wace*, Taylor, 214.
[1] Ord. Vit., I, 425 ; Duchesne, 181 ; Jumièges, 127 ; *Wace*, Pluquet, ll. 10173 and fol. [2] *Florence of Worcester*, Forester, p. 214 ; Eadmer, *Hist. Nov. Rolle*, Rule, p. 184 ; *Outline Itinerary of King Henry I*, Farrar, 38 ; Ord. Vit., III, 381, 383, [3] *Ibid.*, Ord. Vit. and III, 430. [4] *Ibid.*, III, 430 ; IV, 20, 26. [5] *Ibid.*, III, 381, n. ; Freeman, V, 174, 843-9. [6] *Ibid.*, III, 359, n.

ROBERT FITZ ERNEIS. " Robert

ki fu filz Erneis " is mentioned by Wace (l. 13751). He was the son of Erneis, a collateral descendant of the family of Tesson, by his wife Hawise, sister of Fouque d'Aunou (the elder), also nephew of Raoul Tesson I and cousin germain of Raoul Tesson II. Robert Fitz Erneis likewise married a lady Hawise. He was killed at the battle of Hastings, which fact is recorded by Wace and attested to in a charter of his son Robert Fitz Erneis, printed in the *Gallia Christiana*,[1] who was named after him, which reads thus, " Eodem vero patri meo in Anglia Acciso."

Plan., II, 185. *Wace*, Taylor, 239. Le Prevost, *Notes, Wace*, II, 265. *Nor. Peo.*, 147.
[1] *Gall. Christ.*, IX, 334 Instr.

ROBERT GUERNON, SIRE DE MONTFIQUET. The "sire de Montfichet" of Wace (l. 13675) came from Montfiquet in the arrondissement of Bayeux. Gilbert de Montfichet was stated by Le Prevost to have been one

of the "most authentic personages that can be named as assisting at the battle of Hastings," but fails to give his reason for so believing.[1]

Dugdale quotes in the *Monasticon* on the authority of an ancient history of the family the statement that Gilbert de Montficquet was a noble Roman by birth and a relative of duke William who always stopped with him on his visits to Rome, and "That he was privy to all of his (William's) councils, especially to that design of king Edward the Confessor to make him his successor to the realm of England." This is considered pure fabrication by Planché, Cleveland and other commentators on the subject, who attribute it to a priest for whom Gilbert had great esteem.[2] Since it seems highly improbable, if not impossible, for duke William to have gone to Rome without it being recorded, they discard the whole statement. If, however, duke William did have Roman blood in his veins, it necessarily came through the female line. This narrows it down to Papa, Poppa or Poupe, as she is variously called, the mother of the children of duke Rollo,[3] daughter of count Berenger of Bayeux, Sprota, who emanated from a Breton lineage,[4] by whom William Longsword, the second duke of Normandy, had his son Richard I, and Gonnor (de Crépon), of Danish extraction, mother of duke Richard II, all of whose antecedents beyond the facts here mentioned are extremely obscure.[5] Judith, mother of Robert (I) the Magnificent, half-sister of Geoffry, count of Brittany, and daughter of Conan le Tort, count of Rennes[6] and Arlette, by whom duke Robert had William the Conqueror,[7] need not be considered in this connection. Concerning this *vide* 181.

The Guernons were a branch of the barons of Montfiquet in Normandy, so named from their Scandinavian ancestors, and the castle of Montfiquet long existed, as did the church of St-Catherine in the castle, founded by the family. Robert, surnamed Guernon "mustache," baron of Montfiquet, generally conceded to have been the individual indicated by Wace as present at Senlac, about 1050, witnessed a charter of duke William.[8] He had issue William de Montfiquet, who died with-

out children, when the barony went to William, the son of his brother ; another son, Robert de Guernon, held a great barony in Essex in 1086 (Domesday). From this family descended two branches : one, the barons Montfitchet, seated at Stanstead-Mountfitchet, Essex, and Montfitchet tower, London, of which the Montfitchets were the hereditary standard-bearers in times of war ; the other branch retained the name of Guernoñ, from whom descended the celebrated family of Cavendish, the dukes of Newcastle, Devonshire, and other great families.

Plan., II, 49. *Nor. Peo.*, 191. Cle., II, 103, 267. *Wace*, Taylor, 233.
[1] Le Prevost, *Notes, Wace*, II, 255. [2] *Mon.*, ii, 236. [3] Dudon de Saint-Quentin, lib. II, Duchesne, 77D ; Jumièges, 24 ; Ord. Vit., I, 38 ; *ibid.*, ed. Le Prevost, II, 7 ; *vide* App. 16, n. 6 ; Poppea Sabina, the wife of Rufus Crispinus, a Roman knight, was eventually married by the emperor Nero (*Classical Dictionary*, Lempière ; *Seneca his tenne tragedies*, fos. 161–81, translated by Thomas Newton and others, pub. 1581). [4] Dudon de Saint-Quentin, lib. III, Duchesne, 97C ; Jumièges, 33 ; Flodoard, A. 943 ; Freeman I, appendix x ; add. (181). [5] *Jumièges Interp.*, de Torigny, 229, 323 ; Des Bois, V, 306 ; *vide* Guil. Crispin, App. 16, n. 32. [6] Jumièges, 88 ; *ibid. Interp.*, de Torigny, 233. [7] Jumièges, 157. [8] *Gall. Christ.*, XI, 229 Instr.

ROBERT DE HARCOURT.

Robert de Harcourt, surnamed le Fort, was the son of Anchetil and younger brother of Errand de Harcourt,[1] whom he accompanied to England at the time of the conquest and succeeded as the head of the family. He built the castle of Harcourt in Normandy and was by his wife Colette d'Argouges the father of seven sons, the eldest of whom, William, having arrayed himself with king Henry I against his brother Robert Courteheuse, rendered his monarch signal service ; he also commanded the troops which defeated the count of Meulent in Normandy in 1124. He was, on this account, rewarded with large estates in England, which were inherited by his second son Ivo, who became permanently settled there. The English Harcourts were seated at Stanton-Harcourt in Oxfordshire, which was obtained through the heiress of the Camvilles, whose mother received it as a marriage gift from her cousin, queen Adeliza of Louvain, the second wife of Henry I. The ruins of the castle show its former magnificence and effigies of members of the family for many generations remain in the parish church. One of dame Margaret Harcourt, wife of sir Richard, who fought for the house of York in the war of the Roses and received the Garter from Edward IV, shows the order worn immediately above the elbow of the left arm with the motto. A very rare honour, which was only conferred upon ladies in two other known instances. Queen Ann appointed sir Simon Harcourt lord keeper of the great seal, when he received a peerage. He was created baron Harcourt of Stanton-Harcourt in 1711, declared lord high chancellor of England the following year and received a viscountcy in 1721. His grandson and successor received an earldom in 1740. With the 3rd earl the male line became extinct and the estates passed through an heiress to the Vernons. The earl, however, left his unentailed estate of St-Leonards near Windsor to the French branch of the family. In 1917 Lewis Harcourt Vernon, who in 1905 had assumed the name and arms of Harcourt, was created viscount Harcourt. He was the son of William George Granville Vernon of Stanton Harcourt. Robert d'Harcourt, the elder brother of Ivo above mentioned, remained in France and was the ancestor of a long list of great houses. From him descended Jean d'Harcourt, vicomte de Chatellerault, in whose favour the barony of Harcourt was erected into a comté by Philip of Valois in 1338 ; the Harcourts, counts of Montgomery ; the Harcourts, barons d'Ollande ; also the Harcourts, counts of Aumale and Harcourt ; the marquises of Montmorency, 1578, and Pierre d'Harcourt, baron de Beuvron, Beauffou, etc., The baronies of La Motte, Mery, Cleville and Vareville were in reward for services rendered by Pierre d'Harcourt erected into the marquisate of La Motte-Harcourt by Henry IV in 1593. Louis XIV elevated the marquisates of Thury and La Motte into a dukedom for his descendant, Henry d'Harcourt, marshal of France. Regardless of the many wars and revolutions, which have occurred in France, the dukes d'Harcourt retain the château d'Harcourt, near the old Norman stronghold that has borne their name for the last eight hundred years at Thury-Harcourt, arrondissement of Falaise. The present head of this illustrious family, the duc d'Harcourt, is a member of the chamber of Deputies for Bayeux (Calvados) and his cousin, the comte d'Harcourt, is one of the three senators representing Calvados.

Hist. genealog. Maison de Harcourt, G. A. de la Roque ; Père Anselme ; *Thury-Harcourt, Essai hist. et Stat.*, Chalopin. Plan., II, 229. Cle., II, 148, 151. Le Prevost, *Notes, Wace*, II, 266. *Wace*, Taylor, 241. Burke, 66. *Dict. de l'Eure*, I, 247.

ROBERT MALET. *Vide* Guillaume Malet de Graville.

ROBERT MARMION DE FONTENAI. Wace (l. 13623) speaks of " li viel Rogier Marmion " and (l. 13776) records " sire de Fontenei," but this is supposed to be either a clerical or typographical error for Robert the father of Roger. These two references are believed to indicate the same person and is one of the instances in which Wace has confused his subject. Robert, to whom the Conqueror gave Tamworth tower and town in the county of Warwick shortly after the conquest, must be the personage intended. He was viscount of Fontenai and had extensive grants, holding seventeen fees in England and five in Normandy, including the castle of Fontenai, near Caen, called from its ancient lords Fontenai le Marmion, to designate it from the eight other communes of the same name in Normandy. Robert witnessed a notitia relating to the abbey of Holy Trinity, Rouen, and died *c.* 1106, when his widow Hawise became a nun in the abbey of Holy Trinity, Caen, granting to that house her husband's lands, with consent of her sons Roger, Helto and Manasses. The witnesses included William Marmion and Herluin de Fontenay. Roger's son Robert held lands in Lancastershire *c.* 1115–18 and rendered an account of £176 10s. 4d. for relief of his father's lands. This

Roger received considerable land from Robert Le Despensier. The Marmions were a branch of the Tesson family.

Plan., II, 167. Cle., II, 230. Nor. Peo., 324. Le Prevost, Notes, Wace, II, 247, 268. Wace, Taylor, 242. M.S.A.N., M. Vaultier, X, 94. Duchesne. Hist. of the Baronial family of Marmion, etc., C. E. R. Palmer, II, 41.

ROBERT MORETON. Vide Corbet Le Norman.

ROBERT MURDAC. Robert Murdac came from Courtonne-la-Meurdrac near Lisieux ; his family were barons of St-Denis and Meurdraquière in Normandy, where it extended its branches as it did in England. Robert Murdac was a tenant-in-capite, holding two manors in Oxfordshire with one in Hampshire, and he is said by Delisle to have been at the battle of Hastings. He witnessed a charter of king William I, when he confirmed the grants made to the abbey of St-Evroult in 1081.[1] A member of this family was Henry, consecrated archbishop of York in 1147, who died in 1153.[2] Robert Murdac, a descendant, confirmed a gift of his grandfather, Hugh de St-Denis, to the abbey of Hambie in 1172,[3] and Robert Murdac, knight, possibly the same, was a benefactor to the abbey of La Luzerne in the diocese of Avranches in 1194.[4] Fulk Murdac occurs in Normandy in 1198.[5]

Nor. Peo., 341. [1] Ord. Vit., II, 258. [2] Mon., vi, 1172 ; Chron. de Torigny, I, 246. [3] Stapleton, I, lxix. [4] Ibid., II, vi. [5] Ibid., ccxxxviii.

ROBERT COMTE DE MORTAIN. Robert, count de Mortain, the half-brother of duke William, is known to have been at the battle of Hastings and is so reported by the historians of this event. He was the son of Herluin de Conteville and Arlette. His history is so well known that it would be superfluous to repeat it here. Suffice it to say, that he received from king William 797 manors in different parts of England and two castles in Cornwall, of which county he was created earl. He married Matilda, daughter of Roger de Montgomery, by whom he had three

daughters and one son, William, who inherited his earldom. After the death of count Robert, his son William demanded of king Henry I, besides his own inheritance, the earldom of Kent, which had belonged to his deceased uncle, bishop Odo. On being refused the request, he started a revolt in Normandy, was captured at the battle of Tenchebrai, thrown into prison, had his eyes put out and died there. Wace mentions[1] (l. 13765) " Li Quens Robert de Moretoing," and his name occurs three times on the Bayeux tapestry.

Plan., I, 114. Cle., II, 339.

ROBERT D'OUILLI. Robert d'Ouilli, favoured and trusted follower of duke William, came from Ouilly-le-Basset, near Falaise, and was the son of Foque d'Aulnay (Fulco de Alneto), a son of Osmond de Centville, viscount of Vernon and a niece of the duchess Gonnor.[1] He is referred to by Wace (l. 13659), as " E cil d'Ouillie," who with Jean (by some called Roger) d'Ivri,[2] his sworn brother-in-arms, followed duke William to the conquest of England. He received the baronies of Waleries (St-Valery) and Oxford, also called Hokenorton, and in the latter he built his castle which was completed in 1073.[3] Previously at king William's command he had erected a new castle at Wallingford which was commenced in 1067 and finished in 1071.[4] He was a tenant-in-chief in Oxfordshire, and possessed sixty-one manors with forty-two habitable houses, of which county he was constable. According to Kelhame (Domesday), " He was so powerful a man that no one durst oppose him," and he apparently used his powers, judging from the vast possessions acquired by him there. Duke William tarried at Wallingford before his occupation of London and while there gave to Robert in marriage Algitha, daughter and heiress of the wealthy and powerful Wigod de Wallingford. They had an only daughter, Matilda, who married Milo Crispin [5] prior to 1084, on which date she was less than eighteen years of age, for in that year king William spent his Easter at Abingdon and was the guest of Robert d'Ouilli on this occasion. It is recorded concerning this event that Milo Crispin was at the time his son-in-law.[6] King William held Robert in very high esteem, which is made evident by the fact that when this monarch departed he left his young son, afterwards king Henry I, to be educated at the convent of Abingdon under this lord's personal supervision.[7] Wigod's only other child, a son Toking, was killed by an arrowshot in 1080, at the siege of Gerberai. He saved the life of the Conqueror, whose horse had fallen upon him in battle, by giving the king his own,[8] and it is presumed that Wigod died shortly after. Robert d'Ouilli was a benefactor to the abbey of Abingdon[9] and witnessed two charters concerning Westminster during the reign of king William.[10] He died in September 1090 in the opinion of Hedges, but which event the late Armitage Robinson places at 1094, and was buried in the abbey of Abingdon. He was succeeded in his own estates by his brother Nigel. These, including the honour of Wallingford, which he had acquired through marriage with Wigod's daughter, then passed to his son-in-law, Milo Crispin,[11] who died in 1107 without legitimate issue.[12] Milo's widow in 1113 married Brian Fitz Count, who had inherited from his uncle, Hamelin de Balon, the strong castle and vast barony of Abergavenny.[13] They had issue two leper sons, who were kept in Abergavenny priory, but later were apparently transferred to the abbey of Bec, where they seemed to have died, and in which monastery their mother before her death, having made donations to that abbey, is reported to have taken the religious habit, c. 1149.[14] Brian, saddened and broken-hearted at the pitiful plight of his sons, died on a pilgrimage to Jerusalem about 1155.[15] In the *Saxon Chronicle* Brian is called an illegitimate son of Alain Fergant, count of Brittany, by Lucie, daughter of Dreu de Balon, lord of Overwent in Wales. He also inherited a considerable estate in Cornwall from an uncle named Brian,[16] while others say his father was Alain Le Roux. It is more probable that his father was count Brian of Brittany (comte de Vennes), elder brother of counts Alain Le Noir and Alain Le Roux, and that the estates

in Cornwall came from him.[17] The name of Robert d'Ouilli appears on the rolls of Guillaume Tailleur, Leland and Dives.

Plan., II, 213. Cle., I, 328, 330. *Nov. Peo.*, 151, 228. Le Prevost, *Notes, Wace*, II, 252. *Wace*, Taylor, 231. *Rech. Domesd.*, 136.
[1] *Vide* Fouque d'Aulnay. [2] *Vide* Jean d'Ivri. [3] *Hist. of Wallingford*, Hedges, I, 196; *Wood's Antiq. Oxon.* [4] Peter Langtoft, II, 603. [5] *Introd. Domesd.*, I, 458; *Hist. of Wallingford*, Hedges, I, 191; *Hist. of Bucks.*, Lipscomb, I, 18; *Hist. of the House of d'Oyly*, Bayley, I, 6–7; *Hist. Swyncombe and Ewelme*, Napier, p. 1; Jumièges, 136. [6] *Parach. Ant.*, Kennet, I, 94; *Ex. Lib. Monas. Abing.*, Twine MS., C2; Hedges, *ibid.*, I, 219; Freeman, IV, 728. [7] *Berksh.*, Lysons 220. [8] Freeman, IV, 642; Hedges, *ibid.*, I, 199. [9] *Hist. Abing. Rolls*, S. ii, 25. [10] *Westm. Domesd.*, fo. 100b and *ibid.*, fo. 529; *Faustina*, A. iii, fo. 64. [11] Hedges, *ibid.*, I, 222; *Gilbert Crispin, Abbot Westm.*, J. Armitage Robinson, 127. [12] *Vide* Mile Crispin. [13] *Itinerary of Archbishop Baldwin through Wales* in 1188. [14] *Itinerary of Archbishop Baldwin*; *Parach. Antiq.*, Kennet, I, 135, 138, 153; *Mon.*, i, 582, ed. note 6, 1068; Testa de Neuville, 115; Roger Dodsworth's ms. in Bibl. Bodl., vol. IV; Dugdale, I, 469. [15] Hedges, *ibid.*, I, 263. [16] *Mon.*, ii, 702. [17] *Saxon Chronicle*, translation, p. 223; *Hist. of Bucks.*, Lipscomb, I, 18; Hedges, *ibid.*, I, 228; *vide* Comte Alain Le Noir.

ROBERT DE PIERREPONT.
Vide Geoffroi de Pierrepont.

ROBERT DE SAINT-LÉGER.
Robert de St-Léger from St-Léger near Avranches, Normandy, held land in Sussex in 1086 (Domesday), and settled in Kent. He succeeded the earl of Eu in the manor of Ulcomb in that county where his descendants flourished for many generations. There is a legend in the family that the Conqueror first leaned upon his arm when he landed in England. He appears to have been the father of William de St-Leger, who with his son Clarembald, granted lands to Battle abbey during the reign of Henry I.[1] A descendant Ralph de St-Leger, attended Richard Cœur de Lion to the siege of Acre; hence the St-Legers of Kent and Devon and the viscounts Doneraile. The Dives roll carries Robert de St-Leger and it is

also inscribed upon the lists of Holinshed, Duchesne, Scriven and Brompton.

Burke, 95. *Nor. Peo.*, 389. Cle., III, 100. *Hist. Arch. des Bocains*, Rich. Seguin. [1] *Mon.*, i, 318.

ROBERT DE TOENI. Robert de Toeni was a younger brother of Raoul II, the hereditary standard-bearer of Normandy,[1] who received from the Conqueror 131 manors in different counties and took his name from the newly built castle of Stafford, of which king William appointed him the first castellan. He founded the Augustan priory at Stoke in Staffordshire, which became the burial-place of the family. By his wife, Avice de Clare, he was father of Nicholas, sheriff of Staffordshire, and the male line terminated with his grandson Robert. The barony with a great inheritance was carried, by the latter's sister Millicent, to Hervey Bagot. Hence the great house of Stafford, the earls and dukes of Buckingham, so renowned in the history of England. Nigel de Toeni, a younger brother of Robert, also assumed the surname de Stafford. He held Drakelow, Gresley and other manors in Derbyshire and Staffordshire 1086 (Domesday). Castle Gresley took its name from his castle and from him descended the Gresley family. His name appears on the roll of Delisle.

Cle., III, 172, 177. Plan., I, 226. *Nor. Peo.*, 147. *Domesd.*, sub-title *Derbysh.*, p. 323. *Dugdale-Norry*, p. 156. *Baronetage of England*, Wotton, p. 55. Burke, 44. *Magna Britannia Derbysh.*, Lysons, V, 53. *The origin of the Shirleys and of the Gresleys*, Round. [1] *Vide* Raoul de Toeni.

ROBERT DE VASSY. From Vassy, arrondissement of Vire. Wace records "sire de Vaacie" (l. 13660) as having been present at Hastings. It is conceded that Robert and Ivo were in duke William's expedition and settled in England but what their relationship was has not been established. Robert held an extensive barony in Northampton, Warwick, Lincoln and Leicester, comprising nineteen lordships. Ivo was given the hand of Alda, granddaughter of Gilbert Tison, lord of Alnwick, in Northumberland, who had obtained this

barony from Edward the Confessor, and he was the brother of Raoul Tesson of Val-des-Dunes fame. The family was of considerable prominence in England and was later connected with the Lacys, earls of Lincoln, and Cliffords, earls of Cumberland. The viscounts of Vasci and lords Fitz Gerald and Vesci claim descent from a collateral branch of the family which settled in Scotland. Guillaume Tailleur records the presence of members of the family at Hastings, as does Holinshed, Leland and Worcester. Dives carries Robert de Vesci and l'abbé de La Rue in his *Researches of Bayeux Tapestry* registers the name, which is also referred to by Dugdale.

Plan., II, 157. Cle., III, 216. Le Prevost, *Notes*, *Wace*, II, 253. *Wace*, Taylor, 232.

ROBERT de VAUX. The baronial family de Vaux or de Vallibus held the castle of this name in Normandy and in 1080 Robert de Vaux gave part of his tithes of Berners to St-Evroult.[1] He held fiefs in the eastern counties of England, and was a mesne-lord in Norfolk in 1086 (Domesday), besides which, by the gift of Ranulph le Meschin, he possessed Dalston in Cumberland.[2] Hubert de Vaux his brother also by gift of Ranulph held Gillesland, from whom descended the lords Vaux. Another brother Aitard de Vaux held in Norfolk in 1086, as did Ranulph de Vaux in Cumberland. From them descended the families of Strickland and Dalston. Godard occurs in a charter in favour of Mont-Saint-Michel, 1155-9,[3] and Richard vidame of Philip, bishop of Bayeux, at the same period.[4] The name appears on the rolls of Leland, Scriven, Brompton, while Dives carries Robert and Aitard de Vaux.

Cle., I, 294. *Nor. Peo.*, 430. [1] Ord. Vit., II, 190. [2] *Mon.*, i, 400. [3] *Chron. de Torigny*, II, 256. [4] *Ibid.*, II, 258.

ROGER D'ABERNON. Probably from the parish of Abernon, canton of Orbec, arrondissement of Lisieux, Calvados. Roger d'Abernon followed duke William to England and was a subtenant of Richard de Tonbridge (Bienfaite) in Suffolk and Surrey in 1086 (Domesday), under whose banner he

H

probably came to the conquest. He received from the Conqueror the manor of Stoke in the latter county, known as Stoke d'Abernon. His descendants remained there for 300 years. Eguerrande de Abernon witnessed a charter of Savigny, Normandy, in 1112. Ingelram de Abernon in 1165 held four fees of the honour of Clare and was a benefactor to Stoke-Clare, Suffolk.[1] The family spread to other counties and from them descended the viscounts Sidmouth.[2] The name appears on the rolls of Leland, Holinshed, Duchesne and Dives.

Cle., III, 320.   Nor. Peo., 135.
[1] Mon., i, 1067.   [2] Harl. ms., 1080.

ROGER ARUNDEL. It is difficult to establish this family in Normandy, either its origin or its descent. The identity of Roger Arundel is obscure, but the generally accepted opinion is that he was a kinsman of Roger de Montgomery first earl of Arundel. He came to the conquest and settled in Salop, where the Arundels held Habberley and Ondeslawe from the baron Corbet.[1] He held a barony of twenty-eight manors in Somerset in 1086 (Domesday) and was appointed castellan of the castle of Arundel. Roger de Busliaco held Sutton in Somerset under him at the compilation of Domesday, and his son Wido Arundel possessed Pourton, Dorset, from him at this time. From this family descended the earls and baronets Onslow, the lords Arundel of Wardour and the great western families of Lanherne and Trerice.

Burke, 15. Cle., I, 13. Nor. Peo., 143, 348. Rech. Domesd., 85, 216, 251.
[1] Eyton, IV, 351.

ROGER BIGOT, SEIGNEUR DE **MALTOT.** Wace (l. 13677) chronicles "L'ancestre Hue le Bigot ki avoit terre a Maletot ét as Loges et a Chanon." Maletot is near Caen, Canon (Chanon) is in the arrondissement of Lisieux, and Loges may have been either Les Loges, near Aunay, or another commune of the same name, near Falaise. The original name of the family was Wiggott, Wigott, or Bygod. The family of Bigot **or Wigot, was** descended from Wigot

de St-Denis, one of the greatest nobles in Normandy, who made grants to Cerisy abbey in 1042, and in 1050 witnessed a charter of duke William at the head of the Norman barons. He married a sister of Turstin Goz, father of Richard d'Avranches, by whom his younger son, Robert Wigot or Bigot, was ingratiated into the good graces of duke William. His son Roger, was present at Senlac and received large grants for his services at the conquest, comprising 123 manors in Essex and Sussex, only six being in the latter county. It is quite possible that Robert, as well as his son Roger, accompanied duke William to England; the latter must have been a young man at that time, as he did not die until 1107, when he was buried in the abbey of Thetford in Norfolk, which he had founded in 1103. He married Adeliza, daughter of Hugh de Grentemesnil, by whom he had seven children. William, his eldest son and heir, was dapifer to the king and perished in the wreck of the "White Ship," and was succeeded by his brother Hugh, who was also steward of the king's household. Hugh was created earl of Norfolk and his descendants, through a marriage with Maud, eldest daughter and co-heiress of the Marshals, earls of Pembroke, became marshals of England, which office is held to-day by the duke of Norfolk. William Bigot, the younger brother of Roger Bigot here mentioned, went to Apulia, from where he returned with Geoffry Ridel to the conquest of England. He had a grant of Dunmow and Finchingfield, Essex, where he made gifts to Thetford abbey.[1] He had a son, Ilger (Bigod d'Ige), who in 1096 was chief commander in Palestine under Tancard, who left him in command of 200 knights to defend Jerusalem.[2]

Plan., II, 54. Cle., I, 66; III, 57. Nor. Peo., 318. Le Prevost, Notes, Wace, II, 256. Wace, Taylor, 234.
[1] Mon., i.   [2] Ord. Vit., III, 178.

ROGER de BRETEUIL. Breteuil is a canton in the arrondissement of Evreux. Roger de Breteuil was the second son of William Fitz Osberne, first earl of Hereford, whom, according to Delisle, he accompanied to England at the conquest. On the death of his

FALAISE ROLL 99

father in 1071, Roger inherited the earldom and the English estates, and he
thus became the second earl of Hereford.
He " shortly afterwards lost it by his
perfidy and folly " toward his sovereign.
In 1075, during the absence of king
William in Normandy, he joined a
rebellion against that monarch with
Raoul de Gael, earl of Norfolk, who had
taken advantage of the king's absence
to marry Roger's sister, Emma, which
union the king had positively forbidden.[1]
Roger was captured, his properties
confiscated and he was thrown into
prison where he died.

Ord. Vit., II, 60, 78, 82. Plan., I, 80 ;
II, 2. Cle., III, 268.
[1] Vide Raoul de Gael and William Fitz
Osberne.

ROGER D'AMONDEVILLE. From
Amondeville near Caen, spelt Amonder-
ville in the Norman Exchequer rolls of
1198. The first of the name who came
to England at the conquest in 1066
was Roger, sometimes called Humfries,
one of the compilers of the Domesday
survey. He was seneschal to Remigius,
bishop of Lincoln, from whom he
received four Lincolnshire manors,
Kingerby, his principal seat and that
of his successors, Auresby, Ellesham
and Croxton. He married a daughter
of sir Gerard Salvin of Thorpe-Salvin
in Yorkshire, and left issue Jolland,
John and Robert. Jolland married
Beatrice Painel, by whom he had six
sons, two of whom, William and Adam,
received grants from Gilbert de Gand,
earl of Lincoln, while another, Ralph,
obtained from the earl of Albemarle
the Yorkshire manor of Carlton. Helias
de Amondevilla occurs in a roll of the
Infeudationes Militum of 1172.[1] The
family continued of consequence in
various parts of England. Hence the
Irbys, lords Boston. The name occurs
on the lists of Scriven, Holinshed,
Duchesne and Worcester.

Nor. Peo., 293. Cle., I, 31.
[1] Stapleton, I, clii.

ROGER DANIEL. The family was
probably derived from Asnières, in the
arrondissement of Bayeux, Normandy.
Rogerus Daniel, an under-tenant in
the county of Sussex in 1086, was
beyond doubt the ancestor of the great

Cheshire family of Daniel or De Anyers
of Daresbury and Over-Tabley, from
whom, through the female line, the
Willis family of Halsnead park, Lancashire, descend. Petre and Ralph
Daniel occur in Normandy in 1198,[1]
Hugh, Ralph and others in England,
c. 1272.[2] A member of this family was
recorded at the conquest by Léopold
Delisle and the name also appears on the
Battle abbey roll, which may well have
been Roger. The Daniels continued of
importance in England for many centuries, as well as in Normandy, where the
family was represented at the great
assembly of the Norman nobles in 1789.

Cle., I, 291. Nor. Peo., 221. Burke, 42.
[1] M.R.S. [2] R.H.

ROGER D'EVREUX. Roger d'Evreux came to England in 1066 with
his brother William. They were the
sons by a second marriage of William
d'Evreux, the youngest brother of
Richard, count d'Evreux, who was the
son of Robert, count d'Evreux and archbishop of Rouen. They were the first
cousins of William, count d'Evreux,
who was also at Hastings.[1] Roger
married Helewysa, sister of Walter de
Lacy of Hereford, who gave lands to
Gloucester abbey.[2] Her son Robert de
Evrois was a benefactor to Brecknock,
temp. Henry I.[3] There were two
branches in Hereford in 1165 and from
one house descended the viscounts of
Hereford, and the other from Walter
d'Evreux of Rosmar, Normandy, who
held lordships in the counties of Dorset,
Somerset, Surrey, Hants, Middlesex,
Hereford, Buckingham and Wilts, and
the lordships of Salisbury and Ambresbery. He was a companion of the
Conqueror at Hastings and the ancestor
of the Devereux, lord Ferrers of Chartley
and earls of Essex, of whom the second,
one Robert Devereux, was so celebrated
and ill-fated in the reign of queen
Elizabeth.

Burke, 47. Cle., I, 323. Nor. Peo., 225.
[1] Vide Guillaume, comte d'Evreux.
[2] Mon., i, 115. [3] Ibid., 320.

ROGER DE MONTBRAY. Roger
de Montbray, referred to in Wace (l.
13706) as "cil de Moubrai," was a brother
of Geoffry de Montbray, bishop of
Coutances, whom he accompanied to

the battle of Hastings. He witnessed a charter in Normandy, 1066,[1] and was the father of Robert de Montbray or Mowbray, earl of Northumberland, who died c. 1125 and is therefore not believed to have attended the conquest of England. He joined the conspiracy against William Rufus and died in prison.[2]

[1] *Gall. Christ.*, XI, 60.   [2] *Vide* Geoffroi, Evêque de Coutances ; Freeman, IV, 41.

ROGER DE MONTGOMERI. The ancestry of the family of Roger de Montgomery II, seignior of Montgomery in the arrondissement of Lisieux, and count of Alençon and Belèsme in the right of his wife, was quite definite at the time of the conquest. Jumièges [1] informs us that Roger had four brothers, viz. Hugh, Robert, William and Gilbert, stating that William murdered Osberne de Crépon, guardian of the young duke William, who was the son of Herfast, brother of the duchess Gonnor, in revenge for which act the vassals of Osberne murdered Hugh, Robert and William. Gilbert, the youngest son, was unintentionally poisoned by a sister-in-law. This left only Roger, the trusted councillor and follower of duke William. Wace tells us that Roger de Montgomery was in command of a wing of the army at Senlac and Orderic Vital [2] definitely states that he remained in Normandy with queen Matilda and the young duke Robert, as the head of the council which governed the duchy, and that he went to England with king William in 1067. William of Poitiers,[3] who was living at the time, and transcribed the events which transpired at that period, positively states that Roger de Beaumont was the person at the head of the council, appointed by the king to assist queen Matilda in the government of Normandy. To increase the confusion, Wace (l. 13462) chronicles "Rogier li viel, cil de Belmont," which is the usually accepted version. Mr. Edgar Taylor, however, in his translation of the manuscript of the poem in the British museum,[4] points out that the name there is Robert (son of Roger) and not Roger as above indicated, though the epithet le viel is not appropriate to Robert's then age. It is quite possible that le viel is a

clerical error for de Vielles, the name of Roger de Beaumont's father, Humphrey de Vielles, latinized into de Vitulis. Robert de Beaumont would, of course, have been de Vielles as well as his father. Both Orderic Vital and William of Poitiers [5] say that Robert, son of Roger, "a novice in arms," went to England at the conquest, and it seems logical to assume that they would have mentioned Roger's name also, if he had been there. A reason given by some historians for believing Roger de Beaumont was at Hastings is because a man with a beard is shown on the Bayeux tapestry continually at the side of duke William, and since Roger de Beaumont had one he is concluded to have been this individual, which opinion is shared by Fawke as recorded in his work *The Bayeux Tapestry*.[6] Roger was an old man in 1066, which makes it highly improbable, even though he had been present in the battle, that the duke would have placed him by his side, as he would have preferred a younger and more vigorous man who could have defended him should the necessity arise. It seems almost incredible for Orderic Vital to be mistaken about the movements of Roger de Montgomery, as his father was a vassal of this noble. It also appears impossible for Wace to explain at such great length the exploits of Roger de Montgomery in the battle of Hastings on not only one but on two occasions and be wrong about it. Mr. Freeman, the illustrious historian, has undoubtedly hit upon the solution. He accepts the statement of William of Poitiers that Roger de Beaumont was the head of the council in Normandy, instead of Roger de Montgomery, and sets down the assertion of Orderic Vital as "a plain, though very strange confusion between Roger de Montgomery and Roger de Beaumont." The failure of any mention to be made of so powerful and influential a lord as Roger de Montgomery elsewhere from the time of the battle of Hastings until king William's return from Normandy in 1067 is indeed very curious. King William always surrounded himself with a very imposing array of nobles on his visits to Normandy, and if Roger de Montgomery accompanied him on this journey, returning to England with him, it could account for the statement of his first having entered that country at this time. However, whether he attended the conquest or not, he contributed sixty ships to duke William's fleet and received from him, in addition to the earldoms of Arundel and Shrewsbury,[7] the honour of Eye in Suffolk and various estates in other counties amounting to 157 manors, the cities of Chichester and Shrewsbury and the castle of Arundel. He was also quite as powerful in Normandy.

Roger de Montgomery was the son of another Roger; this is proven by the act of foundation of the abbey of Troarn in Hiemois, wherein he acknowledges and distinguishes his father in the following words: " Ego Rogerius ex Normannis, Normannus magni autem Rogerii filius." The eldest son of Roger I was Hugh, which appears at the foot of a charter of his during the time of duke Robert the Magnificent in the following words: " Signum Hugonis filii ejus," and it is confirmed in the *Interpolations of Jumièges* by Orderic Vital.[8] The name of the father of Roger I was undoubtedly Hugh, since a Hugh de Montgomery is reported as the husband of one of the nieces of the duchess Gonnor, viz. Sibell, the fifth daughter of Herfast her brother, which fits in properly with the number of generations required for Roger de Montgomery II, earl of Arundel and Shrewsbury, to have lived at the time of the Conqueror. This genealogy was set up by Robert de Torigny in his *Interpolations of Jumièges*, although he erroneously said Hugh was the father of Roger de Montgomery II, instead of Roger I.[9] Roger de Montgomery II died in 1094, having left numerous progeny by his wife, Mabel de Belèsme, daughter of William Talvas, lord of Belèsme, and a niece of Ivo, bishop of Séez, whom he married in 1048. They had issue, Robert, count of Alençon and seignior of Belèsme, Hugh, earl of Arundel and Shrewsbury, Roger, surnamed de Poitou, who married Almodis, countess of March, and called therefore earl of Lancaster, Philip, who accompanied duke Robert to the Holy Land and died at Antioch and Arnoul, married to Lafracta, daughter of the king

of Ireland, called earl of Pembroke. The daughters were Emma, abbess of Almenathe, Maud, wife of Robert, count of Mortain and earl of Cornwall, Mabel, wife of Hugh de Château-Neuf, and Sibil, wife of Robert Fitz Hamon, lord of Creulli in Normandy. By his second wife he had only one son, Everard, chaplain to king Henry I. Hugh inherited the estates of his father in England, thus becoming earl of Shrewsbury, Chichester and Arundel. Robert de Belèsme received his Norman possessions and on the death of his brother Hugh, c. 1098, purchased his English earldoms from William Rufus for £3,000, which he forfeited in 1102, when he rebelled against king Henry I and was banished from England. King Henry, when he married Adeliza of Louvain, gave to her the earldom of Arundel.[10]

Plan., I, 181, 203. *Introd. Domesd.*, I, 479. Le Prevost, *Notes, Wace*, III, 13. Burke, 83. *Wace*, Taylor, 171.
[1] *Jumièges Interp.*, Ord. Vit., 156. [2] Ord. Vit., II, 14. [3] William of Poitiers, 1267; Freeman, III, 386. [4] *Wace*, Taylor, 102, 206; *Introd. Domesd.*, I, 380. [5] William of Poitiers, *ibid.*; Ord. Vit., I, 484; Plan., I, 181, 203. [6] *The Bayeux Tapestry*, Fawke, Pl. V, No. 49. [7] Ord. Vit., II, 14. [8] *Jumièges Interp.*, Ord. Vit., 156. [9] *Jumièges Interp.*, de Torigny, 329; *Catalogue of Brooke*. [10] Ord. Vit., II, 195; III, 220, 334, 336; *Chron. Henry of Huntingdon*, 241; *Roger of Wendover*, 452.

ROGER MORETON. *Vide* Corbet Le Normand.

ROGER DE MUSSEGROS. Mussegros is a canton of Fleurigny-sur-Andelle in the arrondissement of Les Andelys. The name is presumed to have been derived from Musgrave or Mewsgrave, " the keeper of the king's hawks, or the king's equerry." Roger de Mucelgros, who is said by Delisle to have been at Senlac, was a tenant-in-chief in Herefordshire in 1086 (Domesday), where he gave his name to Lude-Muchgros. He witnessed a charter of Raoul de Toeni in favour of the abbey of St-Evroult in 1080.[1] His descendants spread to many parts of England and in the 13th century the family held estates in Somerset, Dorset, Gloucester and Hereford. Charlton Musgrove in Somerset is named from it. Hence the baronets Musgrove. The name appears on the Dives roll.

Burke, 15. Cle., II, 269. *Nor. Peo.*, 241. [1] Ord. Vit., II, 189.

ROGER D'OISTREHAM. Oistreham is near Caen, Normandy, and at the time of the conquest was an important port, which supplied a great number of ships and sailors to the fleet of duke William. Rogerus de Ostreham, a tenant-in-chief in Kent in 1086 (Domesday), was the companion of the Conqueror, according to Delisle, who inscribed his name on his Dives roll, and Antoine Dupont, in his *Recherches*, subscribes to his presence at Senlac.[1] Duke Robert Courteheuse gave to the church of Holy Trinity at Caen, *c.* 1090, " a market in the vill of Oistreham and the toll and whole extent of territory of the said vill." [2] It is mentioned in the Exchequer rolls, 1180, concerning shipping for the king, and in 1220.[3]

[1] Dupont, I, 56.   [2] Stapleton, II, xxxiii.   [3] *Ibid.*, I, clii.

ROGER PICOT. Roger Picot was the ancestor of the Cheshire branch of the Picot family, in which county he held Broxton as tenant in fee. There are authentic records showing that Gilbert Picot, his grandson, was mesne-lord of Broxton at a period approximating the conquest, who acquired several other Cheshire manors through his wife, Margaret, daughter and heir of Robert de Rullos. Robert Pigot and William, his son, by charter granted to the monks of St-Werberg in Chester the town of Chilleford, and another Gilbert Pigot was a benefactor to the abbey of Pulton in that county in 1210. For many generations their descendants were lords of Butley, and great benefactors to the abbey of Chester. This branch of the family still exists. The name appears on the rolls of Leland, Duchesne, Holinshed and Scriven.

Rech. Domesd., 91. Burke, 87. Cle., II, 371. *Nor. Peo.*, 363.

ROGER LE POITEVIN. *Vide* Guillaume Le Poitevin.

ROGER DE RAMES. The family has its derivation from the castle of Rames, which was situated on the edge of a forest in a valley to the west of Bolbec in the arrondissement of Havre. Robert d'Estouteville, to whose family this castle belonged, received a grant of 200 acres of land from Henry II adjoining it. Roger de Rames, undoubtedly of this family, who is reported to have been at the battle of Hastings by Delisle, held considerable lands in England in 1086 (Domesday), among which were possessions in Essex and Suffolk. In the former county Anschetillus held from him as an undertenant sixteen acres of land in the domain of Metinges, as well as land at Ramesdune, under Robert de Grenon. Anschetillus also held under Roger at Breseta in the hundred of Babenberg in Suffolk.

Rech. Domesd., 155. Stapleton, I, cxxii.

ROGER DE SAINT-GERMAIN. Roger de Saint-Germain held lands in Suffolk in 1086 (Domesday), and the lands of Osbert de Saint-Germain were granted to Troarn abbey by Roger de Montgomery. The family was frequently mentioned in England and long flourished in Normandy. Mathew, Ralph and Richard de Saint-Germain appear in Normandy in 1198.[1] William de Saint-Germain in England in 1199.[2] Henry, John and Simon Germeyn appear also in 1272.[3] The name occurs on the *Researches of the Bayeux Tapestry* by l'abbé de La Rue and is carried on the Dives list.

Nor. Peo., 259.
[1] *M.R.S.*   [2] *R.C.R.*   [3] *R.H.*

SERLON DE BURCI. Burci, or de Bercy, is from Burcy, in the canton of Vassy, arrondissement of Vire, Normandy. Serlon de Burci, who is stated by Delisle to have been at the conquest of England, was a baron in Somerset and Dorset in 1086 (Domesday). Robert Fitz Serlon, his son, had grants in Cheshire from Hugh Lupus.[1] These appear to have descended to Nigel de Burci, who confirmed lands to Chester abbey and in 1165 held lands in Wiltshire, as Nigel de Morden.[2] Hence the

Mordens of Suffield (now Harbord, lords Suffield). Through the similarity of names, Serlon de Burgh or Pembroke, has sometimes been confused with Serlon de Burci. The former was a powerful baron at the time of the conquest, who built the castle of Knaresborough in Yorkshire and appears to have taken his name from the manor of Burgh there. He accompanied Arunulph de Montgomery to the conquest of Pembroke c. 1090. He was descended from Manno or Pontius, baron or prince of Pons in Saintonge, a noble of Gothic race, who was a benefactor to Savigny abbey.[3] A descendant Pontius, or Ponce, prince of Pons, in 1079 granted a church to the abbey of Cormery in the presence of his sons Anselm, Garnier and Philip-Milo.[4] From the first descended the lords of Pons in Aquitaine, one of the most powerful families in France. Ponce had other sons, who went to England. Drogo Fitz Ponce and Walter Fitz Ponce held baronies of importance in 1086 (Domesday) and two younger brothers, Richard Fitz Ponce, who was the ancestor of the de Cliffords, earls of Cumberland, and Osbert Fitz Ponce, are both mentioned in a charter of Henry I, confirming gifts to Malvern priory.[5] Osbert was the father of Serlon de Burgh or Pembroke above mentioned, who was succeeded by Eustache Fitz John his nephew, the son of his brother John, baron of Alnwick, a great favourite of Henry I, which barony he received through marriage with Beatrice, daughter of Ivo de Vesci. Their son William assumed the name de Vesci, hence this branch of the family of that name. Adelm of Aldfield, Yorkshire, who probably bore the name of Burgh, was a brother of Eustache Fitz John, whose son Ralph gave lands at Fountains to the abbey, which were confirmed by Roger de Mowbray [6] and as Ralph de Burgo, *temp.* Henry II, witnessed a charter of Trentham priory.[7] From this branch descended the earls of Ulster, earls and marquesses of Clanricarde and earls of Mayo.

Nov. Peo., 179, 201, 277, 433.
[1] *Mon.*, i, 201.   [2] *Lib. Nig.*   [3] Bouquet, XI, 200.   [4] *Gall. Christ.*, XII, 14.
[5] *Mon.*, i, 266.   [6] *Mon. Ebor.*, Burton, 166.
[7] *Mon.*, ii, 261.

SIMON DE SENLIS. From Senlis in Normandy. Raundoel le Ryche was the father of Simon de Senlis and his brother Garnerius, who came to the conquest of England.[1] Their lineage is obscure, yet Simon must have been held in very high esteem by the Conqueror, since he offered him the hand of the countess Judith his niece, dowered with the earldoms of Huntingdon and Northampton, who had been widowed by the execution of Waltheoff, the son of Siward, earl of Northumberland, which occurred in 1076. The countess refused because Simon " halted on one leg " and, with her three daughters, was forced to flee from her uncle's wrath. King William seized forthwith her possessions and gave to Simon the town of Northampton, with the whole hundred of Falkeley. In 1089 Simon married Maud, the countess's eldest daughter, who brought him the two earldoms above mentioned, which her mother, the countess, had forfeited. They had issue three children, Simon, who succeeded his father, Waltheoff, abbot of Melrose, and a daughter, named Maud, who was married to Robert Fitz Richard, son of Richard de Quincy, who was present at Hastings.[2] Simon was the founder of the castle of Northampton and the priory of St-Andrews, and died in 1115 on his return to the French abbey of Our Lady of Charity from Jerusalem. Maud, his wife, then married David of Scotland, a son of Malcolm, who became one of the most renowned kings of that country. Through this marriage came the connection between the earldom of Huntingdon and the royal house of Scotland. Simon II succeeded to the earldom of Northampton only. The earldom of Huntingdon was by special grace of king Henry I conveyed to David of Scotland, who, on ascending the throne in 1124, transferred it to his only son, Henry, but on Henry's death in 1152, it reverted to Simon. The latter married Isabel de Beaumont and died about 1154, leaving a son and heir, Simon III. Again the earldoms were divided. Simon became earl of Northampton and the earldom of Huntingdon was given by Henry II to Malcolm IV, king of the Scots, the eldest son of prince Henry, who predeceased his father, and therefore the grandson of king David I. The controversy over the earldom still continued, and the king of England, angered by the continual strife and dissension concerning it, ordered the castle demolished. The name appears on the rolls of Holinshed and Duchesne, and Dives carries Simon de Senlis.

Burke, 97. Cle., III, 123. Dugdale. *Nor. Peo.*, 147.
[1] *Mon.*, v, 90.   [2] *Ibid.*, ii, 75.

LE SIRE DE REBERCIL. Rebercil, now Rubercy, is in the arrondissement of Bayeux. The lords of Rebercil belonged to the family of Wac. Geoffry Wac witnessed a charter to Bernay of duke Robert the Magnificent in 1027, at which time he held Rebercil.[1] He was probably the father of the "sire de Rebercil," whom Wace (l. 13777) mentions as one of the five knights at Hastings, who challenged Harold "to come forth." In 1168 Hugh Wac (Wake), lord of Rebercil, made grants to the abbey of Longues.[2] He had married Emma, daughter of Baldwin Fitz Gilbert, or de Gand, founder of the abbey of Bourne in Lincolnshire as well as Deeping priory, and Adelaide de Rullos. Hugh's son Baldwin appears in the *Monasticon* and in a charter of Longues.[3] Another son Geoffry de Ribercy, or de Clifton, was the ancestor of the house of Clifton. Wac was one of the most important Anglo-Norman families, hence the baronets and lords Wake, also the archbishop of this name. Rebercil appears on all of the rolls excepting Dives.

Plan., II, 290. Le Prevost, *Notes, Wace*, II, 269. *Wace*, Taylor, 242. *Nor. Peo.*, 202, 436. Cle., III, 259. *Mon.*, ii, 235.
[1] *M.S.A.N.*, IV, 381.   [2] *Gall. Christ.*, IX, 83–4 Instr.   [3] *M.S.A.N.*, VIII.

LE SIRE DE RUPIERRE. Rupierre is near Caen, Normandy. The family is said to have been descended from the house of Musard, but the statement has not been substantiated. The lords of this house were of great consequence in the 11th and 12th centuries.[1] William de Rupierre came to England with the Conqueror, and was in command of the forces of duke Robert in 1090 before

the castle of Courci in Normandy, by which garrison he was taken prisoner with William de Ferrers.[2] In 1099 William possessed Trenouville, Grenteville and Fremont, and was a benefactor of Troarn.[3] In England Robert de Rupierre paid fines in Nottingham and Derby [4] and the heiress of John Rooper of Turndish, Derby, married De Fourneaux, who assumed her name.[5] Roger de Rupers of the Norman line held lands in Warwick and Leicester, *temp.* John, where he made a grant to Tewkesbury abbey.[6] The counts of Rupierre continued in Normandy until the 18th century. From this family descends the Roopers and the barons Teynham. The name appears on the roll of Leland and on Magny's Ad. to the Dives roll.

Cle., III, 79. *Nor. Peo.*, 382.
[1] Des Bois.   [2] Ord. Vit., II, 508.
[3] *Ibid.*; *M.S.A.N.*, XII, 53.   [4] *Rot. Pip.*
[5] *Mon.*, i, 503.   [6] *Testa de Neuville*, 87.

LE SIRE DE SAINT-MARTIN. Probably from the commune of Saint-Martin in Caux or Brai, Normandy. The sire de Saint-Martin of Wace (l. 13565) was undoubtedly descended from Walter de Saint-Martin and a niece of the duchess Gonnor, from whom were derived the family of Saint-Martin in England and Normandy,[1] but the personage at the conquest has not been identified. Tailleur in the *Norman Chronicle* also lists the seigneur de Saint-Martin. Geoffry, son of Rainauld, lord of Saint-Martin-le-Gaillard in the arrondissement of Dieppe, is mentioned in a charter of Tréport.[2] Roger de Saint-Martin was lord of Hempton, Norfolk, in the reign of Henry I, and founded a priory for Black canons of the order of St-Augustine, dedicated to St-Stephen. He was enfeoffed by his kinsman, earl Warren,[3] and appears in the *Monasticon* in 1119. Alured de Saint-Martin held of the earl of Eu in Sussex, and William de Saint-Martin of the abbess of Winton in Wiltshire, as entered in the *Liber Niger*. The former appears in a number of charters and acts of the period, and married the widowed countess Alice, eldest daughter of William d'Albini, earl of Arundel, and the former queen Adeliza. In 1176, with his brother Robert, he founded the monastery of St-Mary's near Salehurst.

Nor. Peo., 338. Plan., II, 291. Cle., III, 131. Le Prevost, Notes, Wace, II, 238. Wace, Taylor, 215.
[1] Mon., ii, 950. [2] Gall. Christ., XI.
[3] Norfolk, Blomfield.

LE SIRE DE SAINT-SEVER. From Saint-Sever, in the arrondissement of Vire, Normandy. Renouf de Bricasard, vicomte de Bessin, frequently called de Bayeux, whose war-cry at the battle of Val-des-Dunes was " Saint-Sever, sire Saint-Sever," married Matilda, daughter of Richard d'Avranches by Emma de Conteville ; their son and heir Ranulph le Meschin became earl of Chester. Ranulph le vicomte is said to have been the " cil de Saint-Sever " named by Wace (l. 13649), which is the only connection between Saint-Sever and the vicomtes d'Avranches. M. Le Prevost does not believe there existed a seigneur de Saint-Sever in 1066, since it belonged to the house of d'Avranches at that period. Mr. Edgar Taylor, in his translation of Wace, observes, however, that he may have here referred to Hugh d'Avranches, surnamed Lupus, earl of Chester, and son of Richard d'Avranches, who, if at the conquest, is not elsewhere mentioned. The name appears on the rolls of Holinshed, Leland, Brompton and Worcester.

Plan., II, 292. Le Prevost, Notes, Wace, II, 249 ; III, 19. Wace, Taylor, 228.

LE SIRE DE SOLIGNY. This family derives from Subligny near Avranches, and the companion of the Conqueror, whom Wace (l. 13602) refers to as "sire de Solignie," has not been identified. Richard de Subligny, a member of this family, consecrated bishop of Avranches in 1143, executed a charter in favour of Mont-St-Michel about the middle of the 12th century, at which period occurs also in charters of that abbey, Hascoul, Gilbert and John. The name existed in Cornwall, Devon and Somerset, and a marriage with the Painels caused the property of a branch in Normandy to pass to that family. Guillaume Tailleur records the

name as does Scriven, while the Dives roll carries Raoul de Savigni.

Rech., de Gerville, 83, 93. Plan., II, 295. Le Prevost, Notes, Wace, II, 231. Wace, Taylor, 219–31. Avranchin Monumental et Historique, Le Hericher, II, 136. Stapleton, II, clxxxiii. Chron. de Torigny, I, 229 ; II, 12, 242, 297.

TAILLEFER. Henry of Huntington in his Chronicle states that Taillefer, who was supposed to be the jester of duke William, before the armies closed for the fight at the battle of Hastings, " sportively brandishing swords in front of the English troops, while they were lost in amazement at his gambols, slew one of their standard-bearers. A second time one of the enemy fell. The third time he was slain himself." On the other hand Wace (l. 13194) says that Taillefer called to duke William, " A boon, sire. I have long served you and you owe me for all such service. To-day, so please you, you shall repay it. I ask as my guerdon and beseech you for it earnestly that you will allow me to strike the first blow in the battle." To which the duke answered, " I grant it." Then Taillefer put his horse to a gallop, charging before all the rest. The family appears later in England. William, Fulco and Robert Tailefer occur in Normandy in 1180–95[1] and Ralph Tailefer in England in 1202.[2]

Wace, Pluquet, II, 214–15. Nor. Peo., 415. The Chron. Henry of Huntingdon, Forester ed., 211. Guy of Amiens, Carmen de bello, Hastingensi. Wace, Taylor, 189, 299. Geoffry Gaimar's Poem, Arch., XII. Benoît, III, 209.
[1] M.R.S. [2] R.C.

THIERRI POINTEL. Tedricus Pointel appears in 1086 (Domesday) as a tenant in capite in Essex and is said by Delisle to have been at the conquest of England. William Pointel, probably his grandson, is twice mentioned as one of the judiciaries of Amaury de Montfort, comte d'Evreux, in judicial proceedings at Gaillon. In 1118, when count Amaury was in arms against king Henry I, William Pointel put him in possession of the citadel of Evreux and the following year he, with others, defended the citadel against the king.[1] He was the nephew of Ralph de Vitot (near Neubourg), who must have been a grandson of Robert de Vitot, one of the assassins of Gilbert, count of Brionne.[2]

[1] Ord. Vit., III, 449, 478.   [2] *Ibid.*, I, 450.

TOUSTAIN BASSET. *Vide* Osmond Basset.

TOUSTAIN FITZ ROU. Master Wace (ll. 12773–4) records "Tosteins filz Rou le Blanc," whose abode was in Bec-en-Caux.[1] He was also called Toustain du Bec, and said to have been a younger brother of Geoffroi du Bec, which is quite possible, but it has not been satisfactorily verified. There is nothing recorded concerning Toustain prior to the conquest excepting the statement of Wace and the contention of Stacey Grimaldi that his father Rou or Rollo was the brother of Gilbert Crispin I, seigneur de Tillières.[2] Raoul de Toeni was the hereditary standard-bearer of Normandy, but when he refused to officiate in this capacity at Senlac duke William gave the honour to Toustain. Wace writes, "He bore the gonfanon boldly with a good heart, high aloft in the breeze and rode beside the duke, going wherever he went," on which account his family had "quittance for all service and his heirs were entitled to hold their possessions forever." Orderic Vital[3] states Turstin, son of Rollo, bore the standard of Normandy. The banner was the one that the pope Alexander II had blessed and sent to William, duke of Normandy, by Gilbert, archdeacon of Lisieux. Duke William had sent him to Rome to intercede with the pope for his approval of his claim to the throne of England. Gilbert, having succeeded in the mission, returned with the gonfanon. Toustain Fitz Rou received large estates in England, where he held in-chief and by barony in Hampton, Berks, Dorset, Somerset, Devon, Buckingham, Gloucester and Hereford, and as an under-tenant in Wilts, Somerset, Buckingham and Gloucester.[4] Robert Fitz Rou, probably his brother, is likewise written in Domesday as holding possessions in Wilts.[5] In Normandy a noble house, descended from him, took the name of Toustain or Turstin. Walter Turstain held Brocton, Stafford, in the 13th

century from the see of Chester.[6] Léopold Delisle carries his name on the Dives roll.

Plan., I, 227. *Nor. Peo.*, 175. Le Prevost, *Notes*, *Wace*, II, 198. *Wace*, Taylor, 170. *Rech. Domesd.*, 99. *Rech.*, de La Rue, 70.
[1] This was Bec-aux-Cauchois in the arrondissement of Ivetot, not Bec-Crispin in that of Havre.   [2] *Vide* Geoffroi du Bec, Mile Crispin ; Ord. Vit., II, 198.   [3] Ord. Vit., I, 483.   [4] *Introd. Domesd.*, I, 497 ; II, 398.   [5] *Ibid.*, I, 479–97.   [6] Testa de Neville.

TUROLD. The name Turold is woven upon the Bayeux tapestry, between two lines to give it prominence, above the head of a dwarf, with a long beard and clean-shaven neck, which renders him ridiculous in appearance. He is holding two horses, is French and apparently of the house of Gui de Ponthieu. The inscription is obviously not intended for him, but is the name of one of the ambassadors of duke William. Turold is entered in Domesday as a vassal of bishop Odo and the *Researches* of Fowke inform us that Turold was an important personage, constable of Bayeux, where he was very highly esteemed. He witnessed a charter in favour of the abbey of St. Père de Chartres executed prior to 1060. In the archives of St-Lo exists a charter, in which his mark instead of a signature is near that of duke William. Later on there were alliances between the family of Turold and that of the Conqueror, and a Turold became bishop of Bayeux after the death of bishop Odo, the half-brother of king William.

Rech., de La Rue, 57–8. *Bayeux Tapes.*, Fowke, p. 41. *La Tapis. de Bayeux*, Leve, p. 42. *Introd. Domesd.*, II, 397. Stapleton, II, cclxx.

LE CHAMBERLAIN DE TAN-CARVILLE. From Tancarville, arrondissement of Havre. The family probably sprung from Tancred, *c.* 912, whose fief in Normandy was named Tancardivilla and Rabel his son left his name to Rabel's Isle and Rabel's Foss, mentioned in the early records.

Gerold, sire de Tancarville, was father of three sons. Ralph the eldest who is said by Le Prevost to have been guardian of duke William, which is doubtful, as no proof is given and no record can be found to substantiate it.

In a charter regarding the small church of St-Georges de Boscherville, first endowed by duke William and rebuilt by Ralph, are named his father Gerold and his sons Ralph and Rabel (Radulfo filio Gerold uxoreque et filiis ejus Radulfo et Rabello).

Ralph was the duke's first chamberlain, as witness William's own statement in his confirmation of this charter. "My Major-domo or Master of the Household and First Chamberlain" (meus magister Aulaque et Camera mea Princeps). Ralph gave the church of Miraville to the abbey of Jumièges in 1079.

He had a brother Gerold who was the dapifer of duke William and is so recorded in a document concerning St-Georges which was witnessed by the same Gerold and his son Robert (Gerold dapifero meo).[1]

The third brother was Amaury d'Abbetot.[2] Ralph was succeeded by his son William as chamberlain of Normandy, who so appears in 1082 when he witnessed the foundation charter of Holy Trinity at Caen (Willelmi Camerarii filii Radulfi).[3] He became treasurer of king Henry I and justice of England, and in 1114 elevated the collegiate church of St-Georges to an abbey. This act was witnessed by his sons Rabel and Ralph and a daughter Lucia,[4] who were the children by his marriage with Matilda, daughter of William, vicomte d'Arques.[5] Lucia later married William de Vernon and had a son Richard de Vernon as stated in a charter of the abbey of Montebourg in 1157.[6]

He is reported to have had another son William de Graham from whom descended the famous marquess of Montrose, the viscounts of Dundee and the Graham family. He was with king Henry's forces before Laigle in 1118, where he withdrew, and in the following year he supported the king at the battle of Bremule.[7] William witnessed a royal letter in York in 1123[8] and was reported in command of the English at the battle of Bourgteroude in 1124, which is disputed.[9] He was deceased before 1128, since in that year his son and successor Rabel confirmed a donation of his uncle Odon Stigand and

other members of his family to the priory of Ste-Barbe-en-Auge as head of the house.[10] He held lands in Lincolnshire and this priory had there gifts of his lands in the soke of Grantham at Colslerworth, Oston and Somerly.[11] Rabel witnessed a charter of Henry I in favour of the abbey of Fontevraud, 13 January 1131,[12] and in 1137 with other Norman barons rebelled against king Stephen,[13] but peace was arranged in the same year.[14] He married Agnes de Mesidon[15] and Robert de Torigny records his death in 1140.[16] Rabel was succeeded by his son William, who appears as chamberlain in acts of the abbey of Mont-St-Michel of 1154[17] and 1172.[18] The next year[19] William came to Normandy where he, with Joscelyn Crispin, Gilbert de Tillières and other powerful barons, swore allegiance and delivered their castles to the young king. He was governor of Poitou after the death of Patrick of Salisbury[20] and married Theophania, daughter of Stephen of Brittany, earl of Richmond, which occurs in a document found by the jurors of the wapentake of Boothby in 1242 concerning land in Coleby.[21] From this marriage issued Ralph, the next chamberlain, as a charter for the exchange of Andely in 1197 records, who died without children before 1204,[22] William, who succeeded his brother Ralph as chamberlain, and Olivia, both mentioned in the Coleby document (Olivia sorore Willi Camerarii de Tancarvill).[23] The latter married Henry, baron of Fougères, and had a son William.[24] Another daughter, Lucia, is given by Stapleton[25] as married to Richard de Vernon, but this has the appearance of confusion with Lucia the daughter of William the chamberlain of Henry I.

Marcelle Crispin, daughter of Joscelyn Crispin,[26] is stated by La Roque,[27] Père Anselme,[28] Moreri[29] and others to have married the baron of Tancarville, but they do not identify him. This statement is correct because William Crispin VI, grandson of Joscelyn, sire de Dangu, in April 1225 executed a charter in favour of the brothers of the Temple at Bourgoult wherein he refers to "our relative of pious memory, the chamberlain of Tancarville."[30] Marcelle was born after 1050, since she is not mentioned in a charter of about that date of the abbey of Mortemer [31] in which Joscelyn names his children. She would therefore have been the second wife of William the chamberlain who died after 1173 or of Ralph his son, the latter being the most probable, since there was apparently no issue from this marriage. The English branches of the Tancarvilles usually adopted the name Chamberlain, and this family of Lincolnshire bore three escallops which were the arms of the former.

Rech. Domesd., 46. *Nor. Peo.*, 193, 266. Le Prevost, *Notes, Wace,* II, 237, 353. Cle., III, 194. Plan., II, 148. *Wace,* Taylor, '214. *Hist. du Château et des Sires de Tancarville.*
[1] Stapleton, II, cli, clii. [2] *Vide* Ours d'Abbetot. [3] *Opera Lanfranci,* Giles, I, 401. [4] Stapleton, II, cclxxv, cclxxvi. [5] *Jumièges Interp.*, de Torigny, 325 ; Chron. de Torigny, II, 197 ; *vide* Guillaume d'Arques ; *Rech. Domesd.*, 198. [6] Stapleton, II, cclxxv. [7] Ord. Vit., III, 457, 474. [8] *Ibid.*, IV, 56. [9] *Vide* App. 14. [10] *Rech. Domesd.*, 47. [11] Stapleton, II, cxlii. [12] Bibl. nat. lat. 5481, vol. I, 277–8. [13] Ord. Vit., IV, 175 ; *Chron. de Torigny,* I, 206. [14] *Ibid.*, 177. [15] *Hist. du Château et des Sires de Tancarville,* 121–4. [16] *Chron. de Torigny,* I, 218. [17] *Ibid.*, II, 297. [18] *Ibid.*, 302. [19] *Ibid.*, 39. [20] *Ibid.*, and n. 3. [21] Stapleton, II, cxlii. [22] *Ibid.*, cxl. [23] *Ibid.*, cxlii. [24] *Ibid.*, ccxlviii. [25] *Ibid.*, cxlii. [26] *Vide* Guillaume Crispin. [27] La Roque, I, 268. [28] Père Anselme, VI, 633. [29] Moreri, II, 287. [30] Arch. nat. s. 5194, Nos. 26 and 27, box marked, s. 5193. [31] *Cart. de Mortemer,* 57 ; Bibl. nat. lat. 18369.

LE SIRE DE TOUCHET.

From Notre-Dame du Touchet near Mortain, Normandy. Mr. Collins informs us that "The family of Touchet hath been of great note and came in with William the Conqueror as is very evident, the name being on the roll of Battle abbey and in the chronicles of Normandy." In 1082 Ursinus de Touchet granted lands to the church of St-William, Mortain.[1] The name still remained in Normandy in the latter part of the 18th century.[2] Joslin de Touchet was seated in Cheshire during the reign of king William I and was father of Henry, father of another Henry to whom Ranulph Gernons, earl of Chester, gave Tatenhall.[3] Hence the Touchets, lords of Audley, earls of Castlehaven. The name

is inscribed on the rolls of Leland, Scriven, Holinshed, Duchesne, Worcester, and is mentioned by Dugdale. It appears also in the *Researches of the Bayeux Tapestry* by l'abbé de La Rue.

Nor. Peo., 424. Burke, 99.
[1] *Rech.*, de Gerville. [2] *M.S.A.N.*, XII, 23. [3] Oremond, II, 393.

LE SIRE DE TOUQUES.

From Touques, at the mouth of a river of that name, in the arrondissement of Pont-l'Evêque, where the castle stood. Wace (l. 13555) records "cil de Touke," and Guillaume Tailleur in the *Norman Chronicle* mentions le seigneur de Touque, as among the companions of the duke William at the conquest of England. The ancient family of Toque of Godington of Kent claimed descent from this Norman lord. A branch was seated in Nottingham in the reign of William Rufus,[1] and were benefactors to Rufford abbey, in which county they continued for 300 years. Jordan, Roger, Robert and Henri de Touques appear in Dugdale's *Monasticon.* Roger de Touques occurs in Hampshire 1130,[2] Humphrey in Derby, Roger in Dorset in 1165.[3] Other branches were seated in York, Cambridge, Hereford, etc.

Burke, 103. *Nor. Peo.*, 421. Plan., II, 206. Cle., III, 183. Le Prevost, *Notes, Wace,* II, 235. *Wace,* Taylor, 212.
[1] *Nottingham,* Thornton. [2] *Rot. Pip.* [3] *Lib. Nig.*, 90.

LE SIRE DE TOURNEBUT.

Tornebu was a barony near Falaise. William de Turnebu accompanied duke William to the conquest in 1066 [1] and with Adda his wife and William his son made a donation to the abbey of Bec before 1070.[2] His name appears in the *Researches of the Bayeux Tapestry* by the abbé de La Rue. Simon, Thomas, and Amaury de Turnebu occur in Normandy in 1180–1195.[3] The heir of Amaury is mentioned in Hampshire in 1202.[4] The barony of Tournebu held by Thomas de Tournebu in 1165 consisted of twenty fees.[5] Guy, baron of Tournebu, married Jeanne Crispin, granddaughter of William Crispin, the marshal of France *c.* 1325, who brought to him the baronies of Motte-Celny and of Grimbosc.[6] The name appears in

Dugdale, and upon the rolls of Holinshed, Duchesne and Dives.

Nor. Peo., 425.
[1] M.S.A.N., 181.   [2] Bibl. nat. lat. 13905 et 12884.   [3] M.R.S.   [4] R.C.   [5] Duchesne. [6] Père Anselme, VI, 634 ; vide Guillaume Crispin.

LE SIRE de TOURNEUR. From Le Tourneur near Vire, Normandy. Wace (l. 13661) mentions "del Torneor," concerning whom very little is known. However, he also appears in the Norman Chronicle of Guillaume Tailleur as present at Hastings. He may have been killed in that engagement for he is not entered in Domesday but he probably left issue as the earl of Winterton claims descent from the sire de Tourneur, who is here recorded. A branch of the Brittany family of Houel settled at an early date in the parish of Tourneur. It is stated in Nobiliaire de Normandie that "Houels are descendants of the race and estates of the sires du Tourneur."

Plan., II, 296. Cle., II, 151. Le Prevost, Notes, Wace, II, 253. Wace, Taylor, 231. Vide App. 25.

LE SIRE DE TOURNEVILLE. From Turnaville near Evreux, Normandy. Radulphus de Tournavilla is inscribed in Domesday as a sub-tenant in Norfolk. At the time of the conquest this parish had a particular seignior and in fact the title and patronage of Tourneville were joined with the parish of Evreux in the 11th century by le sire de Tourneville, who accompanied the duke Robert to the Holy Land. Delisle in the Dives roll mentions Raoul de Tourneville. Roger de Turville held Weston-Turville in Buckingham of bishop Odo (Domesday) ; another manor in this county is called Turville after him. William de Tourville in the opinion of Burke accompanied duke William to the conquest, soon after which the Tourvilles became large landowners in the counties of Warwick and Leicester. Geoffry de Turville in 1124 had grants from the earl of Leicester and Meulent in England, but having rebelled against king Henry I, was captured and had his eyes put out.

Ord. Vit., IV, 75. Mon., i, 519 ; ii, 309. Cle., III, 191. Burke, 103. Nor. Peo., 213.

LE SIRE DE TRACY. From Tracy near Vire, arrondissement of Caen, Normandy. Turgis de Tracy, who with William de la Ferté, was defeated and driven out of Maine by Fulk le Rechin, count of Anjou, in 1073 [1] was probably the "cil de Tracie" whom Wace (l. 13605) mentions as present at Hastings. In 1082 William and Gilbert de Tracy subscribed to a charter at Tracy, which is recorded in Gallia Christiana.[2] A natural son of Henry I was called William de Tracy, probably because he was born in that castle. Henry de Tracy received from king Stephen the barony of Barnstaple. William de Tracy in 1170 was one of the murderers of Thomas à Becket, archbishop of Canterbury, and is asserted to have been the youngest son of John de Sudeley, lord of Sudeley and Toddington, and Grace, only child and heir of the aforementioned Henry de Tracy. He took his mother's name of Tracy and possessed Toddington in Gloucester, the barony of Barnstaple in Devon, and held twenty-six knights' fees in Normandy in 1165. From him descended the Tracys of Toddington, viscounts Tracy of Rathcoole, and the Tracys, baronets of Stanway. The name is listed by Guillaume Tailleur, Scriven, Holinshed, Brompton, Worcester, de Magny's addition to Dives, and in Dugdale and Banks.

Nor. Peo., 422. Plan., II, 297. Cle., III, 155. Burke, 99. Le Prevost, Notes, Wace, 244. Wace, Taylor, 221.
[1] Ord. Vit., II, 75.   [2] Gall. Christ., XI, Instr. 107. Norman People believe that William de Tracy was at Senlac.

LE SIRE DE TREGOZ. Troisgots is in the arrondissement of St-Lo, where the ruins of a castle exist at the junction of the Vire and the brook of Marqueran, which king John visited in the beginning of the 13th century. The family became seated in Hereford at the time of the conquest [1] and Wace (l. 13669) mentions "E cil ki dunc teneit Tregoz," while Guillaume Tailleur in the Norman Chronicle calls him "sire de Tresgoz." In 1131 Geoffry de Tregoz, son of William, is said by Dugdale to have held lands of William Pevrel of London. His successors were benefactors of Hambye and one of them signed the foundation charter in 1145. Robert de Tregoz, sheriff of Wiltshire, was the distinguished warrior in the time of Richard I, whose place of residence was Lidyard-Tregoze. The seigniory in Normandy was confiscated by Philip Augustus, but the family long remained there. Pierre de Tregoz was among the knights summoned for the service of Mont-St-Michel in 1271. From this family descends the barons Tregoze, viscounts Bolingbroke and St. John.

Plan., II, 298. Cle., III, 403. *Nor. Peo.*, 422. Le Prevost, *Notes, Wace*, II, 255. *Wace*, Taylor, 233. *M.S.A.N.*, de Gerville, V, 215.
[1] Testa de Neville.

LE SIRE DE TROUSSEBOT.

The original seat of the family of Troussebot (" Trossebot " of Wace, l. 13711) is supposed to have been in the north-western part of the district of Neubourg, Normandy, near the domain of the Harcourts. Pagan Troussebot is the first known member of the family and was probably the warrior at Hastings. His son Geoffry Fitz Payne (Pagan) held estates in Yorkshire before the reign of Henry I, where he was seated at Wartre in Holderness. He founded a priory there [1] and the family was afterwards known as Trusbutt of Wartre. William, son of Geoffry, was a stalwart soldier, which was undoubtedly the reason for the interest taken in him by king Henry I.[2] He was hereditary castellan of Bonneville-sur-Touquet in 1138, one branch of whose family possessed domains in the neighbourhood of Bonneville, which was a royal residence. In this same year, Orderic Vital [3] remarks, " William, surnamed Troussebot, governor of Bonneville, having discovered the enemies want of caution " (Geoffry, count of Anjou and his forces, who were quartered in Touque), " set fire to the town in forty-five different places," at which time he and " his garrison in full armour sallied forth from Bonneville and fell upon the enemy, who were completely routed and put to flight." He married Albreda, daughter of Robert de Harcourt, by whom he had issue Richard, Geoffry and Robert and Stapleton adds another, named William,[4] all of whom

died without issue, and three daughters : Rose, married to Everard de Ros, a great baron in Holderness, Hillaria to Robert de Bollers ; and Agatha to Hamo Meinfelin. The two latter died childless and the estates were inherited by William de Ros, grandson of Rose. The family were great benefactors to the church. The name appears on the rolls of Guillaume Tailleur, Scriven, Brompton, Holinshed and Duchesne.

Cle., III, 157. Plan., II, 299. Le Prevost, *Notes, Wace*, II, 260. *Wace*, Taylor, 237.
[1] *Mon.*, ii, 43. [2] Ord. Vit., III, 328.
[3] *Ibid.*, IV, 207. [4] Stapleton, I, clxv.

DE VENOIS.

From Venoix near Caen, Normandy. The barons of Venoix, Verbois or Venois held their fief as hereditary marshals of the stable (master of the horse) of the dukes of Normandy,[1] hence they bore the name of le Marescal or Mareschal of Venois. Milo le Mareschal and Lasceline his wife, were living in 1050, when the duchess Matilda purchased lands at Vancelles from them for Holy Trinity at Caen.[2] They had issue Ralph le Mareschal and other sons, who came to England at the conquest. Ralph was living in 1086 and had issue Robert, Roger le Mareschal, who had lands in Essex, Gerald, owner of estates in Sussex, and Goisfred, a baron in Hampshire and Wiltshire in 1086 (Domesday). The latter was the father of Gilbert, ancestor of the Mareschals. Robert the eldest son, sometimes styled Fitz Ralph, de Hastings, and le Mareschal,[3] was lord of Venoix and the king's sheriff or seneschal at Hastings, where, and at Rye, his descendants long held the revenue in farm from the crown. He had issue William de Hastings who *c.* 1100 married Juliana, granddaughter and heir of Waleran, a great baron in Essex, living in 1130.[4] With Robert de Venoix his brother, he instituted a suit against his cousin, Gilbert Marescal and his son John, to recover the office of hereditary marshal, which Gilbert or Goisfrid his father had obtained and successfully held, although it could not have been theirs by right of birth.[5] The suit failed, but William in compensation was created dapifer.[6] Hence the celebrated and renowned family of Hastings, who married into the royalty of England and were so famous in history. From this line descended the Hastings, barons of Abergavenny, the marquesses of Hastings, the earls of Pembroke, and earls of Striguil in Ireland, as well as the earls of Huntingdon. This latter great branch of the family still exists in the male line, which was ennobled in the person of sir William Hastings, created baron Hastings of Ashby-de-la-Zouch, by king Edward IV, in 1461, under which title he was summoned to parliament. He was one of the most powerful persons in the kingdom and erected at Ashby a magnificent castle, where afterwards Mary queen of Scots was kept in captivity. He possessed tremendous estates, the honours of Pevrel, Belvoir, Hagenet, and Huntingdon, the lands of viscount Beaumont, Belvoir castle, with a great part of the possessions of lord Ros, Ashby-de-la-Zouch, which had belonged to the earls of Wiltshire, the castle and rape of Hastings. He was invested with many high offices ; was ambassador to France, chamberlain to North Wales, constable of six castles and many more honours, too numerous to mention. Upon the death of king Edward IV, his greatness came to a sudden end, as he was lured to the tower of London by the new protector, Richard, duke of Gloucester, and beheaded forthwith in 1483.

Burke, 63. Cle., II, 131 ; III, 244. Nor. Peo., 280.
[1] M.S.A.N., XII, 15.   [2] Ibid.
[3] Domesday, 17, 73, 74B, 160B ; Essex, 107B.   [4] Rot. Pip.   [5] Dugdale.
[6] Blomfield, I, 68, 399.

LE SIRE DE **VESLI.** Vesly-en-Vexin Normand is near Gisors in the diocese of Rouen, anciently called Velli, Velly, Verlei and later Wailley, Vely, etc. The priory of Vesly, depending from the abbey of Marmoutiers near Tours, was according to dom Martene in his history of that famous monastery founded and dedicated to St-Martin by Jean de la Val, a monk in that religious institution, son of Guy II sire de la Val, c. 1060. He gave half of the seigniory of Vesly for this purpose ; the other half belonged to the seigneur de Dangu and his vassals.[1] The confirmation of a charter was executed by Ernoulf de Villanis, giving property in Vesly to the monks of Marmoutiers before 1064 [2] and another was made in 1076 by Richard de Miry (de Miriaco) also confirming possessions in Vesly, given to them by his father, Onfroy, presumably about 1066.[3] Hunfredus de Merai also occurs in the grand charter of William the Conqueror in favour of the abbey of Bec. Osberne de Vesly gave lands to the monks of Vesly, just before 1064, which shortly after 1066 Milo de Vesly, his son, confirmed. The latter therein states that he was in England at the time of the execution of the charter and his father's death, which leads to the conclusion that his absence was occasioned by his participation in the battle of Hastings.[4] MM. Charpillon and Caresme are of the opinion that William, Huges and Robert de Vesly accompanied duke William to England in 1066, in which they are supported by Delisle, who inscribed the latter two on the Dives roll.[5] Hunfridus was a vassal of Ibert de Laci in Yorkshire in 1086 (Domesday) and appears as Umfrido de Villeio before 1100, giving two garbs from the harvest yearly towards the endowment of St. Clement's chapel in Pontefract castle, as recorded by A. S. Ellis. He held in Snidal, Newton and Ackworth, and two centuries later his descendants continued to be tenants of the Lacys in Yorkshire. The charters of Marmoutiers suggest the thought that the Humfridus of Domesday was a member of the family there recorded and came from Vesly-en-Vexin.[6] The Crispin family, lords of Dangu, were large donors to the priory of Vesly in the 12th and 13th centuries, among which were two of William Crispin, lord of Lisors and Dangu, son of Joscelyn, made in 1180–1224, and 1216. In 1260 his grandson, William Crispin, then lord of Dangu, was the sole patron of this priory, which was held by his descendants until revolution, with the exception of a short period during the 15th century.[7] Sir Humphrey de Vesly, c. 1270, held Thorner in Yorkshire of the earl of Lincoln and was also the lord of the manor of Owston, from whom descended the family of Wyly or Wylie.

Cle., III, 272. *Histoire de Vesly-en-Vexin*, Louis Otter, Evreux, 1920, pp. 2 to 201. *Vide* App. 23.
[1] Bibl. nat. lat. 12878 et 12880.   [2] Bibl. municipale de Tours, 1387-8-9 ; also dom Anselme le Michel, who died 1644, in his *History of Marmoutiers* in Latin.   [3] Bibl. nat. lat. ms. 5441 ; extracts from the *Cartulary compiled by Robert de Gaignières*, p. 91 ; Bibl. nat. lat. 12884 and 13905. [4] Bibl. nat. lat. 12878, fo. 162—*Collections*, Etienne Baluze, p. 50 ; Bibl. nat. lat. 5441, p. 91 ; *Chart Majorie Monast.*, I, fo. 98 v°. [5] *Dict. de l'Eure*, II, 981.   [6] Bibl. nat. lat. 5441, p. 99.   [7] *Ibid.*, p. 100 ; *Le Prevost Mem.*, II, 6 ; *vide* Guillaume Crispin. This William Crispin was the marshal.

VITAL. Vital was a vassal of Odo, bishop of Bayeux, as is inscribed in Domesday, and was doubtless the individual of this name who witnessed an act proving that this bishop bought ground to enlarge his palace at Bayeux in 1078. His name is woven in the Bayeux tapestry, where he is clearly indicated as having command of the scouts of duke William's army on its arrival in England, keeping him constantly informed of the movements of the enemy. He was apparently a person of considerable importance, although not mentioned by the chroniclers of the day. A Vital who was a native of Tierceville, near Bayeux, and had formerly been chaplain of Robert, count of Mortain, founded the celebrated abbey of Savigny in Normandy.[1] The name is inscribed on the Dives roll.

Nor. Peo., 433. *La Tapis. de Bayeux*, 101. *Rech.*, de La Rue, 57-8.
[1] Ord. Vit., III, 51-2.

WADARD. Wadard came to England in 1066 with duke William and held estates under Odo, bishop of Bayeux, in Kent and several other counties.[1] His name is clearly woven in the Bayeux tapestry and the question arises as to the identity of this personage who was not mentioned by the historians of the period, to whom such prominence is given in this ancient souvenir. He is depicted as directing the foraging of the duke's troops. His arms and his roll indicate him to have been a superior officer, entrusted with the sustenance of the invading forces. It has been suggested that he was a Norman established in England in the neighbourhood of Hastings, who brought duke William the news of the coming of Harold. It is more probable that he came from Bayeux, where he was of much consequence and well known, having been charged with the general supervision of the army. It would have been his duty to arrange for the assembling of the supplies at Saint-Valery and to see them safely placed on the ships. A very vital part of the expedition. It will be noted that the eminent commentators, Fowke, Freeman and Steenstrup, all consider one proof that the tapestry was designed and made shortly after the conquest, when the personages represented thereon were living, or fresh in memory, is the fact that the names of Turold, Vital and Wadard are inscribed upon it. They may perhaps have been persons of no very great importance, but had made themselves extremely popular by the distinguished services which they had rendered to the army. They would have been forgotten twenty or thirty years later, since no contemporary historians have recorded their deeds. Henry and Simon Wadard in 1278 in Essex were distrained to compel them to be knights.[2] Hence the family of Woodward. M. Léopold Delisle carries his name on the Dives roll.

Rech., de La Rue, 56-7. *The Bayeux Tapestry*, Fowke, 23. *Die Bayeux Tapete*, Steenstrup, 42. Freeman, III, 572. *La Tapisserie de Bayeux*, Leve, 189. *Nor. Peo.*, 449.
[1] *Introd. Domesd.*, II, 404.   [2] *Parliamentary Writs*, Palgrave.

PERSONAGES RECORDED

in the

BIOGRAPHIES

at the

CONQUEST OF ENGLAND

not inscribed

upon the

FALAISE TABLET

PERSONAGES MENTIONED IN THE TEXT

TABLET

WHEN THE HISTORICAL DATA WAS BEING COMPILED CONCERNING THE PRESENCE AT HASTINGS OF THE PERSONALITIES INSCRIBED UPON THE FALAISE ROLL THERE NECESSARILY CAME UNDER OBSERVATION OTHER MEMBERS OF THESE FAMILIES OR PERSONAGES CONNECTED WITH THEM WHO WERE NOT RECORDED UPON THE TABLET. SINCE THEY ARE MENTIONED IN THE TEXT AS COMPANIONS OF THE CONQUEROR WHERE THE INFORMATION IS GIVEN FOR THIS CONCLUSION THEIR NAMES ARE ENROLLED HERE.

M. J. C.

Adam de Brix
Adelolfus de Mert
Aitard de Vaux
Baudri de Limesi
Brient de Bretagne, comte de Vannes
Enisand Musard
Garnier de Senlis
Gautier de Saint-Valéry
Gautier du Bec
Germond de Saint-Ouen
Gilbert de Montfichet
Goisfrid de Ros
Gui, comte de Ponthieu
Guillaume d'Aubigny Ier
Guillaume de Brix
Guillaume de l'Aune
Hervé d'Hélion
Hubert de Rie " le Jeune "
Hugue Bourdet
Hugue de Vesly
Maurin de Caen
Mile de Vesly
Néel de Monneville

Raoul d'Asnières
Raoul de Beaufou
Raoul Painel
Renouf de Saint-Valéry
Renouf Pevrel
Richard de l'Aigle (de Aquila)
Richard de Flandre
Robert Bigot
Robert d'Armentières
Robert Fitz Picot
Robert Fitz Richard
Robert Le Archer
Robert Le Blond
Robert de Todeni
Robert de Vesly
Robert de Vieuxpont
Robert de Vitot
Robert de Vitrie
Roger d'Ivri
Ruaud l'Adoubé (Musard)
Serlon de Ros
Tihel de Héron

SUPPLEMENTAL BIOGRAPHIES
OF COMPANIONS OF
DUKE WILLIAM

THE AVAILABLE FACTS CONCERNING THE PERSONAGES HERE GIVEN
PERMITS THE ASSUMPTION OF THEIR PRESENCE AT SENLAC, WHOSE
BIOGRAPHIES HAVE BEEN INTENTIONALLY CONDENSED. IT WOULD
BE SUPERFLUOUS TO REPEAT THE INFORMATION ALREADY RE-
CORDED CONCERNING THEM WHICH CAN BE ASCERTAINED BY
CONSULTING THE REFERENCES. THE SELECTION WAS MADE FROM
MANY NAMES FOR WHOM PARTICIPATION AT HASTINGS HAS BEEN
SPECIFICALLY CLAIMED, BUT IS LIMITED BECAUSE THERE WAS NOT
TIME FOR FURTHER RESEARCHES.

M. J. C.

ADAM FITZ DURAND. From Maloures, or Malesoures, near Saint-Brieux, in Brittany. Durand de Malesoure lived *c.* 1040 and had two sons, who came to England in 1066, named Adam Fitz Durand, a tenant-in-chief in Essex in 1086, and Fulcher de Maloure. The name Durand occurs on the rolls of Duchesne, Holinshed and Lelànd. Fulcher possessed in barony in Rutland as well as Walgrove in Northamptonshire from the countess Judith in 1086 ; from whence the Walgrave family. The name is carried on the rolls of Holinshed and Brompton.

Northamptonsh., Bridges, II, 127. *Nor. Peo.*, 195. Cle., II, 281. *Rech. Domesd.*, 51.

AMFROI DE CONDÉ. The name of Amfrid Camerarine is recorded as a witness to a charter in Normandy in 1066 [1] who held a barony of 26 lordships in chief in England, 1086 (Domesday). Robert, his son, gave his estate of Condé to Holy Trinity, Caen, in 1082, [2] and is called Robert de Condy, in England in 1103. [3] His brother, Audin de Condé, was bishop of Bayeux in 1112 ; another brother, Richard de Condé, accompanied duke Robert to Palestine in 1096, and Turstin de Condé was archbishop of York in 1119. [4] William de Condé (Willm' de Conden), mentioned in a charter concerning a donation of land to the church of Ste-Marie of Rouen in 1105, immediately following the names of William Crispin junior and his brother Manasses, [5] suggests that he was akin to Pierre de Condé, the son of Emma, daughter of Gilbert Crispin I, both doubtless here connected. Robert de Condé, a descendant of this Pierre, rendered in 1131 an accompt for relief of land of his father in Lincolnshire. [6] Pierre probably was the father of Roger de Condé, husband of the heiress Adelaide de Cheney referred to in a charter of king Stephen (1141) as " Adelais de Condie " when he reinstated her in the possession of her lands. [7] One speculates upon a relationship between Amfroi and Emma, but it is perplexing because the *Crispin genealogy* only chronicles her son Pierre.

Nor. Peo., 207.
[1] *Gall. Christ.*, XI, instru. 60.   [2] *G.C.* 70.   [3] *Mon. Angl.*, i, 514.   [4] Des Bois. [5] Arch. Seine Inf. G. fonds du chap. 8740. [6] *Sub. tit.* Lincoliescira ; *vide* Gilbert Crispin.   [7] Stapleton, II, cliii, cliv. *Hist. and Antiq. of Horncastle*, Wier, and Cle., II, 59 ; *vide*, 185.

ANCHETIL DE GRAI. From Grai between Bayeux and Caen. M. de Ste-Marie in *Researches sur le Domesday* states that this Anchetil belonged to a family of considerable importance in the Bessin, who were sires de Luc and Grai. In 1082 Gisla, daughter of Turstin de Grai, made a donation to Holy Trinity at Caen, which convent she entered. [1] He was the son of Hugh, brother of another Turstin de Grai who remained in Normandy, both sons of Turgis. Anchetil came to England with the Conqueror and held lands in Oxford, 1086 (Domesday), viz. Redrefield (Rotherfield) and five other lordships from William Fitz Osberne (Domesday). Columbanus de Gray, his son, witnessed a charter of Raoul de Limesay, *temp.* Henry I, [2] whose sons Robert and Roger held extensive lands in 1165 as recorded in the *Liber Niger*. Hence the lords of Grey, earls of Kent and Stamford, marquesses of Dorset, dukes of Suffolk and the Greys, earles of Tancarville. The Greys were also the ancestors of lady Jane Grey. The claimed Grey descent from Arlette's father said to have held the castle of Croy in Picardy is incorrect.

Rech. Domesd., 163-70. *Nor. Peo.*, 270. Cle., II, 87.
[1] *Gall. Christ.*, XI, Instr. 71.   [2] *Mon.*, i, 331.

ANSFROI DE **VAUBADON.** The name Vaubadon, Valbadon, Vaberon or Vabadune occurs thrice in Domesday. Ansfrid de Vaubadon, apparently the head of the family, was a baron in Northamptonshire, where he also held under Odo, bishop of Bayeux. Osmond "de Valle Badonis" was a sub-tenant in Herefordshire and is mentioned in England during the reign of King William.[1] Renouf the third under-held' in Kent, some of whose descendants occur later at Shipborne. They were seated at Hatcham, Surrey, *temp.* Henry II, under the name Vabadune. The family probably came to the conquest under the banner of bishop Odo, and Delisle records all three at Hastings. The name also occurs on the roll of Holinshed.

Cle., III, 250.
[1] *Hertfordsh.*, Chauncy.

ANSGER DE **CRIQUETOT.** From Criquetot (now Cristot), near Dieppe. Cribett stands for Cricket, Criquet or Criquetot. This is a baronial family in England, and Ansger, who came over with the Conqueror, held lands in Suffolk from Mandeville in 1086. Hugo Fitz Ansger occurs in 1130[1] and his son, Hubert de Criketot, held two fees from Mandeville in 1165.[2] From them descends the family Hobart. The name appears on the rolls of Holinshed, Duchesne, Leland.

Cle., I, 217. *Nor. Peo.*, 287.
[1] *Rot. Pip.* [2] *Lib. Nig.*

ANSOLD DE **MAULE.** From Maule, five leagues from Paris in the French Vexin. Duchesne records Guarin de Maule, living *c.* 960, possibly the grandfather (but never the father as stated by *Norman People*) of Peter, seignior of Maule, "the rich Parisian" mentioned by Orderic Vital.[1] He informs us that Peter made a donation to the priory of Maule, a cell of Saint-Evroult, in 1076, with the consent of his wife Widesmouth and his sons Ansold, Theobald and William.[2] Peter had another son Guarin, also four daughters, and died *c.* 1100, having "lived to a good old age."[3] Ansold, the son of Peter, went to Greece, where he fought under Robert Guiscard in 1081,[4] and made a donation in 1106 to

the church of Sainte-Mary of Maule. He married Adeline, daughter of Raoul Malovisin, who held the castle of Mantes, by whom he had seven sons and two daughters, among whom were Peter the eldest, his heir, Guarin and Ansold.[5] We are further informed by Vital that Ansold (son of Peter) died in 1118, "having borne arms for 53 years,"[6] which dates back to 1065, and permits the assumption taking in conjunction with the other known facts that he was at Senlac. Guarin de Maule, his son, is stated by Burke and Cleveland to have been at Hastings. This is impossible, since he was an infant, if even born, at that time. Therefore the Guarin de Maule at the conquest was the brother of Ansold and the son of Peter. However, the Domesday tenant of this name, who could have been either one of these Guarins, acquired the lordship of Hatton in Yorkshire and other grants in Cleveland. Robert, his son, was a follower of David, later King of Scotland, and Robert's son fought in the battle of the Standard in 1138. From this family sprung the earls of Panmore (Douglas). The name occurs on the rolls of Holinshed and Leland.

Burke, 81. Cle., II, 295. *Nor. Peo.*, 326.
[1] Ord. Vit., II, 216. [2] *Ibid.* [3] *Ibid.*, 232. [4] *Ibid.*, 223. [5] *Ibid.*, 224. [6] *Ibid.*, 228.

ASCELIN GÖEL DE **PERCIVAL.** *Vide* Robert de Breherval.

AUBRI DE **VER.** Ver, a baronial name derived from Ver, near Bayeux and Caen, was included in the dowry of the duchess Judith. It was granted to this family before 1058, in which year Aubri was in possession of it.[1] He was the father of another Aubri de Ver who accompanied the Conqueror in 1066, and was in 1086 one of the great landowners of Domesday, who held his castle from the king at Hedingham, Essex, and founded Colne priory in that county, as a cell of Abingdon. He also held Kensington in Middlesex and was shorn a monk at Colne in his late years, having had five sons. He was ancestor of the earls of Oxford. Dives has Guillaume de Ver, and the name occurs on the rolls of Scriven, Holinshed, Brompton, Leland and Duchesne.

Dugdale. *Nor. Peo.*, 431, 440. Burke, 105. *Rech. Domesd.*, 86.
[1] *Gall. Christ.*, XI, 108.

AUVRAI D'ESPAGNE. From Espagne, near Pont-Audemer. In 1080 Gautier d'Espagne was a witness to a charter in favour of Saint-Evroult by Raoul de Toeni,[1] and may have been Raoul's uncle, viz. the brother of Roger de Toeni, surnamed d'Espagne. Gautier's sons, Hervé and Alured (Auvrai) d'Espagne, occur in England, 1086 (Domesday). The latter was a great baron and appears as tenant-in-chief in Devonshire, Wiltshire, Dorsetshire, Somersetshire, Herefordshire and Gloucestershire. Twenty-two of his lordships were in Somersetshire, and he was also an under-tenant in Wiltshire, Somersetshire and Gloucestershire. His male line became extinct with Isabella, probably his daughter and eventual heiress, who married Robert de Chandos I. Richard de Demeri held of him at Isle Brewers, Somerset (Domesday). From Hervé descended the Spains of Essex, who long continued to flourish. Dives records Richard, Auvrai and Hervé d'Espagne.

Cle., I, 223; III, 355. *Nor. Peo.*, 403. *Hist. of Essex*, Morant, 363. *Rech. Domesd.*, 132.
[1] Ord. Vit., II, 189.

AUVRAI DE LINCOLN. *Vide* Appendix 20.

AUVRAI MAUBENC. The name occurs as Malbeding, Malebanc, Maubant and Maubenc. Alured (Auvrai) and his brother William, both written in Domesday, came to the conquest doubtless in the train of Robert, count of Mortain. The former was pincerna to this house and held under count Robert thirty-five lordships in various counties. He was a tenant-in-chief in Lincolnshire and an under-tenant in Kent, Sussex, Berkshire, Dorsetshire, Somersetshire, Devonshire and Cornwall. We find among the charters of the abbey of Troarn in 1068 and another of the bishopric of Bayeux in 1083, Alured Malbeding, brother of William. Another was executed by Roger, son of this William Maubenc, dated 1105, in which occurs Ranulf,

vicomte de Vire, parent of Robert Maubant, and in the same year one of Alured de Combray, nephew of the same Ranulf. About 1122 there appears an Alured Pincerna and William his son in a charter of Henry I for the restoration of the abbey of Grestain.[1] Delisle carries Guillaume Maubenc on his roll.

Rech. Domesd., 128–9.
[1] *Mon.*, ii, 984.

AUVRAI DE MERLEBERGE. The great Domesday baron, Alured (Auvrai) de Merleberge, had been a landowner in England prior to the conquest, and was the nephew of one Osberne, who held two manors in Herefordshire during the time of Edward the Confessor. He probably fought at Hastings under the banner of William Fitz Osberne, by whom he was greatly enfeoffed. At the compilation of Domesday he was tenant-in-chief in Herefordshire and Wiltshire and held manors in Surrey, Hampshire and Somersetshire. Agnes, the daughter of Alured who married Thurstin, is also recorded in Domesday. Merleberge is the ancient name of Marlborough. Leland carries this family on his roll and Delisle records Auvrai de Merleberge.

Castles of Herefordshire and their Lords, Robinson. Cle., III, 384. Eyton.

BAGOD D'ARRAS. Wago, Bago or Bagod de Arras was descended from the Carloviginian counts of Artois, whose descendants were advocates of Arras, lords of Bethune and castellans of Saint-Omer, and were among the greatest nobles of Flanders. In 1075, Robert sire de Bethune, or Wethume, advocate of Arras, died, and had issue Robert, ancestor of the advocates of Arras, earls of Albemarle and dukes of Sully; second, Bagod d'Arras, who, in 1075, witnessed a charter in Flanders[1] and came to England at the conquest, where his descendants were of the line of Bagod and Stafford, dukes of Buckingham. He held, 1086, Bromley in Stafford from Robert de Toeni. This same " Bagod (Bagot) Bromley " is still held by his descendants in the male line. The name occurs on the rolls of Scriven, Holinshed, Worcester and Brompton.

Nor. Peo., 146. Cle., I, 194.
[1] Bouquet, XI, 106.

BLUNDEL. The family of Blunden, Blundel or Blondel were seated in Lancashire from the time of the conquest,[1] where they were lords of Ince Blundell. They came to England in the train of William Malet, and William Blondel still held three knights' fees under the honour of the Malets at Eye in 1165.[2] A branch were barons of Edenderry, viscounts of Blundell in Ireland. The name is recorded on the rolls of Holinshed, Duchesne, Leland, Brompton and Scriven.

Nor. Peo., 163. Cle., I, 109.
[1] *Lancash.,* Baines.   [2] *Lib. Nig.*

DAVID D'ARGENTAN. The town and castle of Argentan, Berry, was held in 1080 by Geoffry sire d'Argentan, perhaps the brother of this Norman companion of Duke William at the conquest of England. David was a Domesday baron in Cambridgeshire and Bedfordshire and his manor of Wymondley in the former county was held by grand serjeanty " to serve the king upon the day of his coronation with a silver cup." He married the daughter of Fitz Tek, and his son or grandson William was the father of Reginald, the first member of the family of prominence who died about 1139.

British topogr., 186, ms. Dugdale, I, 614. Camden, 353. *Black Book,* 316, 322. Burke, 14. *Nor. Peo.,* 142. Cle., I, 11. *Rech. Domesd.,* 208.

EUDES FITZ SPIRWIC. The Domesday baron Eudes Fitz Spirwic or Sperwin was probably a Breton and, according to Banks and *Norman People,* came to England in 1066, where he obtained Toteshall, Lincolnshire, with other estates in that county as well as in Norfolk and Suffolk which he held in barony and in chief 1086 (Domesday). From him descended the barons of Toteshall and the family of Denton.

Nor. Peo., 414.

FITZ BERTRAN DE PELEIT. The identity of this noble Breton who followed duke William to Senlac has not been determined, but he must have been of high degree and much consequence. Wace, in referring to the contingent which came in the train of Alain Fergant, count of Brittany, remarks : " Alain Felgan (Fergant) also

came to the crossing and brought with him great baronage from among the Bretons. De Peleit le filz Bertran (l. 11510) and the sire de Dinan (Alain Fitz Flaald) came also ; and Raoul de Gaël and many Bretons from many castles." Wace must have considered him the most important of the count of Brittany's barons, otherwise he would not have mentioned his name first ; nevertheless, nothing else is known about him. The manner in which Wace has recorded him may be interpreted as the son of Bertram de Peleit, Bertran the son of Peleit or de Peleit, the son of Bertran (*vide* Robert Bertram Le Tort).

Wace, Taylor, 118. Plan., II, 280.

FULCHER DE MALOURE. *Vide* Adam Fitz Durand.

GAUTIER DE DOUAI. From Douai, near Lille. Walter de Douai was sometimes called Walter de Bahantune, and in 1065 as castellan of Douai he witnessed a charter of Philippe I.[1] He and Hugh his brother occur in 1066,[2] when Walter participated in the invasion of England, and in 1072 witnessed a charter of Wattignies abbey, Flanders, wherein he appears as the son of Urso de Douai.[3] He held a great barony in Devonshire and Somersetshire, 1086 (Domesday). From him descended the barons of Bampton, Devonshire. Dives has Fouque and Goscelin de Douai.

Cle., II, 392. *Nor. Peo.,* 233. *Devonsh.,* Pole, 22.
[1] Bouquet, XI, 111.   [2] *Ibid.,* 345.
[3] *Ibid.,* 106.

GAUTIER LE EWRUS. Gautier the Fortunate, Le Ewrus (Heureux) erroneously called de Ewrus and de Evreux by Père Anselme, Le Brasseur and others, was of the family of Roumare (Rosmar) as proven by Bowles. Gautier accompanied duke William to the conquest, receiving extensive grants of land, including the lordships of Salisbury and Ambresbery. His hereditary possessions were inherited by his eldest son, Walter, and his younger son, Edward de Evreux (Edwardus vicecomes, Sarisbriensis), as he is inscribed in Domesday, received his estates in Buckinghamshire, Dorsetshire, Hampshire, Herefordshire, Middlesex, Somersetshire, Surrey and Wiltshire. He bore the standard of Henry I in the battle of Brémule with distinction. His grandson, William Fitz Patric, was created by empress Matilda earl of Salisbury, whose only daughter and heiress, Ela, married William Longue-Epée, natural son of Henry II by the fair Rosamond. From this family descended Robert Devereux, the ill-fated favourite of queen Elizabeth, also the Devereux's lord Ferrers of Chartley and earls of Essex.

Cle., I, 324. Burke, 46. *Vide* 3, 50, 188.

GAUTIER FITZ AUTIER. Aother, a great noble of Aquitaine, occurs about 660,[1] and a grant was made to the abbey of Fleury, near Orleans, by another Aother *c.* 987.[2] Autier, his son, was lord of the castle of Mortaine, Aquitaine, *c.* 1030, and had Gautier Fitz Other (Autier), who came to England at the conquest and was castellan of the castle of Wildesore (Windsor), which is mentioned in a charter of the abbey of Abingdon.[3] Ayor the Saxon held under him in Middlesex at the compilation of Domesday.[4] His son Gerald was castellan of the Welsh castle of Carew, whose grandson by deed of 1212 received Molesford in Berkshire. Hence the Fitzgeralds, the earls of Kildare, dukes of Leinster, the earls of Desmond, the marquesses of Lansdowne, the barons and viscounts of Windsor, the barons of Decies, earls of Totness, barons Carew, etc.

Cle., II, 169. Nor. Peo., 62, 243. *Rech. Domesd.,* 253.
[1] Bouquet, X, 342. [2] *Ibid.* [3] Harl. ms. 294, no. 3324. [4] *Domesday,* Middlesex, fo. 130.

GUARIN DE MAULE. *Vide* Ansold de Maule.

GUI DE CRAON. This noble lord was descended from Hunrok, said to have been the last king of the Lombards, the son of Desiderius, and also from Adelbert II, king of Italy, 950,[1] whose son became count of Burgundy, *c.* 1000. The latter's son, Reginald of Burgundy, had Robert, who received the barony of Craon in Anjou from Geoffry Martel in 1052, and from his elder son descended the barons of Craon.[2] His

younger son, Gui de Craon, accompanied the Conqueror to England and held sixty-one lordships by barony in 1086, and was ancestor of the Crowne family in England. Ingelram Peisson, *temp.* Henry I, acquired from de Craon lands in Neuton, Trinkingham and in Lincoln.[3] The Dives roll carries Gui de Craon.

Nor. Peo., 217, 344.
[1] *Art. de ver. les dates.* [2] *Mais. Bretagne,* Du Paz, 735. [3] *Mon.,* i, 753.

GUIDO DE SAINT-MAUR. Saint-Maur, near Mortain, Normandy. Guido came to England in 1066 and was deceased before 1086, when William Fitz Guido, his son, held a barony in Wiltshire, Gloucestershire and Somersetshire (of which Portishead was one) from Geoffroi, bishop of Coutances.[1] He made conquests in Wales, which his family afterwards held. From this family sprung queen Jane Seymour; the dukes of Somerset and the marquesses of Hertford. The name is inscribed upon the rolls of Holinshed, Duchesne and Scriven.

Nor. Peo., 395. Cle., III, 147.
[1] *Mon.,* ii, 530.

GUILLAUME CORBON. *Vide* Hugue Corbon.

GUILLAUME MAUBENC. *Vide* Auvrai Maubenc.

GUILLAUME DE VALECHERVILLE. From Valecherville, also designated Wallichville, or Warlanville, in Caux. Fulco de Valecherville was living 1063, and his son William de Wallichville came to the conquest in 1066, holding grants in Derbyshire, but died before 1086. Robert, his oldest son, held Stanley, Derbyshire, 1086 (Domesday) and several lordships in Nottinghamshire from the king, and was, as "Robert de Stanley," sheriff of Staffordshire, 1124-9.[1] Ralph, the second son, received estates in Nottinghamshire from Henry I, and Walter (de Valiquerville), the third son, was in charge of the troops of Henry I at the castle of Vatteville, Normandy, in 1124, where he was captured.[2] Shortly afterwards it was demolished by the command of king Henry.[3] Hence the baronets Stanley, the celebrated earls of Derby, and the lords Monteagle.

Nor. Peo., 406.
[1] *Rot. Pip.*, 31 Hen. I.   [2] Ord. Vit., IV, 72.   [3] *Ibid.*, 77.

GUILLAUME DE VATTEVILLE. Vatteville-sur-Seine belonged to Hugh, bishop of Bayeux, who gave it to William, count of Talohu (d'Arques), but he lost it when he rebelled against duke William. It then reverted to the dukedom, but later was given to Roger de Beaumont, whose son, Robert count of Meulent, inherited it, where he owned a castle. On the rebellion of Waleran, the young son of Robert, in 1124, who had then succeeded his father, this castle was demolished by the command of king Henry I. Three of the name are entered in Domesday. William, head of this house, held in barony and in chief in Essex and Suffolk and also possessed Percinges under William de Warren with several manors. Robert held lands in Surrey with five manors elsewhere of Richard de Tonbridge, and Richard, the third member of the family was an under-tenant in Surrey. It is most probable that it was represented at Hastings, and the name occurs on the rolls of Holinshed, Duchesne, Leland and Delisle records all three. This family must not be confused with that of Valecherville.

Ord. Vit., III, 474, IV, 72, 77.   Stapleton, I, cliv, clv, clvi.   Cle., III, 270.

HAMON DE CLERVAUX. From Clairvaux, near Rodez, Aquitaine, or of the castle of Clairvaux in Anjou. Hamon de Clervaux is said to have come to England in the train of Alan Le Roux of Brittany, " and this tradition is confirmed by an illumination in Coll. mss.[1] that represents the earl receiving from the Conqueror the grant of his honour of Richmond, for among the banners displayed behind him is delineated the golden saltire of Clervaux." The name occurs on the rolls of Brompton, Leland and Duchesne.

Cle., I, 233.   *Nor. Peo.*, 201.
[1] Faustaina B. 7.

HERVÉ DE BOURGES. Geoffry Papabos was made viscount of Bourges 920.[1] Geoffry III, his grandson, re-built the abbey of Saint-Ambrose,

Bourges, 1012. He had issue Geoffry whose son Stephen was viscount of Bourges and Maldalbert, father of Hervé, de Bourges (Bituricensis). The latter accompanied the Conqueror to Senlac and held a great barony in Suffolk 1086 (Domesday). Henry Fitz Hervé, his son, witnessed a charge of Roger de Clare.[2] Hervé, brother of Henry Fitz Hervé, held in Suffolk under Péché and his son paid a fine in 1130.[3] The barony passed from the family *temp.* Stephen, and from them descended the marquesses of Bristol and the baronets Bathurst.

Nor. Peo., 284.
[1] Père Anselme, III, 216.   [2] *Mon.*, i, 731.   [3] *Rot. Pip.*

HERVÉ D'ESPAGNE. *Vide* Auvrai d'Espagne.

HUBERT HEUSÉ. An ancient French manuscript said to have been found in the abbey of Glastonbury when it was dissolved as well as the visitation of Dorset (1623), records that Hubert Heusé, a noble Norman, married the countess Helen, daughter of the fifth duke of Normandy (Richard III), and accompanied duke William to England, where he was invested with the dignity of high constable and extensive estates. From him descended the Husseys of Dorset and Kent. The name occurs on the rolls of Leland, Holinshed, Duchesne and Delisle.

Burke, 64.

HUGUE LE BOUTEILLIER. The feudal butler of the counts of Meulent (Robert de Beaumont) was Hugo Pincerna, who accompanied Robert to England in 1066 and in 1086 was a baron in Bedfordshire (Domesday). His son Ralph had the custody of his souzerain's estates in 1130 [1] and was a benefactor of Kenilworth priory.[2] Henry I confirmed his grants. His descendants were styled Le Boutiller and Butler of Waresley. From him issued also the earls of Lanesborough. The family continued to be hereditary butlers of the earls of Leicester and Meluent for a long time. The arms of the descendants of this family in various branches are those of the Butlers of Wemme.

Two other Pincernas are entered in Domesday : Richard, an under-tenant in Shropshire and Cheshire, where he held great estates and was the ancestor of the Butlers (Botelers) of Chester and made grants to Chester abbey about 1090,[3] and Robert, who was an under-tenant in Shropshire and was the butler of the earls of Shrewsbury in that shire. All of the above families retained the name Pincerna until some time after the conquest. Richard and Robert are sometimes referred to as " de Corcella."

Cle., I, 89. *Nor. Peo.*, 182, 198.
[1] *Rot. Pip.* [2] *Mon.*, ii, 115. [3] *Ibid.*, i, 201.

HUGUE CORBON. From the Corbon or Corbonnais, the ancient name of a district in Maine, bounded by Commanche l'Huisne and the Sarthe, also called Perche.[1] Four of the name are entered as under-tenants in Domesday, on which account the various rolls, as well as Burke and Delisle, are probably correct in recording this family at the battle of Hastings. Hugh Corbon was an under-tenant in Norfolk and Suffolk holding under Roger Bigot, William in Essex, another in Kent holding Peckeham of bishop Odo, and one in Warwickshire. The family spread to Derbyshire, Somersetshire, Devonshire and many other parts of England, and in the time of Henry II their seat was Corbin's Hall in Staffordshire, which was held by Robert Corbin. The name occurs on the rolls of Holinshed, Duchesne, and Leland and Delisle records Guillaume and Hugue.

Burke, 39. Cle., I, 219.
[1] Ord. Vit., I, 452, II, 108 and ed. n.

HUGUE DE GUIDVILLE. From Viville, Widville, Guidville, which was held of the Toeni family in Normandy. Hugue de Guidville came to England in 1066 and in 1086 held in Northampton and Leicester (Domesday). Robert, his son, *temp.* Henry I, granted the tithes of Guidville to Conches abbey, with the consent of Ralph·de Toeni.[1] Elizabeth Widville, sister of the celebrated earl Rivers, was the queen of Edward IV, from which family descends the baronets Wyville. The name occurs on the rolls of Holinshed, Leland, Worcester, Dives.

Nor. Peo., 451. Cle., III, 251.
[1] *Gall. Christ.*, XI, Instr. 132.

JUHEL DE MAYENNE. From Maine, a Breton noble who held vast

baronies in Devonshire, 1086. He appears in Domesday as Judhel de Totenais (Totness), so styled from his barony of that name, the possessor also of Barnstaple, he was greatly esteemed by the Conqueror. This Juhel, son of an Alfred (Alvred, Alured), was father of Aiulf (Alfred), a Domesday tenant-in-chief who held land under him before the conquest.[1] This fortifies the conclusion of Juhel's presence at Senlac, and in addition, Testa de Neville[2] affirms that Warin Fitz Juel held a knight's fee which had been granted to Judael de Mayenne by the earl of Mortain at the conquest. From whence the Jewells, and the lords of Newhaven. Delisle mistakenly takes Judael for a member of the family of Toeni. From Juhel descended Juhel de Meduana, who witnessed empress Matilda's charter to Geoffry de Mandeville.

Nor. Peo., 327. Lysons. Cle., II, 301. *Rech. Domesd.*, 68. *Feud. Eng.*, Round, 329.
[1] Add. *Exon Domesday*, fo. 426. [2] I, 184.

NÉEL DE TOENI. Néel de Toeni, surnamed de Stafford, was probably a younger brother of Raoul the standard bearer. He held Dakelow, Gresley and some other manors in Derbyshire and Staffordshire, 1086. His son William founded an Augustinian priory *temp.* Henry I, and Roger, the next heir, was the first to bear the name of Gresley. From him descended the Gresleys, and Castle-Gresley took the name from his castle.

Cle., III, 177. Plan., I, 226. *Domesd.*, sub-title, Derbysh., 323. Dugdale, 156. *Baronetage of England*, Wotton, ed. Kimber & Johnston, 55. *Magna Britannia*, vol. 5, 53, Derbysh. *Gresley of Drakelow*, Lysons. *Vide* 97.

NOËL. The foundation of the priory of Raunton in Staffordshire makes it clear that Noël came to the conquest of England, for which he received the manors of Ellenhall, Wiverstone, Podmore and Milnese. Robert, lord of Ellenhall, was granted, *temp.* Henry I, the greater part of Gainsborough from the prior of Coventry. He founded the monastery of Raunton in Staffordshire. From him descends the Nöels of Hilcote, those of Rutland and Leicester, as well as the earls of Gainsborough.

Burke, 84.

NORMAN D'ARCY. From Arci, Normandy. Norman D'Arcy held direct from the king thirty-three lordships in Lincolnshire, of which Nocton was the chief seat of his barony where his son Robert founded an Augustinian priory. Camden compiled a pedigree which is still in possession of the family, which descends from the celebrated John, lord D'Arcy, summoned to parliament in 1322. The name is recorded by Holinshed, Duchesne, Leland, Worcester, Guillaume Tailleur and Dives.

Cle., I, 33. Burke, 75.

RAOUL DE BRANCHE. From Saint-Denis de Branche. Raoul de Branche of the Norman family of Branches, whose estates lay in Caux, accompanied William de Warren to England in 1066, where he received a grant of two knights' fees, of which Gresham was the chief seat. Barsham was also held from the de Wancis, tenants of Warren. Raoul and his son Richard occur in the charters of Walshingham abbey. Walter, son of the latter, in 1165 held half a knight's fee of the king in Caux, Normandy, and his grandson Richard occurs *temp.* Henry II.[1] From them the Gresham family descends. The name is listed by Holinshed and Duchesne.

Nor. Peo., 268. Cle., I, 190. Vide *Norfolk*, Blomfield.

[1] *R.C.R.*, ii.

RENAUD DE VAUTORT. From Vautortes in Mayenne. Reginald de Vautort or Valletort accompanied other barons of Maine to the conquest and received thirty-three lordships in Cornwall from Robert, count of Mortaine (1086, Domesday). Roger de Valletort, baron of Huberton, Devon, his grandson, was the ancestor of the Valletorts of North Tawton and those of Acland, from whence this family. They also held extensively in Devon. *Norman People* are of the opinion that his brothers Hugh and Goisfrid came also with him to the conquest.

Nor. Peo., 134, 317.

RICHARD D'ENGAGNE. From Engen or Ingen, near Boulogne. Richard accompanied the Conqueror to the conquest, and possessed a barony of the king in Buckingham with Redinger in Huntingdon (Domesday). Vitalis d'Ingen, his son, *temp.* Henry I, had Richard, who married a daughter of Alberic de Ver, earl of Oxford, and was baron of Blatherwick. From him descended the lords of Brickhill, Buckinghamshire, and in the female line the earls of Feversham and the baronets Duncombe. *Norman People* says his brother William was at Hastings also. The name occurs on the rolls of Holinshed and Duchesne and Delisle records Richard.

Cle., II, 9. *Nor. Peo.*, 232.

ROBERT DE BREHERVAL. This potent lord was one of the eight sons of Eudo, count of Brittany, who held the castle and barony of Ivry in Normandy by the service of three knights' fees. He came to England, accompanied by his son Ascelin Göel de Percival, with the Conqueror and fought at Senlac, for which service he received the lordships of Kary and Harpetre in Somersetshire. He soon after returned home and died a monk in the abbey of Bec. He is referred to in the Battle abbey roll as Lovell. His son, Ascelin Göel de Percival, received his father's estates in England and is entered in Domesday as a large landowner in Somersetshire, where he held the barony of Castle-Cary.

Ord. Vit., II, 487. Cle., II, 188. Burke, 93. *Vide* Jean d'Ivri, 190.

ROBERT DE GRENVILLE. From Grenneville in the Côtentin, fief of the baron of Saint-Denis le Gaste, of which noble family this, with the family of Bigod, Trailly, Beauchamp, Montague, Saint-Denis and Meurdrac, are believed to have been branches, and the supposition is confirmed by their arms. Robert and his father, William de Grenville, witnessed a charter of Gautier Giffard for Bolbec abbey in 1061.[1] The former accompanied the Conqueror to England and received from Gautier Giffard three knights' fees in Buckinghamshire, which passed to his descendants. His son Richard married Isabel, daughter and eventual co-heir of Gautier Giffard I, earl of Buckingham. Burke, Cleveland and *Norman People* all agree that Robert accompanied the Conqueror. The name appears on the rolls of Leland, Brompton, Worcester and Holinshed.

Nor. Peo., 268. Cle., II, 113. Burke, 61. *Vide* 90.

[1] *Neustria Pia*, 402.

ROGER DE COURCELLES. Hugh Pincerna witnessed a charter in favour of Saint-Amand, Rouen, Normandy, before the conquest,[1] and William de Courcelles, his son,[2] was the father of Roger de Courcelles, who held a great barony in chief in Shropshire, Somersetshire, Wiltshire, etc., 1086 (Domesday). Roger is said to have been the brother of Robert Pincerna, butler of the earls of Shrewsbury, and Richard Pincerna, holding the same dignity of the earls of Chester. This companion of the Conqueror espoused the claim of duke Robert to the throne of England against his brother Henry, and the latter on his ascension to the throne deprived Roger of his vast estates. His son, Roger de Courcelles, later received from king Henry I a grant of the hundred of Frome, Somersetshire, held by the service of one knight's fee. Hugh, his son, was living in 1165, from whom descended the Churchills and the great duke of Marlborough. Delisle carries Robert de Courcelles, which refers to Robert Pincerna (*vide* Hugue Le Bouteillier).

Rech. Domesd., 119. *Nor. Peo.*, 198, 437. Cle., I, 93.
    [1] *Mon.*, i, 996.   [2] *Gall. Christ.*, XI, 64.

TURCHIL LE ROUX. The family Le Rufus, Le Rous or Le Roux was Norman and held lands near Rouen from the county of Breteuil.[1] It was represented at the conquest of England, according to *Norman People*, by Turchil Le Roux, who held lands in Norfolk from Allen Fitz Flaald,[2] which statement is published by Cleveland without comment. Burke is of the opinion that this personage was Radulfus Le Rufus. Be this as it may, the representative at Hastings was probably the father or grandfather of Ralph the Red (Le Roux), who stood very high in the favour of king Henry I, to whom he rendered great service. He went to the Crusade in 1106[3] and on his return was in command of king Henry's forces which opposed Amaury de Montfort[4] and William Crispin III in their bitter feud with the king. He operated from his castle of Pont-Echanfré, near Bernai in the Norman Vexin, in their war early in 1119[5] and during the same year saved the life of Richard, king Henry's son.[6] He perished in the wreck of the *Blanche-Nef* with the king's two sons, and his death was more greatly lamented by that monarch than any of the many others of the English nobility who were drowned in that unfortunate accident.[7] The name is carried on the rolls of Holinshed, Duchesne and Scriven.

Nor. Peo., 383.   Cle., III, 63.   Burke, 94.
    [1] Duchesne.   [2] *Mon.*, i, 627.   [3] Ord. Vit., III, 367.   [4] *Ibid.*, 457, 471.   [5] *Ibid.* [6] *Ibid.*, 472.   [7] *Ibid.*

APPENDIX

APPENDIX

OF

ADDITIONAL INFORMATION

ON THE

BIOGRAPHIES

Appendix 1

GUI COMTE DE PONTHIEU

NOTE 2.—There is a difference of opinion to whom Guy, bishop of Amiens (537), referred in recording the presence of "The noble heir of Ponthieu" (Pontivi nobilis haeres) at the battle of Hastings. Guy I, count of Ponthieu, succeeded his brother Enguerrand II, slain before Arques in 1053, who had married Adélaide (sister of the Conqueror), and in 1062 captured Harold inadvertently driven by a storm upon his coast. His wife Ada died during his lifetime, by whom he had a daughter Agnès, married to Robert de Belèsme, still living at the date of her father's death c. 1100. He is reputed to have had a son Ivo, associated with him in the government of Ponthieu, who predeceased him. It is taken by Freeman for granted that Ivo is intended while Planché wonders whether it was not Guy, bishop of Amiens, himself. Others say that Ivo is a defective reading for Guy.[1] Latter-day researches indicate that it was count Guy I who was at Senlac and the name should have appeared upon the roll.

Ord. Vit., Coll. Gizot, XXVI, 151.   [1] Plan., I, 157-9 ; Freeman, III, 499 ; Historians' History, XVIII, 155, 5th ed. Vide Eudes, comte de Boulogne.

Appendix 2

GUILLAUME, COMTE D'EVREUX

NOTE 3.—Matthew Paris calls William Crispin III, who fought in the battle of Brémule in 1119, count of Evreux, " Willelmus Crispinus consul Ebriocensis," [1] and Père Anselme, who apparently copied him,[2] remarks that William called Crispin, count of Evreux, died in 1118 ; both are mistaken, as William, count of Evreux, and William

Crispin III were separate and distinct personalities. Orderic Vital [3] is quite clear about it. The error undoubtedly occurred from the following passage in the Chronique of Robert de Torigny,[4] referring to the winter of 1111-12, " Henry king of England banished the count of Evreux and William Crispin from Normandy " (Rex Anglorum Henricus expulavit consulem Ebroicensem et Willerum Crispinum a Normannia). Matthew Paris probably overlooked the " et " and read count of Evreux William Crispin (Consulem Ebroicensem Willerum Crispinum).

[1] Matthaei Parisensis Historia Anglorum, sir Frederick Madden, I, 227 (Chron. and Mem. of Great Britain and Ireland Rolls, series no. 57) ; Roger of Wendover, Giles, I, 471.   [2] Père Anselme, II, 478.   [3] Ord. Vit., III, 443 ; vide Guillaume Crispin.   [4] Chron. de Torigny, I, 142.

Appendix 3

GUILLAUME MALET (CONTEVILLE)

NOTE 1.—About 990 Robert the son of Maleth with Osborn de Longueville, William de Breteuil, Gilbert de Menill and others gave the church of Pictariville to religious uses.[1]

NOTE 6.—Conteville in the arrondissement of Pont-Audemer-sur-Risle, department of the Eure, Normandy, was from ancient times the property of the dukes of Normandy and was only given to Herluin de Conteville, the husband of Arlette, mother of the Conqueror, for life.[2] After his death it was probably possessed by Arlette, or if not, it doubtless reverted to the duchy. In any event, William Malet II, son of William Malet I, gave in 1121 the " Manor of Conteville with the church and with all the dependencies of the church and of the manor " to the abbey of

Bec.[3] This was confirmed by both kings Henry I and II. The original charter is preserved amongst the archives of the department of the Eure (H. 28) and the text was reproduced by dom Jouvelin.[4] Conteville was held by this monastery until 1571, when the " abbey of Bec gave as a fief the land and seigniory of Conteville to the lord of Ouilli for sixty pounds rent."[5] How the property was acquired by the Malet family is not clear, unless Gilbert Crispin obtained it from Arlette through a marriage or an alliance, who, at his death, bequeathed it to his daughter Esilia, wife of William Malet I.[6] It would then have passed to her son, William Malet II, the monk of Bec, directly from her.[7]

[1] *Gall. Christ.*, XI, Instr. 139.   [2] *Le Prevost, Mem.*, I, 538.   [3] " Ex dono Will. Malet manerium de Contevilla, cum ecclesia et omnibus, ejus dem ecclesiae et manerii pertinentiis " from the confirmation of Henry II ; *Neustria Pia*, 424 ; *Mon.*, ii, ch. no. 2, 1068. [4] Bibl. nat. lat. 13905, fo. 45.   [5] *Le Prevost Mem.*, I, 538.   [6] *Vide* Gilbert Crispin. [7] *Ibid. Vide* addenda.

Appendix 4

HEREDITARY   VISCOUNTS   OF VEXIN

The hereditary viscountcy of Vexin was granted by duke William c. 1045 to William Crispin I for the purpose of defending it against the French, who were continually invading that part of Normandy. The Crispin family were, beyond doubt, definitely deprived of it by king Henry I of England after the capture of William Crispin II at Tinchebrai, where he was one of the commanders, for his support in that battle of Henry's brother, duke Robert Courteheuse.[1] There is nothing on record to indicate that his son and heir, William Crispin III, or any other of his descendants, ever possessed it, and this may have been one of the reasons for the bitter hatred which this latter powerful seignior consistently held for king Henry. Many of the Norman nobles looked upon Henry as an impostor, for Robert was the oldest, and he had usurped the throne while his brother was returning from a crusade which he had led to the Holy Land.

[1] *Vide* 37, 170 ; c. 8, l. 11 ; photograph charter facing 170, l. 17 ; 174 ; c. 13, l. 11. *Vide* Guillaume Crispin 1re ; Ord. Vit., III, 264.

Appendix 5

SIRE DE GACÉ

NOTE 4.—Robert de Sablé, who revolted against Geoffry Plantagenet, count of Anjou, in 1136,[1] was lord of Gacé and son of Lisard de Sablé and Thiephaine de Briollay la Chevrière, eldest daughter of Warmaise

de Jarzé by her first husband, Geoffry de Briollay. Thiephaine received Jarzé from her mother, whose second husband was Amaury Crispin, lord of Châteauceaux.[2] Lisard was the son of Reginald de Sablé and grandson of Solomon de Sablé and Adélaïde, fourth daughter of Giroie and Gisla, daughter of Turstan de Bastembourg.[3] Giroie was the son of Arnold le Gros of Courcerant and grandson of Abbo le Breton, descended from the highest nobles of France and Brittany.[4] Robert and Hugh, sons of Giroie, with Robert de Vitot murdered Gilbert, count of Brionne, and their brother Fulk who were quietly riding with their brother-in-law Wacelin de Pont-Echangré,[5] as already stated.

[1] Ord. Vit., IV, 156.   [2] *Vide* Geoffroi du Bec.   [3] *Rech. Domesd.*, 245.   [4] Ord. Vit., I, 389.   [5] Jumièges, 156.

Appendix 6

HAMON LE SENESCHAL (ASNEBEC)

NOTE 3.—Wace chronicles (l. 13749) " Cil d'Onebec." Asnebec is a commune near Vire. It is not at present known to whom he refers. However, there is evidence to show that it had no particular seignior at the time of the conquest, but belonged to Robert de Crévecœur, in which event Wace probably referred to him, since he has not done so otherwise, and Robert is generally conceded to have been at Hastings. On the other hand, from a charter in favour of the abbey of Saint-Wandrille, it apparently was possessed by the seigniors of Beaumont-le-Roger at about this time, as Roger de Beaumont in the presence and by the consent of his sons, Robert and Henry, gave to it the church of Asnebec, which leaves it an open question. It was in the latter family c. 1200 when Robert de Neubourg, first of the name, baron of Asnebec, in part, son of Raoul de Neubourg and his wife Amaurie Painel, married Isabeau Crispin, lady of Livarot, daughter of William Crispin son of Joscelyn Crispin, who brought him that barony. Livarot had descended to her directly from William Crispin I. This Robert was the grandson of Robert de Neubourg, who was buried at the abbey of Bec in 1159, a younger son of Henry de Beaumont, earl of Warwick, the second son of Roger de Beaumont. The arms borne by Robert were bendy, or and gules, with label, azure, by some described as bendy, or and azure with a label, gules. The arms of Isabeau were given by La Roque (I, 269), Père Anselme (VI, 633), *Le Prevost Mem.* (II, 6), *Statistique du Calvados*, de Caumont (V, 673), as lozengy argent and gules, but they were undoubtedly fusils the same as her father bore.

Appendix 7

RICHARD DE VERNON (SIRE DE NEAUHOU)

NOTE 6.—Wace (l. 13556) chronicles "sire de Neauhou" from Nehou, arrondissement of Volognes, which fief belonged to the Saint-Sauveur family, but passed to that of Reviers-Vernon, probably at the time of or shortly after the banishment of Néel by duke William, with whom it remained until the end of the 13th century. Wace may here refer to Richard de Vernon, as stated under that paragraph, if not, with the information available it is impossible to identify this personage.

Ord. Vit., II, 40. Le Prevost, *Notes, Wace,* II, 236. *Wace,* Taylor, 212. Plan., II. 206. *Rech.,* de Gerville, 17. *Vide* Richard de Vernon.

Appendix 8

RAOUL DE GAEL
(Concerning the counts of Vexin)

NOTE 2.—The treaty of Saint-Clair-sur-Epte in 911 [1] divided the Vexin into the Norman Vexin (capital, Gisors) and the French Vexin (capital, Pontoise). The former was bounded by the Andelle, the Seine and the Epte, and the latter embraced the territory from the Oise, on both banks of the Seine, including Amiens, Chaumont and Pontoise, to the Epte also, thus making the last-named river the frontier between them.[2] On the death of Robert, king of France, Henry the eldest son was opposed in his rights to the throne by his step-mother, queen Constance, who supported Henry's younger brother Robert, duke of Burgundy. Robert (I) the Magnificent, duke of Normandy, came to the aid of Henry in 1032, at which time he invaded France with a strong army ; this assistance permitted Henry to place himself securely upon the throne. For these services, he ceded to duke Robert the whole of the French Vexin, to which arrangement, Dreu, who was then count of Vexin, readily agreed, because duke Robert had previously given to him in marriage his cousin Goda, sister of Edward the Confessor, who came under his protection after Canute the Great had taken possession of the English throne.[3] By this marriage Dreu had issue : Gautier le Vieux, count of Pontoise, Chaumont and Mantes,[4] Ralf, earl of Hereford (or the East Angles),[5] Fouque, bishop of Amiens,[6] and Amaury of Pontoise, the Delicate.[7] Dreu accompanied duke Robert on his pilgrimage to the Holy Land, where they both died in 1035.[8] King Henry of France soon afterwards, taking advantage of the youth and helplessness of duke William, re-annexed the French Vexin [9] in which he was supported by Gautier, count

of Pontoise, who claimed for himself also the Norman Vexin.[10] This caused a bitter feud between them, and duke William confided the defence of this part of Normandy to William Crispin I, whom he invested with the dignity of count of Vexin prior to 1048.[11] He doubtless did this not only to reward him for his military achievements but also to keep in conspicuous prominence Normandy's justified claim to the whole of the Vexin, which duke William was unable to enforce, being too much occupied elsewhere. M. Le Prevost [12] observes that the history of the counts of Vexin at this period was obscure and that Gautier did not immediately succeed his father in this capacity, nor do any of the contemporary chroniclers so record him. William of Poitiers refers to him as count of Mantes,[13] Orderic Vital [14] and Milo Crispin [15] as count of Pontoise, while Benoît de Sainte-More [16] calls him count of Maine. Be this as it may, the conflict between duke William and Gautier was not confined to this district, for the latter had married Biote, sister of Hugh, count of Maine, on whose death, count Hugh, his son, placed himself and his estates under the protection of duke William. Gautier, in the right of his wife, claimed the whole *comté* and actually possessed part of it. Duke William therefore in 1063 invaded and subdued Maine, at which time he captured Gautier, and his wife, who were carried to Falaise, where they died of poison.[17] Raoul (III) the Great, count of Valois and Amiens, after the death of Gautier, whose cousin he was, re-united Pontoise, Mantes and a great part of the French Vexin.[18] William, when king of England, demanded the French Vexin from king Philippe of France, and upon the latter's refusal with insolence and contempt, king William attacked Mantes with a strong force in 1087, on which occasion his horse stumbled in a ditch, injuring him so severely that he died from its effect in Rouen.[19]

[1] Stapleton, I, lii. [2] *Chron. de Torigny,* I, 267 and n. ; *Hist. Gen. de Normandie,* du Moulin, 113. [3] Ord. Vit., I, 148 ; II, 161 and n., 399 ; Wace, I, 385. [4] Ord. Vit., II, 79 and n. [5] Plan., II, 1. [6] Ord. Vit., II, 399. [7] *Ibid.,* ed. note. [8] *Ibid.,* I, 148 ; II, 400. [9] *Ibid.* [10] *De nob. Crispin. gen.,* I, 342. [11] *Vide* Guillaume Crispin and n. 8. [12] Wace, III, 6 sup. [13] *Patrol.,* CXLIX, Migne, col. 1234 ; Ord. Vit., I, 448 ; II, 79. [14] Ord. Vit., I, 448 ; II, 79. [15] *De nob. Crispin. gen.,* I, 342. [16] Benoît de Sainte-More, III, 137. [17] Ord. Vit., I, 448-9 and n. ; II, 79. [18] Ord. Vit., Le Prevost, III, 234, n. 4. [19] Ord. Vit., II, 398-9, 400-18.

Appendix 9

RAOUL DE TOENI

NOTE 5.—Raoul de Toeni II was born *c.* 1024 because his death occurred on

24 March 1102 and Orderic Vital (II, 190) informs us that he served for nearly sixty years in the wars under duke William and the latter's son Robert Courteheuse. If eighteen years of age when he first bore arms, he would have been seventy-eight when he died.

NOTE 6.—These marriages took place before 1058 or after 1063, the period of Raoul's banishment; the former date fits in best with the known facts.[1] Two of Simon de Montfort's children by this marriage were Amaury, eventually count of Evreux, born c. 1065, as he led the forces of William Rufus against Montfort and Espernon in 1098, was fighting before Gisors in 1123 and died in 1137,[2] and Bertrade, the sister of Amaury, was born probably about 1068-70, since she married Fulk le Réchin, count of Anjou, in 1089.[3] At the time of Simon's marriage his wife Agnès was quite young, for her parents were not married before 1038.[4] He must have been approaching sixty years of age then for his daughter Ève by his first marriage, wife of William Crispin I, was married not later than 1045, her younger son Gilbert, abbot of Westminster, having been born before 1050.[5] Simon died in 1087.[6]

NOTE 7.—M. Le Prevost [7] is of the opinion that Godehilde, who died c. 1096, daughter of Raoul de Toeni II, was first married to Robert de Neubourg, second son of Henry de Beaumont, earl of Warwick, instead of to Robert, count of Meulent, as recorded by Orderic Vital.

The eminent historian is in error because Robert de Neubourg died in 1159 at the abbey of Bec where he was buried,[8] and if he had had his four sons by this Godehilde, allowing nine years for their births, the eldest was born not later than 1080. Assuming that Robert was only eighteen years of age at the time of his marriage, it would place his birth in 1062 and he would have been ninety-seven years old at his death. This assertion is rendered still more intenable by several charters executed by him in favour of the abbey of Bec, with the consent of his wife Godehilde and his sons Henri and Raoul, which would make the date of Robert's birth still earlier.[9]

Orderic Vital's statement can, therefore, be accepted as correct and the Godehilde who was the wife of Robert de Neubourg was the daughter of Raoul de Toeni III or of some other person.

[1] Ord. Vit., I, 431, 441; Le Prevost, ed. II, 89, 93; V, 426.   [2] Ord. Vit., IV, 70; *vide* Robert de Chandos; *Dict. de l'Eure*, I, 733. [3] Ord. Vit., III, 3 and n.   [4] Plan., I, 249. [5] *Vide* Guillaume Crispin, n. 13.   [6] Ord. Vit., II, 426.   [7] Ord. Vit., II, 404; *Le Prevost Mem.*, II, 450-1.   [8] *Chron. de Torigny*, I, 322. [9] *Le Prevost Mem.*, II, 451.

Appendix 10

RICHARD VICOMTE D'AVRANCHES

NOTE 2.—Orderic Vital (II, 444) recites the following narrative concerning Hugue d'Avranches (Hugh Lupus) : " Robert (de Rhuddlan), son of Umfrid, came over to England with his father when quite young and was in the service of king Edward both in his household and army until he was knighted by the king. Then . . . (he) returned to his own country. After the battle of Senlac, while king William was engaged in making head against repeated insurrections, the young knight, with his cousin Hugh, son of Richard d'Avranches, surnamed Goz, came over to England."

While their discourse of Ordericus is susceptible of argument as to the exact date intended, still it casts doubt upon the attendance of Hugh at the battle of Hastings when taken in conjunction with the entry in the cartulary of the abbey of Whitby, quoted by Dugdale in the *Monasticon*.[1] It says that Hugh, earl of Chester, and William de Percy, his sworn companion-in-arms, came into England with William the Conqueror in 1067. MM. Le Prevost, Planché, Taylor and the duchess Cleveland apparently do not believe in the correctness of this charter.

[1] I, 72.

Appendix 11

RICHARD   DE   BIENFAITE   ET D'ORBEC

NOTE 6.—Nothing authentic has been discovered to show that the members of the ducal family of Normandy adopted the surname Crispin other than Gilbert seigneur de Tillières, his immediate family and descendants. Its use in connection with Gilbert, count of Brionne, the Grimaldi genealogy and William, count of Evreux, great-grandson of duke Richard I, are all incorrect. Gilbert Crispin, abbot of Westminster, the grandson of Gilbert Crispin I, in his *Life of Herluin*, abbot of Bec, refers to Gilbert, count of Brionne, as the grandson of Richard I, duke of Normandy, and son of " consul " Godfry. (Giselbertus Brionensis comes primi Ricardi Normanniae ducis nepos ex filio consule Godefrido.) If count Gilbert had been abbot Gilbert's grandfather, he certainly would have mentioned it, and the *Crispin genealogy* of Milo Crispin [1] which recites the family history, would have done so without doubt, but both are silent on the subject.

NOTE 17.—Mr. Stapleton (I, lvi) names the seven sons of duke Richard I thus : Richard II, who succeeded him, Robert, archbishop of Rouen and count of Evreux,

William, who signed as count the foundation charter of Richard I to the abbey of Fécamp in 990, whose honour he could not locate, Godfry, count of Eu, William, count of Exmes and later Eu, Mauger, count of Corbeil in France, whose son William Warlenge was count of Mortain, and Robert (Robertus comes) named in a charter of Richard II as having abstracted by violence from the church of Mont-Saint-Michel all that his grandfather William Longsword had given it. Unless there is additional information concerning the first William other than contained in the charter there is no reason to believe that it was not William, count of Exmes, who witnessed it.

NOTE 21.—The county of Auge has sometimes been confounded with Eu, which latinized is Augum, also Aucensis and Ocensis.

NOTE 22.—The William here recorded could scarcely be William Busac, count of Soissons, the second son of William, count of Eu, who held the castle of Eu for a period prior to 1054.[2]

NOTE 24.—Robert de Torigny entered the abbey of Bec in 1128, where he became librarian in 1149 and was ordained abbot of Mont-Saint-Michel in 1154, for which reason he was also called du Mont. He was therefore in possession of very definite information concerning count Gilbert, who, he says, held Eu for a long time before his death.[3]

NOTE 27.—It is certainly very strange that the name of the wife of so powerful and prominent a noble as Gilbert, count of Brionne, has not been mentioned by any of the contemporary historians, if he had one, when so much has been recorded concerning him. This creates the impression that the mother of his sons may have been intentionally suppressed. If Arlette was their mother, which is so recorded in the *Royal genealogies* by Anderson,[4] and the *Genealogical table of the Courtenay family* by viscount Courtenay and others, then they were born shortly after Arlette's children by Herluin de Conteville, which would be *c.* 1035,[5] because the records preclude her having had children before the birth of duke William.[6] Count Gilbert was murdered before 1040, consequently his sons, if by her, would have been babies at this time. This does not fit in with Richard de Bienfaite's age, for he attested charters of Richard II executed in 1024 and 1025 in favour of the abbeys of Fontenelles and Fécamp, showing, as pointed out in the *Dictionnaire de l'Eure*, that the youngest children then witnessed the most solemn acts.[7] There is nothing tangible to support such a marriage ; on the contrary, the great interest taken in the sons of count Gilbert by Baldwin, count of Flanders, for

fourteen or fifteen years, who trained and educated them at his court, suggests more than the generosity of a kindly prince. It rather indicates a Flemish ancestry for their mother, if not indeed relationship to count Baldwin. This statement concerning count Gilbert can, therefore, be discarded, but as regards Gilbert Crispin I,[8] a rumour of this kind persistently permeates the writings of the chroniclers on this subject.

[1] *De nob. Crispin. gen.* [2] *Vide* Robert, comte d'Eu. [3] *Chron. de Torigny*, and Delisle, note I, 25. [4] Table CCCCXC. [5] *Vide* Eudes Evêque de Bayeux. [6] *Ibid.* [7] *Dict. de l'Eure*, I, 585. [8] *Vide* App. 16, n. 6. App. 3 n. 6. *Vide* addenda.

Appendix 12

PROUZ, CHUDLEIGH, HÉLION, HÉRION

NOTE 11.—Peter Prouz, Pruz or Prouse, of Estervale, afterwards of Chagford, Devonshire, was the second husband of lady Mary de Vernon, daughter of William de Redvers (Riviers), surnamed de Vernon, earl of Devon and widow of Robert de Courtenay. Lady Mary through her mother lady Maude or Mabel de Beaumont, daughter of Robert, count of Meulent or Meulan, was descended from king Henry I of England through his illegitimate son Reginald, earl of Cornwall. She was also from this source a descendant of Henry I, king of France, and Bernard the Dane. By her second marriage she had a son William Prouz, heir of his father whose arms were : Sable three lions rampant argent. He, in turn, was followed by Walter Prouz, who married a daughter of John, lord Dinham. William Prouz, his son and successor, espoused the daughter and heiress of Giles de Gidley and was followed by sir William Prouz of Gidley castle, Devonshire, high sheriff of that county, who married Alice, daughter and heiress of sir Fulk Ferrières or Ferrers of Throwleigh. He died in 1314. Fulk had married Mary, daughter and heiress of sir Alan de Hélion, a descendant of Hervé d'Hélion (sometimes called Ailion) a compagnon of William the Conqueror, who should have appeared upon the Falaise roll. Hervé came from Hillion, near Saint-Brieux, Brittany, and held by barony and in chief in Devonshire, 1086 (Domesday). His descendants were lords of Asseriston, Assheton or Ashton and Credy-Hélion in Devonshire. Léopold Delisle records Hervé d'Hélion on his Dives roll.

The wife of Fulk de Ferrers, seventh in descent from Hervé, brought to her husband the manor of Ashton, Devonshire, known as " Place Barton." Sir Richard Prouz of Ashton, son and heir of sir William, husband of Alice, daughter of Fulk aforementioned, left an only daughter, Thomasine, who married *c.* 1330 sir John de Chudleigh, ancestor of the distinguished family of that name in Devonshire.[1] His arms were Erminois three lions salient gules. Their son, sir John Chudleigh, married Johanna, daughter of sir John Beauchamp of Ryme, and Alicia, daughter and heiress of sir Roger Nonant, lord of Broadclist. Sir James Chudleigh, their son, married Johanna, daughter of sir Henry de la Pomeroy, sister and heiress of sir John de la Pomeroy, who died 14 June 1416. A daughter and heiress of this marriage, Johanna Chudleigh, married first sir John St-Aubyn ; she died 8 December 1423, leaving a son, John St-Aubyn, who married Catherine, daughter and heiress of sir Robert Challons of Challonsleigh, Devonshire. Their daughter, Johanna, aged 17 in 1428, married, second, William Dennys, by whom she had a daughter and heiress, Alice, who became the wife of John Bonville, son of William, lord Bonville of Chewton, deceased in 1491. A daughter Florence from this marriage espoused Thomas Fortescue of Wimpstone, Devonshire, the son and heir of John Fortescue, aged 29 at his father's death, 22 May 1519. They had a daughter Isabella who married Anthony Honeychurch of Tavistock and Aveton Gifford, esq., son and heir of William Honeychurch of Tavistock. The former died 20 June 1573. John Honeychurch, their son and heir, aged 30 at the time of his father's death, 2 May 1605, married Mary, daughter of Edmund Rowland of Bow, Devonshire, and their daughter Joan (wrongly called Mary in the visitation of Devon) married 9 November 1595 Robert Crispin of East Portlemouth, who was baptized there in September 1565.[2] Captain William Crispin of the English navy affixed to his official reports to the Admiralty office, 1660–70, a seal bearing three lions rampant which is identical with those of Prouz and Chudleigh.[3]

The family of Hélion has sometimes been erroneously confounded with that of Hérion, Hérioun or Héron, which emerged from Héron, near Rouen. Tihel de Héron occurs in Essex in 1086 (Domesday) and Odonel Héron, *temp.* William Rufus, witnessed a charter in Durham. Some think that this Tihel was identical with Tihel Brito of Essex and Norfolk (Domesday) whose family gave its name to Burnsted-Hélion. In 1100 king Henry I granted the barony of Héron in Northumberland to this family where they were of great consequence. William de Héron, governor of the castle of Bamborough, Pickering, and Scarborough, lord warden of the forests of the north of Trent and sheriff of the aforesaid county under Henry III, married the daughter and heir of Odonel de Ford and built the castle

of that name in 1227. A descendant, another William, was summoned to parliament as baron by Edward III in 1371. Still another William held a fief in Normandy, *temp.* Philippe Auguste. This family appears on the roll of Battle abbey, having been mentioned by Holinshed and Leland, and John Bernard Burke believed it was represented at the battle of Hastings, to which the known facts point.[4] Whether this was Tihel is not clear. While there appears to be no positive evidence of this assertion, there certainly is nothing to disprove it.

[1] *Extinct and Dormant Baronetcies*, Burke, 115–16 ; *Worthies of Devon*, Prince, 216–18 ; *Nor. Peo.*, 454 ; *Devon*, Pole ; *The Complete Peerage*, Cokayne, IV, 309 and fol. [2] *Visitations of the County of Devon*, Vivian, 189, 190, 478, 626. [3] *The Pennsylvanic Magazine*, published by The Historical Society of Pennsylvania, Vol. LIII, April, 1929, no. 10, M. Jackson Crispin, 131. [4] *Roll of Battle Abbey Annotated*, Burke, 65 ; Cle., II, 144 ; *British Family Antiq.*, VII, 214 ; *Nor. Peo.*, 279, 283, 284 ; *New Baronetage of England*, Miller, 701. From Richard de Redvers.

Appendix 13

ROBERT DE CHANDOS (ESTRÉPAGNY, DANGU)

NOTE 9.—After Dangu came into possession of the Crispin family, who held Estrépagny adjoining it, which had the seigniorial right of " high justice," its seigniors claimed it also for the former.[1] Their efforts to enforce it, which they apparently did for a time, give rise to frequent conflicts with the " high justice " of Gisors. " High justice " alone was entitled to deal with any criminal charges bringing on the death punishment or mutilation, with the right for the " spilling of blood " and " tear," with or without the " hue and cry " and with the civil trials from which a " judiciary duel " could originate. The high judiciary did not judge by himself, but presided over the assizes which were held by his order. " Low justice " dealt with all that was not of the jurisdiction of the " high justice." In the 14th century " middle justice," an intermediary court, came into existence. After the 12th century the seigniorial justice was lessened in power by new institutions such as " the call of the king," " the royal cases," and by the 16th century the seigniorial courts were totally powerless. The " custom of estamps " of the year 1270 forbade a seignior the right to keep a gibbet standing all the time unless he held " high justice." If he had " low justice " he could not let anyone die for thievery and could only put up his gibbet for an execution.[2]

It is curious that out of 1,109 acres of which the baron of Dangu had the seigniory on the actual land of Vesly, 558 were enfeoffed to the lords of Ruelle and Taillis, 535 to commoners which constituted his fief properly speaking. He had from the 16th century only 16 acres non-enfeoffed which was considered at the time of the Revolution the personal property of the lord of Dangu. One knows that the contract of " fieffé " was a real contract of sale made for an invariable and perpetual income, rent in nature or money, sometimes both. As for the vassal, he was really proprietor, but always encumbered with the seigniorial rent. These same rents formed the invariable revenue of the seigniory. The non-enfeoffed domain which the lord exploited or often rented was likely to bring more. The vassal's rights were :

(1) To go, he and his men and his family, to his lord's court of justice.

(2) The right of enjoying the revenues of the domain.

The lord's rights were :

(1) The duty of fidelity given by the vassal ; the vow given by the vassal not to injure his lord or his rights or his goods, and to yield him assistance.

(2) The exaction of military service and monetary assistance levied when the lord's son was made a knight, when his daughter married, when he set out on a crusade.

The fiefs became hereditary from the 10th and 11th century.

The tenure of knight service soon followed the perpetuity of the fief and was connected with it. Each grant, whether to a baron or a gentleman, was computed as so many fees, and each fee gave the service of a knight. A tenant of the crown who was not created into nobility but enjoyed a grant of land furnished also his knights in proportion to his fees.

[1] *Le Prevost Mem.*, II, 58. [2] *Arch. de l'Empire*, Boutaric, I, 320 ; Restitution, no. 65 (D23), Conf. Beugnot, I, 841.

Appendix 14

LE CHAMBERLAIN DE TANCARVILLE

NOTE 9.—Robert de Torigny,[1] Henry of Huntingdon [2] and others say that William de Tancarville was in command of king Henry's troops at the battle of Bourgteroude in 1124, but Orderic Vital [3] ignores him, giving the honours to Ranulph le Meschin,[4] earl of Chester, and William de Harcourt. In this engagement the king's forces defeated Waleran, earl of Meulent, Hugh de Montfort, Amaury de Montfort, William Crispin III [5] and other Norman barons. The first two lords were captured

and Amaury de Montfort, count of Evreux, although taken prisoner by William de Grandcourt, son of William, count d'Eu, who " touched for a man of such bravery," and " rather than entangle a count of such distinguished worth in the meshes of a net from which he could never extricate himself " conducted him to safety and " found an honourable refuge in France " for himself.[6]

[1] *Chron. de Torigny*, I, 164–5 and n. [2] *Chron., Henry of Huntingdon*, Forester, 251. [3] Ord. Vit., IV, 74–5. [4] *Vide* Guillaume Malet and Le Sire de Saint-Sever. [5] *Dict. de l'Eure*, II, 52. [6] Ord. Vit., IV, 75.

Appendix 15

CRISPINS OF CHÂTEAUCEAUX

NOTE 3.—Châteauceaux was anciently in possession of the counts of Nantes, but about 986 was a mesne-fief belonging to the counts of Anjou.[1] At this time, Renaud de Thuringe, viscount of Anjou, built with the help of Fulk Nerra, count of Anjou, and with the consent of the count of Nantes, a feudal fortress upon the ruins of a Gallo-Roman castle, which had existed from the 7th century.[2] He left by Richilde, who was his wife before 969 [3] three sons, Renaud, bishop of Angers,[4] Fouquois de Rochefort (after 993 viscount of Anjou [5] and of Rochefort-sur-Loire[6]), and another son who became seignior of Châteauceaux and ancestor of a noble family of that name.[7] The lords of Châteauceaux had the right to collect toll from the navigation of the Loire, for which purpose they stretched a chain across the river.[8] In 1040, Geoffry de Châteauceaux, its seignior, undoubtedly grandson of Renaud de Thuringe,[9] founded the priory of Saint-Jean-Baptiste of Châteauceaux, which he gave to the monks of Saint-Martin of Marmoutiers of Tours and its abbot Albert, with the approbation of his brothers Hardouin, Orderic, Guiscelin and Raoul. This charter was witnessed by Geoffry Martel, count of Anjou.[10] Geoffry de Châteauceaux was mortally wounded at Ambroise [11] about this time and was succeeded by his brother, Orderic, 1040-9,[12] who lost the favour of Geoffry Martel, *c.* 1060, and was supplanted in the possession of Châteauceaux by his son-in-law Thibaud de Jarzé.[13] The latter assumed the name de Châteauceaux and died *c.* 1074, having left by his wife, daughter of Orderic, a son Geoffry de Jarzé.[14] This Geoffry married Annila and died *c.* 1090,[15] leaving a son Thibaud, who died between 1105,[16] when he signed a document (Tetbaldus de Castello Calso), and 1112 when his sister, Warmaise (Germasia) appears in a charter as possessor of Châteauceaux.[17] She married, first, Geoffry de Briollay [18] and second, Amaury Crispin, grandson of William Crispin I, and probably son of William Crispin II, although the latter had brothers, little known, one of whom could have been his father. It will be recalled that William Crispin I was the brother-in-law of Philippe I, king of France, Fulk le Réchin, count of Anjou, Raoul de Toeni II and Amaury de Montfort, count of Evreux. They all married daughters of that powerful noble Simon, seigneur de Montfort l'Amauri, excepting the latter, who was Simon's son by his third marriage.[19] William Crispin III, William, count of Evreux, and Amaury de Montfort, were in banishment in Anjou just before 1112, in which year they were pardoned by king Henry I of England.[20] It was about this time, or shortly thereafter, that Amaury Crispin came to Anjou and married the widow Warmaise, for, in 1118, Amaury Crispin, then lord of Châteauceaux, and his wife Warmaise, great-granddaughter of Orderic (Orricus) and heiress of Châteauceaux, confirmed a donation to the abbey of Saint-Aubin of Angers, which was witnessed by " Florus, son of king Philippe " (I of France), and sometime later, the same was obtained from count " Fulcho " (Fulk the younger count of Anjou) and his young son " Gaufrid " (Geoffry Plantagenet).[21] Amaury and Warmaise had issue at least two sons, Thibaud and Geoffry, as appears in several charters, c. 1124–5. Theobald occurs later, but nothing further is known of Geoffry.[22] Warmaise died shortly before 1137.[23] Amaury and Theobald joined Robert de Sablé, who had previously revolted, in a rebellion against Geoffry Plantagenet, count of Anjou, in 1141, when Châteauceaux was besieged, captured and destroyed.[24] They made peace with their suzerain, the castle was rebuilt and they died between 1154 and 1157, as their names occur then in a ratification of a previous act by Engelbaud, archbishop of Tours,[25] and neither are heard of thereafter. Robert Crispin was the next seignior of Châteauceaux c. 1060, whose exact identity in the family is obscure. He married Garsie and died without issue, when his inheritance passed to his nephew Simon, who married Etiennette de Chantocé, and at his death, leaving no direct heir, was succeeded by his brother Geoffry.[26] The latter is said to have been the grandson of Amaury, in which event Robert and Geoffry's unknown father, whose wife was a lady by the name of Giberge, were sons of Amaury.[27] Simon was buried in the abbey of Saint-Père de Chartres, where Geoffry paid the monks for taking care of lamps for his soul (quod lamp adas quas ego anima fratris mei Simonis Crispini reddere solebam Monachis Carnuti). Which

creates the thought that he may have been born in Normandy where his parents had lived and that the seigniory of Châteauceaux had reverted to the Norman Crispins after the death of Amaury and Theobald. Robert Crispin of Normandy, a younger brother of Joscelyn, little known, whose age fits in perfectly with this period, could have been identical with Robert of Châteauceaux, which leaves it an open question.[28] Geoffry Crispin was besieged at Châteauceaux in 1172 by the three sons of king Henry II of England and obliged to go to that country, during which period his castle was confided to Maurice de Craon, seneschal of Anjou, who destroyed it.[29] Châteauceaux was rebuilt and again in possession of Geoffry Crispin by 1175.[30] Shortly after 1185 he donated land within the castle walls to the monks of Marmoutiers, near the chapel of Saint-Pierre, for a monastery in which he mentions his wife Marguerite, his mother Giberge, his deceased brother Simon, his sons Théobald (my first born), Simon and Robert. It is witnessed among others by Théobald Crispin, probably his son, and William Crispin.[31] To this charter dom Morice in publishing it erroneously appended (which he later corrected) portions of two others.[32] One was executed by Geoffry de Châteauceaux (grandson of Renaud de Thuringe) c. 1040,[33] and in the other, made after 1065, appears Geoffry, lord of Châteauceaux, who was Geoffry de Jarzé.[34] These additions imply that the Geoffrys there mentioned were identical with Geoffry Crispin, who executed this charter which is without date, indicating that all three were made about the same time. Confusion was added because Geoffry de Brihéri appears in the earlier charters, while his descendant, also named Geoffry de Brihéri, executed another in 1185.[35] Geoffry Crispin occurs in a charter 1189–90 concerning the construction of a chapel for the leper colony of Châteauceaux to which he affixed his seal.[36] It has been reproduced in Varia ad Historiam Britanniæ [37] and by dom Lobineau [38] and dom Morice.[39] The shield is quartered by a cross nowy, the first and second being checky, while the third and fourth are plain. Dom Noël Mars, transcriber of the Cartulaire de Marmoutiers, records another seal of the same epoch, substituting an abbatol cross for the silver cross.[40] These arms are quite similar to those of the Norman Crispins, and when colours were added, both bore argent and gules. L'Armorial d'Anjou, by M. J. Denais (vol. I), records—Of . . . a cross, starred argent, quartered to the first and second of a fretty argent and gules, to the third and fourth full argent. (De . . . à la croix étoilée d'argent cantonnée aux premier et deuxième d'un fretté d'argent et de gueules ; au troisième et au quatrième d'argent plein.)

Geoffry Crispin died about 1199 and was succeeded by his son Théobald,[41] who witnessed the truce between king John of England and Philippe, king of France, in 1206 on behalf of the former,[42] in which year Châteauceaux had been taken by king Philippe, who was by this treaty compelled to relinquish it. In 1214 king John again took it, but in the same year it was lost definitely to England.[43] Théobald Crispin, in addition to Châteauceaux, possessed the castle of Montfauçon in Anjou and Maroiel (now Mareuil) in Poitou, of the king of England as count of these provinces.[44] Far from emulating the actions of his distinguished ancestors, he became a real tyrant, apparently following the tactics of his English sovereign, since Peter, count of Brittany, besieged and captured Châteauceaux in 1224 and drove him in exile to England because " for almost 25 years he had devastated the surrounding country and robbed the navigation of the Loire." Châteauceaux then left the Crispin family for ever.[45] Nevertheless, his relative, king Henry III of England, complained to the pope on account of the conduct of count Peter regarding the castle which Théobald Crispin had " held of us of the comté of Anjou and the castle of Maroeil, held of the comté of Poitiers,"[46] and compelled Ranulph de Blundeville, earl of Chester, to make amends for " his transgression of the previous year in occupying the castle of Théobald Crispin at Châteauceaux." Théobald was pensioned by the king and granted lands at Chalgrave, Oxfordshire, which is significant as this is within five miles of Milo Crispin's castle of Wallingford, but later in 1235 appears as holding the castle of Haroyl in Châtelleraut (Vienne), France.[47] The loss of his ancestral inheritance was no doubt brought about more on account of his consistent support of king John and his well-known sympathy for the cause of king Henry III, descendants of the ancient counts of Anjou, to whom he was related by ties of blood,[48] than to his lawlessness. Châteauceaux was one of the strongest fortresses in Anjou which Théobald, their most ardent and trusted follower, ever held at their disposal, with whose expulsion passed the last remaining vestige of English influence in that comté. This is attested by the king himself who said in 1235 that Théobald had " the keeping of Anjou " (tenuit de nobis de comitatu Andegavensi et castrum de Haroyl).[49] He is last heard of in 1238, when he received from the king his annual fee.[50]

[1] Les Origines Féodales de Châteauceaux, published in the Bulletin de la Société Archéologique de Nantes, Sept. 1913, by l'abbé Bourdeaut, vicaire à Sainte-Anne et Chapelain à Châteauceaux, p. 213. M. l'abbé Bourdeaut, who composed this valuable and complete history of Châteauceaux, is the recognized authority on the subject and has been of great assistance in furnishing information for this biography. [2] Ibid., xxviii ; Le Comté d'Anjou au XIe Siecle, Halphen, 249, 349–50. [3] Le Comté d'Anjou, 347. [4] Archives d'Anjou, Livre Noir de Saint-Florent, I, 116 ; Le Comté d'Anjou, 249, 349–50. [5] Cartulaire de Saint-Aubin, Bertrand de Broussillon, I, 130. [6] Le Comté d'Anjou, Halphen, 347. [7] Bourdeaut, xxviii and 216. [8] Ibid., 214. [9] Ibid., 216. [10] Original Arch. du Maine et Loire; H. Prieuré de Saint-Jean de Châteauceaux; Cart. de Marmoutiers, Bibl. nat. lat. 5441, II, fo. 288, 3 ; Morice, I, col. 385. [11] Original Arch. Maine et Loire ; H. Prieuré de Saint-Jean de Chat. ; Copy Cart. de Marmoutiers, Bibl. nat. lat. 5441, II, fo. 381, vo. [12] Original Arch. Maine et Loire ; Cart. de Saint-Aubin, I, 230 ; Copy Bibl. nat. lat. 5441, II, fo. 381. [13] Cart. de Saint-Aubin, I, 138. [14] Bourdeaut, 221. [15] Ibid., 222. [16] Cart. de l'Abbaye Cardinale de la Trinité de Vendôme, abbé Charles Métais, II, 174, no. 412. [17] Ibid., III, 197–200, no. 427. [18] Ibid. [19] Vide Guillaume Crispin ; App. 9, 17, n. 13 ; Raoul de Toeni II. [20] Vide Guillaume Crispin. [21] Morice, I, 540 ; Cart. de Saint-Aubin, Broussillon, I, 230. [22] Arch. du Maine et Loire, G. 789 ; Hist. de Marmoutiers, Martene, II, 61. [23] Cart. du Ronceray, charter, 115, p. 85, ano. 1125–33, says Warmaise was still alive and another, Arch. du Maine et Loire, G. 789, about 1137, records her deceased. [24] Chron. Angevins, Halphen, 10, 99 ; Chron. des comtes d'Anjou, Halphen, 206, 209 ; Hist. de Sablé, 32, 44. [25] Bibl. nat. lat. 5441, II, fo. 373 ; Arch. d'Anjou, Marchegay, II, 71 (between 1154 and 1157) ; Gall. Christ., XIV, 89 ; Chron. de Torigny, I, 301, n. ; Mém. de la Soc. Archeol. de Touraine, XVII, 58. [26] Notre-Dame Angevine, Grandet, 542 ; Cart. de Craon, Broussillon, I, 70 ; Arch. d'Anjou, II, 68, 72 ; Dict. du Maine et Loire, Port, I, 606 ; Bourdeaut, 231 ; Bibl. nat. lat. 5441, II, fo. 376–7. [27] Bourdeaut, XXIX. [28] Bibl. nat. lat. 5441, II, fo. 376 ; vide App. 17, n. 44. [29] Hist. de Sablé, second part, G. Ménage, 40 ; Chron. de Saint-Aubin ; Recueil d'Annales Angevines, Halphen, 38. [30] Bourdeaut, 235. [31] Bibl. nat. lat. 5441, II, fo. 376–7 ; Original Arch. du Maine et Loire ; Morice, I, cols. 384–5. [32] Preuves, Morice, ibid. [33] Arch. du Maine et Loire, etc., ibid., n. 10. [34] Original Arch. du Maine et Loire; H. Prieuré de Saint-Jean de Chat. ; Bibl. nat. lat. 5441, II, fo. 381, vo. [35] Bibl. nat. lat. 5441, II, fo. 380 vo ; Arch. du Maine et Loire (copy of original). [36] Ibid., fo. 375 ; Arch. d'Anjou, II, 92 ; Morice, I, 715. [37] Bibl. nat. fr. 22322, fo. 306, No. 269. It is quite impossible to identify the transcriber of this charter as the manuscript is a 17th-century document of which a copy was made by the monks of the Blancs Manteaux in Paris. [38] Lobineau, Preuves, II, table of seals, No. 32. [39] Morice, I, table no. 32. [40] Bibl. nat. lat. 5441, II, fo. 382. [41] Arch. d'Anjou, II, 68 ; Bibl. nat. lat. 5441, II, fo. 372 ; Gall. Christ., II, col. 1182 ; Bourdeaut, 235. [42] Recueil des Hist. des Gaules, XVII, 91, dans les Œuvres de Rigord le Breton ; De Gestis Philippe-Auguste. [43] Bourdeaut, XXIX. [44] Morice, I, 851. The original concession of Châteauceaux and Montfauçon can be found in Archives nationales

(J.J., 26, fo. 182, v°, col. 2), which was first published by dom Martene in *Amplissima Collectio* (I, 1191).   [45] *Chron. de Saint-Florent*, Halphen, 125 ; *Chron. de Marmoutiers*, Mabille, 305 ; *Recueil des Historiens des Gaules*, XVIII, 305 ;   Morice, I, 851.   [46] Morice, I, 899 ; Rymer, I, 335.   [47] *Close Roll* quoted in *Victoria Hist. of Yorksh.*, 1/5.   [48] *De nob. Crispin. gen.*, I, 346.   [49] *Ibid.*, n. 47. [50] Liberate rolls.   Vide Geoffroi du Bec.

Appendix 16

GILBERT CRISPIN 1er

NOTE 1.—Gilbert was called Crispin because his hair was curly, stiff, and stood straight upwards like bristling pine (Crispus pinus).[1]

It is very curious that the name in the middle of the 12th century was spelled Crespin. It is Crispin in all of the extant latin charters from 1035, for one hundred years, some of which are reproduced at the end of this work, and Gilbert Crispin, abbot of Westminster, and Milo Crispin of Wallingford so occur. Crespin first appeared in the poem of Wace which is not significant as he was inaccurate in his names. Joscelyn Crispin in two latin charters out of ten in the *Cartulary of Mortemer* dated 1146(92) and 1168(39) is thus recorded. From about then this spelling was used in this branch of the family until the extinction of the male line in the 17th century. It is therefore quite apparent that the original and correct spelling was Crispin.

[1] *De nob. Crispin. gen.*, I, 342.

NOTE 3.—Jumièges is perfectly clear about the identities of Gilbert, count of Brionne, and Gilbert Crispin, he speaks of the former, who held both Brionne and Eu, as the count of Eu (Ocensis siquidem Comes Gislebertus).[1] Immediately afterwards, in the following chapter, he mentions Gilbert Crispin, to whom duke Robert had formerly confided the castle of Tillières, thus : (Tegulensi Castro . . . sed Gislebertus cognomento Crispinus cui illud commiserat olim dux Rodbertus.) [2]

[1] Jumièges, liv, VII, ch. 1 (I–IV), Marx ed., 116. [2] Jumièges, liv, VII, ch. II (V), Marx, 117.

NOTE 9.—Orderic Vital (I, 152) should doubtless have said that Baldric the Teuton married a sister or aunt of Gilbert, count of Brionne, instead of his niece (*vide* Fouque d'Aunou).

NOTE 16.—Concerning Arlette (*vide* 128, 131, 150; addenda). Gilbert Crispin I beyond doubt possessed Conteville for his grandson, Gilbert Crispin III, Laurentia his wife and his son Gilbert confirmed in 1130 its donation by William Malet II to the abbey of Bec,[1] as previously recorded.

François Carré, continuator of the *Chronique du Bec*, following the year 1526 states that Gilbert Crispin contracted a second marriage with Arlette, for which reason she received from her son duke William part of the confiscated lands of Tustain Goz, son of Ansfrid the Dane, viscount of Exmes.[2] Père Anselme observes in referring to Herluin de Conteville, "Others name him Gilbert de Crépon" (II, 470), concerning which Planché remarks: "There may be more in this than meets the eye " (I, 14 ; II, 196). Doufoury says it was " Guillebert de Crépon " and Le Prevost "Guillebert Crespy," but Richebourg in *Essai sur l'Hist. de Neustrie* (321) thinks both are mistaken. The *Courtenay genealogy* subscribes to Gilbert, count of Brionne, which is not correct. The marriage of Arlette to Herluin de Conteville apparently took place shortly before 1030 (*vide* Eudes Evêque de Bayeux).

[1] *Dict. de l'Eure*, II, 914.   [2] Porée, 187 ; *Mon.*, vi, part ii, 1068.

NOTE 17.—" The first abbess of the place (Montivilliers) was the aforesaid Béatrice, aunt of duke Robert." (Prima ejus loci abbotissa fuit praedicta Beatrix, Rotberti ducis amita.)

(Robert exchanged St-Taurin near Evreux with John, abbot of Fécamp, for Montivilliers which Richard II had given to this abbey and established a nunnery there.)

NOTE 18.—" The abbess Béatrice, with the approbation of her sons William, Robert and Gilbert, whom she had by marriage with Gautier de Lescelina " (Abbatissa Beatrix a conjuge Walweii qua De Lesselina annuentibus filii suis Willelmo, Roberto, et Gilleberto).[1] The abbess Béatrice, aunt of duke Robert I, was beyond doubt one of the unidentified natural daughters of Richard I, duke of Normandy.[2] Gautier de Lescelina was identical with Gautier, the second son of Turquetil de Neufmarché-en-Lions, and therefore the brother of Anchetil de Harcourt, and Lesceline, who married William comte d'Eu.[3] " She (Beatrice) was consecrated to God and Ste-Marie under witness of these, namely ; Robert (archbishop of Rouen, her half-brother, who died in 1037), Hugues, (later) bishop of Lisieux (her nephew), the abbot Jean, Gilbert Crispin (I), with the approbation of the count (duke) William (her great-nephew) and the encouragement of her sons for this endowment." [4] These were all descendants of Richard I excepting the abbot, which is very strong presumptive evidence that Gilbert was also, especially when considered with the corroborative facts previously mentioned (*vide* 28). If not, why was he called upon to witness this ceremony at the abbey of Montivilliers which was strictly an affair of the ducal family?

[1] Bibl. lat., Rouen, 1305. [2] *Jumièges Interp.*, de Torigny, 229; Benoît, II, 322. [3] *Vide* 14. [4] *Vide* charter no. 2.

Note 21.—Gilbert V lost the castle of Damville, arrondissement Evreux, canton of Damville-sur-l'Iton, in 1183, when peace was made following the death of Henry Court-Mantel, son of Henry II of England, because Gilbert had joined a revolt of the former against his father, at which time it was given to Simon d'Anet [1] and it was never regained by the Crispins. Bourth, arrondissement of Evreux, canton of Verneuil, remained in the family until 1371, when it passed with Tillières to that of Le Veneur.[2] Both the church and manor of Thiel-Nolent, arrondissement of Bernay, canton of Thiberville, were given by Gilbert Crispin II to the abbey of Bec. This domain left the Crispin family at an early period, the exact date being unknown,[3] and William Crispin II also donated property from there, which is confirmed in a charter of Henry II.[4]

[1] *Le Prevost Mem.*, II, 3; *Dict. de l'Eure*, I, 928. [2] *Dict. de l'Eure*, I, 544. [3] Bibl. nat. lat. 12884, etc. [4] *Le Prevost Mem.*, I, 236.

Note 26.—Gilbert Crispin I, who had been given Tillières by duke Robert I, died between *c.* 1040, when he defended it against Henry I, king of France, and this monarch's defeat at the battle of Mortemer in 1054, because duke William then gave this fortress to his son, Gilbert II. (*Vide* 29, n. 1 and n. 25.)

Note 30.—Gilbert Crispin II donated the entire fief of Hauville to the monks of Jumièges for the salvation of the souls of " the great prince Richard (I), of my glorious master William, duke of Normandy, of my father and my mother, my wife and children " (pro remediis animarum Ricardi magni principis, scilicet Willelmi quoque Normannie domini mei gloriosi ducis . . . atque patrie mei et matris necnon mee meeque Conjugis ac natorum). (*Vide* 167.)

Gilbert mentions duke Richard I because of his descent from him, through his mother, which is emphasized by the fact that he omitted Richard II and Robert, who followed, and then named William his reigning duke. The importance of this gift is attested by the fine which is raised to an almost incredible figure. " Should anyone try to infringe this charter of donation which I think hardly possible, may he be cursed and let him pay to the count one thousand livres of gold and to the church sixty thousand livres of silver." (Original, Arch. Seine-Inf., fonds de Jumièges, series H, for reproduction, *vide* charter no. 5.)

Note 31.—Gilbert Crispin I or II witnessed a deed of duke William in favour of the abbey of Saint-Wandrille between 1035 and 1053.[1]

Between 1054 and 1078 Robert III, abbot of Jumièges, who had to preside at a duel between vassals of the abbey which should have taken place at Vieux-Verneuil, upon the advice and with the consent of Gilbert Crispin II had it transferred to the château of Tillières.[2]

Gilbert Crispin occurs in many charters of the abbey of Saint-Père de Chartres as Gilbert de Tillières, and attested the charter of duke William donating the barony of Nonarit to the church of Saint-Pierre de Lisieux between 1050 and 1066.[3]

In 1086 Gilbert de Tillières II was a witness to a concession of king Philippe [4] and in 1090 Gilbert de Tillières senior (II) with Hersende his wife, and Gilbert junior attested another of Fouques de Vardes.[5] Gilbert de Tillières, Hersende his wife, Gilbert and Ribold his sons, appear in a charter of Geoffry de Berou in 1096 [6] and Gilbert de Tillières II also witnessed three others in 1102.[7] Gilbert de Tillières junior and Hersende his mother appear in a charter of 1107–16 [8] and confirmed a gift made by them in 1107.[9] This latter charter establishes the death of Gilbert Crispin II at about this time, when taken in conjunction with two others in favour of the abbey of Jumièges. One dated 1109 mentions Gilbert III with his wife and noble mother Hersende on which date this Gilbert as judge passed sentence at Tillières concerning a dispute between the monks of Jumièges and Gaurin de Gauville.[10] His father would have acted, if alive, in this capacity. Another after 1102 and in or before 1107 [11] records Gilbert II with his wife (Hersende) and his sons Gilbert and Ribold. Gilbert de Tillières III and his wife Laurentia are named in a charter of Geoffry de Berou, 1107–29 [12] and in 1107–35 are recorded Gilbert de Tillières and Laurentia his wife,[13] while about 1115, in another concerning Geoffry de Berou, are found Gilbert de Tillières, his son Gilbert, and Laurentia his wife.[14]

[1] *Etudes Critiques sur l'Abbaye de Saint-Wandrille*, Ferdinand Lot, p. 64. [2] Original lost; copy in Cartulary A, p. 89, no. 143 (Arch. Seine-Inf., fonds de Jumièges, series H, not classified. *Vide* charter no. 3, p. 191. [3] *Les anc. abb. de Norm.*, D'Anisy, II, 25, no. 893. [4] *Cartulaire de Saint-Père de Chartres*, Guérard, I, 246. [5] *Ibid.*, II, 529. [6] *Ibid.*, II, 557, 559. [7] *Ibid.*, I, 141, 227, 253. [8] *Ibid.*, II, 520–1. [9] *Ibid.*, II, 518–19. [10] *Chart. Abb. Jumièges*, I, 143; *Le Prevost Mem.*, II, 172. [11] *Ibid.*, *Jumièges*, I, 140. [12] *Cartulaire de Saint-Père de Chartres*, II, 559–60. [13] *Ibid.*, II, 538. [14] *Ibid.*, II, 603.

Note 32.—Just how Gilbert Crispin II

was descended from Raoul, count of Ivry, has not been established. William de Breteuil's grandfather, Osberne de Crépon, son of Herfast the brother of the duchess Gonnor, married a daughter of count Raoul, and while there is nothing known on record to indicate that Crispin and Crépon may have been the same name, they are nevertheless very similar.—This charter, in favour of the abbey of Saint-Evroult, the constant association of these families in the ownership of property and the fact that the great seigniories of Tillières and Breteuil adjoined not only each other but Ivry as well, which castles were the greatest fortresses of Normandy on the frontier to France, attests this relationship.[1] Herfast, whose family name was Crépon, was a son or grandson of a Danish knight of this name who followed Rollo into Neustria ; he had a brother William, lord of Pacy and Breteuil as recorded by William de Walthingham, the *Chronicle of Normandy*, the *Dictionnaire de la Noblesse*, and *Gallia Christiana*. The latter published a charter concerning the church at Pictariville about 990 [2] wherein he occurs, and nothing beyond this is known of him. Whether he left offspring or not is unrecorded, but Pacy and Breteuil were in possession of Herfast's descendants although William Crispin I owned considerable property in the former as evidenced by his large donations to the abbey of Bec from there [3] (*vide* Le Sire de Pacy).

[1] *Jumièges Interp.*, de Torigny, 287. [2] Des Bois, V, 306 ; *vide* App. 3 for full charter; *Mon.*, xi, instr. 139. [3] *Vide* Le Sire de Pacy.

NOTE 33.—The signature of Gilbert Crispin II to the foundation charter of Holy Trinity at Caen immediately following the family of king William (William de Warren's) and preceding Roger de Beaumont and the other great nobles of Normandy shows the Conqueror's desire to honour him and attests their consanguinity.

NOTE 35.—This pedigree taken from *Dictionnaire de l'Eure* (11, 914) and *Miscellanea Genealogia et Heraldica* (5th series, vol. 5, part viii, 251) is substantially correct, but a generation seems to be missing between Gilbert Crispin I and Gilbert IV, for Gilbert II was born about 1020 (*vide* Guillaume Crispin) and Gilbert V was not married until 1185. A careful perusal of the charters executed before 1130 by these seigniors supports this opinion, but lacking corroborative information and to avoid confusion, this genealogy has been followed. From Gilbert and Laurentia the generations are correct, but the others need proof before they can be considered accurate. Considerable information on this branch of the family was compiled by the late Emile Gentil and his son Paul Gentil, both of Tillières.

NOTE 36.—" There came from Normandy . . . Gilbert (Crispin) de Tillières with a strong body of warriors " (*Chron. of the Crusades*, lord John de Joinville, Richard of Devizes, and Geoffrey de Vinsauf, ch. XLII, vol. V, series V).

Appendix 17

GUILL. CRISPIN 1er Comte du Vexin

NOTE 1.—" The Miracle whereby Blessed Mary succored William Crispin senior wherein is an account of the noble family of the Crispins " (*Miraculum quo B. Maria Subvenit Willelsmo Crispino Seniori ubi de Nobili Crispinorum genere agitur*) is a manuscript of the early part of the 12th century published with the works of Lanfranc by dom Luc d'Achery, Paris, 1648, and by J. A. Giles, London, 1844. It is found in manuscript 499 du fonds de la Reine de Suède in the Vatican library, pp. 152-7, and a manuscript copy 5427 lat., fo. 116 to 120, v°, in the National library of Paris. The treatise is attributed to Milo Crispin, cantor of the abbey of Bec, at the beginning of the 12th century, grandson of William Crispin I. He died at a great age before 1150 and Gilbert Crispin, abbot of Westminster, probably collaborated in the work. Milo also wrote the lives of the first five abbots of Bec. (Preface, Giles ed. ; *Litt. Hist. de la France*, X, 192-209 ; Porée, I, 104.)

The *Crispin genealogy* was apparently started by Milo Crispin in the first years of the 12th century and added to as events transpired, for he says concerning the viscountcy of Vexin, " and his son (William II) after him (William I) we see as holding the same up to now "; and later in referring to William Crispin III states : " Their grandson from their son William, the third William Crispin . . . joined to the count of Anjou by close ties of blood. . . . William fought for him as far as he could." This was in 1135 (*vide* p. 38).

NOTE 2.—Abbot Gilbert Crispin was born not later than 1050. Dr. Armitage Robinson, late dean of Westminster, records it in 1045. Saint-Anselme became a monk at the abbey of Bec in 1060 and his name is the ninth on the roll of the monks, preserved in the library of the Vatican, following that of Gilbert,[1] who " at an early age " (filium suum interrera ætate) had been placed there by his father.[2] Since he had an elder brother or brothers, William Crispin I, his father, was married not later than 1045.[3] Gilbert Crispin remained at Bec until *c.* 1080 when archbishop Lanfranc sent for him to assist him at Canterbury under whose service and direction he continued until 1085 when he succeeded Vitalis as abbot of Westminster. This date, although generally accepted, has not been conclusively proven. It is more certain that he ruled this abbey for 32 years, for the *Crispin genealogy* just mentioned says so. He was very learned and greatly esteemed as a theologian and was the author of a number of works, the principal of which was the *Life of Herluin, abbot of Bec* (Vita domini Herluini abbatis Beccensis). He was also the author of the following extant treatises : *De disputatio Judaei cum Christiano,*[4] *De Simoniacis,*[5] *De Spiritu Sancto,*[6] *De Casu diaboli,*[7] *De Anima, Sermo in ramis palmarum, Versus ad Anselmum,* and *Disputatio Christiani cum gentili.* Other tracts have been ascribed to him which lack substantiation. The slab of black Tournai marble which lies on the top of Gilbert's tomb, the oldest sculptured monument in Westminster abbey, bears the date of 1114 as that of his death, but it was placed there probably centuries later and is incorrect although it is thus recorded in the *History of Westminster,* by Flete, a 15th-century document. Dr. Robinson, who edited Flete's *History,* wrote to us concerning this much-disputed matter as follows : 29 March 1928 : " This is certainly wrong (1114), for Gilbert made a convention which was attended by Bernard, bishop of Saint-David's, who was not consecrated till 19 September, 1115." He placed Gilbert's death 6 December, 1117, which is also so recorded in the *Anglo-Saxon Chronicle* and the *Winchester Annals.* Gilbert was supposed to occur later in several documents, but this is incorrect (*vide* addenda). In any event he was positively dead before 16 October, 1122, the date of the death of Vitalis, abbot of Savigny, who visited England and on his return entered Gilbert Crispin's name on his mortuary roll (Robinson, 27 ; this mortuary roll was published by Delisle).

The abbey of Bec, now Bec-Herluin, was founded in 1034–5 by Herluin of noble lineage, a vassal of Gilbert, count of Brionne, concerning which no more fitting words can express its past fame than those of Le Prevost : " Bec-Herluin is one of the most famous in the annals of science and religion ; one of which not only our department and our province but France and occidental Europe as well may be proud. We can never be sufficiently emphatic in reminding our compatriots that it was in this small quiet town, to-day deserted and desolate, that the first light was brought from Italy ; and it was from here that it shone over the surrounding countries for several generations. This place, where one can hear now only the voices of soldiers and the neighing of horses, was an inexhaustible nursery which Pro-

vidence seems to have created for the purpose of regenerating the occident and filling its cathedrals and abbeys with sainted and learned personages." To this humble monastery came in 1040 Lanfranc the Lombard, later archbishop of Canterbury, and one of the most astute and trusted advisers of king William in both church and state. He was a former teacher who crossed the Alps a few years before to visit the schools of France. Chance drew him to Bec, where Herluin, writes Gilbert abbot of Westminster, through " his humility of mind and dignity of speech won Lanfranc's veneration and love." The fame of this learned man spread near and far, and Bec was invaded by the youths of the noble families from all parts of Christendom. Lanfranc was ordained prior and the modest abbey of Herluin suddenly became famous. One of those thus drawn thither was Anselme of Aostia, of noble birth, who found himself in 1059 at the age of 25 in the lecture room of Lanfranc. The latter became abbot of St-Stephen at Caen in 1063 at its foundation, when the brilliant Anselme succeeded him as prior. On the death of Herluin in 1078, he was made abbot, which dignity he held until *c.* 1090, when he became archbishop of Canterbury. Much of this information has been preserved to us by Eadmer the monk in his *Life of St-Anselm.* Théobald, also a monk at Bec, was consecrated archbishop of Canterbury in 1138. This abbey was partly burnt and rebuilt several times, and most of the early books unfortunately perished in the fire of the French revolution. Many illustrious personages retired there or became monks, among whom were the Empress Matilda, daughter of king Henry I of England, as well as many warriors mentioned in the text. Following the custom of the period, they were inspired with a desire to expiate their sins particularly for the terrible atrocities and cruelties inflicted by them upon their enemies. They believed that similar torture awaited them eternally unless absolved by the church. This they secured by penance, but chiefly through the donation of much property. Few of the great personages of this barbarous age escaped such terror, not even the duke-king William, as attested by his death-bed discourse. The immense properties of Bec abbey gave rise to the saying :

" From any part the wind blows
The Bec abbey has rent."

It possessed the rights on 30 priories and 120 churches. Its enormous archives with very few exceptions were burnt at the main office of the " sous-prefecture " of Bernai early in the 19th century. The seals attached to these ancient documents were severed therefrom and used to make candles. Fortunately the great Colbert had an inventory made of the abbey's charters which, although very indifferently transcribed, are still to be found in the National library at Paris under the title *Inventaire de titres de l'Abbaye Nostre-Dame-du-Bec-Hellouin fait en l'an* 1670. During the time of the French revolution, in 1789, the abbey was partially demolished, and all of the belongings were then removed, and at present the buildings are used by the government to stable horses for breeding purposes, " dépot remonte de chevaux."

Le Prevost Mem., I, 225 and fol.; Porée; Robinson, 2 and fol.
[1] *Gilbert Crispin, Abbot of Westminster,* J. Armitage Robinson, p. 1.   [2] Bibl. du Vatican no. 499 du fonds de la Reine de Suède.   [3] *De nob. Crispin. gen.*, I, 343.   [4] Brit. mus. addit. 8116 and many ms.   [5] Saint-John's, Oxford, 149.   [6] Vesp. A., XIV.   [7] *Ibid.*, n. 4, and for the fol. tracts.

NOTE 3.—The domain of William Crispin I in the vicinity of Livarot included among other properties Blangy, arrondissement de Pont l'Evêque in Calvados, which was still in possession of his descendants 27 November 1291, when Jean Crispin, knight, confirmed the donation of his ancestors to the monks of Saint-Ymer, and Raoul Crispin (identity unestablished) still held it in 1384.[1] Bournainville,[2] Duranville, Drucourt [3] and Thiel-Nolent, all in the arrondissement of Bernay, canton of Thiberville, belonged to this group, from which seigniories William Crispin II made donations to the abbey of Bec.[4] Duranville was held by Raoul d'Astin under the Crispin family about 1055, when he witnessed a charter of William Crispin I, in which the latter offered his young son Gilbert to that abbey.[5] William Crispin II confirmed in 1087 the donation of Duranville [6] to the Bec abbey and this seigniory passed to Roger of Esserts with Bournainville early in the 13th century.[7]

[1] Bibl. nat. lat. 13905, fo. 68 ; Porée, II, 120 ; *Cart. de Saint-Ymer*, 78.   [2] *Vide* Guillaume de Bourneville.   [3] *Vide* Sire de Driencourt.   [4] Bibl. nat. lat. 12885 et 13905, etc.   [5] *Œuvres de Saint-Anselme*, p. 560 ; *Dict. de l'Eure*, I, 958.   [6] *Annuari Normand*, 19 ; *Le Prevost Mem.*, II, 19.   [7] *Dict. de l'Eure*, I, 958.

Concerning the participation of William Crispin in the battle of Mortemer, William of Poitiers (1231) writes : " Urgebat namque cervices eorum non meritas leniora mucro Roberti Aucensis comitis, ut natalibus ita virtute magni una Hugonis Gornacensis Hugonis Montisfortis, Gualterii Giffardi, Willelmi Crispini aliorumque nostrae partis fortissimorum virorum."

NOTE 11.—The month and day of the death of William Crispin I is ascertained from the *Necrology of Bec* and of *Beaumont-le-Roger* by dom Jouvelin in the National library of Paris (latin 13905). This document records the death of " William Crispin I, monk of our congregation," on 8 January (Januarius 6 des ides (i.e. 8th) O(-biit) Ius (i.e. primus) Will. Crispinus monachus nostrae congregationis).

The year is derived from the *Nomina Monachorum Becci* in the Vatican (ms. no. 499, du fonds de la Reine de Suède). It gives no date but states at what points changes in the abbots take place. Abbot Herluin, who admitted William Crispin to the abbey, died in 1078. The monks moved into their new buildings on 1 November 1073,[1] and the first admission after that is thus given : " Tedinus, first monk of the new church " (Tedinus primus monachus, novae ecclesiae). Four places lower down stands " Willelmus." After him follow twenty-nine other names which still belong to Herluin's time. It can therefore be concluded in the absence of other evidence that William Crispin's death occurred in 1074, although Martin Rule [2] does not give the authority which suggested it.

One can see a remarkable picture at the museum of the Belvédère at Vienna named " All the Saints," by Albert Durer in 1511. The upper part of the painting shows the Trinity adorned by angels and saints. Kneeling underneath, with eyes raised towards the celestial splendour, are people from all walks of life : the clergy, a pope, an emperor, cardinals, priests, kings, princes, a doge, knights, the laic society and, in the midst of these sparkling robes, a poor peasant. The names of the great people he portrayed there are enrolled, most of whom were living in the 11th and 12th centuries, among which were William the Conqueror, queen Matilda, Robert duke of Normandy, Henry I king of England, Henry IV the Roman emperor, Philippe I and Louis VI of France. Of the nobility, William Crispin and his wife Ève; Baldwin, count of Flanders ; Stephen and Théobald, counts of Blois ; Fouque and Geoffry, counts of Anjou, and many others.

[1] Porée, I, 131.   [2] Anselme, I, 166 n.

NOTE 12.—Abbot Gilbert Crispin in his *Life of Herluin* says his death occurred 26 August 1078. (*Vita Herluini* in *Opera Lanfranci*, Giles, I, 260.)

NOTE 13.—Lady Eve, wife of William Crispin I, was the daughter of Simon, sire de Montfort l'Amauri, by his first wife, Isabeau de Broyes, lady of Nogent, and by his third wife Agnès, daughter of Richard, count of Evreux, was half-sister of Amaury de Montfort, count of Evreux, and Bertrade, married first to Fulk le Réchin, count of Anjou and second to Philippe, king of France.[1]

[1] Ord. Vit., III, 3, 433 ; IV, 70 ; Père Anselme, VI, 73, 632 ; *vide* Guillaume, comte d'Evreux ; Geoffroi du Bec, app. 15.

NOTE 17.—Fulco Crispinus attested the Bath abbey charter of 1090 executed at Winchester, and four of the other witnesses were members of or connected with the family of William Crispin I, namely Gilbert Crispin, abbot of Westminster, Robert d'Ouilli, Eudo Dapifer and Alured de Lincoln. Fouque d'Aunou I was the uncle of William Crispin I, and probably the namesake of this Fouque Crispin.[1]

[1] *Mon.*, ii, 266–7 ; *Bath Chartularies* (Som. Rec. Soc.), I, no. 37.

NOTE 20.—Dom Jouvelin[1] places the date of the execution of the Grand charter of the abbey of Bec at about 1070. Le chanoine Porée[2] favours 1077, because archbishop Lanfranc who witnessed it was then in Normandy, but he was also there in 1071, having accompanied William Fitz Osberne from England, at which time he witnessed a confirmation and additional donation to the abbey of Lyre executed by the aforesaid lord.[3]

[1] Bibl. nat. lat. 13905, fo. 115.   [2] I, 645.
[3] *Dict. de l'Eure*, I, 553.

NOTE 22.—Duke Robert Courteheuse held his court at Neaufles about 1090[1] when it possessed the title of barony. The register of Philippe Auguste *c.* 1210 states that William Crispin held his barony of Neaufles for the service of two knights.[2]

[1] *Dict. de l'Eure*, II, 576.   [2] T. Duplessie ; *Dict. de l'Eure*, I, 936 ; II, 516.

NOTE 24.—Manasses Crispin does not have " Dangu " affixed to his name in the charter of Sainte-Marie of Rouen, although he is so designated in the *Dict. de l'Eure*[1] and by others,[2] probably because he may have been castellan of that fortress under his elder brother William Crispin II, who held it in hereditary custodianship as head of the house. The seigniory of Dangu belonged to another family at this period.[3]

[1] I, 934.   [2] *Hist. de la Ville de Gisors*, 329 ; *Hist. de Vesly-en-Vexin*, Otter, 15 ; *Commanderie de Bourgoult* in *Revue Catholique de Normandie*, by l'abbé Guéry in 1903.   [3] *Vide* Robert de Chandos.

NOTE 26.—That William II died shortly after the battle of Tinchebrai is supported by a gift which his wife Agnès made to the abbey of Bec in the first years of the 12th century, for the anniversary of his death (' ad anniversarium ejus faciendum ').[1] Pierre de Langtoft in his *Chronicle* says :
" And William Crispin to be led forth

with the duke (Robert) years and days there the king caused them to be confined. " He finds them clothes, drink and provisions until at length death comes to claim them."
(Pris est le duc Robert, le ray ly fet Maunder A corne son chaustel illoqes va sojourner William de Mortaine ne peut eschaper. Robert d'Estuterile fet ly roy ferger. Et William Crispine ous le duk mener A nuz et jours illoques le roy les fet garder A vestire les trove à manger et bayver Deques taunt qe mort lee veent chalanger.)
Chronique Anglo-Normands, Michel, I, 160.

William was of a proper age to have attended the conquest, and he may have done so, but there is no known evidence to this effect.

[1] Bibl. nat. lat. 1905, fo. 19, v°, et lat. 12884, fo. 215, v°.

NOTE 27.—As early as the 7th century there was a royal villa at Estrépagny. The seignioral rights of high justice were exercised by its lords from time immemorial, and it was a barony from the 13th century.[1] William Crispin II, contrary to the generally accepted opinion, received the laic seigniory of Estrépagny from his father through his rank of military governor and not from his wife, because we are informed in the *Works of Saint-Anselme* that Estrépagny was at that time a fortified market-town, that it was a " lieu de passage " with market-duty and that William Crispin I sojourned there. The wife of William Crispin II received as part of her dowry fifty *s.* levied on the mill of Estrépagny.[2]

[1] *Le Prevost Mem.*, II, 54–60.   [2] *Œuvres de Saint-Anselme*, 36 ; *Dict. de l'Eure*, I, 51, 525.

NOTE 34.—The enmity of William Crispin III toward king Henry was not lessened at this time by the fact that " The king of England rode at the head of a gallant troop of men-at-arms and caused the harvest in the fields about Estrépagny to be reaped by his rapacious soldiery." [1]

[1] Ord. Vit., III, 480.

NOTE 35.—In the battle of Brémule (or Brenneville) in 1119 four hundred French knights attacked five hundred Norman knights ; the former were beaten and one hundred and forty of their number were captured by the enemy. According to Orderic Vital only three knights were killed in the engagement. In those days battles were not very deadly, less on account of the armour with which the knights covered themselves from head to foot than because of the sole aim they kept in mind, to take prisoners and have them ransomed at their pleasure and upon their own terms. Each knight tried to unsaddle his adversary. Moreover, between the French and Normans bonds were many, alliances between families frequent and both spoke the same language. In spite of the rivalry between the two kings (Louis le Gros and Henry I) there was nothing national in such a war.

Ord. Vit., II, 339 ; VI, 358, 359, 369 ; Le Prevost ed.

NOTE 41.—The lady of Lisors was rather the wife of William Crispin III than identical with the wife of William Crispin V, son of Joscelyn, said to have been Ève d'Harcourt,[1] lady of Lisors, daughter of William d'Harcourt by Père Anselme, La Roque, Moreri, and others.[2] Joscelyn was himself in possession of the fief of Lisors, which he had probably inherited from his mother.[3] In any event if Ève d'Harcourt really was the wife of William Crispin V and bore the title of lady of Lisors, it was through the right of her husband and not her own, for there is nothing on record to show that the Harcourts had ever possessed that domain.

[1] Dict. de l'Eure, II, 440 ; vide n. 47. [2] VI, 632 ; I, 270 ; II, 287. [3] Cart. de Mortemer, 49, 55, 56, 76, 78 ; Bibl. nat. lat. 18369 ; Le Prevost Mem., II, 315 ; Dict. de l'Eure, I, 733.

NOTES 42, 43, 44, 45.—La Roque, Père Anselme, Moreri, Bérée, Le Prevost, etc., have not recorded William Crispin III, the son of William Crispin II and father of Joscelyn, probably because Orderic Vital (IV, 70) erroneously called the William Crispin who fought before Gisors in 1123, the nephew instead of the great-nephew of Amaury de Montfort, count of Evreux. They also ignored or overlooked the confirmation charter of Joscelyn to the abbey of Bec, wherein he confirms the gifts of his predecessors[1] : namely, William Crispin I and Ève, his wife, William Crispin II, their son and his wife Agnès, and William Crispin III, son of the latter. The Crispin genealogy by Milo Crispin[2] gives exactly the same pedigree. The aforementioned charter recorded by dom Jouvelin was published in the Histoire de l'Abbaye du Bec by the venerable and beloved chanoine Porée, former curé of Bournainville, correspondent of the Institute, director of the society of Antiquaries of Normandy, etc., chevalier of the legion of Honour, and recognized authority on the history of that abbey, who concurs in the opinion that Joscelyn was the son of William Crispin III. The guidance and services of chanoine Porée in the investigation of the early Crispin family has been of inestimable value, for in producing this work and his edition of the Chronique du Bec he was brought in contact with the extant charters and records of the abbey. Much history of the first Crispins was necessarily interwoven with that of this celebrated monastery from its foundation

until the end of the 12th century since they were its principal benefactors and the jealous guardians of its secular rights during this period.

If Joscelyn had been the son of William II as the aforementioned say, then the third William would have been Joscelyn's brother whom the latter succeeded. This is untenable because Gilbert Crispin, abbot of Westminster, younger brother of William Crispin II, is known to have been born c. 1045, while Joscelyn lived until c. 1197. Joscelyn's birth appears to have taken place about 1115-20, when William II, if alive, would have been 70 to 75 years of age besides, he made extensive donations to the abbey of Bec before 1070, when he certainly was of full age.

The following charter gives the names of the known sons of William Crispin III : " Joscelyn Crispin, by the concession of my brothers, William and Robert . . . which I, William, the eldest of the Crispins have ceded and confirmed with my token " (Joscelinus Crispinus concessione fratrum meorum Willelmi et Roberti . . . hoc ego Willelmus Crispineorum primogenitus concessi et signo meo confirmavi). This charter is reproduced in the Commanderie de Bourgoult by the abbé C. Guéry (almoner of the college of Evreux), published in the 15 September 1901 issue of the Revue Catholique de Normandie, Evreux (p. 114), who received it from the abbé Humbolt, curé of Lisors. It does not appear in the Cartulary of Mortemer, but there is no reason to doubt its authenticity, as the oldest son of this branch of the Crispin family was always named William. Both Joscelyn Crispin and his brother Robert occur in the " great Pipe roll," the former under Essex and Herts, 4 Henry II (1160), " Joscelyn Crispin Xs et iiii^{d}," and the latter in London and Middlesex, 2^{d} Henry II (1158), " Et in libat Robti Crispi(n) pbatoris xvi, s. et iii^{d} " :

Agnès, a sister of Joscelyn Crispin, married Goel de Baudemont, a powerful baron of the Norman Vexin as appears in charters in favour of the regular canons established at Sausseuse and the abbey of Jumièges.[3]

Emahius, Joscelyn and Gilbert Crispin occur in the confirmation of the privileges of the ville of Rouen by Henry, duke of Normandy, which had been granted by duke William. La Roque,[4] quoting John of Brompton, places the date in 1106, and says it was executed by duke William's son, Henry I, then king of England and duke of Normandy. This is an error ; the confirmation occurred between 1149 and 1159.

Hugh, archbishop of Rouen, who was consecrated in 1130,[5] and Philippe d'Harcourt, bishop of Bayeux in 1142,[6] attested this document. Since Henry I died in 1135 it could not have been him, the next of the name, duke of Normandy, was Henry, son of Geoffry Plantagenet, count of Anjou and duke of Normandy, who gave up that duchy to his son in 1149,[7] the latter also becoming Henry II of England five years later. Robert de Neubourg, another witness of this confirmation, died in 1159, which fixes the date as stated.

Joscelyn Crispin (count) seignior of Estrèpagny, Blangy, Neaufles, Lisors, Livarot and Dangu,[8] which latter he acquired through his wife Isabel du Plessis de Dangu, daughter of Robert and Eufémie de Dangu, had by her the following children, between 1141 and 1150 : William, Robert, Eustache, Agnès, Èva and Emeline,[9] and later another, Marcelle, who married, first, the baron of Tancarville (probably Ralph, who died c. 1204) and, second, Jean de Gisors.[10] Joscelyn is mentioned in many charters of the abbey of Mortemer, to which he gave extensive possessions. At one time he and his father-in-law donated 128 acres equally, and it is the confirmation of this gift wherein his children just named occur. It was made in atonement for the violent death of Adam Aiguillon (Adam Aculei), seignior of Trie in the French Vexin near Gisors, and to escape the revenge of his family which was the outcome of a feud between them. (Jos. Crispinus gener ipsius Roberti alias LX pro concordia de morte Aculei.) [11] These dates are fixed because Hugh, archbishop of Rouen, in a confirmatory charter dated there in 1141 concerning the abbey of Mortemer, and preserved in the Cartulary of that monastery (29), refers to land given to it by Robert de Dangu : " The land with all its appurtenances which was given by the noble man Robert de Dangu at the place called Pommeraie " (Terram quoque cum omnibus pertinentiis suis que vobis a nobili viro Roberto de Dangu donata est, in loco qui de Pomeria nominatur . . . anno ab incarnatione Domini M⁰C⁰XL⁰I⁰). This donation was confirmed by Joscelyn Crispin in an undated charter wherein he names his children which is placed in the Cartulary immediately after one of 1150 (55-6-7). The next charter which bears a date is the fifth following that of Joscelyn which was executed in 1152 (60). It may thus be assumed that his confirmation occurred about this time.

Toward the latter part of the 12th century Joscelyn gave lands from his fiefs of Livarot and Blangy to Notre Dame de Beaulieu.[12]

Joscelyn's castle of Estrépagny in 1150 had eleven fortresses depending from it, which included Dangu, Neaufles, Gisors, Baudemont, Bray, Nogent beyond the Andelle, Harachiville, etc. At that time

Henry Plantagenet, duke of Normandy, with the consent of his father, Geoffry, count of Anjou, gave his suzerainty of this stronghold to the king of France.[13]

[1] Vide Guillaume Crispin, n. 37 text.   [2] De nob. Crispin. gen., I, 348.   [3] Stapleton, II, cxii ; Chart. Abb. Jumièges, I, 223.   [4] IV, 1275.   [5] Chron. de Torigny, I, 183-4 and n.   [6] Ord. Vit., IV, 213 and n. ; Chron. de Torigny, I, 229 and n.   [7] Roger of Wendover, Giles, 503.   [8] Vide Robert de Chandos.   [9] Cart. de Mortemer, 12 and fol.   [10] Père Anselme, VI, 633 ; La Roque, I, 268 ; Moreri, II, 287 ; vide Le Chamberlain de Tancarville.   [11] Ibid., n. 9 ; Dict. de l'Eure, I, 935, II, 443.   [12] La Roque, IV, 966.   [13] Hist. de la France, XII, 187 ; Le Prevost Mem., I, 188.

NOTE 46.—Joscelyn Crispin is named in a charter in favour of the abbey of Mortemer of 1180-9,[1] in one by his son, William Crispin V, temp. Philippe Auguste of the priory of Vesly-en-Vexin between 1180 and 1197,[2] and occurs in the Exchequer rolls of 1180.[3]

The rolls of 1198 have the following record : " The heir Joscelyn Crispin rendered account of 14 pounds for his father on account of debts of Raoul Bishop of Lisieux. In donation to the said heir of Joscelyn 14 pounds by order of the king. Account discharged." (Heres Joscelin Crispin reddit Compotum de 14 lib. Pro patre suo de debitis Radulphi episcopi Lexovii. In perdonatione ipse heredi del Joscelini 14 lib. per breve Regis. Et quietus est.) [4] This indicates that Joscelyn died about 1197. Some think it should read " The heir of Joscelyn " (Heres Joscelini).

He was deceased by this time, for his son and successor, William V, then held Dangu. Philippe Auguste had taken it in 1196 and in 1197 Richard I of England compelled William Crispin V to deliver it to him. It passed back and forth between these monarchs until peace was made in 1199.[5]

[1] Cart. de Mortemer, 22.   [2] Bibl. nat. lat. 5441, I, fo. 101.   [3] Stapleton, I, cxxii ; II, ccviii ; Grands Rôles de l'Échiquier, L. d'Anisy, Part I, 23, col. 2, 28, col. 2.   [4] Ibid., d'Anisy, Part II, 12, col. 2.   [5] Stapleton, II, xliii ; Dict. de l'Eure, I, 935.

NOTES 47-9.—Robert d'Harcourt II, son and heir of William d'Harcourt, married, as is shown by Stapleton,[1] Ève, daughter of Joscelyn Crispin, sister of William Crispin V, and not Joanna, daughter of Robert, count of Meulent, as stated by La Roque.[2] Robert d'Harcourt died between 1199 and 1208 [3] and Ève Crispin d'Harcourt occurs in a charter of the abbey of Mortemer, with her father and mother, of 1180-9 (Dña Evā de harecort filia ei),[4] which speaks of a large donation of her mother Isabel and of one by her. William Crispin V may have as claimed married a sister of Robert d'Harcourt named Ève, but it has the appearance of confusion on the part of the historians and genealogists with William's sister Ève, and can be so considered pending documentary substantiation of this statement. His wife at the time of his death shortly before 1223 was Amicie, daughter of Barthélemy de Roye, grand chamberlain of France, and of Péronnelle de Montfort. She was the mother of his children, at least of William Crispin VI, for the obituary of Joyenval says so [5] and places the death of the latter on 28 June : " William Crispin of Dangu." [6] William V had a daughter also, Isabeau, lady of Livarot, who married Robert de Neubourg, baron of Asnebec, a great grandson of Henry de Beaumont, first earl of Warwick.[7] Amicie is said to have been the first wife of William Crispin VI, son and heir of William V, by Père Anselme,[8] Moreri,[9] Le Prevost,[10] and others who have not given the following charter due consideration. She died between 1221, the date of the foundation of the abbey of Joyenval by her father,[11] and 1224, because in the latter year he confirmed a donation made to that abbey by her wherein he speaks of his daughter as deceased. " Know that our daughter of good memory A., wife of William Crispin, for the salvation of her soul and her mother's had given," etc. (Noverit universitas vestra quod cum bone memorie A., filia nostra, uxor Guillelmi Crispini pro Salute anime matris sue et sua legasset in perpetuum . . . redditus). To the charter is affixed an equestrian seal checky with two lozenges in chief, of green wax with red and green silk ribbon, bearing the inscription " Barthélemy de Roye chamberlain of France " (Sigill. Bartholomei de Roie camerarii Francis).[12] After the death of her husband Amicie became a nun and abbess of Premy at Cambray,[13] to the church of which ville her ancestors had been identified for generations.[14] Thus she could not have been the wife of William Crispin VI, which is substantiated below. Furthermore, William VI in 1224 made a donation to Joyenval " for the salvation of my soul and of my parents and friends " (Pro remedio anime mee parentum et amicorum meorum),[15] and another in the following year, " which I give and concede for the salvation of my soul and the souls of my ancestors " (Quod ego dedi et concessi pro remedio anime mee et antecessorum meorum).[16] Since he does not mention a wife or children it can be assumed that he had neither up to that time.

[1] Stapleton, II, ccix. [2] La Roque, I, 269. [3] Stapleton, II, ccviii, ccix. [4] Cart. de Mortemer, 22. [5] Père Anselme, VI, 633. [6] Bibl. nat. lat. 17048, fo. 717. [7] Vide Hamon Le Seneschal ; La Roque, I, 269 ; Père Anselme, VI, 633. [8] VI, 634. [9] II, 287. [10] II,

58. [11] Bibl. nat. lat. 17048, fo. 704. [12] Ibid. [13] Moreri, IX, 414 ; Dict. de l'Eure, I, 936. [14] Père Anselme, VIII, 7, 8. [15] Arch. Seine-et-Oise, series H, abb. de Joyenval 9 ; Bibl. nat. lat. 17048, fo. 709. [16] Arch. nat. S., 5193, nos. 26–7, charter marked 5194.

NOTE 50.—William Crispin VI having become a French subject fought at the king's side in the battle of Bouvinnes in 1220.[1] In a document of July 1223, with no title attached to his name, concerning Bourgoult, he speaks of his uncle, Robert Crispin, then deceased, son of Joscelyn, whose heir he was and Agnès du Rouvray, his aunt, the wife of Robert.[2] He occurs in another of the same year in a controversy with the archbishop of Rouen, wherein he refers to a fief which apparently came to him from the chamberlain of Tancarville (his uncle).[3] In another of 1224 as sire de Dangu he again refers to his uncle Robert,[4] which appears to be the first time the Crispins claimed this title for Dangu. William Crispin VI married Alix de Sancerre by 1230, for in that year he confirmed the donations of his predecessors to the priory of Saint-Ymer-en-Auge as sire de Mauny,[5] which domain he possessed in her right. She was the daughter of Etienne, count of Cârillon-sur-Loing, grand bouteiller of France, of the illustrious house of the counts of Champagne,[6] and of Elonore de Soissons his first wife, and as is recorded in an act of parliament Alix was living in 1263.[7] They had issue, William VII, who followed, Jean, lord of Lisors and Saint-Clair-sur-Epte, and Hugues, ancestor of the seigniors of Bourri. Jean married Amicie or Anne de Ferrières, who died in 1292 and he followed in 1297. They had Jean, lord of Lisors, deceased in 1316, William d'Arquency and Etienne dead in 1327, all of whom were buried in the abbey of Mortemer.[8] William VI died prior to 1254, when his son William VII, the marshal, paid homage to the king for his patrimony, the domain of his wife, and the lapsed constableship of Normandy.[9] Indeed, there is evidence that he died shortly before 1248, as Drocon de Montigny, bailiff of Gisors in an account of the ascension, 1248, mentions the tutelage of William's children.[10] This indicates that his son, who succeeded him, William VII, the marshal, was probably quite young at the date of his marriage six years later.

[1] Dict. de l'Eure, II, 53. [2] Arch. nat., S. 5194, no. 19, box numbered 5193. [3] Cart. Normand., Delisle, 307. [4] Arch. Seine-et-Oise, series H, abb. de Joyenval, 6049. [5] Cart. de Saint-Ymer-en-Auge et Bricquebec, Breard, 34. [6] Le Prevost Mem., II, 58. [7] Père Anselme, II, 847 ; VI, 686 ; Le Prevost Mem., II, 7. [8] Dossiers Bleus, 78 ; Moreri, II, 287 ; IX, 414 ; La Roque, I, 629 ; Hist. de la Ville de Rouen, II, 57. [9] Cart. Normand., 519 ; Dict. de l'Eure, I, 936. [10] De Baulo puerorum Gellemi

Crispini pro tertio II, c. l. Compte des Dracon de Montigny, Bailli de Gisors Ascension, 1248 ; *Hist. de la France*, XXI, 277F.

NOTE 51.—William Crispin VII who married Jeanne de Mortemer, was the grandson of William V, brother of Robert Crispin, both sons of Joscelyn, because in a charter regarding Bourgoult of 1256 he mentions " Monseigneur Robert Crespin, uncle of my very dear father, monseigneur William Crespin (knight)," which document bears a fusiled seal. This establishes beyond question that he was the third William in direct male descent, following Joscelyn.[1]

William Crispin in 1263 and his wife made a donation to the monks of Jumièges which occurs in a document of William chamberlain of Tancarville.[2] He appears in two more of the same year, one concerning the land of Hommet [3] and the other the forest of Mauny.[4] In 1264, William Crispin, seigneur d'Estrépagny, occurs relative to certain rights of the citizens of Estrépagny,[5] and in 1266 he made a donation to the abbey of Saint-Wandrille.[6] Two years later, he and his wife appear in a document concerning the monks of Sainte-Catherine of Rouen,[7] and he is mentioned in a decree of this year referring to the abbey of Montivilliers.[8] In 1270, William Crispin, knight, was maintained in his rights to hunt big game in the wood of Saint-Poer.[9] On 31 January 1274 he is recorded in a document relative to his fief of Mauny as sire d'Estrépagny,[10] and the following year he was sustained in certain claims to the forest of Lions.[11] He had a lawsuit against the abbey of Saint-Ouen of Rouen,[12] 10 October 1277, and in 1283 received a favourable decree regarding his rights of high justice in his barony of Estrépagny [13] and another in 1286 concerning these rights in his back fiefs and Dangu.[14] He occurs in 1292 in an agreement with reference to the ground of Berri,[15] and in the same year he was in conflict with the high justice of Gisors on account of Dangu.[16] In 1293 he again occurs regarding the land of Berri.[17]

William Crispin VII after the death of his wife, between 1269 and 1272, claimed in the latter year the constableship of Normandy during the minority of his children, which lapsed when his wife died, pretending that it was hereditary and not individual, being joined and annexed to the glebe and to the domain of Varanguebec.[18]

Nevertheless, the court at Rouen held that the title was personal and not transferable, it was therefore withdrawn from William Crispin's children [19] and in 1275 it again so ruled,[20] but later in the same year William proved his claim to the hereditary constableship,[21] and the court records in 1277 show that it was given to him until the majority of his children.[22] At

this period there were three kinds of majority :

First, *The legal majority*, generally fixed at twenty for both sexes. It gave the power to administer and dispose of personal property.

Second, *The feudal majority* dealt with tenure of the fee, was at twenty for males and fifteen for females.

Third, *The perfect majority* gave the entire capacity to dispose of the estate and personal property and was almost universally fixed at the age of 26.

A decree of 1278 confirmed William Crispin in the " seisin " of all of the land which formerly belonged to Jourdain (du Hommet), constable of Normandy,[23] which shows that the pedigree given by William de Meulan following was correct. Thus entrenched in this office, William Crispin apparently held it until the time of his death, at least he so appears in a deed of 1293,[24] when his children were certainly of full age, and king Philippe-le-Bel gave the title to him in letters of 1297.[25]

Jean de Meulan III, count of Tancarville, of the blood royal, whose family had acquired this office through marriage with the granddaughter of William Crispin the marshal, emulating him in the desire to prove that the constableship was attached to the soil, used his tremendous influence at court to this end. He succeeded in having it admitted in a declaration of 1381 that he held " Varanguebec by reason of which he was constable." [26]

William de Meulan, count of Tancarville, brother and successor of the aforementioned Jean, in an action given at the parliament at the Royal palace, 20 July 1398,[27] thus recites the manner in which the constableship came to William Crispin : Jourdain du Hommet, brother of William du Hommet mentioned below,[28] possessed " the land of Varanguebec, a noble barony to which the constableship of Normandy was annexed " as well as the baronies of La Haie-du-Puits and La Luthumière, all carried by his daughter through marriage to Robert de Mortemer, baron of Bec de Mortemer-en-Caux. Their son William, baron of Bec de Mortemer, La Luthumière, and Varanguebec, and therefore constable of Normandy, had an only daughter Jeanne, who married William Crispin. The defendant in the suit, Roger de Bricqueville, also descended from the family du Hommet, while agreeing in the essential parts of the pedigree said the name of Jeanne's father was Robert, in which event she was the sister of William de Mortemer, whom she succeeded (*vide* appendix 19, Constables of Normandy).

M. de la Mare Chenevarin, auditor of the chamber of accounts at Rouen, says in the ms. Memoirs in his library dated 1417,[29] the

"Constableship of Normandy went with the domain of Varanguebec," but there exists a charter of Henry II made at Caen among the archives of Our Lady of Aunay confirming a donation of Richard du Hommet, wherein he is called constable of Normandy, to which office king Henry constituted him [30] in letters of concession, and made it hereditary for his posterity.[31] William du Hommet, his son, possessed it hereditarily after 1173 [32] and it was confirmed to him and his descendants by the same king.[33] Richard du Hommet II, son of the last-named William, brought Varanguebec into the family through marriage, as recorded in appendix 19, but the constableship had already been possessed by his father and grandfather. On 31 December 1563 the land of Varanguebec was given by Leonor d'Orleans, duc de Longueville, who had inherited it from the Tancarvilles through the Harcourts, to his natural brother François, marquis de Rotelin.[34] The former retained and joined to the land of Tancarville the constableship of Normandy and it was still there in 1718 when it was acquired by the count of Evreux, which was confirmed by letters patent from the king and verified without opposition by the parliament of Rouen, 18 November 1719.[35] Thus the constableship was attached to the person and not the land, for while Varanguebec and the vast domain of du Hommet, with this hereditary office, passed to the descendants of Richard du Hommet together, it was not because the one was attached to the other but by right of birth.[36]

[1] Arch. nat. S. 5192, no. 15, first folder. [2] Recueil de jugement de l'exch. de Norm., Delisle, 191-2, no. 827. [3] Archives de l'Empire, Boutaric, 67, no. 731. [4] Ibid., 90, 91, no. 967. [5] Ibid., 81, no. 888. [6] Dict. de l'Eure, I, 936. [7] Ibid. [8] Boutaric, 113, no. 1255. [9] Ibid., 147, no. 1561. [10] Cart. Normand., Delisle, 835. [11] Boutaric, 118, no. 1963. [12] Cart. Normand., 907. [13] Boutaric, 236, no. 2484. [14] Ibid., 250, no. 2567. [15] Ibid., 276, no. 2798. [16] Ibid., 278, no. 2817. [17] Ibid., note 15. [18] Arch. de l'Empire, Boutaric, 169, no. 1852, Olim, I, fo. 191 r°; La Roque, I, 630, III, 388; Arch. Seine Inf. fonds du abb. de Valasse, not classified. [19] Ibid. [20] Boutaric, 332, no. 212 (D 27). [21] Ibid., 334, no. 229 (D 27, v°); Grands officiers de la Couronne, Doufourny, I, 494. [22] Boutaric, 187, no. 2022, Olim, II, fo. 32 v°. [23] Ibid., 202, no. 2151, Olim, II, fo. 41 r°. [24] Copy Arch. Seine Inf.; La Roque, I, 653. [25] Hist. du diocèse de Bayeux, 233. [26] Hist. du comté d'Evreux, Le Brasseur, 4; Le Prevost Mem., II, 58. [27] La Roque, II, 1459, 2013; Ibid., Le Prevost Mem. [28] Neustria Pia, 758-61. [29] La Roque, I, 630, III, 388. [30] Ibid., I, 653. [31] Ibid., IV, 2181-2; Stapleton, I, cxxxv. [32] Red Book, Saint-Martin de Seez, fo. 85; Stapleton, I, cxxxv; La Roque, I, 653. [33] Ibid., La Roque; Stapleton, I, cxxxv. [34] Le Brasseur, 5; La Roque, III, 718. [35] Le Brasseur, 2. [36] Le Brasseur, app. 1 to 28.

NOTE 52.—Bretteville la Chaussée, Seine-Inf., arrondissement of Havre canton of Goderville, enjoyed the privilege of high justice and power of barony. It was held by William Crispin VII, the marshal in the right of his wife under the baron of Tancarville, and was therefore independent of the barony of Bec-Crispin.

Cart. Normand., Delisle, 241, no. 953; Olim, I; Boutaric, I, 365, no. 425B.

NOTE 54.—At first there was only one marshal of France who, under Philippe Auguste (1180-1223), led the advance guard and directed the battle. From Saint-Louis (1226-70) to François I (1515) there were two who were subordinate to the constable, passed the troops under review and maintained discipline in the armies.[1]

[1] Dict. hist. des instit. Moeurs et Coutumes de la France, A. Cheruel, I, 211; II, 733; Guillaume Le Breton, book VIII of the Philippeide.

NOTES 55, 56, 57, 58, 59, 60.—William Crispin VIII, eldest son of the marshal, baron of Estrépagny, etc., married Mahaut de Baumez, daughter of Thibaud, seigneur de Baumez, and of Marguerite de Villebon, which is confirmed in a decree of 1322 where occurs "Guillelum Crispini militem dominum d'Estrepigny," showing that he was then the head of the family. His wife obtained her dowry over his lands in Normandy in 1330 when he was necessarily deceased.[1] They had issue two daughters only; Jeanne Crispin, the eldest, married Jean II de Meulan, grand master and grand chamberlain of France, governor of Champagne, Brie, Bourgogne and Languedoc, count of Tancarville and lord of Montreuil-Bellai and through her constable of Normandy, baron of Estrépagny, Varanguebec and Neaufles. The latter domain had left the Crispin family about this time, for it was possessed by queen Blanche (d'Evreux), wife of king Philippe VI (de Valois), c.1350, but prior to 1398 part of it was returned to the Tancarvilles. The château was destroyed c. 1647 by the order of cardinal Mazarin and only part of the tower still remains.[2] The younger daughter Marie married Jean de Chalons III, count of Auxerre and Tonnerre, high cup-bearer of France, who carried to him the baronies of Bec-Crispin, La Luthumière and the seigniories of Boutavant and Louves.[3] An epitaph in the abbey of Mortemer said to refer to the marshal places the death of "William Crispin, formerly lord of d'Angu" on 26 August 1333 and that of his son Jean, 10 September of the same year.[4] The date cannot be reconciled with the known facts, difficult as it is to disbelieve this record. M. Le Prevost in fixing it in 1313 is substantially correct, and it is significant that the day and month recorded by him is the same as that of the epitaph.

M. Valutien, dean of the faculty of Rouen, in an article on the Crispin family published in 1836 in the *Mémoires de la Société des Antiquaires de Normandie*[5] says the marshal died in 1283 and others favour this period.[6] The reason for their conclusion undoubtedly was because William Crispin styled himself marshal in a number of documents of Philippe le Hardi dated 1283–4[7] and does not so occur thereafter. In 1292 William Crispin gave "liege-homage" for the land of La Loupe formerly held by the "lady of Dangu his mother." (Guillaume Crespin chevalier fit hommage lige de la terre de la Loupe que tenoit la Dame de Dangu sa mère.)[8] This could only refer to Alix de Sancerre, the mother of the William Crispin who married Jeanne de Mortemer as the Sancerre family owned the castle and domain of La Loupe, which proves that it was William Crispin, the constable and marshal, who executed the document. He occurs as constable of Normandy and sire de Dangu, concerning a lease of certain fiefs in an act of August 1293[9] and as sire de Dangu in another in favour of the priory of Vesly-en-Vexin in 1296.[10] A concession to the nuns of Montevilliers was made in 1299 by his oldest son "William Crispin, the young, seigneur du Bec de Mortemer," which seigniory he had inherited from his mother. He affixed an equestrian seal with shield and saddle-cloth charged with fusils of exactly the same design as that used by his grandfather, William Crispin VI. Père Anselme says the marshal was called "the young," it was rather his son as this is the only charter where this designation has been found.[11] William Crispin, lord of Dangu, and his son William are recorded in an act of 1302 in the cartulary of Saint-Wandrille,[12] where he is also referred to as seigneur de Sainte-Marie du Mont, de Saint-Martin and de Saint-Germain de Varaville.[13] William Crispin "the father," "the old" and "the eldest," and William Crispin "the young" and "the son," are recorded several times in 1303 and 1304 concerning convocations for the war of Flanders,[14] who it can be presumed were the marshal and his son. The marshal's power was so great that he did not even fear excommunication. In December 1309 "the noble man sire William Crispin knight" (nobilis sir Guillume Crespin) occurs in a bull of pope Clement V, who instructed the dean of the church of Paris to excommunicate him unless he settled a controversy with the canon of the church of Rouen over a toll tax which William exacted of him for crossing his property at Saint-Clair-sur-Epte with belongings. William claimed this as his hereditary right, but the

following year on the fifth of October he gave satisfaction to the canon adjusting the matter. This agreement was attested with his seal, bearing fusils.[15] He last occurs "Item foedum Domini Guillelmi Crespin" in the register of requests presented to parliament in 1312.[16] Jean, first of the name, sire de Dangu, the marshal's second son, also inherited from his parents Lisors and Mauny, and married Jeanne Tesson Bertrand, lady of Thury, by whom he had Jean II and William IX. The marshal was dead before 1315, for in that year his son "Jean" I as "sire de Dangu" executed a document in favour of the abbey of Gomerfontaine with the consent of his sons "Jean II and William"[17] which shows that he did not die at the same time as his father. This charter also establishes that Jean II was older than his brother William or his name would not have preceded the latter's in the charter; furthermore, Jean II received Dangu, Lisors, and Thury, a much more important inheritance than Mauny, which was bequeathed to his brother.

The opposite opinion has been registered by Anselme, Moreri, and others who have overlooked these details. In 1320 Jean I, or his son Jean II, as "sire de Dangu" confirmed to the abbey of Joyenval the donation of his ancestors.[18] One of these Jeans occurs as "sire de Lisors" in 1330.[19] Jean II, seigneur de Dangu, de Lisors and de Thury, eldest son of Jean I, married Jeanne, daughter of Henry III, baron of Avangour,[20] by whom he had William X, seigneur, de Dangu and de Thury, who appears with the former title in a charter of 8 May 1334 with his wife Agnès de Trie, daughter of Renaud de Trie, seigneur de Vaumain (Oise) and Jeanne Hodunc.[21] Hence both Jean I and II were deceased by this time. La Roque[22] without giving his reason says, this William, who was the only sire de Dangu of this name following the marshal, died in this year; in any event, however, he was dead before 1353, without issue, when his wife is recorded as a widow.[23] The epitaph of the abbey of Mortemer of 1333 might refer to him, assuming that he had a son Jean unrecorded elsewhere because they both died at the same time. The date even then would be incorrect, although La Roque's statement, if it can be credited, signifies that his death occurred in the following year.

His sister Blanche, who married, first, Louis, seigneur de Ferrières, and, second, Pierre or Jean, seigneur de Préaux, succeeded to his inheritance.[24] Jeanne, a younger sister, married Guy, seigneur de Tournebu, to whom she brought the barony of Motte-Cesny and of Grimbosc.[25] The male line now reverted to William Crispin IX, seigneur de Mauny, second son of Jean

I, who occurs in a decree of parliament in 1323 and one of the king in the following year.[26] He is called patron of the chapel of Mauny in 1337[27] and is recorded in a war receipt of 1352 for his services in command of bow-shooters.[28] Three dated 1353, 1354 and 1356, of William Crispin, "esquire," undoubtedly his son, indicates that he was still alive. In any event he was dead before 1368[29] since his widow, Jeanne de Moy, had married Jean de Mericourt by this time who had a lawsuit with her son whose widow in turn she became in this year.[30] They had issue William XI, who followed and Jeanne, married, first, to Raoul Herpin, seigneur de Saint-Sauflieu and, second, to Jean, seigneur de Crévecœur and de Thois whose widow she became in 1380.[31] William Crispin XI, seigneur de Mauny, inherited Lisors from the heirs of Jean Crispin I, sire de Dangu, probably through his father William IX, after whose death he sold it c. 1367.[32] By his wife Jeanne de Calletot, lady of Fleury, Lilly and Morigny in the forest of Lions, called the three cities of Saint-Denis, daughter of William de Calletot, seigneur de Darneval-en-Caux, he had issue William XII, and Ide married to Louis de Thibouville, who became a widow in 1419.[33]

William XI made a donation to Saint-Omer 19 June 1369 and occurs in a charter of 1371, on both of which documents his arms are attached. An inclined fusiled shield, supporters, a lion or leopard rampant on the dexter and sinister sides. Crest, a helmet at the top, a wisp.[34] William Crispin rendered signal service to the king of France in his wars from 1368 to 1381, and is recorded in eight of them.[35] It is uncertain, however, whether it was this William or his son and heir William XII, who participated in the last few campaigns. On 6 January 1376 during the reign of Charles V the records of the chamber of accounts show that Bec-Crispin was sold by Louis de Chalons I, count of Auxerre, son of Jean III, to William de Bordes.[36]

The Crispins tried to regain it and Père Anselme says William Crispin XI "took it from the hands of those to whom the count of Auxerre sold it," but by what means he obtained it is not clear.[37] If this be true, then William died and his son and heir William XII inherited it from him before 1386, as will be shown later on, for, by a decree of parliament[38] in that year, William de Bordes was maintained in his possession of it.

William Crispin XII supported the king in his campaign in 1388 at the frontiers of Germany.[39] The Exchequer of the year 1391 informs us that William Crispin XII tried to regain the barony of Bec-Crespin

and another act of the same year speaks of "the late noble man messire William Crispin" and his son "Jean Crispin esquire minor," establishing the death of the former at this time.[40]

He had married Jacqueline d'Auvricher, daughter of Jean d'Auvricher and Marie de Braente.[41]

Jean Crispin, their oldest son and heir, occurs in a document of 1404, as sire de Mauny, signifying that he was then of age and had succeeded to his father's estates.[42] In a lawsuit of 1410 it is stated that Bec-Crispin was then in the possession of John de Bordes, son of the above-mentioned, and another of 1413 says Jean Crispin is baron of Bec-Crispin.[43] How he acquired it is again unrecorded. It was therefore held by him in 1418 when Henry V of England confiscated, and sold it, to John Fastolf, an English knight, at which time he also seized the adjoining baronies in that part of Normandy.[44] Jean had regained it by 1447, when he appears as baron du Bec-Crispin in a charter then executed by him and still held it at the time of his death.[45]

King Henry's act of confiscation declares "these grounds (Bec-Crispin) had belonged to William Crespin (XII) and Jacqueline d'Orchet (Auvricher), his wife,"[46] and therefore only applied to possession of it by them sometime previous to 1386 and after 1376 as it could not have been at a later date. King Henry, 17 January 1420, in an act executed at Rouen, confiscated Maudestour, Villores, Heuville and Coudray and half of the domain of Bellebœuf and the fiefs of Margotes with their dependencies situated in the bailiwick of Rouen and Gisors which belonged to William Crispin, knight, "on account of his disobedience," viz. because he had remained loyal to the king of France. King Henry gave these lands to Marie de Bréante, widow of Jean d'Auvricher, who apparently had faithfully supported the English for the king calls him "our liege-man."[47] This was not William Crispin XII, husband of Jacqueline d'Auvricher, who was seigneur de Mauny and d'Angerville.[48] Jacqueline in 1425 received 300 livres from the king Charles VII, the reason for which payment was not disclosed, but it was assumed by the historians to have been for war services rendered by her husband, then deceased,[49] who thought he was the William Crispin whose properties had been confiscated. These circumstances caused Père Anselme, Moreri, and others to confuse this William with William Crispin XII, the husband of Jacqueline. The former was a cadet of the house whose identity remains unestablished, who may be identical with the "William Crispin, knight, and actual verdier of the woods of La Ferté Macé," living at this period, who occurs in charters of 1398, 1401 and 1408. His arms differ from those of the main line of the family.

A chevron on an inclined shield. Supporters, two griffins segreant, one on the dexter side and the other on the sinister. Crest, a griffin's head.[50] While the confiscated properties of William Crispin, the cadet, were in the immediate vicinity of those of the Crispin and Auvricher families, signifying close relationship, nevertheless, none of them were key fiefs of either.

Jacqueline d'Auvricher Crispin was the mistress of king Charles VII and died in 1440.[51] Her son Jean by William Crispin XII inherited from her the domain of Auvricher (now Orcher, canton of Montevilliers), to which was attached the title of hereditary marshal of Normandy. Jean married Marguerite, daughter of Pierre d'Ambroise, seigneur de Chaumont and of Anne de Bueil, by whom he had no issue, who after his death married Jean de Rochechouart, seigneur de Mortemer, 25 August 1457.[52] Jacqueline Crispin was the mother also of Antoine Crispin the archbishop, Jeanne, admitted to have been the daughter of king Charles, and another daughter, Jacqueline. Antoine after the death of his brother Jean, whose heir he was, sold all of this inheritance, which included Bec-Crispin, Angerville, Auvricher, Mauny, Plasne, Ferrières, Grumesnil, and Barneville, to Pierre de Brézé, husband of his sister Jeanne for 9,000 livres, and 2,000 gold pieces for the dower of Jeanne d'Aunou, widow of Jacques d'Auvricher his uncle, of Marguerite d'Ambroise, widow of his brother Jean and of Jacqueline his sister, married to Robert de Folques.[53] Antoine was one of the two ambassadors of king Louis XI to the duke of Burgundy in 1462 and was either a very old man at the time of his death or he was not the son of William Crispin XII. In any event, he was the recipient of most unusual favours and honours from both king Charles VII and his son Louis XI, among which was a pension of 3,000 livres of tournois annually granted in 1467 by the latter,[54] which creates the thought that Antoine may also have been the offspring of Charles VII.

Pierre de Brézé, seignior of Varenne and Brechessac, count of Maulévrier, etc., grand seneschal of Anjou, Poitou and Normandy, was killed at the battle of Montlhéry in 1465. He and his wife Jeanne Crispin sold the three cities of Saint-Denis situated in the forest of Lions to Louis de Harcourt,[55] which she had received from her brothers Jean and Antoine. This in-heritance came to Jean through his father, William Crispin XII, who received it from his mother, Jeanne de Calletot, wife of William Crispin XI, which proves that she married the latter and not William Crispin, sire de Dangu and de Thury, the son of Jean II, sire de Dangu, as stated by La Roque and others.[56] Pierre and his wife who died shortly before 1488, lie buried in the cathedral of Rouen, where their magnificent sarcophagus exists in the chapel of the Holy Virgin.[57] Their son and heir, Jacques de Brézé, married Charlotte, daughter of Charles VII by his morganatic wife, the beautiful Agnès Sorel[58] and, having caught her in the act of adultery with his huntsman, Pierre de la Bergne, he killed her,[59] for which act of violence he was never punished. His son by Agnès, Louis de Brézé, count of Maulévrier, baron of Bec-Crispin and Mauny, grand seneschal, lieutenant-general, governor of Normandy, died 23 July 1531 and was buried in the cathedral at Rouen. His wife, Diane of Poitiers, mistress of king Henry II, erected a mausoleum for him, which is one of the finest works of renaissance sculpture of its kind of the 16th century, made entirely of alabaster and black marble and enhanced with gold, where at her death she was likewise interred.[60]

Bec-Crispin definitely left the possession of the Crispin family through the marriage of Françoise, daughter of Louis de Brézé, to Robert de la Marck IV in the first half of the 16th century.[61]

[1] Boutaric, 432, no. 6719 ; Père Anselme, VI, 632 ; Moreri, II, 287.   [2] Père Anselme, VI, 633 ; Le Prevost Mem., II, 58.   [3] Ibid. and La Roque, II, 1460.   [4] Hist. de la ville de Rouen, II, 58 ; vide n. 23.   [5] Second series, IV, 110.   [6] Dict. de l'Eure, I, 936 ; Lechevalier, 7.   [7] Mem. de la chambre des comptes de Paris, cote 13, from 1330 to 1339, destroyed in the fire of 1737 ; Olim, I, Boutaric, I, 388, 389, no. 357 ; La Roque, II, 2005 ; III, 240, 246, 247 ; Père Anselme, VI, 631–2 ; Dossiers Bleus, Bibl. nat. 5675, vol. 222.   [8] Cartulary or Register of the fiefs of the Bishopric of Chartres ; La Roque, IV, 1018 (old no. 2132).   [9] Record of Colart de Basqueville, guardian of the seal of the castle of Gisors for the king, 2 December 1398 ; Arch. de l'Empire, Boutaric, J., 217, no. 20 ; "Copy" Arch. Seine Inf. at Rouen.   [10] Bibl. nat. lat. 5441, I, fo. 101–2.   [11] Arch. Seine Inf. fonds du abb. de Montivilliers (not classified).   [12] Cart. de abb. de Saint-Wandrille, fo. 290.   [13] Ibid.   [14] Hist. de la France, XXIII, 791, D. 798E, 792B, 735G, 802F.   [15] Arch. Seine Inf., G. 3611.   [16] La Roque, IV, 1018.   [17] Ibid., I, 629.   [18] Arch. Seine-et-Oise, series H, abb. de Joyenval, box 9.   [19] Dict. de l'Eure, I, 936.   [20] La Roque, II, 2012 ; Père Anselme, VI, 634 ; Moreri, II, 287.   [21] Ibid. ; Arch. Seine Inf., G. 4106 ; Le Prevost Mem., II, 8.   [22] La Roque, II, 2013.   [23] Ibid., Père Anselme, Moreri, and Le Prevost ; Dict. de l'Eure, I, 937.   [24] Ibid.   [25] La

Roque, III, 786 ; *ibid.*, Père Anselme and Moreri. [26] *Ibid.* ; Boutaric, II, 551, no. 7397. [27] *Pou-ille de la Province de Rouen*, Longnon, 5D. [28] Bibl. nat. *Collection* Clairmbault, 37, p. 2788, no. 93. [29] *Ibid.*, n. 24 ; Bibl. nat. fr. 27412, *Pieces Originales*, 928, fo. 44, no. 2–3 ; *Collection* Clairmbault, 37, 2789, no. 98. [30] *Ibid.*, Père Anselme. [31] *Ibid.*, Père Anselme and Moreri. [32] *Dict. de l'Eure*, II, 440. [33] La Roque, III, 559 ; *ibid.*, Père Anselme and Moreri. [34] *Inventaire des Sceaux de la Coll.* Clairmbault, Demay, I, 317, no. 2994 ; *vide* Mile Crispin ; app. 18. [35] *Ibid.*, Père Anselme ; B.n. *Coll.* Clairmbault, 37, 2789, no. 97, 99. [36] *Noticèe hist. sur les Barons et la Barronniae du Bec-Crespin*, Lechevalier, 10 to 15 ; *Register des Fiefs et Arriere-Fiefs du Bailliage de Caux, Beau-cousin* ; La Roque, II, 2012. [37] *Ibid.*, Père Anselme. [38] Lechevalier, 10 ; Arch. Seine Inf., B. 188. [39] *Ibid.*, Père Anselme. [40] *Ibid.*, La Roque. [41] *Ibid.*, n. 47, 51. [42] *P.O.* 928, no. 27. [43] *Ibid.*, Lechevalier. [44] *Ibid.*, Père Anselme and Moreri. [45] *P.O.* 928, no. 31, 33, 41, 42. [46] *Mem. de la Soc. des Antiquaires de Norm.* [47] *Rôles Normands et Francais tires des Arch. de Londres*, Brequigny, 121. [48] William Crispin XI appears on the tomb of Pierre de Brézé in the Cathedral of Rouen as seigneur de Mauny and d'Angerville, *Tombeaux de la Cathed. de Rouen*, A. Deville, 63. [49] *Ibid.*, Père Anselme. [50] *P.O.* 928, 18, 19, 20. [51] *Estraits sur les derniers Mélanges hist. oriques et archéologiques concernant le départment de la Seine Inférieure et plus Spécialment la ville de Rouen*, Chas. de Beaurepaire, archevist, Sein-Inf., 271–4 ; *Inventaire des dessins exécutés por Roger de Gaignières conservés au départ. des Estampes et des Manuscrits*, H. Bouchot, I, 73, no. 579. [52] *Ibid.*, Beaurepaire, Père Anselme and Moreri ; *Hist. de Charles VII* ; Dufresne de Beaucourt, IV, 411 ; V, 67. [53] Bibl. de Rouen, ms. Y 10 mart. [54] *P.O.* 928, no. 46. [55] Père Anselme, VI, 635 ; La Roque, III, quoting ms. of Duchesne ; *vide* n. 60 text ; Moreri, II, 287 ; *Dossiers Bleus*, 78, fo. 1 ; *Les Chron. de Norm.*, Hellot, 278, 301. [56] La Roque II, 2013. [57] *Tombeau de Rouen*, 53–9. [58] *Dict. de l'Eure*, I, 206. [59] *Ibid.* [60] *Ibid.*, n. 57. [61] Lechevalier, II.

NOTE 62.—Charles de Venasque-Ferriol is the authority for the statement that Hugues Crispin was a younger brother of William Crispin VII the marshal, and the progenitor of the seigneurs de Bourri and de Villebon and the marquis de Vardes.

Père Anselme,[1] Moreri[2] and *Dossiers Bleus*[3] have accepted it, while La Roque ignores it entirely. Little or nothing is known of the first three or four generations given and while these powerful and distinguished seigniors were quite possibly descended from William Crispin I doubt is cast upon the accuracy of this part of the pedigree because its author produced it at the same time as the Crispin-Grimaldi genealogy. Le Brasseur also was apparently unconvinced.[4]

[1] II, 84. [2] II, 288. [3] 78. [4] *Hist. du Comté d'Evreux*, 18, 19.

Appendix 18

MILE CRISPIN

NOTE 1.—Milo Crispin appears more frequently in Domesday as Wigod de Wallingford's successor than does Robert de Ouilli. There are reasons for believing that Milo was the son of Gilbert Crispin I and Arlette, and there is fairly good evidence that he had two natural children named Hugh and Cecilia dealt with in the addenda. (*Vide* 28, 66, 81, 128, 131–6, 150–8, 181, 185.)

NOTE 20.—If Herluin and Gilbert Crispin I had been full brothers, Gilbert Crispin, abbot of Westminster, would have mentioned it in his *Life of Herluin* (*Vita Domini Herluini Abbatis Beccensis*),[1] wherein he names Herluin's father Ansgot of Danish origin and his mother Héloïse, a relative of the dukes of Flanders. (Mater proximam ducum Flandriae consanguinitatem attigit. Ansgotus ille, ista Helois nomen habebat.) Héloïse was said to have been the granddaughter of the count St. Paul, probably Herbert (died 951), obscure brother of Baldwin III, count of Flanders,[2] descended from the kings of Italy, Charlemagne and Alfred the Great. Herluin confirmed the donation of all of his possessions with their dependencies for the foundation of the abbey of Bec, consisting of one-third of the domains of Burneville (Bonneville-sur-le-Bec), Taville (Cavilleio the Petit-Quevilli), and Surceio (Surci, hamlet of Mezières), as well as the entire domain of Cernai (near Orbec), which had belonged to Ansgot during his lifetime as a dowry of his wife and was bequeathed by her, at his request, entirely to Herluin. Concerning this the latter said, " I abbot Herluin son of Ansgot in the presence of my approving brothers Odo and Roger give," etc. (Ego abbas Herluinus filius Ansgoti, astantibus et laudantibus fratribus mei Odone et Rogerio . . . donavi Sanctae Mariae.)[3] Thus Herluin had only these two full brothers living, who each inherited equal parts of their father's lands, making it evident that Gilbert Crispin I was not Ansgot's son, as asserted by Stacy Grimaldi, but this does not prove that Gilbert was not a son of Héloïse and, therefore, Herluin's half-brother. The profound interest taken in Herluin and his abbey by William Crispin I and his family for generations, its greatest benefactors, strongly suggests consanguinity. This would explain the failure of the *Crispin genealogy* to name Gilbert's parents ; although it very pointedly stresses the fact that he was " renowned for his race and nobility," why this curious omission ? This would give him Roman ancestry usually accorded him through Bernard, king of Italy.

[1] *Opera Lanfranci*, Giles, I, 261; *Gilbert Crispin, Abbot of Westminster*, Robinson, 87. [2] Père Anselme, II, 714. [3] Bibl. nat. lat. 13905, fo. 74.

NOTE 26.—Gilbert Crispin I did not possess Bec-Herluin, which was never a lay barony; it belonged solely to the abbey of Bec, having been given by abbot Herluin and Gilbert, count of Brionne, whose vassal Herluin was. Count Gilbert had inherited the surrounding country direct from the dukes of Normandy, through his father Godfry. Robert de Torigny in his *Interpolations of Jumièges*, who was librarian of the abbey of Bec in 1149,[1] is the authority for this statement.[2] If Gilbert Crispin was baron of Bec, it was another of the name in Normandy. Notre-Dame-du-Bec · and Saint-Martin-du-Bec belonged to the fief of Bretteville-la-Chaussée and came into the Crispin family at the same time as Bec-de-Mortagne and Bec-Crispin, *c.* 1250.[3] Le Bec-Thomas, arrondissement of Louviers, was created a barony in the 12th century.[4] This leaves Bec-aux-Cauchois, arrondissement of Yvetot, but there is no evidence that it ever was a barony.

Montivilliers adjoins Bec-Crispin while Fécamp, from whose abbey that of Montivilliers had formerly depended, is near Bec-aux-Cauchois, Bec-de-Mortagne, and Estouteville, all closely grouped in Caux. The early history of Bec-Crispin is very obscure, its first known possessor having been Vauquelin-du-Bec, in the 12th century, therefore, Gilbert, who was closely identified with Montivilliers,[5] could have held it previously.

The evidence to the contrary is, however, most convincing, for if so, why was it never mentioned in the records of the abbey of Bec-Herluin or in the *De nobile Crispinorum genere*? Still here is a possibility even though remote.

The Chron. de Normandie and the *Dict. de la Noblesse* says Toustain Fitz Rou held Bec-Crispin, but Wace's version that he came from Bec-aux-Cauchois is correct and supports the belief that Gilbert and Rou (supposed brother of Herluin), Toustain's father, were brothers.[6] The Estoutevilles, here also, said to descend from Roger, an authentic brother of Herluin,[7] strengthens the observation that Herluin and Gilbert may have been half-brothers, but never full brothers, as the Grimaldi genealogy records.

[1] Porée, I, xix. [2] *Jumièges Interp.*, de Torigny, 288. [3] *Recueil des Hist. des France*, Rigaud, vol. XXII. [4] *Le Prevost Mem.*, I, 227. [5] *Vide* 136. [6] *Vide* 24, 67, 106. [7] *Vide* 190.

NOTE 28.—Renée du Bec-Crispin was the daughter of René du Bec I, marquis de Vardes and Bosse, councillor of the state, captain of 50 men-at-arms of the king's regiment, governor of Capelle and the county of Thierache, knight of the order of the King, married 20 January 1592 Helen d'Or, daughter of Charles d'Or, lord of Baillet and Francanville, and Madeleine l'Hospital-Vitry, married 3 June 1545.[1] After the publication of the Grimaldi genealogy the head of this branch of the family, nephew of countess Renée, annexed the name. He occurs in an act of 1673 as François René du Bec-Crispin de Grimaldi, marquis of Vardes and Bosse, count of Moret, knight of the order of the King, councillor in all his councils, lieutenant-general in his armies, captain-colonel of a hundred Swiss guards of his majesty's body-guard, and governor of the city of Aigues-Mortes. He continued to use this designation until his death, 3 September 1688.[2]

[1] *Description de la Haute Normandie*, Toussaint de Plessis, I, 717. [2] *Dict. Critique de biographie et d'histoire*, A. Jal, 1224.

NOTE 31.—An equestrian seal of Rainier Grimaldi, founder of the dynasty of that name of Monaco, *c.* 1300, shows fusils on both the shield and saddle-cloth,[1] which arms his descendants have continued to bear until the present day. A charter concerning the church of Coudraye executed by William V son of Joscelyn (Willelmus Joscelini Crispini filius), states that his father was then living. Unfortunately it is undated and the seal is lost, but as he mentions king Philippe (Auguste) it was necessarily between 1180 and the time of Joscelyn's death. Another of 1216 in favour of Vesly-en-Vexin has been fully described by Le Prevost and reproduced in the notes of Guillaume Crispin Ier of the text. This charter and seal cannot now be located and whether Le Prevost actually saw it or made his description of it from a copy carelessly drawn in the *Collection*[2] of Roger de Gaignières is unknown. In any event the original has disappeared and it was probably either destroyed with the other records of Vesly or is privately owned. The equestrian seal attached to this charter is charged with fusils[3] which have frequently been mistaken for lozenges. Père Anselme,[4] Le Prevost[5] and others fell into the same error and La Roque was not immune. He records William's arms as lozengy argent and gules and his reproduction of them shows squares or checks inverted while in another chapter he describes those of William's daughter, Isabeau married to Robert de Neubourg, as fusily argent and gules, the design of both being identical.[6] This indicates that he made no distinction between the two and indeed in olden times the Norman and French seigniors did not either. The oldest and original charge was the fusil. In English heraldry the lozenge is slightly elongated in relation to an inverted check, and the fusil is longer and narrower than the lozenge. A green equestrian seal of William Crispin VI, son and heir of William V, attached to a document concerning the knights of the Temple of Bourgoult, dated 1225, preserved in the National archives,[7] if only casually observed, might be mistaken for lozenges, but the charges are really fusils and this is the opinion of Douet d'Arcq.[8] In another charter executed by him in 1227 concerning the same brotherhood [5] on the equestrian seal of white wax the figure and horse differ slightly from that attached to the former charter, but the charges are more elongated and distinctly fusils. The use of these different seals leads to the assumption that the one of 1225 belonged to his father William V, then deceased, and was identical with the one the latter used in the 1216 charter.

There are preserved also seals of William Crispin VI identical with that of 1227 in the National archives dated 1230 concerning the safe conduct of the countess of Ponthieu,[10] in 1234 regarding the countess of Boulogne,[11] and in 1237 one of brown wax in favour of the abbey of Gomerfontaine.[12] Cristian Crispin (identity unknown) and his wife, Ermentru, affixed a flowered seal to a charter of Bourgoult in 1238.[13] A plain fusiled shield occurs on a document by William Crispin VII, the marshal, dated 1256,[14] incorrectly called lozenges by Le Prevost,[15] and the same charges appear on a charter by his wife, Jeanne de Mortemer Crispin, in 1269 in favour of the abbey of Valasse, where their arms are quartered.[16] Standing, a lady with cape lined with vair ; falcon on her dexter wrist and at her feet on the dexter side a dog standing (rampant) ; counter seal quartered with her husband's arms ; fusily, of a fesse of six pieces charged with fleurs de lys on the one and the other. Fusils appear on his equestrian seal of 1296 concerning the priory of Vesly-en-Vexin.[17] In 1299 William Crispin, seigneur du Bec de Mortemer, his son also used an equestrian seal identical with those of his grandfather William, as previously stated.[18] In 1302 Jean Crispin,[19] the second son of the marshal, bore fusils, but his equestrian figure of the same design as his brother's just mentioned faces in the opposite direction from those of the senior members of the family. William Crispin X, seigneur de Mauny, husband of Jeanne de Calletot, head of the house in 1371,[20] affixed a seal with the same charges to a charter, and on one of 1398 of William Crispin, a cadet of the family, a chevron occurs on the shield.[21]

Jean Crispin, hereditary marshal of Normandy, etc., executed many documents, to which the seals are still attached.

In 1410 the inclined fusiled shield is supported on both the dexter and sinister sides by a female figure standing upright.[22] On a charter of 1447 he used only an inclined fusiled shield.[23] Usually he affixed a very elaborate seal. Fusily an inclined shield ; supporters, a lion rampant on the dexter side and a griffin segreant on the sinister ; crest, a helmet, at the top, a wisp. This occurs on a charter of 1448,[24] three of 1450 [25] and four of 1451.[26] In the latter year he used an entirely different design ; fusily, an inclined shield ; supporters, a lion rampant on the dexter side and a goat rampant on the sinister ; crest, an unicorn's head couped. This seal does not seem to occur elsewhere.[27] The following year he attached a simple fusiled shield,[28] and in 1453 on two charters he reverted to the lion and griffin type mentioned.[29]

The arms on the cover of this work are those of the descendants of king William I, two leopards or lions passant guardant. King Richard I added another leopard on which the royal arms of England were founded and when colours existed, red and gold were adopted (gules, two leopards or lions passant guardant or).

Charles du Bec II, baron of Bourri and Villebon, the eldest direct male descendant of Hugues Crispin, supposed brother of the marshal and founder of this branch of the family,[30] in 1558 attached a fusiled quartering to a document. His brother Pierre, who succeeded him, was the grandfather of countess Renée du Bec-Crispin [31] and the great-grandfather of François-René, the last of his branch of the family, who also bore fusils. Hence the armorial bearings of the main line of the Crispins of Normandy and France from the earliest known records were fusily argent and gules.

As has been previously recorded under appendix 15, the Crispins of Châteauceaux bore checky argent and gules, which it will be observed are only slightly different from these arms.[32] Those of the English Crispins vary considerably because the family there did not obtain in one distinguished line, as it did in Normandy and Anjou, but spread into numerous branches, or was absorbed in the female line by other prominent families. Lozengy, argent and gules are ascribed to Milo Crispin on the walls of the church of Swyncombe,[33] and Banks and Burke attribute to Milo, barry of eight, argent and gules with a bordure engrailed sable.[34] Since arms were not borne until after the middle of the 12th century and colours later, it is difficult to understand these claims. An unidentified shield mascally argent and gules in Westminster abbey, *temp.* Henry III, probably belonged to a cadet of the Norman Crispin family.

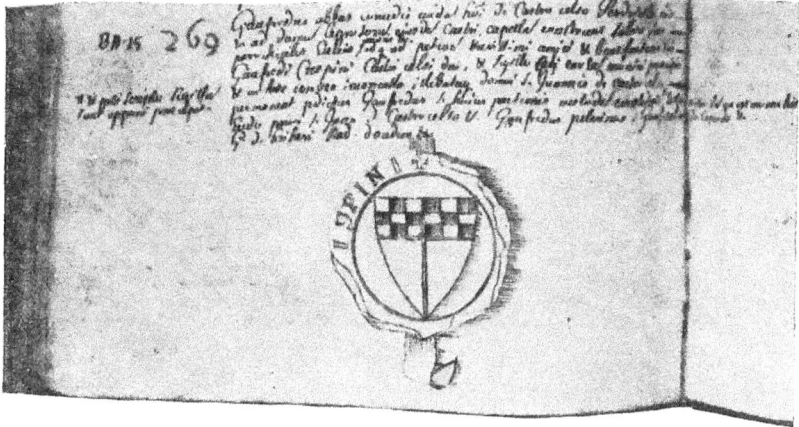

SEAL REDUCED.

CHARTER OF GEOFFRY CRISPIN; SEIGNEUR DE CHÂTEAUCEAUX, 1189–1190

THE SEAL HAS BEEN LOST, BUT THE COPY HERE REPRODUCED OCCURS IN VARIA AD HISTORIAM BRITANNIÆ (Bibl. nat. fr., fo. 306).

(*Vide* 23, 38, 152)

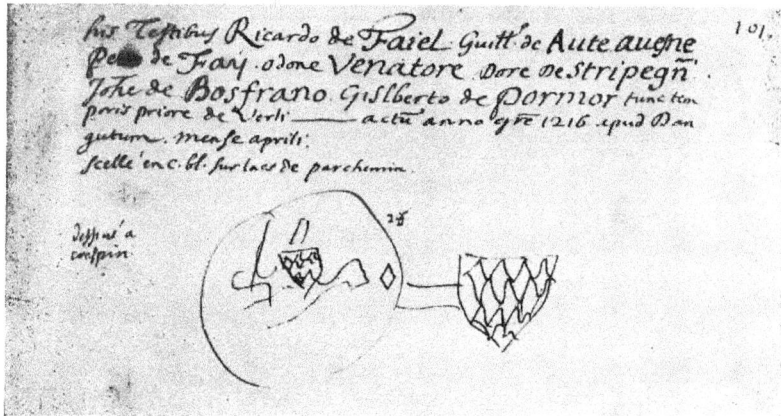

CHARTER OF WILLIAM CRISPIN V, SON OF
JOSCELYN CRISPIN, DATED 1216

THE ORIGINAL HAS DISAPPEARED, BUT THIS COPY IS TO
BE FOUND IN GAIGNIÈRES COLLECTION (Bibl. nat. lat.
5441, 1, 100, 101).

(*Vide* 38, 40, 151.)

Charter a

SEAL SLIGHTLY REDUCED.

This seal is attached to a charter
dated 1219 of Robert Crispin,
seigneur d'Arquency, younger
brother of William V, and is the
oldest known extant seal of the
family. The spelling of the name
had apparently by this time been
changed to Crespin (Arch. nat. S.,
nos. 20 and 21).

(*Vide* 143, 144, 152

COUNTERSEAL

CHARTER DATED 1225 OF WILLIAM CRISPIN VI, SIRE DE DANGU, SON OF WILLIAM CRISPIN V

THIS IS THE OLDEST EXTANT SEAL OF THE DIRECT MALE LINE. THE DATE IS UNDER THE FOLD

(Arch. nat. S. 5193, no. 26 r° 5194, no. 27 v°)

(*Vide* 152)

Charter b

COUNTERSEAL   SEAL CONSIDERABLY REDUCED

CHARTER DATED 1227 OF WILLIAM CRISPIN VI, SIRE DE DANGU

THE DATE IS UNDER THE FOLD

(Arch. nat. S. 5194, no. 29)

(*Vide* 152)

Charter 6

SEAL CONSIDERABLY REDUCED

CHARTER DATED 1234 OF WILLIAM CRISPIN VI, SIRE DE DANGU

THE DATE IS UNDER THE FOLD

(Arch. nat. J. 238 v°, no. 20)

(Vide 152)

Charter d

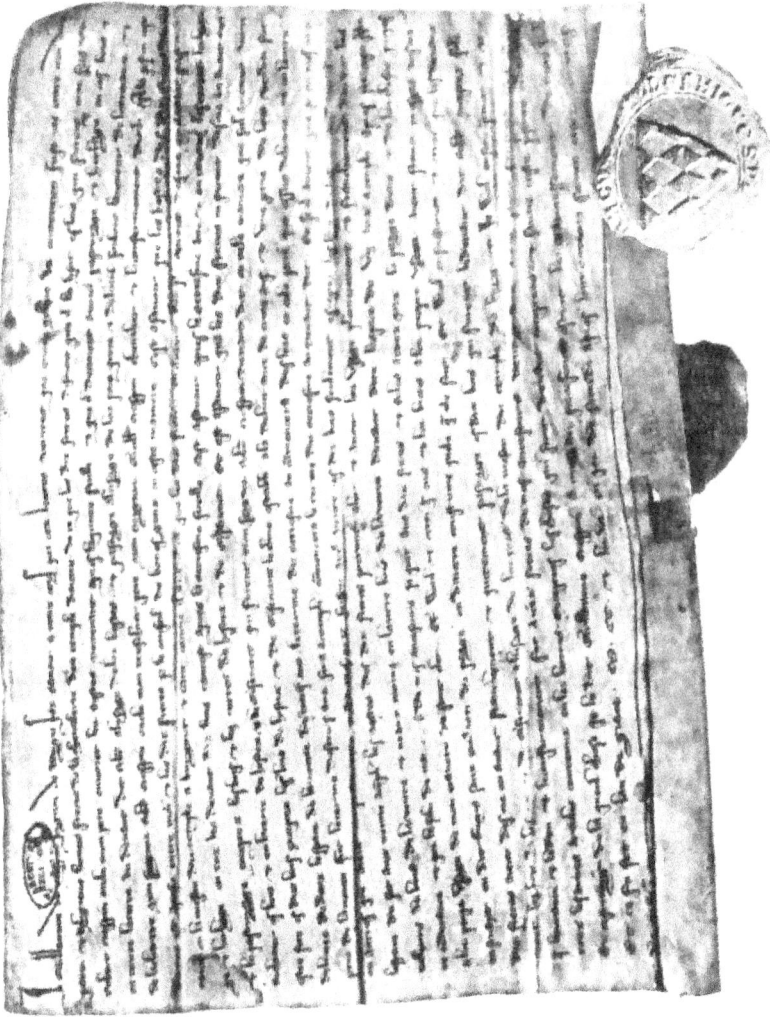

CHARTER OF WILLIAM CRISPIN VII, CONSTABLE OF NORMANDY, 1256

(Arch. nat. S. 5192, no. 15)

(*Vide* 145, 152)

Charter e

SEAL
COUNTERSEAL

CHARTER EXECUTED BY JEANNE DE MORTEMER DATED 1269 IN FAVOUR OF THE ABBEY
OF VALASSE

THE COUNTERSEAL IS QUARTERED WITH THE ARMS OF LADY JEANNE AND THOSE OF HER HUSBAND, WILLIAM CRISPIN VII,
CONSTABLE OF NORMANDY

(Arch. Seine-Inf. fonds du abbaye de Valasse [not classified])

(Vide 152)

Charter f

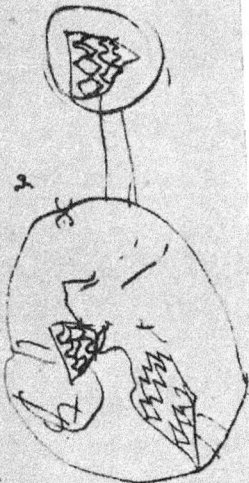

WILLIAM CRISPIN VII, CONSTABLE OF NORMANDY AND MARSHAL OF FRANCE

ORIGINAL SEAL HAS DISAPPEARED, BUT THIS COPY IS IN GAIGNIÈRES COLLECTION

(Bibl. nat. lat. 5441, I, fo. 102)

(*Vide* 39, 152)

Charter g

CHARTER OF WILLIAM CRISPIN, THE YOUNG, SEIGNEUR DU BEC DE MORTEMER, ELDEST SON
OF WILLIAM CRISPIN, THE MARSHAL, 1299

(Arch. Seine Inf., fonds du Abbaye de Montivilliers [not classified])

(*Vide* 152)

SEAL CONSIDERABLY REDUCED

THE SIMILARITY OF THE CHARGES
AND THE EXACT DESIGN OF THE
SEALS OF THESE FAMILIES, AT THE
SAME DATE, IS HERE SHOWN

SEAL OF RAINIER GRIMALDI c. 1300,
FOUNDER OF THE DYNASTY OF THE
PRINCES OF MONACO
Reproduced by Gustave Saige, their
former archivist (Monaco ses Origines
et son Hist. 49)

(*Vide* 68, 151; add.)

Charter h

SEAL ENLARGED THREE TIMES

CHARTER OF JEAN CRISPIN, SEIGNEUR DE MAUNY, BROTHER OF ANTOINE THE ARCHBISHOP

1410

(Pièces originales 928, no. 27)

(*Vide* 152)

ANOTHER CHARTER OF JEAN CRISPIN, SIRE DE MAUNY, THEN ALSO BARON OF BEC-CRISPIN, AND HEREDITARY MARSHAL OF NORMANDY, 1453

(Pièces orig. 928, no. 40)

(*Vide* 152)

SEAL SLIGHTLY ENLARGED

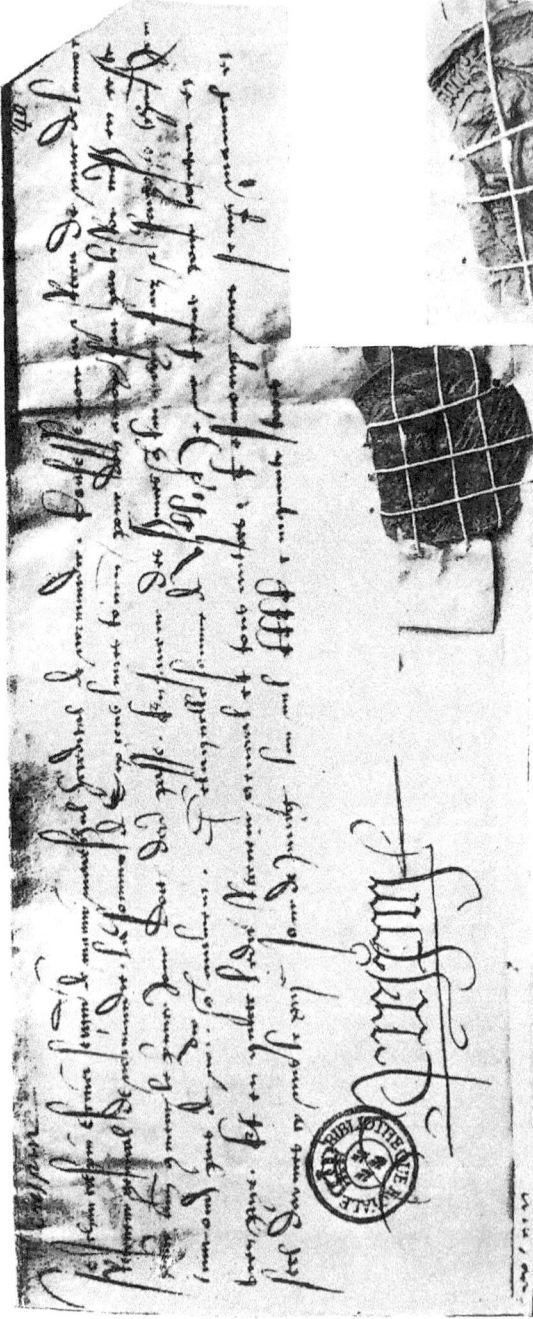

COPY OF A DIFFERENT SEAL OF THE SAME BARON, 1451
(*Les anc. abb. de Norm., Ardennes, d'Arrisy I, 42, no. 511, pl. xxii, no. 5*)

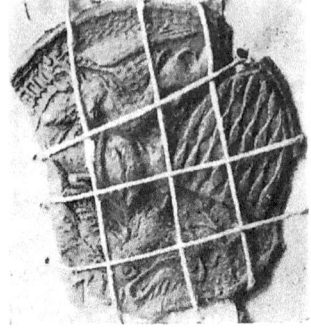

Charter j

Some of the other armorial bearings of the family in England are :

Crispin of Devonshire : Gules, ten lozenges argent, four, three, two and one.[35]

Crispin or Crespine : Gules, ten lozenges argent, four, three, two, and one, crest, a hydra seven headed.[36]

Cryspyn : Gules, ten lozenges ermine, four, three, two and one.[37]

Crispin : Barry and lozenges countercharged argent and sable. Crest, a hydra verted seven headed.[38]

Crispin of Cheshire (quartered ; with Hatton) : Barry of four argent and gules lozengy countercharged.[39]

Crispin of Essex (quartered with Rich) : Barry of four argent and gules three fusils conjoined in fess in chief and as many in base, all countercharged.[40]

Crispin of Salisbury (Berkshire) : Barry of ten argent and gules, a bordure engrailed sable.[41]

Crispin of Lincolnshire : Barry bendy argent and gules countercharged.[42]

Crispin of Hampshire : Barry bendy in the shading of a bunch of grapes.[43]

Crispin of Nottinghamshire : Barry of eight or barry of ten.[44]

William Cryspyng of Suffolk 1359 : Three bars, a bend over all.[45]

William Crepin (c. 1280) : Argent three bars gules engrailed.[46]

Crispin of Todwell (quartered with Sent Clere) : Gules ten mascules argent, four, three, two and one.[47]

Crispin of Tittleshall, Norfolk, 1598 : Argent, a chevron azure between three chaplets gules.[48] Crisping of Happisburg [49] and the Ashton [50] family (intermarried with the Crispins), both of the same county, bore these arms and colours. Thomas Holme mentioned below did also, excepting they were within a bordure sable with ten roundels.[51]

Crispin of Halton, Huntingdonshire : Sable, two arms in fess, habited argules joining the hands proper, one issuing from the dexter side, the other from the sinister, between three crescents of the second.[52]

Crispin of Hampshire : Argent, a cross flory gules.[53]

Sir John de Creppenge of Yorkshire, 1307 : Gules, a lion rampant argent, billitty or.[54] He was high sheriff of Yorkshire and the son and heir of Sir Robert de Creppinge. These arms are identical with those of Gilbert Crispin VII, baron of Tillières, which he affixed to a charter in favour of Saint-Père de Chartres in 1259, referred to under the text of Gilbert Crispin 2°, Seigneur de Tillières, excepting the colours differ. Sir Robert may have been his brother or one of his younger sons. Crispin of Kingston-on-Hull (Yorks) : Three

lions rampant. Crest, a demi-griffin erased with wings addorsed.

Captain William Crispin bore these arms in 1650 which were later confirmed to him by the college of Arms, England, and the office of Arms, Ireland, thus : Erminios three lions rampant azure armed and langued purpure. Crest, demi-griffin erased with wings addorsed azure. Motto, Dum clavum rectum teneam.[55]

William Crispin, captain in the English navy under the Commonwealth and Charles II and acting rear-admiral in the East Indian expedition in 1654, commanded by admiral sir William Penn, affixed these arms to his official documents to the Admiralty office.[56] His father bearing the same name had also been a sea-captain under Oliver Cromwell and died aboard his battleship the *Fellowship*, from which he was buried in the chancel of the church of Carrickfergus, Ireland, in 1645.[57] Captain Crispin married Rebecca Bradshaw, granddaughter of captain Giles Penn [58] of the Royal navy, who was also the grandfather of William Penn, the founder of Pennsylvania. The latter sent captain Crispin to that province in 1681 at the head of the commission " For the settling of the colony," was appointed chief justice, assistant to the governor, and surveyor-general of Pennsylvania. He was the progenitor of the Crispins of America, for while he died on the voyage and was buried either at sea or in the Barbados, his son Silas, who accompanied him, continued to Philadelphia, where he established the family. He married first Hester, daughter of captain Thomas Holme, provincial councillor, first assistant to the governor and surveyor-general of Pennsylvania, who plotted and laid out the city of Philadelphia and the province of Pennsylvania, by whom he had eight children. By a second marriage with Mary, daughter of Richard Stockton, of the distinguished family of New Jersey of that name, he had seven additional children.[59] Thomas Holme in his will bequeathed an acre of ground in Holmesburg, Philadelphia, for a family cemetery where he and the early Crispins, who were Quakers, lie buried. It is within the city limits and Philadelphia to honour them surrounded it by the Holme-Crispin park. There are emblazoned upon the walls of the chapel in the chateau of William the Conqueror at Falaise where the tablet is hung the oldest known arms of some of the families whose names are inscribed upon it.

The shields and the armorial charges thereon were designed and embellished under the direction of colonel F. G. Langham of Hastings, member of the committee Guillaume le Conquérant.

Milo Crispin appears on the Battle abbey

roll as Valingford, as stated in the text, and Delisle records him upon that of Dives.

[1] Saige, 49. [2] Bibl. nat. lat. 5441, vol. 2, fo. 99, 100, 101. [3] *Ibid.* [4] Père Anselme, VI, 633. [5] *Le Prevost Mem.*, II, 6. [6] La Roque, I, 269–71 ; II, 2011–14. [7] Archives nationale, S. 5194, nos. 26, 27, box is numbered S. 5193. [8] *Inventaire des Sceaux des Archives de l'Empire*, I, 557, no. 1960, 1961. [9] *Ibid.*, S. 5194, no. 29, box is numbered S. 5193. [10] Arch. nat., J. 395, no. 122. [11] *Ibid.*, J. 238, no. 20. [12] Arch. Seine Inf., G. 1815. [13] Arch. nat., S. 5192, no. 13. [14] *Ibid.*, no. 15 ; *Cart. Normand.*, Delisle, 519 ; *vide* Guillaume Crispin, app. 17, n. 51. [15] *Le Prevost Mem.*, II, 7. [16] Arch. Seine Inf. fonds du abb. de Valasse (not classified). [17] Bibl. nat. lat. 5441, II, 102. [18] Arch. Seine Inf. fonds du abb. de Montivilliers (not classified). [19] Original in Bibl. nat. *Cabinet of* Clairmbault, *Inventaire des Sceaux de la Normandie*, G. Demay, I, 317, no. 2995. [20] *Ibid.*, 2994 ; *vide* Guillaume Crispin, app. 17, no. 55. [21] *Pièces Originales*, 928 ; Crispin chartes 20484, no. 18 ; Bibl. nat. fr. 27412 ; *vide* Guillaume Crispin and n. ; app. 17, n. 55. [22] *P.O.*, no. 27. [23] *Ibid.*, no. 31. [24] *Ibid.*, 32. [25] *Ibid.*, 35, 36 ; British museum charter, no. 4456. [26] *Ibid.*, 37, 38, 39, 41. [27] *Les Anc. Abb. de Norm.*, Ardennes, L. d'Ainsy, I, 42, no. 511, pl. XXII, no. 15. [28] Arch. Seine Inf., G. 1040. [29] *P.O.* 928, no. 40, 41. [30] Bibl. royale, C. 259. [31] Moreri, II, 288 ; *Hist. Gen. et Chron. de la Maison Royale de France*, De Courcy, II, 88 ; IV, 242 ; *vide* Guillaume Crispin. [32] *Vide* Geoffroi du Bec. [33] *Hist. Notices of Swyncombe and Ewelme*, Napier, 239. [34] Banks ; *The General Armory*, Burke. [35] *Ibid.*, Burke. [36] *Ibid.* [37] British museum Harleian ms. 752. [38] *G.A.*, Burke. [39] *Visit of Cheshire*, Harl. soc., 276. [40] *Visit of Essex*, Harl. soc., 276. [41] *G.A.*, Burke. [42] *Hist.* [43] B.m. Cot. Ch. V, 67, deed B. 3692. [44] *Red Book*, I, 331. [45] Add. ch. 9677. [46] B.m. Harl. ms. 6589. [47] *Ibid.*, 2129. [48] *Hist. of Norfolk*, Blomefield, 10, 69. [49] College of Arms. [50] *Ann. and Antiq. of Lacock Abbey*, Bowles. [51] *Captain William Crispin* in *The Pennsylvania Magazine of History and Biography*, M. Jackson Crispin, vol. LIII, Apr., July, Oct. (p. 314), 1929, published by the Historical Society of Pennsylvania, Philadelphia. [52] *G.A.*, Burke. [53] *Ibid.* [54] Yorksh. lay subsidies, Yorksh. Ach. soc., vol. XVI. [55] M. Jackson Crispin, *ibid.*, April, LIII, 131. [56] *Ibid.*, 97, 98. [57] *Crispins of Kingston-on-Hull* in *Publications of the Genealogical Society of Pennsylvania*, Philadelphia, M. Jackson Crispin, vol. X, no. 2, Mar. 1928, p. 117. [58] Parish register, Stepney, co. Middlesex, vol. II (Canterbury, 1899), 83 ; *Visitation of Lancash.*, 1654–5, by *Dugdale*, Raines, p. 53. [59] M. Jackson Crispin, *Pennsylvania Magazine*, LIII, 289 and fol.

Appendix 19

CONSTABLES OF NORMANDY
(Du Hommet, de Mortemer, Crispin)

The local designation of the constableship of Normandy was derived from Humetum (Le Hommet), a castle in the diocese of Coutances (de Honore de Humeto), for which the service of Richard du Hommet in 1172 was three and one half knights' fees and 18 men at arms.[1] The pedigree of the family was recorded by William du Hommet, who describes himself (Gillelmus de Humeto, constablarius Normanniae, filius Ricardi de Humeto junioris) constable of Normandy in 1239, who renewed the charter of Saint-Fromond granted by his ancestors [2] which dated back to the time of duke Richard II before 1025. It was founded by Robert du Hommet (Robertus de Humeto), who, the charter informs us, was succeeded by his grandson William. The latter left a daughter, his heiress, who married John, son of Odo, bishop of Bayeux (genuit filium nomine Johannem),[3] from whom he acquired the honour of Hommet, which name he assumed. Robert du Hommet his son succeeded him and occurs as the grandson of the bishop (Robertus nepos Episcopi) in the roll of the Exchequer 31 Henry I—1130. His son and heir, Richard, in 1172 owed service for the honours of Hommet and of Beaumont-le-Richard in the Bessin, whose son William in that year neglected to make any return for the fief of Say. This property came into the family through Agnès de Beaumont, wife of Richard and mother of William, who was the daughter and heiress of Jourdain de Say by his wife Lucy.[4] Richard is also mentioned by Henry II in a confirmation to the abbey of Notre-Dame d'Aunay, as constable of Normandy, with his wife Agnès.[5] King Henry in 1173 granted to " Richard du Hommet his constable " the castle of Stamford,[6] which he confirmed to him and his descendants,[7] with Meisy and La Haie de La Luthumière in Normandy to hold as a fief.[8] Richard du Hommet I about this time relinquished this high office and became a monk in the abbey of Aunay which he had founded and where he died in 1181.[9] He had by his wife Agnès in addition to William who succeeded to the constableship, two other sons, Enguerrand I, father of William de Semilly and Geoffry du Hommet,[10] and Jourdain.[11] Henry II confirmed to William the grant made to his father Richard of his " Constabularia " to hold to him and his posterity " in feodo et hereditate." [12] William married Lucia, probably the granddaughter of Adam de Brix, and they had Richard du Hommet II, William de Say, Henry, Jourdain, bishop of Lisieux, Thomas, Enguerrand and several daughters, one of whom, Clementina, married Ranulph de Blundeville sixth, earl of Chester, *temp.* king John.[13]

Richard II, his eldest son, married, first, Aegidia or Gila de la Haie [14] before 1185,[15] through which source he received vast possessions, later recorded, and king Richard I confirmed, 20 June 1189, some lands in the Cotentin to him which had been seized by the crown at the death of his wife's father, Richard de la Haie, 26 April 1169.[16] Aegidia died young and was buried in the abbey of Saint-Nicholas de Blanchelande, to which a grant was made for her soul by her mother, Matilda de la Haie, née de Vernon, consented to by her husband, Richard du Hommet (II).[17] Secondly, Richard du Hommet II married Alienora, relict of Robert de la Haie, elder brother of Richard de la Haie, who made a gift to the abbey of Montebourg with the consent of her husband, Richard du Hommet, (II) and her son, Robert de la Haie (II).[18] Richard du Hommet II predeceased his father William in 1200,[19] who just before 1205 in the presence of Thomas his son and William his grandson made a donation to the priory of Sainte-Marguerite de Vignats.[20] He probably died about 1209, in which year his son Thomas made a donation to the abbey of Longue from Beaumont-le-Richard of the succession of his father.[21] His grandson William, son of Richard du Hommet II, appears as constable in a charter dated 1213 concerning the chapel of Sainte-Catherine in the parish of Le Désert (Gillelmus de Humeto constabularius, avus meus . . . antequam filiam suam maritasset Ricardo) which he gave in 1238 to the brethren of Holy Trinity, for whom his wife Eustachia there founded the priory of La Perrine. This William was of age in 1200 and so far as is known died issueless.[22] Roger de Bricqueville, in a lawsuit in 1398 referred to under Appendix 17 of William Crispin, in relating the pedigrees of the families du Hommet and La Haie, says that both Enguerrand I and Jourdain, sons of Richard du Hommet I and brothers of William senior, the constable, held this office successively. If so, it was after 1239, when they must have been very old men, because they were probably full grown when their father took the monastic garb in 1173. Their elder brother William, who succeeded his father in this hereditary office, was of age then, which would place his birth not later than about 1050. Enguerrand I and Jourdain, who were the great-uncles of William II the constable, living in 1239, would probably have been close to ninety years of age at this time. Enguerrand is recorded in the register of Philippe Auguste by Guérin in 1220 as having performed service due the king on behalf of William du Hommet the constable, son of Richard du Hommet (II), for the honour of Remilly " by the command of the constable the eldest born." He held it with him " in equal part of the line of the eldest born " (per manum constabularii antenati sui in paragio), which did not extend to his posterity according to Norman

law. The truth of the matter seems to be that this was Enguerrand II, younger brother of Thomas, who when he witnessed the aforementioned charter of his father, William senior, was his eldest living son. Thomas had no issue, and if dead by 1220, Enguerrand II, his heir, childless also, may have been constable, succeeding William II after 1239, but Enguerrand I, who left sons, was not, or one of them would have inherited this dignity. Jourdain was certainly constable, for he is said to have been in an act dated 1278,[23] as recorded on page 145, and it is certain that his immediate heirs succeeded to this office, at which time they must have been the oldest surviving branch of the family. The pedigree ot La Haie commences with Richard Turstain, called Haldub, which is referred to under Eudes Le Seneschal, sire de La Haie, also called Ivan, surnamed al Chapel. Eudes received through marriage the barony of La Haie-du-Puits, which formerly had belonged to the ducal domain. His daughter Murial had issue : Cécilia, Robert, Raoul and Richard, seigneur de La Haie-du-Puits, which latter, dapifer of Normandy (Dapifer Normanniæ) under Geoffry Plantagenet,[24] was born early in the 12th century and died in 1169.[25] He married Matilda de Vernon, daughter of William de Vernon, who died before 1174,[26] and they jointly founded in 1154 the abbey of Saint-Nicholas de Blanchelande in the parish of Varanguebec.[27] Matilda brought to her husband in marriage the baronies of Varanguebec, and it is said La Luthumière, but it has been shown that the latter was possessed by Richard du Hommet I, at least a part of it, although through what channel he acquired it is unrecorded. They had issue three daughters, Aegidia before mentioned married to Richard du Hommet II, to whom she carried these extensive domains since her sisters Nicole, living temp. King John,[28] who married the earl of Lincoln, and Isabel, wife of the baron de Roullon, both died without issue.[29] Now, as previously recorded, William Crispin the marshal, William de Meulan, count of Tancarville, whose family were hereditary chamberlains of Normandy, which office was attached to the domain and county of Tancarville,[30] Roger de Bricqueville and La Mare Chenevarin [31] claim that the constableship was attached to the land of Varanguebec. The latter two further state that Richard de la Haie was on this account constable of Normandy. The first statement is false, and regarding the second there is no other mention of Richard in this capacity. He is not so designated in his foundation charter of Blanchelande or in the Exchequer rolls 14 Henry II, 1168, wherein he occurs as " Ricardi de Haia," and the constableship was held by the du

Hommets long before they possessed Varanguebec. William, son of Richard du Hommet II, is last heard of in 1239, when he made the confirmation to Saint-Fromond and died without direct heirs. The constableship, with Varanguebec, La Haie-du-Puits, and La Luthumière, reverted to Jourdain du Hommet, the son of Richard du Hommet I, the constable or his heirs. Jourdain had three daughters, one of whom married Robert, baron of Bec de Mortemer, whose castle of Mortemer (Mortum Mare) was at Saint-Victor-en-Caux.[32] This family was descended from that of the same name represented at Hastings, and the pedigree of this branch starts with Roger de Mortemer, who married, first, Milesaunt, daughter of the earl of Derby, by whom he had Hugh, who died without issue 1227, and, second, Isabella, daughter of lord de Ferrers of Lechelade, from which union issued Ralph, deceased in 1246, leaving an heir Roger, Robert (above mentioned) and Philip.[33] Roger de Mortemer I died 24 June 1215,[34] and through the descendants of Robert his third son, the constableship eventually came to William Crispin VII, the marshal, as recorded in Appendix 17.

[1] Stapleton, I, cxxxv.   [2] *Ibid.*, II, clxxxi.
[3] Ord. Vit., II, 429; IV, 94.   [4] Stapleton, I, cxxxv; Ord. Vit., IV, 94, ed. n.   [5] La Roque, I, 653.   [6] Stapleton, II, clxxxiii.   [7] Rymer, I, 12; *ibid.*, Stapleton.   [8] *Ibid.*, Stapleton.
[9] Stapleton, I, cxxxv.   [10] Stapleton, II, lxxix.
[11] *Ibid.*, I, cxxxv.   [12] *Ibid.*   [13] *Ibid.*, I, clxxiii.   [14] *Ibid.*, II, clxxxiv.   [15] *Ibid.*, I, cxlv.   [16] *Ibid.*   [17] *Ibid.*, II, clxxxiv.   [18] *Ibid.*   [19] *Ibid.*   [20] *Ibid.*   [21] *Ibid.*   [22] *Ibid.*, I, cxlv; II, clxxxi, clxxxiv.   [23] Boutaric, 202, no. 2151; Olim, II, fo. 41 r°. *vide* c., X.   [24] Stapleton, I, xxxiv, *vide* 184.   [25] *Ibid.*, I, cxlv.   [26] *Ibid.*, II, cclxxix; Ord. Vit., I, 453, and ed. n.; Plan., II, 49.   [27] Stapleton, II, xxxi, ccxxvi.   [28] *Ibid.*, I, cvi.   [29] *Ibid.*, I, cxlv; La Roque, II, 1459-60.   [30] La Roque, I, 654; *vide* app. 17.   [31] *Ibid.*, I, 630, III, 388.   [32] Stapleton, II, cxix.   [33] *Ibid.*, cxxi.   [34] *Ibid.*, II, cxxv; *vide* app. 17, Guillaume Crispin.

Appendix 20

AUVRAI DE LINCOLN

The potent lord Alured (Auvrai) de Lincoln witnessed a charter in Normandy in 1180[1] and was a great Domesday baron who attended duke William on his expedition to England in 1066. He held in chief in Bedfordshire and North Riding Lincolnshire, in which latter county he possessed fifty lordships, and was an under-tenant in Rutland and Cheshire.[2] He probably married Esilia, daughter of Gilbert Crispin I, widow of William Malet I, who contracted a second marriage after the death of her husband.

This is made evident by an original charter in the Cottonian collection dated at Devizes in 1152 by Henry, duke of Normandy and count of Anjou, in which he made a grant to Ranulph de Gernon, earl of Chester, and in various entries in Domesday. This earl was the son of Ranulph le Meschin,[3] the third earl palatine of Chester, and Lucia, daughter of Ivo Taillebois by a marriage with a daughter of William Malet I, who was also named Lucia.[4] From a charter of Spalding priory, this marriage of Ivo and Lucia is quite evident.[5] The countess Lucia, daughter of Ivo, had previously married Roger de Roumare, son of Gerald de Roumare, shortly before 1100, by whom she had a son William de Roumare.[6]

In the list of tenants in Lincolnshire prior to 1120, the date that Ranulph le Meschin succeeded to the earldom of Chester after the death of his first cousin Richard, earl of Chester, who perished in the shipwreck of the *Blanche Nef*, there occurs " Rannulphus Meschinus," above which appears " Comes Linc." interlined. The words were added subsequently as the facsimile of the manuscript shows, nor is there any other record or authority to prove that he was earl of Lincoln. Neither can the statement of Stapleton and others that Ranulph de Gernon, his son, held it conjointly with his half-brother, William de Roumare be justified.[7]

An extract of the Cottonian charter referring to Ranulph de Gernon, the earl, follows : " The whole honor of Eye as well and fully as Robert Malet uncle of his mother at any time held it and I have given to him the fee of Alan de Lincoln who was the uncle of his mother and the fee of Erneis de Burum as his inheritance " (totum honorem de Eia Sicut Robertus Malet avunculus matris sue illum melius et plenius tenuit . . . Et fœudum Alani de Lincolia ei dedi, qui fuit avunculus matris sue, et fœudum Ernisii de Burum sicut suam hereditatem).[8] This indicates clearly that the wife of Ivo Taillebois, who was the mother of the countess Lucia, was the sister of both Robert Malet and Alan de Lincoln. The latter would then have been the son of Esilia Crispin Malet by a second marriage. Mr. Stapleton suggests that Alured may have been the brother of this Alan [9] because Alan was his successor, but this is not agreeable with the known facts which support the generally accepted opinion that this Alan (II) was the son of Alured.

Alured occurs in Domesday as the grandson or nephew of Thorold the sheriff in the time previous to Domesday (Aluredus nepos Toroldi) concerning land of the Saxon Sybi in the city of Lincoln, which he held direct from the king.[10]

Alured held Thorold's lands of the fief of

Colsuan of Lincoln, a favourite of king William, as his homager.[11] " Nepos " here undoubtedly means grandson, which Alured possibly was by a daughter of Thorold and a Breton husband, since he was contemporary with William Malet. The latter was probably the grandson of the earl Leofric, discussed later on, who married Godiva, the supposed sister of Thorold.[12] This relationship of the sheriff is recorded in a charter of the Monasticon,[13] where he occurs as " Thorold of Bucknall," a hamlet situated about ten miles from Lincoln, which reads thus : " I, Thorald of Bucknall, in the presence of my most noble lord, Leofric, earl of Leicester, and his most noble countess lady Godiva, my sister, and with the goodwill and consent of my lord and near kinsman earl Algar, their firstborn son and heir, have given . . . ."

" Ego Thoraldus de Bukenhale coram nobilissimo domino meo Leofrico comite leicestriae et noblissima comitissa sua domina Godiva sorore mea cum consensu et bona voluntate domini et cognati mei comitis Algari primogeniti et heredis eorum donavi . . . ." Thorold also appears in a grant of a survey of the city of Lincoln as " Turaldus de Greteville,"[14] undoubtedly for Greetwell, several miles from there, and " Turoldus vicecomes " (sheriff) is written in Domesday as a benefactor of Crowland (S. Gutlaco) not Spalding as Freeman said.[15]

The consanguinity of Robert Malet and Alan de Lincoln with the countess Lucia is also attested in Domesday, where it shows that the manor of Aulkborough in 1086 was possessed by Ivo Taillebois, the father of the countess, which land is recorded to have been previously owned by William Malet. He possibly gave it to his daughter Lucia, wife of Ivo, during his lifetime, otherwise it would not have been separated from the barony of his son and heir Robert. Furthermore, a manor in Ludford was held by Ivo, which, prior to the Domesday compilation, was owned by Thorold, wherein the latter appears as the " antecessor " of the former.[16]

The kinship of the earls of Chester with Esilia Crispin Malet is further verified by a charter of king Stephen reproduced in the addenda, to Ranulph de Gernon, the fourth earl, wherein the king restores the estates in Lincolnshire of " Adelais de Condé,"[17] descended from Pierre de Condé, son of Emma Crispin, the sister of Esilia. It corroborates a relationship between these earls and the family of Condé and also signifies that both were of the lineage of Crispin.[18] In regard to this, Freeman[19] most unconvincingly attempts to show that Esilia Crispin was not the wife of William Malet, as his wife is mentioned in Domesday several times, only as " the mother

of Robert Malet,"[20] without giving her name.

For Esilia Crispin to have been the mother of both Robert Malet and Alan de Lincoln she must have been born about 1030, and if married by 1047 was then only 17, and Robert could not have been older than 18 in 1066.

That Robert was of a proper age to have attended the conquest is made evident in several ways. He appears as a donor of lands in the Grand charter of the abbey of Bec executed c. 1070,[21] when he was certainly of full age, and this is substantiated farther on. Alan could not have been born before 1072 or 1073, when Esilia would have reached the age of 42, after which time she would have had at least one other child, Alured de Lincoln II. There is nothing in these statements which by themselves could not have happened, but when taken collectively they are very unusual. Should this theory be incorrect, then William Malet may have been the father of Robert Malet by a previous marriage or alliance with a woman named Asa, who occurs in the clamores de Euruicscire in Domesday.[22] She had been divorced or separated from her husband, one Beornwulf (cf. p. 51), and all of her lands which she held in her own right (ut domina) free from all control of her husband were given to William Malet, who held them " donec invasum est castellum." The jurors attested that the lands ought to belong to Robert Malet. This suggestion of Freeman is supported to a certain extent by the recorded statement of Simeon and Durham that William Malet, with his wife and two children, were captured with him at the siege of York in 1069. (Willelmo Malet [qui tunc vicecomitatum gerebat, Sim.] cum suâ conjuge et duobus liberis.)[23] These would have been William, his second son, and Lucia, because at that time Robert would not have been called a child. The latter shortly after claimed some of his father's lands,[24] which also indicates that he was then of age. William lost the office of sheriff of Yorkshire during his captivity, for an entry in Domesday shows that it was held by Hugh, the son of Baldric (298), which was in 1070.[25]

Since William Malet had these two children by Esilia, his daughter Lucia by this marriage, the wife of Ivo Taillebois, was the half-sister of both Robert Malet and Alan de Lincoln, if it be true that Robert was William's son by Asa, or an unknown lady. The countess Lucia, her daughter, would then have been the niece of each of them, although Alan and Robert would not have been related.

There is nothing in this inconsistent with the Cottonian charter and it must be admitted that Asa fits in with the known facts more smoothly as the mother of Robert Malet than does Esilia, which leaves it an open matter.

There has not been a suspicion of irregularity on the part of the parents of Robert, although the constant omission of his mother's name in Domesday is very curious. Another argument used by Freeman, equally as groundless, calls attention to the statement in the *Crispin genealogy*, (*De nobili Crispinorum genere*), that Esilia Crispin was "the mother of William Malet." [26] He declares this referred to a "William Malet, a monk at Bec," who died shortly after 1121, at a very advanced age. This is correct, and for that reason he says Esilia could not have been the wife of the William Malet (I) of the conquest. He deliberately ignored or was unaware of the fact that the William of Bec was a younger son of William I and Esilia who inherited the Norman estates of his father. [27] He lived at this monastery for many years, to which he made large donations, at the time when the *Crispin genealogy* was being composed by Milo Crispin, himself a monk there. It was therefore perfectly natural that the latter in recording the family pedigree should mention the son who was his uncle then living there, instead of the father, deceased for many years and not a benefactor to that abbey. Had he turned to the *Grand charter of William the Conqueror* to that monastery he would have found therein recorded a gift of lands by Robert Malet to it before 1070 with the consent of Gilbert Crispin II. William Malet II, his younger brother, the monk, gave Conteville to Bec in 1121, [28] shortly after which year he died, because it was confirmed by Gilbert Crispin III in 1130. [29] Attention is here drawn to these gifts which show the lands of both were held under the Crispin family.

The close connection of the English ancestors of William Malet and Alured de Lincoln and the attendant circumstances permit the assumption that their activities were closely interwoven. Under these conditions the latter would be frequently thrown in contact with the Malet family and therefore a logical successor in the affections of the widowed Esilia.

Now an Alan de Lincoln (I) attended the counsel of the barons in the fifteenth year of the reign of king William I, 1081, [30] and attested a Durham charter in 1084 and was succeeded by Alured I, probably his brother, before 1086, as Alan I, does not appear in Domesday. Alured I was followed by his son, the Alan (II) of the Cottonian charter, for it is apparent that the other Alan I could not have been the son of Esilia Crispin Malet, who was certainly not a widow before 1069.

Alan II appears in the great Pipe roll of

Henry I in Lincolnshire [31] on the page opposite to entries concerning the countess Lucia and her son earl Ranulph in 1131, which demonstrates that he could not have been the Alan of 1081.

Alured had another son, Alured II, whose son Robert held the castle of Wareham against king Stephen for the empress Matilda in 1138, as recorded by Orderic Vital [32] (Rodbertus Alveredi de Lincoliâ filius), and who occurs in the same Pipe roll in the county of Dorset. [33] Since he was alive and fighting at this time, it is evident that he could not have been the son of Alured I as claimed by Freeman. From a grant made by William de Roumare, [34] son of the countess, Freeman though, Colsuan or Coleswegen as he calls him, therein named was the son of Alured I also, [35] but this is not agreeable with the previous mention of his fief.

"Avunculus matris" is susceptible of the translations, "uncle of his mother" or "his maternal uncle." The former, to have the generations fit in properly, is intended here, for if it had been the latter there would only have been one Lucia, the wife successively of Ivo Taillebois (by whom she had no issue), Roger Fitz Gerold and Ranulph, earl of Chester. It is recorded in the great Pipe roll that her eldest son William de Roumare was of age in 1122, and Ranulph, earl of Chester, her younger son, in 1131, [36] who must have been born not later than 1101 and 1110 respectively.

Now since it has been established that Ivo Taillebois married in 1072 and died in 1114, [37] and as Ranulph le Meschin was alive until 1128, [38] it is very apparent that Ivo, according to this theory, could not have been either the first or the last husband of the countess Lucia who died c. 1148. This suggestion of Dugdale, [39] Ellis, [40] and others needs no further consideration, neither does the assertion of Edmonson [41] and Dugdale [42] that the countess Lucia was the daughter of earl Algar, for no evidence is known to substantiate this conclusion as pointed out by Freeman. [43] The earl is said by Edmonson, [44] sir Alexander Malet in a note in his translation of Wace [45] and writers upon the subject, to have married a sister of William Malet I, and Freeman [46] again disagrees. The name of Algar's wife gives no indication of Norman extraction, for it was Ælfigifu or Elfgiva, which is thoroughly English and is so recorded several times in Domesday. [47]

The mother of William Malet probably was, as already stated by Ellis, [48] a sister of Algar, although there is no authentic record to support their supposition. The claim of the earls of Chester of descent from the ancient earls of Mercia through the countess Lucia among other things, renders this deduction the most plausible, even though they did not seem to know just how it occurred.

They certainly should have known from whence they sprung and there can be no doubt that William Malet was English on his mother's side and closely connected with king Harold, who married the daughter of earl Algar, for Guy of Amiens says so [49] (Quidam partim Normannus et Anglus, Compater Heraldi).

Compater means joint sponsor, godfather to the same child,[50] but coupled as it is with the reference to William's English descent doubtless here implies a closer relationship between them. Furthermore, William Malet witnessed immediately after the earls a charter recorded by Dugdale, of William the Conqueror in favour of the church of Saint-Martin le Grand in London, to which he affixed " Princeps " after his name.[51] His Mercian blood could have been one of the reasons for thus honouring him, although the title was not hereditary as sometimes happened at that period.

Earl Leofric died an old man in 1057 and his wife [52] Godiva was alive after the conquest, but deceased before the Domesday survey,[53] when she must have been of great age. Algar, their son, was dead just before 1064,[54] and of his sons, Burhhard died in Normandy before 1066,[55] Edwin was slain in 1071 [56] and Morcar was living in 1087.[57] This indicates that William Malet and Alured de Lincoln were of the same generation as the sons of Algar. The latter gave the priory of Lapley in Staffordshire as a cell to Saint-Remigius of Rheims, quoted in a charter preserved in the local history of that city,[58] where his son Burhhard was buried, suggesting Norman affiliations. Howbeit the countess Lucia eventually succeeded to a portion of the possessions of the sheriff Thorold and to those of her father, Ivo Taillebois, whose heiress she was. It is also made clear by Nichols in the Lincoln volume of the *Archaeological Institute* that she was the kinswoman of both the sheriff and William Malet.[59]

This most perplexing and unsolved matter was discussed at great length by Round and Kirk in *The Genealogist*, who came to no definite conclusion, although the latter agreed to the two Lucias. In a document of 1076–9 occurs " Lincoliensis Turoldus," which was Thorold the sheriff, therefore, of Lincolnshire. Consequently he was not, as Round says, an " English sheriff " of the days before the conquest, but a foreigner, who died before Domesday.[60]

That Alured de Lincoln was only partly of Anglo-Saxon extraction is attested by the fact that he was not written among the tenants of Edward the Confessor, neither does he appear as one before the

compilation of Domesday, from which it can be taken for granted that he was a foreigner.

The Grand Charter of the abbey of Bec where one might reasonably look for him if Norman reveals only Alured, brother of Warren de Manmulin, whose name immediately precedes that of Gilbert Crispin (II). This is the company in which Alured de Lincoln would be expected to be found, nevertheless there is no evidence whatever that it was him.[61] His name and that of Alan imply a Breton origin, which is probably correct, although it has not been proven. He is known only as Lincoln taken from his English barony, and he must have been of distinguished lineage which his honours and possessions indicate.

The pedigree would then be, which slightly differs from that given in *Recherches sur le Domesday* [62]:

Alan I and Alured I, parentage unknown, grandsons or nephews of Thorold.

Alan I occurs as a witness with Robert, earl of Mortain, William de Redvers, Robert Fitz Gerold (brother-in-law of the countess Lucia), and others to a charter of William, bishop of Durham, to Saint-Cuthbert's, Durham,[63] and in another of William the Conqueror to Durham monastery with Robert, count of Mortain.[64]

Alured I succeeded Alan I between 1081 and 1086, who died without issue.

Alured I by a marriage with Esilia Crispin Malet had Alan II, his heir, and Alured II.

Alan II died without male issue, whose daughter Margareta married Ranulph de Bajocis (Bayeux).

They were living 1141–6 and the latter is named in the *Book of Fees* as the " heir of Alan de Lincoln " and Hugh is mentioned as the heir of Ranulph. They had at least four sons, Hugh, Alan, William, and Robert, as evidenced by several charters in the *Monasticon*. The foundation charter of the abbey of Newhouse, Lincolnshire, reads in part, " dominibus meis Randulfo, uxore ejus Margareta et filiis ejus Hugone et Alano." Among the witnesses were Acardus de Lincoln and Suspir de Bajocis.[65]

Another charter of Hugh (Hugo de Bajocis) in which he gives to the priory of Sempringham, Lincolnshire, lands in Sempringham and Billingbrunc, witnessed by Acardus, my uncle (avunculus meus), Alan, William, and Robert, my brothers, and Suspirius de Bajocis.[66] This is curious because Lucia was sometimes termed " countess of Bolinbroke." Hugh in another made a donation for the soul of Alan de Lincoln (II), his grandfather (pro anima de Alani de Lincolnia avi mei).[67] The family de

Bajocis, Baiocis, or Bayous, prevailed for several centuries and held the barony of Bayeux. This leads one to suspect that Ranulph de Bayeux, husband of Margareta, may have been the son of Renouf de Bricasard, viscount of Bayeux in the Bessin [68] and, therefore, the brother of Ranulph le Meschin, third earl of Chester, the husband of the countess Lucia, whose son, Ranulph de Gernon, fourth earl of Chester, in her right received the fee of Alan de Lincoln (II) as recorded in the Cottonian charter.

This perplexing array of facts makes it extremely difficult to understand why this fee passed to Ranulph de Gernon when Alan de Lincoln II apparently had living male descendants.

Alured II witnessed a charter at Nottingham erroneously dated 1119 making a grant to Saint-Cuthbert's, Durham. [69] This was attested by Gilbert Crispin, abbot of Westminster, [70] but the date really was 1109 (vide 192).

Robert, son and heir of Alured II, married Benta, by whom he had Alured III, his successor (Ailredus de Lincolnia filius Bentae and Bente mater Aluredi de Lincoln). [71]

Alured III married Albreda and was sheriff of Dorsetshire. Leland informs us that Alured de Lincoln was friendly with the holy hermit Wulfric, monk of Haselbury, who died in 1154, and that Alured had an uncle by the name of Sampson, who was the brother of the wife of William, lord of Haselbury, apparently William Fitz Walter (Aluredus de Lincolnia familiaris Wulfrici . . . Sampson de Lincolnia, vir non parvi nominis, avunculus Aluredi de Lincolnia, qui nunc superest, frater fruit uxoris Guilielmi domini de Haselberge . . . Durandus de Mohun, miles, frater uxoris Gulielmi filii Gualteri). [72] Leland probably secured his information from a history of Wulfric of Haselbury by John, monk, later abbot, of Ford. It is uncertain whether this refers to Alured II or III. Alured III died in 1198 and was succeeded by a son of the same name.

Alured IV married Matilda and was one of those who defended and held the castle of Winchester for king John in 1200.

Alured V, last of the name, son and heir of Alured IV, married Joan and died without issue in 1264. [73] He was succeeded in his possessions by his sisters Margery, who married Robert Fitz Payn, Beatrice, wife of William de Gouiz, and Albreda, who died childless. From Margery descended Margaret Fitz Payn, wife of Roger Crispin of Devon, who died in 1313 and left a son, Thomas Crispin, and a daughter Elizabeth married to sir John

Streche, whose son, sir John Streche, was sheriff of Devon in 1379. The female descendants of Elizabeth married into the families of Beauchamp, Bonville, Cheyne, Saye, Pudsey, Babington, etc. There were numerous collateral branches of the Lincoln family in England, from one of which it is believed Abraham Lincoln, president of the United States, descended. William d' Aubigny (de Albini), pincerna, is recorded as earl of Lincoln in a cartulary of Lewes priory which Eyton [74] discards as an error of the scribe, but Cocayne [75] found it so recorded in the original charter in the Public Record office. In a cartulary of Reading [76] he again so appears and the original charter is also there to support the cartulary. [77] No one seems to believe it, but here the records are. In any event, Alan de Lincoln (II) was connected in some important way with the family de Albini. See also Feudal England, Round. [78]

[1] Gall. Christ., XI, 139 ; Nor. Peo., 311. [2] Domesday, Bedford, fo. 215b ; Clamores, N. Riding Lincoln., fo. 375b ; Rutland, fo. 293b ; Clamores in Chester, fo. 377b. [3] Vide Le Sire de Saint-Sever. [4] Mon., iii, 216. [5] Stapleton, II, cliii–iv ; Cle., II, 263. [6] Ibid., Stapleton. [7] Stapleton, II, clxi ; G.E.C., v, 85 ; Feudal England, Round, 184. [8] British museum, Cotton, ch. XVII, 2. [9] Stapleton, II, cliii. [10] Domesday, Lincolnsh., fo. 336b. [11] Ibid., Domesday, fo. 357 ; Thirty-fifth report of the Deputy Keeper, p. 8 ; Stapleton, II, cliii. [12] Roger of Wendover, Giles, 341 ; Henry of Huntingdon, Forester, 206, 207, 213, 214 ; William of Malmesbury, Giles, 215–85. [13] II, 119 ; Cod. Dipl., IV, 126. [14] The charter of Thorold of Bucknall is one of those in the spurious work of Ingulf and Peter de Blois, his continuator, in the Crowland Chronicle. Ingulf was its abbot and former secretary to duke William (Ord. Vit., II, 101). This of itself does not disprove that the statement therein made is incorrect so far as Thorold having been the brother of Godiva is concerned, for it was evidently founded on contemporary memoranda and has generally been accepted. Freeman bases his pedigree on this assumption ; Stapleton, II, cliii. [15] Domesday, Lincolnsh., fo. 346b. [16] Domesday, Lincolnsh., fo. 351, Cart. of Spalding, Mon., iii, 216. [17] Vide addenda, 185. [18] Stapleton, II, cliii–iv. [19] III, 777. [20] Domesday, II, 305, 317b, 323b, 324, 326. [21] Bibl. nat. lat. 13905. [22] p. 373. [23] 85 Hinde ; Roger of Wendover, II, 6 ; Historia Ange., I, 12 ; Matthew Paris. [24] Domesday, Yorksh., 247 ; Suffolk, 332b ; Norfolk, 133b. [25] Domesday, Yorksh., 298. [26] I, 341 ; The Genealogist, VIII, 89. [27] Plan., II, 98 ; Cle., II, 263. [28] Bibl. nat. lat. 13905, fo. 116. [29] Dict. de l'Eure, II, 914 ; Vide Gilbert Crispin, n. 16. [30] Rech. Domesd., 135. [31] p. 111 ; Stapleton, II, cliv ; Ord. Vit., IV, 44. [32] VI, 201. [33] p. 15. [34] Dep. Keep., thirty-fifth report, 8. [35] III, 779–80. [36] Ibid., n. 23. [37] Chronicle of Ingulphus of Croyland,

Peter de Blois, continuator. [38] *Ibid.*, n. 23 ; *Annals and Antiq. of Lacock Abbey*, Bowles, 72. [39] *The Baronage of England* (I, 10), quoting Ingulph of Croyland. [40] Ellis, I, 490 ; Freeman, II, 682. [41] *The Peerage*, VI, 22. [42] *The Baronage of England, ibid.* ; *Annals de Peterborough, Mon.*, i, 306 ; *Chron. of Croyland* ; *Cart. of Spalding.* [43] II, 682. [44] *The Peerage*, VI, 23. [45] pp. 268-9. [46] II, 679 ; III, 778-9. [47] *Domesday*, fo. 231b ; Suffolk, II, 286b ; Nottinghamsh., II, 280b. [48] I, 490 ; Cle., III, 344. [49] p. 588 ; H.B., 809D. [50] *Parallel Chronicles*, Earle, 318. [51] Plan., II, 98 ; Cle., II, 263. [52] *Henry of Huntingdon*, 207 ; Freeman, II, 466. [53] Freeman, II, 682. [54] *Ibid.*, II, 476. [55] *Ibid.*, II, 466 ; *Henry of Huntingdon*, 207. [56] *Henry of Huntingdon*, 213. [57] Freeman, IV, 475. [58] *Domesday*, Northamptonsh., 222b, should be Staffordsh. ; *Mon.*, vi, 1042 ; Ellis, I, 325. [59] p. 255. [60] New Series, vols. 5 to 9 ; Round, 329. [61] *Vide* 169, line 28. [62] 135. [63] *Mon.*, i, 237 ; O.V. II, 434. [64] *Ibid.*, i, 238. [65] *Ibid.*, vi, 865. [66] *Ibid.*, vi, 947. [67] *Ibid.*, vi, 866. [68] *Vide* 105. [69] Dep. Keep., thirtieth report, 201. [70] *Vide* 139. [71] *Collectanea*, Leland. [72] Leland, *ibid.* [73] Inquisition No. 19 in 48 Henry III (1264) ; *Rech. Domesd.*, 135. [74] *Hist. of Shropshire*, II, 273. [75] *Complete Peerage*, V, 85. [76] *Harl. MS.*, 1708, fo. 97. [77] *Add. Cart.*, 19586. [78] 187.

Appendix 21

BAUDOIN DE MEULES ET DU SAP

The sons of Baldwin were born in the following order : " Willelmus filius Baldwini," indicated sheriff of Devon 1096 [1] ; Robert, who held Brionne, 1090,[2] and occurs 1101,[3] Richard who succeeded, and Guiger, a monk at Bec. As Richard died in 1137 and his sister Adeliza in 1142,[4] both were born late in Baldwin's life.

[1] *Tavistock Cart.*, in *Mon.*, ii, 497. [2] Ord. Vit., II, 490-3. [3] *Feud. Eng.*, Round, 472. [4] Ford abbey.

Appendix 22

NÉEL DE MONNEVILLE

NOTE I.—Néel de Monneville was the son of Raoul de Montville and Avica his wife who with his mother and brothers Raoul and William made a donation to the canons of Saint-Georges de Boscherville for the soul of his father Raoul. The latter occurs in a charter of Gerold de Roumare to Sainte-Marie and Saint-Amand of Rouen to whom he was probably akin. He received his surname from Montville, Monneville, Man-

ville or Monville, a vill in the Roumois.[1] *Norman People*, who report Néel at Senlac, erroneously state that he was a brother of Roger d'Amondeville. The families were separate and distinct. Néel held extensive possessions by barony and in chief in Yorkshire 1086 (Domesday). Delisle records him upon the Dives roll as Néel de Munneville.

Nor. Peo., 293 ; Cle., II, 321. [1] Stapleton, II, clii. *Vide* Guillaume d'Arques.

Appendix 23

LE SIRE DE VESLI

Robert de Verli (Vesly) occurs in Norfolk 1086 (Domesday), while Hugh and William de Vesly held in Essex and Yorkshire. Turold de Verlai held thirteen lordships under Roger de Montgomery in Shropshire and from him descended the family of Chelwynds.

Appendix 24

GUILLAUME DE MOULINS SIRE DE FALAISE

William de Falaise died 19 October 1100 at his castle of Moulins and was buried in the chapter house of Saint-Evroult, leaving to Robert his son and heir his Norman barony (Stapleton, I, cxxxiii–iv).

Appendix 25

LE SIRE DE TOURNIÈRES

Tournières is in the arrondissement of Bayeux. Wace (l. 13664) speaks of " sire de Tornières," but the companion of the Conqueror of this name has not been identified by any of the chroniclers of the subject. We do not profess to know anything about him and have only recorded his name because Wace did so, whom we have no reason to disbelieve. He in all probability can be classed among those who were killed in the battle of Hastings or died soon after, which would account for his obscurity. Richard de Tourneriis occurs in the foundation charter of Kenilworth, *temp.* Henry I. It is possible that Wace may have confused him with the sire de Torneor.

Le Prevost, *Notes, Wace*, II, 254 ; *Wace*, Taylor, 232 ; Plan., II, 296.

M

THE FOLLOWING CHARTERS ARE NOT
TO BE FOUND IN THE AMERICAN
LIBRARIES AND ARE THEREFORE
PUBLISHED HERE.

M. J. C.

No. 1. CHARTER OF ROBERT, DUKE OF NORMANDY, IN FAVOUR OF THE MONASTERY OF MONTIVILLIERS
1035[1]

(Annales Ordinis S. Benedicti occidentalium monachorum patriarchæ. Johanne Mabillon. IV, 399, 400, Paris, 1707)

ANN. CHR.
1035.
XLVIII.
Monasterium
Villare
instauratur.
* Montivilliers.

Ineunte anno MXXXV. *Rotbertus dux Nortmannorum*, principum sui temporis exemplo Jerosolymitanum iter aggressurus, Willelmum seu Guillelmum filium suum, vixdum septennem, ex concubina ortum, *Gisleberti Crispini Brionensis comitis* tutelæ commisit, & utrumque Heinrici regis patrocinio commendavit. Id factum in procerum conventu Fiscamni habito, ubi in fidem pueri omnes jurarunt. Ibidem etiam actum de instaurando puellari Monasterio-villari*, in Caletis quondam, suggerente Filiberto abbate, a Warattone præfecto palatii haud procul ab opido Harefloto, prope ostia Sequanæ constructo, quod commune ceterorum fere Neustriæ monasteriorum excidium tempore Danicæ persecutionis tulerat. Hunc locum Richardus secundus, ipsius Rotberti parens, Fiscamnensibus monachis contulerat, ut ex eo facerent quidquid vellent, tamquam ex proprio alodo. at Rotbertus locum istum in priorem statum restituere volens, Johannem abbatem rogavit, ut ipsi eum concederet, dato in commutationem monasterio sancti Taurini *apud Ebroas*, ut eodem jure illud in alodum tenerent Fiscamnenses, & *sit cella prædicti monasterii sanctæ Trinitatis in sempiternum*, ut Rotbertus ipse loquitur in litteris hac de re conditis, in quibus ait, se id aegre ab Johanne abbate obtinuisse. Recepto itaque Villari in suam potestatem, Rotbertus monasterium puellarum ibidem mox instaurare cœpit, idque in prædicto Fiscamnensi conventu a suis proceribus confirmari curavit. Legimus in archivo Monasterii Villaris litteras Rotberti ducis, in quibus ait, se doluisse tam sancti loci dejectionem, quem sancto Filiberto a Warattone duce eo pacto concessum fuisse acceperat, ut illic in honore " sanctæ Mariæ monasterium construeret, & virgines, sub regulari disciplina Domino militaturas, multis terrarum possessionibus beneficiato ordinaret. Proinde se decrevisse hunc locum in priorem statum redintegrare, consentientibus fidelibus suis, & *maxime quadam amita mea*, inquit, *nomine Beatrice, id agente & studente, quæ postea habitu mutato, Domino illic militare elegit.* Tum varias eidem monasterio possessiones assignat princeps, vetatque ne in eodem loco alterius sexus ordo habeatur ; & *si status sanctæ Regulæ depravatus* illic *aliquando defecerit, eodem sexu, eodemque ordine reparetur.* quod sub æternæ damnationis anathemate ratum esse jubet auctoritate *Rotberti archiepiscopi, Hugonis quoque Ebroicæ episcopi, alteriusque Hugonis episcopi Abrincavum civitatis, Jahannis etiam Fiscamnensium abbatis, necnon Gradulfi abbatis Fontinellensis cœnobii, hujus operis maxime procuratoris, cui eadem amita mea,* ait ille, *sanctæ professionis firmitatem professa est ; comitis Balduini & Engelramni, Osberni-Nigelli vicecomitis, Gotselinii, & Richardi, ac ceterorum nobilium. Facta est hæc privilegii auctoritas Fiscamni in conventu celebri, idus Januarii, octavo anno regni nostri, quo & Jerusalem petiturus, ibi licentiam eundi a Deo & sanctis ejus petii ; anno ab incarnatione Domini millesimo trigesimoquinto, regnante Heinrico rege Francorum anno IIII. indictione IIII. lege III.* His litteris apponuntur cum Rotberto signa *Villaris ecclesiæ, Willelmi comitis, Hugonis Lixoviensis episcopi, Johannis abbatis, Gisleberti-Crispini, & Willelmi-Crispini.* Subsequuntur in pancharta variæ donationes Willelmi Nortmannorum comitis, sororis Adelogiæ, quæ sanctimonialis ibidem facta, terram de Bello-monte Villari dedit ; Hatvidis itidem sanctimonialis mediam partem terræ Dot concessit. *Prima ejus loci abbatissa fuit prædicta Beatrix, Rotberti ducis amita :* secunda Elizabeth, cui consuetudinem terræ de Calvelvilla Willelmus comes impertiit. Hoc monasterium exemtione gaudet & jurisdictione in quasdam ecclesias, habetque officialem, cui archiepiscopus vices suas committit. De hac jurisdictione gravis controversia tempore Innocentii III exorta est. . . ."

[1] This Charter and those following are not indexed.

No. 2. EXTRACT OF THE FOUNDATION CHARTER OF ROBERT, DUKE OF NORMANDY

GIVEN AT FÉCAMP, 13 JANUARY, 1035, AND CONFIRMED BY PHILIPPE LE BEL IN 1304

(Bibl. lat. Rouen, 1035)

In nomine S^{tte} et Individuæ Trinitatis Robertus Divinæ Authoritatis normanerum Dux & rector ðibus . . . .

Presentis cartæ privilegio confirmamus ut sine contradictiones molestia ea quæ infra memorantur vel a me vel a patre meo comite Ricardo dedita sine concessa supradicto monasterio perpetualiter serviant . . . .

Pertinent, quæ autem sequntur a victoriosissimo rege anglorum invictissimo que Duce normannorum Willelmo Data, sive ab abbatissa seu a moniatibus tempore suæ conversâôis eo permittente sunt concessa emit vero *Abbatissa Beatrix* a conjuge *Walterii quæ De Lescelina* annuentibus *filiis suis Willelmo, Roberto & Gilleberto* partem terræ quam habebat in villa quæ dicitur Helinis sub testimonio quidem suorum & nostrorum hominum quorum nomina sunt hæc Robertus capellanus, Ansgotus, Rainaldus et alii plures & hoc siquidem authoritat—et licentia Comitis actum est . . . .

. . . loco S^{tae} Mariæ Deo dedicata sub horum testimonio scilicet Roberti *Hugonis Luxoviensis* Épi, *Joannis abbatis, Guisleberti Crispini* Annuente Willelmo comite et faventibus filiis suis beneficium . . . .

. . . roboratur insuper subscriptis testium nominibus Osmundi Basset ac fratrum suorum *Willelmi de Linsoreus, Roberti* atque *Fulni, Rainaldiq ;* de Nonant. . . . .

. . . . . . Hugo prædictæ ecclia audiente Renaldo Regis capellano et Rainaldo de monasterio Villarensi et Aluredo et Gisleberto de Ceuron & Willelmo nepote ejüsdem, Hugonis et Wimondo Gaillart abejuredum unum molendinum cum terra molendinarii dedit Tetbaldus pro filia sua Aduenia . . .

(We had this original confirmation photographed, which does not record William Crispin (I), but dom. Mabillon does in his version on the preceding page. Perhaps he secured his data from the original papers of duke Robert.)

No. 3. CHARTER OF THE ABBEY OF JUMIÈGES ATTESTED BY WILLIAM CRISPIN I, AS COUNT OF VEXIN

1045–1048 [1]

Roger de Montgomery releases his vassal Geoffry, Monk of Jumièges, from service for the fief of Fontaine, which the latter gave to this monastery.

1   Original (Arch. Seine Inf., Fonds de Jumièges, Série H non classée). Vide Mabillon IV, 509–10 ; *Gall. Christ.*, XI, 194 ; *Hist. Abb. Royale de Saint-Pierre de Jumièges*, Loth I, 167.

In nomine summe et individue Trinitatis. Ego Rogerius quem dicunt de Monte Gummeri, notum esse volo fidelibus cunctis presentibus atque futuris quod quidam meus fidelis, Goisfredus nomine, filius Gotselini Stantuin, presentem vitam omnimodo despitiens futuramque adquirere cupiens, Spiritu sancto sibi inspira(nte), seculum istud sua sponte meoque consensu dereliquid [*sic*] transitorium atque in Gemmetico monasterio habitum suscepit monachicum. Is itaque Goisfredus alodum possidebat in villa que dicitur Fontanas et inde michi serviebat pro eo quod ipse alodus in mea ditione manebat. Quem ego, illius rogatu atque precatu, solidum ac quietum Deo concedo et sancto Petro in Gemmetico monasterio, ubi monachus effectus est. Pro hac quoque donatione accepi ab abbate loci illius, Godefredo nomine, atque ab ipso Goisfredo unum equum. XXX. librarum necnon unum halberc .VII. librarum. Et ut hæc mea donatio firma semper perseveret, manu propria eam firmavi dominoque meo comiti ac ejus fidelibus firmandam tradidi.

S(ignum) *Willelmi co+mitis Normannorum.* Signum *Roge+rii Montemgomerii.* S(ignum) *Widonis+comitis.* S(ignum) *Willelmi comitis + Vilcasini.* S(ignum) *Willelmi Archensis comitis +.* S(ignum) *Willelmi filii Osberni +.*

Au dos d'une ecriture du XI siecle : Fontanas.

[1] Geoffry died, according to the necrology of the Abbey of Jumièges, 24 May 1048.

WILLIAM CRISPIN I WITNESSES AS COUNT OF VEXIN

(*Vide* charter no. 3)

CHARTER OF GILBERT CRISPIN II

(*Vide* charter no. 5 on the following page)

No. 4. CHARTER OF THE ABBEY OF JUMIÈGES
1048–1078

ROBERT III, ABBOT OF JUMIÈGES, BY CONSENT AND ADVICE OF GILBERT
CRISPIN, TAKES TO TILLIÈRES HIS DUEL OF VIEUX VERNEUIL

A. Original lost—B. Copy of the beginning of XIII Century in the Cartulaire A, p. 89, no.
143 (Arch. of Seine Inférieure, fonds of Jumièges, series H).

Notum sit omnibus tam futuris quam presentibus quod dumnus abbas Robertus de
Jumeges, assensu Gilleberti Crispini et ejus consilio, quoddam suum duellum de Veteri
Vernolio ex propria voluntate sua ad Tillerias adduxit. Ipse abbas duellum in castello
tenuit. Ita quod *Gillebertus Crispinus* in duello abbatis nichil clamavit nec clamat super
isto duello ; nec consuetudo Gilleberti nec consu (e)tudo abbatis lucrata nec perdita
fuit. Hec scripta Gillebertus Crispinus adsignavit et sigillo suo inscrixit.

No. 5. CHARTER OF THE ABBEY OF JUMIÈGES
c. 1054

DONATION OF THE FIEF OF HAUVILLE BY GILBERT CRISPIN II TO THAT
MONASTERY

A. Original (Arch. of Seine Inférieure, fonds of Jumièges, series H).

Cum apud christianissimos non pauci, inter primates regni cælestis concives, vere
pro benefitiis habentur, quique vero hoc mereantur pro sue conversationis modulo, quoquo
modo fiat, Deus, cujus providentia que sunt sancta proveniunt, illo elemosinis instantes
gloriosius sublimare ac remunerare non desistit. Dum enim acheus elemosinam, latinus
autem misericordiam sonat : " Beati misericordes, inquit, id est elemosinam sectantes,
quoniam misericordiam consequentur " rursemque Dominus : " Agite elemosinam, et
omnia munda sunt vobis," et alibi " Benefacit anime sue vir misericors." Quorum
igitur et aliorum divinitatis verborum reminiscens, ego Gislebertus deicola et sanctorum
servus sub hujus regni principis Willelmi potestate constitutus, mortisque periculorum
non oblitus, benefitium, Alsvillam scilicet, quam a predicto meo domino militans obtineo,
sancto Petro apostolorum principi tribuo. Et quoniam inestimabilis pro quantitate sui
ipsa terra a vicinis loci dicitur, a monachis Gemmeticensibus ducentas denariorum libras
et unum equum viginti librarum atque untias auri duas accepi ; et hæc pro pauco, quoniam
transitiva habenda sunt. Sed quod carius in rebus computatur et quod melius eligitur,
pro remediis animarum Richardi magni principis scilicet, Wilelmi quoque Normannie
domini mei gloriosi ducis, nunc in vita gratia Dei viventis, atque patris mei et matris
necnon mee meeque conjugis ac natorum, devotius hoc ago quam cupidus aviditate muneris
detineor. Nam notum fore tam presentibus quam futuris viventium cupio quatinus
omnia superius et inferius ipsi ville adjacentia sive pertinentia ea ratione dono ut si quis
hanc donationis cartulam infringere quod minime credo, presumpserit, omni maledictioni
subjaceat, atque mille libras auri comiti et sexaginta milia argenti æclesie persolvat, et
decetero in perpetuum cum omni posteritate sui servus fiat. Ut autem haec scriptio
firma maneat, istorum manibus traditur roboranda quorum ista sunt nomina. Signum +
Gisleberti + Crispini et conjugis ejus. Signum Vuillelmi + Nortmannie comitis. Signum
+ Vuillelmi Ebroicensis episcopi. Signum Stigandi + dapiferi. Signum Hugonis +
pincerne. Signum Vuillelmi + filii Osberni. Signum Salomo + nis. Signum + Ricardi
Vuarini filii + + + + +

On the back of the charter in the writing of the 11th *century is the name,* Alsville ; *of a posterior
writing :* Hauville.

No. 6. GRAND CHARTER OF WILLIAM THE CONQUEROR TO THE ABBEY OF BEC

c. 1070

(Bibl. nat. lat. 13905, f° 115 r°, 201; 115 v° 202; 116 r° 203, and lat. 12884, f° 85)

In nomine Patris et Filii et Spiritus Sancti. Amen. Beccensi cœnobio sanctæ De genitricis Mariæ dederunt vel vendiderunt subscripti : Willelmus rex Anglorum, tunc tantum dux Normannorum, filius Roberti comitis, decimam denariorum totius census Brionniæ, partem quam cohæredes Baldrici habebant in Servavilla, cum omnibus consuetudinibus de ipsa villa ad se pertinentibus ; licenciam faciendi burgum circa cœnobium ; ecclesias de Algia quæ fuerunt comitis Gisleberti, quas habebat in suo dominio, et decimas. —Herluinus filius Ansgoti, abbas ejusdem cœnobii, tertiam partem Bornevillæ et Surcei et Cavillei ; totum Sarnaium ; quod habuerat mater ejus in Malavilla.—Gislebertus comes, servitia alodiorum fratrum Herluini abbatis, aquam Rislæ a vadis usque sub ponte Altoi ; quod habebat in Malavilla ; molendinum Normanni.—Baldricus, quod habebat in Sarvavilla et Ermentruvilla in marcherboht.—Drogo, filius Rodulfi, quod pater in alodium ubique habebat, consensu Roberti Gaufridi filii.—Escalwisus, Ildeberti filius, quod habebat in Becco, præter domum et molendinum, et quod habuit Surcei.—Willelmus comes de Augo, terram Escalwisi filii Rodulfi Goscelini venatoris. Terram quam habuerunt filii Turstini a domo Casalwisi usque Calvomontem commutavit abbas Becci, concessu abbatis Gemetici Roberti et capituli.—Guido comes, de vicina silva quod separat via ab ecclesia S. Martini per criptam Senseu (?) usque Novam villam ; aquam a parco usque ad fontem ejusdem aquæ, cum sanguine, teloneo cunctis consuetudinibus ; hagiam de Monte Malo.—Hugo filius Wascelini, ecclesiam Fraisnosæ, tertiam partem decimæ, duos hospites, terram quam ibi in dominio habebat, medietatem pratorum ad se pertinentium, duas tertias partes gorgi : in Ulmo duos hospites, decimam tertiæ partis villæ.—Gislebertus et Hugo, filii Ogerii, duas partes ecclesiæ et decimæ Fraisnose.—Ascelinus, filius Rogeri, ecclesiam Buxeti, decimam, hospitem unum, terram ad unam carrucam concessu Hugonis de Monte Forti, quod habebat in ecclesia et decima de Maretot, residuum Baldricus frater ejus.—Ricardus de Harolcurt, quod habebat ad Siccas fontanas.—Ivo, quod habebat in Apletot. Ricardus filius Herluini concessit quod Ivo de Apletot dedit in ecclesia et decima S. Germani et decima S. Cristofori.—Adda, filia ejusdem Ricardi, cum viro suo Willelmo concessit quæ data erant de iis quæ ad se tenebant.—Rogerius de Bellomonte, decimam de silva Brionnii, nisi quod dederat ecclesiæ de Novoburgo.—Robertus filius Anchitilli, decimam Haiæ de Tilio.—Guido de Gloz et Ansereda uxor ejus, quod habebant in Tierevilla et Fontancurte de Rogerio de Bellomonte.—Rogerius filius Turoldi, servicium de alodiis Drogolini et Escalwisi filii Ildeberti.—Johannes filius Rodulfi comitis, ecclesiam S. Georgii de Veuvra cum decima, decimam de eodem burgo et XII hospites, aquam, domos, insulam quæ est a Ponte Altoi usque ad molendinum episcopi Ebroicensis, terram Walcot de Liveht.—Ricardus, filius Gisleberti comitis, ecclesias de Orbec et Benefacta cum decimis et de Luceio, decimam telonei de Orbec, et quod Willelmus Calcion dedit in ecclesia de Avesnis cum decima, et terram sacerdotis in Fulgereto.—Balduinus frater ejusdem Ricardi, decimam de Bosco Ranulfi, terram unius carrucæ in Sapo, decimam scrutlandre de Molis.—Robertus filius Gradulfi, quod habebat Hairan.—Willelmus filius Turgisi, moltam de Bervilla, excepta domo Rogerii de Toit.—Willelmus filius Geroii, villam quæ dicitur Rosseria, sedem unius molendini in Calvilla.—Hugo de Bolbec, dimidiam moltam de Bosco Girardi.—Hugo de Gornaco et filius ejus Girardus, dominium suum in eadem villa, exempto bosco qui dicitur ramerius, et bosco sub domo Rodulfi.—Willelmus de Britolio concessit ea quæ pater ejus Willelmus dederat, id est quod habebat de illo Rogerius filius Helgoti, Robertus filius Ebroini, Robertus Manducans, Robertus Ricuzonis, et quod habebat in leuga Brionnii, et quod *Willelmus Crispinus* dederat de his quæ ab eo tenebat, et dedit unam domum in Ponte S. Petri cum omnibus consuetudinibus.— Rogerius, filius Helgoti, omnem terram suam præter . . . de Maretou et de Linbueht.— *Willelmus Crispinus*, quod de illo habebant Osbernus filius Walonis et Goiffridus canonicus Lexovii, et in Cromanvilla Walo Brito ; in Blangeio ecclesiam, decimam sui dominii, et quod sui homines ibi dederunt, decimam molendinorum suorum de Œillia, de Bernaco, decimam carrucæ suæ de Falco, ecclesiam de Livaroht, cum decima molendinorum et dominii sui, et quod . . . aitardus de *Roberto Crispino* tenuerat, in Strepineio decimam denariorum burgi, clausum Blancardi post mortem Evæ uxoris suæ, decimam omnium silvarum quas in Normannia habebat, XL solidos de teloneo Blangei et de theloneo

Livaroht, sextam partem molendinorum Pacei, dimidium silvæ ibidem ad se pertinentis, C solidos de Paceio, XX de Strepineio, et decimam ibidem totius annonæ suæ.—Walterius filius Vingoris, in Blangeio terram Rainerii . . ., in Livaroht decimam dominii sui.— Maurinus de Pinu, terram Rogeri filii Girardi ; Rainaldus filius Normanni, decimam de Coldreto.—Odardus de Vernone, consuetudines de clauso Blancardi, juxta Blancardum tantumdem terræ. *Willelmus Crispinus junior,* decimam molendinii et sui domini quod habebat in Maisnillo Fulberti ; in Druolcurt ecclesiam, decimam, et quod habebat de eo Robertus Malcovenant, unam domum in Livaroht cum cunctis consuetudinibus ; dimidium ecclesiæ et decimæ de Bornenvilla, alterum dimidium Ricardus filius Rainfredi.— Hugo Pipart, quartam partem ecclesiæ de Tilio, duas acras terræ, decimam omnium quæ ibi habebat.—Gislebertus filius Rainaldi, IIII viginti acras juxta Tiliolum.—Gislebertus d'Astin, ecclesiam et decimam Durantvillæ.—Osulfus, decimam dominii sui de Livaroht.—Erchembaldus de Faverolis, quod habebat de Ricardo filio Rainfredi.— Rodulfus de Cromanvilla, suam partem ipsius villæ, decimam terræ quam habebat sub strata.—Hæc omnia quæ *Willelmus Crispinus* major dedit vel homines ejus dederunt.— *Gislebertus Crispinus,* ecclesiam, decimam, moltam de Tilio ; ecclesiam S. Hilarii de Tegulariis cum decima omnium redituum ipsius villæ, dimidium feriæ piscariæ, licentiam piscandi per totam aquam, terram unius carrucæ, capellam de castello ; ecclesiam de Danvilla, decimam omnium reddituum ipsius villæ, terram dimidiæ carrucæ, dimidium molendinum, furnos ejusdem villæ, terram Rainaldi Gotleurat.—Lambertus de Tegulariis, terram ad unam carrucam.—Gislebertus Guolt, XL acras terræ in Maisnillo Herberti, concessu ejusdem *Gisleberti Crispini.*—Berengerius Barsot, quod habebat in Pelevilla, ejusdem concessu.—Rodulfus de Cunella et filius ejus, aliquantulum terræ in Tegulariis, et circa Danvillam circa dimidiam carrucam ejusdem concessu.—Robertus Malet, concessu ejusdem Gisleberti, sedem unius molendini in Maisnillo Goscelini et acram terræ unam, et viam ad molendinum.—Pascua ejusdem molendini dedit Geroius d'Escalfo, et ripam et unam acram et dimidiam terræ quam Herfredus de Rolvilla contulerat.—Emma de Condeto, in Tiliolo ecclesiam, decimam, terram unius carrucæ, et terram Rodulfi de Livet.—Petrus filius ejus, dimidium residui ejusdem villæ de Tiliolo, excepta molta, unum molendinum in Apevilla.—Fulco de Alnou, juxta S. Julianum terram unius carrucæ, unum molendinum ; ecclesiam de Maisnillo Scimunt, et terram quam habebat Ivelinus in eadem villa.—Albereda soror Fulconis, terram Groisselers.—Willelmus de Paceio, in Maisnillo Scimunt circa novem acras terræ.—Hadwis mater ipsius, ejusdem concessu, in Calceisse villa, terram unius carrucæ, et quod Hunfredus de Merai ibi habebat ab ea.—Walterius Broc, terram suam in valle juxta Brotonam.—Comes Simon, tertiam partem aquæ de Vuellebuoht, quantum pertinet ad piscationem et ad forisfacturas furti vel ablationis piscium.—Willelmus filius Ascelini, ecclesiam Bosci Ascelini cum decima. —Giroldus de Vernone, unum arpentum vineæ. Osmundus faber de Vernone, IIII arpentos vineæ, duo molendina, IIII gorgos. unam domum.—Anschitillus Grammaticus cum uxore et prole sua, consuetudines quas habebat in rebus ejusdem Osmundi.—Has donationes Vernonensium Willelmus de Vernone concessit, et dedit consuetudines quas ibi habebat et quatuor arpentos vineæ in plantis de Bucolen, et ut res præfati cœnobii sine omni exactione transeant per potestatem ipsius castri.—Hugo de Grentemaisnillo, ut res ipsius monasterii per Novum Mercatum sine exactione transeant quantum ad eum pertinebat.— Paganus de Neelfa, in Marboht quod dedit Godefridus et Walchelinus frater ejus, et Guimundus cognatus eorum, et terram juxta ecclesiam ad habitandum.—Warnerius de Manmulinis, dimidium eorum quæ habebat in Manmulinis, et Alveredus dimidium quod frater ejus ab eo tenebat, si frater ejus concesserit.—*Gislebertus Crispinus,* molendinum in Lonsaltu.—*Willelmus Crispinus,* terram unius carrucæ in Papia.—Teudo de S. Dionisio, quod Goiffridus dederat de iis quæ ab eo tenebat, et decimam de sua terra de Coheria et de bosco . . . et pastionem in eodem bosco.—Willelmus de Tornebu et Adda uxor ejus, et Willelmus filius ejus, quod habebant in ecclesia et decima de Cricheboht.—Hugo, filius Ascelini, terram Fulberti sacerdotis de Buxeto.—Rogerius et fratres ejus filii Croc, terram quam habebant in Furcis, et decimam de sua terra de Nazandis, et in bosco et in alneto.—Paganus de Neelfa, decimam quam habebat in suo dominio in Marbueht.— Goiffridus de Berou, cum sorore sua Agnete, ecclesiam de Donna Maria cum decima, et quod habebat in aqua Arve, et sedem molendini. *S. Willelmi regis Anglorum.*—*S. Matildis reginæ.*—*S. Rotberti comitis filii eorum. S. Will. filii eorum.*—*S. Lanfranci Cant. arch.* —*S. Odonis Baj. episcopi et comitis.*—*S. Rogerii de Bellomonte. S. Will. Crispini.*— *S. Milonis Crispini.*—*S. Will. comitis Ebroicensis.*—*S. Ricardi filii Gisleberti comitis.*

Testes confirmationis regis et Roberti filii ejus in Londonia : Lanfrancus archiepiscopus Cantuariensis ; Odo Bajocensis episcopus ; Walchelinus de Wintonia ; Osbernus de Elcestra ; Guido de Pont . . . : Will. de Britolio ; Will. de Tornebu ; Walterius Broc, et multi alii.

No. 7. CHARTER OF PHILIPPE I, KING OF FRANCE, CONCERNING THE ABBEY OF CHARTRES
1086

(*Cartulaire de l'abbaye de Saint-Père de Chartres*, Guérard, II, 245–6)

De vineis Herberti, concessis a Philippo rege in Area Braca.

" In nomine sanctæ et individuæ Trinitatis, Patris et Filii et Spiritus Sancti. Cum regalis solium dignitatis multiplex virtutum cultus exornet, liberalitas tamen atque munificentia præcipuum locum tenet, quarum effectus multorum necessitabus condescendat et vis eorum petitionibus satisfaciat. Notum ergo esse volumus, ego Philippus, gratia Dei rex Francorum, omnibus sanctæ Dei æcclesiæ fidelibus et nostris, tam præsentibus quam futuris, quod Eustachius, abbas videlicet sancti Petri cœnobii Carnotensis, nostræ serenitatis adiit præsentiam, obnixe postulans, ut munificentiæ nostræ aurem ejus precibus inclinare regali pietate dignaremur, quatinus, pro incolumitate nostra et statu regni nostri liberalitatis nostræ assensum preberemus cuidam Herberto atque ejus uxori, Ingelburgi nomine, ut quod, Deo inspirante, longo tempore maturaverant implere, nostra licentia ducere quivissent ad effectum ; scilicet ut de rebus propriis quas habebant in area Braca, sanctum Petrum et monachos ejus heredes facerent : videlicet de duobus aripennis et dimidio vineæ, de domo sua, horreo et furno, omnique supellectili eorum. Cujus justam petitionem judicantes, cum nostris fidelibus qui nobiscum præsentes aderant, dignum duximus, pro anima patris mei Hanrici regis atque pro nostra salute, assensum prebere donationi prædicti viri et uxoris ejus. Placuit etiam serenitati nostræ regia interdicere actoritate, ne quis umquam per succedentia tempora huic nostræ munificentiæ operi, quod cudimus, aliqua temeritate præsumat contraire, neque de concessis jam dictis rebus, neque in parvo neque in magno, quicquam minuere audeat ; neque custodem, quem ibi monachi posuerint, qualibet corveda seu exactione premat vel gravet ; sed, liber ab omni consuetudine seculiarium hominum, secure ibi maneat, et monachis serviat : tantummodo, statuto tempore, quindecim denarii, quatuor vini cantari, mina avene, panis et gallina una, nobis habenda, officio nostro reddantur. Quod si ni reddendo monachi tardi exstiterint, emendent, et res nominatas non perdant, mandavimus itaque have cartam nostro nomine nominibusque primatum nostrorum atque regiæ dignitatis sigillo corroborari, ut rata et inviolata permaneat in evum. *S. Philippi regis.* Gausfridi, episcopi Carnotensis. Amalrici clerici. Frogerii de Catalaunis. Rodberti de Rupe Forti. Guausfridi, comitis Maritaniæ. Gervasi, dapiferi regis. Philippi capellani. Tedbaldi, stabularii regis. Lancelini, pincerne regis. *Gisleberti de Tegulariis.* Hugonis de Curte Sexaudi. *Fulconis pincernæ.* Udonis, dapiferi episcopi. VVibaldi clerici. Adventii. Johannis Brustini. Arroldi. Richerii et Girardi de sancto Georgio. Actum est hoc Drocis castro publice, ante portam sancti Vincentii ; anno ab incarnatione Domini millesimo LXXX°VI°. Ego Gislebertus notarius, ad vicem Gaufridi, Parisiorum episcopi, summi cancellarii regis, relegendo subscripsi."

No. 8. WHEREIN WILLIAM CRISPIN II IS CALLED VISCOUNT OF VEXIN (1084–1095)

(Bibliothèque nationale, Département des manuscrits, Fonds latin, ms. lat. 5441, I, fo. 100)

Noverint quod Radulfus et Rogerius frater ejus dederunt in elemosinam monachis Majoris Monasterii cunctam decimam de Noiers. Rogerius autem vendidit de sua parte unum vavassum cum toto fevo ejus in Verriaco, Osbertum nomine, cognomento Peregrinum. Mortuo Rogero, Radulfus frater ejus dedit filiam suam Bagillam Roberto de Faiel in uxorem. Qui Robertus calumpniatus est quod dederat Radulfus et Rogerius frater ejus. De calumpnia ad hunc finem venit. Testes sunt de laicis : Hernulfus de Villanis ; Hugo, frater ejus ; Rainaldus Botet ; Guillelmus Dapifer ; Robertus, filius Alberici ; Guillelmus de Quadrivio ; Garnerius, filius Geltrudis ; Herbertus Durus Denarius ; Hugo Faber. Dominus Kadilo, remissus ad obedientiam Verliaci, dedit predicto Radulfo de Noers triginta solidos denariorum pontisarensium ut in curia Roberti, Normannorum comitis, *apud Nielfam castrum coram Guillelmo Crispino, illius terre vicecomite*, quicquid dederat vel vendiderat monachis Majoris Monasterii firmaret. Quod factum est. Testes sunt : *Guillelmus Crispinus et duo filii ejus, Guillelmus et Simon ;* Radulfus de Cromanvilla ; Radulfus, filius ejus ; Bernardus de Porcomortuo ; Hugo, filius ejus ; Ingerannus de Calvi-

...petus consilio patris mei et amicorum —— totum B martino
et monachis majoris monrij In perpetua elemosina ———
possidendum concessi —— et sigillo meo feci corroborari huius rei
testes —— Johannes Tuelou. Gaufrid de Granavilla
Stephanus prepositus Danguti et plures alij'
(Sans datte.) le sceau est perdu

Nouerint —— quod Radulfus et Rogerius frater ejus
dederunt In elemosina monachis majoris Monrij cunctam
decimam de Noiers —— Rogerus aute vendidit de sua parte
IV avasse cum toto feu ejus In vorriaco offertu nomine
cognom peregrinum. mortuo Rogero Radulfus frater
ejus —— dedit filiam suam Bagillam Roberto de
Faiel In uxorem qui robertus Calumpniatus est quod
dederat Radulfus & Rogerius frater ejus —— de Calumpnia ad
hunc finem venit —— testes sunt —— de laicis hermulfus
de Villanis, hugo frater ejus. Rainaldus Botet
Guillms Dapifer. Robertus filius alberici. Guillelmus
de Quadriuio. Garnerius filius Geltrudis. herbert
Durus Denarius. hugo faber. —— Dns Kadilo
remissus ad obedientiam Verliaci —— dedit prefecto Radulfo
de Noers 30 sol. den pontis. ut In Curia Roberti norman—
norum Comitis apud Mielfam Castrum coram Guillo
Crispino Illius terre Vicecomite, quicquid dederat vel
vendiderat monachis maj monrij —— firmaret quod factum est
—— Testes sunt Guillms Crispinus et duo filij ejus Guil=
lelmus, et Simon. Radulfus de Cromanvilla Ra=
dulfus filius ejus. Bernardus de Porcomortuo.
hugo filius ejus. Ingerrannus de Caluicurte.
alueredus de Eamachijs. miles de Verli.
Goffredus de Riana asceelinus popinot
—— Guillms de Quadriuio. Godifrid. filius
adelent petrus filius olberti. ascho filius alueret. Gar=
nerius filius Geltrudis. Goffridus de Suntaico.
(Sans datte et sans sceau)

Sciant —— Quod Ego Guillelmus Crispinus do—
—— monachis majoris Monrij apud Verliacum quicquid
juris habere me dicebam in muris Granchiæ atlis ——
In fosis vero ejusde ville. et In mensuris vini, in
viis et semitis —— per me et eos debet coiter emendari
—— presentem Cartam sigilli mei munimine confirmaui

curte ; Alveredus de Gamachiis ; Milo de Verli ; Goffredus de Riana ; Ascelinus Popinot; Guillelmus de Quadruvio ; Godifridus, filius Adelent ; Petrus, filius Osberti ; Ascho, filius Alverez ; Garnerius filius Geltrudis ; Goffridus de Suntaico.

(Sans datte et sans sceau)

No. 9. CHARTER OF THE ABBEY OF SAINT-PÈRE OF CHARTRES (1090)

(*Cartulaire de l'abbaye de Saint-Père de Chartres*, Guérard, II, 530–1)

Quod Fulco de Vadis concessit nobis ecclesiam de Belchia, cum decima et terrula quadam et cimiterii medietate et moltura proprie annone.

" Ego Fulco de Vadis volo ut, hujus legitimi scripti recitatione, subsequentium fidelium doceatur noticia, quia, propter predarum ablationes quibus terram sancti Petri tirannica hostilitate opprimens, vastaveram, anathematis vinculo a cetu fidelium sum sequestratus, et, divina ultione acrius perurgente, usque ad mortis ultima sum pertractus. In hujus igitur extreme necessitatis positus augustia, accersitis ad me monachis sancti Petri, ad satisfactionis remedium confugiens, de violentiis quas ei immerito intuleram impetrata ab eisdem absolutione, ad placationem satisfaciens tandem perveni, et, pro redemptione anime mee predecessorumque meorum, annuentibus conjuge mea et filio Godefrido, uxoreque ejusdem cum proprio filio, nomine Fulcone, et Willelmo de Ferreia, sub cujus dominatu extat eadem ecclesia, necnon duobus *Gislebertis de Tegulariis*, scilicet patre et filio, concedo sancti Petri apostolorum principi, firmissima donatione, ecclesiam sancti Martini de Belgica, liberam et quietam, cum terra duorum boum, terrulaque ad ipsius ecclesie altare pertinente ; addita decima quam ibidem hereditaria antiquitate tenebam, et ut monachi ejusdem loci ad meos molendinos suam annonam, absque moltura, molant. His quoque addidi cimiterii medietatem. Quod si aliquis, etc. Willelmo de Ferteia ; Godefrido, ejusdem Fulconis filio ; *Gisleberto de Tileriis seniore ; Hersende, ejus uxore ; Gisleberto juniore.*"

No. 10. CHARTER OF THE ABBEY OF SAINT-PÈRE OF CHARTRES (1096)

(*Cartulaire de l'abbaye de Saint-Père de Chartres*, Guérard, II, 557–8–9)

De molendinis de Bero a Gaufrido nobis per medium communicatis ; et de carrucata terre apud Aliarium, cum licencia piscandi in aquis suis, et uno arpenno terre cum hospicio uno nobis datis.

" In nomine Patris et Filii et Spiritus sancti. Notum sit omnibus unius ac universalis ecclesie filiis, quia ego Gaufridus de Bero, de malefactis meis penitens, hujus rei gratia, de rebus meis quas ab ignotis predecessoribus jus hereditarium mihi commendaverat, monachis sancti Petri Carnotensis cenobii eodem jure per secula possidendas, uxore mea, filiis filiaque, necnon fratre, parentibus ac dominis meis concedentibus, concedo et confirmo. Hec autem omnia, ne sub hujus proemioli serie indiscussa remaneant, singula subterius assignata sequens pagina revelabit. Sed ne interim, aliquibus de medio amputatis, hec nostra donaria in aliquo ideo infirmata videantur, huic carte inserendum decrevimus, quod, abbate et predictis monachis horum donariorum stabilitati previdentibus, ab eisdem, hujus rei gratia, ego, nomine Gaufridus XII libras Carnotensium, et filius meus Gaufridus pullum, XXX solidis appreciatum, accepimus. His igitur diffinitis, que sint donaria et qualiter data, dantia et concedentium nomina videantur. Apud Bero, duorum molendinorum retinens medietatem, ut eam mihi heredibusque meis solidam ac quietam retineo, ita aliam eorundem molendinorum medietatem ipsis monachis, tam in piscaria quam in ceteris aliis utilitatibus sive consuetudinibus, quiete ac solide possidendam concedimus. In reliquis vero gurgitibus, ad minutias et anguillas tantum capiendas, per omnia omnibus diebus unius piscatoris assiduam piscariam, concedimus. Concedimus etiam priori et ceteris monachis de Bruerolis quando ad opus sue comestionis piscari voluerint, ut prescriptum per omnia piscatorem, aut alium si voluerint, ad omnes pisces cum custodia piscari faciant. Si autem abbas ejusdem Carnotensis cenobii in partibus ipsis affuerit, quotiens et cum quibuscunque piscatoribus voluerit, cum igne et aliis omnibus modis, as omnes pisces per omnia piscari faciet. Sciendum etiam, quia quotquot molendinarii saltus in prefatis gurgitibus inveniri poterint, eos inter nos et ipsos monachos ita participes esse concedimus, ut, si nos et ipsi unum aut plures molendinos inibi confor-

mabimus, uno aut pluribus conformatis, sicuti in prescriptis molendinis per omnia com-
participabimur, sic erit in istis. Si autem ipsi soli, aut ego et non ipsi ; qui solus eos
preparabit, solus eorumdem redditus, donec justum fuerit, possidebit. Restat itaque,
apud Bero, agripennum terre cum hospiciali, et, ad Aliarium, sufficiens carrucata terre ;
que, ut superiora, illis concedimus. Concedimus etiam eisdem, de silva proxima huic
terre, pasquale propriorum porcorum suorum, et medietatem pascualis omnium quos-
cunque in eadem silva hospitari sibi voluerint. Quos ita illis relinquimus omni inquietate
absolutos, ut nichil omnino unquam ab eis requiramus, preter illud quod dictum est
medietatem videlicet pascualis eorum. Hec igitur sunt acta anno ab incarnatione MXCVI⁰,
indictione IVᵃ. Dantes : Godefridus de Bero ; Eufemia, uxor ejus ; Gaufridus, filius
ejus ; Radulfus ; Gislebertus, Richardus, filii ejus ; Adelina, filia ejus. Testes ex parte
dantium : Petrus, frater G. ; Gislebertus filius Aicardi ; Willelmus, filiaster G. de Bero ;
Geraldus de Transbosco, Sulpicius, Chotardus, Gauterius Richardi, Willelmus Aivardus ;
Fulco, filius G. de Vadis ; Vitalis de Trembleio, Willelmus de Curtellis. Testes monachorum : Herveus de Menovillari, Bartholomeus de Fontanis, Odo prepositus, Robertus
de Matunvillari, Robertus filius Frodonis ; Robertus de Belfo ; Germundus famulus
Huberti monachi ; Stephanus, filius Rogerii ; Robertus portarius, Gaudius et Teduinus,
fratres ; Odo, filius Herberti ; Robertus infirmerius, Adventius sartor ; Rainaldus, filius
Arnulfi ; Stephanus de Canfolio, Durandus faber, Tescelinus de Reconvillari ; Ivo, filius
Hatonis. Concedentes ; *domni Gislebertus de Tileriis ; Hersendis, uxor ejus ; Gislebertus
et Ribaldus, filii ejus.*"

No. 11. CHARTER OF THE ABBEY OF JUMIÈGES
IITH CENTURY

DONATION BY RICHARD OF ALL HIS POSSESSIONS AT VERNEUIL TO THE
ABBEY OF JUMIÈGES, WHEN HE ENTERED THAT ABBEY AND BY
CONSENT OF HIS SONS GILBERT, GAUTIER, GARIN, RAOUL AND
RAOUL THE YOUNGER

A. Original (Arch. of Seine Inférieure, fonds of Jumièges, series H)

Ego Ricardus, sancti Benedicti accipiens habitum apud Gemmeticensem cœnobium,
dono ecclesie prelibate quicquid in villa que Vernuelei nuncupatur habueram, excepta
annone decimatione. Filii autem mei Gislebertus atque Gualterus, Guarinus, Rodulfus,
alter Rodulfus, hanc donationem fore ratam concedunt. *Gislebertus + Crispinus ejusque
+ uxor atque eorundem filius Gislebertus* + idipsum annuunt. Guarinus + De Reimalast
identidem concedit. Hujus igitur rei testis est Isnardus + de La Ferteit ejusque nepos,
nomine Hugo, multique alii, Rotbertus +, Normannus +, filii Hugonis + de Mortvilerz,
Rodulfus +, Hugo + filii Airardi, Guazo + de Alneiz, Totart + de Druis, Sulpicius +

No. 12. CHARTER OF WILLIAM, ARCHBISHOP
OF ROUEN
1105

(Original, Arch. Seine Inf., fonds du Chap. no. 8740)

Anno ab Incarnatione Dñi M.C.V. Willmo Archiepo in Sca Rotomagensi Ecclia
presidente. Radulf fili Walbti de Bodriz reddidit Sce Marie Rotomagensis eccle tra
de Gisorz qua idem Walbt, ipse fili ej Radulf post morte patris in excommunicatione
tenuerant. auferendo ea eide eccle. Hanc redditione fecit prefat Radulf apud Roth-
omagu p cultellu in dieb ; pentecostes sup altare Sce Marie du missa ibi celebraret
presente Willmo archiepo presentib ; archidiaconis. videlicet Benedicto. Fulbto.
Goisleno. Ursello. Ricardo. Rogero secretario cu omi congregatione eccle presentib ;
etia quaplurib ; civib ; Rotomagi. ibiq ; cora altari. absolvit archieps Walbtu, Radulfu
filiu ej culpa sua culpaq ; patris cognoscente confitente. Ex hinc comuni consensu
statuto tmino ab ultraq ; parte convenenert ap Verlein ta archieps qua ide Radulf
fili Walbti. necnon mat ej frs. ibiq ; Radulf renovavit hanc redditione. reddiditq ; to

ANNO AB INCARNATIONE DNI M̄ C̄ V · WILLᵒᵒ ARCHIEP̄O IN SC̄A ROTOMAGENSI ECCL̄IA
p̄sidente · Radulſ fili' walbti de bodriz · reddidit Sc̄e MARIE rothomagenſiſ eccl̄e t̄r̄a de giſorz ·
q̄ idem wualbt' ⁊ ipse fili' a radulſ post morte patriſ in excomunicatione tenuerunt · auferendo
ea eide eccl̄e · hanc reddicione fecit p̄fat' radulſ apud rothomagu̅ p cultellu̅ in dieb· pentecoſteſ
ſup alcare sc̄e MARIE du̅ miſſa ibi celebraret̄ · p̄sente willoo archiepo · ⁊ p̄sentib: archidiaconiſ ·
uidelicet Benedicto · ſulbto · coiſleno · ursello · Ricardo · ⁊ rogero ſecretario cu̅ omi congregatione eccl̄e ·
⁊ p̄sentib: etiā quāplurib; ciuib; rotomagi · ibiq; coru̅ altari · abſolui archiepſ walbtu̅ ⁊ radulfu̅
fili̅u̅ ei· culpa ſua · culpa̅q; patriſ cognoſcente ⁊ confitente · Exhinc comuni conſenſu · ſtatuto timino
aliquātu̅ partę · conuenerent ap uerlehu̅ tā archiepſ quā ide radulſ fili' walbti · necnon mat' ei
⁊ fr̄ibuſq; radulſ renouauit hanc reddicione · reddidit̄q; t̄r̄ę sc̄ę MARIŞ p̄fatā t̄r̄a de giſorz · p
baculu̅ in manu̅ archiepi · Ubi t̄r̄ę int̄fuert̄ hanc reddicione cocedenteſ ex parte radulſi ·
mat' ei' ⁊ fr̄ſ · uidelicet walbt' euſtachi' Albic' ingelrann' nepoſ ei fili' willmi de carz · hommeſ
ſui · uidelicet ricard' deſontanū · odard' p̄ſteual · joheſ de bodriz · ragan' de corcelſ · hucbt' de
uerlei · oſmund' de fauel · bernard' fili' raineri · drogo ſentier · Rainald' ſorel · Radulſ fili' odardi ·
Exparte u̅ archiepi · cu̅ p̄fatiſ archidiaconiſ · int̄fuert̄ caſati sc̄ę MARIŞ ⁊ hommeſ ei' ſcilicet
oſmund' de caluomonte · pagan' de mielſa · Robt' de fauel · ⁊ gaſzo · hugo dapiſer pagani ·
⁊ willm' fr̄ ei' · guidard' fili' ineri · euſtachi' de fraſneuſ · Robt' fili' belinandi · oiſlebt' de uerlei ·
willm' filiu̅ iuueniſ · ⁊ manaſſeſ fr̄ ei' · willm' de condet · willm' fili' hucbti · hugo de pormort ·
⁊ joheſ fr̄ ei' · walter' torel · hugo de boſemont · Robt' fili' ernulfi de uillaniſ · Radulſ de liſorz ·
hugo fili' ſerloniſ · willm' fili' euſtachi · aſcelin fili' andreę · roger de p̄elliſ · Radulſ de uilerſ ·
florenti' canonic' · Ricard' p̄br' de giſorz · monachu̅ ⁊ de uerlei · Radulſ' mordant · ⁊ anſchetill' ·
Cu̅ hiſ · hommeſ plurimi ibi affuert̄ · ⁊ de giſorz · ⁊ de mielſa · ⁊ de caluomonte · ⁊ de uerlei ·
⁊ de danguz · ⁊ de uilerſ · Pro hac itaq; reddicione · dedit p̄fat' archiepſ eide Radulfo
filio walbti in cognicione · xx̄ marcaſ argenti · eode m̄ /ſo in hertin ⁊ auro · ſub teſtimonio
omiu̅ · q̅ m̄ hac carta ſcripti habent̄ ·

WILLIAM CRISPIN II, HIS BROTHER MANASSES AND
WILLIAM DE CONDÉ APPEAR AS WITNESSES

(*Vide* charter no. 12)

Sce Marie prefata tra de Gisorz p baculu in manu archiepi. Ubi tc intfuert hanc redditione concedentes ex parte Radulfi. mat ej frs. videlicet Walbt. Eustachi. Albic. Ingelrann nepos ej fili Willmi de Carz. Homines sui videlicet Ricard de Fontanis. Odard Presteval. Jones de Bodriz. Pagan de Corceles. Hucbt de Verlei. Osmund de Faiel. Bernard fili Raineri. Drogo Sentier. Rainald Sorel. Radulf fili Odardi. Ex parte u archiepi cu pfatis archidiaconis intfuert casati Sce Marie, homines ej scilicet Osmund de Calvomonte. Pagan de Melsa. Rotbt de Faiel, Gaszo. Hugo dapifer Pagani : Willm fr ej. Guidard fili Imeri. Eustachi de Fraisneus. Rotbt fili Helinandi Gislebt de Verlei. *Willm C'spin juvenis, Manasses fr ej. Willm de Condeit.* Willm fili Hucbti. Hugo de Pormort, Jones fr ej. Walter Torel. Hugo de Bosemont. Rotbt fili Ernulfi de Villanis. Radulf de Lisorz. Hugo fili Serlonis. Willm fili Eustachii. Ascelin fili Andree. Roger de Ptellis. Radulf de Vilers. Florenti canonic. Ricard prbr de Gisorz. Monachi u de Verlei. Radulf Mordant, Anschetill. Cu his homines plurimi ibi affuert, de Gisorz, de Melsa, de Calvomonte, de Verlei, de Dangut, de Vilers. Pro hac itaq ; redditione. dedit pfat archieps eide Radulfo filio Walbti in cognitione xx marcas argenti. eode Radulfo in tc ituro. Sub testimonio omiu q in hac scripta habent.

No. 13. MIRACULUM

QUO B. MARIA SUBVENIT GUILLELMO CRISPINO SENIORI ;—UBI DE NOBILI CRISPINORUM GENERE AGITUR

(Patrologiæ cursus completus, Migne, tome CL, 736–43)

This is a better manuscript than the one of Giles quoted on page 138, which is the reason for reproducing it.

Beata Domini Mater et perpetua Virgo Maria, singulare præsidium Christianorum, per quam salus mundi apparuit, quo majorem apud Deum præ cæteris gratiam invenisse dignoscitur, eo frequentius ab hominibus, et fiducialius atque familiarius in necessitatibus invocatur ; et ipsa celer clementiæ suæ multis impendere solet beneficium. Unde nonnulla illius subventionis exempla inveniuntur scripta, plurima passim jugi sentiuntur effectu ; quæ propter multitudinem non sunt commendata memoriæ. E quibus unum referre volumus, quod dignum memoria videtur, quodque pro sui magnitudine non potuit latere illius hominibus. In quo facto ostendit beatissima Dei parens quam benignum gerat erga miseros ad se confugientes affectum Nam cuidam nobili viro et sibi devoto, nomine Willelmo, cognomento Crispino, ejus misericordiam deprecanti in magna anxietate adfuit, et miserabiliter illum eripuit de instanti periculo mortis, sed priusquam hujus miraculi ordinem pandamus, dignum videtur paucis indicare quis fuerit ille Willelmus, et unde cognomen Crispini sibi et suo generi contigerit.

Antequam Northmanni duce Willelmo Angliam debellarent, fuit in Neustria, quæ nunc Northmannia vocatur, vir egregius, nomine Gislebertus, genere et nobilitate præclarus, qui ab habitudine capillorum, primus Crispini cognomine dicitur insignitus ; nam in sua primæva ætate habebat capillos crispos et rigidos, atque sursum erectos, et, ut ita dicam, rebursos ad modum pini ramorum, qui semper tendunt sursum, quare cognominatus est Crispinus, quas, *crispus pinus ;* quam capillorum rebursionem adhuc videmus in iis qui de ipsius Gisleberti genere descendunt. Unde et ipsi eodem cognomine a cæteris Northmannorum familiis dirimuntur. *Iste Gislebertus qui, ut diximus, Crispini cognomen primus est adeptus, accepit uxorem Senioris Fulconis de Alnov germanam, nomine Gonnorem, de qua tres filios genuit, Gislebertum Crispinum, pro quo scribere ita suscepimus, et Robertum, duasque filias Emmam Petri de Condeto genitricem, atque Esiliam matrem Willelmi Malet, qui miles strenuus, in senectute factus est monachus Becci, et transactis aliquot annis honorifice in cænobiali observatione, ut talem virum decebat, bono fine quievit. Robertus Crispinus minor frater, Northmannia egressus, plurimas peragravit regiones, donec Constantinopolim veniret ; ab imperatore cum honore susceptus, magnique nominis apud omnes effectus, ibi, ut fertur, invidia Græcorum veneno periit. Gisebertus Crispinus major horum trium fratrum, a duce Northmannorum, castrum Tegularias in hæreditate custodiendum accepit,* quod hæredes ejus tenent usque ad præsens tempus. Prædictus Willelmus Crispinus medius frater, generis nobilitate, et morum probitate atque militia famosissimus, inter Northmannorum primos habebatur, qui, ut diximus, de primo Crispinorum patre Gisleberto optimus filius, ad totius generis sui gloriam felicibus auspiciis prodiit, et sicut inter Romanos olim Fabii, vel Anicii, sive Manlii, insignes habebantur ita Crispini inter Northmannos et Francos honoratiores reputabantur. Sed iste Willelmus inter omnes nominatissimus fuisse fertur, qui suo tempore, militiæ titulis, insignes pene super omnes ejusdem tempestatis viros enituit. Unde præclara ejus probitas plures sibi effecerat invidos, atque hostes reddiderat atrocissimos. Ea tempestate Franci, *auctore Walterio Vetulo comite de Ponte-Ysare*, qui totam terram intra *Ittam et Andelam, atque Sequanam suam debere esse dicebat*, crebras irruptiones ultra fluvium Ittam faciebant, et prædas de Vilcasino agebant ; et ideo dux Northmannorum Willelmus, qui postea rex Anglorum fuit, prædictum *Willelmum Crispinum*, quia erat probatissimus in re militari, collocavit in castro Melfia, contra Francorum incursus, ad coercendas eorum præsumptiones, *donans illi castrum ipsum et Vilcasini vicecomitatum jure hæreditario custodiendum, et filius ejus post eum, sicut usque hodie videmus*. At ille ibi mansionem sibi constituit familiam et milites in loco posuit contra irruptiones Francorum ; qua de re Franci, vehementer irati, in tantum odium contra illum exarserunt ut mortem ejus tota aviditate appeterent. '

His de ortu Crispini cognominis prælibatis, nunc jam ad rem veniamus, quam, ut a veracibus relatoribus accepimus, simpliciter, referre curabimus. Et est res memoriæ digna, et beatæ Domini Matri congrua, quæ humano generi post Deum singulariter est amabilis et per sæcula cuncta laudabilis.

Inspirante Domino Deo nostro Jesu Christo, omnium bonorum auctore, quidam miles, strenuus et dives Herluinus, postposita nobilitate terrena, abjecta sæculi pompa, qua ante juxta modum suum non parum defloruerat, deposito quoque militiæ cingulo ad Christi paupertatem tota devotione se contulit, ut in monachica conversatione soli Deo liberius vacaret. Hic itaque renuntians sæculo sibi ad votum arridenti, in fundo sui juris, qui Burnevilla dicitur, volens cœnobium construere, ecclesiam ædificavit, in honore sanctæ Mariæ ; ibique religionis habitum suscepit, cum esset annorum quadraginta, nec multo post presbyter ordinatus, et abbas constitutus est. Quia campestris et inaquosus est locus, per soporem monitus a beata Domini Matre Maria, in vallem ad rivum qui vocatur Beccus secessit ; ibique nobile ædificare cœpit in honorem ejusdem sanctæ Mariæ Matris Domini monasterium, quod Deus perfecit ad sui nominis gloriam, et multorum hominum salutem et solatium. Cui Deus ad auxilium et consilium adduxit juxta desiderium cordis sui Lanfrancum, virum in liberalibus artibus undecunque peritissimum ; quem cum magno suscipiens gaudio, dedit ei habitum religionis. Tunc confluebant ad prædictum locum certatim multi sæculares litterati et alii cervices suas levi jugo Domini, et obsequio regularis vitæ humiliter inclinare. Alii liberos suos a Lanfranco erudiendos in liberalium artium philosophia, et informandos per Herluinum in regulari disciplina tradere, nonnulli ipsum locum rebus suis studebant amplissime ditare. Inter quos egregius vir prædictus Willelmus Crispinus, filium suum in tenera ætate nomine Gislebertum prædictis Patribus Deo nutriendum sub regulari disciplina obtulit, et malta de rebus suis temporalis vitæ subsidia cum puero ministravit. Quorum informatus doctrina et sanctæ conversationis exemplis, sic cum divino profecit auxilio in divinis et philosophicis institutis ut omnes artes, quas liberales vocant, ad unguem addisceret, et earum rivulos pluribus ipse perfectus in religione propinaret. Cujus tanta fuit in activa et speculativa vita perfectio ut cum Deus Lanfrancum Cantuarensi Ecclesiæ in summo pontificatu præficeret, eum Lanfrancus ad regimen West-Monasterii, Deo vocante, provideret ; tantaque sanctitatis gratia, ut credimus, Deo et hominibus placuit ut humilitatem præ cunctis sui temporis prælatis et specialiter prætenderet, et sublimius prædicaret. Hic triginta duobus annis loco magis profuit quam præfuit, et in senectute bona, plenus dierum, et sanctitate, patribus suis appositus, hujus vitæ terminum clausit. In hujus Patris genitore Willelmo, scilicet Crispino, jam superius sæpe nominato, res gesta est, excellentia insignis, relatu mirabilis, et quæ deceat Domini Matrem B. Mariam semper Virginem, quam pro suis magnis et multis beneficiis, indesinenter laudat universus terrarum orbis. Hic enim nobilis vir, ut jam diximus, a duce Northmannorum Willelmo in castro Melfia marchisus fuerat constitutus contra Francos, qui transeuntes Ittam fluvium, subitis rapinis Vilcasinum devastabant ; ibique posuerat suam familiam ad castelli custodiam. Verumtamen terram quam habebat in Northmannia, in Lexoviensi pago, certis temporibus revisebat, et dispositis rebus revertebatur Melfiam ; in eundo autem, vel redeundo Beccum non transibat, quin venerabilem Patrem Herluinum videret, et cum eo loqueretur. Accidit autem ut rediens juxta morem de terra sua, Domino disponente, quadam die Dominica, vir ille devotus, Beccensem inviseret ecclesiam, et cum abbate licentius de negotiis suis ageret. Qui cum inter se familiariter contulissent de iis quæ res postulabat necessaria, licentiam abeundi postulavit, et cum gratia festinus discessit ; cumque aliquantulum processisset, substitit, et protinus ad abbatem revertitur. De cujus reditu admiratus homo Dei, resalutatus ab illo cur rediisset inquisivit. " Ad hoc redii. Crispinus ait, alme Pater, ut me benedicas meque tuis fratrumque tuorum orationibus commendem, quatenus nos Deo et ejus piæ Genitrici me suppliciter commendare studeatis." Mox vir Domini Herluinus, pietatis visceribus in ferventem viri devotionem miro charitatis affectu præcordialiter motus. " Deo, inquit, te et sanctissimæ Matri ejus commendamus ; quorum te tuitio protegat. et a cunctis adversitatibus potenter defendat." In hac benedictione confisus, osculatis abbate et fratribus, cum sociis ad locum properat, quo ire cœperat, ad castrum, suæ scilicet custodiæ deputatum. At vero Franci, qui e regione ultra Ittam commanebant, audito quod Willelmus Crispinus transiens Sequanam in Northmanniam descendisset, conglobati in unum, sollicite observabant ejus reditum, cumforte, ipsa die qua revertebatur, in vicina silva in insidiis occultati operiebantur, ut venientem aut caperent, aut trucidarent. Crispinus ad locum properans, cum jam non longe a Castro esset, transivit juxta silvam, in qua Franci latitabant ad eum interimendum parati : qui mox cernentes quem quærebant, surgentes de insidiis audacter illum invadunt : tunc socii relicto eo omnes fugerunt ; ille præsidium fugæ attentare volens, densitate silvæ præpediebatur ; sicque interceptus, quia nec fugere, nec resistere valebat, de equo exiliit ; et necessitate compulsus super radicem excisæ arboris quæ juxta erat, insedit ; habenas, quibus equum regebat, ut quidam dicunt, vicinæ arboris ramis appendit ; et ut alii volunt, ad augmentum miraculi, manu retinuit. His arctatus angustiis, Willelmus Crispinus cor ad Deum levat, Matremque misericordiæ magna devotione mentis reclamat : " Domine Jesu Christe, ait, miserere mei, et per merita Patris Herluini et fratrum ejus, quibus me suppliciter hodie commendavi, libera me de hoc imminenti periculo mortis. O generosa Virgo, intacta Domini Mater, suscipe indignas tui peccatoris [f. precatoris] preces, et contribulati cordis sacrificium ante Deum, et ante te ascendat in odorem suavitatis. Virgo virginum, Domina angelorum, si qua tibi cura est de tuo Beccensi Herluino, suppliciter obsecro ut a præsenti me liberare digneris exitio. Instant undique hostes, jam de mea morte, vel cautione insultando triumphantes ; imminet hostilis manus, quam non licet effugere ; et in ipso mortis limine interceptus, cogor de vita desperare. Quid faciet iste tuus servulus, o intacta Parens Dei, sacrarium Spiritus sancti, quid faciet quem hostilis cuneus lanceis insequitur et gladiis. Succurre itaque, Domina piissima, per potestatem qua es apud cœlestes gloriosa, apud terrigenas imperiosa, apud inferos terribilis ; ubique propitia, ubique magnifica, ubique præeminens auctoritate et majestate regia, et innova in me antiquæ subventionis tuæ beneficia, quia non patet effugiendi via. Mater misericordiæ, per orationes servorum tuorum Becci, Herluini, et fratrum ejusdem loci, quorum orationibus me mane commendavi, libera me ab hac præsenti jam imagine mortis." Hujusmodi oratione in conspectu Domini, et ejus gloriosæ Matris Mariæ cum tota mentis devotione, et magno contriti cordis dolore, sine sono vocis emissa, anxiatus est spiritu pene usque ad sudorem mortis, cum subito a sinistris astitit ei ad vitæ solatium quædam virago præclara, vultu jucunda, ornatu regio speciosa, subtili et candida sindone amicta, quæ manicam suam dexteram expandit super eum, et hoc velamine ejus fere corpus cooperuit totum, nam ad tibias usque medias hoc tegmen descendebat, et ultra pertingere non valebat. Habebat autem rubeas caligas et ideo contrahebat se et stringebat, et totus in seipso curvatus, laborabat quatenus tibias et pedes sub manica regiæ puellæ absconderet, nec poterat. Accedunt hostes, et virum inquirere lanceis et mucronum cuspidibus accelerant, et pungendo sub frontibus, et arbustis, atque fruetis, usque ad ejus pedes vel ad corpus undique infestant, sed nullomodo ipsum tangebant. Ipse vero per munitionem beatæ Dei Genitricis, inimicis suis factus est invisibilis, et admirantes dicebant : " Quo abiit ? Quid devenit ? Nunquid eum viventem terra absorbuit ? Huc venit, hic fuit. Quo fugit et abscessit ? Ecce equus illius dependet, quem insequimur : hunc, eo non invento ad detrimentum illius subripiat qui vult." At illi quibus erat sanior mens responderunt non se venisse equum rapere, sed hostem, si possent, infestum jugulare. Cumque diu investigando illum laborassent in vacuum, vesperascente jam die, confusi ad propria redieruut. Tunc illa piissima domina : " Scisne, inquit, homo, in mortis angustia, unde tibi provenerunt vitæ subsidia ? Nosti nomen meum, quæ tibi ministravi in mortis angustia respirandi solatium ? Ego sum bona Dei Mater, cui te abbas Herluinus toto corde commendavit, quando hoc tua intentio devote postulavit." His dictis, Virgo, discessit. Sic spargit Regina cœli sperantibus in se odorem vitæ, sic attrahit ad se innumerabiles copiosa charitate, et neminem relinquit inglorium, qui devote ejus implorat auxilium. Comites Crispini, qui timore hostium ab eo profugerant, venientes domum tristi rumore repleverant oppidum quod eorum dominus aut càptus esset, aut mortuus. Dolor ingens omnium, luctus incomparabilis erat per totum castellum, cum subito prospiciunt Willelmum Crispinum super equum venientem, et cum magno gaudio occurrentes suscipiunt illum lætantes. Hic heros, cum antea plurimum Beccensem amaret Ecclesiam, deinceps hac de causa super omnes dilexit, et de rebus suis multa in ea Deo servientibus contulit. Quam dilectionem posteris suis, quasi hæreditariam reliquit, ita ut videatur quod infantes, de ejus progenie venientes, Beccensem diligant naturaliter Ecclesiam ; ac si cum lacte carnis biberint ipsius dulcedinem amoris ; ipsam quoque Domini Genitricem, quæ per totum mundum venerabilis habetur, quasi solum Becci colatur, sanctam Mariam Becci invocant, et deprecantur, et multoties ejus auxilium experti sunt in necessitatibus suis. De quibus dicitur quia Beccensem Ecclesiam, mox in ipso ortu, quasi in cunis nuper natam exc̀eperunt, et educaverunt, atque ad perfectam ætatem perduxerunt ; sumptibusque suis pro posse extulerunt. Hic egregius vir, sæpe fatus Willelmus Crispinus, ad extremum veniens misit, et rogavit sanctum Patrem Herluinum venire ad se, ut daret sibi religionis habitum ; tardante autem abbate, vidit dæmones ad se venisse, et duas macerias nimium excelsas circa se ædificare. Quibus ita arctabatur ut non se putaret inde posse evadere, cum ecce aspiciebat sanctum Benedictum, signum Dominicæ crucis manibus ferentem, ad se accedere ; ad cujus adventum illa dæmonica phantasia tota evanescebat. Nec mora, nuntiatur adesse Beccensis abbas venerabilis Herluinus, et cum eo quidam monachus, nomine Willelmus, qui postea fuit abbas Cormeliensis, a quo hæc audita dicuntur. Narravit ergo Crispinus abbati ludificationes dæmonum, et Dei adjutorium per sanctum Benedictum sibi impensum. Tunc factus, est monachus et post paucos dies vita discessit et humatus juxta ecclesiam ubi claustrum ædificandum erat, confidens se per sanctam Domini Matrem Mariam suam liberatricem, et per beatum Benedictum gratiam Christi, et misericordiam consecuturum.

EPITAPHIUM WILLELMI CRISPINI SENIORIS

Nobiliter natus miles fuit hic tumulatus,
  Providus, et fortis, moribus atque probus.
Qui ne mundus eum posset submergere secum,
  Huc portum subiit, monachus hic obiit.
Jani post Nonas, ac tres et quatuor horas,
  Cum jam complesset, quintaque jam fieret.
Parvus erat Beccus, cum parvum nomine rebus,
  Sumptibus esse suis, extulit ut potuit.
Noto Crispinus fuerat cognomine dictus,
  Nomine Willelmus, cui, Deus, esto pius.

Iste Willelmus Crispinus habuit uxorem, nomine Evam, genere et moribus sibi competentem, de qua genuit Gislebertum, prædictum West Monasterii abbatem, et alios plures Hæc Eva de gente Francorum, claris natalibus progenita, postquam prædicto nupsit Willelmo, ejus se aptans moribus cœpit Beccensem ecclesiam præ omnibus amare, abbatem et monachos, quasi ex se genitos totis visceribus amplecti, magna devotione venerari. Vestes et quæcunque in ornamentis pretiosa habebat, in usus ecclesiæ et fratrum expendit ; ipsamque Domini Matrem, et ejus Beccensem ecclesiam, toto corde dilexit. Defuncto viro ejus Willelmo totam se ad Dei servitium convertit, vivens in sancta viduitate, jejuniis, vigiliis, et orationibus intenta, quantum sexus vel ætas patiebatur, carnem, et sanguinem usque ad finem vitæ non gustans, elcemosynas multas indigentibus faciens ; post aliquot annos a Willelmo Rothomagensi archiepiscopo velata, in subjectione Beccensis cœnobii permansit usque ad mortem, et defuncta sepulta est juxta virum suum.

Horum nepos de filio Willelmo tertius Willelmus Crispinus, originalem amorem trahens erga Beccensem ecclesiam miro eam coluit affectu. Iste Willelmus sanguinis propinquitate jungebatur comiti Andegavorum ; ideoque familiaris illi erat ; ad quem cum se aliquando contulisset, ut ad amicum, et comes contra quosdam suos bellum gereret, qui in terra sua contra illum rebellabant, pugnabat Willelmus pro eo, quantum poterat. Quadam die reperiens hostes, irruit audacter in eos ; at illi terga verterunt, sive timore, ut fugerent, seu industria, ut eum longius abductum capere possent. Quos ille insecutus aliquantum, a suis disjunctus est ; inimici videntes illum se persequentem solum, unus eorum conversus equum, cui insidebat, percussit, et per latera transforavit. Ille, sciens equum ad mortem vulneratum, mox vertit habenas, et conversus retrorsum, calcaribus urgens cornipedem, celeri fuga ad suos reverti conabatur. Beatam Domini Matrem inclamitans, voce magna : " Sancta Maria Becci, adjuva me, sancta Maria Becci, adjuva me." Sic vociferando pervenit ad quoddam fossatum, quo perpeti saltu transmisso, quasi jam securitate potitus cecidit mortuus. Hoc idem Willelmus Crispinus pro magno miraculo, ad honorem Dei et ejus sanctæ Genitricis, narrare solitus erat, quod equus pene mortuus, profluente hinc inde ubertim sanguine a lateribus, per duo fere milliaria portavit eum ad tutum locum. Equidem equus ipse, ut aiebat, nimia velocitate vigebat, sed tam velocem nunquam eum invenerat. Idem Willelmus, postea captus, cum in carcere diu teneretur ferro constrictus, timore et angore coactus, vovit, si Deus eum de hac tribulatione liberaret, quod iret Jerusalem Nec multo post egressus, liber de carcere, accepit crucem, signum videlicet eundi Jerusalem. Mox ita mutatus est verbo et opere ut totus subito videretur alteratus, cunctis qui hoc videbant mirantibus. Proficiscendi terminum posuit ad primam festivitatem sancti Michaelis ; sane rogabat Deum et sanctam Matrem ejus, quatenus, si in via moriturus erat, antequam proficisci inciperet, moreretur, quo Beccum delatus, inter antecessores suos jaceret humatus.   Quod Deus juxta bonitatem suam, sicut petebat, illi concessit Nam infirmitate correptus, hominem exuit in vigilia sancti Michaelis quarto Kalend.   Octobris, et sicut desideraverat, utque moriens præceperat, die qua profecturum se dixerat.   Portatum est corpus ejus ad dominam suam sanctam Beccensem Mariam, et juxtasuos patres sepultum.   Talibus beneficiis beata Dei genitrix genus Crispinorum, et alios quamplures cujusque ordinis, et generis, ad suam familiaritatem adduxit, ut firmiori fide et ardentiori amore ejus audeant implorare in suis necessitatibus auxilium, quatenus per ipsius, intercessionem recuperare valeant Filii sui Domini nostri Jesu Christi gratiam, qui vivit et regnat cum Patre, et Spiritu sancto Deus in sæcula.   Amen.

No. 14.   CHARTER OF ALBERT, MONK OF JUMIÈGES
1107
RECORDING THE PURCHASE OF THE DIME OF GAUVILLE FROM FOULK, SON AND HEIR OF TETBOLD DE GAUVILLE

A.   Original (Arch. of Seine Inférieure, fonds of Jumièges, series H)

Albertus monacus sancti Petri Gemmeticensis emit a quodam milite, nomine Fulcone, decimam Gauville et ea que pertinent ad ecclesiam prefati maisnelli.   Insuper emit ab eodem milite tantum terre quantum.   IIII^{or}. boves possunt arare in tribus temporibus anni juxta consuetudinem agricolarum.   Dedit autem pro his omnibus.   VI. libras denariorum frater jam dictus.   Emptionem siquidem hujusmodi Gislebertus senior, in cujus honore illa villa sita est, stabilem fore inperpetuum concessit.   Mortuo autem Fulcone, Guarinus, frater illius, totam emptionem jam dictam auferens nostre ecclesie, tamquam heres, in dominio suo saisivit.   Denique sepe et multum apud Deum, item apud homines querimoniam fecimus : nec tamen, quamdiu vixit ille, id quod nostrum erat habere potuimus.   Postmodum, illo defuncto, ad filium ejus nomine Gislebertum paterna hereditas transiit.   Qui, sicut pater suus, nobis eandem injuriam et ipse intulit.   Hic vero, sagitta percussus cum militibus insidias faceret, quicquid nobis auferebat reddidit ; deinde jam proximus morti, monachilem habitum postulans suscepit ; ex ipsius vulneris ictu occubuit ; Gemmeticum delatum, sicut nostrum monachum, sepulture tradidimus.   Hanc cartulam *ego Gislebertus manu mea* + *confirmo, et itidem uxor mea* + *et duo* + *filii mei Gislebertus et Riboldus* + *astruunt.*   Ego Hugo, frater defuncti, hoc ipsum confirmo + et frater meus Gausfridus.   Hujus autem rei sunt testes Willelmus de Curtellis, Berardus de Carnellis, Baldricus, Walterus filius Ricardi, Fulcone [*sic*] Willelmus de Falc et alii plures.   Ex parte sancti Petri, Gervasius, Vivianus et Gausfridus nepos Gervasii.   Signum + Hugonis.

No. 15.   CHARTER OF THE ABBEY OF SAINT-PÈRE OF CHARTRES
1107
(Cartulaire de l'abbaye de Saint-Père de Chartres, Guérard, II, 518–19)

De uno furnorum de Bruerolis a Gervasio de Castro Novo nobis donato uxore et filiis ejus necnon et *Gisleberto de Teleriis concedentibus.*

Anno 1107 " ... Gervasius et uxor ejus Mabilia, annuentibus filiis eorum Hugone, Petro, Gervasio, Guascone, et filia Mabilia, dono perhenni, pro redemptione animarum suarum, attribuerunt sancto Petro et sancto Germano quendam furnum in Bruerolensi vico, et aream ipsius domus que de super eum est constructa, eadem firmitate et libertate qua alium ibidem habemus furnum, et qua cetera que nostra sunt in eodem castro tenemus.   Prefatum quoque *donum Gisleberti de Tegulariis*, materque ejus Hersendis, sui assensus munimine confirmaverunt.   Actum est hoc anno dominice incarnationis MCVII^o, Philippo Francorum regni sceptrum obtinente, Ivone Carnotis in episcopalem cathedram residente.   Testes ex parte Gervasii fuere hii : Thomas senescallus, Robertus de Trunche Villari, Hugo de Vilerio ; Willelmus, frater ejus ; Willelmus de Regimalastro, Boldinus Nutritius, Garinus Galetus.   Testes sancti Petri : Sulpitius decanus ; Drogo, Adelelmus presbiteri ; Godefridus de Nemore ; Odo de Ulmis, Andrée ; Germundus famulus ; Rainaldus, filius Aventii ; Odo de Gisiaco, Gauterius cocus ; Gauterius et

N

Huboldus, de familia sancti Petri. Isti sunt testes de assensu *Gisleberti de Tegulariis :* Willelmus de Curtellis, Godardus de Mineriis ; *Gislebertus filius Rogerii ;* Gunherius, Gollinus de Torrourio, Bernerius de Bruerolis ; Richerius, filius ejus ; Isoius, Guimundus ; Radulfus, filius ejus ; Ernulfus pedagearius. Isti autem affuerunt Mabilia assensit huic dono : Gervasius, pater ejus et mater ; Thomas dapifer, Willelmus de Regimalastro, Robertus de Trunco Villari ; Radulfus, nepos ejus ; Odo de Plano Campo, Galo camerarius. Sciendum autem quod, in predicta villa, nemo, preter nos monachos sancti Petri, potest clibanum construere, sicut in nostro regali privilegio continetur.

No. 16. CHARTER OF URSO, ABBOT OF JUMIÈGES
1109

CONCERNING THE CIRCUMSTANCES BY WHICH THE DIME OF GAUVILLE
WAS ACQUIRED

A. Original (Arch. of Seine Inférieure, fonds of Jumièges, series H) A.[1] Duplicate (*ibidem*)

Anno ab incarnatione Domini. M^{mo}. centesimo nono, conventionem recuperationis Gauville factam ego Ursus, abbas Gemmeticensis, ad firmitatem posterorum notam fieri volo. Monachi Gemmeticenses emerunt in Gauvilla tantum terre quantum. IIII^{or}, boves arare possunt in tribus temporibus anni, a quodam milite nomine Fulcone, simulque ecclesiam cum decimis suis, annuente et confirmante Gisleb(erto se)niore, de cujus ditione prefate res sunt. Defun(cto autem) Fulcone, Gaurinus, heres ejus effectus, abstulit nobis quicquid in villa illa habuimus. Post hec, Gislebertus, filius et heres Gaurini, casu vulneratus, eternam damnationem timens pro violentia rerum nostrarum a patre suo facta, ad misericordiam sancti Petri confugit, injuste ablata reddidit, et habitum monachilem expetiit et accepit. Post hec vero, malis pejores succedentes, fratres ipsius Gisleberti eadem retraxerunt, multis precibus et placitis intervenientibus et pro discordia et permutatione bellorum ad effectum non pervenientibus. Pace vero redeunte hoc predicto termino, frequentibus clamoribus monachorum Gillebertus junoir permotus, possessores predictarum rerum compulit ad justiciam, et, causis utrinque dictis et examinatis, res nostre nobis adjudicate sunt. Unde de predictis rebus ecclesiam cum decimis et duo arpenta juxta ecclesiam nobis reddiderunt. Hec facta sunt apud Teulerias, judicante et confirmante Gisleberto et veneranda matre ejus Hersinte, que hujus rei emptioni et recuperationi affuit, et militibus ejus. *Signum + Gisleberti Crispini. Signum + uxoris ejus. Signum + matris sue Hersinde.* Signum + Guillelmi (de) Curtellis. Signum + Guarini f(...)rdi. Isti concesserunt Richerius et frater ejus Gausfridus. Ex parte mona(chorum) ...(Gaus)fridus, ...rdus Corp, Godefredus filius Viviani, Hugo et Gausfridus ......rdus rater, presbiteri .....tus nepos Alberge, Go......... (fili)us Heriberti, G......... obertus filius.

No. 17. EXTRACT FROM CHARTER OF HENRY DUKE OF NORMANDY AND COUNT OF ANJOU CONCERNING THE ABBEY OF MORTEMER
1150

(*Cart. de Mortemer*, Bibl. nat. lat. 18369, fo. 53)

Carta dua. h. de augmto lande de Belfuiss, de cetis p foresta Enricus dux Normannor et comes Andega necessariis uor, Archiepo Rothomag et epis Normannie et omnib ; Baronib ; Baillivis et amicis et fidelib ; suis : Salt.................
Test. Arnulfo Lexovien epo. Willo cancellar. Rainaldo de Sco Valerico dapifero meo. Waltero Giffart comite de Longavilla. Alexandro de Bohun. Osberto de Cailleio. Robto de Wennesual. Rogero de Pauliaco. Ricardo de Humez. Willo filio Hamonis. Warino filio Geroldi. Hugone de Dovera. Wachelino Maingnoti Heirieio de Novilla. Engerranno Pontario. Act apdt Roth. anno ab incarn Dñ. M°.C°.L°.

No. 18. CONFIRMATION CHARTER OF JOSCELYN CRISPIN TO THE ABBEY OF MORTEMER

c. 1150

(*Cart. de Mortemer*, Bibl. nat. lat. 18369, fo. 55–6–7)

Hos a nomine Sce individue Trinitatis notu sit oib ; fidelib ; ta presentib p futuris qd *ego Goscelinus crispinis p salute anime mee et Robti de Dangu et Eufemie uxoris ej et Isabelis filie ej videlicet uxoris mee* atq omniu amicor meor concedo Deo et Sce Marie et conventui frm de Mortuomari in Leonib CXXVIII acras de terra mea cura Pomeria in elemosina absolute : absq omni cuilibet servicii vel consuetudinis vel exactionis retentione in ppetuu libere possidendas. Ex qb LX. predictus Robtus de Dangu in elemosina illis donavit et alias LX supaddimus p concordia qua fecim p morte e de aculei et reliquas VIII p terra de Bertholomei de Neafla. Et pret hoc terra ad curia et ad edificia sua facienda et qd hoies mei de feodo meo illis dederunt vel in futuro dabunt saluo servicio meo illia similit concedo. Insup et concedo eis qcqd de feodo meo habet in terra de Mesengera qua Belotus filius Hiteri de Noum donavit filiis Ricardi de Piaissio. Hugoni scilicet Radulfo atq ; Waltero ppter pace restituenda int se : illo qui ppter interfectione patru suor contra muice dissidebant. qua terra predictus Hyter de Nojun pater Beloti precio emerat ta sibi q heredib ; suis libe in ppetuu possidenda exceptis VII solidis Rothomag vavassorib ; de Warchua et de Lisorz qui illi terra vendiderant singlis annis ad festu Sci Remigii p solvendis. Quor nomina sunt hec. Hugo Guerner. Robtus Marcafessa. Ebroinus de Altavesna, Hugo Pinel et Radulfus fr ejus et Radulfus de Mucegros. Eo aute pacto donavit Belotus terra predictis filiis Ricardi ut et ipsi Deo et Sci Marie, frib ; de Mortuo mari eande terra in elemosina donarent ppt eor videlicet animas ob quor intfectione dissensio erat : libere omino in ppm possidenda exceptis VII solidis Rothom predictis vavassorib et heredib ; eor annuatim ad festu Sci Remigii p solvendis. Qd ita fecerunt. *Ut aute hec omia semper rata pmaneant sigilli mei impressione confirmo, concedente Isabele uxore mea. Willo et Robto filiis meis. Eustachia, Agnete, Eva, Emelina filiab meis.* Test Waltero Torello. Anschero de Salcheio et Eustachio filio ej. Godefrido de Strepeneio. Sarracheno de Geniis. Reginaldo filio Godefrido de Estrepeneio. Grimaldo de Nealfla. Waltero de Grainvilla. Hugone de Lisorz. Robto de Neuis. Odone de Gisencurte. Odone Buschet.

No. 19. CONFIRMATION CHARTER OF JOSCELYN CRISPIN AND ROBERT DE DANGU TO THE ABBEY OF MORTEMER

c. 1150

(*Cart. de Mortemer*, Bibl. nat. lat. 18369, fo. 57)

N nomine Sce et individue Trinitatis notu sit omnib ; fidelib, ta presentib ; q furutis quatin ego *Robt de Dangu* p salute anime mee *et uxoris mee Eufemie* et antecessor omniuq ; amicor meor dono atq ; confirmo Deo, Sce Marie, conventui frm de Mortuomari LX acres terre de dmco meo apud Pomeria in elemosina absolute et absq ; omi cuilibet servicii vel consuetudinis vel exactionis retentione in ppm libe possidendas. Et pret hoc terra ad curia et ad edificia sua facienda. et qd hoies de feodo meo illis dederunt in presenti vel in futuro dabunt. simili modo illis firmit concedo. S ; et Eufemia uxor mea, *Goscelinus Crespins, Ysabel uxor illi filia mea videlicet illud idem concedunt.* Qd totu ut ratu atq ; omino in convulsu semp pmaneat mei et supradicti Goscelini sigilli impressione signavimus. Huj doni et concessions testes sunt hii. Engelrannus sacerdos. Hugo Malevesin. Richardus de Roca. Hugo de Lisorz. Gualterus Porcus. Arnulfus ppositus de Lisorz. Robtus Pinel.

No. 20. CONFIRMATION CHARTER OF JOSCELYN CRISPIN AND HIS SON WILLIAM TO THE ABBEY OF BEC

1155

DOM JOUVELIN IN RECORDING THIS CONFIRMATION CHARTER STYLES
JOSCELYN CRISPIN, *COUNT* (GOSCELINUS CRISPINUS COMES
SIT ET CONFIRMAVIT DONATIONS . . .)[1]

(Bibl. nat. lat. 13905, fo. 215 v°, 68 ; 216 r° 69 chapter XLVIII; *Le Prevost Mem.*, II, 19)

Notum sit omnibus præsentibus et futuris quod *ego, Goscelinus Crispinus*, pro salute mea et omnium antecessorum et heredum meorum concessi et hac presenti carta confirmavi Deo et S. Mariæ Beccii et monachis ejusdem loci, omnes donationes quas antecessores mei et homines eorum eis fecerunt, videlicet in terris, in hominibus in reditibus, in ecclesiis et decimis et molendinis et pratis et in quibuslibet aliis rebus scilicet : ex dono primi *Guillelmi Crispini*, ecclesias de Livarrot, de Blangeio cum omnibus pertinentibus ad eas, et decimam dominii sui, et deciman carucæ suæ de Falco, ecclesiam de Livarrot cum patronatu et omnibus pertinentibus ad eam ; in Strepigneio, decimam denariorum burgi et 20 solidos ad luminare ecclesiæ, et decimam ibidem totius annonæ suæ, et unum hospitem cum omnibus consuetudinibus ; in Longavilla clausum Blanchardi ; in teloneo de Blangeio, 10 solidos ; in teloneo de Livarrot, decimam et unam domum cum omnibus consuetudinibus suis, et sextam partem molendinorum de Passeio, 100 solidos in teloneo ejusdem villæ. Ex dono Evæ, uxoris ipsius, unam acram prati in Blangeio et unum hospitem cum omnibus consuetudinibus. *Ex dono Guillelmi Crispini secundi, filii dicti Guillelmi et Evæ, decimam* molendini et dominii sui de Mesnillo Fulberti ; in Drolcort, ecclesiam cum decima et patronatu et omnibus alii pertinentiis, et quod habebat de eo Robertus Malconvenanus. In Burnenvilla, medietatem ecclesiæ et decimæ et patronatus. Ex dono Richardi filii Reinfredi, aliam medietatem ejusdem ecclesiæ, decimæ et patronatus. In molendino de Blangi, unum modium annonæ et dimidium modium frumenti, et dimidium grossæ annonæ. Ex dono Gisleberti Dastin, ecclesiam de Duranvilla et decimam cum patronatu et omnibus ad eam pertinentibus, et terram ad domum ædificandum ubi decima ejusdem villæ reponatur. Ex dono Erchembaldi de Faverolis, quod habetat de Richardo filio Reinfredi. Ex dono Agnetis uxoris ejusdem Guillelmi, ad annualiarium ipsius faciendum, dimidium molendini de Bernayo, et 50 solidos in molendino Strepigneio. *Ex dono Guillelmi Crispini tertii, filii dicti Guillelmi secundi et Agnetis*, 30 acras terræ in Falco, et in furno de Blangi 10 solidos, et alteram medietatem molendini de Bernayo, ecclesiam de Sefrevilla cum decima et patronatu. In Livarrot, decimam fœni sui et decimam gardini sui ejusdem villæ. Hæc omnia quæ scripta sunt, *ego, Goscelinus Crispinus Beccum veniens cum filio meo Guillelmo adhuc parvo*, dictis monachis in liberam et perpetuam eleemosynam concessi, assensu et voluntate dicti Guillelmi filii mei, et hac præsenti carta mea sigilli mei munimento roborata confirmavi, et, propter, unum candelabrum ego G. et dictus Guillelmus filius meus, præsenti toto conventu, super majus altare Beccii posuimus, anno ab Incarnatione M°C°LV°, coram his et aliis.

---

[1] If it be true that he held this title, which so potent a noble may have, it was not hereditary, for his son and heir, William V, does not so occur.

ADDENDA

CONCERNING OSMOND DE CENTVILLE, HERBERT II COUNT OF VERMANDOIS AND CHAMPAGNE AND BERNARD, COUNT OF SENLIS

Richard I, duke of Normandy, after the death of his father, when only 10 years of age, was placed under the protection and custody of Louis (IV) d'Outremer. king of France. Osmond de Centville, his governor in 944–5, hiding him in a large basket used for carrying wood, succeeded in taking him unobserved past the castle guards and, leaping upon a horse awaiting him, conducted the young duke to Bernard, count of Senlis, and the seignior of Coucy,[1] who are reputed to have been his uncles. This was doubtless the Osmond, son of Norman, from Ouilly-Basset or Normanville, viscount of Vernon, who married a niece of the duchess Gonnor.[2] The statement by Jumièges[3] and Orderic Vital[4] that Bernard was the uncle of duke Richard is disputed, although Lauer[5] and others unconvincingly tried to explain it. Forester observed that he was the cousin germain of Leudegarde, wife of William Longsword, second duke of Normandy, who was the daughter of Herbert II, count of Vermandois and Champagne,[6] which latter died in 942–3.[7] Duke William probably repudiated her because she later married Thibaud (I) le Tricheur, count of Blois and Chartres,[8] while Sprota, the Breton mother of his son, duke Richard, outlived him.[9] The nationality of Sprota is recorded by Flodoard, canon of Rheims, and since he was a contemporary writer, it is very direct (natus de concubina Britanna).[10] The prevailing opinion held by Freeman[11] and others, which is probably correct, that Bernard was the brother of Poppa, daughter of Berenger, count of Bayeux, the wife of Rollo, first duke of Normandy, would make him the great uncle of young Richard II.[12] Be this as it may, since Bernard was the cousin of Herbert II, count of Vermandois,[13] one can be more certain that he was descended from Bernard d'Italia (king of Italy), the grandson of Charlemagne through his son, Pépin I, king of Italy. If this hypothesis be true, it would seem to be the only source through which William the Conqueror could claim an Italian connection[14] dealt with under Robert Guernon, sire de Montfiquet (93).

[1] Jumièges, 48, 49; *Hist. de Norm.*, de Moulin, III, 55 to 60.   [2] *Vide* 19; T. VII.
[3] Jumièges, 48, 49.   [4] II, 299.   [5] *Op. cit.*, 5.   [6] Dudo, 97c; *Jumièges Interp.*, de Torigny, 223, T. IV.   [7] Jumièges, 34 n.   [8] *Ibid.*, 35 n.; Freeman, I, 223.   [9] Jumièges, 33; *Jumièges Interp.*, de Torigny, 258, 259.   [10] A. 943.   [11] Freeman, I, 214.   [12] Freeman, I, 180, 214; Jumièges, 49 n.   [13] Jumièges, 49 n.   [14] *Vide*, 187.

MILO CRISPIN'S PARENTAGE

The parentage of the great Milo Crispin, warrior at Hastings, baron of the honour of Wallingford and possessor of that most important castle to which we have drawn attention in his biography, has not been satisfactorily determined. There are many extenuating circumstances which indicate that he was the son of Gilbert Crispin I, and Arlette, the mother of the Conqueror, for while there is nothing definite to substantiate such a conclusion there are many things to support it. The high favour and esteem in which he was held and the many positions and honours showered upon him by the Conqueror and his sons, William Rufus and Henry I, mentioned in his biography, are indeed very significant. The Conqueror gave to him as previously observed one of the richest heiresses of England, the granddaughter of Wigod de Wallingford, who had been cupbearer to Edward the Confessor. Duke William, therefore, knew him well before the conquest, having met him on his visits to king Edward. Milo witnessed the *Grand charter* of the Conqueror in favour of the abbey of Bec, immediately following William Crispin and preceding the potent nobles William, count of Evreux, and Richard de Bienfaite, son of Gilbert, count of Brionne, both of the latter having been direct descendants of duke Richard I. Milo was thus honoured for some particular reason which is made all the more apparent because he did not make a donation of any kind to that monastery until a considerably later date. To these pertinent observations must be added the silence accorded him in the *Crispin genealogy*. Milo Crispin, its author and doubtless named after the warrior, probably did not refer to him in that pedigree for the reason that he did not dare or did not think it advisable to name his mother. As it gives all of Gilbert Crispin's children by his wife Gonnor, it would have been awkward to record Milo if he were not Gilbert's son by her.   This leads to the supposition that Milo, if the son of Gilbert and Arlette, was the offspring of an alliance rather than a marriage, wherefore, and through deference to the Conqueror, his name was suppressed in that genealogy, which is interwoven in the Miraculum, a religious record of the church.   If a marriage had occurred there would have been no reason to have ignored it.   This would account for the references to such an affiliation coming down through the centuries in the writings of the historians and genealogists on the subject which must also be accorded due consideration.   This presents its difficulties too for Conteville having been held by William Malet II under Gilbert Crispin III, probably through Arlette, points rather to a marriage than an alliance, but if so, why was it totally ignored ?

Now these facts by themselves have no particular value, but when taken collectively are very convincing.   (*Vide* 28, 66, 128, 131, 136, 150, 158.)

WILLIAM DU HOMMET I,   The wife of William du Hommet I, constable of
HIS WIVES AND GUIL-   Normandy, elder son of Richard du Hommet I, was
LAUME DE SEMILLY   Lucia, granddaughter and heir of Adam de Brix,[1] which
                                        is so recorded in a charter in favour of the abbey of
Longues [2] wherein this William makes a donation for the peace of her soul who therefore predeceased him.   *Recherches sur le Domesday*,[3] on the other hand, say the name of his wife was Agnès, daughter of William de Semilly I, and that their son William assumed this name.   It is possible that Agnès may have been the second wife of William, but she was apparently not the mother of his children.   The name of the son of William du Hommet I, the constable, was not William de Semilly but William de Say.[4]   William de Semilly II and Geoffry du Hommet, his brother, were the sons of Enguerrand du Hommet I, and Cecilia, his wife, daughter and heir of William de Semilly I,[5] as recorded under appendix 19.   (*Vide* 50, col. 2, line 53 ; 154, col. 2, line 53 and Table X.)

[1] Stapleton, I, clxxiii ; Héritière des biens d'Adam de Bruys (Brix) son ayeul.   Anc. Châteaux de l'Arrd., de Valognes Mém. par de Gerville.   Who cites an act 1232 from the cart. of St-Sauveur-le-Vicomte.   [2] Stapleton, II, clxxxiv.   [3] 94.   [4] Stapleton, I, clxxiii.   [5] *Ibid.*, I, clii.

CONCERNING THE AGES   The revolt of William, count of Exmes and later Eu,
OF THE SONS OF   against his half-brother Richard II, duke of Normandy,
RICHARD I, DUKE OF   creates the thought that there may have been something
NORMANDY   underneath this seditious affair of greater significance
                                        than merely his desire to be freed from complying with
the customary fealty due his brother as head of the ducal house.   Jumièges, to whom we are indebted for this information, remarks that William " became proud and rebellious " and " in order to carry out the rules of his chivalry, urged on by the schemes of wicked men, defied his lord and withdrew the respect which he owed him."   The ancient historian may for some unknown reason have purposely suppressed the real cause of this treasonable act.   Whatever it may have been his brother, the duke, took a very serious view of it, for he captured and imprisoned William and kept him confined for five years.   Jumièges adds concerning it, " some of his satellites having persevered in their seditious design were overcome and put to death, others were exiled from the limits of the duchy."   William only gained his freedom by escaping, and after great suffering and distress at an opportune moment " throwing himself on the ground at his feet he begged his forgiveness with tears. The duke, moved with pity at the supplication of count Raoul " (of Ivry their uncle), forgave him.   If William had attempted to supplant his brother as duke of Normandy, the punishment meted out would be more in keeping with the offence committed than the mere caprice of a dissatisfied or wayward brother.   If this be true, there could scarcely be any other grounds for William's claim than seniority of birth, and indeed evidence is not lacking to this effect.   William witnessed, as early as 990, the foundation charter of the abbey of Fécamp, Godfry, his elder brother, was apparently born not later than 960, while Richard II is recorded as having married in 1008, about which time William married also.   Godfry was then dead and had left a son born not later than 1000.   Richard's marriage is placed in the year mentioned because the contract for it with Judith is said to have been executed on this date.   She was the only child of Conan le Tort, count of Rennes, by his second wife Ermengarde, daughter of Geoffry Grisegonelle, count of Anjou, married according to the *Chronique de Mont-St-Michel* in 970.   Conan was slain in 992 at the battle of Conquereux.   This marriage date is disputed, for in this event Judith would have been under the ordinary laws of nature about 35 years of age at her marriage

and the mother of five children before her death in 1017. Her sons, Richard III and Robert, would have been 17 and 18 in 1026-7 when their father Richard II died. The conclusion entertained in some quarters that they were nearly of full age then seems the more probable, especially as her third son, William, died a monk at Fécamp in 1025. In any event, these children were born about this time and after Godfry's son Gilbert. This proves nothing of itself, but it does show that Richard II married late in life, at least 45 to 48 years of age, if he was older than Godfry. It seems rather unusual for the head of such an important dukedom to have delayed his marriage for so long a time, but unless he did he was Godfry's junior. The solution may be that Richard I, when he eventually married Gonnor, by whom he had numerous progeny, thereby legitimizing them, at that time named Richard II, the eldest son of this union, his successor, even though he may have been younger than Godfry and William. This left Godfry, William, and the remainder of his offspring illegitimate.

The former received from his father the important comté of Brionne c. 980 when he must have been at least of full age, and his brother Richard II, after he succeeded to the dukedom, gave him the equally important comté of Eu. These extensive possessions no doubt placated and satisfied him. He died shortly after the council held at Fécamp in 1006, which act he and his brother William witnessed immediately after the duke. It was then that his younger brother William, who possessed only the comté of Exmes, revolted. This rather definitely fixes it at this time, for had William's elder brother Godfry been alive when it occurred he would undoubtedly have attempted to intercede for him, which Jumièges would have mentioned. It may be that William then claimed the dukedom as the oldest surviving son of duke Richard I, even though illegitimate, which in those days was not much of an objection. The truth of the matter is, as pointed out by Moulin, the peasants had revolted because they wanted the privilege of using the streams and forests, to be released from paying rent to their over-lords and to have their freedom. While they toiled incessantly and suffered great privations, the seigniors pillaged their crops and robbed them, meanwhile living in idleness and luxury at court where the duke would have no one in his household beneath the rank of a noble. The peasants attempted to draw the bourgeoisie in their insurrection, who, while not actively supporting it, ignored the nobles.

This enterprise was brought to a speedy close by Raoul, count of Ivry, at the behest of the duke, and the peasants returned to their ploughs.

Richard, rendered uneasy by their insubordination and fearing for the loyalty of the seigniors and counts, demanded that they reacknowledge him as their sovereign lord. This homage was accorded to him by all with the exception of William and his friends, whose names Jumièges has entirely ignored. The reason is said to have been because they wished to continue robbing the people, but the real cause may have lain deeper. It is difficult to believe that the partisans of William would have taken such great risks for anything short of a very momentous enterprise in which category the circumstances narrated by Jumièges can scarcely be classified. This anxiety of Richard to have all of his subjects proclaim him anew as their reigning duke, coupled with the dissent of William, rather suggests a desire to fortify his rights in the possession of the dukedom than a fear of disloyalty from a less sinister cause. (Vide 51, 80, 130, 136 ; Jumièges, 74 ; Hist. de Normandie, Moulin, IV, 94.)

ANCESTRY OF WILLIAM DE WARREN I AND ROGER DE MORTEMER   The ancestry of William de Warren I and Roger de Mortemer is difficult to establish in detail as the information available is conflicting. Robert de Torigny in his Chronique [1] records them as the sons of Gautier de St-Martin, while in his Continuation of Jumièges [2] he says William de Warren I was the father of Roger. Later on in the same work [3] he states that "their father" (without naming him) married a niece of the duchess Gonner, from which union they issued. To add to the confusion, on the same page he remarks that Nicholas de Bacqueville was the father, by another niece of the duchess, of William Martel and Gautier de St-Martin. The known facts are these : In 1054 after the battle of Mortemer, Roger de Mortemer was deprived of his castle of this name by duke William,[4] which was given to young William de Warren I. The solution is to be found in a charter of the Cartulary of St-Wandrille,[5] where is recorded "Roger, son of Raoul de Warren" (Signum Rogerii, filii Rodulfi de Varechna), which establishes quite clearly that this Roger de Mortemer and William de Warren were the sons of Raoul de Warren. It is, nevertheless, very strange that Orderic Vital styles William the cousin or kinsman of Roger instead of his brother.[6] He was in a position to get very direct information, because he tells us himself that Roger de Warren, son of Erneis de Coutances and nephew of William de

Warren I, became a monk at St-Evroult, the monastery where Orderic wrote his history.[7] However this may be, there is no reason to doubt Robert de Torigny's statement of their having been descended from a niece of the duchess Gonnor, and the truth of the matter seems to be that Raoul de Warren's father really was the husband of one of these nieces, whether he was Gautier de St-Martin or some other person. (*Vide* 52, 76, 104.)

[1] II, 211.   [2] 253.   [3] 328.   [4] Ord. Vit., Le Prevost ed., III, 316 ; Plan., I, 132.   [5] Lot, I, 98 ; Ord. Vit., *ibid.*, 316 n.   [6] *Vide* 52.   [7] Ord. Vit., Forester ed., II, 185.

CRISPIN-GRIMALDI   The arms of the Crispin and Grimaldi families, as can
ARMS AND ANCESTRY   be readily observed from the photographs of them repro-
                           duced in this work and referred to in the biography of Milo
Crispin, were absolutely identical in 1300. This applies not only to the charges but to
the design of the seals, and later to the colours, which were argent and gules. Just a
few years prior to this date the Grimaldi had first established themselves in Monaco, while
the Crispins had already been using these arms for about a century. Whether they were
the armorial bearings of the Grimaldi before they left Genoa or were adopted by them
after their occupation of Monaco is not clear. In either event, although fusils are a simple
charge which of itself would not signify relationship, nevertheless the fact that the designs
of the seals were exactly alike, as well as the colours, demands serious consideration. It
may indeed be that these powerful families had intermarried at this or some earlier period,
the memory of which is lost, but it was certainly not in the manner recorded in the spurious
Crispin-Grimaldi genealogy by Venasque-Ferriol. Possibly some such tradition existed
then, and not knowing the facts they had this pedigree composed in accordance with their
ideas and wishes. Prevalent as the custom was at this time for noble families to record
fantastic lineages it seems incredible that two of such distinction would make up the whole
genealogy without any support whatever. If these arms had first appeared after the
composition of this false pedigree, then the entire matter could be discarded. However,
inasmuch as the seals were attached to charters centuries before, this similarity assumes a
peculiar significance, which it is difficult to explain save by some family connection. (*Vide*
66, 68, photograph of Charter H.)

ANCESTRY OF RICHARD   In the action 20 July 1398 concerning the tenure of
DE LA HAIE   the barony of La Haie-du-Puis [1] the defendants claim
                           descent from Richard Turstain Haldub, son of Turstain
de Bastembourg, son of Anslac de Bastembourg,[2] and his wife Emma, parentage unknown,
but here and elsewhere erroneously confused with the half-sister of William the Conqueror,
of the same name. They begat Ivon (or Eudes) al Chapel, who had three sons, Robert,
Raoul and Richard de la Haie, which latter married Matilda de Vernon.[3] This pedigree
differs from that of Stapleton [4] supported by Planché,[5] who say Eudes Dapifer (of
Normandy) left issue a daughter and heir Muriel, wife of Robert de la Haie,[6] her cousin,
son of Raoul de la Haie. This Raoul would then have been the brother of Eudes, which
descent is correct, as the following extract from a charter in the *Gallia Christiana* sub-
stantiates. (Robertus de Haya filius Radulfi senescalli Roberti comitis Moritonii, nepos
Hudonii dapiferi Willelmi Regis.) Robert, Raoul (who married Olivia, the sister or
daughter of William d'Aubigny (II), pincerna [7]) and Richard were not the sons of Eudes
but of his daughter Muriel, for this latter Richard de la Haie did not die until 1169,[8]
when he was killed by pirates, leaving only daughters.[9] (*Vide* Table X.)

[1] 145, 155.   [2] 155 ;   *Rech. Domesd.*, 249.   [3] La Roque, II, 1459–60. [4] I, clxxvi.
[5] II, 124.   [6] 17.   [7] *Wace*, Taylor, 235 ; Planché, II, 124 ; Stapleton, II, xxxiii.   [8] 155.
[9] *Ibid.*, Taylor.

SEIGNIORS AND MARQUISES   The branch of the Crispin family claimed to have
OF BOURRI, BOSSE AND   descended from Hugues, reputed to have been a
VARDES OF THE LINE OF   younger brother of William Crispin VII, the marshal
DU BEC AND BEC-CRISPIN   of France, was first published by Charles de
                               Venasque-Ferriol, author of the spurious Crispin-
Grimaldi genealogy. It is interesting to note that no authentic record exists of any
members of this house having used the name Crispin until after this time when Countess
Renée, the ambassadress, occurs as du Bec-Crispin. These lords previously occur only as
du Bec in documents of record, some of which follow :
        Charles du Bec I, lord of Bourri in 1533–4.
        Charles du Bec I or II in 1558.
        René du Bec I in 1592.

Philippe, bishop of Nantes, later archbishop of Rheims 1594 and 1612.

Countess Renee's brother, René du Bec II, then head of the family, did not adopt it, and appears in a document of 1627 as René du Bec, but his son and successor, François René, does occur as du Bec-Crispin de Grimaldy in documents executed in 1668–73 and thereafter.

These facts prove the name Crispin was assumed after the composition of the Crispin-Grimaldi genealogy, and places this pedigree in the same precarious category. (*Vide* Bibl. nat. (royale), C. 259, Nos. 29, 38, 41, 63, 67, 68.)

RELATIONSHIP OF THE CRISPIN, CONDÉ, CHENEY FAMILIES WITH THE EARLS OF CHESTER

Emma Crispin, daughter of Gilbert Crispin I, the mother of Pierre de Condé,[1] apparently had a grandson Roger, who seems to have been the issue of Pierre, her only recorded son. This Roger married Adelaide de Cheney, daughter and heiress of William de Cheney, lord of Cavenby and Glentham (Lincolnshire) *temp.* William the Conqueror. Their daughter, Agnès, whom Weir records their only child, " resided at her castle of Horncastle " [2] in Lincolnshire, married Walter Clifford, lord of Clifford castle. " Hórncastle sometime belonging to Adeliza de Condé was laid even with the ground in king Stephen's reign ; after that it was a barony of Gerard de Rodes but now of the Bishops of Carlisle." [3] It was sold to the latter *temp.* Henry III. During the revolt of Adelaide's relatives, Ranulph, earl of Chester, and his half-brother, William de Roumare, earl of Lincoln, against king Stephen, her possessions were confiscated but were returned to her, after these brothers had defeated that monarch, as recited in a charter by this king to earl Ranulph, " and lastly, for the special respect that the king bore unto him (earl Ranulph), he not only restored to Adelais de Condie all her lands, viz. Horncastle (in Lincolnshire), when the castle should be demolished, but all other his own lands " [4] (*Vide* Tables III, VIII, XIII.)

Another branch of the Cheney family was related to Milo Crispin, baron of Wallingford, in the following manner. Ralph de Langetot I, from Longuetot, canton of Bolbec, Normandy, was a domesday tenant in Buckinghamshire, Bedfordshire, Oxfordshire and Suffolk, all held under Gautier Giffard, count of Longueville, probably a near relative.

He witnessed a charter of William Rufus confirming a grant of Gautier Gifford,[5] and another confirmation of Conan, duke of Brittany.[6]

He had a son Ralph II, quite probably the issue of Ralph de Caineto of Norfolk,[7] and a daughter named Alice who became the wife of Roger de Cheney. In the cartulary of Eynsham abbey is recorded a charter of Aliz de Langetot, who made a gift to it " for her salvation, for that of her sons and daughters . . . and the soul of her lord Roger de Chaisnei [8] (1142–8).

Ralph II married Cecilia and had Ralph III, their heir, and probably Milo. " Ralph de Langetot (II) gave to St. Mary and the monks of Reading one hide in Lineberg (Bucks) . . . and I made this grant with counsel and consent of my mother Cecilia of whose dower the same land is." [9]

Their son Milo de Langetot and Milo, his son, witnessed a grant to Eynsham abbey of 1155–62,[10] and Milo de Langetot attested another to this abbey, also witnessed by Roger de Oili,[11] related to Milo Crispin.

Ralph de Langetot III had a daughter and heir, Emma de Langetot, thus described in 1185 :

" Emma de Langetot, aged 60, is the widow of a tenant in chief of the king and is of the kindred of those of Chedney and of Joscelyn Crispin (de genere illorum de Chedney et Joscelini Crispini). . . . Her heirs are the wife of Alan de Dunstanville (Muriel) and the wife of Alard Fitz William (Cecilia)." [12]

Emma married Geoffry Fitz William,[13] whose identity we have been unable to satisfactorily establish. Cecilia, their younger daughter, inherited from her mother Gethampton, which had belonged to Milo Crispin at Domesday.

Its possession by this Cecilia occurs in a return of the fees of the honour of Wallingford in 1213, where it is stated that Alard Fitz Willima held the fee of one knight of the inheritance of his wife (Cecilia) in Gatehampton.[14]

It, therefore, descended to Cecilia directly from Milo Crispin through her great-grandmother Cecilia, and her mother Emma, whose husband Geoffry occurs in a carta of 1166 for one knight's fee under the honour of Wallingford, probably Gatehampton.

The relationship of Emma to Cheney was through her great-aunt Alice, wife of Roger de Cheney.

The Crispin connection immediately suggests Milo Crispin, who held Gatehampton at Domesday.

This is very strong presumptive evidence that Cecilia, wife of Ralph II, was a natural daughter of Milo Crispin, who had no legitimate issue,[15] when coupled with the fact that she had a son and grandson Milo, then an uncommon name.

Furthermore, Milo Crispin was a great landowner in all of the counties where Ralph de Langetot (I) of Domesday held lands excepting Sussex.

[1] *Vide* 28, 116, 157. [2] *History and Antiquities of Horncastle*, Weir, Cle., I, 259. [3] Camden, Cle., *ibid.* [4] Stapleton, II, cliii, n. ; *vide* 157. [5] *Mon.*, i, 583. [6] *Ibid.*, 811. [7] *Vide* 21. [8] *Cart. of Eynsham*, Salter, 124. [9] *Reading Cart.*, Harl. ms. 1708, fol. 90. [10] *Cart. Eynsham*, Salter, 1, 417. [11] *Ibid.*, no. 17. [12] Rot. de Dom. (P.R.S., 21, 35). [13] *Red Book of the Exchequer*, 312 ; *Pipe Roll*, 11, 25, 26 Henry II. [14] Testa de Nevill. [15] *Vide* 66.

CONCERNING JOSCELYN CRISPIN — Joscelyn Crispin swore allegiance to Geoffry Plantagenet, count of Anjou, as duke of Normandy, at Rouen in 1144, with which prince he stood in the highest favour. He quarrelled with his new sovereign, king Louis (VII) the Young, about 1155, and king Henry II of England reconciled him to that king in 1160. However, Henry again took possession of the Norman Vexin four years later.[1] Bound as Joscelyn was by the ties of blood to the kings of England, he was forced by these Anjou relatives at times to swear fealty to the king of France. The boundary of the Norman Vexin was constantly under dispute and, therefore, the usual battle-ground of the two countries, when indeed they were not fighting for the same reason in the vicinity of Tillières. His sympathies were traditionally with Normandy and the counts of Anjou, consequently when he was compelled to acknowledge the French king as his sovereign, he did so with the utmost reluctance.

The reference to Joscelyn Crispin in the *Rotulus de Dominabus* of the year 1185 referred to in the preceding *addenda* indicates that he was then alive. His son, William, unfortunately without date, executed the following confirmation charter : " Know ye all men present and to come that I, William Crispin, give and with this present charter confirm to God and the church of Notre Dame du Bec ten pounds of Anjou to be received annually from my land of Blangy which my father, Joscelyn Crispin, when he came to his last days, bequeathed to the afore mentioned church " (Sciant . . . quod ego Willelmus Crispinus . . . do et presenti carta confirmo Deo et ecclesiae Sanctae Mariae Becci decem libratas andegavensium annuantim in praepositura mea de Blangeio quas pater meus Gocelinus Crispinus cum ad extrema adveniss et predictae ecclesiae delegavit) sans datte.[2]

We have been unable to find any other reference than that mentioned on page 143 which would give light on this matter and, therefore, must be content with the knowledge that Joscelyn was alive 1180–5 and dead before 1197. William Crispin V, his son and heir, suffered the same experience as his father did, only to a much greater degree. The possession of his castles of Estrépagny and Dangu was constantly changing during his life-time between kings Richard Cœur de Lion, John and Henry III of England on the one hand, and Philip Augustus of France on the other.

Joscelyn's great-grandson, William Crispin VII, marshal of France, was commissioner for the reformation of the bailiwicks of Amiens, Lillie and Tournay.[3]

[1] *Dict. de l'Eure*, 1, 935. [2] Bibl. nat. lat. 13905, fo. 97 v⁰ (rouge), 186. [3] Book II of the *Memoirs of the Chamber of Accounts* of Paris, fo. 186, quoted no. 13 from 1330 to 1349.

ANCESTRY OF LADY MABEL DE BEAUMONT AND HER PROUZ, CHUDLEIGH, AND HÉLION DESCENDANTS — Peter Prouz, Pruz, or Prouse of Eastervale, afterwards Chagford, in the shire of Devon, was the second husband of Mary de Vernon, widow of Robert de Courtenay, baron of Okehampton, daughter of William de Redvers, surnamed de Vernon, sixth earl of Devon, by his wife, Mabel de Beaumont, the progenitors of the Devon family of Chudleigh.

The ancestry of this noble lady was indeed most lofty since her father, Robert, count of Meulan (Meulent), was descended from Waleran I, count of Meulent, Bernard the Dane, Henry I, king of France, and Hugue the Great, count of Vermandois.[1] Her mother's ancestry was still more imposing, who was descended from Henry I, king of England, and, therefore, the Conqueror and Queen Matilda, daughter of Baldwin V, count of Flanders. From Alfred the Great, king of England, Bernard and Pépin, kings of Italy, and the emperor Charlemagne.

Henry I, king of France, was the father of Hugue the Great, count of Crépi or Vermandois, younger brother of Philip I, king of France,[2] whose daughter, Elizabeth Vermandois, became the wife of Robert de Beaumont, count of Meulent and earl of Leicester [3] ; their son, Waleran II,[4] count of Meulent, married Agnès de Montfort,[5] by whom they had Robert, count of Meulent, who married Matilda, daughter of Reginald, earl of Cornwall,[6] by his wife Beatrix, daughter of William Fitz Richard, a potent lord in Cornwall. Reginald was the natural son of Henry I, king of England, by Elizabeth, his mistress, daughter of the aforementioned Robert, count of Meulent and earl of Leicester. Henry I, king of England, through his mother, Matilda of Flanders, was descended from the emperor Charlemagne.

Charlemagne, king of France, emperor of the East, died 28 January 814 at Aix-la-Chapelle. He was succeeded by his son, Louis I.

Pépin, king of Italy, his second son, conquered Venice and died shortly after at Milan, 8 July 810, succeeded by:

Bernard, king of Italy, crowned 810, aged 12. Took up arms against Louis I, king of France, and died 17 April 818. The next in succession was:

Pépin II, seigneur de Péronne and St-Quentin, who was succeeded by his son:

Herbert I, seigneur de Péronne and St-Quentin. Killed in 902, by the followers of a count of Flanders, succeeded by:

Herbert II, count of Vermandois. He arrested at St-Quentin, Charles the Simple, king of France, and sent him prisoner to Péronne. Died 943. He married Hildegrante, daughter of Robert II, duc de France, later king. Their daughter, Alix or Adelle, who died at Burges 960, became the wife of:

Arnoul I, count of Flanders, who died 27 March 965. He was the son of Baudouin II, count of Flanders, of Boulogne and of St-Paul, who died 2 January 918 or 919, and was buried in the abbey of St-Pierre, whose wife was Ethelswitha, whom he married in the year 884. She died 7 June 929. She was the daughter of Alfred the Great, king of England, who was born at Wantage in the county of Berks 850. Crowned at Winchester 871. Founded the University of Oxford and died there in 901, buried at Winchester. His wife was Elswitha, daughter of the earl of Mercia.

Baudouin III, count of Flanders, died 1 January 961. He married Mahaud de Bourgogne, daughter of Conrad I, duke of Burgundy. He predeceased his father, Arnoul, who either associated himself with Baldwin in his government or else resigned in his favour, and on the death of his son again took possession.[7] Succeeded by:

Arnoul II, count of Flanders, buried 23 March 988, at the chapel of St-Laurent in the abbey of St-Pierre de Gand, whose wife was Rosele, daughter of Bérenger II, king of Italy. Died 26 January 1003. He was succeeded by:

Baudouin IV, count of Flanders, died 30 May 1036, buried in the chapel of St-Laurent, whose wife was Ogive or Cunegonde, daughter of Frederic I, count of Luxemburg, who died 21 February 1030. Buried with her husband. Succeeded by:

Baudouin V, count and marquis of Flanders, married Adèla, daughter of Robert the Good, king of France. Died at Lille 1 September 1067, buried in the Collegiate church of St-Pierre, whose daughter, Matilda, became the queen of:

William the Conqueror, king of England, duke of Normandy. Born at Falaise 1027. Crowned at Westminster abbey 25 December 1066. Died at the abbey of St-Gervais, Rouen 1087.

[1] *Vide* 14, 87; T. VI, XI. [2] Ord. Vit., II, 348. [3] Ord. Vit., *ibid.*; *Jumièges Interp.*, de Torigny, 332. [4] Ord. Vit., *ibid.* [5] Ord. Vit., IV, 157, ed. n. [6] Stapleton, II, cxcvii. [7] *L'Art de Verifier les Dates*, III, 3.

SEIGNEURS DE "Sire de Tillières" (Gilbert Crispin II) occurs on the rolls of
TILLIÈRES Guillaume Tailleur and de Magny's addition to that of Dives.
Gilbert and William Crispin witnessed charters in 1050 and 1066 of Mont-St-Michel and St-Julien-du-Manz.[1]

Landry, son of Gilbert, occurs in a charter of the abbey of Chartres before 1102 concerning Brueroles, which domain was partly in possession of the seigniors of Tillières. This charter names Hildeburge, his wife, Isnardo and Raoul, his sons, and Adelina, his daughter. (Ego Landricus filius Gisleberti, una cum uxor mea Hildeburgi . . . teristrum unum duorum solidorum filiique mei Isnardus et Radulfus . . . et filia mea Adelina . . . S. domini Hugoni. S. Gisleberti de Tilerias.[2]) Another charter concerning the same mentions also a son Renaud (Rainaldus et Isnardus filii Landrinci).[3] The fact that Gilbert Crispin II attested this document alone, with the exception of Dominus Hugh, an officer of the church, leads one to believe that this Gilbert, father of Landry, was Gilbert Crispin II.

Dom Jouvelin recorded a charter in which Gilbert Crispin III, *c.* 1148, gave one-tenth of the ground of Brueroles to the abbey of Bec, which was confirmed in that year by Hughes de Châteauneuf and his son, Hugues.[4] The chapel of St. Nichols in the château of Tillières was given by Gilbert Crispin to the church of Saint-Hilaire de Tillières, which belonged to the abbey of Bec.[5]

King Louis VII burned part of the citadel of Tillières in 1152.[6]

Gilbert Crispin IV was included in the peace signed in 1154 by Louis (VII) the Young, king of France, and Henry, count of Anjou, second of the name king of England.[7]

In 1160 Gilbert IV witnessed a charter of Richer de l'Aigle, his father-in-law, in favour of the abbey of St-Evroult.[8] Gilbert, being at war with Hugh de Châteauneuf II, called duke Henry to his assistance, who hastened to his aid and they burned Hugh's castle at Brueroles.[9]

In 1172 "Gillebertus (Crispin V) de Tegulariis" made return of the service of his fief of Tillières (Teuleriae) at three knights and *ad suum servitium* four knights.[10] This Gilbert was a strong partisan of king Henry the Younger.

After the death of Gilbert Crispin V in the Holy Land his children came under the guardianship of Philippe de Creully, eldest son of Richard, first baron of Creully, son of Robert de Caen and Mabel, daughter of Robert Fitz Hamon, son of Hamon Le Seneschal, viscount of Kent, sire de Crevecœur and de Creully. Robert de Caen was a natural son of Henry I of England, who created him earl of Gloucester. To understand this line thoroughly it must be borne in mind that Eleanor de Vitrie, the widow of Gilbert Crispin V, married after his death, William Fitz Patric, earl of Salisbury, descended from Gerold, *dapifer* of duke William, founder of the house of Roumare, whose daughter and heiress, Ela, countess of Salisbury, married William Longue-Epée, a natural brother of kings Richard I and John of England.[11]

During the minority of Gilbert Crispin VI, heir to the honour of Tillières, it was for some time in the hands of Philip de Creully, who renders account on the exchequer roll of the year 1198 of £394 10s. of the residue of his proffer in respect of this honour. Upon the decease of Philip, the land of his own inheritance also became an escheat, 25 August 1202, and in 1219 his honour of Creully was held by Gilbert (Crispin VI) de Tillières, who had obtained it in marriage with his daughter and to whom he had probably been espoused while yet a ward in the custody of her father. Of that date, in the month of May, is a charter of Gillebert (Crispin VI) de Tillières, *Dominus de Croleio*, granting to Peter de Tilly, for his services and homage, certain lands in the parish of Maton (Matthieu). In the year following he was entered among the holders of fiefs, in the bailiwick of Renard de Ville-Thierry, *Gillebertus de Telleres iii feoda apud manerium* (Le Manoir) *cum pertinentis, sed pertinentia sunt in diversis balliviis*; and in the bailiwick of Bartholomew de Drouais, the lord of Tillières, *Dominicus Tileriarum*, had two fiefs *pro Tileriis* by the service of two knights in the *ost du Roi*. On the same register Richard de Creully, younger brother of Philip, is put down as holding three parts of one knight's fee at Le Mesnil-Bus and Monthuchon in the bailiwick of Coutances *de Gisleberto de Croili antenato suo*.

In England the elder Gilbert (Crispin V) de Tillières had held, of the honour of Clare, the vills of Headley and Westcote, county Surrey, and had also inherited twelve librates of land in Compton, county Berkshire, which Henry II had given to his father, Gilbert Crispin (IV), all which inheritance vested in the descendants of the marriage with Eleanor de Vitre.[12]

Gilbert VI died without issue and the succession from this point is clouded. His sister Juliana, wife of Baldwin Rastel, probably succeeded him for she was lady of Tillières some time prior to 1227 when she was a widow. This is recorded in a deed in the cartulary of the abbey of St-Martin de Mondaye entitling her, lady of Tillières, wherein her mother, Eleanor, made a donation for her soul to that monastery. Another sister, Joanna, married Thomas Malmaines.[13]

Juliana occurs in a charter of St-Père de Chartres (533) as lady of Tillières, *Juliana domina de Tilleriis*, which Le Prevost says was dated in 1228. This must have been a year earlier according to the deed just mentioned. Her daughter, Hylaria, or Hilaria, succeeded as lady of Tillières,[14] whose husband, sir James de Bovelingham, knight, through her right, became seignior of Tillières. This is verified in a number of charters and acts. In 1232 James de Bovelingham, lord of Tillières, and Hilaria, his wife, confirmed as " sovereign lords " the donation of the living of Chéronvilliers.[15] (Ego Jacobus de Bouelingehan miles dominus Tilleriarum et ego Hiliaria uxor ejus.)

In 1234 Jacques, seigneur de Tillières, and Hilaria, his wife, confirm donations to the abbey de l'Estrée.[16] They apparently held Tillières as late as 1247, for a precept for an extent of the lands of James de Bovelingham in Headley, dated 10 April 1247, was issued to the sheriff of Surrey.[17]

The member or members of the family who possessed Tillières from then until 1259 remains to be established. This seigneur in 1264 approved the restoration of the patronage of Bourth to the convent of St-Sauveur of Evreux.[18] The statement by the *Dictionnaire de l'Eure* and others that Gilbert VI was succeeded by Robert de Tillières, his younger brother, is an error, as the records just recited prove. M. Pazet recorded the opinion that Robert de Tillières succeeded Gilbert V, possibly a younger brother, but there is no evidence of this succession ; indeed, it is to the contrary, as has been demonstrated. However, Gilbert V may have had a brother, Robert, whose grandson could have succeeded Hilaria and have been Gilbert Crispin VII, who was certainly in possession of Tillières in 1259 when he executed a charter in favour of the abbey of Chartres.[19]

He is said to have lived until 1314 (which statement we have not substantiated), when he was succeeded by his son, Gilbert VIII. In 1328 this latter Gilbert abandoned certain rights of Tillières,[20] and in 1337 this abandonment was ratified by his sons, Gilbert, seignior of Brueroles-Aubert in part, Jacot and Jehan.[21] In 1370 he exchanged with king Charles V his seigniory and castle of Tillières for Longchamp and six thousand pounds gold.[22] King Charles VI, according to the *Dictionnaire de l'Eure*, gave Tillières to Gui de Baveux in 1376, while Le Prevost says he presented it in 1386 for bravery at the battle of Cocherel.[23] We find in the *Archives de l'Empire* the following entry :

Guy de Baveux (I) was lord of the fief of Tillières in the latter year and Robert de Baveux, his son, was seigneur de Tillières in 1391. In 1406 Guy de Baveux (II), his son, rendered an account for his fief of Tillières, in which year he died without issue.[24] Jean, his brother, succeeded and held it in 1419, but the English captured him at Dreux and hanged him in 1420.[25] Jean died childless and Jeanne, his sister, widow of Jean Le Veneur,[25] became dame of Tillières. Philippe, her son, was only two years of age when his father died, but he held that barony in 1450 and died in 1486. François I, his son and heir, is recorded living in 1503 and the *Dictionnaire de l'Eure* says he died two years later. Jean II, who followed, is recorded living in 1534, but was dead by 1565, for in this year Tillières was raised to a comté for his son, Tanneguy I,[26] who, according to the *Dictionnaire de l'Eure*, died in 1596. Anselme says Jacques, eldest son of Tanneguy, was count from 1592 to 1596, while Charpillon states that he predeceased his father, which is apparently correct. However, Tanneguy II, son and heir of Jacques, who succeeded, was named ambassador to England in 1619 and died 12 February 1653. From here the succession was as follows : Henry I, 1653–87 ; François II, 1687–1704 ; Jacques-Tanneguy I, count of Tillières, 1704–40 ; Jacques-Tanneguy II, marquis of Tillières, 1740–8 ; François-Jacques-Tanneguy, marquis of Tillières, 1748–89.[27]

Those who believe that Gilbert Crispin I had a Roman ancestry point to the many noble Romans who bore this name before his time, B.C. 361 T. Quinctius T. F. Pennus Capitolinus Crispinus was made dictator to conduct war against the Gauls. During the reign of Diocletian the two brothers Crispin and Crispinian, of a noble Roman family born about the middle of the 3rd century, are reputed to have left home to escape persecution on account of their religious beliefs and went to Soissons (now in Normandy), then the capitol of Gallia, in the ancient Gallo-Roman empire. They preached the gospel, meanwhile making shoes in order that they might not be an expense to the people. This drew upon them the displeasure of their monarch at Rome, and they met the martyr's fate, having been executed 25 October 287 A.D. by emperor Maximian, hence Saint Crispin, the patron saint of shoemakers.[28]

There were many other distinguished Romans bearing the name, among which was Hilaire (Hilary) Sarde, son of Crispin, a pope who sat on the throne of Saint-Peter for six years and ten days (461–8 A.D.). He spread letters of the Catholic faith throughout the whole East, confirmed the three councils of Nicæa, Ephesus and Chalcedon, condemned and set his anathema upon all heresies ; he assembled numerous ornaments in the basilica of the saints and ordained twenty-two bishops. After numerous good work he was buried in the church of Saint-Laurent in the same crypt with pope Sexte III.[29]

[1] *Dict. de l'Eure*, I, 927.   [2] *Cart. de St-Père de Chartres*, I, 253.   [3] *Ibid.*, II, 515.   [4] Bibl. nat. lat. 13905, fo. 97, v⁰ (rouge), 186.   [5] Bibl. nat. lat. 12884, fo. 173.   [6] *Le Prevost Mem.*, III, 227.   [7] *Dict. de l'Eure*, I, 928.   [8] Vangeois, 275 ; *Dict. de l'Eure, ibid.*   [9] *Ibid.* [10] Stapleton, I, cxx.   [11] *Vide* 50, 54, 107, 120 ; Stapleton, II, xlvii ; *Ann. and Antiq. of Lacock Abbey*, Bowles, 39, 65.   [12] Stapleton, II, xlv to xlix ; *Misc. Genea. et Heraldica*, article Col. Tyler, 5th Series, vol. V, part VIII, 258.   [13] Stapleton, II, xlv, xlviii.   [14] *Le Prevost Mem.* III, 278.   [15] *Ibid.*   [16] *Ibid.*   [17] Stapleton, II, xlix.   [18] *Dict. de l'Eure*, II, 914.   [19] *Dict. de l'Eure*, II, 914 ; *Les Barons de Creully*, Pezet, 57 ; *vide* 29.   [20] *Le Prevost Mem.*, III, 278 ; *St-Père de Chartres*, 584.   [21] *Ibid.*   [22] *Le Prevost Mem.*, III, 277 ; *Dict. de l'Eure*, II, 914. [23] *Ibid.*   [24] 308, no. 173 ; *Dict. de l'Eure*, II, 914.   [25] 308, no. 186 ; *Dict. de l'Eure, ibid* ; Père Anselme, VIII, 257.   [26] Père Anselme ; *Dict. de l'Eure, ibid.* ; *Le Prevost Mem.*, II, 277 ; *Arch. de l'Empire, ibid.*   [27] Père Anselme, 259, 260, 261 ; *Dict. de l'Eure*, II, 914, 915.   [28] *Lives of the Saints*, VII, 210, 212 ; *Dict. Greek and Roman*, 892.   [29] Ord. Vit., I, 335.

HEREDITARY MARSHALS   This hereditary title was attached to the domain of
OF NORMANDY   Auvricher (now Orcher), canton of Montivilliers, and
                        came into possession of Jean Crispin, " counselor and
chamberlain of the king," baron of Bec-Crispin, seignior d'Angerville, d'Auvricher, de

Mauny, de Plasnes, etc., "grand master inspector and general reformer of waters and forests of the king in the duchy of Normandy and the county of Picardy, captain of Pont de l'Arche," sometime knight-banneret, etc.

Jean Crispin became invested with the dignity of hereditary Marshal sometime towards the middle of the 15th century, acquired in the right of his mother, Jacqueline d'Auvricher, wife of William Crispin XII, sire de Mauny and d'Angerville. Jean dying without issue, it passed to his brother, Antoine, archbishop of Narbonne, and was held by Robert de Folques in the right of his wife, Jacqueline, youngest sister of Antoine, to whose descendants it passed. She was lady of Grusmenil, Ferrières, Hausse and necessarily Auvricher, which domains were, therefore, not included in the sale by Antoine of his inheritance to Pierre de Brézé, as we have erroneously stated (149). Their daughter, Jeanne de Folques, married first, Gilles de Rouvray de St-Simon, second, Louis de Villiers de Mesnil-Madame-Rance. Her grandson by her first marriage, Louis de St-Simon de Rasse, married Charlotte-Armande of the celebrated Rohan-Chabot family. (Bibl. nat. fr. 27412, P.O. 928, no. 31, 33, 35, 36, 38, 39, 42; vide 149; Père Anselme, IV, 407.)

HEREDITARY CHAMBERLAINS OF   The Tancarvilles, hereditary chamber-
NORMANDY: THE TANCARVILLES   lains of Normandy, eventually became the
                                chamberlains of France, and through mar-
riage into the Crispin family they acquired the hereditary constableship of Normandy. (Vide 106.)

ANCESTRY OF THE   Roger, brother of Herluin, founder and first abbot of
ESTOUTEVILLE FAMILY   the abbey of Bec, was the ancestor of the family of Estoute-
                            ville, according to Genealogie de quelques Familles Issues
Des Ducs de Normandie. entre autres les Stutt Comtes D'Assay et Marquis de Tracy Cadets d'Estouteville issus par des Puines des du Bec des Comtes de Brionne issus de Rollon 1er Ducs de Normandie par le Comte L. de Clement de Blavette.

ANCESTRY OF   This companion of the Conqueror at Hastings, who was the
SIMON DE SENLIS   recipient of so many unusual favours from this monarch, was
                            probably a descendant of Bernard de Senlis, which would explain
this consideration for him on the part of the duke-king. (Vide 181.)

THE IDENTITY OF   The reference to Robertus filius Willelmi has erroneously
ROBERT FILIUS   been placed in the biography of William L'Acher, page 33.
WILLELMI   Robert, the tutor of Henry I, was Robert, son of Achard and,
                            therefore, should have been recorded under Achard (Acard)
d'Ambrières, page 1. He was so named by that king in a charter wherein he grants to Robert five manors in Berkshire, which may be translated as follows : " Know ye that I have given and granted to Robert Achard, my master, and to his heirs in fee and hereditarily Aldermaneston (Aldermaston) and Finchamstede (Finchampstead) and Colsthorpe (Coldrop) and Speresholt (Sparsholt) and Cewehlewe (Challow) with all their appurtenances in churches and in mills, etc. . . . for the service of one knight." " Sciatis me dedisse et concessisse Roberto Achard, magistro meo et heredibus suis in feudo et in hereditate Aldermaneston et Finchamstede et Colsthorpe et Speresholt et Cewehlewe cum omnibus appendiciis suis in ecclesiis et molendinis . . . per servicium unius militis."

This discards the prevailing theory held by the authorities mentioned under these two biographies.

NOTE.—This information was brought to our attention through the courtesy of General John Ross Delafield, who has been of great help to us. (Calendar of Charter Rolls, vol. III, 1300–26, p. 360, dated 30 July 1317.)

This also applies to the data concerning Cecilia, natural daughter of Milo Crispin, and the justification of the Langetot pedigree recorded on the preceding page. Grant, 14 February 1229, to " Robert Achard, son and heir of William Achard of manors (above named), which king Henry, grandfather of king Henry, grandfather of the present king, gave to Robert Achard, grandfather of the said William, father of the said Robert, to hold the same with the churches by the service of one knight." (Ibid., vol. I, p. 91.)

CONCERNING BRIENT DE   Brian (Brient) of Brittany was the younger
BRETAGNE, COMTE DE VANNES   brother of Geoffry (II) de Botherel, comte de
                                 Penthièvre, and the older brother of Alain Le
Roux, Alain Le Noir, Etienne and Robert. There is plenty of evidence to substantiate this which Lobineau, Morice, Père Anselme and others attest. The Cartulary of Marmoutier which records a donation of Geoffry and his brothers to that abbey reads in part (Hoc donum concesserunt etiam omnes fratres ejus Brientius videlicet comes Anglicæ

terræ et Alanus Rufus ejus scilicet successor, atque alter Alanus qui et Niger decebatur hic etiam tertius successit in rego, et quidam qui sororem ejus bastardum usorem duxerat, Guifandus de Pleveno).[1] This would seem to signify that Brian was the first earl of Richmond, which is incorrect, as the records are quite clear that it was Alain Le Roux, assuming, of course, that Richmond was then an earldom. Cocayne [2] quoting *Registrum Honoris de Richmond* by Gale, believes it was only an honour until king Stephen's time, when Alan, second of the name, styled le Noir, became the first earl. The aforementioned brothers were the sons of Eudes, comte de Penthièvre and d'Avaujour, grandsons of Geoffry, comte de Bretagne and great-grandsons of Richard I, duke of Normandy, all of whom bore the title of count,[3] and this may possibly be the only implication intended in the Marmoutier charter. Vital records Brian fighting in 1068 and 1069, which suggests presence at Senlac, " two sons of Harold . . . encountered by Brian, son of Eudes, count of Brittany " (Protinus illis Briennus Eudonis comitis Britanniæ).[4] He occurs in Suffolk Domesday [5] " Comes Brienus " and was deceased before the survey when his lands were held by Robert, count of Mortain, which accounts for his obscurity in England. Consequently he did not fight at Cardiff, unless the battle occurred before that date, which seems improbable.[6]

[1] *Preuves*, I, col. 459 ; Père Anselme, III, 52 ; *vide* 2.   [2] *Complete Peerage*, Cokayne, VI, 342.   [3] *Ibid.* ; *Rech. Domesd.*, 74.   [4] II, 23, 26 ; *vide* 2.   [5] II, 291.   [6] *Vide* 2, 59 ; *vide* Alain Le Noir.

CONCERNING WILLIAM BOTONER, ALIAS WILLIAM OF WORCESTER (WYCESTRE)

Hearne, who published the roll of William of Worcester in the *Liber Niger*,[1] believed it was a copy of some noted record of Battle Abbey. It was sent to William of Worcester with this inscription written across the back, " To my most welebeloved and trusty friend, William Worcetre." Hearne placed CCCLIII in a marginal note, indicating that he considered it written 353 years after the battle of Hastings, which would place it in 1419. This is incorrect, for William of Worcester was born at Bristol *c.* 1415, was living in 1480, and his death is placed in 1490.[2] He was educated at Oxford by sir John Fastolf, who was a great baron in the reign of Henry V of England, which monarch he accompanied to Normandy during the wars in that duchy. Sir John in 1417 was captain of the town and castle of Meulent and " Comes Lieutenant " of the king in the bailiwicks of Rouen, Evreux, Alençon and took over the government of the countries of Anjou and Maine.[3] It was this same Fastolf who purchased in 1418 the barony of Bec-Crispin from his sovereign, who had confiscated it from the Crispin family.[4] After the English withdrew from this part of Normandy this barony again came into possession of Jean Crispin, the hereditary marshal of Normandy (*vide* 148). William of Worcester lived at Caister in Norfolk, the English home of sir John, after his graduation, when he became the latter's esquire, historian, and executor.[5] He was a man of great and various literary talents and an extremely ardent antiquarian. Among his many works were the *Acts* of his patron, sir John, and *A Fragment of the Chronicle of Normandy* from the years 1414 to 1422 taken from his manuscripts and those of sir George Chastelain.[6]

[1] II, 522–4.   [2] *Henri Quinti Angliæ Regis Gesta*, Benj. Williams, x.   [3] *Ibid.*, 277–8.   [4] *Vide* 148.   [5] *Ibid.*, n. 3.   [6] *Ibid.*, pp. 215–62 inclusive.

CONCERNING THE DATE OF THE DEATH OF GILBERT CRISPIN, ABBOT OF WESTMINSTER

Gilbert Crispin, abbot of Westminster, was comparable with the greatest men of his century not only for his piety, learning, and writings, but as a theologian of rare distinction which we have drawn attention to in the appendix (139). In his thirst for knowledge he visited the academies of France, travelled throughout Italy, went to Rome, and passed through Germany on his return to England. We will deal here only with the generally accepted opinion that his death occurred on 6 December 1117, concerning which there has been much controversy on account of the many conflicting and perplexing circumstances surrounding it, but which has a most distinguished following (139).[1] Vitalis, the predecessor of Gilbert, as abbot of Westminster, ruled this abbey according to John Flete from 1073 to 1082,[2] who says he died 19 June of the latter year.[3] Flete appears on the chamberlain's roll in 1420 and was a monk there from then until 1465, during which time he wrote a *History of Westminster Abbey*.[4] Richard Widmore, who wrote a *History* of the abbey three centuries later,[5] disputes this date, but he was unaware of a grant by abbot Gilbert to William Baynard in 1083. (Anno dominice incarnationis millesimo LXXX°III°. Nos Gilbertus abbas et conventus Westm' concessimus Willelmo Baynard . . .[6]) This was, however, written in " Westminster " Domesday by a 15th-century hand and may have been wrongly copied. To add to the dilemma, Vitalis witnessed the confirmation of a Durham charter of king William I in 1084 (anno regno mei XVIII [7]) which also is a copy. Here is an anachronism, but the latter date has generally been conceded.

The commencement of the rule of Vitalis is placed by the *Winchester Annales* in 1076, and by the *Anglo-Saxon Chronicle* in 1077 (1076), which date dean Robinson accepts in his edition of Flete [8] and he places Vitalis' death 19 June 1085.[9] Accordingly this year has been decided upon as the beginning of the rule of Gilbert. The statement in the ancient *Crispin genealogy* by Milo Crispin (*De nob. Crispin. gen.*), the monk at Bec, that Gilbert governed Westminster for 32 years, which was well known and believed by all of the aforementioned, is why Flete, who thought that Vitalis died in 1082, placed Gilbert's death in 1114 (Gislebertus cognomento Crispinus . . . iste quidem Normannus, nobilis genere. . . . Obiit autempater iste et misericors sexto die Decembris anno domini millesimo CXIV° [10]). To-day it so incorrectly appears on his tomb in Westminster abbey in the south cloister and is the reason why those who believe he first went there in 1085 place his death in 1117. The black Tournai marble slab which had covered his tomb for centuries was removed from the stone floor in the 18th-century and placed on the side of the wall. This was necessary to preserve it, as the constant treading of the feet of Westminster boys was obliterating his features. It is very easy to prove 1114 incorrect, for Gilbert executed a document after 19 September 1115. . . . G. abbatem et con-ventum Westm' et Willemum de Bocholanda . . . testes : . . . Bernardus episcopus de Sancto David.[11] There is a record in the history of Croyland by its continuator, Peter of Blois (spurious though this work may be), that Henry I in 1118 sent Gilbert of West-minster with Geoffry of Croyland to Thibaud, count of Blois, to propose an interview on the subject of the division which existed then between the count and the king of France.[12] This difficulty can be gotten over, however, by the method of commencing the year then in use. There appears a charter in the 30th report of the deputy keeper on page 201 dated 1119 to St-Cuthbert's, Durham, which is witnessed among others by Gilbert, abbot of Westminster. This was incorrectly translated by the authorities. The date is mcix (1109) as shown by a confirmation of May 1413 printed in Calendar of charter rolls,[13] which is confirmed by Raine.[14] The rule of Gilbert's successor at Westminster, abbot Herbert, commenced according to Eadmer in January 1121.[15] The date is attested by a grant confirming privileges to Herbert in this year from Peter of Cluny, the papal legate.[16] We have to ask, why this delay of three years in appointing Gilbert's suc-cessor ? Was his non-appearance in any known documents during this period due to incapacity, removal from office, or elevation to a higher dignity ? If for any of these reasons, why is it nowhere recorded ? The fact that king Henry was absent in Normandy from 1116 to 1120 continuously [17] does not seem a sufficient explanation for leaving this great monastery without a head for such a prolonged period, but in lieu of a better explanation this needs must suffice. In disagreeing with the date of 1117 dom. Mabillon refers to an anonymous dedicatory epistle to Alexander, bishop of Lincoln, who was nominated at the Easter court in 1123 and consecrated in the following July.[18] This epistle Mabillon attributed to abbot Gilbert, while others believed it was written by William de Champeaux, but it was not from the pen of either. The latter, a notable figure in the history of philosophy in the first years of the 12th century, became bishop of Chalons-sur-Marne and is said to have died in January 1121, but even if it was 1122, it would eliminate him.[19] Gilbert dedicated his "De disputatio Judæi cum Christiano " (139) to St-Anselme, and while the one to Alexander follows closely his phraseology at the beginning, it finishes in a very different style and was undoubtedly written by some admirer of Gilbert who desired to curry favour with the bishop Alexander.[20] If the foregoing were not enough to prove Mabillon incorrect, the mortuary roll of Savigny show-ing that Gilbert was dead before 1122, which we have previously recorded, surely would.[21]

TITVLVS : SCI : PETRI : WESTMONASTERII

Anima eius et anime omnium fidelium defunctorum Requiescant in pace

Offa. rege. Ædgaro. rege.   Matilda. regina.   crispin.
AMEN.   Orate pro nostris. ∧ ÆDWARDO. REGE. ∧ Vital'. abb. Giselberto.   abb'.

These insertions were made later so that all could recognize the well-known personages.

Therefore, since the statement of the Bec chronicler regarding the length of Gilbert's rule of Westminster is so direct that it has not been doubted, and as he is nowhere recorded after 1117, this year must be accepted as that of his death pending evidence to the contrary.

---

[1] *Gilbert Crispin, abbot of Westminster*, Robinson, 19, 26 ; *The History of Westminster Abbey, John Flete*, ed. Robinson, 142 ; Jean Picard, canon of St-Victor, Paris, following Florence of

Worcester, also agreed (*Hist. Litt. de la France* X, 195). [2] Flete, 141. [3] *Ibid*, 22.
[4] Flete, 2 ; *G. C., abbot*, 181. [5] Flete, 1, 181. [6] "*Westminster*" *Domesday*, fo. 82 ; *G. C., abbot*. [7] *Historiæ Dunelmensis Scriptores Tres* (Surtees soc.), canon Raine, app., pp. v, vi. [8] Flete, 139. [9] *Ibid*. [10] *Vide* charter no. 13 ; Flete, 85. [11] *Vide* app. 17 (139) ; *West. Domesd.*, fo. 528. [12] *Hist. Litt. de la France, ibid*. [13] Charter rolls, V, 454. [14] Raine, app., p. xxxii. [15] Eadmer, *Hist. Nov. Rolls*, ser., 291 ; Flete, 142. [16] *West. Domesd.*, fo. 411 ; Flete, 142. [17] *G. C., abbot*, 126. [18] *Ibid.*, 61. [19] It is interesting to note that a later member of this distinguished family, Louis Boivin-Champeaux, was the author of "Notice sur Guillaume de Long-Champ, Évêque d'Ely, Vice-Roi d'Angleterre," published in 1885. This monograph deals with a decree of Richard I (Cœur de Lion), who needed money so desperately that he demanded the resealing of all charters previously granted by him during his reign. For this purpose Richard had a third lion added (152) to the royal arms of England (unchanged to-day). Senator Jean Boivin-Champeaux of the " Comité Guillaume le Conquérant," also of this family, is president of the " Conseil général du Calvados " ; *G. C., abbot*, 61. [20] *Hist. Litt. de la France, ibid.* ; *G. C., abbot, ibid.* [21] *Vide* (139) ; *G. C., abbot, ibid.*

CONCERNING SEVERAL FORTIFIED CASTLES OF THE 11TH CENTURY

BEC-CRISPIN (arrd. of Hávre, dép. Seine-Inférieure)

The barony of Bec, surnamed Bec-Vauquelin, Bec-de-Mortemer, and Bec-Crispin, belonged successively to the families named. Of the Vauquelin little is known. In the 12th century Vauquelin-de-Becco was almoner at the priory of Longueville, which had 70 acres of ground at Bretteville and at Martenbosc, but in 1180 it is certain that the Mortemers were seigniors of Bec. It passed to the Crispin family from them through marriage, *c.* 1254, with the constableship of Normandy and other extensive possessions. As previously stated, the title of barony was attached to the ground testifying the importance of the property and the singular services rendered by its first owners.

Of the ancient fortress of Bec, one can only see the cellars of the Roman epoch, of a primitive pointed gothic style. The walls, which are not less than one meter in thickness and pierced with loopholes, are well preserved.

From the donjon with two towers, next to the pond formed by the source of the Lézarde, was a wall surrounded by water and fortified by five other towers, of which three are still existing. Two of them overlooked the postern and the drawbridge. In the bottom of the third, named " Tower of the blackhole," was the place where the seignioral justice kept the obstinate vassals.

The foundation walls of the two towers which had disappeared have been found. Bec-Crispin was a real fortress. Its situation in the middle of the inexhaustible waters made it a place easy to keep, and to resist assaults.

The deeds of the Mortemers and of the Crispins do not leave any doubt of the importance that the castle had in the history of the province. When Rouen surrendered, 13 January 1419, so did also Bec-Crispin, Caudebec, Montivilliers, Avricher, Fécamp, and Tancarville, which king Henry V of England garrisoned.

The rebellion of 1435 delivered up a second time Bec-Crispin. The following year, the duke of York took back the country while in 1440 the troops of Talbot were. The occupation ended in 1449 ; after that Charles VII took the town of Harfleur.

During the following years, the barons tried to repair the disasters of this hundred years' struggle. Chiefly Jean Crispin, the hereditary marshal of Normandy, attracted the farmers by giving them considerable rebates. At the same time the castle was rebuilt. The accounts of the barony of which M. de Beaurepaire published important notes in " the state of the County " mentioned several payments for work done to the castle and its outbuildings. But if this work made a part of the castle and its outbuildings habitable, it did not save it from the revolution which was happening in the art and especially in the architecture.

The beauty of the scenery drew the attention of the rich barons, admirers of the Renaissance. On the old donjon they built on a smaller scale a castle such as those which were erected by the kings of the 16th century. At that time the historical rôle of the castle of Bec stops. The new castle was a country place belonging to people having their residence at Rouen or Paris, where their business was.

A decree of 1612 pictures it as follows : The castle of Bec-de-Mortemer, surnamed Bec-Crispin, is very old, built with towers, with several buildings surrounded by walls and ditches full of running water with a drawbridge. Around it were 60 acres of ground, a yard surrounded with walls and the farmers' buildings. On the non-enfieffed property there was a farm with 55 acres of ground, situated at St-Martin and Notre-Dame-du-Bec, with two fields where the mills of the barony were, also 1,200 acres of cut wood situated on the hill of d'Hermeville, which belonged to the castle.

The lands which comprised the barony were very little smaller than the king's.[1]

BLANGY (arrd. of Pout l'Evêque, dép. Calvados)

The fortified castle of Blangy apparently existed in the middle of the 11th century when this domain was in the possession of William Crispin I, its first recorded seignior. Some of the walls and a portion of the keep, which was evidently square, still remain. The stones are of ashlar, regularly cut so as to form a facing, and as no moulding or aperture is left, it is impossible to determine from this mass the date of the château of which it formed a part. The barony of Blangy remained in the Crispin family until the middle of the 14th century, when it passed through the marriage of Jeanne Crispin with Jean de Meulan, count of Tancerville, etc., to that family.[2]

CHÂTEAUCEAUX—now CHAMPTOCEAUX (arrd. of Cholet, dép. Maine et Loire)

Aptly termed the "eagle's nest," the fortress was first erected by the Romans on the top of a cliff which rises almost perpendicular from the banks of the Loire to a great height on the top of which is a plateau of many acres where have been erected several fortresses by the seigniors of Châteauceaux. The ancient privilege of its seigniors to collect toll from the extensive navigation passing up and down this river, gateway to the important city of Nantes, led to many ferocious disputes. The chain which was stretched across the river directly beneath the castle was at first guarded by men-at-arms of sufficient numbers on the shore, with boats ready for instant attack, to collect by force their tribute. Later in the days of gunpowder it was watched over by men stationed night and day in a tower which still remains on the spur of the hill where they could readily pour bullets into any boat refusing to stop. With this hereditary right descending through so many generations, small wonder that at the time of Théobold Crispin we find him branded justly or unjustly a brigand. The extensive ruins of Châteauceaux have such great proportions that neither wars nor time could obliterate them, attesting the magnitude of this castle and fortress. Occupied successively by Renaud de Thuringe, viscount of Anjou, and his descendants, the families of Jarzé and Crispin which latter commenced with Amaury Crispin, c. 1119, and ended with Théobald Crispin, a century later, when it passed from this family for ever. A latter-day château now graces a portion of the old enclosures overlooking the beautiful river and valley below. (*Les Origines Feodales de Châteauceaux*, l'Abbe Bourdeaut ; *vide* App. 16.)

DANGU (arrd. of Andelis, dép. Eure)

In very early times a stronghold was constructed at Dangu to command the ford of the Epte which separated Normandy and France. The first castle was built by the Normans about the 10th century.[3] We have observed, as recorded in the *History of the lords and castles of Dangu*, written in 1714, by Berée de Courpont and deposited among the archives of the department of the Eure,[4] that the castle was not erected where it is to-day, but in the woods and on the summit of a slope toward Gisors, where one can see three high mounds of earth without any stone work. William Rufus fortified it in 1092,[5] when the Crispin family were installed as its castilians, and in the first half of the next century Joscelyn Crispin acquired the domain of Dangu as well, through marriage, and it remained in this family until the early part of the 14th century.[6] It was continually the seat of very violent struggles between Normandy and France on account of its strategic position. M. Malte-Drun in an article on Dangu [7] describes the ancient castle as follows : " The castle comprised in the 12th century (and during Joscelyn Crispin's time) a keep and a double line of walls. The inner rampart in the form of a circle surrounding the keep was composed of high thick walls flanked by towers and protected by a moat. The outer not so strong was in the form of an arc, the extremities of which were supported to the south-west by the inner fortifications. In the outer wall two doors gave access to the surrounding country : one was on the side of the village in front of the church of Saint-Jean, the other was on the opposite side, facing towards the west and leading to the open country. This wall surrounded the dwellings and the slope. From this fortification one could gain access to the second, which dominated it by crossing the moat on a drawbridge and entering through a door constructed in a great square tower ; this opened into the court or the place of arms of the castle. The buildings in which the people lived were against the circular wall which protected it in the centre and the keep whose imposing mass dominated the two ramparts, the other buildings, and the neighbouring countryside was on an artificial hillock or mound. From the platform of the keep one could see the fortified walls of Gisors and its castle, the towers of Neaufles, of Bouri, or Courcelles, and of Gamaches. This fortified castle and domain left this family in the early part of the 14th century." Later the fortifications were destroyed, the moats levelled and the keep demolished, so that to-day almost no vestige of the ancient feudal manor remains.

ESTRÉPAGNY (arrd. of Andelis, dép. Eure)

Estrépagny was the centre of a royal villa in the 7th century.[8] King Dagobert gave this important domain to the abbey of St-Denis, c. 630.[9] Just when it became a fortified castle is uncertain, but not later than the middle of the 11th century, when William Crispin I had the guardianship of that fortress. As recited elsewhere in this work, it eventually came into possession of the illustrious house of Orleans-Longueville in the middle of the 15th century. In 1689 a part of Estrépagny was protected by a moat about 33 feet wide and there was a drawbridge at the porte du Thil on the Rouen side.[10] In 1704 the town was still surrounded by walls.

LIVAROT (arrd. of Lisieux, dép. Calvados)

The Château of Livarot, the original construction of which may go as far back as the 11th century, was one of the most remarkable feudal edifices of the district. The enceinte, circular in form, built in the hardest sandstone, carefully trimmed, was surrounded by deep moats supplied with water from the river Vie ; moreover, Livarot was long regarded as an important stronghold. But this old castle having been dismantled in the wars of the 14th century, only a few portions of its original walls remained, unequal in height, on which several wooden constructions had been fixed, devoid of all uniformity or regularity. The most remarkable part of this ancient dwelling and the best preserved was a pavilion, or turret, giving access into the interior, and where formerly was a drawbridge. The whole of the enceinte must have had a circumference of 252 feet within the moats.[11]

NEAUFLES (arrd. of Andelis, dép. Eure)

Neaufles was one of the most ancient villages of the Norman Vexin. It was a Roman camp prior to c. 1040–5, when William Crispin I built there a fortified fortress at the behest of duke William, which he made his chief seat. About 50 years later during the reign of William Rufus the castle was rebuilt and brought up to date under the direction of Robert de Bélesme. There remains nothing of this château excepting part of the tower which still stands and a portion of the foundation walls. It was demolished c. 1647, when cardinal Mazarin ordered the destruction of the majority of the strongholds of Normandy. This domain passed from the Crispin family in the middle of the 14th century to that of Tancerville through marriage.[12]

TILLIÈRES (arrd. of Evreux, dép. Eure)

Deep in the centre of France on the southern border of Normandy there lie the remains of the ancient castle of Tillières-sur-Avre, in its day one of the strongest fortresses of the Norman dukes, built by them more than 900 years ago. The castle, donjon, or keep have long since disappeared, having been replaced by an imposing château, which in turn was supplanted by the present villa. It was erected on the spur of a hill commanding the valley of the river Avre, on the frontier of France. A comprehensive idea of its construction can be obtained from its present remains, the walls of which are built in two tiers, one inside and rising perpendicularly to a great height above the other. This made it a fort within a fort which had flank defence on account of a bastion at each corner. Perched high above this imposing defence towered the castle, threatening menace to the kings of France whose territory it overlooked. With the passing of the intervening centuries and the ravages of the hundred years of English occupancy this ancient fortress has disappeared with the exception of a portion of the lower and upper walls. The Crispin family acquired the hereditary guardianship of this fortress c. 1030 as well as the fortified castle of Damville and Bourth in the adjoining country, which were built at that time. They held Tillières and Bourth until the middle of the 14th century, but lost Damville definitely in 1183, as already observed.[13] They were known usually by the name de Tillières, later sometime corrupted into Tyler and Taylor.

WALLINGFORD (Berkshire, England)

The castle of Wallingford dates back to the days of the Roman occupation, when it is believed a fortified encampment existed there, which régime held sway in England for a period of 400 years.[14] This honour and castle was successively in the possession of Wigod, the Anglo-Saxon, Robert d'Ouilli, and Milo Crispin, the Norman warrior companions of duke William, and of Brian Fitz Count, which became one of the strongest and most important fortified castles in England. Its importance in ancient times is attested by the fact that during the reign of Athelstan [15] coins were minted there bearing the moneyer's name, Beornwald. Ruding disputes this and gives the reign of Edgar as that in which the earliest coin was struck here, but they were minted at Wallingford 35 years earlier, because several are now in the cabinet of the British museum.[16] The mint at Wallingford in 1017, during the reign of Canute, is styled Weli ; Welin ; three of these coins are also in the British museum and there are several of king Harold I there who died in 1039.[17] Wallingford is first mentioned in history in 1006 when the Danes marched there and " burned it all down." If a castle existed then it also fell at this time. They returned and repeated the devastation in 1010.[18] After this it is believed a castle was not built until shortly after the Conquest when a reconstruction of the old or a new castle destined to become famous in English history was erected by Robert d'Ouilli at the command of the Conqueror.[19] The grand and spacious residence of Wigod at Wallingford was not a castrum of the Roman type, although it may have had the character of a fortress, approached by drawbridges through projecting portals and double gates, but it was not a fortified castle, lacking the towers and impregnable walls of more ancient times. The Saxons made no military works of their own, but used the existing Roman earthworks.[20] Consequently when the Conqueror arrived fortified castles were extremely rare, which rendered the Conquest comparatively easy. Wigod was one of the few great Englishmen who took sides with William, which places him more or less in the class of a traitor.[21] The mint of Wallingford still continued active in the time of the Conqueror.[22]

Wallingford became a great storm centre about the time when the empress Matilda, the daughter of Henry I, attempted to secure the throne of England which Stephen had usurped after the death of this monarch.[23] It was then in possession of Brian Fitz Count, who had married the widow of Milo Crispin, where Matilda had taken refuge in 1141,[24] in which year she was proclaimed queen. For eight months she was acknowledged sovereign, but never crowned, and Stephen, though a prisoner, had not abdicated. Wallingford had extensive donjons, the buried ruins of which may be seen to-day, where prisoners, not sent to the tower of London, were frequently placed in custody.[25] There remains little of this ancient and historic fortress to-day ; it has almost entirely disappeared with the exception of a few walls. A dignified mansion of later date now adjoins these ruins, all of which are enclosed within high stone walls. The picturesque and quaint town of Wallingford still bears a feudal appearance and the curfew rings at 9 o'clock at night, as of yore.

[1] Noticè-Historique Sur les Barons et la Baronnie du Bec, dit Bec-Vauquelin, Bec-de-Mortemer et Bec-Crispin, A. Lechevalier, 1898, vide 39 ; App. 17.   [2] Statistique Monumentale du Calvados, de Caumont, IV, 382 ; vide 37, 140.   [3] Le Prevost Mem. & Notes, II, 4.   [4] Hist. des Seigneurs et Châteaux de Dangu, ms. archives de l'Eure.   [5] Le Prevost, ibid.   [6] Vide 37, 90 ; App. 13, 17. [7] France illustrée, Eure, 26.   [8] Le Prevost, ibid., II, 54.   [9] Hist. de St-Denis, Doublet, 674. [10] Le Prevost, ibid., II, 56.   [11] Ibid., de Caumont, V, 678.   [12] Le Prevost, ibid., II, 438 ; 38 ; App. 17.   [13] Vide 28, App. 16 ; addenda.   [14] History of Wallingford, Hedges. This most excellent and thorough work in two volumes gives a complete history of the castle from the early Roman occupation to the 20th century, I, 169.   [15] Ibid., 171.   [16] Ibid., 171.   [17] Ibid., 175. [18] Ibid., 175.   [19] Ibid., 181 ; vide 95.   [20] Ibid., 182.   [21] Ibid., 194.   [22] Ibid., 220. [23] Ibid., 234.   [24] Ibid., 237.   [25] Ibid., 275.

ANCESTRY OF HÉLOÏSE, MOTHER OF THE ABBOTT HERLUIN

Arnoul I, count of Flanders, married Adelle, daughter of Herbert II, count of Vermandois, and had issue : [1]

Baldwin III, who succeeded as count of Flanders.

Herbert, of whom nothing is known excepting his name and the date of his death in 951.

Lietgarde of Flanders, who married Wieman, count and chatelain of Gand, died 29 September 961 and was buried in the abbey of St-Pierre-lès-Gand, to which her husband gave great benefactions.[2]

Edelgarde of Flanders, wife of Valeran, count of Crespy, following David Blondel.

Elstrude of Flanders, wife of Sifrid, Danish seignior, who was the origin of the counts of Guines.[3]

Herbert was probably count of St-Paul and may have been the grandfather of Héloïse, the mother of Herluin, abbot of Bec, referred to on page 150. If Héloïse was not descended from Herbert, then she was from one of his sisters, of whom the most probable would be Elstrude, since she was the wife of Sifrid, the progenitor of the counts of Guines, which title her grandfather is supposed, following Grimaldi, to have held. Sifrid was a Dane and so was Ansgot, the husband of Héloïse.

[1] Père Anselme, II, 714.   [2] History of the House of Guines, Duchesne, II, chapter I ; Wredieus, page 22, of his proofs ; Père Anselme, ibid.   [3] Duchesne, ibid. ; Père Anselme, ibid.

AUVRAI MAUBENC

Page 118, *col.* 2, *l.* 7 : The foundation charter of Montacaute priory by William, count of Mortain, was witnessed by Alured Pincerna and William, his son, to which priory the de Lincoln family were afterwards great benefactors. This must have been the same Alured (presumably surnamed Maubenc) and his son William who witnessed the charter of Grestin in 1122. In the cartulary of the priory of Montacaute we find this entry recorded : " Alured the butler, for his own welfare and that of his lord, William, count of Mortain, grants to Montacaute two parts of the tithes of Acford." Among the lands of Robert Fitz Payne, grandson of the last Alured de Lincoln, in 1281 was found " Acford Aluredi," evidently the Acford, above referred to, now known as Okeford Fitzpaine. This has raised the query if the Alured Pincerna of the Montacaute charter may have been Alured de Lincoln II, but he is not known to have had a son William, his heir and son having been Robert. The Additamenta to Exeter Domesday shows that Alured Maubenc (Malbeding) of the Conquest was pincerna to the house of Mortain. William, his brother, a palatine baron of Hugh " Lupus," was progenitor of the barons Wich-Malbank of Cheshire. The statement that this Alured and William came to England with Hugh is contrary to the facts regarding Alured, who probably accompanied William, count of Mortain, and who does not appear to have been connected with the house of d'Avranches.

AUVRAI DE LINCOLN

Page 160, *col.* 2, *l.* 23 : The connection between the de Lincoln and de Albini families was through marriage. In the Pipe roll of 1213 (quoted *in part* on page 158), there is an entry that " Ranulph de Bajocis pays 20 silver marks for a daughter of Alan de Lincoln and 40 marks for the lands of Onfrey de Albini. And the said Ranulph will owe 200 marks after the death of Alan which could not be claimed in Alan's lifetime. Alan de Lincoln pays a claim of half a gold mark for the lands which he gave to Onfrey de Albini with his daughter." This makes it evident that Margareta, daughter and heiress of Alan de Lincoln, married firstly, Onfrey de Albini, and secondly, Ranulph de Bajocis (Bayeux)

GUILLAUME CRISPIN VI, SIRE DE DANGU

The statement in *appendix* 17, *page* 144, *column* 2, at *line* 44, that William Crispin VI died prior to 1254 is incorrect, as an obituary entry of the abbey of Joyenval had been overlooked (*Obituaire de l'Abbaye de Joyenval*), which occurs on page 296, volume II, of *Obituaires de la Province de Sens, Diocèse de Chartres*, published by August Molinier, Paris, 1906. " 19 June commemorates the seignior William Crispin junior, knight, son of Dame Amicie de Roye who made many donations to us and died in the year 1266." (19 [Junii] C[ommemorato] domini Guillelmi Crispini junioris, militis, filii dominae Amiciae de Roya qui nobis plura donavit et obiit anno Domini 1266.) Since he was the son of Amicie de Roye he is definitely located as William Crispin VI. This is very confusing because his son and heir, William Crispin VII, the constable of Normandy and marshal of France who married Jeanne de Mortemer, declares himself seignior of Dangu in a charter of 1256 referred to on page 145, column 1, there photographically reproduced following page 152, designated as charter " e." " I, William, called Crispin, seignior of Dangu . . . that since a contention arose between us on the one hand and the religious men, brethren of the Knightly Order of the Temple . . . by which the ten brethren declared that they had the right of gathering the wood from the possessions of my lord, Robert Crispin, uncle of my father . . . the charter of Monseigneur Robert Crispin, uncle of my very dear father, Monseigneur William Crispin, knight. . . ." (Je, Guillaume, dit Crispin, Seignor de Dangu . . . comme matire de contention fust née entre moi, d'une post, et religieus homes, frères de la chevalerie deu Temple . . . de ce que les dix frères disoient que il lor lisvit ès bois qui furent monseignor Robert Crespin, oncle de mon père . . . de la charte monseignor Robert Crespin, oncle mon très chier père, monseignor Guillaume Crespin, chevalier.) It is just as certain that this was William Crispin VII, for, as will be observed, he mentions in this charter Robert Crispin, the uncle of his father, in connection with the " Commanderie de Bourgoult " or Knight Templars, of which order Robert Crispin was the chief founder. His charter of donation to the Templars reads in part : " To all those sons of the Holy Apostolic See to whom these presents should come, Robert Crispin gives greeting in the name of the one God. You should all know that Robert Crispin has donated out of love of God and the safety of my Soul, also that of Agnes, my wife, and with her wish to God and the brethren of the Temple of Solomon into free and eternal alms, sixty acres of land . . . all situated in the holdings and woods of Bourgoult. . . . Done in the year of the Incarnated Word 1219." (Omnibus Sancte Ecclesie Apostolice filiis ad quos presens scriptum pervenerit, Robertus Crespin salutem individuo deo perpetuam. Noverit universitas vestra quod ego Robertus Crespin pro amore dei et salute anime mee, necnon Agnetis uxoris mee et ipsius voluntate donavi et concessi deo et fratribus templi Salomonis in liberam et perpetuam elemosinam sexaginta acras terre . . . sitas totas in uno tenemento et in boscho de Bourgoult. . . . Actum fuit hos anno Verbi Incarnati millesimo ducentesimo decimo nono.)

The original of this charter is in the Archives Nationales in Paris, and a reproduction of Robert's seal attached to it is reproduced following page 152. This Robert Crispin was the brother of William Crispin V (father of William Crispin VI), both sons of Joscelyn Crispin. M. Le Prevost was puzzled by the 1256 charter, as was Léopold Delisle and Louis Passy, for in reproducing it in the *Memories and Notes of the Department of Eure,* of the former the statement is made that they do not know which of these Williams executed it. They were, therefore, unaware or ignored the 1219 charter of Robert, otherwise it would have been quite apparent that the 1256 charter was executed by the third William from Joscelyn, the father of Robert. The entry in the Obituary of the abbey of Joyenval must have escaped them also, otherwise they would have mentioned it, which they failed to do.

Since, therefore, William Crispin VII was seignior of Dangu in 1256, his father must have relinquished this seigniory in his favour for some reason prior to this date. Perhaps he was incapacitated, for if the record of Drocon de Montigny, bailiff of Gisors, referred to on page 144, column 2, can be trusted concerning the tutelage of his children in 1248, some credence may be given to this thought. Howbeit, William VII had succeeded his father, William VI, by this time, since both were then living. William VII is further identified in this connection by the entry in the *Register of the Fiefs of the Bishopric of Chartres* dated 1292 and quoted on page 147, column 1, line 13, as the son of Alix de Sancerre (wife of William VI), "Lady of Dangu, his mother."

GUILLAUME CRISPIN (CONCERNING CHÂTEAUCEAUX)

A charter of the Anjou branch of this family, seigniors of Châteauceaux, has just been brought to our attention by l'abbé Bourdeaut of Nantes, France, the authority on this subject. It is here reproduced because the opinion has been accepted that Theobald Crispin was the last of the name who was seignior of Châteauceaux, having been driven in exile to England by Peter, count of Brittany, in 1224. While there seems to be no good reason to discount this conclusion, nevertheless, the following charter indicates that the Crispin family were prominently identified with Châteauceaux, at least a century and a half later.

" Aimery d'Argenton, seignor of Hérixzon, lieutenant general in Anjou and in Maine, of the very powerful prince, Monseignor the Duke of Anjou, count of Maine, son of Monsieur the King at Colin de Tours, salut.

" We ask you and tell you that the sum of 100 sheeps in gold which you have raised or ought to have raised and received from the inhabitants of the seigniory of Châteauceaux to have Jeh. Chaperon or Guille Crespin go to England to . . . of the said castellany the said sum and if it has not been raised, do so hastily and deliver it to Jehan or Guille for the cause above stated, by taking from them an acknowledgment together with these letters you will be free from obligation and deliver the said sum as always. See that this is done without mistake. Made at Angers the 12th day of October in the year of 1361."

By Monseignor the lieutenant Lefeuvre.

(Lettres d'Aimery d'Argenton, lieutenant général en Anjou, ordonnant de porter cent moutons d'or en Angleterre.

Archives de la Loire Inf. E 232

13 October 1361 Angers.

Aimery d'Argenton, seigneur de Hérixzon, lieutenant général en Anjou et en Maine de très puissant prince Monsgr. le Duc d'Anjou, comte du Maine fils du Roy Messire, a'Colin de Tours, salut. Nous vous mandons et estroitement enjoignons que la somme de cent moutons d'or que vous avez ou devez avoir levée et fait lever et reçu des habitants en la castellenie de Chasteauceaux pour bailler à Tch. Chaperon ou Guille Crespin pour aller en Angleterre pour la bien tran . . . de lad. chastellenie vous icelle somme, si elle n'est toute levée levez et faictes levez hastivement et tantost la bailliez et délivrez aux.d. Jehan ou Guille pour la cause dessus dicte en prenant (d'eulx) lectre de recognoissance de ce par laquelle avec ces présentes, vous demourez quictes et délivré d'icelle somme a'tousjours. Sigardez qu'il n'y ait faute. Donné a'Angers le XIIᵉ jour d'Octobre l'an de grâce 1361.

par Monsgr. le lieutenant,
Lefeuvre)

" I do not know the land of which William Crispin of 1361 was seignior, but he belonged to the first nobility of the county of the Manges as well as his companion, Jean Chaperon, one of the principal families of Anjou of whom one finds every where the souvenir in the Manges" (Letter of l'abbé Bourdeaut, 29 July 1938 ; *vide* app. 15).

Page 146, *col.* 2, *l.* 34 : In a booklet by M. L'Abbé F. Blanquart of Rouen entitled " Fiefs et Arrière Fiefs du Vexin Normand et du Vexin Français " is given the texts of three lists drawn up in 1330, 1366, and the extreme end of the fourteenth or beginning of the fifteenth century respectively, and which give the names of the fiefs depending either directly or indirectly from the archbishop of Rouen. The lists were established to give assistance in the collection of the seignorial taxes due to the archbishop.

Members of the Crispin family are mentioned only in the first list, that is, the one drawn up in 1330, and a translation of the complete extract relating to them is given below :

Bernouville . . . 18 . . . 19 . . . 20.—Jehan de Meleun, esquire, holds, on account of damoiselle Johanne, his wife, daughter of monseigneur Guillaume Crispin, chevalier, sire of Estrépagny and constable of Normandy, by homage, from monseigneur the archbishop, the following fiefs :

Herquenchie (d'Arquency), the fief of Lisors. Worth vij^{xx} livres of Paris in revenue or thereabouts.
The fief of Fontenil, at La Buscaille. Worth .c. livres of Paris in revenue or thereabouts.
The fief of messire Guillaume Daubeuf, at La Buscaille. Worth ij^{cc} livres in revenue.
Corbie, the whole town. Worth about .c. livres of Paris in revenue.
Hennesiez, almost the whole town. Worth about .ij^{a}. livres in revenue.
A part of Guiseigniés. Worth about .c. livres in revenue.
Travailles, the whole town. Worth about .l. livres in revenue. Held by half fief.
A part of Feuguerolez. Worth about .xl. livres in revenue.
The fief of Thorel, at Villers in Veuguessin (Vexin). Worth about .c. sous of Paris in revenue.

GUILLAUME MALET, THE MONK AT BEC

William Malet, the monk at Bec in 1121, was the grandson of William Malet I, the warrior at Hastings, and not his son as has been stated on page 28 and in several other places in the " Falaise Roll." This error occurred because the following charter had been overlooked, which establishes this conclusion with reasonable certainty. William Malet I died before 1086, the date of the compilation of Domesday.[1] William Malet (II) about 1117 gave to the abbey of Bec " for his son, William, who had become a monk at Bec and for the salvation of his soul, for that of his wife and for his children and for the soul of his father and his mother and his brother Robert, properties which are situated in the bishopric of Evreux, near the river Carentan at the place called Mesnil-Joscelyn " (pro filio suo Willelmo qui factus est monachus Becci . . . pro salute anime sue et conjugis et liberorum suorum et pro anima patris et matris sue et fratris sui Roberti . . . in episcopatu Ebroicensi juxta Carentonam fluvium, que vocatur Maisnillum Joscelini). This donation was confirmed by Gilbert Crispin III and Laurentia, his wife, in 1130.[2] Therefore, William the monk here referred to was William Malet, third of the name. Robert Malet mentioned in the charter as brother of William Malet (II) was slain in the battle of Tinchebrai in 1106.[3] He gave to the abbey of Bec about 1070 " a mill at Mesnil-Joscelyn, an acre of land and the path leading to this mill with the consent of Gilbert Crispin " (II).[4] In 1121, as already observed, William Malet gave the manor and church of Conteville to the abbey of Bec.[5] We do not know whether this was William Malet II or III. We were misled into believing that Gilbert Crispin III confirmed this donation.[6]

The ownership of these Mesnil-Joscelyn properties under the Crispin family is fairly good evidence that the Malets of these charters were related and descendants of William Malet I as this Robert was certainly his son and successor. The statement in the *miraculum* in the ancient Crispin genealogy (*De nob. Crispin, gen.*) that " Esilia (Crispin, one of the daughters of Gilbert Crispin I, was the) mother of William Malet who was a brave soldier and in old age became a monk at Bec and after living a few years . . . he died a quiet death," [7] cannot be substantiated, for William Malet of Hastings fame was her husband and not her son as has been shown.[8] However, there is nothing to prove that he did not become a monk at Bec as well as his grandson and died there as the date and manner of his death are unknown.[9] Since the first part of this statement is erroneous, the latter part may be also, but this is the only instance in this genealogy found incorrect. The remainder has either been proven or cannot be refuted. Unfortunately, the *necrology of Bec* and of *Beaumont-le-Roger* do not reveal the name of Malet.[10]

It has been claimed that Esilia was the daughter of Gilbert Crispin I and Arlette, the mother of the Conqueror, rather than the offspring of Gilbert and his wife, Gonnor, as recorded in the *miraculum* [11] and that Milo Crispin, the warrior at Senlac, was born of this union also. There is much presumptive evidence to warrant this deduction,[12] and, if true, would satisfactorily explain how William Malet III came in possession of Conteville.[13]

[1] *Vide* 43.   [2] Bibl. nat. lat. 13905, fo. 21 v°; Chron. de Torigny, I, 138.   [3] Cle., II, 263. [4] *Vide* charter 6, line 24; Bibl. nat. lat. 13905, fo. 165 v°., 175 v°.   [5] *Vide* 127.   [6] *Vide* 136, 158.   [7] *Vide* charter 13, line 25; Bibl. nat. lat., fo. 161 to 120 v°.   [8] *Vide* app. 3, 20. [9] *Vide* 43.   [10] Bibl. nat. lat. 13905.   [11] *Ibid.*, note 7.   [12] *Vide* 181-2.   [13] *Vide* app. 3.

FURTHER CONCERNING HÉLOÏSE, MOTHER OF THE ABBOT HERLUIN

(Vide 150, 196)

Trying to identify Héloïse, mother of Herluin, abbot of Bec, only on the statement that she was a blood relative of the dukes of Flanders made by Gilbert Crispin, abbot of Westminster, who wrote the life of Herluin (150), must necessarily, with the available facts, be merely conjecture. Arnold II, count of Flanders, son and heir of Baldwin III, count of Flanders, married Roselle, daughter of Bérenger II, king of Italy. Philippe de Mornay, seigneur de Plessis-Marlay, La Roque, and others whom Grimaldi followed, say Héloïse, mother of the abbot Herluin and the wife of Ansgot, was the daughter of Raoul, count of Guines and Boulogne, and Roselle de St-Paul, otherwise the daughter of Baldwin (III), count of Flanders, as La Roque (I, 629) would have it. While the dates do not preclude Roselle de St-Paul having been the daughter of either Baldwin III or Herbert, his brother, elsewhere observed (196), nevertheless, since the same applies to Arnold II it is more probable that he was her father on account of her name having been Roselle, which does not previously occur in the family of the dukes of Flanders. Père Anselme (II, 712), following Duchesne (A. du Chesne, *Hist. de la Maison de Guines*, pp. 13, 14), says that Sifrid the Dane, who married Elstrude, daughter of Arnold I, count of Flanders, was the first count of Guines and, again (vol. 2, 715) quoting the same authority, states that Arnold II, count of Flanders, gave Guines to their son Adolph. However this may be, Adolph, son and heir of Sifrid and Elstrude, apparently espoused Mahaud, daughter of Arnold or Ernulfe, count of Boulogne (Père Anselme, VI, 247), among whose offspring was Raoul, count of Guines, aforesaid. Père Anselme does not give the parents of this Arnold (Ernulfe), progenitor of this branch of the counts of Boulogne whose descendants later became so famous, and admits he did not know who was his wife. The name Arnold is suggestive, but even more so is the fact that he held the comté of Boulogne which had belonged to Arnold I, count of Flanders, father of Baldwin III, and lived at the same period as the children of Arnold I. Arnold I, count of Flanders, also held the comté of St-Paul, which with Boulogne he acquired on the death of his brother, Adolph, in 933. Père Anselme says Arnold II, grandson of Arnold I, was count of Flanders, Boulogne and Guyenne. How could he have held Boulogne when it was then in possession of Ernicle, son and heir of Arnold (Ernulfe), count of Boulogne, which comté had been in this family since the time of Baldwin III, count of Flanders? Eustache I and his celebrated son, Eustache II, companion-in-arms of William the Conqueror, succeeded Ernicle as counts of Boulogne in the order named. It would seem, therefore, that Père Anselme was mistaken and that Arnold II of Flanders never held Boulogne. The same authority does not mention the successor of Raoul as count of Guines and differs with Duchesne regarding the parentage of Roselle, supposed mother of Héloïse. He records her, not Roselle de St-Paul, as Duchesne does (*ibid.*), but Roselle de Boulogne, daughter of Ernicle, count of Boulogne, and sister of Eustache I, count of Boulogne (VI, 248). In this event Roselle de Boulogne would have been the niece of Mahaud de Boulogne, mother of Raoul, count of Guines, her husband, and, therefore, his first cousin. Neither Duchesne nor Père Anselme mentions Héloïse as the daughter of either Roselle, if there were two, and we are unable to prove or disprove this assertion.

RIOUFE, COUNT OF EVREUX OR CÔTENTIN

Orderic Vital (ed. Le Prevost, I, 162-3) informs us that Rioufe, count of Evreux (Rithulfus Ebroicensis), revolted against William Longsword, second duke of Normandy, while Wace (ed. Pluquet, I, 107) calls him count of Côtentin (Riouf Quens fu de Costentin entre Vire è la mer). Robert, son of Richard I, duke of Normandy, was count of Evreux and archbishop of Rouen. If Ordericus is correct, which Le Prevost quite convincingly points out, one wonders just where Rioufe fitted into the ducal family of Normandy.

FURTHER CONCERNING SIMON DE SENLIS

Père Anselme (VI, 250-1), quoting from the manuscripts of Duchesne, gives a different ancestry for Simon de Senlis, the companion of the Conqueror, from that of Dugdale in the *Monasticon* (V, 90), followed in his biography (103). The pedigree begins with Rothold de Senlis, seigneur de Chantilly and de Ermenouville, whose son and heir, Fouques de Senlis, seigneur de Senlis, was living in 1027. The name of the wife of Fouques was not known to Père Anselme, but he records Laundry de Senlis, seigneur de Chantilly, his successor, who married Ermengarde, paternal aunt of Robert Vidame de Senlis, seigneur d'Acy and de Sourvilliers, the parent of Simon de Senlis of the Conquest. Garnier de Senlis is here made the uncle of Simon instead of his brother. This does not alter the observation (190) that Simon de Senlis may have been a descendant of Bernard de Senlis, supposed brother of Poppa, mother of the children of Rollo, first duke of Normandy.

NAMES AND ROLLS OF COMPANIONS OF
DUKE WILLIAM PREVIOUSLY PUBLISHED

GUY, BISHOP OF AMIENS

Gui, comte de Ponthieu (Pontivi nobilis haeres)
Eustache, comte de Boulogne
Gautier Giffard
Hugh de Montfort
Taillefer

Widonis Carmen de Hastingæ Proelio, in *Chron. Anglo-Normands*, Michel, III, 25.

WILLIAM OF POITIERS

Odo, bishop of Bayeux
Geoffry, bishop of Coutances
Robert, son of Roger de Beaumont
Eustache, comte de Boulogne
William, son of Richard, comte d'Evreux
Geoffry, son of Rotrou, comte de Mortain

William Fitz Osbern
Aimeri de Thouars
Gautier Giffard
Hugh de Montfort
Raoul de Toeni
Hugh de Grandménil
William de Warren

(Folio 1246, *vide* abbrevations.)

BAYEUX TAPESTRY

(Names woven in it)

Odo, bishop of Bayeux (ODO EPS: BACVLV.)
Robert, count of Mortain (ROTBERT)
Wadard (VVADARD)
Turold (TVROLD)
Eustache, count of Boulogne (E... ΓIVS)
Vital (VITAL)
Duke William (VVILLELMI DVCIS)
Harold (HAROLD)
Ælfgyva (ÆLFGYVA)
Guy, count of Ponthieu (VVIDO)
Lewine (LEVVINE), brother of Harold
Gyrth (GYRD), brother of Harold

Toustain Fitz Rou (not woven in tapestry but shown carrying the ganfanon)

ORDERIC VITAL

Eustache, count de Boulogne
William, son of Richard, comte d'Evreux
Geoffrey, son of Robert, comte de Mortagne, son of Rotrou, seig. de Mortagne, comte de Perche
William Fitz Osberne
Robert, son of Robert (Roger) de Beaumont, a novice in arms
Aimer, vicomte de Thouars
Earl Hugh, the constable (de Montfort)
Walter Giffard
Ralph Toni

Hugh de Grant-Mesnil
William de Warren
Turstin, son of Rollo (Toustain Fitz Rou)
Odo, bishop of Bayeux
Geoffrey, bishop of Coutances
Engenulf, lord of Laigle (Engenoulf de l'Aigle)
William Mallet (Malet)
Robert de Vitot
Guilbert d'Aufay
Stephen, son of Airard (Etienne Erard)

ROBERT WACE

Wiestace d'Abevile (Eustache, comte de Boulogne)
Engerran de Laigle (l'Aigle)
Sire d'Aubemare (Eudes, comte de Champagne)
Alainz Ferganz
Li jovente d'Anisie (Le sire)
Gilbert d'Asnières
Li boteillier d'Aubignie
Cil d'Alnei (Aulnay)
Sire d'Alnou (Aunou)
Sire d'Auviler
Richarz d'Avrencin
Rogier de Belmont (Robert de Beaumont)
Robert sire de Belfou
De Peleit le fitz Bertran
Robert Bertram, torz
Avenals des Biarz (Guillaume)
L'ancestre Hue li Bigot
Onfrei de Bohon
Luce de Bolbec (Hugue)
Sire de Bonnesboz
Botevilain
Guillaume fils Osber de Bretuil
Sire de Briencort
De Chaaignes
Seignor de Caillie
Onfrei de Cartrai
Maugier de Carterai novel chavelier
Willame de Columbières
Cil de Combrai
Raol de Conches (Tesson)
Giffrei, Eveske de Constances
Cil de Corcie
Willame Crespin ✓
Sire de Crievecoer (Hamon Le Seneschal)
Sire de Dinan (Alain Fitz Flaald)
Sire de Driencort
Cil d'Espiné
Sire d'Estotevile
Quens d'Ou (Robert)
Sire de Ferrières
Sire de la Ferté (Macé)
Robert filz Ernéis
Tostein filz Rou li Blanc
Cil de Felgières
Raol de Gael
Sire de Saint Galeri (Saint-Valéry)
Willeme de Garenes (Warren)
Cil de Gasie
Galtier Giffart
Cil de Gloz
Hue de Gornai
Cil de Goviz
Un vassal de Grentemesnil
Sire de la Haie (Eudes Le Seneschal)
Sire de Herecort
Cil de Jort
Chevalier de Lacie (Ibert)
Cil de Lacie (Gautier)

Sire de Litehare
Sire de Magnevile
Guillame Mallet
Cil de La Mare
Baron Rogier Marmion (Robert Marmion de Fontenai)
Martels de Basquevile (Geoffroi)
Gifrei de Meanie (Geffroi seigneur de Mortagne)
Sire del viez Molei (Guillaume Bacon sire du)
Cil de Monceals (Monceaux)
Cil de Monbrai (Roger)
Sire de Monfichet (Robert Guernon sire de)
Hue sire de Montfort
Rogier de Montgomeri
Quens Robert de Moretoing
Hue de Mortemer
Dam Willame des Molins (sire de Falaise)
Willame de Moion
L'Eveske Odun (of Bayeux)
Dam Richart Orbec (de Bienfaite et)
Cil d'Oillie
Sire de Pacy
Paienals des Monstiers-Hubert
Willame Patric de la Lande
Sire des Pins
Chevalier de Pirou
Cil de Port
Sire de Praères
Cil de Praels (Eudes Dapifer sire de Préaux)
Sire de Rebercil
Sire de Reviers
Dam Willame de Romare
Cil de Saint Cler
Cels de Saint Johan (Guillaume)
Sire de Saint-Martin
Néel de Saint-Salvéor (vicomte)
Seignor de Saint-Sever
Cil de Sap (Baudoin de Meules et)
Cil de Sacie
Cil de Saie
Cil de Sainteals (Cintheaux)
Sire de Semillie
Sire de Solignie
Taillefer (ménestrel)
Chamberlene de Tancharvile
Baron Raol Teisson de Cingueleiz
Baronz Tillières (Gilbert Crispin II)
Visquens de Toarz (also Dam Ameri de)
Del Tornéor
De Tornières
Cil de Touke (Touques)
Cil de Tracie
Cil de Trégoz
Trossebot
Cil d'Urinie (Origni)
Cil de Val de Saire (Guillaume d'Anneville)
Sire de Vaacie
Dam Willame de Vez-Pont
Cil de Vitrie

Cil d'Onebac (identity confused. *Vide* app. 6, Hamon Le Seneschal)
Le sire de Fontenai (Duplication for Robert Marmion)

Sire de Néauhou (identity confused. *Vide* Richard de Vernon, Néel de Saint-Sauveur and app. 7). De Courci and de Vitrie occur twice.

BENOÎT DE SAINTE-MORE

Robert, son of Roger de Beaumont
Comte Eustache (de Boulogne)
William Fitz Osberne
Count de Toarz (Eimeris)
Gautier Gifart
William de Warren

Taillefer
Hugh, count de Montfort
Robert comte d'Eu
Richard (William) comte d'Evreux
Roger de Montgomery
Robert, count of Mortain

Chronique de Benoît de Sainte-More, in *Chronique Anglo-Normands*, Michel, I, 167 to 303.

JOHN OF BROMPTON [1]

Maundevyle et Daundevyle
Seint-Aubyn et Seynt-Omer
Ounfravyle et Downfrevyle
Seynt-Fylbert Fyens et Gomer
Bolvyle et Baskarvyle
Turbevyle et Turbemer
Evyle et Clevyle
Gorges et Spenser
Morevyle et Colevyle
Brus et Boteler
Warbevyle et Carvyle
Crevequel et Seynt-Quinteyn
Botevyle et Stotevyle
Deverouge et Seynt-Martin
Deverous et Cavervyle
Seynt-Mor et Seynt-Leger
Mooun et Boun
Seynt-Vigor et Seynt-Per
Vipoun et Vinoun
Avynel et Paynell
Baylon et Bayloun
Peyvere et Peverell
Maris et Marmyoun
Rivers et Rivel
Agulis et Aguloun
Beauchamp et Beaupel
Chaumburleys et Chaumbursoun
Lou et Lovell
Ros et Druell
Vere et Vernoun
Mountabours et Mountsorell
Verdyers et Verdoun
Trussebot et Trussell
Cryel et Caroun
Bergos et Burnell
Dummer et Dommoun
Bra et Boterell
Hastyng et Cammois
Biset et Basset
Bardelfe Botes et Boys
Malevyle et Malet

Warenne et Wardeboys
Bonevyle et Bonet
Rodes et Deverois
Nervyle et Narbet
Auris et Argenten
Coynale et Corbet
Botetour et Boteveleyn
Mountayn et Mounfychet
Malebouch et Malemeyn
Geynevyle et Gyffard
Hautevyle et Hauteyn
Say et Seward
Danvey et Dyveyn
Chary et Chaward
Malure et Malvesyn
Pyryton et Pypard
Morten et Mortimer
Harecourt et Haunsard
Braunz et Columber
Musegrave et Musard
Seynt-Denis et Seynt-Cler
Mare et Mantravers
Fernz et Ferers
Ylebon Hyldebrond Holyon
Bernevyle et Berners
Loges et Seint-Lou
Cheyne et Chalers
Maubank et Seint-Malou
Daundon et Daungers
Wake et Wakevyle
Vessi Gray et Graungers
Coudree et Knevyle
Bertram et Bygod
Scales et Clermount
Traylliz et Tragod
Beauvys et Beaumount
Penbri et Pypotte
Mouns et Mountchampe
Freyn et Folyot
Nowers et Nowchaumpe
Dapisoun et Talbote

[1] This roll and those following are not indexed.

Percy Crus et Lacy
Sanzayer et Saunford
Quiney et Tracy
Vadu et Vatorte
Stokes et Somery
Montagu et Mounford
Seynt Johan et Seynt-Jay
Forneus et Fornyvaus
Greyle et Seynt-Walry
Valens Yle et Vaus
Pynkeney et Panely
Clarel et Claraus
Mohant et Mountchensy
Aubevyle et Seynt-Amauns
Loveyn et Lucy
Agantez et Dragans
Artoys et Arcy
Malerbe et Maudut
Grevyle et Courcy

Brewes et Chaudut
Arras et Cressy
Fizowres et Fiz de lou
Merle et Moubray
Cantemor et Cantelou
Gornay et Courtnay
Braybuffe et Huldbynse
Haustlayng et Tornay
Bolebeke et Molyns
Husee et Husay
Moleton et Besyle
Pounchardon et Pomeray
Richford et Desevyle
Longevyle et Longespay
Watervyle et Dayvyle
Peyns et Pountlarge
Nebors et Nevyle
Straunge et Sauvage
Hynoys Burs Burgenou

Roll published in his *Chronicle,* 1436.

WILLIAM OF WORCESTER

Bastard	Seintbrewel	Haket	Wilbi
Baignard	Trainel	Trivet	Mornele
Brassard	Clarel	Burdet	Sacchevile
Maignard	Fresel	Bret	Bernevile
Berard	Wadel	Luci	Greinvile
Mawreward	Trussel	Laci	Boitevile
Boignard	Condrel	Limeci	Frivile
Hansard	Burnel	Simeli	Lungevile
Hasard	Burfel	Munteni	Fressevile
Ayelard	Peverel	Barri	Folmile
Achard	Avenel	Berri	Brevile
Swiward	Viel	Courti	Canvile
Soilard	Spigurnel	Traci	Carevile
Ward	Toret	Braci	Cardevile
Doreward	Tainet	Aukeni	Asprevile
Wichard	Tupz	Parli	Colevile
Musard	Butet	Cunli	Torevile
Hard	Bonett	Cicerli	Barvile
Giffard	Malett	Cresci	Stuntevile
Pipard	Bluet	Arci	Butevile
Pichard	Brachet	Perci	Hunsrevile
Gerard	Belet	Veili	Nevile
Fassard	Ledet	Soleni	Grenvile
Ailard	Pilet	Vesei	Turbevile
Morelle	Palet	Muntchanensi	Spinevile
Martelle	Touchet	Meisi	Arvile
Painelle	Basset	Gangi	Sandervile
Pinel	Buket	Herci	Amundevile
Putrel	Duket	Moungomeri	Wivile
Purcel	Piket	Someri	Osevile
Chainel	Mulet	Akeni	Grounvile
Ridel	Baret	Pleisi	Abbevile
Russelle	Mounfichet	Paveli	Somervile
Blundel	Punchet	Auden	Senevile
Maunsel	Pachet	Quinsi	Baskervile
Torchapelle	Corbet	Tonni	Hanvile
Charnel	Biset	Hai	Hantevile
Tirel	Hanet	Sai	Andevile
Torel	Livet	Darci	Dunstervile
Sourel	Hacket	Masci	Sourvile

Widevile	Sentoiner	Clare	Coubrei
Maundevile	Archer	Fenis	Sancei
Albemarle	Maleverer	Punegsyce	Annei
Lungchampe	Bou.hchier	Eurons	Bussei
Nuncchampe	Husier	Mauns	Keines
Feskampe	Ver	Waldebef	Freignes
Beauchampe	Sintleger	Gras	Curcei
Mounford	Gunter	Bardulf	Lescei
Mountagu	Travers	Fantulf	Delamare
Mounbrai	Mautervers	Rochele	Zetche
Ferebrace	Vilers	Fizbrian	Camage
Feteplace	Prers	Mareis	Gauter
Bars	Morins	Britoñ	Hubert
Quartermars	Bigood	Frisoñ	Lambert
Perpunt	Bagot	Grauntsoñ	Mareschal
Fizsimunds	Talbot	Valens	Drumassal
Aubrei	Tibotot	Lovel	Nizunt
Fisgesrai	Cabot	Courthose	Trussbert
Fizpers	Gaunt	Feriters	Seignes
Fizwater	Passeauaunt	Foliambre	Rennes
Passemer	Lincot	Richemont	Chawis
Mortemer	Lovetot	Roos	Sintchiz
Poer	Pikot	Gurnai	Sintmoriz
Renger	Muelent	Corateis	Cantlou
Roter	Duredent	Santmareis	Bozmr
Beler	Tiptot	Beaumeis	Bran
Boner	Fornivale	Bleis	Escot
Botener	Drival	Greis	Kirketot
Butler	Surdeival	Wasteneis	Tailpais
Seler	Orival	Courteneis	Martimas
Despenser	Meigne	Pulein	Kusas
Budler	Cheine	Malmani	Murdas
Saucer	Niemarche	Chastelein	Gorge
Chaucer	Burle	Chamberlein	Sintgorge
Ferrer	Savage	Butevilein	Yvoire
Gorger	Sintjon	Mortein	Sintjour
Miler	Garmmemil	Carli	Leini
Sanzaver	Barl	Brok	Mortein
Gower	Fizhu	Heris	Figarvi
Leverer	Fizurs	Morlei	Kosni
Sentcler	Fizherberd	Monfrei	

Hearne stated that this roll was compiled in 1419, but William of Worcester was only four years of age then (*vide* addenda).

GUILLAUME LE TAILLEUR

I haue thought good to publish the names of them as heretofore I haue done, out of the Chronicles of Normandie, gathered by William Tayleur of Rhoane. (Stowe).

To wit Odo Byshoppe of Baion: Robert Earle of Mortaigne: These two were brethren of Duke William by his mother: Bandonni of Buillou: Roger Earle of Beamont, that was surnamed with the Beard, of him came the linage of Mellent.

Guilliam Mallet	Le sire de Feugiers
Guilliam Fitz Osberne	Henry sire de Ferrers
Le sir de Montfort sus Rille	Le sire Dambemare
Guilliam de vielz Pont	Guilliam sire de Romare
Neel de Saint-Saueur le vicont	Le sire de Lichare

Le sire de Tonque
Le sire de la Mare
Le sire de Nehabon
Le sire de Piron
Le sire de Beauson
Le sire de Damnon
Le sire de Soteuile
Le sire de Margneuille
Le sire de Tankeruille
Eustace Dambleuille
Le sire de Magneuille
Le sire de Grimsuille
Guilliam Crespin
Le sire de Sainct-Martin
Guilliam de Moulinous
Le sire de Pins
Gieffray sire de Mayenne
Affroy de Behunt
Affroy & Mauigr, de Cartaict
Guilliam de Garennes
Hue de Gournay sire le de Bray
Le Conte Hue de Gournay
Enguemount le Laigle
Le vicont de Touars
Richart Donnemchni
Le sire de Biars
Le sire de Salligny
Le Boutellier Daubegny
Le sire de Marre
Le sire de Victry
Le sire de Lacy
Le sire du vall Darie
Le sire de Tracy
Hue sire de Montfor
Le sire de Piqgny
Hamon de Brayen
Le sire de Spinay
Le sire de Port
Le sire de Torchy
Le sire de Iort
Le sire de Riuers
Guilliam Moyon
Raoul Tesson de Chignelois
Rogier Marmion
Raoul de Gael
Aue Neel de Biars
Parnel du Monstier
Bertram le Tort
Hubert Robert
Le sire de Seukee
Le sire de Dormal
Le sire de Brenall
Le sire de Sainct-Iehan
Le sire de Bois
Le sire de Homme
Le sire de Saussay
Le sire de Cailly
Le sire de Semilly
Le sire de Tilly
Le sire de Romely
Martell de Basqueuill
Le sire de Praux
Le sire de Gonys
Le sire de Sainteaulx
De Mullox

These Archers of the vale of Rueill, *and of* Bretueill, *and of many other places.*

Le sire de Sainct-Saen
Le sire de la Rimer
Le sire de Salnarinlle
Le sire de Tony
Eude de Beaugien
Le sire de Ollie
Le sire de Sacy
Le Sire de Vassye
Le Bisquams de Chaymes
Le Sire de Sap
Le sire Duglosse
Le sire de Nime
Le sire de Blamuille
Le sire de Brencon
Le vidam de Partenay
Raoult de Mormont
Pierre de Bailleul
Sir de Fescamp
Le sire de Beaufault
Le sire de Tillieres
Le sire de Pacy
Le Seneschall de Torchy
Le sire de Gacy
Le sire de Doully
Le sire de Sancy
Le sire de Bacy
Le sire de Tourneur
Le sire de Praores
Guilliam de Colombiers
Hue sire de Bollebec
Richart sire Dorbec ╲_ ?
Le sire de Donnebos
Le sire de trois gros
Le sire Mont Fiquet
Hue le Vigot *alias* Bigot de Maletot
Le sire de la Haye
Le sire de Bracy
Le sire de Moubray
Le sire de Say
Le sire de Lasert
Bonteuillam Tronsebours
Guilliam Patris de la Land
Hue de Mortemer
Le sire Donuiller
Le sire Donnebant
Le sire de Sainct-Cler
Robert le fits Herneys duke Dorlians
Le sire de Harecourt
Le sire Creuecure
Le sire de Dancourt
Le sire de Brunetot
Le sire de Cambray
Le sire Dauncy
Le sire Fonteney
Le Counte Deureux
Le sire de Roberchil
Alan sergent Counte de Britaigne
Le sire de Sainct-Wallery
Le Counte Deden
Gualtar Guisart, Counte de Longneuille
Le sire de Scouteuille
Le Counte Thomas Danbinale

Guilliam de Hoimes & Darques
Le sire de Barreuile
Le sire de Breante
Le sire de Freanuile
Le sire de Panilly

Le sire de Clere
Tostamdubec
Le sire de Mangny
Roger du Mont Gomery Comes
Almary de Touaers

Annales or Generall Chronicle of England, begun first by maister John Stowe, continued and published by Edmond Howes in 1615 (pp. 103–4–5).

Copies of this roll were made by Fox, Holinshed and Stowe concerning which Fuller says: " This catalogue is taken out of Guilliam Tayleur, a Norman chronicler of good credit. But the worst is we want Tayleur's French original ; and I fear it hath passed through some butcher's hands before it came to us. For there be three editions thereof in our English historians, which like the feet of a badger, fall out of unequal length, so different the number of names therein " (*Church History of England*, 245–6).

Guillaume le Tailleur published the *Cronicques de Normandie* in 1487.

LELAND

[Alphabetically arranged]

Aumarill et Deyncourt
Audel et Aungeloun
Argenteyn et Avenele
Sainct Amande et Adryelle
Avenel et S-Amary
Aimeris et Aveneris

Bertrem et Buttencourt
Biard et Biford
Bardolf et Basset
Bigot et Boown
Baillof et Boundeville
Briansoun et Baskerville
Burnel et Buttevillain
Bruys et Dispencer
Boys et Boteler
Brabasoun et Bevers
Braund et Baybof
Bruys et Burgh
Bavent et Bussy
Bretonn et Blundet
Baius et Bluett
Banestre et Bekard
Bealum et Beauchamp
Baudyn et Bray
Burdet et Boroun
Baudewyn et Beaumont
Blundet et Burdoun
Barray et Bretevile
Blounte et Boseville
Benny et Boyvile
Broth et Barbedor
Baret et Bourte
Byngard et Bernevale
Bonet et Barry
Brian et Bidin
Buscel et Bevery
Bernevile et Bretevile
Belew et Bertin
Broy et Bromevile
Bleyn et Breicourt
Busard et Belevile

Camoys et Cameville
Chavent et Chauncy
Chaumberlayn et Chaumberoun
Comyn et Columber
Corby et Gorbet
Chaundoys et Chaward
Challouns et Challeys
Clerevalx et Clarel
Chapes et Chaudut
Cauntelow et Coubray
Cresry et Courteny
Constable et Tally
Champeneys et Chanceus
Coursoun et Courtevile
Chartres et Chenil

Deyville et Darcy
Daubenay et Deverelle
Denyas et Druel
Delahay et Haunsard
Dodingle et Darell
De Lalaund et de l'Isle
De la Pole et Pinkeney
De Wake et De la War
De la Marche et De la Mare
Dakeny et Dautre
Diseney et Dabernoun
Damary et Deveroys
Daverenges et Duylly
De la Rivers et Revel
Destraunges et Delatoun
Dulee et De la Laund
De la Valet et Veylaund
Damot et Damay
Duraunt et Doreny
Disart et Doynell
De la Huse et Howell

Estraunge et Estoteville

Fererers et Foleville
Fiz Walter et Werdoun

Fenes et Felebert
Fitz Roger et Fitz Robert
Fovecourt et Feniers
Fitz Philip et Fliot
Fourneux et Fournivau
Fitz Alayne et Gilebof
Fitz William et Watervile
Fitz Robert et Fitz Aleyne
Fitz Ralph et Rosel
Fitz Brian et Bracy
Fryville et Fressel
Fitz Rouf et Filiol
Fitz Thomas et Tibol
Fitz Morice et S-More
Fitz Hugh et Fitz Henry
Fitz Arviz et Esturmy
Fitz Raynald et Roscelin
Fitz Marmaduke et Mountrivel
Fitz Eustace et Eustacy
Fermbaud et Frisoun
Fichent et Trivet

Gurnay et Greilly
Graunson et Tracy
Gorgeise et Gower
Griketot et Grevequer
Gaunt et Garre
Genevile et Gifard
Gaugy et Gobaude
Gray et Graunson
Galofer et Gubion
Grymward et Geroun
Glancourt et Chaumont
Graundyn et Gerdoun

Hautein et Hauville
Hastings et Haulley
Hurell et Husee
Hercy et Heroun
Heryce et Harecourt
Hayward et Henour
Hameline et Hareville

Jardin et Jay

Kymarays et Kyriel
Kanceis et Kevelers

Loveyne et Lascy
Lymesey et Latymer
Lungvilers et S-Ligiere
Loveday et Lovel
Lenias et Levecote
Lascels et Lovein
Longvil et Longespe
Loverak et Longchaump
Lifford et Osevile
Loring et Loterel
Lisours et Longvale
La Muile et Lownay
Liof et Limers

Mohaut et Mooun
Morley et Moundevile
Moubray et Morvile

Meneville et Mauley
Malebuche et Malemayn
Morteine et Mortimer
Muse et Martine
Mountburgh et Mounsorel
Maleville et Malet
Mounfey et Mounfichet
Maleberge et Marre
Mussegros et Musard
Maingun et Montravers
Merkingfel et Mourreis
Montagu et Mountfort
Mautalent et Maudict
Maunys et Meulos
Mortivaux et Monthensy
Mallop et Marny
Maihermer et Muschet
Menyle et Maufe
Maucovenant et Mounpinson
Maoun et Mainard
Malebys et Mounceus
Myriet et Morley
Mauliverer et Mouncy
Mauclerk et Maners
Musteys et Merlay
Mauches et Mascy
Movet et S-Martine
Male Kake et Mauncel
Mangysir et Mauveysin
Maulovel et Maurewarde

Neners et Nereville
Newmarch et Newbet
Neville et Newburgh
Nairmere et Fitz Neel

Otinel et S-Thomer
Onatule et Cheyni
Oysel et Olifard

Pygot et Percy
Power et Panel, *alias* Paignel
Peche et Peverelle
Perot et Pykarde
Poynce et Pavely
Paifrer et Plukenet
Peverel et Fitz Payne
Pikard et Pinkadoun
Perpounte et Fitz Peris
Pugoys et Paiteny
Perrers et Pavillioun
Percehay et Pereris

Quincy et S-Quintine
Querru et Coigners

Ros et Ridel
Ryvers et Ryvel
Rugetius et Fitz Rohaut
Ry et Rokell
Rysers et Reynevil
Rivers et Ripere

Soucheville, Coudray et Colleville
S-Cloyis et S-Clere

Sainct Amande et Adryelle
Someraye et Howarde
Saunzaver et Saunford
Sainct Tese et Sauvay
Souley et Soules
Sorel et Somery
S-John et S-Jory
S-Leo et Luscy
Saunzpour et Fitz Simon
Salvayn et Say
Sesee et Solers
Sovereng et Suylly
Surdevale et Sengryn
S-Barbe et Sageville

Tregos et Treylly
Tuchet et Trussell
Takel et Talbot
Tourbeville et Tipitot
Thays et Tony
Tuk et Tany
Thorny et Thornille
Tyriet et Turley
Tolimer et Treville
Tourys et Tay

Tingez et Gruyele
Tinel et Traville
Tolet et Tisoun
Tarteray et Chercourt

Vipount et Umfraville
Veer et Vinoun
Vuasteneys et Waville
Vescy et Verders
Valence et Vaus
Vavasør et Warroys
Verbois et Wacelay
Vallonis et Vernoun
Vendour et Veroun
Venables et Venour
Vilain et Valeris
Vernoun et Waterville

Warenne et Wauncy
Waville et Warley
Waloys et Levele
Wace et Wyvile
Warde et Werlay
Walangay et Fitzwarin
Wemerlay et Wamervile

Roll published in Leland's *De Rebus Britannicis Collectanea,* edited by Hearne and published in 1715 (163 years after his death), and reprinted in 1770.

THE BATTLE ABBEY ROLL

OF

HOLINSHED AND DUCHESNE

HOLINSHED	DUCHESNE	HOLINSHED	DUCHESNE
A		**B**	
Aumarle	Aumerle	Bertram	Bertram
Aincourt		Buttecourt	Buttecourt
Audeley	Audeley	Brebus and Byseg	Bræhus
Adgillam	Angilliam		Byseg
Argentoune	Argentoun	Bardolfe	Bardolf
Arundell	Arundell	Basset and Bigot	Basset
Auenant	Auenant	Bohun	Bohun
Abell	Abel	Bailif	Baylife
Auuerne		Bondeuile	Bondeuile
Aunwers		Brabason	Barbason
Angers	Avvgers	Baskeruile	
Angenoun	Angenoun		Beer
Archere	Archer	Bures	Bures
Anuay		Bounilaine	Bonylayne
Asperuile	Asperuile	Bois	
Abbeuile		Botelere	
Andeuile		Bourcher	
Amouerduile	Amonerduile	Brabaion	Barbayon
Arcy and Akeny	Arey	Berners	Berners
	Akeny	Braibuf	Braybuf
Albeny	Albeny	Brande and Bronce	Brand
Aybeuare			Bonuile
Amay		Burgh	Burgh
Aspermound	Asperemound	Bushy	Busshy
Amerénges		Banet	
		Blondell	Blundell

HOLINSHED	DUCHESNE	HOLINSHED	DUCHESNE
Breton	Breton	Blundell	Blundel
	Belasyse	Burdet	Burdet
	Bowser	Bagot	Bigot
Bluat and Baious	Bayons		Beaupount
	Bulmere	Beauuise	
Browne	Broune	Belemis	
Beke	Beke	Beisin	
Bickard		Bernon	
	Bowlers	Boels	Bools
Banastre	Banestre	Belefroun	Belefroun
Baloun		Brutz	
	Belomy	Barchampe	Barchampe
	Belknape		
Beauchampe	Beauchamp		C
Bray and Bandy	Bandy		
Bracy		Camois	Camos
Boundes		Camuille	Chanuille
Bascoun		Chawent	Chawent
Broilem		Chauncy	Chancy
Broleuy	Broyleby	Conderay	Couderay
Burnell	Burnel	Coluile	Coluile
Bellet	Belot	Chamberlaine	Chamberlaine
	Beufort	Chamburnoun	Chambernoune
Baudewin	Baudewine	Comin	
Beaumont		Columber	
Burdon	Burdon	Cribett	Cribet
Berteuilay	Bertevyley	Creuquere	
Barre	Barte	Corbine	Corbine
Busseuile	Busseuile	Corbett	Corbet
Blunt	Blunt		Coniers
Beaupere	Beawper	Chaundos	Chaundos
Beuill			Coucy
Barduedor		Chaworth	Chaworthe
Brette	Bret	Cleremaus	Claremaus
Barrett	Barret	Clarell	Clarell
Bonrett		Chopis	
Bainard			Camnine
Barniuale	Barneuale	Chaunduit	Chaunduyt
Bonett			Claruays
Barry	Barry	Chantelow	Chantilowe
Bryan		Chamberaye	
Bodin	Bodyt		Colet
Beteuile	Berteuile	Cressy	Cressy
Bertin	Bertine	Curtenay	Courtenay
Bereneuile		Conestable	Constable
Bellewe	Belew		Chancer
Beuery		Cholmeley	Cholmelay
Busshell	Buschell		Corleuile
Boranuile		Champney	Champeney
Browe			Carew
Beleuers	Beleners	Chawnos	Chawnos
Buffard	Buffard	Comiuile	
Boteler	Boteler		Claruaile
Bonueier		Champaine	Champain
Boteuile	Botuile	Careuile	
Bellire		Carbonelle	Carbonell
Bastard		Charles	Charles
Bainard		Chereberge	Chareberge
Brasard	Brasard	Chawnes	Chawnes
Beelhelme	Belhelme	Chaumont	Chawmont
Braine		Caperoun	
Brent		Cheine	Cheyne
Braunch	Braunche	Curson	Cursen
Belesuz	Bolesur	Couille	Conell

HOLINSHED	DUCHESNE
Chaiters	Chayters
Cheines	Cheynes
Cateray	Cateray
Cherecourt	Cherecourt
Cammile	Chaunuile
Clerenay	Clereney
Curly	Curly
Cuily	
Clinels	
Chaundos	
Courteney	
Clifford	Clyfford

D

HOLINSHED	DUCHESNE
Denauille	Deauuile
Dercy	Dercy
Diue	Dine
Dispencere	Dispencer
Daubeny	
Daniell	Daniel
Denise and Druell	Denyse
	Druell
Deuaus	Devaus
Dauers	Dauers
Dodingsels	Doningsels
Darell	Darell
Delaber	Delabere
Delapole	De la Pole
Delalinde	De la Lind
Delahill	De la Hill
Delaware	De la Wate
Delauache	De la Watche
Dakeny	Dakeny
Dauntre	Dauntre
Desny	Desuye
Dabernoune	Dabernoune
Damry	Damry
Daueros	Daueros
Dauonge	
Duilby	
Delauere	De la Vere
Delahoid	
Durange	
Delee	De Liele
Delaund	
Delaward	De la Warde
Delaplanch	De la Planch
Damnot	
Danway	Danway
Dehense	De Hewse
Deuile	
Disard	Disard
Doiuile	
Durant	Durant
Drury	Diury
Dabitot	
Dunsteruile	
Dunchampe	
Dambelton	

E

HOLINSHED	DUCHESNE
Estrange	Estrange
Estuteuile	Estutauille
	Escriols
Engaire	Engayne
Estriels	
	Euers
Esturney	Esturney

F

HOLINSHED	DUCHESNE
Ferrerers	
Foluille	Foluile
Fitz Water	Fitz Water
Fitz Marmaduke	Fitz Marmadux
Fleuez	
Filberd	Fiberd
Fitz Roger	Fitz Roger
	Fitz Robert
Fauecourt	Fanecourt
Ferrers	
Fitz Philip	Fitz Philip
Filiot	
Furniueus	
Furniuaus	
Fitz Otes	
Fitz William	Fitz William
Fitz Roand	
Fitz Pain	Fitz Paine
Fitz Auger	
Fitz Aleyn	Fitz Alyne
Fitz Rauff	Fitz Raulfe
Fitz Browne	Fitz Browne
Fouke	Foke
Freuil	Freuile
Front de Boef	
Facunberge	Faconbrige
Fort	
Frisell	Frissell
Fitz Simon	
Fitz Fouk	
Filioll	Filioll
Fitz Thomas	Fitz Thomas
Fitz Morice	Fitz Morice
Fitz Hugh	Fitz Hugh
Fitz Henrie	
Fitz Waren	Fitz Warren
Fitz Rainold	
Flamuile	Faunuile
Formay	Formay
Fitz Eustach	
Fitz Laurence	
Formibaud	Formiband
Frisound	Frison
Finere and Fitz Robert	Finer
	Fitz Vrcy
Furniuale	Furniuall
Fitz Geffrey	
Fitz Herbert	Fitzs Herbert
Fitz Peres	
Fichet	
Fitz Rewes	
Fitz Fitz	
Fitz Iohn	Fitz Iohn
Fleschampe	

HOLINSHED	DUCHESNE	HOLINSHED	DUCHESNE
		Ierconuise	
	G	Ianuile	Ianuile
Gurnay		Iasperuile	Iasparuile
	Gargraue		
Gressy			**K**
Graunson	Graunson	Kaunt	
Gracy	Gracy	Karre	Karre
Georges		Karrowe	Karron
	Glanuile	Koine	
Gower	Gouer	Kimaronne	
Gaugy		Kiriell	Kyriell
Goband		Kancey	
	Gascoyne	Kenelre	
Gray	Gray		
Gaunson			**L**
Golofre	Golofer		
Gobion			Lestrange
Grensy		Loueny	Leuony
Graunt	Grauns	Lacy	
Greile		Linneby	
Greuet		Latomer	Latomere
Gurry		Loueday	Loueday
Gurley	Gurly		Logenton
Grammort		Louell	Leuel
Gernoun			Lescrope
Grendon		Lemare	Lemare
Gurdon	Gurdon	Leuetot	
Gines			Litterile
Griuil		Lucy	Lucy
Greneuile		Luny	
Glateuile			Lislay, or Liele
Gurney		Logeuile	
Giffard		Longespes	Longspes
Gouerges		Louerace	
Gamages	Gamages	Longechampe	Lonschampe
	Gaunt	Lascales	Lastels
		Lacy	
	H		Lindsey
Haunteny		Louan	
Haunsard	Hansard	Leded	
Hastings	Hastings	Luse	
Hanlay	Haulay	Loterell	Loterel
Haureil		Loruge	
Husee	Husie	Longeuale	Longuaile
Hercy			Lewawse
Herioun		Loy	Loy
Herne	Herne	Lorancourt	
Harecourt		Loions	
Henoure		Limers	
Houell		Longepay	
Hamelin	Hamelyn	Laumale	
Harewell	Harewell	Lane	Laue
Hardell	Hardel		Le Despenser
Hakett	Hecket	Louetot	
Hamound	Hamound		
Harcord	Harecord		**M**
		Mohant	
	I	Mowne	
		Maundeuile	
Iarden	Iarden	Marmilon	Marmilon
Iay	Iay	Moribray	Moribray
Ieniels		Moruile	Moruile

HOLINSHED	DUCHESNE	HOLINSHED	DUCHESNE
Miriell		Mountlouel	
Manlay	Manley	Mawreward	
Malebraunch	Malebranche	Monhaut	
Malemaine	Malemaine	Meller	
	Muschampe	Mountgomerie	
Mortimere		Manlay	
	Musgraue	Maulard	
	Mesni-le-Villers		Menpincoy
Mortimaine	Mortmaine	Mainard	Mainard
Muse	Muse	Menere	
Marteine	Marteine		Morell
Mountbother	Mountbocher	Martinast	
Mountsoler		Mare	
Maleuile	Maleuile		Morley
Malet			Mountmartin
Mounteney	Mountney		yners
Monfichet			Mauley
Maleherbe	Maleherbe	Mainwaring	Mainwaring
Mare		Matelay	
Musegros	Musgros	Malemis	
Musard	Musard		Mantell
Moine		Maleheire	
Montravers	Mautrauers	Moren	
Merke	Merke	Melun	
Murres	Murres	Marceans	
Mortiuale		Maiell	Mayel
Monchenesy		Morton	Morton
Mallory			
Marny		**N**	
Mountagu	Montagu	Noers	
Mountford		Neuile	Neuile
Maule		Newmarch	Neumarche
Monhermon			Norton
Musett		Norbet	Norbet
Meneuile		Norice	Norece
Manteuenant and		Newborough	Newborough
Manfe		Neiremet	
Menpincoy		Neile	Neele
Maine		Normauile	Normanuile
Mainard		Neofmarch	
Morell		Nermitz	
Mainell		Nembrutz	
Maleluse			
Memorous		**O**	
Morreis		Oteuell	Otenel
Morleian Maine		Olibef	Olibef
Maleuere		Olifant	Olifaunt
	Montalent	Osenel	
Mandut	Mandute	Oisell	Oysell
Mountmarten		Olifard	Oliford
Mantelet		Orinall	
	Manle	Orioll	Oryoll
Miners			
	Malory	**P**	
Mauclerke		Pigot	Pigot
	Merny	Pery	Pecy
Maunchenell		Perepount	Perecount
Mouet		Pershale	Pershale
Meintenore		Power	Power
	Muffet	Painell	Paynel
Meletak		Perche and Pauey	Peche
Manuile		Peurell	Peuerell
Mangisere		Perot	Perot
Maumasin			

HOLINSHED	DUCHESNE	HOLINSHED	DUCHESNE
Picard	Picard	Seucheus	
	Pudsey	Senclere	
Pinkenie		Sent Quintin	Seint Quintine
Pomeray	Pimeray	Sent Omere	Seint Omer
Pounce	Pounsey	Sent Amond	Seint Amand
Pauely		Sent Legere	Seint Leger
Paifrere		Someruile	Soueruile
Plukenet		Siward	
Phuars		Saunsouere	
Punchardoun	Punchardon	Sanford	Sanford
Pinchard	Pynchard	Sanctes	
Placy	Placy	Sauay	
Pugoy		Saulay	
Patefine	Patine	Sules	
Place		Sorell	
Pampilioun	Pampilion	Somerey	Somery
Percelay		Sent Iohn	
Perere and Pekeny		Sent George	Seint George
Poterell	Poterell	Sent Les	Seint Lés
Peukeney	Pekeney	Sesse	
	Perwinke	Saluin	Sauine
Peccell		Say	
Pinell		Solers	
Putrill		Saulay	
Petiuoll			Seint Clo
Preaus		Sent Albin	Seint Albine
Pantolf		Sent Martin	
Peito		Sourdemale	
Penecord	Penicord	Seguin	
Preudirlegast		Sent Barbe	Seinte Barbe
Perciuale		Sent Vile	
		Souremount	
Q		Soreglise	
Quinci	Quincy	Sanduile	Sandeuile
Quintiny	Quintine	Sauncey	
		Sirewast	
R		Sent Cheueroll	
		Sent More	Seint M
Ros	Rose	Sent Scudemore	Seint S.
Ridell	Ridle		
Riuers		**T**	
Riuell	Rynel		
Rous	Rous		Tows
Rushell	Russel	Toget	Toget
Raband			Talybois
Ronde	Rond	Tercy	
Rie		Tuchet	Tuchet
Rokell		Tracy	
Risers			Truslot
Randuile		Trousbut	Trusbu
Roselin		Trainell	Trayne
Rastoke		Taket	Taket
Rinuill		Trussel and Trison	
Rougere		Talbot	Talbot
Rait		Touny	
Ripere		Traies	
Rigny		Tollemach	
Richemound	Richmond	Tolous	
Rochford	Rocheford	Tanny	Tanny
Raimond	Reymond	Touke	
		Tibtote	Tibtote
S			Trussell
Souch	Seuche	Turbeuile	Turbeuill
Sheuile		Turuile	Turuile

HOLINSHED	DUCHESNE
Tomy and Tauerner	
Trencheuile	
Trenchelion	
Tankeruile	
Tirell	
Triuet	
Tolet	
Trauers	
Tardeuile	
Turburuile	
Tineuille	
Torell	Torel
	Tauers
Tortechappell	
	Torel
Trusbote	
Treuerell	
	Tirell
Tenwis	
Totelles	Totels
	Tauerner
V	
Vere	
Vernoun	
Vescy	
Verdoune	
Valence	Valence
Verdeire	
	Vancord
Vauasour	Vauasour
Vendore	Vender
Verlay	
	Verder
Valanger	
	Verdon
	Aubrie de Vere
	Vernoun
lan	
land	Verland

HOLINSHED	DUCHESNE
Valers	
	Verlay
	Vernois
Veirny	Verny
Vauuruile	
	Vilan
Veniels	
	Vmframuile
Verrere	
Vschere	
Veffay	
Vanay	
Vian	
Vernoys	
Vrnall	
Vnket	Vnket
	Vrnall
Vrnafull	
Vasderoll	
Vaberon	
Valingford	
Venicorde	
Valiue	
Viuille	
Vancorde and	
Valenges	
W	
Wardebois	
Ward	
Wafre	
Wake	Wake
	Waledger
	Warde
	Wardebus
Wareine	Waren
Wate	Wate
Watelin	Wateline
Wateuil	Wateuile
Wely	Woly
Werdonell	
Wespaile	
Wiuell	Wyuell

...nshed published his roll in 1577 and Duchesne's appeared early in the 17th century.

SCRIVEN *ALIAS* FOX

followeth the Sirnames of the Cheife Noblemen, and

nen, which came into England, with William *the Conquerour,*

according as I found them fet downe in a very auncient
Role, which Role I receiued of Maifter *Thomas*
Scriuen Efquire, in whofe handes
it remayned at the publication of this Booke. (Stowe.)

	Auenel	Amile	Aubrey
uerenges	Aspreuil	Aunmiduile	Archer
Aielard	Audeny	Abbeuile	
Alard	Akein	Anduile	Bastarde
Aubeny	Arcy	Albemarke	Baignard

Baruile
Brassard
Berad
Boygnard
Barkaruile
Baret
Basset
Bars
Belet
Beil
Breit
Boneit
Bluet
Brachet
Buket
Biset
Blundel
Burdet
Blete
Barry
Berri
Bracy
Brenenile
Bounttuile
Butenile
Beamehampe
Burnel
Bussel
Beleice
Bonere
Bodler
Botiler
Bogod
Burle
Baul
Brenbe
Brus
Butelem
Bricourt
Brian
Boch
Bozim
Bion
Bailoil
Brocheris
Bardulfe
Bancan
Bussey
Beamuis
Bleis
Bauentre

Camule
Carenile
Cardcuile
Condrey
Cursey
Cautlon
Caily
Corbet
Clare
Curtais
Curthose
Chamlin
Costentin

Comthense
Cozmir
Chalenges
Chastlem
Courtueis
Chawers
Curty
Conun
Crioile
Charles
Chen
Chaucer
Chandos
Cunly
Curly
Crely
Colenile
Cabot
Charnel
Chamel
Charel
Cheinie

Darcy
Dunsteruile
Douchampe
Despenser
Duredent
Driuall
Duket
Dreward
Delamare
Drunall
Dela
Denicourt

Eurous
Estotkirke

Faherburt
Fossard
Fresel
Freuile
Fressenile
Folenile
Firmunde
Fizgeffray
Firpers
Fizwaters
Feskampe
Fizhu
Fizurs
Ferrer
Fornitall
Fineis
Fizbrian
Frison
Ferers
Fohamble
Frignes
Fizgariz
Formentin

Gangy
Greminle

Gieunile
Gornumile
Gemule
Gerard
Giffard
Gondrel
Gorger
Goner
Gigod
Gaibit
Giptot
Garin
Gunter
Gras
Grauntson
Gournay
Greis
Gamage
Gautere
Gorge

Hamule
Hantuile
Humchampe
Herebrace
Henile
Herenile
Hauet
Hachet
Haket
Haruy
Hanesy
Hersy
Hai
Hasard
Hausard
Hasser
Hubert
Hamelin
Harecurte
Hus
Hense

Iardin

Kemes
Keines
Kusac
Kosin
Kamais

Laci
Liar
Lunecy
Luret
Lucy
Lidet
Linguenile
Leuener
Licot
Lonecot
Louell
Lescei
Lambert
Lenn

Limare
Lisle
La

Maignard
Maureward
Mountford
Mountague
Mountbray
Maundeuile
Mortmer
Mansel
Maschy
Mungomer
Moruile
Meisy
Munty
Mounteni
Mulet
Mumfichet
Martell
Morell
Musard
Maleit
Milere
Moleuorer
Manturners
Moreijs
Muelent
Meigne
Menul
Manne
Maceis
Mabuom
Mortem
Manfey
Maresthall
Morley
Martinas
Murdacke
Metun
Mameisin
Morin
Mire
Morim

Neemarch
Nepunt

Orniall
Oseuile
Orware

Passemer
Passenaunt
Picot
Pooruanger
Pers
Purcel
Pichard
Pypard
Pamel
Panel
Piterel
Penerel
Pleisy

Paueli	Seintenile	Seintlis	Truan
Pilet	Somery	Seintmoris	Tener
Parly	Say	Seintgorge	Tisiure
Palet	Suncli	Seintiore	Tayleboys
Piket	Sorel	Seint-quintin	
Percy	Seteplace	Seintmore	Verer
Punchet	Spiuenile	Sauntzire	Vilers
Pachet	Saundernile	Saintchy	Vesty
Punis	Sonule	Setuans	Vinframile
Pandulfe	Soler	Seinte-royiz	Veily
Pulem	Sourrile	Seinteleme	Vaieus
Penir	Stutenile		Veisin
Penne	Soleny	Toret	Vorill
Phanecourt	Spigurnel	Tauit	Venur
Pales	Seintbrenel	Turpet	Vauasue
Prouz	Soylard	Tramel	Vaus
Pirim	Swywar	Torchapel	
Peisim	Saucer	Tonny	
Parteben	Sausauer	Trussel	Wydenile
Puntfrait	Seniler	Tuchet	Wimle
	Saintcler	Toreuile	Wilby
Quinsi	Senittomer	Treuet	Wadel
Quatramars	Seintleger	Tirel	Ward
	Saundenall	Trans	Wyschard
Russel	Sauage	Talebot	Waldeboef
Rydel	Semtion	Turbenile	Wastueis
Roter	Saint-mareis	Tracy	Warem
Rochell	Saucei	Trussebut	Weirim
Rooz	Sal	Toc	
Richmount	Seignes	Tailpas	Yuoire

Roll in Stowe's work by Howes.

RESEARCHES OF THE BAYEUX TAPESTRY

Wace did not write down the names of all the seigniors who helped the duke of Normandy in his expedition. From our researches we are certain there exist in our province many families which had branches established in England at the time and since the conquest and have kept the same name and very often the same arms. But as those names are not written on the catalogue of Wace we give hereunder the names we found through our researches (L'abbé de La Rue).

Achard	d'Argouges
d'Angerville	d'Auray
d'Annverville	de Bailleul
de Briqueville	de Montfiquet
de Carnouville	d'Orglande
de Carbonel	de Percy
de Clinchamp	de Pierre Pont
de Courcy	de Saint-Germain
de Couvert	de Sainte-Marie d'Aigneaux
de Cussy	de Touchet
de Fribois	de Tournebu
de Harcourt	de Tillis
d'Héricy	de Vassi
de Houdetot	de Vernois
Mallet de Granville	de Verdun
de Mathon	Le Viconte
du Merle	

Recherches sur la Tapisserie de Bayeux, published in 1824.

DIVES ROLL

OF

LÉOPOLD DELISLE

[Alphabetically arranged]

Ours d'Abbetot
Roger d'Abernon
Achard
Ruaud l'Adoubé
Norman d'Adreci
Engenouf de l'Aigle
Aioul
Bernard d'Alençon
Guillaume Alis
Geoffroi Alselin
Hugue L'Ane
Richer d'Andeli
Ansgot
Guillaume d'Ansleville
Honfroi d'Ansleville
Fouque d'Appeville
Guillaume L'Archer
Arnoul d'Ardre
David d'Argentan
D'Argouges
Guillaume d'Arques
Osberne d'Arques
Robert d'Armentières
Roger Arundel
Robert d'Auberville
Roger d Auberville
Seri d'Auberville
Néel d'Aubigny
Guillaume d'Audrieu
Goubert d'Aufay
Robert d'Aumale
Guillaume de l'Aune
Raoul d'Aunou
D'Auvrecher d'Angerville
Hugue d'Avranches
Rahier d'Avre
Azor

Renaud de Bailleul
Geoffroi Bainard
Raoul Baignard
Guineboud de Balon
Hamelin de Balon
Raoul de Bans
Raoul de Bapaumes
Robert de Barbes
Guillaume Basset
Raoul Basset
Robert Le Bastard
Bavent
Eude, évêque de Bayeux
Hugue de Beauchamp
Guillaume de Beaufou
Richard de Beaumais
Henri de Beaumont
Goubert de Beauvais

Geoffroi du Bec
Guillaume Belet
Ours de Berchères
Raoul de Bernai
Hugue de Bernières
Hervé Le Berrurier
Guillaume Bertran
Néel de Berville
Dreu de La Beuvrière
Richard de Bienfaite
Roger Bigot
Guillaume de Biville
Honfroi de Biville
Guimond de Blangi
Gilbert Le Blond
Guillaume Le Blond
Gilbert de Blosseville
Raoul Blouet
Robert Blouet
Hugue de Bois Hébert
Honfroi de Bohon
Roger Boissel
Hugue de Bolbec
Richard de Bondeville
Guillaume Bonvalet
Guillaume du Bosc
Roger de Bosc Normand
Guillaume de Bosc Roard
Roger de Bosc Roard
Raoul Botin
Guillaume de Bourneville
Hugue Bourdet
Robert Bourdet
Fouque Le Bourguignon
Guillaume de Brai
Hugue de Brébeuf
Auvrai Le Breton
Roger de Breteuil
Gilbert de Bretteville
Osberne du Breuil
De Briqueville
Renier de Brimou
Guillaume de Briouse
Robert de Brix
Raoul de La Bruière
Robert de Buci
Gilbert de Budi
Roger de Bulli
Serlon de Burci
Erneis de Buron
Guillaume de Bursigni

Fouque de Caen
Maurin de Caen
Guillaume de Cahaignes
Guillaume de Cailly

Guillaume de Cairon
Geoffroi Cambrai
De Canouville
Carbonnel
Guillaume de Cardon
Guillaume de Carnet
Honfroi de Carteret
Mauger de Carteret
Roger de Carteret
Guillaume de Castillon
Guillaume de Ceaucé
Eude, comte de Champagne
Robert de Chandos
Roger de Chandos
Raoul de Chartres
Anquetil de Cherbourg
Guillaume La Chèvre
Gonfroi de Cioches
Sigar de Cioches
Fouque de Claville
De Clinchamps
Gilbert de Colleville
Guillaume de Colleville
Baudoin de Colombières
Raoul de Colombières
Renouf de Colombelles
Raoul de Conteville
Robert Corbet
Roger Corbet
Guillaume Corbon
Hugue de Corbon
Ansfroi de Cormeilles
Goscelin de Cormeilles
Aubri de Couci
Raoul de Courbépine
Robert de Courcelles
Richard de Courcy
Robert de Courçon
Gui de Craon
Mile Crespin
Renaud Croc
Robert Cruel
Honfroi de Culai
Eude Cul de Loup
De Cussy

Daniel
Danneville
Guillaume de Daumerai
Guillaume Le Despensier
Robert Le Despensier
Beuselin de Dives
Hugue de Dol
Fouque de Douai
Goscelin de Douai
Amauri de Dreux
Herman le Dreux
Guillaume de Durville

Hardouin d'Écalles
Écouland
Guillaume d'Ecouis
Richard Engagne
Auvrai d'Espagne
Hervé d'Espagne

Guillaume Espec
Raoul L'Estourmi
Richard L'Estourmi
Guillaume d'Eu
Osberne d'Eu
Robert, comte d'Eu
Guillaume, comte d'Evreux
Roger d'Evreux

Guillaume de Falaise
Guillaume de Fécamp
Henri de Ferrières
Robert fils de Geroud
Guillaume fils d'Osberne
Turstain fils de Rou
Toustain fils d'Unspac
Baudoin Le Flamand
Eude Le Flamand
Gerboud Le Flamand
Guinemard Le Flamand
Hugue Le Flamand
Josce Le Flamand
Renouf Flambard
Guillaume Folet
Etienne de Fontenai
Guillaume de La Forêt
Néel Fossard
Guillaume de Fougères
Raoul de Fougères
Eude de Fourneaux
Raoul Framan
Richard Fresle
De Fribois
Robert Froment

Raoul de Gael
Gilbert de Gand
Gilbert Gibard
Berenger Giffard
Fouke Giffard
Osberne Giffard
Girard
Robert de Glanville
Guillaume Goulaffre
Hugue de Gournai
Néel de Gournai
Anquetil de Grai
Aubert Greslet
Gautier de Grancourt
Hugue de Grentemesnil
Turold de Grenteville
Robert Guernon
Toustain de Guernon
Geoffroi de La Guierche

Gautier Hachet
Robert de Harcourt
Raoul de Hauville
Hervé d'Hélion
D'Héricy
Arnoul de Hesdin
Gautier Heusé
Hugue de Hodenc
Hugue de Hoto
D'Houdetot

Gautier d'Incourt
Honfroi de l'Ile
Raoul de l'Ile
Achard d'Ivri
Hugue d'Ivri
Roger d'Ivri

Gautier de Laci
Hugue de Laci
Ibert de Laci
Roger de Laci
    Landri
    Lanfranc
Raoul de Languetot
Guillaume de Lêtre
Raoul de Limesi
Roger de Lisieux
Fouque de Lisors
Biget de Loges
Robert de Lorz
Guillaume de Loucelles
Guillaume de Louvet

Hugue de Maci
Durand Malet
Gilbert Malet
Guillaume Malet
Robert Malet
Guillaume de Malleville
Gilbert Maminot
Hugue Maminot
Geoffroi de Mandeville
Hugue de Manneville
Toustain Mantel
Guillaume de La Mare
Hugue de La Mare
Geoffroi Le Maréchal
Geoffroi Martel
Raoul de Marsi
    De Mathan
Guillaume Maubenc
Gonfroi Mauduit
Guillaume Mauduit
Geoffroi Maurouard
Richard de Méri
    Du Merle
Auvrai de Merleberge
Robert, comte de Meulan
Baudoin de' Meules
Roger de Meules
Hugue de Mobec
Guillaume de Monceaux
Ansger de Montaigu
Dreu de Montaigu
Hubert de Mont Canisi
Geoffroi de Montbrai
Robert de Montbrai
    De Montfiquet
Hugue de Montfort
Robert de Montfort
Hugue de Montgomeri
Roger de Montgomeri
Robert, comte de Mortaine
Mathieu de Mortagne
Raoul de Mortemer

Robert des Moutiers
Guillaume de Moyon
Roger de Moyaux
Gautier de Mucedent
Néel de Munneville
Robert Murdac
Hascouf Musard
Hugue Musard
Roger de Mussegros

Bernard du Neufmarché
Richard de Neuville
Raoul de Noron
Guillaume de Noyers

Roger d'Oistreham
Gautier d'Omontville
Roger d'Orbec
    D'Orglande
    Osmond
Raoul d'Ouilli
Robert d'Ouilli

Raoul Painel
Bernard Pancevolt
Guillaume Pantoul
Turould de Papelion
Foucher de Paris
Guillaume de Parthenay
Osberne Pastforeire
Guillaume Péché
Arnoul de Perci
Guillaume de Perci
Geoffroi, comte de la Perche
Guillaume Pevrel
Renouf Pevrel
Roger Picot
Anscoul de Picquigni
Guillaume de Picquigni
Geoffroi de Pierrepont
Renaud de Pierrepont
Robert de Pierrepont
Raoul Pinel
Raoul Pipin
Roger de Pistres
Guillaume Poignant
Richard Poignant
Guillaume de Poillei
Thierri Pointel
Guernon de Pois
Guillaume Le Poitevin
Roger Le Poitevin
Raoul de La Pommeraie
Robert de Pontchardon
Guillaume de Pont-de-l'Arche
Hubert de Port
Hugue de Port

Gui de Rainecourt
Enguerrand de Raimbeaucourt
Gui de Raimbeaucourt
Roger de Rames
    Ravenot
Hugue de Rennes
Guillaume de Reviers

Richard de Reviers
Robert de Rhuddlan
Gautier de Risbou
Goscelin de La Rivière
Robert de Romenel
Vauquelin de Rosai
Anquetil de Ros
Ansgot de Ros
Geoffroi de Ros
Serlo de Ros
Alain Le Roux
Geoffroi de Runeville

Richard de Sacquenville
Richard de Saint Clair
Roger de Saint Germain
Renaud de Sainte Hélène
Toustain de Sainte Hélène
Robert de Saint Leger
Bernard de Saint Ouen
De Sainte Marie d'Agneaux
Hugue de Saint Quentin
Raoul de Saint Sanson
Gautier de Saint Valeri
Renouf de Saint Valeri
Sanson
Osberne de Saussai
Raoul de Saussai
Raoul de Savigni
Eude Le Sénéschal
Hamon Le Sénéschal
Simon de Senlis
Ansger de Senarpont
Guillaume de Sept Meules
Hugue Silvestre
Roger de Sommeri
Richard de Sourdeval

Guillaume de Taillebois
Ive de Taillebois
Raoul de Taillebois
Geoffroi Talbot
Richard Talbot
Auvrai de Tanie
Guimond de Tessel
Robert Thaon
Raoul du Theil
Honfroi de Tilleul
De Tilly
Toustain Tinel

Gilbert Tison
Berenger de Toeni
Guillaume de Toeni
Ibert de Toeni
Juhel de Toeni
Raoul de Toeni
Robert de Toeni
Renaud de Torteval
De Touchet
Geoffroi de Tournai
Raoul de Tourlaville
De Tournebut
Raoul de Tourneville
Toustain
Raoul Tranchard
Geoffroi de Trelli

Pierre de Valonges
Guillaume de Vatteville
Richard de Vatteville
Robert de Vatteville
Ansfroi de Vaubadon
Osmond de Vaubadon
Renouf de Vaubadon
Guillaume de Vauville
Aitard de Vaux
Robert de Vaux
Ive de Veci
Robert de Veci
Gilbert de Venables
De Venois
Guillaume de Ver
Bertran de Verdun
Gautier de Vernon
Huard de Vernon
Richard de Vernon
Hugue de Vesli
Robert de Vesli
Le Vicomte
Robert de Villon
Honfroi Vis-de-Loup
Raoul Vis-de-Loup
Vital
Robert de Vitot
Hugue de Viville

Wadard
Osberne de Wanci
Guillaume de Warenne
Gilbert de Wissant

Roll published by Léopold Delisle in 1866 and the marble upon which it is inscribed is hung upon the wall of the ancient church of Dives where duke William prayed before his embarkation.

DE MAGNY'S ADDITION TO THE DIVES ROLL

(Nobiliaire de Normandie)

Bernard, fils de Hervé, duc d'Orléans
Alain Fergant, comte de Bretagne
Néel, vicomte du Côtentin
Odon, Evêque de Bayeux
Herbert d'Aigneaux
Eustache d'Ambleville

Avenel des Biards
Martel de Bacqueville
Guillain de Banville
De Barville
De Baynce
Eude de Beaujeu

Toussaint du Bec
De Breauté
De Brécey
Hamon de Cayeu
De Chambray
De Courtenay
De Coville
De Creuilly, issu de la race des ducs de
 Normandie
Doynel
Étienne Érard
D'Espinay
D'Estouteville
De Folleville
De Gacé
Gouhier
Robert Grante
Robert Gruel
Harenc (tige de a maison de Gauville)

Robert de la Haye
De la Haye Malherbe
Hercé
Houel
De Janville
De Malherbe
De Mallebranche
de Mauvoisin
Payen du Montier
De Roumare
De Rupierre
Russel, alias Rozel
De Tancarville
Raoul Tesson
Amaury de Thouars
De Tillières
De Tracy
D'Unfraville
Guillain de Vieux-Pont

ERRATA

Page 3, *col.* 2, *l.* 2 : *for* Longuespee *read* Longue-Epée
,, 3 ,, 2 ,, 19 : *for History of Laycock Abbey read Annals and Antiquities of Lacock Abbey*
,, 7 ,, 1 ,, 32 : *for* Pont Lévêque *read* Pont l'Evêque
,, 8 ,, 2 ,, 24, *note* 8 : *for Vide* App. 24. *read Vide* App. 21
,, 11 ,, 2 ,, 6 : *for* Pont Lèvêque *read* Pont l'Evêque
,, 11 ,, 2 ,, 14 : *for* Troarm *read* Troarn
,, 14 ,, 1 ,, 33 : *for* Herevourt *read* Herecourt
,, 18 ,, 2 ,, 2 : *for* Le Prévost *read* Le Prevost
,, 20 ,, 1 ,, 5 : *for* Godefroy *read* Godfry
,, 22 ,, 1 ,, 7 : *for* Mortimer *read* Mortemer
,, 23 ,, 2 ,, 43 : *for* Bec-aux-Couchois *read* Bec-aux-Cauchois
,, 28 ,, 2 ,, 12 : Emma de Condé (Condeto) occurs in the Grand charter of the abbey of Bec, *vide* 169, also 116, 157, 185
,, 29 ,, 1 ,, 9 : *for* Mortimer *read* Mortemer
,, 37 ,, 1 ,, 36 : Vilcasinus, Vilcassinus, Vilicasinus, Vulcasinus is the latin, and Velquesin, Vulguessin, and Velquessin, the old french, for Vexin
,, 37 ,, 1 ,, 42 : *for* Estrepagny *read* Estrépagny
,, 37 ,, 2 ,, 41 : *ibid.*
,, 37 ,, 2 ,, 56 : *for* Fontenville *read* Fontenelles (Anselme VI, 632)
,, 38 ,, 1 ,, 20 : *for* d'Estrepagny *read* d'Estrépagny
,, 39 ,, 1 ,, 7 : *for* Luthumiére *read* Luthumière
,, 39 ,, 1 ,, 8 : *for* Bretterville *read* Bretteville
,, 39 ,, 1 ,, 25 : *for* Estrepagny *read* Estrépagny
,, 43 ,, 1 ,, 13 : *for* Edward the Confessor *read* William the Conqueror
,, 43 ,, 2 ,, 34 : *for note* 6 *read* 7 *after* Taillebois
,, 43 ,, 2 ,, 48 : *insert at end of note* 6 : App. 20 ; Cle., II, 261
,, 44 ,, 1 ,, 6 : *for* daughter *read* natural daughter
,, 46 ,, 2, *ll.* 36, 45, 46 : *for* Peche *read* Péché
,, 52 ,, 1, *l.* 32 : *for* revised ancestry of William de Warren, *vide* add.
,, 53 ,, 1 ,, 7 : *after* 408. *add Hist., Trinité du Mont*, 17
,, 53 ,, 1 ,, 10 : *for* Godefroy de Villers *read* Godefry
,, 53 ,, 1 ,, 55 : *for* Rechin *read* Réchin
,, 54 ,, 2 ,, 4 : pp. 55 ; 60 ; 71 ; 80 ; 82 ; 83 ; *for* Belesme *read* Belèsme
,, 55 ,, 1, *ll.* 8 and 28 : *Add to note* 2, charter of 1069, *Hist., de L'Abb., Royale de Saint-Denys en France*, F. Jacques Dovelet (Paris, 1625), 840 ; also ed. dom Michel Felibien (Paris, 1706), lxxxviii
,, 55 ,, 1, *l.* 37 : *delete* of
,, 59 ,, 2 ,, 45 : *for* Mortimer *read* Mortemer
,, 63 ,, 2 ,, 26 : *for* to *read* from
,, 66 ,, 1 ,, 39 : *for* Erenis de Burum *read* Erneis de Burun or Burum
,, 66 ,, 2 ,, 51 : *after* Wallingford *read* Milo Crispin (Milonis Crispinis) witnessed a charter of William the Conqueror to the priory of Lewes, executed not earlier than 1080
,, 66 ,, 2 ,, 57 : *for* Gilbert abbot *read* Gilbert Crispin abbot
,, 67 ,, 1 ,, 1 : *for* Gilbert abbot *read* Gilbert Crispin abbot
,, 67 ,, 2 ,, 44 : *for* Pepin *read* Pépin
,, 67 ,, 2 ,, 52 : *ibid.*
,, 68 ,, 2 ,, 56 : *for* constable *read* vicomte
,, 72 ,, 2 ,, 27 : *for* Walern *read* Waleran
,, 75 : For ancestry of Raoul de Mortemer, *vide* 52 ; App. 19 and add. (183)
,, 77 ,, 2 ,, 6 : Planché thought Radulfi Taisson was identical with Raoul Tesson I rather than Radulphus Taxo, as stated

Page 92 *col.* 2, *note* 1 : *for* Gall. Christ., IX *read* XI
  ,,   95 ,,   2, *l.* 29 : *for* St-Valery *read* St-Valéry
  ,,   95 ,,   2 ,, 39 : *for* Kelhame *read* Kelham's
  ,,   96 ,,   1 ,, 39 : *for* seemed *read* seem
  ,,   96 ,,   1 ,, 56 : *for* Vennes *read* Vannes
  ,,   98 ,,   2 ,, 44 : *for* Tancard *read* Tancred
  ,, 104 ,,   2 ,, 30 : *for* Ancestry of St-Martin, *vide* addenda
  ,, 105 ,,   2 ,, 37 : *for* Carmen de bello, Hastingensi, *read* Widonis Carmen de Hast-
                         ingae Proel. in Chron. Anglo-Normands, Michel, III, 24
  ,,   vi ,,   3, 68th name : *for* Tournièr *read* Tournières.
  ,, 114 ,,   2, *delete* Richard de Flandre *add* Le sire de Tournières.
  ,, 157 ,,   2, *l.* 38 : *for* Simeon and Durham *read* Simeon of Durham (Hist., Angl.,
                         Twysden I, 198)
Table VI, wife of Gautier Giffard II *for* Rohais, dau. of Richard de Bienfaite *read* Agnès,
                        sister of Anselme de Ribemont (Ord. Vit. III, 343)

Page xii, *l.* 26 : *for* Ciriæ *read* Curiæ
  ,,   3, *col.* 2, *l.* 10 : *for* Anglican *read* Anglicanum
  ,,   12 ,,   2 ,, 1 : *for* Anglican *read* Anglicanum
  ,,   15 ,,   2 ,, 40 : *for* Poithieu *read* Ponthieu
  ,,   15 ,,   2 ,, 49 : *for* and a daughter also named Adelaide was born from one of these
                       husbands. Adelaide *read* ; however, he left a daughter Judith who
                       later became countess of Northumberland. Adélaïde
  ,,   18 ,,   2 ,, 34 : *for* La Roux *read* Le Roux
  ,,   21 ,,   1 ,, 14 : *for* les-Petit *read* le-Petit
  ,,   24 ,,   1 ,, 46 : *for* Saint-Lo *read* St-Lô
  ,,   25 ,,   1 ,, 15 : *for* Bauté *read* Beauté
  ,,   25 ,,   2 ,, 3 : *for* las Tours *read* la Tours
  ,,   35 ,,   2 ,, 36 : *for* ; he increased *read*, whose son William increased
  ,,   35 ,,   2 ,, 45 : *for* Philip *read* William
  ,,   40 ,,   1 ,, 31 : *for* lydée *read* lycée
  ,,   54 ,,   2 ,, 52 : Concerning Hamon Le Sénéschal and Robert de Crévecœur *vide* Dugdale
                       I, 591 ; Banks I, 60–1 ; Charter Rolls, 13 Edward I, m. 22 ; 41 Edward
                       III, m. 8, Public Record Office ; Registrum Roffense public records of
                       Goudhurst (Kent).
  ,,   72 ,,   2 ,, 16 : *for* Pin *read* Pins
  ,,   82 ,,   1 ,, 18 : *for* Hereford *read* Hertford
  ,,   97 ,,   2 ,, 7 : *for* viscounts of Vasci *read* viscounts of Vesci
  ,, 102 ,,   1, *ll.* 1, 3 : *for* Musgrove *read* Musgrave
  ,, 132 ,,   1, *l.* 56 : *for* Burnsted *read* Bumpstead
  ,, 144 ,,   1 ,, 13 : *for* on 28 June *read* 19 June 1266 (Obituaires de la province de Sens, diocese
                       de Chartres, Molinier, vol. II, 296)
  ,, 156 ,,   1 ,, 54 : *for* 1180 *read* 1080
  ,, 159 ,,   2, *ll.* 38, 39 : *for* Margareta married Ranulph de Bajocis *read* Margareta married
                       firstly, Onfrey de Albini, and secondly, Ranulph de Bajocis (Bayeux)
  ,, 159 ,,   2, *l.* 56 : *for* Billingbrunc *read* Billingbruc
  ,, 160 ,,   1, *ll.* 5, 6 : *for* Renouf de Bricasard, viscount of Bayeux *read* Renouf de Bricasard,
                       viscount of Bessin, sometimes called de Bayeux
  ,, 160 ,,   1, *l.* 42 : *for* fruit *read* fuit
  ,, 160 ,,   2 ,, 14 : *for* Cocayne *read* Cokayne
  ,, 185, *ll.* 55, 58, 61 : *for* Gatehampton *read* Gethampton
  ,, 190, *l.* 32 : *for* L'Acher *read* L'Archer
  ,, 245, *col.* 1, *l.* 13 : *for* Dapiper *read* Dapifer
Table   V : *for* Godfry born c. 1060 *read* 960
  ,,   V : *for* Godfry died c. 1108 *read* c. 1006
  ,,   VII : *for* Richard de Redvers died 1106 *read* 1107
  ,,   VIII : *for* Gilbert Crispin V was slain 1189 *read* 1191
  ,,   VIII : *for* Gilbert Crispin VI was baron of Tillières from 1189 *read* 1191
  ,,   IX : *for* Catherine Challows *read* Challons
  ,,   IX : *for* Thomas Forescue *read* Fortescue
  ,,   XIV : *for* Elizabeth Harrison married 1636 *read* 1626
  ,,   XIV : *for* Margaret Gilbert *read* Joan
  ,,   XIV : *for* Helen Crispin married Charles Owens 1910 *read* 1911
  ,,   XIV : *for* Margaret Owens born 1911 *read* 1912
  ,,   XIV : *for* Erma Marchant married 12 April *read* 3 April
Corrigenda : *vide* Auvrai Maubenc and Auvrai de Lincoln
      ,,   *vide* Further concerning Héloïse, mother of Herluin
      ,,   *vide* Rioufe, count of Évreux or Côtentin
      ,,   *vide* Roselle de Boulogne and Roselle de St-Paul
      ,,   *vide* William Crispin VI, sire de Dangu
      ,,   *vide* William Crispin (concerning Châteauceaux)
      ,,   *vide* William Malet, monk at Bec

INDEX OF COMPANIONS

A—Guy, bishop of Amiens
B—Benoît de Sainte-More
C—Crispin
M—Macary and Prentout
P—William of Poitiers
R—La Rue
T—Bayeux Tapestry
V—Orderic Vital
W—Wace

The number in heavy type indicates page of the biography.

GENERAL INDEX

A

Abbaye-aux-Dames, 20, 26, 36, 83
Abbetot, church of, 70 ; Amaury d', 70, 107 ; Emeline d', 70 ; Jean d', 70 ; Ours d', 22, 70, 91 ; Raoul d', Robert d', 70
Abergavenny, castle, 54
Abernon, Enguerrand de, Ingelram de, 98 ; Roger de, 97, 98
Abingdon, abbey, 96, 117, 120 ; convent, 96
Achard, William, 1 ; Robert, 190
Acre, St-Jean d', 3, 29
Aculei, Adam, app. 17
Adalbert II, duke of Lombardy, 44
Adda, wife of William de Tournebut, 108
Adèla, daughter of Robert, king of France, affianced wife of Richard III, duke of Normandy, and later wife of Baldwin V of Flanders, 71
Adèla, daughter of the Conqueror, 80
Adèla, widow of Roger de Toeni, 41
Adélaïde, daughter of Robert I, duke of Normandy, 15
Adélaïde, wife of Enguerrand II, count of Ponthieu, app. 1.
Adélaïde, wife of Maino de Fougères II, 74
Adélaïde, wife of Solomon de Sablé, app. 5.
Adelbert II, king of Italy, 120
Adelina, wife of Roger de Beaumont, 87
Adeline, wife of Alain Flaald, 2
Adeline, wife of Hugh de Gand, 30
Adeline, wife of both, Roger d'Ivri, 60, 64 and Robert Bigot, 98
Adeliza de Balto, 25
Adeliza, sister of Richard Fitz Baldwin, 8 ; app. 21
Adeliza of Louvain, wife of Henry I, king of England, 6, 47, 73, 94, 101, 104
Adeliza, wife of Geoffry de Mandeville, 25
Adoubé, Ruaud d' (Musard), 55
Aelfigifu (Elfgiva), wife of Algar, earl of Mercia, app. 20
Agnès, wife of André de Vitrie, 3
Agnès, daughter of Guy, count of Ponthieu, app. 1
Agnès, daughter of Richard, count of Evreux and third wife of Simon de Montfort l'Amauri, 41, 78, 130, 140
Aigle, castle of l', 13, 38 ; Engenoulf de l', 13 ; Gilbert de l', 13, 25 ; Juliana de, wife of Gilbert Crispin IV, 29 ; Richard de l', also called de Aquila, 13 ; Roger de l', 13 ; add.

Aigneaux, Corbin d', 57 ; Herbert d', 56, 57
Aincourt (Encourt), Gautier d', parish of, Ralph d', William d', 20
Aiulf, Domesday tenant-in-chief, 122
Alain Le Noir, count in Brittany, earl of Richmond, 2, 96 ; add.
Alain Le Roux, count in Brittany, earl of Richmond, 1, 2, 4, 18, 55, 66, 73, 96, 121 ; add.
Alain, seneschal of Dol, 2
Alberade, wife of Raoul, count of Ivry, 63
Alberdede, wife of Walter de Falaise, 44
Alberic III, earl of Guisnes, 33
Albert, abbot of Marmoutiers, 133
Albreda, wife of Baudoin de Meules, 7
Albreda, sister of Fouque d'Aunou, 20
Albreda, wife of Gerold de Roumare, 50
Albreda, wife of Alured de Lincoln III, 159
Albreda, wife of Renaud de Gournay, 59
Aldermaneston, manor, 190
Aldfield, Adelm of, 103
Alditha, wife of king Harold, 43
Alexander II, pope, 106 ; bishop, Lincoln, 192
Alfonso, king of Aragon, 88
Alfred the Great, king of England, add.
Alfred I, baron of Fougères, 74
Algar, earl of Mercia, 2, 43 ; app. 20
Algernon, earl of Hertford, 48
Aliard, wife of Theobold, the son of Pépin, 67
Alis, Guillaume d', 31, 32 ; Hugh d', 31 ; Philip d', sir Roger, 32
Almodis, countess of March, 101
Alno, castle, 20
Alnwick, fortress, 47 ; John, baron, 103
Alre, Guillaume d', Hubert d', William d', 32
Amaury the Delicate, of Pontoise, app. 8
Ambrières, Achard d', 1, 56
Ambriose, Marguerite d', wife of Jean, baron du Bec-Crispin, 149 ; Pierre d', 149
Amfreville (Umfreville), Gilbert d', Odonel d', baron Riddesdale, 86 ; Robert d', 85, 86 ; Walter d', 86
Amondeville, Adam d', Helias d', John d', Jolland d', Ralph d', Robert d', Roger d', 99 ; app. 22 ; William d', 99
Anceline, wife of Turquetil de Neufmarché, 14 ; T. XI
Anet, Simon d', app. 16
Angerville, Crispin domain, 149 ; T. VIII ; Auvrecher d', 5 ; ibid. ; Benedict d', Huburtus d', Raoul d', Robert d',

Bagot, Hervey, 97
Bailleul, Le sire (of Fécamp) ; Pierre de, Renaud de, 9
Baladon, Drogo de, 54
Baldric the Teuton, 25, 28, 82 ; app. 16, 20
Baldwin II, Baldwin III, and Baldwin IV, counts of Flanders, add.
Baldwin V, count of Flanders (1034–1067), married Adèla, daughter of Robert, king of France, 7, 30, 79, 81 ; app. 11, 17 ; add.
Baldwin VI, count of Flanders (1067–1070), 42
Balon, Dreu de, 96 ; Guinebaud de, 53, 54 ; Guionech de, 54 ; Hamelin de, 2, 53, 54, 96 ; Lucie, 2, 54
Bamborough, castle, app. 4, 12
Banastre, Richard, Robert, 86
Barbatus, Godfrey, 47 ; Hugh, 60
Barbery, abbey, 12
Bardney, abbey, 30
Barneville, Crispin domain, 149
Barnstable, charter of, 13
Basset, duke of Loire, 18 ; Osmond, 19, 70, 73, 106 ; Osmond, viscount of Vernon, vide Centville, 19 ; Ouilli de, 70 ; Ralph, 26, 89 ; Raoul, 26, 70, 73 ; Toustain, 19, 70, 106 ; William, 70
Bastard, John Pallexfen ; Robert le, 86
Bastembourg, Anslac de, 80, 87, 184 ; T. III ; Gisla, app. 5 ; Turstan de, 17, 60, 87, 184 ; app. 5
Bath, priory, 45 ; app. 17
Battle, abbey of, 11, 35, 96, 99, 108, 123 ; app. 12, 18
Baudemont, castle, 143 ; Goel de, 142
Baugency, Hericus de, John de, Landric de, 62
Baumez, Mahaut, wife of William Crispin ; T. VIII ; Thibaud, Seigneur de, 146
Bauquencey, Baldric de, 19, 20
Bayeux (Bajocis), Alan de, Hugh, Ranulph, Robert, Suspir, 159 ; T. XIII
Bayeux, Eudes (Odo) bishop, 2, 4, 15, 24, 33, 41, 44, 50, 52, 54, 57, 60, 61, 66, 95, 106, 109, 112, 117, 118, 122 ; app. 18, 20 ; church, 27
Baynard, William, 190
Béatrice, daughter of Hilduin, 25
Béatrice, abbess of Montevilliers, aunt of duke Robert I, 14, 81 ; app. 16 ; c. 2 ; T. V, XI
Béatrice, wife of William de Gloz, 54
Beatrix, daughter of William Fitz Richard, add.
Beaubec, charter of, 22
Beauchamp, Hugue de, 58 ; Joanna, app. 12 ; Milo de, Pagan de, Simon de, 58 ; sir John, app. 20 ; Walter de, 70 ; descent from Elizabeth Crispin (Streche), 160
Beaufou, Guillaume de, 34, 86, 87 ; Raoul de, 86 ; Richard de, T. IV ; Robert de, 34, 86

Beaulieu, Notre Dame de, app. 17
Beaumais, Hugh de, 80 ; Richard (Belemis), 80, 88 ; Roger de (Beaumez), 80 ; Walter de, William de, 80
Beaumont, the abbey of, 90 ; Roger de, 75, 87, 100, 121 ; T. VI ; his wife, Adeline, daughter of Waleran I, count of Meulent (Meulan) ; T. ibid. ; his eldest son, Robert de, count of Meulent (Meulan) and earl of Leicester, 52, 79, 87, 100 ; app. 6, 9 ; T. ibid. ; his second son, Henry de, earl of Warwick, 87 ; app. 6, 9, 17 ; T. ibid. ; Robert de ; his wives, first Godehilde de Toeni, no issue ; second Elizabeth, daughter of Hugh the Great, count of Vermandois, son of Henry I, king of France, 87 ; add. ; their children, Waleran II, count of Meulent, 30, 72, 87 ; app. 14 ; add. (called by some son of William de Warren II) ; married to Agnès de Montfort, lady of Gournai-sur-Mare ; Robert de, count of Leicester, 87 ; T. ibid. ; Albreda de, Amicia de, Elizabeth de, mistress of Henry I, add. ; Emma de, 87 ; T. ibid. ; and Isabella de, 87, 103 ; T. ibid. ; Robert, count of Meulan, son of Waleran II, 67 ; app. 17 ; add. ; married Matilda, daughter of Reginald, earl of Cornwall, natural son of Henry I, king of England, 84 ; vide add. ; their son, Waleran III, count of Meulan (Meulent), 31 ; T. VI ; their daughter, Mabel, married William de Redever, surnamed de Vernon, sixth earl of Devon, 84 ; app. 12 ; add. ; T. IX ; whose daughter, Mary, married first Robert de Courtenay, second sir Peter Prouz, 84 ; app. 12 ; T. ibid. ; Prouz descent to Chudleigh, app. 12 ; T. ibid. ; Anceline de, 62, Agnès de, 154 ; vide Meulan
Beauvais, Richard de, 88 ; Vincent de, 5
Bec, abbey of, 11, 13, 20, 28, 29, 35, 37, 38, 43, 59, 60, 66, 71, 72, 81, 90, 96, 111, 123, 181, 186 ; app. 3, 9, 16, 17, 18, 20 ; c. 13, 20
Bec, Charles du, I, 184 ; T. VIII ; Charles du, II, 184 ; app. 18 ; T. ibid. ; Gautier du, baron of Eresby, 24, 65 ; app. 18 ; T. ibid. ; Geoffroi du, 23, 67, 106 ; app. 15, 18 ; T. ibid. ; Henry du, 24 ; T. ibid. ; Jeanne du, T. ibid. ; Pierre du, app. 18 ; T. ibid. ; Ralph du, 23 ; app. 18 ; T. ibid. ; René du, I, 184 ; app. 17, 18 ; T. ibid. ; René du, II, 184 ; T. ibid. ; Walter du, 24
Bec, Le Thomas domain, app. 18
Bec-aux-Cauchois domain, 106 ; app. 18
Bec-Herluin, app. 17, 18
Bec-de-Mortemer, barony, 38 ; app. 17, 18 ; add.
Bec-de-Mortagne, 152 (c, h)
Bec-Crispin, William du, 80

Eudes, comte de Champagne (*continued*)—
throne ; is captured with his son,
thrown into prison and dies there ;
his son liberated, 16
Eudes, count of Penthièvre, 2, 191
Eugène III, pope, 34
Eustache I, count of Boulogne, 18
Eustache II, count of Boulogne, 4, 15, 18,
79
Èva, wife of Guy de Brian, 65
Everard, chaplain to Henry I, 101
Evesham, abbey, 53, 70
Evreux, comté, 41 ; parish, 109 ; Edward
de, 119 ; Ela de, 120 ; Gautier d', 119,
120 ; Ralph d', 41 ; *vide* Gacé ; Roger
d', 41, 99 ; Walter d', 99, 119 ; Wil-
liam d', 41
Evrois (Evreux), Robert de, 99
Exeter, castle, 7
Exmes, comté, 81, 183 ; castle, 14
Eye, honour, app. 20 ; priory, 7, 12
Eynsham, abbey, *vide* St-Mary of

F

Falaise, Guillaume de Moulins, sire de, 44,
65 ; app. 24 ; Alan de, Alured de, 45 ;
Hugh de, Robert de, 44 ; app. 24 ;
Simon de, 44 ; Sybil de, 45 ; Walter
de, 44, 77
Fastolf, John, 148, 191
Fécamp, abbey, 4, 6, 9, 14, 16, 20, 29, 51,
182, 183 ; app. 11
Fergant, Alain, count of Brittany, 1, 2, 96,
119
Feritate, William de la, 66
Ferrières, Crispin seigniory, 149 ; Guil-
laume de, 41, 56, 92, 104 ; Alice de,
app. 12 ; Anne de, app. 17 ; Enguenulf
de, 56 ; Henri de, 41, 56 ; John de, 56 ;
Louis seigneur de, app. 17 ; Robert
de, 56 ; sir Julk, 12 ; Walkelin de, 56
Ferte, Hugh de la, 65 ; Richard de la, 66 ;
William de la, 65, 109
Ferté-Macé, Mathieu de la, 56, 65, 66
Filibert, abbot of Montivilliers, c. 1
Finchamstede, manor, 190
Fitz Alan (Alain), Henry, Isabeau, 6, 50 ;
John, 2 ; Mary, 2 ; Walter, 2, 4 ;
William, 2, 50
Fitz Anscaul, Beatrice, 3 ; William, 1, 3
Fitz Ansger, Hugo, 117
Fitz Autier (Other), Gautier, Gerald, 120
Fitz Baldwin, Giger, 7 ; app. 21 ; Richard,
8 ; app. 21 ; Robert, William, 7 ;
app. 21
Fitz Bertran de Peleit, 119
Fitz Count, Brian, 2, 54, 67, 96, 195
Fitz Durand, Adam, 116, 119
Fitz Edith, Maud, Robert, 8
Fitz Erneis, Robert I, 19, 92 ; Robert II,
Robert III, T. XII
Fitz Flaald, Alain, 2, 124
Fitz Geoffry, Odo, 16

Fitz Gerold, *vide* Roumare
Fitz Gilbert, Baldwin, *vide* de Meules
Fitz Giroie, Fulk, Hugh, app. 5 ; Robert,
53 ; app. 5
Fitz Guido, William, 120
Fitz Hamon, Mabel, 55 ; add. ; Robert,
21, 45, 55, 101 ; add.
Fitz Hercie, Ivo, 62
Fitz Hervé, Hervy, 121
Fitz John, Eustache, 77, 103
Fitz Juel, Warin, 122
Fitz Lambert, Henry, Hugh, Matilda,
Richard, William, 75
Fitz Martin, Robert, William, 65
Fitz Norman, Hugh, *vide* Hugh de La Mare
Fitz Osberne, William, 2, 11, 17, 22, 41,
42, 52, 54, 58, 60, 63, 71, 72, 74, 83,
98, 116, 118 ; app. 17 ; Emma, his
daughter, 42, 74 ; his sons, Ralph, 42 ;
Roger and William, *vide* de Breteuil
Fitz Osmond, Anchetil, Hugh, 70
Fitz Patrick, William, second earl of Salis-
bury, 3
Fitz Payne (Payn, Pagan), Geoffry, son of
Pagan Troussebot, 110 ; Margaret,
Robert, 160
Fitz Picot, Isabel, 50 ; Margaret, 160 ;
Robert, 42, 50, 160
Fitz Ponce, Drogo, Richard, Walter, 103
Fitz Renfrid, 63
Fitz Richard, Robert (unidentified), 30, 43
Fitz Richard, Robert (Péché), 46
Fitz Richard, Robert (de Quincy), 103
Fitz Richard, William, add.
Fitz Rou, Toustain, Le Blanc, 23, 67, 106
Fitz Ruald, Alan, 55
Fitz Serlon, Robert, 102
Fitz Spirwic, 119
Fitz Tek, 119
Fitz Walter, Robert, 21 ; William, 160
Fitz William, Alard, Geoffry, William, 185 ;
T. VIII
Flaitel, Emengarde, Gerard, 22
Flamand, Gautier de, 21
Flambord, Ranulf, Thomas, 72
Flèche, Jean de la, 44, 52
Flete, John, monk of Westminster, 190
Fleury, abbey, 120 ; city, *vide* St-Dennis
Folkingham, baron, 30
Folkstone, baron, 33
Folques, Robert de, app. 17 ; Jeanne, add.
Fons Dulcis, abbey, 26
Fontenay, Robert Marmion de, 94 ; abbey,
47, 77 ; T. XII ; castle, Helto de,
Herluin, Manasses de, Roger de, 94
Fontenelles (now St-Wandrille, founded
648) abbey, 37, 57, 87
Fontevraud, abbey, 107
Ford, abbey, app. 21 ; Odonel de, app. 12
Fornelles, Ralph de, 17
Fors, abbey, 73
Fortescue, Isabella, Thomas, John, app.
12
Fortibus, Aveline de, William de, 84

Grenville, Richard de, 123 ; Robert de, 123 ; William de, 123
Grestin, abbey, 36
Grimaldi, Rainer, app. 18
Grimaldi-Crispin genealogy, *vide* Crispin
Grimaldo, duke of Brabant, son of Otto Canella, 67
Grimaldus, count of Flanders, Hugo, 67
Grimaldus I, prince of Monoco, 67
Grimaldy, François René du Bec-Crispin de, 39, 184 ; app. 18
Grisegonelle, Geoffry, count of Anjou, 182
Gros, Arnold le, app. 5 ; Odon le, 53
Grumesnil, Crispin seigniory, 149
Guador, *vide* Gaël
Guerinfroi, 15
Guernon, Robert, sire de Montfiquet, 4, 20, 92
Guernsey, island of, 32
Guierche, Geoffry de la ; Sylvester de la, bishop of Rennes, 24
Guido, prince of Monoco, 67
Guidville, Hugue de, 122 ; Robert de, 122
Guierche, Geoffroi de, 24 ; Sylvester de, Walter de, 24
Guillaume, comte d'Evreux, *vide* William
Guiscard, Robert, 46, 85, 117
Guitmund, lord of Maulins-la-Marche, 44
Gundred, wife of Robert Le Blond, 27
Gundred, wife of William de Lambert, 75
Gundreda, wife of William de Warren, 52, 75
Gunnora, mother of William de Briouse, 35
Guy II, seignior of La Val, Guy III, *ibid.*, 31
Guy, count of Burgundy, 81, 85
Guy, count of Ponthieu, 16, 18 ; app. 1
Guynes (Guines), Sifrid, Count of, 67, 196
Gwinner, Sarah, wife of Frederick E. Crispin I, T. XIV

H

Hachet, Gautier, 22 ; Geoffry, Ricardi, Walter, William, 22
Hadewisa, wife of Raoul de Limesi, 75
Haie, Eudes Le Seneschal, sire de La, 15, 17, 25, 64 ; app. 19 ; T. X ; Cicily de La, 45 ; T. *ibid.* ; Aegidia or Gila de La, app. 19 ; add. ; Matilda de La, app. 19 ; T. *ibid.* ; Murial de La, 184 ; T. *ibid.* ; Ralph de La, 17 ; T. *ibid.* ; Raoul de La, 184 ; T. *ibid.* ; Richard de La, 184 ; app. 19 ; T. *ibid.* ; Robert de, 45, 64, 184 ; app. 19 ; T. *ibid.* ; Robert de La, II, 17 ; app. 19
Haie-du-Puits, La, seigniory, 17 ; app. 19
Hambie, abbey, 3, 95
Hansel, William, 23
Harcourt, Norman castle of, 93 ; English castle, 94 ; Anchetil de, first to assume name of Harcourt, 14, 93, 143 ; app. 16 ; T. XI ; Arnoul de, said to have been slain in battle of Cardiff, Wales, 14, 59, 69, 191 ; Errand de succeeded Anchetil de, present at Hastings (no

issue), 14, 93 ; Ève d', *vide* wife of Robert d', II, Gervais de, 14 ; T. *ibid.* ; Henry d', marshal of France, 94 ; T. *ibid.* ; Jean de, son of Anquetil de, 14 ; T. *ibid.* ; Jean d', created count of Harcourt by Philip VI of France, 94 ; T. *ibid.* ; dame Margaret de, received the order of the Garter from Edward IV, 94 ; T. *ibid.* ; Philippe d', bishop of Bayeux, 34, 97, 142 ; T. *ibid.* ; Pierre d', baron of Beuvron, 94 ; T. *ibid.* ; Renaud de, 14 ; T. *ibid.* ; Robert de (I), le Fort succeeded his brother Errand de, present at Hastings, 5, 14, 93, 94, 110 ; T. *ibid.* ; Robert II d', married Ève, daughter of Joscelyn Crispin, 38, 143 ; T. *ibid.* ; sir Simon, lord keeper of the great seal under Queen Ann, 94 ; William d', strongly supported king Henry I against his brother, duke Robert Courteheuse, 93 ; app. 14, 17 ; Yves de, 14
Harold, king of England, 24, 41, 43, 46, 77, 104, 112 ; app. 1, 20
d'Harquency, *vide* d'Arquency
Hastings, William de, 110 ; sir William, 111
Hauville, fief of Gilbert Crispin I, 29 ; app. 16 ; c. 5
Hawise, of Brittany, 1, 3
Hawise, wife of Erneis and daughter of Baldric the Teuton, 19, 92
Hawise, wife of Ibert de Lacy, 62
Hawise, wife of Robert de Fontenay, 94
Hawise, wife of Robert Fitz Erneis, 92
Hawise, wife of Roger de Mortemer, 76
Headley, vill, add.
Helen, supposed natural daughter of Richard III, duke of Normandy, 121
Hélion, sir Alan de, Hervé d', Mary, app. 12
Helisenda, wife of Gerold de Grantemesnil, 50
Héloïse, wife of Ansgot the Dane, 67 ; app. 18 ; add
Henry I, king of England, 2, 4, 6, 7, 8, 9, 10, 12, 13, 14, 17, 18, 20, 22, 27, 32, 33, 35, 36, 38, 41, 42, 43, 46, 47, 52, 54, 55, 58, 64, 65, 66, 67, 70, 72, 76, 78, 80, 84, 86, 87, 89, 90, 91, 92, 93, 95, 96, 99, 101, 103, 105, 107, 109, 110, 121, 123, 124, 181 ; app. 3, 12, 15, 16, 17, 19, 20, 25 ; add.
Henry I, king of France, 28, 29, 69 ; add.
Henry II, king of England, 2, 3, 10, 33, 35, 44, 46, 54, 55, 56, 59, 63, 67, 86, 89, 102, 103, 117, 120, 122 ; app. 3, 15, 16, 17, 19 ; add.
Henry III, king of England, 16, 48, 56, 57, 84, 185 ; app. 12, 15, 17, 18, 20 ; add.
Henry IV, king of England, 57, 94 ; app. 17 ; Henry V, *ibid.*, app. 17 ; Henry VI, *ibid.*, 21 ; Henry VII, *ibid.*, 49 ; Henry VIII, 62, 88
Henry VI, sire de Lezingen, 1
Henry, earl of Warwick, 25

Tripcovich, count Oliviero, husband of Elizabeth Crispin ; T. XIV
Troarn, abbey, 11, 78, 101, 102, 118
Troussebot, Pagan, 110 ; Agatha, Geoffry, Hillaria, Richard, Robert, Rose, William, 110
Troussil, Guy, 35
Turold, 106
Turstain, Hrolf, 28, 80
Turstain, Richard, 17, 25, 155, 184 ; T. X
Turstain, Walter, 106
Turulph, companion of Rollo, 65
Tutbury, castle, 56

U

Umfreville, Robert de, *vide* Amfreville
Urso, abbot of Jumièges, c. 16

V

Val, Gui de La, 31, 54 ; Gui de La, II, 111 ; Hamon de La, 31, 54 ; Jean de La, 111
Valasse, abbey, app. 18
Val-des-Dunes, battle, 6, 69, 77 ; T. XII
Val-Richer, abbey, 11
Valecherville, Guillaume de, 120 ; Fulco de, Robert de, Walter de, 120
Valenciennes, Béatrice de, 31 ; Christian de, 31
Valognes, conspiracy, 6, 16 ; Pierre de, 18
Vauquelin-de-Becco, 193
Varanguebec, Crispin barony, 39 ; app. 17, 19
Vardes, Fouques de, app. 16
Vareville, Crispin seigniory, 147
Varham, Hughes de, 25
Vassy, Ive de, 63, 65, 77, 97, 103 ; Robert de, 63, 97
Vatteville, Guillaume de, 121 ; castle, 120 ; Richard de, 121
Vaubadon, Ansfroi de, Osmond de, Renouf de, 117
Vaudrey, abbey, 10
Vautort, Renaud de, Goisfrid de, Hugh de, Richard de, Roger de, 123
Vaux, Robert de, Aitard de, 97 ; Godard de, Hubert de, Ranulph de, Richard de, 97
Venables, Gilbert de, 31, 79 ; Walter de, 31
Venator, Gilbert, 79
Veneur, Raoul Le, Walter de, 79
Venois (Venoix) de, 110, 111
Ver, Aubri de, Guillaume de, 117
Verdun, Bertran de, 9
Vermandois, Elizabeth of, daughter of Hugh the Great, count of Vermandois, married first Robert de Beaumont, second William de Warren II, 52, 87
Vernon, castle, 85 ; Richard de, 27, 33, 58, 85, 107 ; app. 7 ; Blithildis, 85
Vernon, Gautier de, 23, 85 ; Huard de, 58, 85 ; Joan de, 84 ; Hugh de, 33, 85 ; Lewis Harcourt, 94 ; Matilda de, 184 ;

app. 19 ; Roger de, 85 ; Walter de, 85 ; William de, 107 ; app. 19 ; William George Granville, 94
Vernon, William de Redvers, surnamed de, sixth earl of Devon, 8, 84, 85 ; app. 12 ; add. ; T. IX ; lady Mary de Redvers surnamed de, 8, 84 ; app. 12 ; add. ; T. *ibid.* ; Baldwin de Redvers surnamed de, Baldwin, his son, 84 ; T. *ibid.*
Vesci, Béatrice de, 77, 103 ; John de, 77 ; Maud de, 65 ; William de, 77, 103 ; barony, 47
Vesli, Le sire de, 111 ; app. 23 ; Mile de, 111 ; Robert de, 111 ; app. 23 ; Huges de, 11 ; app. 23 ; Hunfridus de, Osberne de, sir Humphrey de, 111 ; Turold de, app. 23 ; William de, 111 ; app. 23
Vexin, comté, app. 8 ; count and viscount, *vide* Dreu, count of, and Guillaume Crispin I, count, and viscount of, 37 ; app. 8 ; William Crispin II deprived of this viscountcy, add.
Viellers, Humphrey de, 87, 100
Vieux, Gautier le, *vide* Gautier, count of Pontoise
Vieuxpont, Guillaume de, 43, 51, 52, 60 ; Robert de, 52
Viger, brother of Baldric the Teuton, 19
Villanis, Ernoulf de, 111
Villebon, Marguerite de, app. 17
Villiers, Godefroi de, 53 ; George, Pagan de, 53 ; Louis de Mesnil-, 190
Vital, vassal of Odo, bishop of Bayeux, 112
Vitalis, abbot of Savigny, app. 17
Vitalis, abbot of Westminster, 191, 192 ; app. 17
Vitot, Robert de, 53, 106 ; app. 5 ; Ralph de, 105
Vitray-sous-l'Aigle, 3
Vitrie, André de, 3 ; Robert de, 3 ; Eleanor de, 3, 29 ; *vide* Gilbert Crispin V ; add.; William de, 3

W

Wac, Hugh, 11 ; Geoffry, 104
Wadard, companion of duke William, 112 ; Henry, Simon, 112
Wadsworth, Geoffry de, 78
Waleran, baron of Essex, 110
Wallingford, castle, 95 ; add. ; Wigod de, cup-bearer of Edward the Confessor, 64, 66, 95, 96, 195 ; app. 18 ; Algitha de, wife of Robert d'Ouilli, 66, 95 ; Matilda de, wife of Milo Crispin, 66, 67, 95, 195 ; Toking de, 96
Walshingham, abbey of, 123
Waltheof, earl of Northumberland, 74, 103
Walthingham, William de, app. 16
Wanci, Hugue de, 62 ; Osborne de, 70
Wareham, castle, app. 20
Warkworth, castle, 47

ADDITIONS AND CORRECTIONS

By G. ANDREWS MORIARTY

Reprinted with permission from *The American Genealogist*

Volume XVI, Number 1, July, 1939, pages 56-63

The Falaise roll, by M. Jackson· Crispin, Chevalier de la Legion d'Honneur, etc., and Leonce Macrary, Professeur du College de Falaise. Frome and London, Butler and Tanner, Ltd., 1938. (Obtainable in U. S. from M. Jackson Crispin, Berwick, Pa.)

This very attractive looking volume is an amplification of the bronze tablet recently erected at Falaise containing a roll of the tenants who followed the Great Bastard to the stricken field of Hastings, *not* Senlac, as the authors persist in calling it (*cf.* J. B. Round's *Feudal England*, pp. 333-240).

The book is divided into several sections. After giving the roll and a list of the authorities relied upon, we have the biographies of those whose names appear on the roll, followed by an appendix containing documents and amplifications of the lives, together with reproductions of French charters relating to the Crispins, Lords of Tillières, a collection of former lists and genealogical charts of certain important families. The index is excellent but the biographies are arranged in the exasperating French fashion of giving them according to the Christian name, rather than in the order of the second or distinctive name. One is struck at the outset by the undue amount of space accorded in a book, purporting to be of a general nature, to the Lords of Tillières, to the detriment of other equally important or more illustrious names. . This is the more remarkable as the genealogical chart of Mr. Crispin's ancestry inserted, not very logically, discloses that he does not trace his descent back of a certain John Crispin, who was living in Yorkshire in the reign of Queen Elizabeth. Between this John Crispin and the ancient Lords of Tillières looms a genealogical gulf of some five hundred years, which any serious genealogist knows is quite a space to bridge.

With these general observations I turn to the roll itself. Any competent student of Anglo-Norman genealogy is aware that a list of the proved companions of William at Hastings is a very small one, and the authors admit this at the outset. Such a list would consist only of the names appearing in the poem of Guy of Amiens, in William of Poictiers, Orderic Vitalis and Benoît de Sainte-More, together with the persons depicted in the Bayeux Tapestry. These are the contemporary and, therefore, the primary sources of information as to those who were present on the ever memorable day of Saint Calixtus. Such a list has been compiled by an eminent English scholar of the Anglo-Norman period, Lewis Loyd, Esq., Solicitor of the Treasury. A similar list may be compiled from those given in *The Falaise Roll* on pp. 199 and 201. It may here be noted that the various rolls given in this volume are among its most useful features. Mr. Loyd, in addition, has compiled a list of those who were *probably* at the battle; this is also a small list. It is to be hoped that Mr. Loyd will print these lists in the not too distant future. *The Falaise Roll*, however, is largely based upon that given by Master Wace in his *Roman de Rou*. Now Master Wace lived one hundred years after the battle, being a court poet in the household of Henry Fitz Empress (*i.e.*, Henry II reigned 1154-1189) and besides the space of time which had elapsed since the battle, Master Wace was a good court poet and was prone to flatter the vanity of those who were great and important at the court of the first Angevin. Undoubtedly many of the names listed by him are correct but others are not, and the difficulty of the whole thing is that one cannot to-day separate the sheep from the goats. Our authors recognize the doubt which hangs over the list in the *Roman de Rou*, so I shall not quarrel with them on this point, beyond observing that the names which do not appear in the lists cited by me above, but which are taken solely from Wace cannot be trusted. However, as an essay on the great men on the Morrow of Conquest, such a compilation as *The Falaise Roll* has a very definite value, if carefully compiled.

Let us now consider the formidable array of authorities cited on pp. xi-xii. One notes the names of such great scholars, the pioneers of Anglo-Norman genealogy, as Stapleton and Eyton, but one notes with surprise the omission of such names as Chester-Waters and Mr. Kirk. This surprise turns into amazement to find that the various works of that great scholar of the period, the late Dr. William Farrer, are totally ignored as well as the mass of excellent material to be found in *The Genealogist, The Ancestor* and the *Victoria County Histories*. We find also scant reference to the great mass of record material which has been printed by the Public Record Office. But what is one to say when the name of the greatest scholar of the Anglo-Norman period, the man who has done more than anyone else to put Anglo-Norman genealogy on a sound basis, the author of *Feudal England, Geoffrey de Mandeville* and *Studies in Peerage and Family History*, the late Dr. J. Horace Round, is utterly ignored? Where are the references to the monumental *Complete Peerage*, edited by Vicary Gibbs, now in the course of publication, with its splendid articles by such authorities as G. W. Watson, John Brownbill and Miss Ethel Stokes? Where is my friend, Oswald Barron, F.S.A.; and where is M. Leopold Delisle, by far the premier scholar on the French side of the Channel, whose great works, outside of the *Dives Roll*, are scarcely mentioned? Such omissions augur ill for our roll, especially when one notes reference to such minor works as those of Chesnaye Des Bois and to "that most misleading book," as Dr. Round styled it, *The Norman People*, reliance upon which is only too evident as we proceed. The fact is that in general, both as to the authorities relied upon and the material presented, the French side of this book is far superior to the English and its chief value lies in the material presented from the Norman sources and in the names of the places in Normandy whence the tenants came, which should be useful to those who do not have ready access to M. Dupont's book upon this subject.

We now turn to the list and the biographies. One notes the names of Le Sire de Bailleul and of Guinebaud and Hameline de Balon. As to the former our authors are somewhat vague. Had they studied Dr. Round's *Calendar of Documents Preserved in France* they would have found out that the first Balliol in England, Guy de Balliol, came, not from Bailleul in Normandy, but that he was Sieur of Bailleul-en-Vimeu in Picardy and that he did not arrive in England until the reign of William Rufus (*cf.* also *The Genealogist*, n.s., vol. 8, p. 217). Guy was succeeded both in his English and French fees by his nephew Bernard, the ancestor of the historic house, but Guy left a daughter, Hawis, who became the wife of William Bertram, the first baron of Mitford (*cf. The Falaise Roll*, p. 9). On page 54, under Hamelin de Balon we learn that Dru de Baladon was the ancestor of the de Monmouths and that he had three sons, Hamelin, Guionech and Wynebald or Guinebaud. Here is confusion worse confounded. Belron or Baderon, brother of Guihenoc, a Breton from Epiniac, was the father of William son of Baderon, the Domesday tenant in Gloucestershire and the undoubted ancestor of the de Monmouths (J. B. Round's *Studies in Peerage and Family History*, pp. 121 and 123). As to the Balons our authors are as completely misled, as was the great Dugdale, by the *Genealogia Fundatoris* of the Abergavenny monks. Beginners in mediaeval genealogy should beware of the *Genealogia Fundatoris* of the various religious houses. These monkish pedigrees are as often as not untrustworthy and are responsible for much false genealogy. Hamelin and Wynebaud de Balon first came into England in the reign of William Rufus, from Ballon in Maine and doubtless returned with him after one of his campaigns against Count Helias. Wynebaud was the grandfather of Henry de Newmarch but the greater interest centers around Hameline and his descendants. This question cannot be considered without also considering the fate of the great house of Fitz Osborne. William Fitz Osborne was one of the greatest, if not the greatest, of the nobles of the Conquest, Dapifer of Normandy and Lord of Breteuil; he was Lord of the Isle of Wight, Earl of Hereford and Viceroy of England on the Morrow of the Conquest and was slain in Flanders in 1071. His son, Roger, Earl of Hereford, was undone by his conspiracy hatched at the bride ale of his sister, Emma, with Ralf of Norfolk in 1074. It was for alleged complicity in this plot against the Conqueror that Earl Waltheof lost his head. Great as was the house of Fitz Osborne, its fall was greater. Roger died in prison and by most of the older genealogists he is said to have left no issue male. By a brilliant piece of work, such as only he was capable of doing, Dr. Round has shown that Roger left a son, "Reginald son of the Earl," who married Emmeline, daughter of Hamelin de Balon and whose descendants, under the name of Balon, survived with diminished splendour at Much Marcle for several centuries. All this could have been read in Dr. Round's book, but not one word do we find about it either under Hamelin de Balon (p. 54), under William Fitz Osborne (pp. 41-42) or under Roger de Breteuil (p. 98).

Of those who were most probably at the battle I fail to see the names of Pons, who witnessed a charter of Duke William at St. Valery, just prior to the crossing over to England. Pons is a rare name in Normandy, being far more common in the southwest in Poictou and Aquitaine. It seems most probable that Pons either fell in the battle or was, at any rate, dead before Domesday and that he was the father of Dru, Walter and Richard Fitz Pons, the latter being the ancestor of the great house of Clifford. Another omission of a man from the Western Marches, who, there is every reason to believe, was present at the battle, is Roger de Pîtres or Pistres, who came from Pîtres, a village across the river from Pont de l'Arche, where some four centuries later the descendants of the Normans and the English administered a sound thrashing to the descendants of the Normans and the French. This Roger was a follower of William Fitz Osborne and was by him made the first Norman sheriff of Gloucestershire before he left England forever in 1071. He was the father of that great noble of Henry I, Walter the Sheriff or de Gloucester and the grandfather of Miles, Earl of Hereford, the faithful soldier of the Empress in the wars of the next century, the ancestor, through his daughter and eventual coheiress, of the house of Bohun.

We now turn to the biographies themselves. On p. 4 we learn, under Ansger de Montaigu, that his brother, Dru, was the ancestor of the present Dukes of Manchester, whereas in fact the present ducal house descends from a small yeoman of Henging Houghton, in the middle of the fifteenth century, named William Ladd, through his son Richard Ladd alias Montagu, yeoman, who was living in 1471 and who had no drop of the blood of the ancient Earls of Salisbury in his veins (*cf. Complete Peerage*, ed. Gibbs, vol. 9, appendix D). On the same page we are told that the house of Ros derived its name from Rots, near

Caen, whereas Peter de Ros, the probable son or grandson of Fulc, the Domesday tenant, derived his name from his lordship of Ros in Holderness.

In the account (p. 21) of Walter Giffard, who was, beyond all doubt, present at the battle, we learn that he had brothers Berenger and Osborne Giffard. It so happens that Osborne is an ancestor of this reviewer, who has been engaged for over twenty years on the study of the "sublimi prosapia Giffardi" as they are styled by Orderic. Osborne, the caput of whose barony was Winterburne, Wilts., had his principal place of residence, apparently, at Brimpsfield, Gloucs. He appears in Domesday and also witnessed several charters of the Conqueror towards the end of his reign (*cf.* Henry W. C. Davis' *Regesta Rerum Anglo-Normanorum, 1066-1154*). This Osborne died in 1096, some thirty years after Hastings. Now at the time of the battle we know that Walter Giffard was old and bald-headed and short of breath, so he can hardly have been the brother of Osborne, who survived the battle some thirty years. The word Giffard means "fat face" and was one of those rude nicknames in which the Normans greatly delighted. No relationship has been proved between Walter and Osborne, but the fact that Osborne's son, Ellis, witnessed the great Giffard charter to Longueville points to some relationship. It seems not unlikely, as Mr. A. S. Ellis has pointed out in his *Domesday in Gloucestershire*, that Osborne may have been a younger son of old Walter. The devolution of the Giffard fees in the next century to the descendants of Walter's daughter, Rohese, may be accounted for by the great power of the house of Clare at this time or again Osborne may have been the child of a second marriage of Walter and so excluded under the doctrine of *possessio fratris*, if this doctrine was law at this early date. As to Berenger, the ancestor of the Fronthill Giffards, nothing is known as to his parentage. In connection with the Giffards it is gratifying to note that our authors give the name of the wife of Osburn de Bolbec, the founder of the line, as Wevie, sister of the Duchess Gunor and not Aveline, another sister, a mistake nearly always made by English genealogists. In their discussion of the de Clares under Richard de Bienfaite or de Tonbridge or Fitz Gilbert our authors would have done well to examine Dr. Round's chart of the family in his *Feudal England*, p. 473. Had they done so, their account of this mighty house would have been more correct; and, had they studied the masterly monograph of Mr. Lewis Loyd appearing in App. A of vol. 9 of the *Complete Peerage* (ed. Gibbs) upon the relationship of the families of Warenne and Mortimer they would have avoided some bad errors.

On p. 155 it is stated that Nicola de la Haye, daughter of Richard, the Constable of Lincoln, who married Muriel daughter of Colswegen, the native thegn at Lincoln and not of Eudes the

Sewer as is here stated (*cf.* Wm. Farrer's *Honors and Knights' Fees*, vol. 3, p. 56), "married the Earl of Lincoln and died without issue." This is an error that no English antiquary could make but it was, perhaps, natural for a Frenchman to fall into, as her sister Juliana married Richard de Humet, the Norman, who left issue in Normandy. Nicola was the redoubtable lady, who was made sheriff of Lincoln by King John. She remained faithful to him in all his troubles and held Lincoln Castle for him in 1216. This Nicola married first William son of Erneis and secondly Gerard de Camville. Her granddaughter, Idoine de Camville, was the wife of William le Longespye, the Paladin, who died a hero's death, fighting for the Cross on the disastrous field of Damietta. The account of the Mortimers, p. 156, would have been happier if the account of that family in vol. 9 of the *Complete Peerage* (ed. Gibbs) had been consulted.

On p. 92 the old, long exploded story, as to the descent of the Cavendish family from Guernon, is again retold. Let me point out that the origin of the ducal house of Devonshire is still uncertain, that even their connection with the famous Chief Justice of the reign of Richard II cannot be clearly shown and that their first known ancestor was most probably a respectable mercer, trading in London in the 15th Century (J. H. Round's *Family Origins*, pp. 22-32). As far back as 1712 Mr. Thomas Ruggles, F. S. A., exposed the fictitious Guernon descent. Equally misleading is the statement (p. 91) that "the Earls of Sunderland and Spencer, the Dukes of Marlborough and Barons Churchill" descend from the heroic Chief Justice, Hugh le Despencer, who died beside the Great Earl on the field of Evesham. The first *proved* ancestor of the present ducal house was one William Spencer, a yeoman, living towards the close of the 15th Century. His son, John Spencer of Snitterfield and Hodnell, inherited a fortune from a wealthy uncle, John Spencer, yeoman, of Hodnell, co. Warwick, who prospered as a glazier and died late in 1496, leaving his wealth to the aforesaid John, who in 1506 purchased Wormleighton and in 1508 Althorpe, well known in after years as the family seat. The pedigree tracing their descent from the ancient Despencers was one of the impudent concoctions put out by the Elizabethan heralds (*cf.* "*The Rise of the Spencers*" in J. H. Round's *Studies in Peerage and Family History*, pp. 279-329). The Spencers were typical of the new rich, who rose to importance under the first two Tudors.

The most aggravating article, perhaps, in the whole work is the account of "the Countess Lucy" under Auvrai de Lincoln, in App. 20, p. 156. The Countess Lucy is one of the outstanding unsolved problems of Anglo-Norman genealogy. Mr. Stapleton, Prof. Freeman, Dr. Round, Mr. Kirk and Dr. Farrer (*Honors and Knights' Fees*, vol. 2, p. 154) all have grappled with the question. At the moment a brilliant young American don at

Cambridge is proposing to deal anew with the problem, and this reviewer has it down on his list of things to be considered. The present status of the Countess is, perhaps, best summed up in a monograph by Mr. Brownbill (*Complete Peerage*, ed. Gibbs, vol. 7, App. J), whose conclusions were summarized in *The American Genealogist*, vol. 10, p. 125, *q.v.* Our authors follow Stapleton in placing Lucy as the daughter of William Malet, and wife of Ives Taillebois, who died in 1114 (*sic*),—he actually died in or shortly before 1094. It was their daughter Lucy, according to our authors, who married first Roger Fitz Gerold or Roger de Roumare and secondly Ranulf le Meschin, Earl of Chester, who died prior to 1131. The only difficulty with this is that the charters do not bear out the interpretation that there were two Lucys. We refer the reader to Mr. Brownbill's monograph for the actual history of Lucy.

On p. 35 we are warned against confusing the family of de Brewes or Briouze, here called Briouse, from Briouze near Argentan with that of Brius or Bruce, whose "representative at Hastings" we are told was Robert de Brix, who came from Bruis or Brix in the Contentin. Yet under Brix. p. 88, we are informed that this Robert had sons Adam and William and that the latter received Bramber Castle in Sussex. The actual facts of the case are as follows: William de Brewes from Briouze near Argentan appears in Domesday, when he held the fee of Bramber in Sussex. He was the ancestor of the de Brewes family, usually incorrectly written by English genealogists Braose. Robert de Brus, from Bruis or Brix in the Contentin, first appears in England after the battle of Tenchebrai in the reign of Henry I, the Domesday account of his fee is a later insertion (*cf.* Wm. Farrer's *Early Yorkshire Charters* vol. 2, p. 11). His wife, Agnes, was, apparently, the daughter of Geoffrey Bainard. They had sons Adam, Peter, Robert and probably Hugh. In the account of the Percys, although the parentage of the first William, William aux Gernons or "with the Whiskers," is unknown, we are given the long exploded descent from "Bernard the Dane." Under Nevill, p. 83, we are informed, without any proof being presented, that the Domesday under-tenants in Lincolnshire, Gilbert and Ralph, were sons of a certain Richard de Nevill from Neuville-sur-Touques. We have, moreover, the old nonsense about Gilbert having been "Admiral of the Fleet." A serious account of the Nevills will be found in *Complete Peerage* (ed. Gibbs) vol. 9, p. 491. Gilbert was, beyond all doubt, the ancestor in the female line, of the great native house of Raby.

The above are only a few of the errors noted by this reviewer, but it by no means follows that the book is without merit. There is much valuable source material from the French archives, especially such as concerns the Crispins, Lords of Tillières. The homes of the tenants in Normandy are especially helpful, as are the collection of previous rolls, all brought together in one place. The chief weakness is a totally inadequate knowledge of the English side of the picture and a failure to give proof of various important statements. Some of the biographies are accurate and useful, as, for example, the account of the de Vitre family, p. 3, although our authors seem uncertain whether to ascribe a Breton or Norman origin to the house. It is the indiscriminate mixture of sound facts with fiction and error which is the chief defect. In the hands of an expert the book can be useful, but in the hands of an amateur it is bound to be exceedingly dangerous. For too much use has been made of *The Norman People*, a book containing the same defects.

The use of the word seignior for Sieur or Seigneur strikes one as somewhat quaint.

G. Andrews Moriarty, F. S. A.

GENEALOGICAL TABLES

TABLE I

THE RULERS OF FRANCE

Clovis I (Lodowig) 481–511
  Founder of the empire of the Franks. He is said to have been son of Childeric, who died in 481, the chief of the Salian Franks. At the death of Clovis I the empire was divided into four parts, which were held by his sons: Childebert I (died in 558); Clodomir (d. 524); Clotaire I (d. 561); and Thierri (or Theodoric) I (d. 534). Following upon the deaths of these four, the history becomes somewhat confused by the various successions of sons and nephews. Thierri I was followed by his son, Theudebert I (d. 547), and he was succeeded by his son Theudebald, who died in 553. None of these was sole king, except Clotaire I, who held that position from the death of Childebert I in 558 until his own death in 561. He was followed by his four sons: Caribert (d. 567); Gontran (d. 593); Sigebert I (d. 575); and Chilperic I (d. 584). Sigebert I was followed by his son, Childebert II (d. 596), and Chilperic I was followed by his son, Clotaire II, who at his death in 628 had been sole king for 15 years. To Childebert II succeeded Theudebert II and Thierri II (or Theodoric), who were his sons and both of whom died in 613.
  The foregoing covers the period of 511–628
Dagobert I, sole king 628–638
Sigebert II and Clovis II, joint kings 638–656
Clotaire III, king of Neustria and Burgundy 656–670
Childeric II, king of Austrasia 660–670, sole king 670–673
Thierri III, king of Neustria, 673–679 . . . . 673–687 (?)
Dagobert II, son of Sigebert II, never reigned: murdered in 679.
  From about this date and until 752 the Merovingian kings were merely insignificant figureheads, known as "do nothings" or "rois faineants," and their history is vague. They were under the control of Pippin of Heristal, 687–714; Charles Martel, 715–743; and Pippin (the Short), who became king in 752. The names of these "kings," with approximate dates, are: Clovis III, 687; Childebert III, 695; Dagobert III, 711; Thierri IV, 720, died 737; a space of interregnum, 737–742; Childeric III, last of the Merovingians, deposed in 752; thus covering the period 687–752
  From this period the successions become more settled, and are:

Pippin (the Short) . . .	752–768	John II (the Good) . . .	1350–1364
Charles (Charlemagne) and Carloman (I)	768–771	Charles V (the Wise) . . .	1364–1380
Charlemagne, alone . . .	771–814	Charles VI . . .	1380–1422
Louis I (the Pious) . . .	814–840	Charles VII (the Victorious) . .	1422–1461
Charles I (the Bald) . . .	840–877	Louis XI . . .	1461–1483
Louis II (the Stammerer) . .	877–879	Charles VIII . . .	1483–1498
Louis III (d. 882) and Carloman (II)	879–884	Louis XII (Father of his Country)	1498–1515
Charles II (the Fat) (he was deposed) .	884–887	Francis I . . .	1515–1547
Eudes (Odo), elected by the barons .	887–898	Henry II . . .	1547–1559
Charles III (the Simple) (deposed) .	898–922	Francis II . . .	1559–1560
Robert, elected by barons . .	922–923	Charles IX . . .	1560–1574
Raoul (Rodolf), elected . .	923–936	Henry III . . .	1574–1589
Louis IV (d'Outremer) "from Overseas"	936–954	(Last of the Valois)	
Lothaire	954–986	Henry IV . . .	1589–1610
Louis V (the Lazy) . . .	986–987	Louis XIII . . .	1610–1643
(Last of the Carolingians.)		Louis XIV . . .	1643–1715
Hugh Capet . . .	987–996	Louis XV . . .	1715–1774
Robert (the Good) . . .	996–1031	Louis XVI (he was arrested in June 1791,	
Henry I . . .	1031–1060	and executed on January 21, 1793)	1774–1793
Philip I . . .	1060–1108	Louis XVII never reigned (he died in	
Louis VI (the Fat) . .	1108–1137	prison in 1795)	
Louis VII (the Young) . .	1137–1180	The Republic . . .	1792–1799
Philip II (Philip Augustus) .	1180–1223	The Consulate, Napoleon as First Consul	1799–1804
Louis VIII . . .	1223–1226	Napoleon I, Emperor . .	1804–1814
Louis IX (the Saint) . .	1226–1270	Louis XVIII . . .	1814–1815
Philip III (the Bold) . .	1270–1285	Napoleon I (the 100 days) . .	1815
Philip IV (the Fair) . .	1285–1314	Louis XVIII (restored) . .	1815–1824
Louis X (the Burly, or the Quarreller) .	1314–1316	Charles X . . .	1824–1830
John I, an infant who lived 8 days only	1316	Louis Philippe I . . .	1830–1848
Philip V (the Tall) . . .	1316–1322	The Republic, Louis Napoleon as President	1848–1852
Charles IV (the Fair) . .	1322–1328	Napoleon III, Emperor . .	1852–1870
(Last of the Capets)		The Republic . . .	1870
Philip VI, of Valois . . .	1328–1350		

—— pedigrees proven.
∿∿ pedigrees proven, those intervening, intentionally omitted.
.... pedigrees not proven.

TABLE II

THE RULERS OF ENGLAND

Egbert, king of Wessex	802–827
king of England	827–839
Ethelwulf	839–858
Ethelbald	858–860
Ethelbert	860–866
Ethelred I	866–871
Alfred the Great	871–901
Edward the Elder	901–925
Athelstan	925–940
Edmund	940–946
Edred	946–955
Edwy	955–959
Edgar	959–975
Edward	975–979
Ethelred the Unready	979–1016
Edmund Ironside, reigned 7 months	1016
Canute	1017–1035
Harold I	1035–1040
Hardicanute	1040–1042
Edward the Confessor	1042–1066
Harold II	1066–1066
William the Conqueror	1066–1087
William II (Rufus)	1087–1100
Henry I	1100–1135
Stephen	1135–1154
Henry II	1154–1189
Richard I (Cœur de Lion)	1189–1199
John (Lackland)	1199–1216
Henry III	1216–1272
Edward I	1272–1307
Edward II	1307–1327
Edward III	1327–1377
Richard II	1377–1399
Henry IV	1399–1413
Henry V	1413–1422
Henry VI	1422–1461
Edward IV	1461–1483
Edward V	1483–1483
Richard III	1483–1485
Henry VII	1485–1509
Henry VIII	1509–1547
Edward VI	1547–1553
Mary (Tudor)	1553–1558
Elizabeth	1558–1603
James I	1603–1625
Charles I	1625–1649
Oliver Cromwell (The Commonwealth)	1649–1660
Charles II	1660–1685
James II	1685–1689
William III and Mary	1689–1694
William III alone	1694–1702
Anne	1702–1714
George I	1714–1727
George II	1727–1760
George III	1760–1820
George IV	1820–1830
William IV	1830–1837
Victoria	1837–1901
Edward VII	1901–1910
George V	1910–1936
Edward VIII, reigned 11 months, abdicated	1936
George VI	1936

(*Rech. Domesd.*, 249 to Richard d'Avranches,

Rognwald = Hi
count de Maerc, etc. | d

Thoric, count de Maerc   Hrolf, or Rollon,   Hrollager, = En
                          1st duke of   natural son
                          Normandy   living in 896

Hrolf Turstan, = G
living in 920   c

Anslec de Bastembourg, = N...   Ansfrid de Goz, = N
branch of Briguebec,   or the Danish,
living in 943, died in   first viscount
990   of Exmes till
                                       978

Turstain de Bastembourg = N...   Onfroy, the Danish = N
                                         viscount d'Exmes
                                         in 1013

William Bertram,   Hugh Barbatus de = N...   Turstain de Goz, = Ju
baron of   Montfort-sur-   viscount d'Ex-
Briquebec   Risle   mes since 1035
                                         till 1041

                         Hugh de Montfort =
                         (*Jumièges, Interp.*,   Richard d'Avranches, = E
Robert Bertram,   Hugh de Rosel   Ord. Vit., 163)   living in 1064 and   c
" Le Tort "   in 1082   r

                                 2   3
Richard Turstain = Emma ...   Gilsla, wife of Seig.   Judith, wife of   Elisende, wife of   H
Haldub   Montreuil and   Richer de   Gilbert, count d'Eu   I
                         Echaufour   Laigle   d
                         (*Jumièges, Interp.*,
                         Ord. Vit., 163)

                                   2   3
Eudo al Chapel = Muriel, half-sister   Robert,   Philippe d'Avranches,   Ri
             of d. William   monk of St. Evroult,   died s.p.   s
             (*vide* 155)   abbot of St. Edmond   a
                                                          2
                                                          s
                                                          c
                                                          l
                                                          (

[1] Descent of the earls of Chester from the Crispin family.

TABLE III

IER OF ROLLO, FIRST DUKE OF NORMANDY

d earl of Chester, balance *vide* 158)

r Hildur,
: Rolf Nefio

N.

William Malet = Esilia Crispin,[1] 1st marriage,
dau. Gilbert
Crispin I

e, dau. of Thibaut,
de Blois and de Chartres

Ivo Taillebois = Lucia Malet

William, branch = N...
of the seignors
of Bec-Crespin

Ranulph le Meschin, = Lucia Taillebois
3rd earl, died
c. 1129

Osmont de Goz = N...

Ranulph de Gernon,
4th earl, d. 1153
(*vide* 157)

de Monterolier

Hugh Kevelioc,
5th earl, d. 1181

de Conteville,
f Arlette,
r of the Conqueror

Ranulph de Blundeville,
6th earl, died
s.p. 1232

d'Avranches, = Hermentrude, dau.		4 Isabelle, wife	5 Mathilde = Renouf de Brica-
of Chester,	of Hughes, count	of Gilbert,	d'Avranches	sard, viscount
1101	de Clermont	son of the		de Bayeux
		count de		
		Corbeil		

d'Avranches, = Mathilde, dau.	4 Othewell, governor	5 Giva, married
1120 at the	of Etienne,	of the son of	to Geoffroy
25 years,	count of	Henri I, died in	Rider, died
rl of Chester,	Champagne	in 1120	in 1120
ded by his			
Ranulph			
chin			
above)			

Rognwald, count of Maerc = Hildir, dau. of Rolf Nefio

1. Rollo, Rollon, Row, or Robert, = (1) Gisla, dau. of Charles the Simple, = (2) Poppa, dau. of Berenger,
   d. of N. 911–927   k. of France (no issue)   c. of Bayeux,
      eventually mar. by Roll

2. William Longsword, d. of N. = Sprota   = Asperleng of Vaudreuil
   927–943, [1] mar. Leudegarde, | eventually mar.
   dau. of Herbert II, c. de   by William Longsword
   Vermandois (no issue)

3. Richard (I) the Fearless = (1) Emma,   = (2) Gonnor de Crépon,   Raoul = Alberad
   d. of N. 943–996   dau. of Hugh the Great,   of Danish extraction   c. of Ivry
      c. of Paris (no issue)   and Bayeux

Hugh,
bishop of Bayeux

4. Richard II, = (1) Judith, = (2) Papia   Mauger,   Robert,   Emma = (1) Ethelred,   = (2)
   d. of N.   dau. of Conan   (*Hist. gen.*   c. of   c. of Evreux,   k. of England   k.
   996–1026   le Tort, c. of   *de Nor-*   Corbeil   and arch-
     Rennes, slain   *mandie,*   bishop of   Edmund   Edward
     992, and half-   du Mou-   Rouen | the Confesso
     sister of   lin, 103)   Edward
     Geoffry, c. of
     Brittany, mar.   Edgar
     circa 1008, died
     1017 (*vide*
     Plan., I, 78, 80)

5. Richard III,   Estrith, sister of   = Robert (I) the Magnificent,   Arlette = Herluin   Eleanor = Ba
   d. of N.   Canute the Great   d. of N. 1028–1035   her issue | of Conte-   c.
   1026–1028   (no issue) (*vide*   by d. | ville
     Plan., I, 15 ; Free-   Robert I
     man, I, 472)

7. William the Conqueror = Matilda,   Adele = Odo,   Odo,   Robert
   d. of N. 1035–1087   dau. of Baldwin V,   c. of Cham-   bishop of Bayeux,   c. of
     c. of Flanders   pagne   d. of Kent   e. of C

Nicholas,   Helen   John = N . . . du Hommet
abbot of   (natural   assumed the name
St.-Ouen   daughter)   du Hommet (mother
(natural   (*vide* 121)   unknown)
son)
(Ord. Vit.,   Robert du Hommet
II, 69)   (*vide* 154)

8. Robert Courteheuse = Sibella de   William Rufus   9. Henry I   = (1)   Matilda = (2) Adeliza,
   d. of N. 1087–1106, | Conversana   k. of E.   k. of E. 1100–35;   dau. of   Geoffry Ba
   born 1054, died   1087–1100,   d. of N. 1106–   Malcolm III,   d. of Lorr
   1134 (*vide* Plan.,   born 1060   1135, born 1068   k. of Scot-   and c. of
   I, 86)   (*ibid.*)   (*ibid.*)   land   (*ibid.*)

Daughter = Lambert de   William Clito
(natural)   St-Saens

10. Geoffry Plantagenet = Matilda (empress)
    c. of Anjou ; d. of N.
    from shortly after
    1135 until 1149

11. Henry II   = Eleanor, dau. and heir
    k. of E. 1154–1189, | of William, d. of
    d. of N. 1149–1189 | Aquitaine

12. Richard (I)   = Berengaria   13. John (Lackland)   = (1) Hadwisa,   = (2) Isabella,
    Cœur de Lion,   of Navarre   k. of E. 1199–1216,   dau. of earl   dau. of Aymer,
    k. of E. and   d. of N. 1199–1204.   of Gloucester   c. of Angoulême
    d. of N. 1189–1199   This title became
       extinct 8 June 1795

The pedigrees to William the Conqueror were taken from Jumièges (24–8, 33–4–5, 60–6–8–9,

TABLE IV

Gerlotta = William, d. of Aquitaine
and c. of Poitou

| John, bishop of Avranches, later archbishop of Rouen | Emma = Osberne de Crépon | Daughter = Richard de Beaufou |

| ...anute, Denmark | Hedwig = Geoffry, c. of Brittany | Matilda = Odo, c. of Chartres | | Richard I, his natural children (*vide* T. V) |

| ...vin IV, Flanders | Alisa = Rainald, also called c. of Bur-Judith gundy | William, monk of Fécamp | William = c. of Arques and Talou | Mauger, archbishop of Rouen | Papia = Gilbert, advocate of St. Valery |

Guy of Burgundy

| = Matilda, ...rtain, dau. of Roger ...nwall de Montgomery | Emma = Richard, viscount of Avranches | Muriel = Eudo al Chapel, sire de la Haie |

William the Conqueror,
his natural children

| u. of ...atus, ...e ...abant | Richard, born 1057–8, died young (*ibid.*) | Cecilia, abbess of Holy Trinity, Caen, born 1056 (*ibid.*) | Constance = Alain, born 1061, d. of mar. 1086 Brittany (*ibid.*) | Adela = Stephen, born 1062, c. of Blois mar. 1080 and Chartres (*ibid.*) |

Agatha, born 1064, died before 1080, unmar. (*ibid.*)

| William Pevrel by Maud, dau. of Ingleric, an Anglo-Saxon noble | = Adelina de Lancaster, dau. of Roger de Poitou, e. of Lancaster | Wife of Hugh de Chateau-sur-Loir | [2] Thomas, arch-bishop of York |

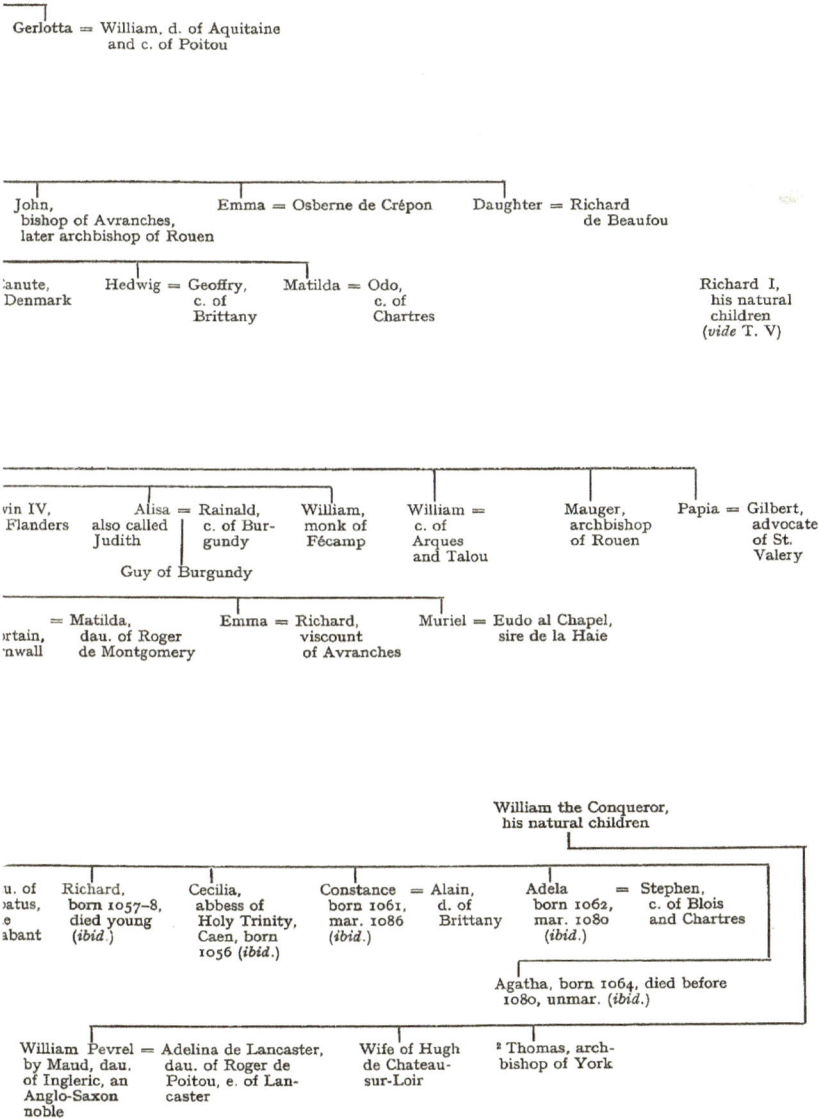

[1] Leudegarde, who married, 2nd, Thibaud (I) le Tricheur, count of Blois and Chartres.
[2] Thomas, archbishop of York, witnessed a Charter of king William I as follows : *Ego Thomas Archiepiscopus Regis filius*, wherein his name appears in capital letters, the same as those of king William, queen Matilda, and their sons Robert and William, while those of primate Lanfranc and the great earls are in ordinary type (*Olivarius Vredius, Gen. Com. Fland. Prob. Tab.* 3), *vide* Père Anselme, Forester, and Planché (I, 73 ; II, 272) concerning these alleged illegitimate children.

Godfrey, count
of Brionne and Eu,
born c. 1060,
died c. 1108
(*vide* 19, 81)

Daughter (unknown),——
possibly mar.
Baldric the Teuton,
aunt of c. Gilbert
(*vide* 19, 81)

William, count = Lesceline,
of Exmes   dau. of Turquetil d
(later Eu)   Neufmarché
                     (*vide* T. XI.)

Gilbert, c.················
of Brionne and Eu,
born c. 1000,
died c. 1040 (*vide* 81)

Sister of c. Gilbert,——
possibly mar.
Baldric the Teuton
(*vide* 19, 81)

Robert, c. of = Beatrix
Eu

William
c. of H
and S

Richard de   Baldwin de
Bienfaite,   Meules
mother
unknown,
probably
Flemish

Niece of c. Gilbert.——
Vital says mar.
Baldric the Teuton,
but it is intenable
(*vide* 19, 81)

William,   Robert
c. of Eu

Fouque d'Aunou I   Gonnor = Gilbert Crispin I   Daughter,   Baldric de   Richard de
                                                         husband   Bauquency   Courcy I
                                                         unknown

Fouque d'A. II,   Gilbert Crispin II,   William Crispin I,   Robert   Milo (2),   Rich
(Hastings)   (Hastings)   (Hastings)   (Hastings)   (Ha

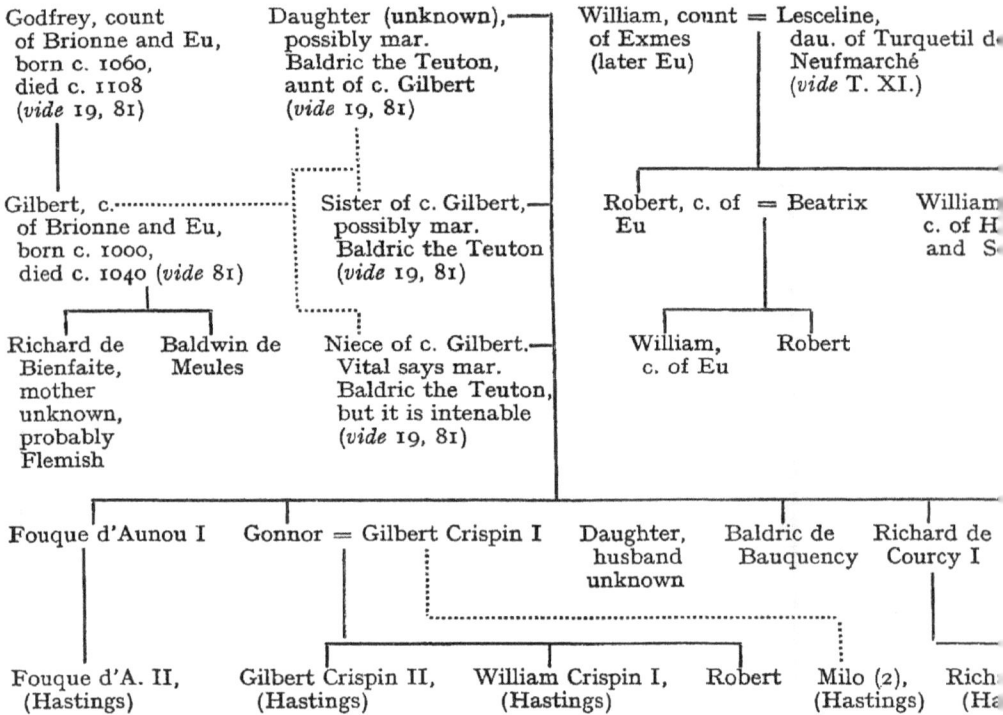

[1] This marriage is not the only indication that the duchess Gonnor had a much younger sister
count Gilbert's sister or aunt.

TABLE V

ARD I, DUKE OF NORMANDY

, 80, 130, 136)

| William, count witnessed foun- dation of Fécamp, 990 (*vide* 131) | Robert, count despoiler of abbey of Mont-St. Michel (*vide* 131) | Daughter, one of the two unidentified daughters was Beatrice, abbess of = Gautier de Lescelina or Montivilliers de Turqueville (*vide* 81, 136) (*vide* T. XI) |

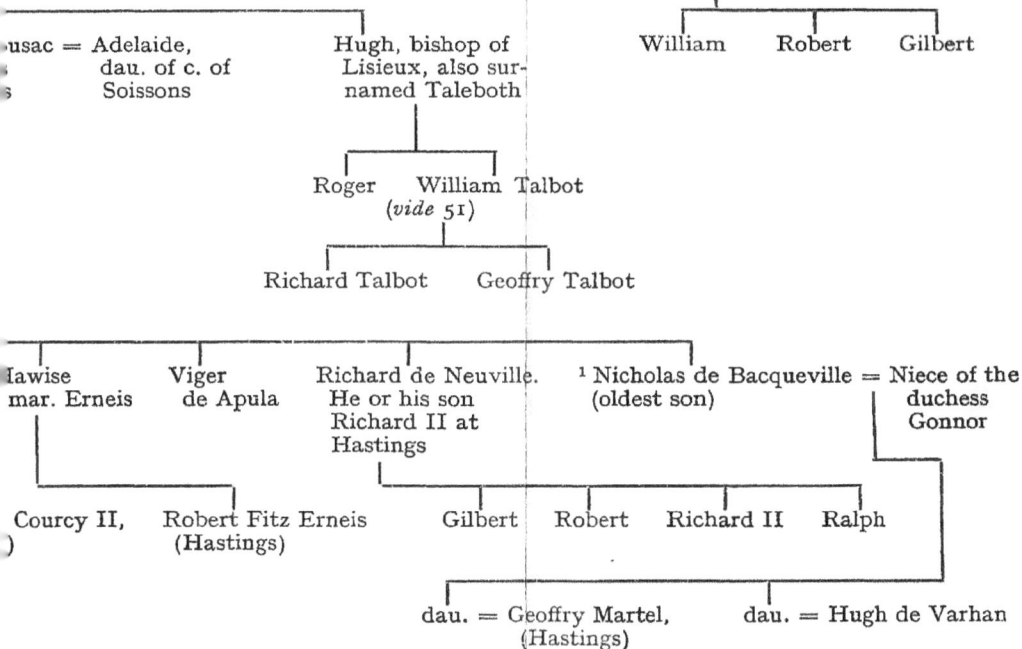

usac = Adelaide, dau. of c. of Soissons

Hugh, bishop of Lisieux, also sur- named Taleboth

William   Robert   Gilbert

Roger   William Talbot (*vide* 51)

Richard Talbot   Geoffry Talbot

| Iawise mar. Erneis | Viger de Apula | Richard de Neuville. He or his son Richard II at Hastings | ¹ Nicholas de Bacqueville = Niece of the (oldest son) duchess Gonnor |

Courcy II,)   Robert Fitz Erneis (Hastings)   Gilbert   Robert   Richard II   Ralph

dau. = Geoffry Martel, (Hastings)   dau. = Hugh de Varhan

Tables VI and VIII).   It also makes it increasingly clear that Vital should have said Baldric marrie(

Herfast de Crépon

Sainfria = The forester
of Scheceville

Wevie = Osberne Giffard,
sire de Bolbec

Aveline =

Osberne de Crépon = Emma, dau. of Raoul,
c. of Ivry

[2] Gautier Gifford I = dau. of Gerard Flaitel

William FitzOsberne = Adelina de Toeni = Richilde, countess
of Flanders

Gautier Giffard II = Rohias, da
Richard c
faite

William de
Breteuil

Ralph,
a monk

Roger,
e. of
Hereford

Emma = Raoul de Gaël,
e. of Norfolk

Matilda = William Chan
of Tancarvill

Eustache = Juliana,
(natural   dau. of Henry I
son)   of England

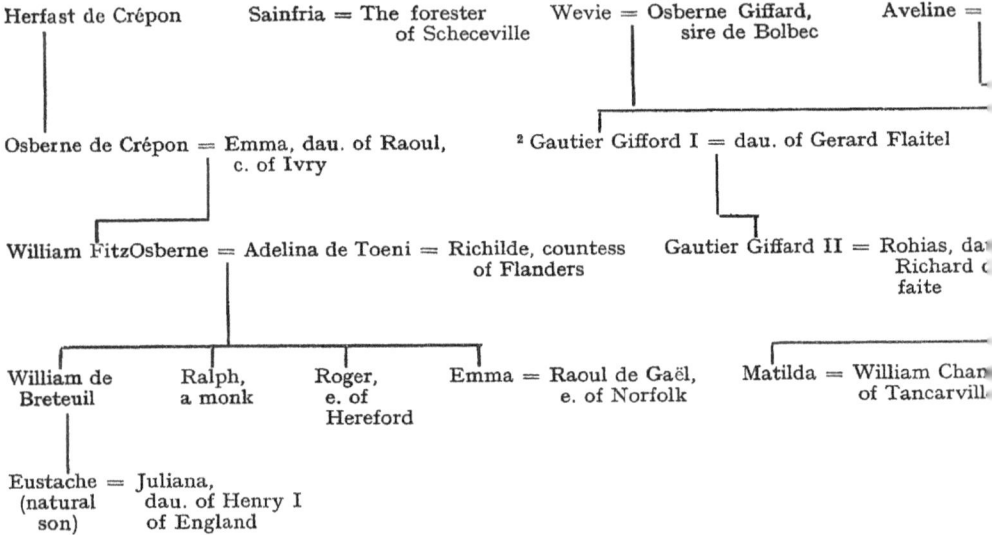

[1] Thurold was the eldest son of Torf, who was the son of Bernard the Dane (*vide* 14; T.
[2] There is evidently a generation missing between Osberne and Gautier II; that of William,
Arques, is correct.

TABLE VI

ISTERS OF THE DUCHESS GONNOR

Torigny, 324, 325)

de Pontaudemer [1]

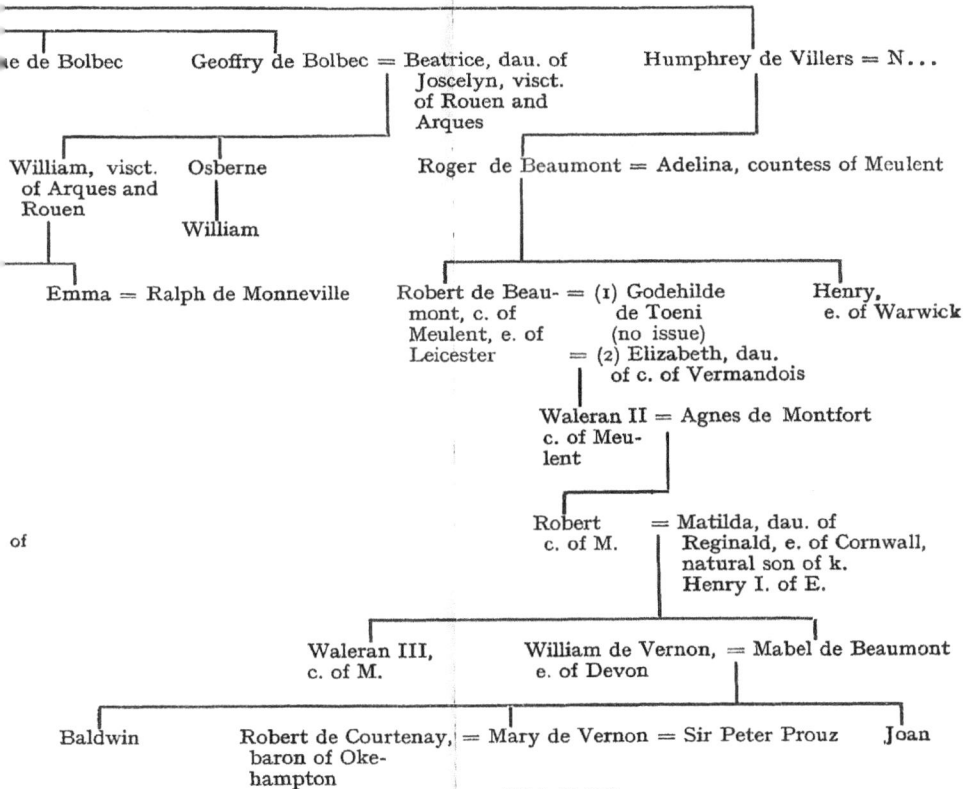

e de Bolbec   Geoffry de Bolbec = Beatrice, dau. of   Humphrey de Villers = N...
                                   Joscelyn, visct.
                                   of Rouen and
                                   Arques

William, visct.   Osberne   Roger de Beaumont = Adelina, countess of Meulent
of Arques and
Rouen
                    William

Emma = Ralph de Monneville   Robert de Beau- = (1) Godehilde   Henry,
                              mont, c. of   de Toeni   e. of Warwick
                              Meulent, e. of   (no issue)
                              Leicester   = (2) Elizabeth, dau.
                                                  of c. of Vermandois

                                              Waleran II = Agnes de Montfort
                                              c. of Meu-
                                              lent

of   Robert   = Matilda, dau. of
                                              c. of M.   Reginald, e. of Cornwall,
                                                          natural son of k.
                                                          Henry I. of E.

                   Waleran III,   William de Vernon, = Mabel de Beaumont
                   c. of M.   e. of Devon

Baldwin   Robert de Courtenay, = Mary de Vernon = Sir Peter Prouz   Joan
           baron of Oke-
           hampton
                                   (*Vide* T. IX)

DESCENDANTS OF THE NIECES OF THE DUCHESS GONNOR RECORDE[

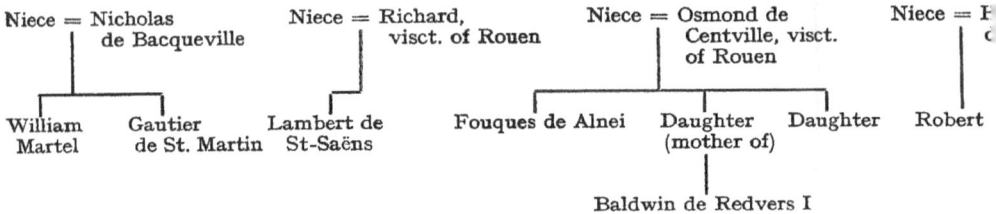

Niece = Nicholas
        de Bacqueville

Niece = Richard,
        visct. of Rouen

Niece = Osmond de
        Centville, visct.
        of Rouen

Niece = F
        c

William   Gautier   Lambert de
Martel   de St. Martin St-Saëns

Fouques de Alnei   Daughter   Daughter   Robert
                (mother of)

Baldwin de Redvers I

PEDIGREES CORRECTED TO

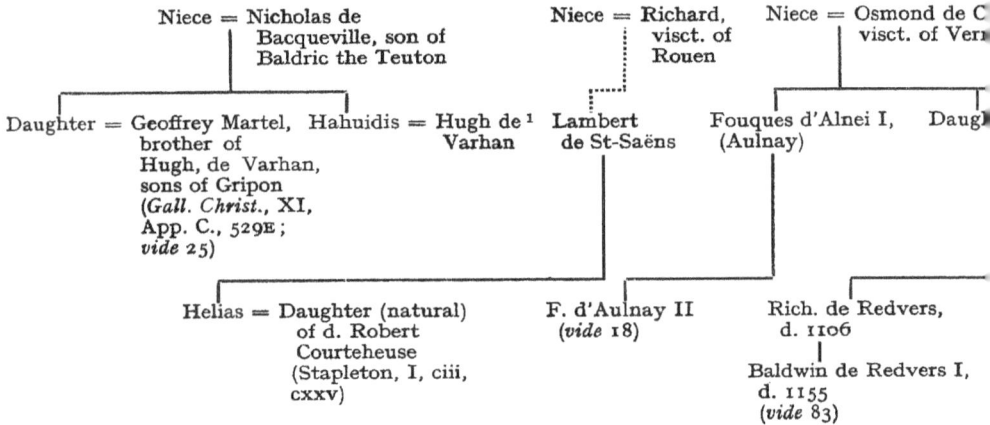

Niece = Nicholas de
        Bacqueville, son of
        Baldric the Teuton

Niece = Richard,
        visct. of
        Rouen

Niece = Osmond de C
        visct. of Ver

Daughter = Geoffrey Martel, Hahuidis = Hugh de [1] Lambert
        brother of   Varhan   de St-Saëns
        Hugh, de Varhan,
        sons of Gripon
        (*Gall. Christ.*, XI,
        App. C., 529E;
        vide 25)

Fouques d'Alnei I,   Daugl
(Aulnay)

Helias = Daughter (natural)
        of d. Robert
        Courteheuse
        (Stapleton, I, ciii,
        cxxv)

F. d'Aulnay II
(*vide* 18)

Rich. de Redvers,
d. 1106

Baldwin de Redvers I,
d. 1155
(*vide* 83)

The details of these pedigrees of Robert de Torigny are incorrect, even that of Richard, viscount of R
duke Robert Courteheuse, and was dispossessed of his estates by Henry I for his adherence to the cause of V
the grandson of viscount Richard.   The statement, however, of descent in some way of these illustrious famil
[1] The lands of Hugh de Varhan (Hugh Fitz Grip) in Dorsetshire passed through his widow Hahuidis to A

TABLE VII

BY ROBERT DE TORIGNY IN HIS *INTERPOLATION OF JUMIÈGES* (328–9)

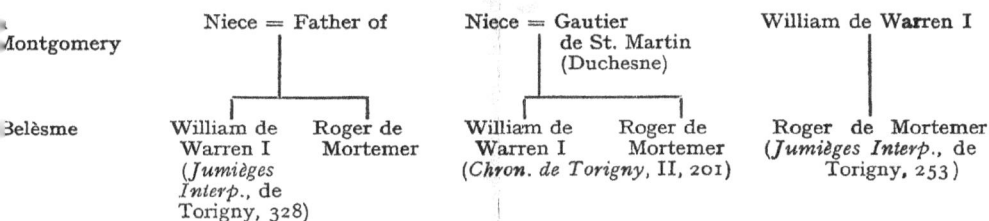

Montgomery	Niece = Father of		Niece = Gautier de St. Martin (Duchesne)		William de Warren I
Belèsme	William de Warren I (*Jumièges Interp.*, de Torigny, 328)	Roger de Mortemer	William de Warren I (*Chron. de Torigny*, II, 201)	Roger de Mortemer	Roger de Mortemer (*Jumièges Interp.*, de Torigny, 253)

CONFORM TO THE KNOWN FACTS

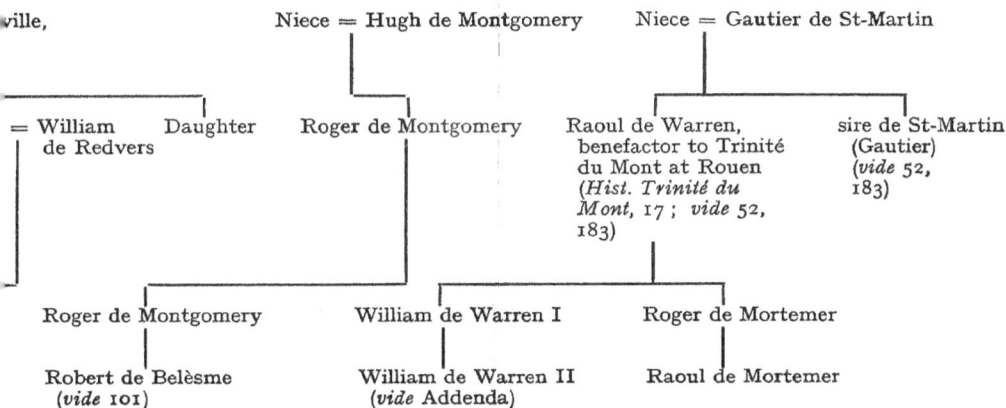

ville,			Niece = Hugh de Montgomery	Niece = Gautier de St-Martin	
= William de Redvers	Daughter	Roger de Montgomery		Raoul de Warren, benefactor to Trinité du Mont at Rouen (*Hist. Trinité du Mont*, 17 ; *vide* 52, 183)	sire de St-Martin (Gautier) (*vide* 52, 183)

Roger de Montgomery	William de Warren I	Roger de Mortemer
Robert de Belèsme (*vide* 101)	William de Warren II (*vide* Addenda)	Raoul de Mortemer

in which a generation seems to be missing. Helias, son of Lambert de St-Saëns, married a natural daughter of Clito, duke of Flanders, duke Robert's son, in 1127. He could scarcely have been, as Stapleton suppose nieces of the duchess Gonnor has generally been accepted and cannot be refuted.
de Lincoln as recorded in a charter of the Conqueror. (*Domesday; Charter of Montivilliers*, back of sheet "C 6."

Gilbert Crispin I = Gonnor,
seigneur de   dau. of Baldric the Teuton,
Tillières c.   descended from Richard I, duke
1030 to 1040,   of Normandy, through
French   her mother
occupation,
c. 1040 to 1045

Gilbert C. II = Hersende   William Crispin I = Eve de Montfort   Robert,   Esilia = (1) Wi
seig. de T.   comte du Vexin,   died s.p.   (*vide*   Ma
1054–1107   seig. d'Estrépagny,   28, 142) = (2) Al
                            etc.   Li

Gilbert III,   Ribold Landry,   William II   = Agnes d'Estrépagny   Gilbert, abbot of
mar. Lau-   mar.   vict. du Vexin,   Westminster
rentia,   Hildeberga seig. d'Estré-   1086–1117
seig. de T.   pagny, etc.
1107–1154

                              William III = N . . . *possibly* Simon   Amaury, seig. de   N
            Isnardo   Raoul   seig. d'Es- lady of   Châteauceaux
                              trépagny,   Lisors   (*possibly*)
                              etc.
       Renaud   Adeline

Gilbert IV = Julienne de Laigle   William IV.   Joscelyn   = Isabel du Plessis   Robe
seig. de T.   seig. d'Estré- succeeded   de Dangu
1154–1171   pagny, etc.   his brother
                                  died s.p.

Gilbert V = Eleanor   Robert   William V = Amicie   Robert = Agnes   Eustache Agne
seig. de T. de Vitrie (*possibly*) sire de   de Roye   Seig.   de Rouvray
1171–1189   Dangu, etc.   d'Arquency

Gilbert VI, Juiliana,   Joanna,   William VI = Alix de   Isabeau = Robert de Neubo
baron of   dame of T. mar.   sire de   Sancerre   lady of   baron of Asneb
T. 1189–   before   Thomas   Dangu, etc.   Livarot
1222, mar.   1227, pos- de Mal-
dau. of   sibly from maines   William VII = Jeanne de Mortemer,
Philippe   1222, mar.   constable of Normandy,   lord of I
de Creully   Baldwin   marshal of France,   mar. c. 1054,   and St-
             Rastel   baron of Bec-Crispin, died c. 1069   sur-Ept
                                                Estrépagny, etc.,   died 12
James de Bovel- = Hilaria, dame of   died c. 1313
ingham   T. 1227, last
                  so recorded   William VIII = Mahaut   Jean I = J
                  1247   constable of N., de Beaumez sire de Dangu, de
                                                died before 1330   Lisors, and de Mauny,
Gilbert VII (possibly grandson of   living 1320–30,
Robert), b. of T. 1259–1314,   died before 1334
possibly from 1247

                                                Jeanne   = Jean de Meulan II,   Marie
Gilbert VIII,   Jacot   Jehan   lady of Estrépagny, grand chamberlain   lady of
b. of T. 1314–   Varanguebec and Neaurles, of France, c. of La Lut
1370, when barony   brought constableship of Tancarville   Boutav
acquired by king   Normandy to husband   Louves
of France

FAMILY OF LE BAVEUX,   William XI = Jeanne de   Jeanne = (1) Raoul Herpin,
   BARONS OF TILLIÈRES   sire de   Calletot,   seig. St.-Sanflieu
Guy Le Baveux I,   Mauny de   lady of   = (2) Jean, seig. de
recorded b. of T. 1386   Lisors, died Fluery,   Crevecœur and
       | before 1256 Lilly and   de Thois
   Robert = Agnès Paynel

TABLE VIII

RMANDY AND FRANCE

, 16, 17, 18, 19, 23)

Emma † = N. de Condé (*vide* 116)	William de Cheney	Milo,† baron of = Matilda de Wallingford, Wallingford held Gethampton (no issue)		Ralph de Langetot I

y)

Fouques *possibly*)	Pierre de Condé (*vide* 28, 185; T. XIV)	Hugh, (natural son)	Cecilia, = Ralph (natural de Langetot II dau.)

f c, *obili* possibly)	Roger de Condé = Adelaide de Cheney, heiress " Horncastle "	Ralph de Milo de Langetot III Langetot I

s = Goël de Baudemont	Agnes = Walter Clifford	Emma = Geoffry Milo de de Langetot Fitz William Langetot II

Robert Emeline Marcelle = Baron of de Tancarville, Harcourt II Wi'iam or Ralph		Muriel = Alan de b. 1155 Dunstanville

Cecilia = Alard Fitz
b. 1161, William
held Gethampton

e de Ferrières, d 1292	¹ Hugh, ancestor of Seigneur de Bourri, de Villebon and marquis de Vardes	Alice = Roger de Cheney, de Langetot son of Ralph de Caineto (*vide* 21)

Jean, lord of Lisors, died 1316	William d'Arquency, dead by 1327	Etienne, dead 1327

Jean de Chalons III, high cupbearer of France, c. of Auxerre and Ton- nerre	Jean II = Jeanne sire de d'Avangour Dangu, de Thury and de Lisors	William IX = Jeanne sire de de Moy Mauny, dead be- fore 1368

William X = Agnes . de Dangu de Trie de Thury, l s.p. be- e 1353	Blanche = (1) Louis, succeeded to seig. de Dangu and Thury Ferrières (2) Pierre or Jean de D·f····	Jeanne = Guy, lady of sieg. de Motte-Cesny Tournebu and Grimbosc

1391

Guy II, b. of T., died s.p. 1406	Jean I, b. of T. 1406–1419, died s.p.	Jeanne, dame of T., then widow of Jean Le Veneur

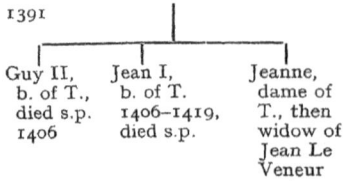

ENGLISH OCCUPATION
Gilbert Halsade,
  b. of T. 1419–1449

FAMILY OF LE VENEUR,
  BARONS OF TILLIÈRES

Philippe I, 1450–1486

François I, living 1486
  and in 1503, probably
  died 1505

Jean II, recorded baron 1508,
  living 1534

Tanneguy I, became count of
  T. 1565, died 1592–96. His
  son and heir Jacques predeceased him

Jacques I (succession questionable)
  claimed by Père Anselme,
  count 1592–1596

Tanneguy II, c. of T.
  1596–1653, son of Jacques

Henry I, c. of T.
  1653–1687

François II, c. of T.
  1687–1704

Jacques-Tanneguy I,
  c. of T. 1704–1740

Jacques-Tanneguy II,
  marquis of T. 1740–1748

François-Jacques-Tanneguy,
  marquis of T. 1748–1789
  (*Vide* seigneurs de Tillières,
  addenda)

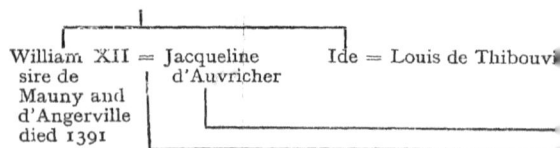

William XII = Jacqueline   Ide = Louis de Thibouvi
sire de   d'Auvricher
Mauny and
d'Angerville
died 1391

Jean = Marguerite d'Ambrois
hereditary marshal of Normandy,
baron of Bec-Crispin, Mauny, etc.,
died s.p. 1453

Jean I = Tiphenne Paon
          (Doss. Bleus., 78

William = N . . .   Michel, canon
                                       created car
                                       died 1316
Jordain = Marie de l'Isle

Geoffry = Marie Postel

William = Catherine de Brillac   Jean,
                                        canon and t

Jean II = Marguerite Roncherolles,   Charles,
councillor of the   lady of Vardes   council
king, 1470   1482–1
                                      the ch

Charles du Bec I = Madeline de Beauvilliers   A
vice-admiral of France,
baron of Bourri and
of Vardres

Charles du Bec II, = Marie de Clercy   Philippe, bishop
living 1558   archbishop of R
                                          and peer of Fra

Georges = Marie Jubert   Jean,   René du
       = Jeanne de Laurens   died   marqui
Their male children of both s.p.   Vardes
  marriages died young   La Bo

Jean III,   René du Bec IV = Jacqueline
  murdered by brigands   countess c
  in Italy 1616

François-René du Bec-Crispin de Grimaldy = Catherine Ni
count of Moret, marquis de Vardes,   dau. Jean N
lieutenant-general of the armies of the   first preside
king, captain colonel of 100 Swiss Guards, chamber of
died in Paris 1688   in Paris

Marie Elizabeth = Louis de Rohan-Chabot,
dau. and sole heir,   duke of Rohan-Chabot,
born 4 April 1661,   prince of Laon, etc.
mar. 28 July 1678

ine,
ibishop of Narbonne,
f Laon, etc.,
d 1472

Jeanne = Pierre   Jacqueline = Robert
succeeded her de Brézé   de Fouques
half-brothers,
was the natural
dau. of king
Charles VII

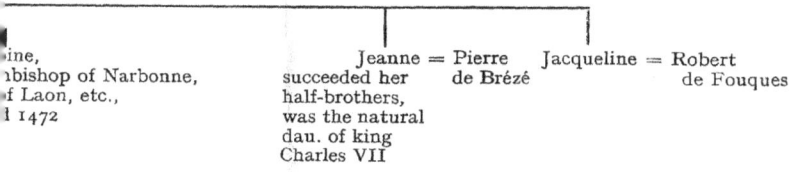

*CRISPIN RELATIONSHIP WITH THE COUNTS OF ANJOU, KINGS OF ENGLAND
AND FRANCE.

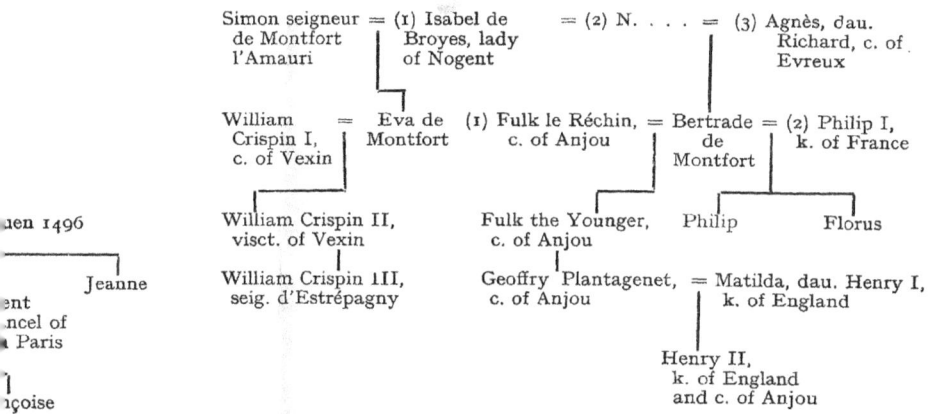

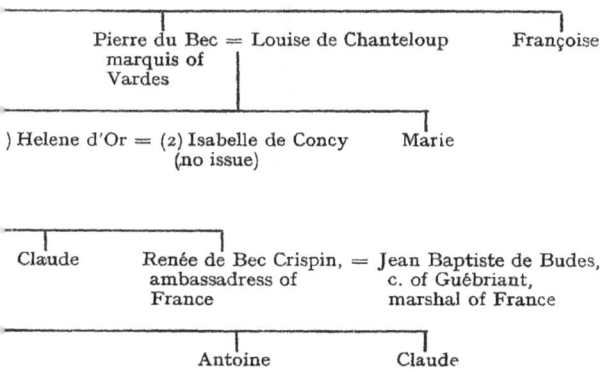

Simon seigneur = (1) Isabel de   = (2) N. . . . = (3) Agnès, dau.
de Montfort   Broyes, lady   Richard, c. of
l'Amauri   of Nogent   Evreux

William   = Eva de (1) Fulk le Réchin, = Bertrade = (2) Philip I,
Crispin I,   Montfort   c. of Anjou   de   k. of France
c. of Vexin   Montfort

uen 1496

Jeanne

ent
ncel of
i Paris

içoise

William Crispin II,   Fulk the Younger, Philip   Florus
visct. of Vexin   c. of Anjou

William Crispin III,   Geoffry Plantagenet, = Matilda, dau. Henry I,
seig. d'Estrépagny   c. of Anjou   k. of England

Henry II,
k. of England
and c. of Anjou

Pierre du Bec = Louise de Chanteloup   Françoise
marquis of
Vardes

) Helene d'Or = (2) Isabelle de Concy   Marie
(no issue)

Claude   Renée de Bec Crispin, = Jean Baptiste de Budes,
ambassadress of   c. of Guébriant,
France   marshal of France

Antoine   Claude

* Thus the Crispin family, the counts of Anjou, and the descendants of Philip I, king of France,
by his marriage with Bertrade de Montfort, were related through their common ancestor, Simon
de Montfort l'Amauri, but they were not descended from each other.
† Relationship of Condé, Cheney, Crispin and Langetot.

[1] William = dau. of Osmond de Centville,
de Redvers | visct. of Vernon and a niece
(*Gall.Christ.*, | of the duchess Gonnor
vol. xi)

[2] Richard de Redvers I = Adeliza   William de Redvers
1st earl of Devon,   de Pevrel   or de Vernon at
lord of the Isle of   Hastings, held
Wight, died 1107   fief of Vernon, 1077

William   Robert   Richard
l. 1096,   l. 1101,   baron of
died s.p.   died s.p.   ton, her
before 1101   of Devo
               died s.p

Baldwin de Redvers I,   William de Vernon,   Robert of   Hadewise = Williar
2nd earl of Devon,   heir to his father's   Ste-Mère   (Stephen II,   R
lord of Isle of Wight,   estates in Normandy   l'Eglise   clvii)
died 1155

Richard de Redvers II,   William de Redvers = Mabel, dau. of Robert,   Hen
3rd earl of Devon,   surnamed de Ver-   earl of Meulent (Meulan),
died 1162   non, 6th earl of   descended from Henry I of
         Devon, lord of the   England, Bernard the Dane,
         Isle of Wight, died   Henry I of France, Charlemag
         1216

Baldwin   Richard,   Baldwin = Margery, dau.   Mary   = (1) Robe
de Redvers,   5th earl of   died   of Warine   de Vernon,   baro
4th earl of   Devon,   v.p.   FitzGerald   at length   ham
Devon,   succeeded   1216   sole heir   died
died s.p.   by his uncle
     William de   (1) William = Joan,
     Vernon,   Briwere   siste
     died s.p.   Baldwin = Amicia, dau. of   Mai
     1166   7th earl,   e. of Gloucester   Ver
          died 1245

               Baldwin,
               8th earl,
               poisoned 1262.
               Line ends

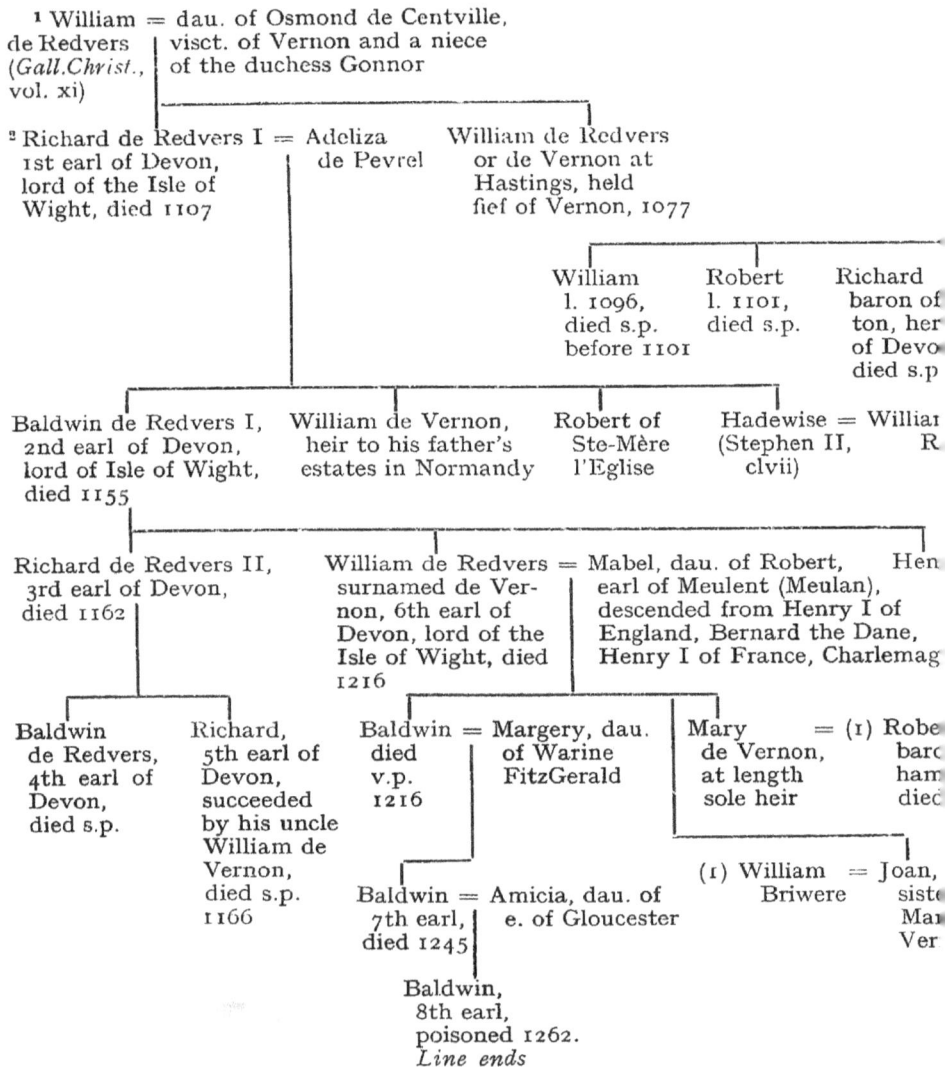

[1] William de Redvers and his brother, Baldwin, were the heirs of their brother, Richa
Père de Chartres of 1060 by its abbot, Landry. This document indicates that Richard di
Chartres, I, 152), while its abbot, Landry, was deceased in 1069 (*ibid.*, I, 210).

[2] Opinion differs whether Richard de Redvers I actually was earl of Devon (*vide*, 84). S
created by king Stephen (II, cclxxiii).

[3] For the wives omitted, *vide* 131.

TABLE IX

.IONNE AND EU, HEREDITARY SHERIFF OF DEVON, AND
RS, EARL OF DEVON

itapleton, addenda)

Baldwin de Meules and du Sap,
   baron of Okehampton,
   hereditary sheriff of Devon

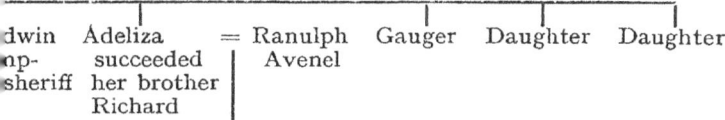

dwin Adeliza = Ranulph Gauger Daughter Daughter
np-   succeeded   Avenel
sheriff her brother
    Richard

(1) Robert d'Abrinces = Matilda = (2) Robert FitzEdith
    or d'Avranches   natural son of Henry I

Reginald de Courtenay = Hawise,   William de Courtenay = Matilda
            lady of   son of sir Reginald
            Okehampton

                                    Sir John de Chudleigh = Johanna
                                                  Beauchamp
                                    Sir James de Chudleigh = Johanna
urtenay = (2) Sir Peter Prouz   de la Pomeroy
 -        of Changford, Devon   Joanna de Chudleigh = Sir John St-
                                                  Aubyn
    ³⋅William Prouz

                                    John de St-Aubyn = Catherine
    Walter Prouz   Challows
                                    Joanna de St-Aubyn = (2) William
    William Prouz   Dennys

    Sir William Prouz   Alice Dennys = John Bonville

    Sir Richard Prouz

                                    Florence Bonville = Thomas
    Thomasine Prouz = Sir John de   Forescue
     mar. c. 1330   Chudleigh

                                    Isabella Fortescue = Anthony
                                                  Honeychurch

lvers, all of whom occur in a charter of Saint-
ly thereafter (*Chart. de l'abb. de St. Père de*   John Honeychurch = Mary
                                                  Rowland
says Baldwin, his son, was the first earl, thus   Joan Honeychurch = Robert Crispin
                                        mar. 1595   bapt. 1565
                                        (*vide* 132)   (*vide* 132)

Robert du Hommet,
living before 1025
|
Son
|
William du Hommet
|
Daughter = John, son of Odo,
bishop of
Bayeux
Robert du Hommet

Jourdain de Say = Lucy

¹Richard du Hommet I = Agnes de Beaumont
constable of Nor-
mandy, died 1181

Guillaume de Semilly I

²William du Hommet I = Lucia,   *Jourdain ³Enguerrand I = Cécilia   Robert de la Haie=
constable of Nor-   g.-dau. of   3rd Son   2nd Son
mandy, died c. 1209   Adam de |
                       Brix   William de   Jourdain   Geoffry   Enguerrand
                                 Semilly II   de Semilly du Hommet   de Semilly

Richard II = (1)⁶Aegidia Gila = (2) Aleinora, William   Henry   Jourdain,
du Hommet,   or Gillette, dau. relict of   de Say   bishop of Lisieux
died 1200   of Richard and   Robert de la
             Matilda de la Haie Haie

William du Hommet II = Eustachia
appears as
constable in
1213 and 1239

F

*Jourdain du Hommet = N . . .
or his heirs succeeded
to the constableship

Daughter = Seigneur   Daughter = Seigneur   Daughter = Robert d
           de Villiers   de Hotot   brought the constableship (younges
                                             of Normandy to her hus-   baron o
                                             band   (La Roq

William de M
baron of Bec
constable of
|
Jeanne de Mo

¹ *Arch. du Calvados*, Aunay col., no. 25.
² *Ibid.*, no. 8 ; *Mon.*, IV, 262.
³ *Black book* of the chapter of Bayeux charters, nos. 87, 88 ; Stapleton I, cliii,
II, lxxix, clxxvii.
⁴ Stapleton, I, cvi.
⁵ La Roque, II, 1460 ; Braceton's *Note Book*, II, 392.
⁶ La Roque, *ibid.* ; *Chron. de Torigny*, II, 12, Delisle N ; Stapleton, I, cxlv ; II,
clxxx, clxxxi, clxxxiv.

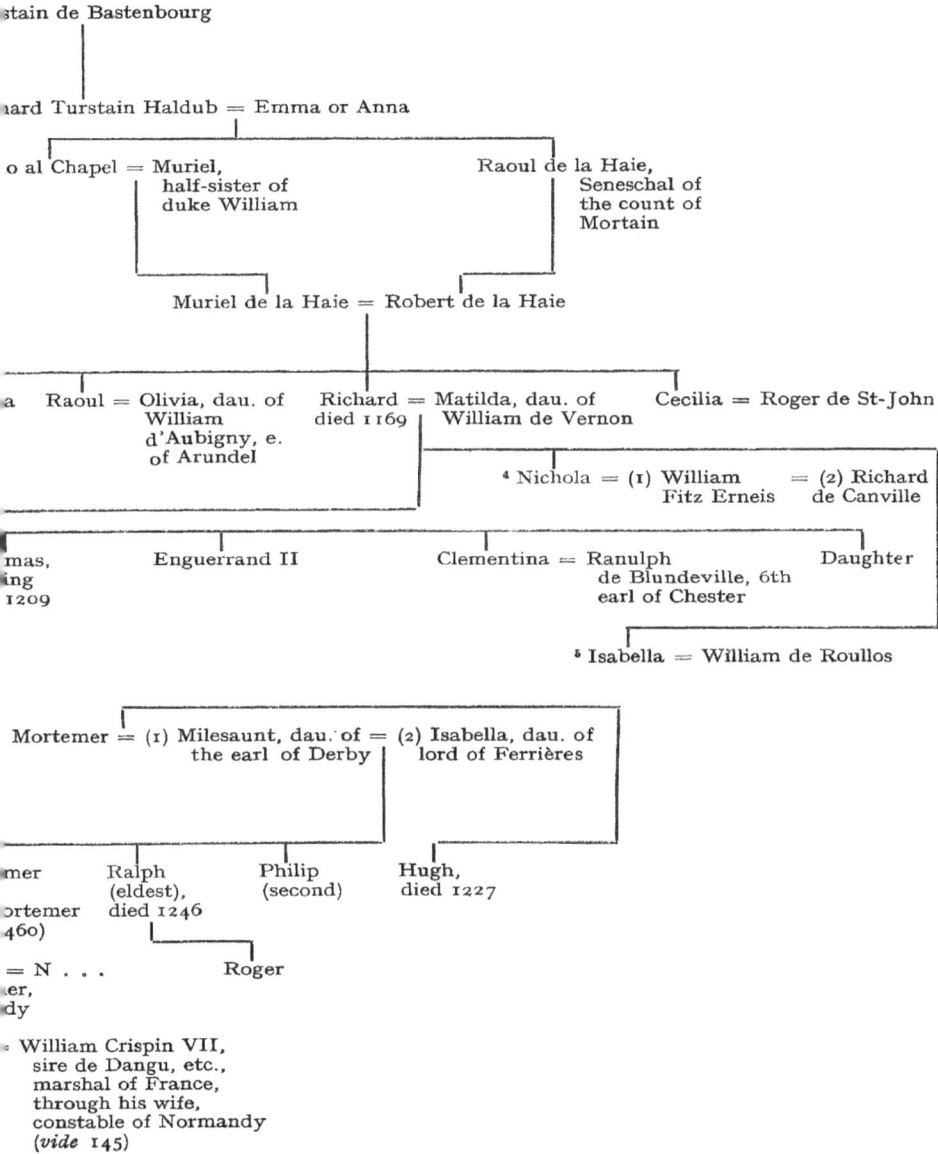

TABLE X

E LA HAIE FAMILIES

, 155)

stain de Bastenbourg

ard Turstain Haldub = Emma or Anna

o al Chapel = Muriel,   Raoul de la Haie,
       half-sister of   Seneschal of
       duke William   the count of
                                Mortain

Muriel de la Haie = Robert de la Haie

a   Raoul = Olivia, dau. of   Richard = Matilda, dau. of   Cecilia = Roger de St-John
        William   died 1169 William de Vernon
        d'Aubigny, e.
        of Arundel

[4] Nichola = (1) William   = (2) Richard
             Fitz Erneis   de Canville

mas,   Enguerrand II   Clementina = Ranulph   Daughter
ing   de Blundeville, 6th
1209   earl of Chester

[5] Isabella = William de Roullos

Mortemer = (1) Milesaunt, dau. of = (2) Isabella, dau. of
           the earl of Derby   lord of Ferrières

mer   Ralph   Philip   Hugh,
      (eldest),   (second)   died 1227
ortemer died 1246
460)

= N . . .   Roger
er,
dy

= William Crispin VII,
   sire de Dangu, etc.,
   marshal of France,
   through his wife,
   constable of Normandy
   (*vide* 145)

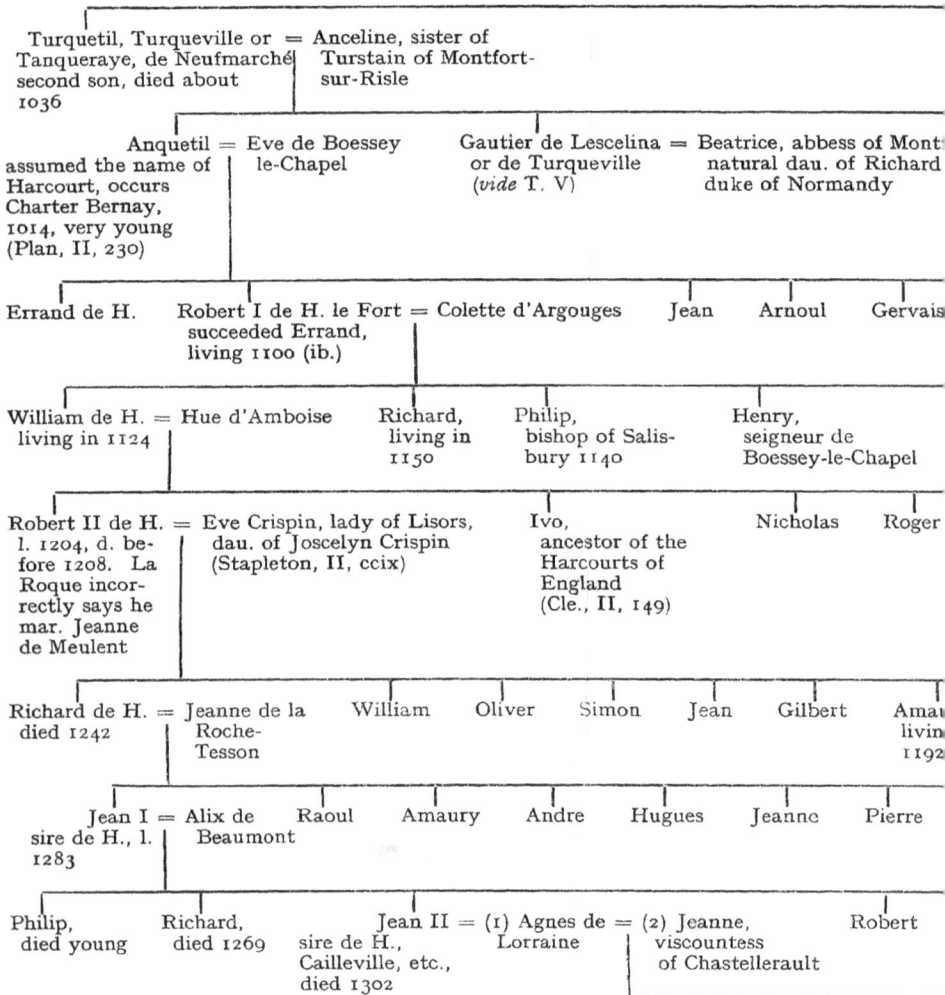

Turquetil, Turqueville or = Anceline, sister of
Tanqueraye, de Neufmarché Turstain of Montfort-
second son, died about sur-Risle
1036

Anquetil = Eve de Boessey   Gautier de Lescelina = Beatrice, abbess of Mont
assumed the name of   le-Chapel   or de Turqueville   natural dau. of Richard
Harcourt, occurs   (*vide* T. V)   duke of Normandy
Charter Bernay,
1014, very young
(Plan, II, 230)

Errand de H.   Robert I de H. le Fort = Colette d'Argouges   Jean   Arnoul   Gervais
   succeeded Errand,
   living 1100 (ib.)

William de H. = Hue d'Amboise   Richard,   Philip,   Henry,
living in 1124   living in   bishop of Salis-   seigneur de
   1150   bury 1140   Boessey-le-Chapel

Robert II de H. = Eve Crispin, lady of Lisors,   Ivo,   Nicholas   Roger
l. 1204, d. be-   dau. of Joscelyn Crispin   ancestor of the
fore 1208. La   (Stapleton, II, ccix)   Harcourts of
Roque incor-   England
rectly says he   (Cle., II, 149)
mar. Jeanne
de Meulent

Richard de H. = Jeanne de la   William   Oliver   Simon   Jean   Gilbert   Amau
died 1242   Roche-   livin
  Tesson   1192

Jean I = Alix de   Raoul   Amaury   Andre   Hugues   Jeanne   Pierre
sire de H., l.   Beaumont
1283

Philip,   Richard,   Jean II = (1) Agnes de = (2) Jeanne,   Robert
died young   died 1269   sire de H.,   Lorraine   viscountess
   Cailleville, etc.,   of Chastellerault
   died 1302

TABLE XI

MILY OF NORMANDY

de Harcourt ; Père Anselme, V, 125 and fol.)

ne = Sprota of Burgundy,
  | mar. 912
  Torf = Ensorberge, mar. 955.

Thurold de Pontaudemer
(*vide* Table VI), eldest son

rs,   Lesceline de Turqueville = William, count of Exmes,
          (*vide* T. V)   later Eu

Yves   Renaud

Baldwin,
seigneur de
Cailleville

William   Renaud   Alberede   Alix   Eve   Beatrix
                                      probably confused
                                      with Eve Crispin
                                      daughter of
                                      Joscelyn

Roger   Raoul

x   Marguerite

iam   Raoul   Guy   Alix   Luce   Isabeau   Blanche   Agnes   Jeanne   Isabel

Jean III   = Alix de   Jeanne   Marguerite
died 1326   Brabant
sire de H.

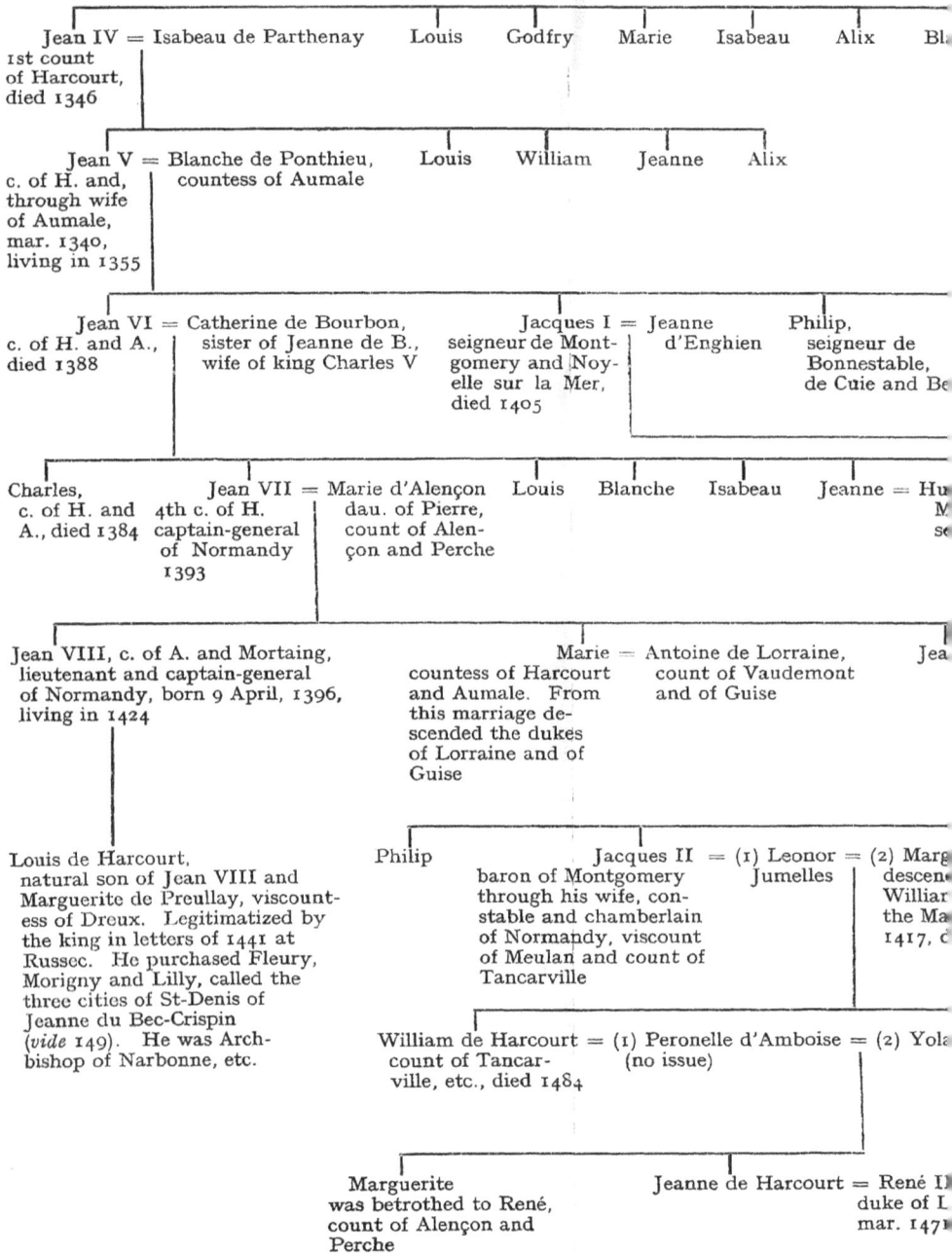

Jean IV = Isabeau de Parthenay   Louis   Godfry   Marie   Isabeau   Alix   Bl
1st count
of Harcourt,
died 1346

Jean V = Blanche de Ponthieu,   Louis   William   Jeanne   Alix
c. of H. and,   countess of Aumale
through wife
of Aumale,
mar. 1340,
living in 1355

Jean VI = Catherine de Bourbon,   Jacques I = Jeanne   Philip,
c. of H. and A.,   sister of Jeanne de B.,   seigneur de Mont-   d'Enghien   seigneur de
died 1388   wife of king Charles V   gomery and Noy-   Bonnestable,
    elle sur la Mer,   de Cuie and Be
    died 1405

Charles,   Jean VII = Marie d'Alençon   Louis   Blanche   Isabeau   Jeanne = Hu
c. of H. and   4th c. of H.   dau. of Pierre,   M
A., died 1384   captain-general   count of Alen-   se
    of Normandy   çon and Perche
    1393

Jean VIII, c. of A. and Mortaing,   Marie = Antoine de Lorraine,   Jea
lieutenant and captain-general   countess of Harcourt   count of Vaudemont
of Normandy, born 9 April, 1396,   and Aumale. From   and of Guise
living in 1424   this marriage de-
    scended the dukes
    of Lorraine and of
    Guise

Louis de Harcourt,   Philip   Jacques II = (1) Leonor = (2) Marg
natural son of Jean VIII and   baron of Montgomery   Jumelles   descen
Marguerite de Preullay, viscount-   through his wife, con-   Williar
ess of Dreux. Legitimatized by   stable and chamberlain   the Ma
the king in letters of 1441 at   of Normandy, viscount   1417, c
Russec. He purchased Fleury,   of Meulan and count of
Morigny and Lilly, called the   Tancarville
three cities of St-Denis of
Jeanne du Bec-Crispin
(*vide* 149). He was Arch-   William de Harcourt = (1) Peronelle d'Amboise = (2) Yola
bishop of Narbonne, etc.   count of Tancar-   (no issue)
    ville, etc., died 1484

Marguerite   Jeanne de Harcourt = René I
was betrothed to René,   duke of L
count of Alençon and   mar. 1471
Perche

ie

Robert   Charles   Errand   Louis   Jeanne   Catherine

on

e   Marie   Catherine   Marguerite de Harcourt = Jean —
gomery,   called by La Roque   Baron of Ferrière,
ur de Beausant   (II, 1694) Yolande   Dangu and Thury, which
                                                              latter two came from
                                                              the Crispin family
                                                              (*Le Prevost Mem.*, II, 14)

te de Meulan,   Christophe   Marie   Jeanne   Autre
  from
ispin VII
i, mar.
  1448

e Laval   Marie = Jean,
               second wife,   count of Dunoir and Longueville,
                mar. 1436   natural son of Louis de France,
                              duke of Orleans, and of
                                Marguerite d'Enghien

                   François d'Orleans,
ne, etc.,   succeeded his uncle, William de Harcourt,
                   as count of Harcourt, Tancarville, etc.

Ticic,
  original name of
  the Tessons, c. 725

Radulphus Taxo,
  witnessed with Fouque, count of Anjou,
  his blood relative (Le Prevost, *Notes, Wace,* II, 30)
  c. 1028, a charter of the abbey of Coulombs
          A

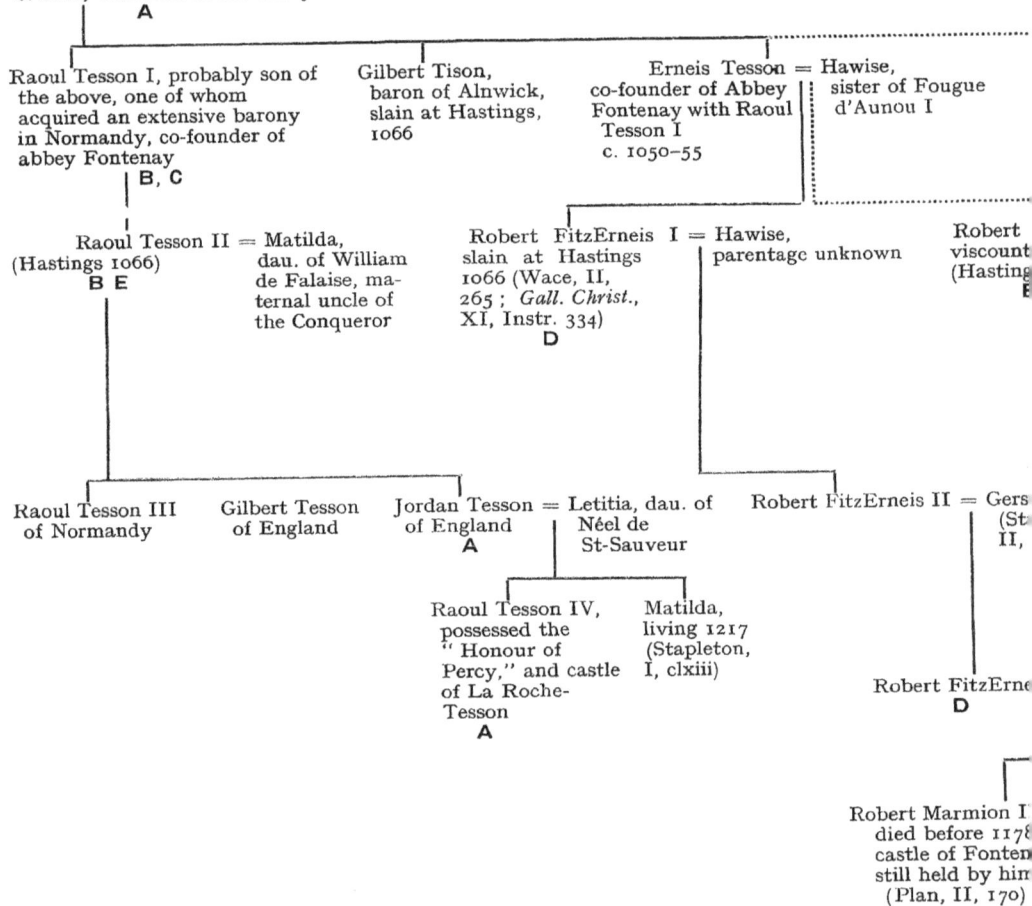

Raoul Tesson I, probably son of   Gilbert Tison,   Erneis Tesson = Hawise,
  the above, one of whom   baron of Alnwick,   co-founder of Abbey || sister of Fougue
  acquired an extensive barony   slain at Hastings,   Fontenay with Raoul || d'Aunou I
  in Normandy, co-founder of   1066   Tesson I
  abbey Fontenay   c. 1050–55
          B, C

Raoul Tesson II = Matilda,   Robert FitzErneis I = Hawise,   Robert
(Hastings 1066)   dau. of William   slain at Hastings   parentage unknown   viscount
      B E   de Falaise, ma-   1066 (Wace, II,   (Hasting
                  ternal uncle of   265 ; *Gall. Christ.,*   **E**
                  the Conqueror   XI, Instr. 334)
                                              D

Raoul Tesson III   Gilbert Tesson   Jordan Tesson = Letitia, dau. of   Robert FitzErneis II = Gers
  of Normandy   of England   of England   Néel de   (St
                                              A   St-Sauveur   II,

                              Raoul Tesson IV,   Matilda,
                                possessed the   living 1217
                                " Honour of   (Stapleton,
                                Percy," and castle   I, clxiii)
                                of La Roche-   Robert FitzErne
                                Tesson   **D**
                                    A

                                                                    Robert Marmion I
                                                                    died before 1178
                                                                    castle of Fonten
                                                                    still held by hir
                                                                    (Plan, II, 170)

A " The Honour of Percy in the Bailiwick of Coutances, designated *curtes,* a domain only in contra-
  distinction to a fortified bourgh or *castellum,* was the land of Ralph Tesson and held of the crown *in
  capite* by the service of a knight : he had also in this district the castle of La Roche-Tesson, which
  had been chosen as the seat of the lords of the fief of La Colombe, belonging to the Honour of St-Pair,
  and for which he had done homage to the abbot of Mont-St-Michel in 1178, after the death of his father
  Jordan Tesson " (Stapleton, I, lxxxiii ; II, xiii).
B Raoul Tesson I gave 12 acres of land *in pago Baiocensi* to the abbey of Fontenay before the conquest
  which he had exchanged with William Marmion (Stapleton, II, xcvi).
C Le Prevost thought the chief seat of Raoul Tesson I was Thury because his battle-cry at Val des Dunes
  was " Tur aie " (*Wace,* l. 9059 ; Le Prevost, *Notes, Wace,* II, 246 ; *Wace,* Taylor, 19).
D Three generations of the Tessons, commencing with Robert Fitz Erneis I, rapidly succeeded each other
  (*Wace,* Taylor, 223 ; Plan., II, 170 ; Le Prevost, *Notes, Wace,* II, 246).
E Wace (l. 13622–3) mentions Raoul Tesson (II) and Roger (Robert) Marmion (I) as fighting side by side
  at Hastings (*Wace,* Taylor, 223 ; Plan., II, 170).
  Round interpolates another Robert here, *Feud. Eng.,* 191.

(*Vide* 47, 77 ; *Nor. Peo.*, 147–8, 441)

Mansfred the Dane

Geoffry de Percy

William de Percy

Geoffry de Percy

William de Percy

Geoffry de Percy

...mion,
...essed charter
...sson I
...., XI, 413)

= Hedgewisa (Hawise),
became a nun at
Holy Trinity, Caen,
c. 1106, to which she
gave land, witnessed
by her dau. Gersenda,
and the latter's son,
Robert FitzErneis III

William de Percy = Emma de Port
died 1096
A

Serlon de Percy,
abbot of
Whitby

Ralph de Perc

...r Marmion   Helto   Manasses
...l extensive
...s formerly
...nging to Robert
...Despensier,
...l 1131
...pleton, II, xcvii)

Alain de Percy = Emma de Gand

Richard de Percy of Dunsl...
Lofthouse, in which
Grendale was located
(*Mon.*, I, 74 ; *Nor. Peo.*, 2

...bert Marmion II = Milisent
...ed 1143
E

William de Percy

Ralph de Grendale

William de Percy   Wa

...e   4 Sons,   Maud   = William,
...hamp   died s.p.   de Percy   earl of Warwick
                        (no issue)

Agnes de Percy = Joscelyn de Louvain,
brother of Adeliza,
queen of Henry I,
adopted the name
of Percy

Ralph

Henry de Percy,
ancestor of the earls and
dukes of Northumberland

ARMS

Tesson	.	.	. gules, a fesse, ermine.
Marmion	.	.	. vair, a fesse, gules.
Percy	.	.	. azure, a fesse indented, or.
Percy of the South		.	fessy or bendy.
Bryon	.	.	. bendy or fessy.
Baird	.	.	. a fesse with three mullets.
Washington	.	.	. a fesse with three mullets.

(*Nor. Peo.*, 147–8, 324, 359, 442.)

(*Crispins of Kingston-on-Hull* * in *Pub. Geneal. Soc. Penna.*, March 1928, and *Captain William Crispin, Penna. Mag.*, Apr., Ju
Family of William Penn, Founder of Penna.,

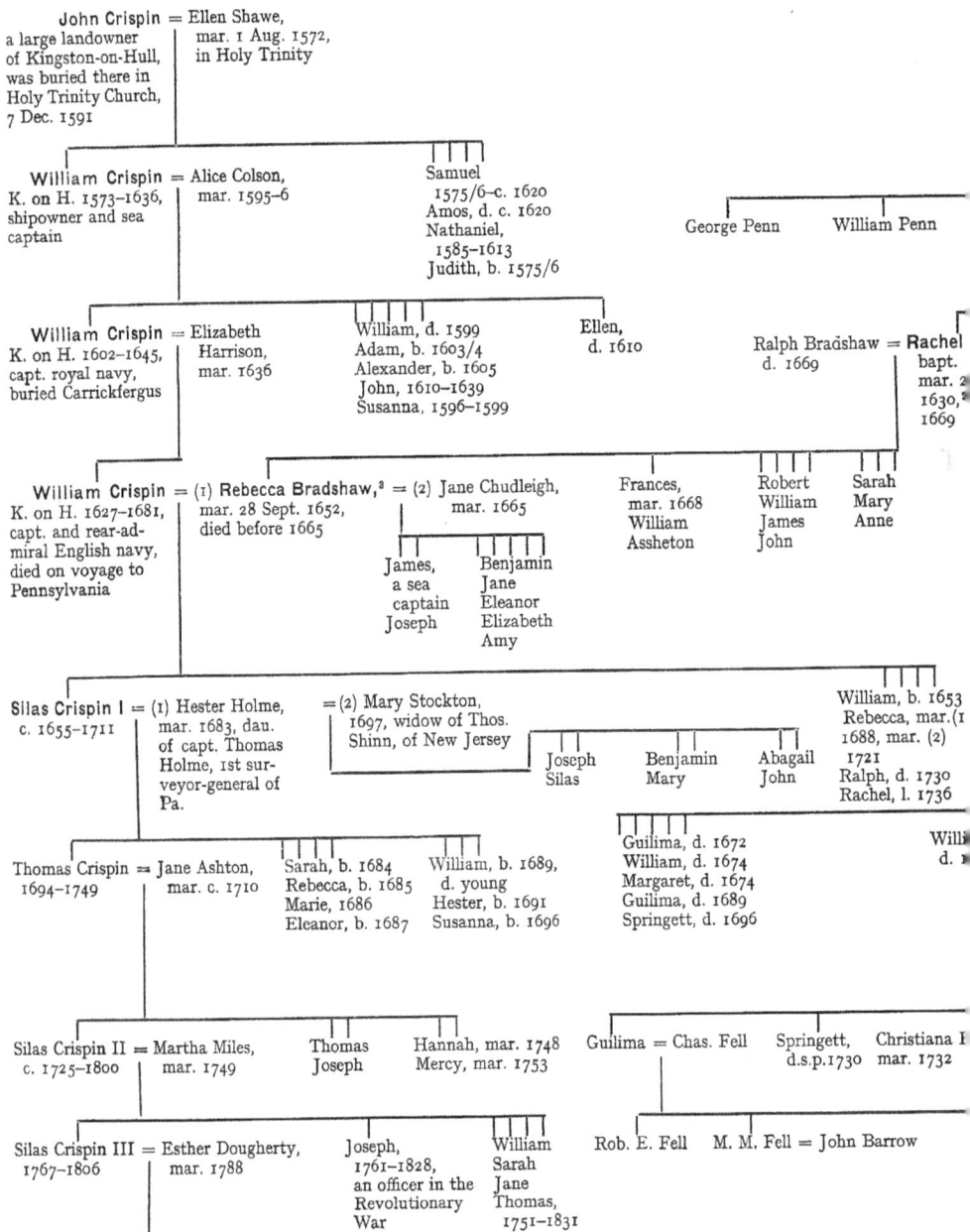

John Crispin = Ellen Shawe,
a large landowner | mar. 1 Aug. 1572,
of Kingston-on-Hull, | in Holy Trinity
was buried there in
Holy Trinity Church,
7 Dec. 1591

William Crispin = Alice Colson,
K. on H. 1573–1636, | mar. 1595–6
shipowner and sea
captain

Samuel
1575/6–c. 1620
Amos, d. c. 1620
Nathaniel,
1585–1613
Judith, b. 1575/6

George Penn   William Penn

William Crispin = Elizabeth
K. on H. 1602–1645, | Harrison,
capt. royal navy, | mar. 1636
buried Carrickfergus

William, d. 1599
Adam, b. 1603/4
Alexander, b. 1605
John, 1610–1639
Susanna, 1596–1599

Ellen,
d. 1610

Ralph Bradshaw = Rachel
d. 1669 | bapt.
| mar. 2
| 1630,
| 1669

William Crispin = (1) Rebecca Bradshaw,[3] = (2) Jane Chudleigh,
K. on H. 1627–1681, | mar. 28 Sept. 1652, | mar. 1665
capt. and rear-ad- | died before 1665
miral English navy,
died on voyage to
Pennsylvania

James,   Benjamin
a sea   Jane
captain   Eleanor
Joseph   Elizabeth
               Amy

Frances,   Robert   Sarah
mar. 1668   William   Mary
William   James   Anne
Assheton   John

Silas Crispin I = (1) Hester Holme, = (2) Mary Stockton,
c. 1655–1711 | mar. 1683, dau. | 1697, widow of Thos.
| of capt. Thomas | Shinn, of New Jersey
| Holme, 1st sur-
| veyor-general of
| Pa.

Joseph   Benjamin   Abagail
Silas   Mary   John

William, b. 1653
Rebecca, mar. (1
1688, mar. (2)
1721
Ralph, d. 1730
Rachel, l. 1736

Thomas Crispin = Jane Ashton,
1694–1749 | mar. c. 1710

Sarah, b. 1684   William, b. 1689,
Rebecca, b. 1685 d. young
Marie, 1686   Hester, b. 1691
Eleanor, b. 1687 Susanna, b. 1696

Guilima, d. 1672
William, d. 1674
Margaret, d. 1674
Guilima, d. 1689
Springett, d. 1696

Willi
d.

Silas Crispin II = Martha Miles,
c. 1725–1800 | mar. 1749

Thomas   Hannah, mar. 1748
Joseph   Mercy, mar. 1753

Guilima = Chas. Fell   Springett,   Christiana
| d.s.p.1730 mar. 1732

Silas Crispin III = Esther Dougherty,
1767–1806 | mar. 1788

Joseph,   William
1761–1828,   Sarah
an officer in the Jane
Revolutionary   Thomas,
War   1751–1831

Rob. E. Fell   M. M. Fell = John Barrow

TABLE XIV

PENN RELATIONSHIP

Oct. 1929, M. Jackson Crispin; *Pedigree and Geneal. Notes of the Highly Distinguished Family of Penn*, James Coleman, London, 1871; *The cestry and Descendants*, Howard M. Jenkins, Philada., 1899.) [1]

William Penn,
of Minety, co. Gloucester, and Penn's Lodge, co. Wilts,
will dated 1591, proved 21 April 1592—lies buried before altar,
church of Minety

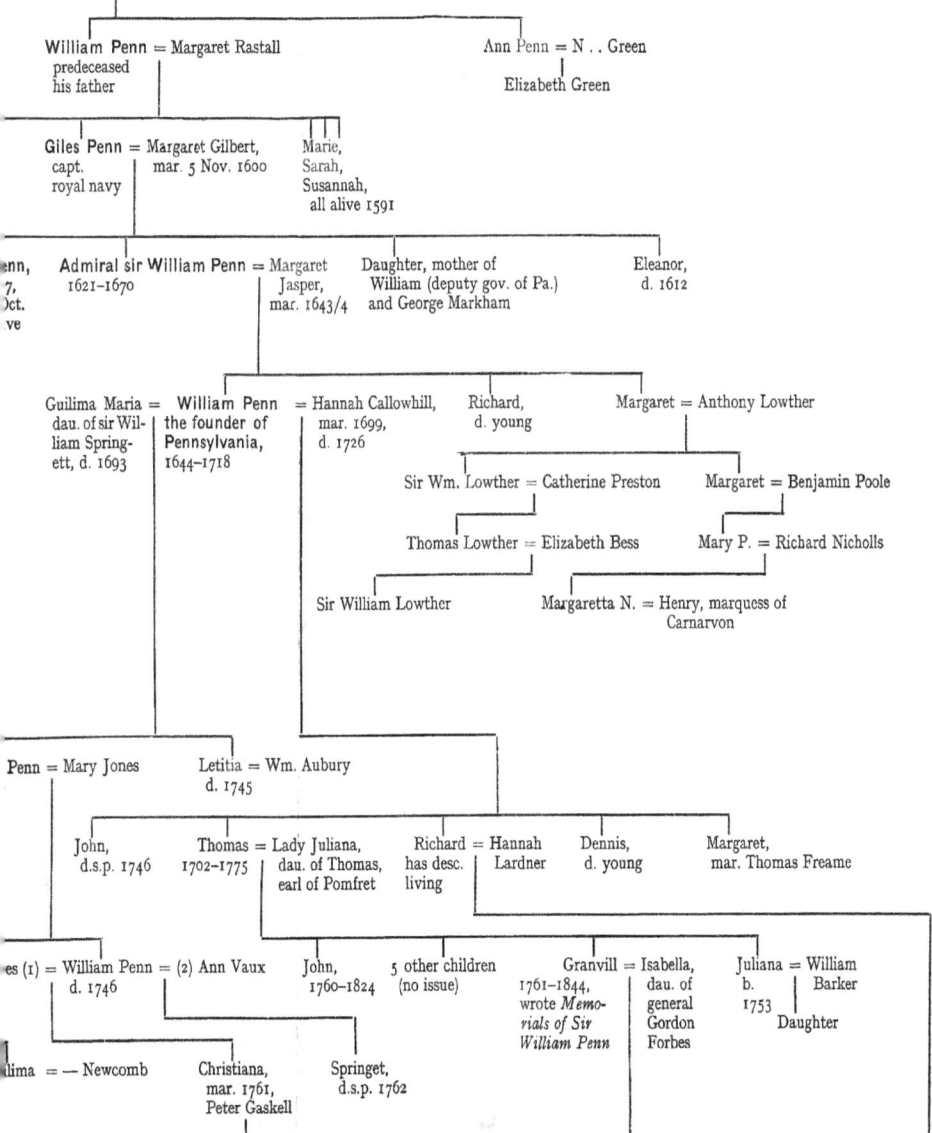

William Penn = Margaret Rastall
predeceased
his father

Ann Penn = N . . Green

Elizabeth Green

Giles Penn = Margaret Gilbert,
capt. | mar. 5 Nov. 1600
royal navy

Marie,
Sarah,
Susannah,
all alive 1591

enn,
7,
Oct.
ve

Admiral sir William Penn = Margaret
1621–1670   Jasper,
mar. 1643/4

Daughter, mother of
William (deputy gov. of Pa.)
and George Markham

Eleanor,
d. 1612

Guilima Maria = **William Penn**
dau. of sir Wil- | the founder of
liam Spring- | Pennsylvania,
ett, d. 1693 | 1644–1718

= Hannah Callowhill,
mar. 1699,
d. 1726

Richard,
d. young

Margaret = Anthony Lowther

Sir Wm. Lowther = Catherine Preston

Margaret = Benjamin Poole

Thomas Lowther = Elizabeth Bess

Mary P. = Richard Nicholls

Sir William Lowther

Margaretta N. = Henry, marquess of
Carnarvon

Penn = Mary Jones

Letitia = Wm. Aubury
d. 1745

John,
d.s.p. 1746

Thomas = Lady Juliana,
1702–1775 | dau. of Thomas,
earl of Pomfret

Richard = Hannah
has desc. | Lardner
living

Dennis,
d. young

Margaret,
mar. Thomas Freame

es (1) = William Penn = (2) Ann Vaux
d. 1746

John,
1760–1824

5 other children
(no issue)

Granvill = Isabella,
1761–1844, | dau. of
wrote *Memo-* | general
rials of Sir | Gordon
William Penn | Forbes

Juliana = William
b. | Barker
1753

Daughter

lima = — Newcomb

Christiana,
mar. 1761,
Peter Gaskell

Springet,
d.s.p. 1762

Hon. Benjamin Crispin = Maria Foster,   Martha,   Mary,   Silas,   Hester,   Ann,   Pau
1792–1864, member   mar. 1816   1789–1817   d. 1865   1798–1823   b. 1803,   b. 1800,   d. 1847
general assembly of   d. 1832   d. 1829
Pennsylvania 1837–8–9,
member senate
1840–1–2–3, speaker
of the senate 1843,
first common council-
man for the 23rd ward
of Philadelphia, 1854

Benjamin Franklin Crispin I = Elizabeth Glenn   Edward   William   Eleanor   Jane   Thomas   Charles
1821–1898

Benjamin Franklin Crispin II = Margaret Jackson, 1853–1931,   Robert,   Charles,   Sarah Frances =
1847–1903, president First   mar. 1874, dau. of hon.   1849–1913,   1856–1926,   1846–1930,
national bank of Berwick,   Mordecai W. Jackson,   mar. 1873,   d.s.p.   mar. 1874
Pa.   founder, Jackson & Woodin   Fannie Bow-   Elizabeth,
                      (1849), now the American Car   man   1873–1891,
                      & Foundry Co.   unmarried

Mordecai Jackson Crispin = (1) Marie Brockway,   = (2) Erma Marchant,   = (3) Andrée Detrez,
b. 13 May 1875, gen. mgr.   b. Beach Haven, Pa.,   b. 1888, mar. 12 April   b. 1898, Paris, France,
and treas. U.S. Metal &   1874 ; mar. B.H.   1916, New York, dau.   mar. 23 Sept. 1931,
Mfg. Co., New York, 1900–   1900, d. 1907 New   of James and Nannie   Paris, dau. of Ernest
16, American Car & Fdy.   York, dau. of capt.   (Mathews) Marchant   and Adrienne Detrez o
Co., New York, 1916–22.   Frank E. and Cora   (no issue), divorced,   Paris and La Baule,
Retired 1922, president   (Campbell) Brockway   now wife of judge   France
First Nat. Bank, Berwick,   Cyrus W. Palmer
since 1909

Count Olivero Tripcovich = Elizabeth,   Jacqueline I
of Trieste, Italy,   countess Tripcovich-Crispin,   b. 5 Aug. 1
ancient title forfeited in his   b. 3 Jan. 1905, New York,
father's time, restored   mar. 30 Jan. 1929,
1 May 1936 by king Victor   St. Patrick's cathedral,
Emanuel III   New York

[1] Other references : *The Crispin Family*, rev. W. F. Crispin, Akron, Ohio, 1901 ;
Captain William Crispin, by Oliver Hough in the *Pennsylvania Magazine*, 1898, vol.
XXII, 34–56 ; *Colonel and Revolutionary Families of Pennsylvania*, J. W. Jordan, New
York, 1911 ; *New Series*, Wilfred Jordan, 1935.
[2] Marriage register (1618–1635), St-Gregory by St-Paul, London (by license of the
Vicar-General) ; *Visitation of co. Lancaster, 1664–5, by Dugdale*, Raines, part I, 53.
[3] Parish register, Stepney, co. Middlesex, vol. II (Canterbury 1899), 83 ; *Dugdale*,
ibid.
* The Kingston-on-Hull pedigree was approved by A. T. Butler, portcullis of the
college of Arms, London, in a letter to the author dated 18 July 1927.

Benjamin Eaton C. II,
b. 19 Nov. 1931

y
er

Alexander Forbes Gaskell | William, d. 1802, infant | Julianna, d. 1804, infant | Granville John Penn, 1802–1867 | Thomas Gordon Penn, 1803–1869 | William, b. 1811 | Sophia d.s.p. 1827 = Col. sir William Gomm, k.c.b. | Louisa, Isabella, Henrietta, all d. infants

James Clayton = Hannah | John Penn, = Ann Allen 1728–1795 of Phila. | Richard Penn = Mary Masters of Phila. | William Penn

William Penn, 1776–1837 | Richard, 1837, d.s.p. | Hannah, d. unmarried | Mary = Samuel Paynter

Silas,
b. 1828, graduated
West Point military academy,
third in his class in 1846,
became colonel ordnance
U.S.A. 1881—d.s.p. 1889 in
New York

orge S. Clark esburg | William = Matilda Mitchell, 1851–1924 mar. 1875 | Louis = Susan Church, 1863–1933 mar. 1881 | Maria = William E. 1858–1933, Smith mar. 1883

Benjamin, 1877–1878
William, 1883–1896 | John Stephenson = Elizabeth 1875–1936 Rowland | Elizabeth, b. 1878, a physician in Philadelphia

(2) Irene Sampson = Charles E. = (1) Elizabeth, mar. 1922 b. 1882 b. 1884, (have issue) mar. 1915, divorced 1922

John Maxwell R. = Mary Loper, mar. 1928 | Arthur, 1883–1936

Eleanor, b. 1917

Frank M. = Emma Weeks, b. 1876 mar. 1905 d. 1937 d. before husband

Clarence Gearhart Crispin = Mae Eaton,
b. 27 Sept. 1879, presi- | b. 1 Mar. 1882,
dent, Multiplex Mfg. Co., | mar. 1904 Berwick, dau. of late
Berwick, Pa., assistant | F. H. Eaton, former president
district manager, Ameri- | Jackson & Woodin Mfg. Co.
can Car & Fdy. Co., | and American Car & Foundry Co.
1907–1921, senior vice-
president, First Nat.
Bank, Berwick, Pa., since
1909, executor, estate of
Frederick H. Eaton

Helen Jean = Charles
b. 11 Jan. 1886, Beland
mar. 8 June 1910, Owens
Berwick

Margaret, b. 17 May 1911 | Elizabeth, b. 4 Nov. 1914

Eaton C. = Laura Clock, t. 1905 mar. 1929 | Frederick Eaton C. = Sarah Louise Gwinner, b. 17 Sept. 1906 mar. 1929

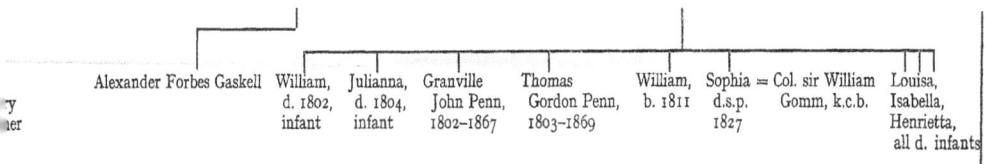

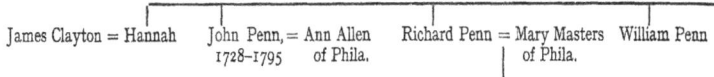

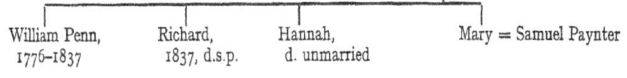

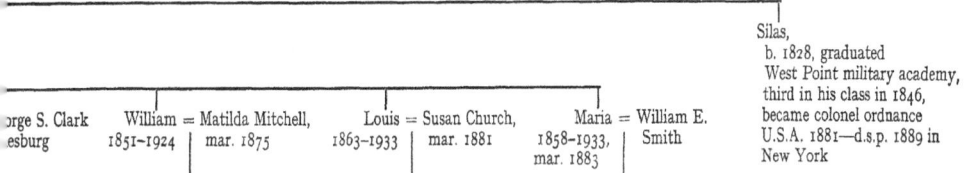

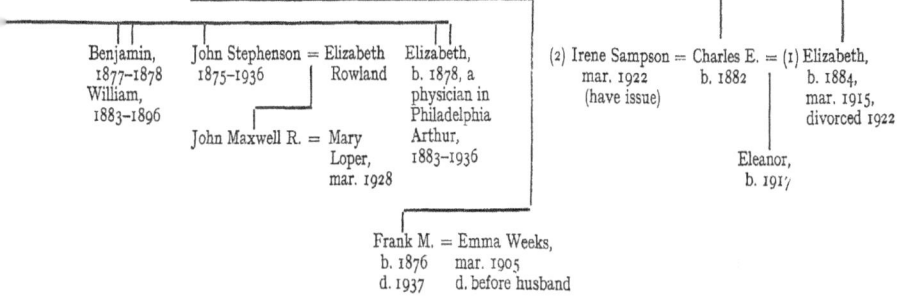

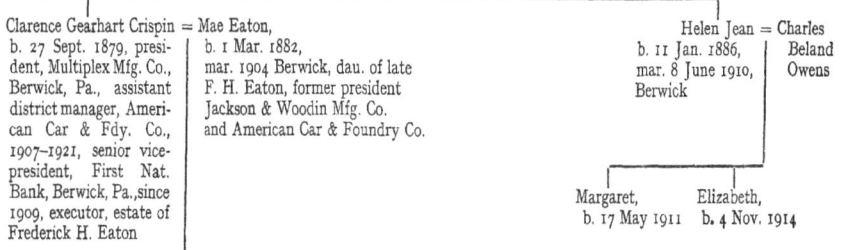

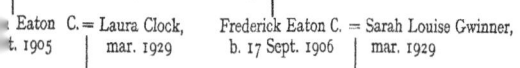

Frederick Eaton C. II,

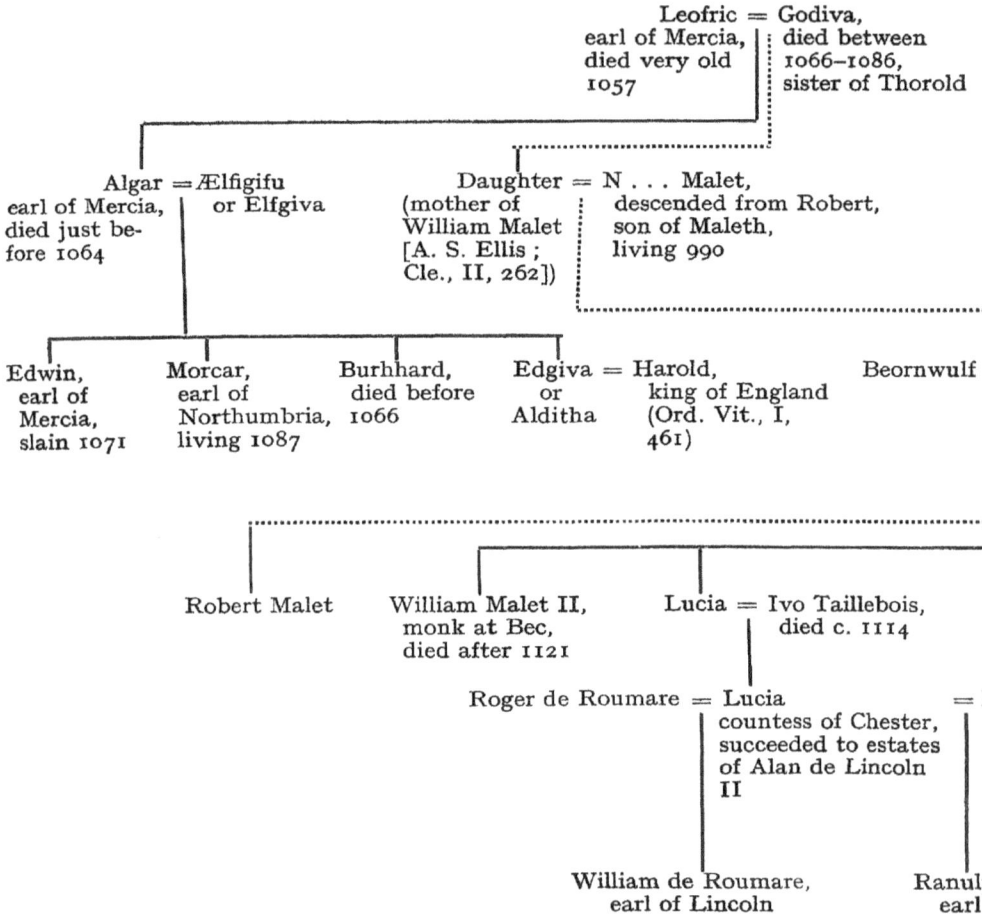

Leofric = Godiva,
earl of Mercia, died between
died very old 1066–1086,
1057 sister of Thorold

Algar = Ælfigifu   Daughter = N . . . Malet,
earl of Mercia,   or Elfgiva   (mother of   descended from Robert,
died just be-   William Malet   son of Maleth,
fore 1064   [A. S. Ellis ;   living 990
                           Cle., II, 262])

Edwin,   Morcar,   Burhhard,   Edgiva = Harold,   Beornwulf
earl of   earl of   died before   or   king of England
Mercia,   Northumbria,   1066   Alditha   (Ord. Vit., I,
slain 1071   living 1087   461)

Robert Malet   William Malet II,   Lucia = Ivo Taillebois,
                monk at Bec,   died c. 1114
                died after 1121

Roger de Roumare = Lucia   =
                         countess of Chester,
                         succeeded to estates
                         of Alan de Lincoln
                         II

William de Roumare,   Ranul
earl of Lincoln   earl

TABLE XIII

FAMILY

p. 3, 20 ; Addenda)

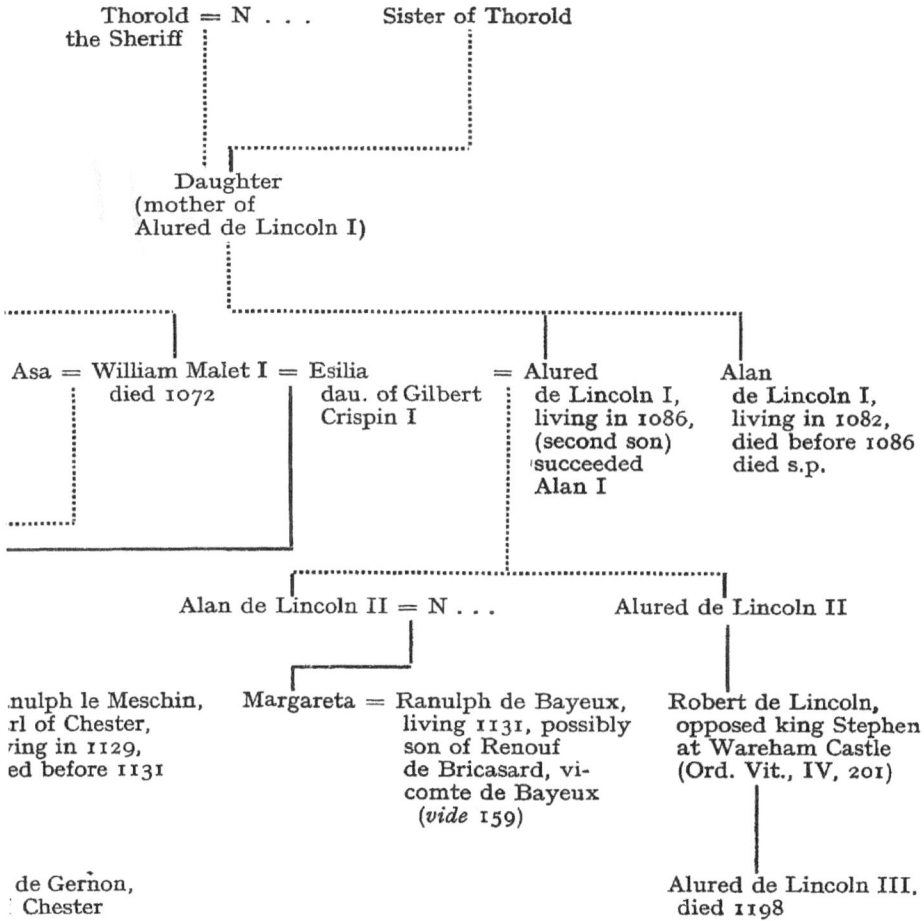

Thorold = N . . .   Sister of Thorold
the Sheriff

Daughter
(mother of
Alured de Lincoln I)

Asa = William Malet I = Esilia   = Alured   Alan
died 1072   dau. of Gilbert   de Lincoln I,   de Lincoln I,
Crispin I   living in 1086,   living in 1082,
(second son)   died before 1086
succeeded   died s.p.
Alan I

Alan de Lincoln II = N . . .   Alured de Lincoln II

.nulph le Meschin,   Margareta = Ranulph de Bayeux,   Robert de Lincoln,
rl of Chester,   living 1131, possibly   opposed king Stephen
ring in 1129,   son of Renouf   at Wareham Castle
ed before 1131   de Bricasard, vi-   (Ord. Vit., IV, 201)
comte de Bayeux
(*vide* 159)

de Gernon,   Alured de Lincoln III.
Chester   died 1198

www.ingramcontent.com/pod-product-compliance
Lightning Source LLC
Chambersburg PA
CBHW031116020426

42333CB00012B/111